WILLIAM JENNINGS BRYAN
I. Political Evangelist, 1860–1908

WILLIAM JENNINGS BRYAN

I. Political Evangelist

1860–1908

by

PAOLO E. COLETTA

UNIVERSITY OF NEBRASKA PRESS · LINCOLN

1964

Publishers on the Plains

UNP

MANUFACTURED IN THE UNITED STATES OF AMERICA

For
Maria, Alicevelyn, Dana Maria, and Michael

Preface and Acknowledgments

WILLIAM JENNINGS BRYAN exemplified what a common man could accomplish in the fluid social structure of democratic America. To rise from humble beginnings to the leadership of a major political party is no mean record; the fact that his party selected him as its presidential candidate three times remains unique.

Born and bred of the soil, Bryan stanchly represented agrarian America of the last frontier. When the election of 1896 posed the question of whether the United States would remain an agricultural nation or adopt the policies and techniques of the industrial state which it had become, he defended the Jeffersonian rather than the Hamiltonian philosophy.

Bryan was less a statesman than a moralist and evangelist. Had he been a missionary, he probably would have dedicated his life to saving the souls of persons and nations that did not know God. A humanitarian, he sought to change men rather than their institutions, to get men to exercise in political, economic, and social fields the righteousness they should show in religious and ethical matters. Not an innovator, his power lay not in radicalism—in seeking to overthrow or to make a sharp break with the past—but rather in his buoyant belief in progressive change that would recapture for the future the equalitarian democracy that characterized early America and would thus fulfill the promise of American life. His evocative rhetoric in popularizing this progressivism, and his "keeping of the faith" in its defense, support his being called a political evangelist.

When the Spanish-American War raised the question whether the United States should remain attached to its isolationist attitude or adopt the "large policy" an emotionally aroused people demanded as befitting a great power, Bryan adhered to the traditional isolationist attitude of his Middle West. History upholds his anticolonialism, and his search for methods short of war for settling international problems has left its mark upon American history.

This volume deals largely with Bryan as a political figure who left his impress on American domestic and foreign policy battles from 1890 to 1908. A subsequent volume will detail his activities as a declining political power, as secretary of state, prohibitionist, and Fundamentalist Puritan.

My grateful thanks are due a large number of persons. My colleague, Professor Richard West, and my former colleague, Dr. Gerald E. Wheeler, read portions of the manuscript and offered constructive suggestions. Professor Emeritus Allan Nevins, of Columbia University, provided unending stimulation; and a sabbatical leave granted by the United States Naval Academy made extended research possible. I am further indebted to Mr. J. Monahan and Miss Mildred Flint, of the Illinois State Historical Society, Springfield, Illinois; Dr. H. Gary Hudson, former president of Illinois College, Jacksonville, Illinois, for use of the *Minutes* of the Board of Trustees, and to Dean Ernest C. Hildner, who read portions of the manuscript dealing with Bryan's college days, arranged interviews for me, and gave access to the college library and student records; to the officers of Sigma Pi, Illinois College, for use of their *Minute Book;* and to Mr. Philip E. Bradish, Clerk of the Circuit Court, Morgan County, Illinois, for legal papers dealing with the life of Silas Lillard Bryan. Both Dr. James C. Olson, former Director of the Nebraska State Historical Society, Lincoln, and his successor, Dr. William D. Aeschbacher, proved indefatigable in helping me with materials in Nebraska history, as have also Frank A. Lundy, Director of University Libraries, the University of Nebraska, and Miss Frances Schneider of the Omaha Public Library. Dr. Milo Bail, president, and Mr. William T. Utley, chairman of the Political Science Department, University of Omaha, facilitated my research by inviting me to be a visiting professor with them for three summers.

For skilled direction in the use of personal papers in the Division of Manuscripts, Library of Congress, I wish to thank Dr. David Mearns, Dr. C. Percy Powell, and Dr. Joseph Vance. Mrs. Woodrow Wilson gave permission to use the Woodrow Wilson Papers, the Honorable William Aldrich permitted use of the Nelson W. Aldrich Papers, and the late Mrs. Ruth Bryan Rohde not only permitted use of the William Jennings Bryan Papers but let me read a large collection of the letters exchanged between her mother and father, and other papers. Professor Henry Steele Commager was extremely generous in turning over to me all the research he had accomplished for a study of Bryan. Miss Juliet Wolohan steered me through the David Bennett Hill file in the George

S. Bixby Papers, New York State Library, Albany, New York; and Dr. Vernon Tate, Librarian, United States Naval Academy, acquired needed literary materials and illustrations. Credit for information received in personal interviews and letters is indicated in the text. The late Charles G. Dawes; the late Mrs. Thomas Stinson Allen, Bryan's youngest sister; the late Silas Bryan, son of ex-Governor Charles W. Bryan; and the late Honorable Homer S. Cummings were particularly gracious. Professor Bennett H. Wall, University of Kentucky, furnished information on the Kentucky election of 1896; Professor H. Wayne Morgan, University of Texas, information on silver and politics in the Far West; Mrs. Frank L. Owsley, Tennessee State Archives and Library, information on the Tennessee election of 1896; and Professor Samuel Horace Merrill, University of Maryland, insight into Bourbon philosophy, particularly that of Grover Cleveland. I am deeply grateful, too, to my wife and daughter for their uncomplaining loyalty and patience when I seemed to live more for Bryan than for them.

Grateful acknowledgment is made the following for the use of copyrighted materials: From the Nebraska State Historical Society, the author's "The Youth of William Jennings Bryan—Beginnings of a Christian Statesman," *Nebraska History*, 31 (March 1950), 1–24; "William Jennings Bryan and the Nebraska Senatorial Election of 1893," *ibid.*, (September 1950), 183–205; "William Jennings Bryan's First Nebraska Years," *ibid.*, 33 (June 1952), 71–94; "The Morning Star of the Reformation: William Jennings Bryan's First Congressional Campaign," *ibid.*, 37 (June 1956), 102–119; "A Tempest in a Teapot?—Governor Poynter's Appointment of William V. Allen to the United States Senate, 1899," *ibid.*, 38 (June 1957), 155–163; "The Nebraska Democratic State Convention of April 13–14, 1892," *ibid.*, 39 (December 1958), 317–333; "William Jennings Bryan's Second Congressional Campaign," *ibid.*, 40 (December 1959), 275–291; and "Bryan, Cleveland, and the Disrupted Democracy, 1890–1896," *ibid.*, 41 (March 1960), 1–27; from the Illinois State Historical Society, the author's "Silas Bryan of Salem," *Journal of the Illinois State Historical Society*, 42 (March 1949), 57–79, and "'Won, 1880—One, 1884'—The Courtship of William Jennings Bryan and Elizabeth Baird," *ibid.*, 50 (Autumn 1957), 231–242; from the Pacific Coast Branch of the American Historical Association for the author's "Bryan, McKinley, and the Treaty of Paris," *Pacific Historical Review*, 26 (May 1957), 131–146, and "McKinley, the Peace Negotiations, and the Acquisition of the Philippines," *ibid.*, 30 (November

1961), 341–350; and to the University of North Carolina Press for permission to condense a short section of Josephus Daniels, *Editor in Politics* (1941).

PAOLO E. COLETTA

United States Naval Academy
Annapolis, Maryland

Contents

PREFACE AND ACKNOWLEDGMENTS   vii

1. Genesis   1

2. College Days   9

3. Love and the Law   21

4. The Morning Star of the Reformation   33

5. Congressman: Tariff Reform and the Income Tax   49

6. Congressman: Currency Reform   62

7. Road to the Nomination   99

8. The "Cross of Gold" and the Triple Alliance   127

9. The Hero of a Lost Cause   161

10. Cuba Libre and America's Mission   213

11. Kansas City   238

12. The Solemn Referendum: The Election of 1900   263

13. Low Ebb: 1901–1904   290

14. Keeping the Faith: 1904   319

15. The Return of the Innocent   353

16. "Shall the People Rule?"   390

    BIBLIOGRAPHY   446

    INDEX   479

A picture section follows page 178.

WILLIAM JENNINGS BRYAN
I. Political Evangelist, 1860–1908

CHAPTER 1

Genesis

I

THE ANCESTORS of William Jennings Bryan on his father's side were of Irish stock. One line flows back to Baron William De Bowbray, who helped wrest Magna Carta from King John; another goes back to a king of Munster known as Brian Borou, "King of the Irish," who was born about A.D. 927. William Smith Bryan, the first Bryan known to rebel against despotic government, suffered banishment to the colony of Virginia during the wars of the Puritan Revolution. A grandson settled near Winchester, Virginia, in 1710. One of his children, William, William Jennings's great-grandfather, accepted a commission from the governor of North Carolina on July 1, 1776 and mustered troops to fight the British. After the war he amassed farm and timber lands and became a leader in the civic and religious life of Culpeper County, south of Winchester. So active was he in the Baptist church that it was popularly called the Bryan Meeting House. Through him the Bryans were related by marriage with the Daniel Boone family.

William had three sons and two daughters. Two sons succumbed to the lure of the West, one going to Ohio and one to Kentucky, starting the movement of the Bryans along a path very similar to that followed by the Lincoln family. The last son, John, William Jennings's grandfather, stayed on the home place for a time and married Nancy Lillard, of English descent. They built a double log cabin and filled it with children. After the seventh child, Silas Lillard, was born, in 1822, they moved across the state to Point Pleasant, on the Kanawha River near its junction with the Ohio. There three more children were born. After eight years on the Kanawha Nancy Lillard died. Two years later, when Silas was twelve, his father died, leaving him to the care of several older brothers and sisters who had not gone to western country.

At eighteen years of age, Silas decided to go west. He walked from Virginia to Troy, Missouri, to live with his brother William, a farmer. He was almost six feet tall, raw-boned, with an aquiline nose and thin lips. His slenderness belied a grim kind of determination, an instinct

1

for seeing things through. First he must obtain an education, a more powerful tool than land or slaves. Then someday he might become a country squire and possess a mansion and a deer park, as did some of the planters of Virginia. He believed that the common individual had the unquestioned right to the completest equality of opportunity to make the most of his abilities. Believing so, there was no reason why he could not perhaps become a member of Congress.

For the next decade Silas toiled unremittingly to obtain the power which is knowledge. He attended various schools until he settled down at McKendree College, a Methodist institution in Lebanon, Illinois. By working as a farm hand and woodchopper he supported himself until graduation, in 1849, at the advanced age of twenty-seven, then persisted until he won a master's degree. For the next two years he taught in the Walnut Hill school, a dozen miles from Salem, and for two years he was elected county superintendent of schools. Meantime he had been studying law, and at the age of twenty-nine he was admitted to the bar and began practice in Salem. The next year, 1852, on his thirtieth birthday, he married Mariah Elizabeth Jennings. The house he built for her, the birthplace of William Jennings Bryan, is now maintained by the city of Salem as a museum.

The roots of the Jennings family can be traced to thirteenth-century England. They intermingle with the Brewsters, who crossed on the *Mayflower,* and with the progenitors of Charles Gates Dawes. There was a John Jennings in America as early as 1659, but the first Jennings about whom much is known is Israel Jennings, born about 1784. He married Mary Waters and in 1819 moved from Maysville, Kentucky, to a farm two miles west of Walnut Hill, Illinois. The third of their eight children, Charles Wayland Jennings, in 1826 married Maria Wood Davidson, of Scottish descent. The fourth of their ten children was named Mariah Elizabeth. By the time of her birth, Israel Jennings had amassed land in Marion County and had served several terms in the General Assembly. It was possibly with his aid that Silas Bryan won election to the state senate soon after he married Mariah.[1]

---

[1] The family trees of the Bryan and Jennings families are traced from the Bryan Family Bible and the manuscript, "Bryan Genealogy," in the Mrs. Thomas Stinson Allen Papers; William Jennings Bryan and Mary Baird Bryan, *The Memoirs of William Jennings Bryan,* pp. 18–21; W. A. Crozier (ed.), *Virginia County Records,* I, 12, 18, 85; Mary J. Seymour, *Lineage Book. National Society of the Daughters of the American Revolution,* VII, 263; XII, 341; XIX, 1; XXI, 321; Charles W. Bryan, Jr., "Morgan Bryan, Pioneer on the Opequon and Yadkin," *The Virginia Magazine of History and Biography,* 70 (April 1962), 154–164.

Mariah, born in 1834, had been one of Silas's pupils at the Walnut Hill school. He was tall, thin, prematurely bald, and twelve years her senior. She was tall and straight, with brown hair and gray eyes, a prominent nose, and high cheekbones. She could not be called beautiful, but Silas saw that she had attributes that would make her a good wife—modesty, simplicity in dress, capacity for household management, particular devotion to the church, and a family of some political influence.

During his eight years in the state senate Silas Bryan saw the crystallization of the issues which provoked the Civil War, the splitting of the Democracy, the death of the Whig party, and the birth of the Republican. He was in contact in Springfield with Lyman Trumbull, who had examined him for the bar, and with Stephen A. Douglas and Abraham Lincoln. In the exciting elections of 1853 and 1859 he naturally supported Douglas, the Democrat, rather than Lincoln for United States senator. In 1860, when the Republicans captured Illinois, he was retired. However, back in "Egypt," [2] safe Democratic country, he won election as a circuit judge and, without giving up his private practice, began a judicial career that lasted twelve years.

Broad and tolerant in most matters, the Judge was occasionally argumentative or hard-headed. A trial lawyer of recognized ability, he believed his decisions, once blessed by prayer, to be immutable. He prayed three times a day, unobtrusively if in the public eye, and he also prayed before opening his court. He was addicted to quoting the Scriptures to juries and in heaping extravagant praise upon the virtues of his clients. In his farewell address to his last grand jury he asserted that he had not grown rich from the spoils of office. That he had of the world's goods "a reasonable competency" was the result not of holding office but of "rigid economy, long and patient professional labor, and the sweat of the face in agricultural pursuits. . . ." He was convinced "that the more we conform our lives and actions, both in private and public relations, to the demands of honor, truth, sincerity, justice, and Christianity, the greater will be our happiness and prosperity, and the better we shall enjoy this present world, and the broader will be the foundations for the enjoyment of the world to come." [3]

Silas added his lawyer's fees to his income from the bench and at the

[2] The earliest Virginia, Kentucky, and Tennessee people who moved into southern Illinois called the area "Egypt" because of the scarcity of food therein during their first years.

[3] Bryan, *Memoirs*, p. 242.

age of forty-four years he bought a five-hundred-acre farm about a mile northwest of Salem. There he built the mansion that served for years as a showplace of Marion County and engaged in the farming he loved so well. He kept a deer park, too, until he was attacked by a buck.

The first two Bryan children, a boy and a girl, had sickened and died within two weeks of each other. In his scrawling hand Silas wrote in the family Bible that he felt he could never be reconciled to his loss, that he was so despondent that he felt he would soon be with them. In 1858 Frances was born, and in 1860, William Jennings. Silas wished to name the boy William; Mariah wanted to call him Jennings. They agreed on William Jennings. Later came Russell Jones, Charles Wayland, Nancy Lillard and, in 1872, Mary Elizabeth.

II

BELIEVING that the home was more potent than the school in the formation of moral values, Mariah taught her children until they were ten years old, when they entered the public schools. William Jennings never forgot how he would recite lessons from a speller, a McGuffey reader, and a geography text, to his mother, the most receptive, appreciative, and enthusiastic audience he ever had.[4] In the public school, perhaps because of his home training, he received his best grades in deportment rather than academics, and in the first two years of high school he did better in the work of the literary and debating societies than in his regular courses. He confessed that he was studious less because he loved learning than because of the "coercive power" of his parents, who were quite stern. He commented later that he sometimes considered that he should have been given greater liberties, and his playmates said that the Judge brought his boys up under closer rules than their own fathers did. Instead of candy or toys the Judge gave his children catechisms and saw to it that they memorized them.[5]

Judge Bryan farmed about half of his acres and rented out the rest. He grew corn and wheat, raised cattle, poultry, and vegetables, and taught his children agriculture by making them practice it. Being the oldest son, William Jennings pulled the "laboring oar." By the time he was fourteen years old he was rated a farm hand, as able as any man to handle a plow or, on horseback, to round up cattle. He later ad-

[4] *Ibid.*, pp. 40–41; see Henry Steele Commager, *The American Mind: An Interpretation of American Thought and Character Since the 1880's*, pp. 33–40.

[5] Interview with H. T. Sweney, Salem, Illinois, June 7, 1947.

mitted that the songs he sang in Sunday School lacked the words needed
to describe his feelings when, in winter, with nose running and fingers
numbed with cold, he had to build the fires in the house, feed and
water the stock, and milk the cows. Yet he believed his years on the
farm invaluable: they taught him industry and obedience, gave him
physical strength to endure fatigue and resist illness, and provided
wholesome sport and amusement. Life was hard, simple, and energetic.
The Bryans were upright, conscientious, and somewhat conventional;
infrequently colorful or charming, they were always moral and religious. The Judge might call himself a commoner and often speak of
the "laboring and toiling masses," yet by the time he retired from the
bench in 1872 he was as close to being an aristocrat as rural conditions
permitted. Few families in Salem owned five hundred acres unencumbered, hired Negro servants, used silver at table, and had a piano
in the parlor.

Judge Bryan reached the peak of his career when William Jennings
was in his most impressionable years, and he inculcated in him the
religious, political, and ethical principles that made William a replica
of himself. William's earliest ambitions were to be a farmer, lawyer,
and preacher. In 1900, when he was forty years of age, he bought a farm
and kept in intimate contact with the soil, although like his father the
major source of his income was derived from nonagricultural pursuits.
Again like his father, William became a lawyer, albeit he practiced law
much less than did the Judge. Both mother and father taught him to
obey them and to fear God. From them he learned that he must follow
the dictates of the Bible in his temporal as well as in his spiritual life.
The prayers the Judge conducted before the family altar became one of
William's "sweetest recollections." The Judge was a faithful member
of the church and spoke often on religious questions. William, too, became an avid reader and propounder of the Bible and one of the greatest lay leaders of his day.

William followed his parents in devotion to Protestant evangelistic
religion. No theologians, they valued the Bible as the inspired source
for salvation and also as a perpetual font for wisdom concerning ethical
conduct. The Protestant evangelistic religion—the gospel service, the
revival, the emphasis upon missions, and the appeal to the heart rather
than to the mind in soul-winning—amply sufficed for them, their community, and the Middle West. They used the Bible and McGuffey to
teach their children the character-forming values of the church, home,
and school; the importance of truth, love, obedience, work, and thrift;

and the dangers involved in drinking, gambling, dancing, swearing, idleness, and dishonesty. The morality the parents implanted in William made an everlasting impression and hardened as the years went by. He never smoked, gambled, danced, or swore, and he began signing the temperance pledge before he knew what temperance meant. When about thirteen years old he was hired to help with a threshing. He carried water to the men but refused to bring them whisky.

Characteristic of the charity and love in Silas's heart was his providing for the less fortunate members of his family. Under his spacious roof he brought two sisters, a niece, and grandmother Jennings. After his own marriage, William Jennings provided a home for his in-laws until they died and made separate arrangements for the care of his own mother.

Until he was twelve William attended a Methodist Sunday School in the morning with his mother and a Baptist one in the afternoon with his father, but he was unaware of denominational differences between his parents. Then Mariah became a Baptist and as stanch an advocate of Baptist doctrine as Silas, now a deacon of his church. These were still years of occasional violent religious emotionalism, and William and his elder sister made it a practice to attend revival meetings. While in a Presbyterian church they were converted, and they became members. The Judge offered no objections. Although conversion can transform one's life, it caused no change in William's. Perhaps because he already felt that he was "saved," he said nothing about his "being saved." Moreover, as he put it, "Having been brought up in a Christian home, conversion did not mean a change in my habits of life or habits of thought. I do not know of a virtue that came into my life as a result of my joining the church, because all the virtues had been taught me by my parents." [6] Not until he was on his deathbed did the Judge tell Mariah that he was disappointed that William had not joined the Baptist church.

The Judge told William that the two classes of men who contributed most to good government and righteous living were a nation's statesmen and its divines, and William agreed. He credited his father with a "definite influence" in the shaping of his political as well as his religious views, and he was so positive that his father was correct that he said shortly before his own death that he saw no reason for deviating

[6] Bryan, *Memoirs*, p. 44. For Bryan as a child of the Middle Border, see Commager, *American Mind*, pp. 165–170, and Paul W. Glad, *The Trumpet Soundeth: William Jennings Bryan and His Democracy, 1896–1912*, pp. 1–20.

from his teachings. His memory erred, however, in one important respect. While the Judge followed Jefferson in claiming that "Too much government in republics is the rock upon which they founder," he was primarily a Jacksonian. Except for schools and libraries, state subsidies for public improvements did not fit in with his tenets of individualism. Capital should seek its own investment, he declared, and the halt and the lame should be succored by the benevolence of fellow men, not by government. Here William differed, for he would use government not only to control forces inimical to the general well-being, like monopoly, but also as a positive agent in improving the welfare of the farming and laboring classes.[7]

When he retired from the bench, in 1872, the Judge ran for Congress. It was a stirring campaign, with the Liberal Republicans challenging the conservatism of Grantism, and cries of "fusion" and "bolting" filled the air. Despite both Democratic and Greenback support, Silas lost to a Republican. This was his last campaign. "What's the use of pounding on the log after the coon's gone?" he asked, as he frequently did when referring to a closed case.[8] There is a story to the effect that William delivered a speech in his behalf and that the excellence of the speech stilled the laughter aroused by William's appearance. The incident may be dismissed as apocryphal, but the campaign provoked enthusiasm unusual in a boy his age and stimulated his interest in public life as a career. The fact that his father had Greenback as well as Democratic support was never lost upon him, and he dreamed of being a United States senator and played the part of a Democratic senator in his high school forensic activities.

The physical powers, capacity for speaking, personal habits, choice of vocation, political tenets, religious beliefs, and ethics of William Jennings Bryan thus derived in great part from his parents, particularly

---

[7] Silas Bryan was elected a member of the Illinois constitutional convention of 1870 and played a creditable part in its proceedings. Among his resolutions were those that provided for the establishment of public libraries; that all offices—legislative, executive, and judicial—should be filled by popular election; and that the new constitution should be offered to the people for ratification one section at a time. *Debates and Proceedings of the Constitutional Convention of the State of Illinois, Convened at the City of Springfield, December 13, 1869* (Springfield, 1870), I, 83, 134–145, 310–312, 545–546; Silas Bryan, *The Compensation of Public Officers Should Be Regulated By Constitutional Provision* (7 pp., n.d., n.p.), Mrs. Thomas Stinson Allen Papers.

[8] J. T. Dorris, "Hon. Thomas E. Merritt," *Journal of the Illinois State Historical Society*, 11 (April 1918–January 1919), 503.

from his father.[9] The determination with which he performed what he considered his duty, the devotion with which he sought to implement his purposes, and the self-righteousness which he exhibited upon many occasions came to him by inheritance. And the philosophy of life which he attained by the time he left home for college remained remarkably unchanged for the rest of his life. By 1874, when he had completed his second year of high school, he had grown into a strong, fairly serious student who merited further education. With his head full of politics, fortified with a protecting insulation of fundamentalism, and armed with his church letter of transfer, he prepared to meet the "mind worshipers" at Whipple Academy, the preparatory school for Illinois College. Whether he would be a minister or a lawyer-politician was a decision he still had to make.

[9] Paolo E. Coletta, "Silas Bryan of Salem," *ibid.*, 42 (March 1949), 57–79.

CHAPTER 2

College Days

I

THE DEPRESSION beginning in 1873 sadly depleted the income from the Bryan farm, but Judge Bryan was determined to keep a promise he had made to himself to obtain the best education available for his six children. His dream of sending William to an Eastern college and then to Oxford having dissolved because of financial stringency, he accepted the offer of a cousin, Dr. Hiram Jones, to look after William as long as he attended Whipple Academy and Illinois College. Thereupon William went to Jacksonville, Illinois, and enrolled at the academy as a "middler," that is, one who had finished only two years of high school. His instructors at first saw nothing to differentiate him from other students, mostly farm boys from the surrounding area. Bryan's geology teacher, Dr. Henry E. Storrs, is best remembered for saying later in his life that it was not he who taught Bryan that man descended from a monkey.[1]

The change from home to academy and college life was made easy for Bryan by Dr. and Mrs. Jones. Jones practiced medicine but also offered courses in the college in medicine and philosophy. Among his friends were Bronson Alcott, Ralph Waldo Emerson, and William T. Harris, and in his home Bryan heard much about Plato, Hegel, and evolution, the last then a hotly debated issue. There is no evidence that Dr. Jones's philosophical beliefs influenced Bryan in any way; in fact they were wholly incompatible with fundamentalism.[2] He acted as a foster father to Bryan while Mrs. Jones, whom Bryan called Cousin Lizzie, furnished him with comforts and helped him with his school work.

[1] George R. Poage, "College Career of William Jennings Bryan," *Mississippi Valley Historical Review*, 15 (September 1928), 168, 173. See also, for descriptions of Illinois College in Bryan's day, Charles H. Rammelkamp, *Illinois College: A Centennial History, 1829–1929*, and Julian M. Sturtevant, Jr. (ed.), *Julian Monson Sturtevant: An Autobiography* (New York, 1896).

[2] Paul Russell Anderson, "Hiram K. Jones and Philosophy at Jacksonville," *Journal of the Illinois State Historical Society*, 33 (March–December 1940), 478–520.

Disturbed by what he learned in his courses in physics and chemistry, Bryan postponed joining a church and wrote to the great agnostic, Robert Ingersoll, for his views on God and immortality. Ingersoll replied, in substance, "I don't know." Bryan wondered how anyone could deny the heart a living faith and substitute for it a despairing "I don't know." [3] Finally, when his instructors resolved his doubts, he took his letter to the Presbyterian church.

At Illinois College itself Bryan studied a classical curriculum little changed since the Judge's days in college, and he enjoyed the religious environment provided by a Protestant denominational school. His favorite subject until he became a senior was mathematics, for he believed that it led to accuracy in thinking and clarity of vocal expression. He also valued his three years of Latin and four of Greek for their training in etymology and diction rather than for themselves. In the English Department, in addition to the regular courses in composition and literature, he took exercises in declamation, oratory, and logic. As a senior his favorite courses were American history, economics, and moral philosophy. In George Bancroft's *History of the United States*, which taught that the nation had reached the acme of perfection during the administrations of Andrew Jackson, he found democracy defined as "the voice of God 'as it breathes through the people,' " and he became convinced, in the words of Bancroft, that "democracy is practical Christianity." In Alexis de Tocqueville's *Democracy in America* he learned about the principle of equality that theoretically underlies the democratic state, that political liberty can work only in the context of relative economic equality, and that "privilege" is an ever constant danger to democracy. Tocqueville may have stimulated his desire to study law and to choose the jury system as the topic for his senior thesis in law school.

In later life Bryan claimed that from his course in economics he learned the arguments he used in opposing the protective tariff and in proposing bimetallism. In the former case he was correct, for Julian Monson Sturtevant, who wrote the text used in class, was an avowed free trader,[4] but he strongly opposed governmental interference with the currency system. Bryan was simply mistaken when he said Sturtevant favored bimetallism, for he thoroughly denounced the attempts

---

[3] William Jennings Bryan, "The Prince of Peace," *The Speeches of William Jennings Bryan*, II, 282.

[4] Julian M. Sturtevant, *Economics, or the Science of Wealth*, pp. 114–128, 135–144, 236–237, 306–308.

being made, even as he wrote his book, to remonetize silver, and he would permit its use only as subsidiary coinage.[5]

A much greater influence upon Bryan than Sturtevant was Wendell Phillips, who spoke on the campus on "The Lost Arts" and stimulated him to read his other speeches. Phillips thought the "money power" a menace to republican government, confessing "that the only fear I have in regard to Republican institutions is whether, in our day, any adequate remedy will be found for this incoming flood of the power of incorporated wealth." Into a notebook Bryan copied a paragraph from Phillips's "A Voice the People Know":

> When slavery was abolished . . . it was settled that the capitalist should no longer own the laborer. . . . This is a step in the Ages, a revolution deeper than that which was sealed at Appomattox. It began when Congress declared all men equal: it will never end till it is settled that the people are the source of all power and safely to be trusted with its exercise over every interest. . . .[6]

These sentiments fitted in well with Bryan's own beliefs; these were words such as he used later in his campaigns for "Equal rights for all, special privileges to none."

During his senior year, when he specialized in the social sciences, Bryan made a brilliant showing. Grades were based on 10, with 8 as passing. The class average for the eleven seniors ranged from a low of 8.01 to Bryan's 8.93. He ranked fourth highest in German; third in Greek, Latin, science, and mathematics; second in English; and an unrivaled first in social studies. "Bryan is the acknowledged hero of his class, he having made one hundred in Moral Philosophy," reported the *Illinois College Rambler,* the school paper. He also received 10 in Tocqueville, and he was selected as the valedictorian of the class of 1881.[7]

Not a profound scholar, Bryan won his grades by persistent applica-

[5] "It is a mischievous delusion for government to enact that debts may be paid in silver dollars, each worth only ninety cents. The experience of the civilized world will still make gold money, though our laws may drive it from circulation; and our exchanges with the human race must, in spite of our senseless and tyrannical legislation, be adjusted in the money of the rest of the world," meaning gold, wrote Sturtevant. *Ibid.,* p. 72. See Joseph Dorfman, *The Economic Mind in American Civilization,* III, 50–63, 73–74.

[6] Most of Bryan's college notebooks are in the William Jennings Bryan Papers.

[7] Courses offered during Bryan's period of attendance are listed in the *Illinois College Catalog* for 1875–1880; his grades are found in *Illinois College Student Records, 1853–1888,* at the college.

tion and industry. He had a retentive memory, was conscientious in the use of time, and thorough in preparations.[8] The average student at college drew three or four books from the library in four years. In six years Bryan borrowed eighteen, mostly fiction, especially novels by Dickens, which may have impressed him with the effects of the Industrial Revolution upon the working class. But he also had Dr. Jones's magnificent library at his fingertips. Of course he credited God rather than himself for his success, saying, "I have not felt much like rejoicing as I have of expressing my gratitude to God, 'for surely goodness and mercy have followed me all the days of my life.' " He concluded that he had been "extraordinarily fortunate" during his years in Jacksonville: "I came unknown, without prestige or the influence of a well known name and have been lifted up (I use the passive voice because I can not believe it has been all my work) until I have been successively recognized as the best in the class in declamation, essay, oratory, and . . . in general standing in studies." [9] Moreover, he had been active on as many as seven school committees at a time. His sweetheart, Mary Elizabeth Baird, noted the "tired, tired face of L[ittle] B[oy] with his eyes all heavy and bloodshot." She chided gently: "You said you would rather wear out than rust out. That's all right, but why not let the wearing be a gradual one?" [10] But to wear out gradually was not the Bryan way.

II

THE STIMULI to which Bryan reacted most forcibly while at Whipple Academy and at Illinois College were the prizes offered for excellence in public speaking. Prizes were given for different classes at the exhibitions which took place each spring—orations for juniors and seniors, essays for sophomores, and declamations for freshmen and for the middlers of Whipple. Besides these school contests there were those of the two literary societies, Phi Alpha and Sigma Pi, in each of which keen competition abounded. Every student had to join a society; Bryan was voted into the older, Sigma Pi.

Sigma Pi's quarters, on the second floor of Beecher Hall, have changed

---

[8] *Illinois College Rambler,* March 5, 1881; Poage, "College Career of William Jennings Bryan," p. 179; Julian S. Wadsworth, "William Jennings Bryan, '81—College Days," *Illinois College Alumni Quarterly,* 15 (1939), 11.

[9] Letter to Mary Baird, April 17, 1881, Mrs. Ruth Bryan Rohde Papers.

[10] Letter of May 3, 1881, *ibid.*

little since Bryan's day. As in a legislature, the chairs are arranged in a semicircle facing the president's desk; between them and the desk is the "well" in which the speakers hold forth. The president wields the gavel. To one side sits the secretary, who writes in the *Minute Book* the names of the speakers and their topics and occasionally comments upon the speakers' abilities and notes the winners of debates. The speeches themselves are not recorded. On the other side a "critic" sits before an unabridged dictionary.[11]

Soon after he joined Sigma Pi it was recorded that Bryan did "himself and the society good."[12] As a tribute he was given a place as a declaimer on the program of the society's open meeting, to which the student body, faculty, and public, including the young ladies of the town's several female academies, were invited. In the Whipple Academy declamation contest he delivered that portion of Patrick Henry's "Give Me Liberty or Give Me Death" speech called "There Is No Peace." The judges rated him near the bottom of the list of speakers, for he was as yet unaccomplished. Yet he was determined to succeed. He had to be prepared on two weeks' notice to discuss such timely topics as "Should the United States Adopt Free Trade?" "Should the State Control the Liquor Traffic by Legislation?" "Should Indian Territory be Thrown Open to White Settlement?" and "Does Foreign Immigration Presage the Overthrow of American Institutions?"[13] He worked on these questions seriously, plumbing them to the depths of which he was capable. He found Sigma Pi an invaluable school in which to practice parliamentary procedure, and like so many of his contemporaries, including Champ Clark, George W. Norris, Mark Sullivan, and Albert J. Beveridge, he held literary societies indispensable in fostering a spirit of progress in politics and interest in responsible citizenship. Sigma Pi permitted him to expound and defend conclusions he had already reached—taxes were too high; monopolies, especially the railroads, should be regulated in the interest of the people; mortgage, tariff, and railroad rates should be reduced; middlemen should be eliminated or forced to lower their charges; there should be an increased amount of money in circulation. His complaints were those of his father; of other farmers who took part in the Granger movement, which engulfed Salem and Jacksonville in its path through the West and South between 1873 and 1876; and of those organized in the Illinois Farmers' Mutual

[11] Visit by the writer to Illinois College, June 1947.
[12] Sigma Pi *Minute Book*, January 14, 1876.
[13] *Ibid.*, 1876–1878, *passim*.

Benefit Association or in the national Greenback movement. Fusion tickets, with which he was already familiar from his father's congressional campaign of 1872, won many Illinois county contests in the mid-seventies, and the money question was the leading issue of the state and congressional campaigns of 1874 and 1875 and the basic plank in the platform of the new Greenback party in 1876.[14] Enough interest in Greenbackism was generated in Jacksonville to cause the formation of a Greenback Club, while at college a twenty-five dollar prize for the best senior essay on "The Currency Question" sent aspirants scurrying to the library heretofore shunned.

Bryan debated the greenback, specie resumption, and national bank questions in Sigma Pi. He debated against the abolition of the national banking system, but he did so merely for effect, for he always preferred the negative side in debate, and later in life he made the abolition of the system a major part of his credo. Sigma Pi also debated "That Paper Money Is the Currency Best Adapted to the Needs of the Country," but Bryan's task that evening was to read an essay, and the tenor of the debate may be judged from the facetious remark of the secretary —"We then decided that hard money was best adapted to our wants, which no doubt will have marvellous influence on those controlling such affairs." [15]

There is no evidence that Bryan possessed a deeper insight into cures for the farmer's ills than his classmates did, but there is ample proof that he was genuinely interested in how political parties proposed to solve them. It was during his years at Sigma Pi, years of depression, that he learned to hold the "money power," represented by the national banks of the East, responsible for the hard times following 1873; and in 1876, when just sixteen years of age, he was interested enough to attend the Democratic national convention in St. Louis—with admission to the hall gained by climbing in through a window.

Upon his return to college in September 1876, Bryan found Sigma Pi in ferment over the forthcoming election. Then, as the Electoral Commission investigated, the Sigma Pi's debated "That Our Government Has Cause to Fear the Unsubdued Spirit of the South." By Feb-

[14] Solon J. Buck, "Agricultural Organization in Illinois, 1870–1880," *Journal of the Illinois State Historical Society*, 3 (April 1910–January 1912), 10–23, and *The Agrarian Crusade*, pp. 47–59; Allan Nevins, *The Emergence of Modern America, 1865–1878*, pp. 169–175; Charles Edward Russell, *Bare Hands and Stone Walls: Some Recollections of a Side-Line Reformer*, pp. 237–255.

[15] Sigma Pi *Minute Book*, November 23, 1877.

ruary 1877 attention had shifted to other matters, and Bryan debated the affirmative of "Resolved, That the United States Government Should Abolish All Protective Duties." The secretary recorded that "Bryan, in the course of the debate, brought down the house by saying, 'The President of the College is for Free Trade, our ex-president is for free trade, and I, myself, am for F.T.' " [16] Few ever "brought down the house" at Sigma Pi.

To his father William appeared a prodigal spender and poor book-keeper. The Judge's eyes were failing him, but he could still see that William was consuming the value of a steer every two months just for incidentals, "a very large advance over the forty three cents spent on my first session of college life." [17] In 1878 he wrote, "We have our corn gathered—crop light and cheap. The complaint of hard times is still pressing on us. . . . Money is much harder to get than formerly— prices have gone down on all commodities." [18] When William returned home for the summer he was as tall as the Judge but not yet possessed of his wit. The Judge weighed 154 pounds and William, 150. "I shall soon be as heavy as you are," said William. "When you have four more pounds of brains we will weigh the same," replied the Judge.[19]

All of Bryan's work in Sigma Pi and at the school forensic activities was undertaken with the goal of class orator in mind. He even took a private course in elocution from an itinerant teacher, who found him determined and zealous but lacking the graces of a good orator. For six years, too, the vision of representing the college in an inter-state oratorical contest spurred him on. As a freshman he worked his way up from the bottom to first place in declamation. Characteristi-cally, he chose as prize an Oxford Bible with Concordance instead of cash. He shared second prize for Latin prose as a sophomore. In por-traying the sufferings of the workers during the railroad strike of 1877 he "moved us all to tears," according to the secretary of Sigma Pi. He gained a reputation with his first oration, "Master Motives," which he delivered on March 5, 1880. With "Individual Powers," given at the spring exhibition, he won first prize and earned the right to represent the college in the interstate contest that fall. He came out second, but as the local hero he made all the arrangements for the interstate

[16] *Ibid.*, February 16, 1877.
[17] See Bryan's *Memorandum Book*, Bryan Papers.
[18] Letters of November 11 and November 25, 1878, Rohde Papers.
[19] William Jennings Bryan and Mary Baird Bryan, *The Memoirs of William Jennings Bryan*, pp. 55, 56.

contest held in Jacksonville in 1881. At graduation, with his mother, his brother Russell, and Mary Baird in the audience, Bryan delivered first the class oration, on "Character," and then the valedictory, in which he "launched all upon the uncertain seas of life."

Meantime Bryan had begun active work in politics. Although not yet old enough to vote in 1880 he helped organize the Hancock Club of Salem during his summer vacation, delivered his first prepared political address, and stumped two counties in behalf of William M. Springer, congressional incumbent from the old Thirteenth District who had studied law under Judge Bryan. His Salem speech, which began with "If ye have tears prepare to shed them now" and ended with "give me liberty or give me death," was too long. When he asked his mother, who heard him, what she thought of it, she replied with wit worthy of the Judge, "Well there were a few good places in it—where you might have stopped!" [20] In a speech in the college chapel in January 1881 he revealed himself a partisan beyond all doubt and made his first known reference to Thomas Jefferson. He told the Republicans that "we can well afford to wait until the Republican party finds its death by suicide." As a Democrat, he added, he supported Jefferson's faith in the rule of the people, a dislike of "one man power," the superiority of civil over military authority, the separation of church and state, a close following of the Constitution, equality before the law, liberty for individual conduct, and intellectual and moral development as the only safeguard against corruption. "The Democrats may have been slaughtered, but like the oxen of the sun, which the companions of Ulysses butchered, the hides crawl after their tormentors," he concluded.[21]

Bryan's success in academics, oratory, and stumping did not extend to his winning of high office in either the student organization or Sigma Pi. He was elected vice president of the freshman class but to no other student office. In Sigma Pi he filled the offices of sergeant-at-arms, chaplain, critic, and vice president. He was also president for five weeks, and by custom should have been re-elected for a similar period, but the wheel of factionalism which had already overturned two elections because of fraudulent ballots whirled him out. It has been suggested that the movement to supplant him was fomented by

[20] Interview with Mrs. Thomas Stinson Allen, Lincoln, Nebraska, July 11, 1948.
[21] "A Defense of Democracy," Bryan Papers, Bryan Museum, Salem, Illinois.

thousand people and Jacksonville fewer than ten thousand, and the staples of his life had been the farmers' problems, the church, and politics. He had no first-hand experience with labor as labor, industry as industry, or finance as finance. His views of democracy were derivative rather than the result of philosophical speculation; yet his speeches and orations show that even at this time, like Jefferson, he opposed not capitalism but such excrescences as corporate power and monopoly, especially the "money power," as well as bossism in politics. Government, he believed, should be controlled by the "producing class," the immense majority that actually applied labor and capital to natural resources to produce wealth, rather than by the few who profited from law-created privilege.

A return to Jefferson's principles had been demanded by such party leaders as Horatio Seymour and Samuel Tilden during Reconstruction days, but Jefferson's name disappeared from the Democracy's national platforms written in the generation before 1892.[29] To his chapel speech of January 1881, which included the major planks of the national Democratic platform of 1880, Bryan added his support of Jefferson's faith in the people to govern themselves. He had already determined, then, that Jefferson would be his political god. Since his entire life had centered about the farmer and his problems, it was logical that he should follow Jefferson and make a defense of agriculture as the most dignified, virtuous, healthful, and important occupation a major weapon in his political armory. Like Jefferson, too, he believed that American society should remain simple, homogeneous, and rural rather than industrial, urban, and stratified along class lines; and that the rights of minorities were best protected by a strict interpretation of the Constitution which would leave the states sovereign in local matters. He thus failed to take into account the fact that the clash of arms in the Civil War had doomed the agrarianism he and Jefferson championed and that the new, industrialized, complex society demanded positive leadership rather than the mere negation of forces apparently irresistible. He was already a partisan Democrat and, although a patriotic nationalist, also a defender of sectional causes. A firm believer in progress by peaceful means, he nevertheless proved rigid rather than pragmatic, and thus appeared to be a conservative because unwilling to compromise.

To a classmate who confided that he felt a call to enter the ministry

[29] Merrill D. Peterson, *The Jefferson Image in the American Mind*, p. 251.

Bryan in turn revealed that he too had felt God calling him, not to the ministry but to a calling no less sacred—that of being a Christian statesman. The two codes Bryan had chosen to direct this future, then, were the spiritual and ethical concepts of the Bible and the political principles of Thomas Jefferson.

CHAPTER 3

Love and the Law

I

IN THE fall of 1879, when he was nineteen years old, Bryan entered his junior year at Illinois College and Mary Elizabeth Baird, aged eighteen years, enrolled at the Jacksonville Female Academy. It was at an "open house" at the "Jail for Angels," as the academy was called, that Bryan first saw Mary. Her features were clear-cut but gently molded into an oval-shaped face. She had full, curved lips, large gray-brown eyes, curly brown hair, lightness of movement, and a ready laugh, but a searching expression revealed that there was an intellect behind her attractive appearance.

Mary's charm proved irresistible to Bryan, but she was not immediately taken with him. He was tall enough, but his face was pale and thin; his brows were heavy, his nose too prominent, and his hair was parted "distressingly straight." On the other hand, his dark eyes were keen, his hair fine in quality, and his thin-lipped mouth and square-cut chin revealed determination. He was neat but not fastidious, carried himself with dignity, and had an expansive and expressive smile.[1]

Bryan's resourcefulness in circumventing academy regulations for callers proved prodigious. When Mary's mother stayed at a local sanitarium during the winter of 1879–1880, he called upon her at the same time that Mary did. In violation of rules, he took Mary for rides in a buggy he rented. Then, after Mrs. Baird returned to her home, he induced the wife of the president of the college to invite Mary to her home for an evening, when he too would call. Several other women fell in with similar requests, with the result that the courtship flourished amidst a merry conspiracy.[2]

[1] William Jennings Bryan and Mary Baird Bryan, *The Memoirs of William Jennings Bryan,* p. 222.
[2] Interviews with Miss Carrie Dunlap and Mrs. Julian S. Wadsworth, Jacksonville, June 28, 1947; Bryan to Mary Baird, March 9, 27, May 2, 4, 12, 1880 and Mary Baird to Bryan, May 11, 1880, Mrs. Ruth Bryan Rohde Papers.

At the end of May 1880, with their meetings discovered by the academy authorities and punishment pending, Bryan and Mary concluded that they cared more for each other than they had suspected. When the principal, E. F. Bullard, declared that the "dignity of the school" would be upheld if she returned home immediately, before the end of the term, but that she could return in the fall rather than be expelled, she submitted graciously. Bullard escorted her to the train and waited until it pulled out. Meantime Bryan was coming forward from the baggage car in which he had hidden. He sat beside her and they exchanged rings, but when he insisted upon going home with her to ask for consent to their engagement she balked: she made him get off at the next stop and return to Jacksonville—she would handle her parents herself! [3]

Mollified by Mary's explanation of her honorable relations with Bryan, by a letter in which Bullard referred to the "thoughtless" rather than "evil" mistake made, and by a letter of apology from Bryan, John Baird concluded that a "sad mistake" had been made but that Bryan was not a "fast young man." Summertime courtship nevertheless proceeded by letter, for Bryan worked on the home farm while Mary took up "domestic science" at her home in Perry.

When school reopened in the fall, Bullard permitted the exchange of letters once a week. In October, when Bryan won fifty dollars for placing second in the interstate oratorical contest, he bought a ring, a garnet set in gold, and had a dedication cut inside the band, "Will to Mamie, June 4th, 1880." The date was that of their exchange of rings on the train. He was expected at her home for the Thanksgiving holidays, at which time he would ask for her hand. "Hope you will not be frightened though I imagine it would be a rather disagreeable task. Being a girl has a few advantages after all. However, you ask J.[ohn] B.[aird] for it, and if he fails to arrange matters satisfactorily there is a party concerned who *can* and will manage him." [4] Mary was a very practical girl.

When Bryan approached Mr. Baird, he almost unconsciously turned to the Scriptures. "Mr. Baird," he said, "I have been reading Proverbs a good deal lately and find that Solomon says that 'Who findeth a wife findeth a good thing and obtaineth favor of the Lord.'" "Yes, I believe Solomon did say that," replied Mr. Baird, no mean student

[3] E. F. Bullard to Bryan, May 22, 24, 1880 and Mary Baird to Bryan, May 25, 1880, Rohde Papers.

[4] Mary to Bryan, October 17, 24, 1880, *ibid.*

of the Bible, "yet Paul suggests that 'he that giveth her in marriage doeth well; but he that giveth her not in marriage doeth better.'" Bryan was stumped for a moment. Then with a flash of inspiration he countered: "Solomon would be the best authority upon this point because Paul was never married while Solomon had a number of wives." [5] Baird took an instant liking to Bryan and approved of the engagement.

Mary now worried about what Bryan's mother, who would be at his graduation, would think of her. "I tell you if I stood in her shoes I would just hate the girl who dared fall in love with my prize, 'the staff of my declining years.' I won't blame her if she tried to make us quarrel and separate. Am afraid it would be rather difficult task." [6] Although Mariah found no objection to Mary as a person, she thought William should become self-supporting before getting married. Since his mother had never "been in his fix" he did not think she knew how many "almighty dollars" he needed, but when Mary suggested they could get married and keep separate accounts he replied with an emphatic "No!" No woman could love a man if she performed her domestic duties and also paid for her support. *He* would earn the money. He looked forward to the time when they could be together "all the time . . . not many years hence." [7]

II

In the spring of 1881, with his father dead less than a year and the estate saddled with debt, Bryan was uncertain whether or not he could attend law school. In March 1880 the ailing Judge had gone to see Dr. Jones in Jacksonville. On the morning of March 29 Jones had found him unconscious from a paralytic stroke. William kept vigil until death came in the afternoon of March 30, a few minutes after Mariah arrived from Salem. On the next day mother and son accompanied the body to Salem. Articles in memoriam appeared in the local press for months afterwards as unsolicited testimonials to a man who, in an age when politics and dishonesty were practically synonymous, had passed his life in politics and remained honest.

Except for fifteen hundred dollars, a horse and buggy, and the piano, which he gave to his "blessed wife," Silas left the rest of his estate to

[5] Mrs. Ruth Bryan Rohde to the author, October 14, 1948.
[6] Mary to Bryan, May 22, 1881, Rohde Papers.
[7] Bryan to Mary, March 27, April 3, 1881, *ibid.*

his children, share and share alike, any rent or proceeds from the sale of land to be applied to their education. But friends for whom he had signed security notes totaling fifteen thousand dollars had defaulted, and he willed that the notes be paid. By following his injunction his heirs deprived themselves of almost all the material substance he left except the farm.

At a family conference after the Judge's funeral it was decided that William should return to college and that an attempt would be made to send him to law school. If Russell Bryan entered college, however, William must stay at home. The death of Russell in August 1880 made it possible for William to go on to law school. A cousin had attended and highly recommended Union Law College in Chicago. It was decided that William would go to Union Law.

Union Law College, then associated with the old Chicago University, later became the law department of Northwestern University. In Bryan's day it offered a two-year course at least as good as the average [8] and so arranged that students could work in a law office part of each day, a boon for Bryan because his mother could pay the tuition but he had to earn his keep. As soon as he found an inexpensive room —he walked the four miles to school to save the five-cent trolley fare— he called upon Judge Lyman Trumbull, who had admitted his father to the bar, and asked him for a job. Trumbull hired him, and for five dollars a week Bryan swept floors, filled inkwells, copied and filed, and read law.

As at Illinois College Bryan took an active part in school politics, in debating, in the church, and in the Y.M.C.A. He was elected president of the junior class and also class orator. Among other topics, he debated the prohibition question, woman suffrage, and the tariff, arguing in the last instance that internal revenue taxes should be taken off all articles of domestic manufacture except tobacco and liquor, a position which followed that of the Democratic tariff reformers in

[8] In 1881 the school had five men on its faculty and forty-three students. The junior year included a study of the *Commentaries* of Blackstone and of Kent, Gould's *Pleadings*, Cooley's *Torts*, and Washburne's *Criminal Law*. During the senior year, in addition to texts—Chitty's *Pleadings*, Bishop's *Equity*, Washburne's *Real Property*, Story's *Equity*, and Cooley's *Constitutional Limitations*—lectures were given on medical jurisprudence, patents, criminal law, and on statutes and practice in the United States courts. Moot courts were held on Saturday mornings. *Circular of the Union College of Law for the Year 1883–1884* (Chicago, 1883); Arthur Herbert Wilde, *Northwestern University, A History, 1855–1905* (4 vols., New York, 1905), IV, 29–54.

Congress. He led the negative side on the question that England's interference in Egypt's affairs was warranted (after bombarding Alexandria and occupying Cairo, England took control of Egypt in November 1882), but he argued in the negative only for the sake of argument, for he intensely disliked England's imperialistic foreign policy. "However much we admire England's power in war or her eminence in peace I can not but feel that her foreign policy is mercenary, tyrannical and iniquitous in the extreme and a disgrace to her boasted civilization," he wrote Mary Baird.[9]

In his graduation oration, "Eternal Vigilance Is the Price of Safety," Bryan revealed concern with current political affairs. He followed Andrew Jackson, who had stated that "You must remember . . . that eternal vigilance by the people is the price of liberty; and that you must pay the price if you wish to secure the blessing." Bryan noted that corruption in the suffrage and in the administration of justice was rife in Chicago. Although he disliked Carter Harrison, mayor since 1879 and dictator of the Cook County Democracy, he was such a partisan that he wrote Mary that "it will take more than fusion between corruption and ignorance to defeat the Democratic party, the embodiment of intelligence and honesty." [10] His letters to Mary made it amply clear that he was unfavorably impressed with big city life and with the position of industrial labor. He noted that small business was giving way to big business, that giant corporations already existed in coal, steel, railroads, and oil, and that the day of the monopolistic trust was at hand. He believed that a few persons were enriching themselves at the expense of the masses, that the men who worked in factories, packing houses, and railroad yards were creating wealth for others to enjoy. They certainly lacked the sense of independence relished by the farmers of Salem and Jacksonville, and he believed that those who worked in George Pullman's shops, which he visited, were ready to rebel against poor conditions of labor and low standards of pay. They did so a few years later. He also pointedly noted that most of the Robber Barons were Republicans.[11]

Bryan's belief in the need for reform was strengthened by Lyman Trumbull. Trumbull had helped push the Thirteenth Amendment through the Senate and had introduced the Freedman's Bureau and

[9] Letters of November 30, 1881 and January 14, 1883, Rohde Papers.

[10] Letter, June 8, 1882, *ibid.*

[11] Letters of October 9, November 30, 1881, February 26, 1882, and January 28, February 11, and April 4, 1883, *ibid.*

Civil Rights bills. He told Bryan to speak out against injustice, whether racial, political, or economic, and Bryan freely admitted that he had a decided influence upon his subsequent career.[12] At Union Law, too, Bryan was known to have a burning interest in problems of government, and upon some of his classmates at least he impressed the thought that the evils attending the encroachment of wealth upon the rights of the commonwealth spelled trouble for the country.

As at college, Bryan won high grades as a result of persistent and diligent application. Beyond the general principles of law, which he found to be moral principles, he did not care to go, for law would be merely the means to the ends that he might marry and engage in politics.

Strenuous undertakings and a miserly existence during most of his two years in Chicago caused Bryan to be ill for extended periods, and once he had to leave school for a short time. Only when he returned to the farm for the summer did he really feel well. A great deal of his trouble stemmed from his attempting too much, and a worried Mary wrote him that "I will measure your love for me by the time you take for rest and recreation." [13] Bryan received five dollars a week from Trumbull and earned a dollar or two a week by making debt collections, but he allowed himself only four dollars a week for both room and board during the first year. Moreover, he had extremely bad eating habits. It was not unusual for him to eat fried pigs' feet for breakfast, corned beef and parsnips or veal cutlets and buckwheat cakes for lunch or dinner, and pie or pastry for "tea" in the afternoon. And at all times his appetite for radishes, which he liked best with butter, remained insatiable.

Soon after the beginning of his second year Mariah wrote that the defaulted notes were being taken up and that she would soon be square with the world. Meantime he had spent part of the summer of 1882 seeking a place in which to practice. He visited Troy, Missouri; it was too small. He fled Kansas City because it was too big and the saloons were running full blast. Then he went to Jacksonville and had a long talk with Dr. Jones. By Christmas time Jones had placed him with one of the city's prominent firms, Kirby, Brown, and Russell. He could have joined two cousins to form the firm of Bryan, Jennings, and Bryan in Salem, as his mother wished, but he preferred Jacksonville.

[12] Willis J. Abbot, "William Jennings Bryan—A Character Sketch," *American Review of Reviews*, 14 (August 1896), 164.

[13] Letter, October 4, 1882, Rohde Papers.

"It is best you should go where you can do best," she declared patiently, and in the same breath promised him a thousand dollars as a wedding present. Once he was earning five hundred dollars a year, he replied, he would make the wedding bells ring.

During his second year in Chicago Bryan wrote Mary that he had but two ambitions in life, professional success and marriage. He also prayed that "I may develop powers that exert a great influence for good." He did not desire wealth as such, for "Success is the greatest perverter of virtue," but as soon as he earned enough to provide for her they would marry.[14] She, meantime, continued her studies in housekeeping. She had her troubles. "You would laugh to see me tugging away," she wrote. "I now milk indiscriminately—sometimes the stream hits Pa, sometimes the cow's legs occasionally goes [sic] in the bucket. Pa says my object is to remove the milk—saving it is of no consequence." Yet she was earnest about learning domestic science, writing Bryan that "I am practical enough to see that repeated avowals of affection would not hold your devotion as effectually as a neat, tidy, house and well cooked food." [15]

Bryan's insistence upon becoming self-supporting was only one reason that postponed marriage. Another was the rivalry for Mary on the part of her mother, a psychoneurotic whose complaints of real or imagined ills increased as the time of Mary's marriage approached. Any criticism by Bryan, however, provoked great loyalty from Mary and the response that she willingly undertook to care for her mother, although she confessed that she found the going pretty tough. ". . . there's no use talking about it for it only makes the tears chase each other down my nose till I can hardly write, and doesn't do any good either," she wrote Bryan, who wondered often if Mrs. Baird would ever give Mary up.

III

Because he liked to do important things on important days, Bryan arrived in Jacksonville on July 4, 1883, shortly after acquiring admission to the bar. On July 5 he nailed his shingle to the entranceway, hauled a battered rolltop desk up to the offices of Kirby, Brown, and Russell, and put it just inside the door, where all could see him when they entered—as impressive as a man of twenty-three in a full beard

[14] Letters of January 15 and October 22, 1882, and February 11, 1883, *ibid.*
[15] Letter, November 8, 1882, *ibid.*

could look. He would have starved in quiet dignity had he not had ability to sell himself, a winsome smile, a hearty handshake, and a name easily converted to "O'Brien." He needed a stroke of luck, which he would perceive as God's favor, but for weeks clients of the firm passed him on the way to the inner offices, and he despaired about his prospects. "Don't be discouraged in your work, dearie. Father and I were talking about you . . . and he said you were going 'through the narrows' and would have it pretty hard for a while," but they both thought he would "come out all right," Mary wrote him.[16] Finally a barkeeper who had a cousin who was a lawyer asked Bryan to collect a debt. The barkeeper had been an odd-job man Bryan had befriended at the Jones's, and he now saw the return of bread cast upon the waters. He collected the note, and when the debtor remained a customer the barkeeper noted that Bryan could collect debts "without making a man mad" and sent him more business. Bryan's first work, at 20 per cent commission, netted him exactly fifty-two cents, and his first month brought him $9.60.[17]

Bryan acted as an insurance agent, collected rents, sold real estate and books on commission, and kept Dr. Jones's accounts, but he had to draw upon his share of the family estate during the first six months in Jacksonville. Not until Robert D. Russell left the firm to establish an independent practice in Minneapolis did the first ray of hope pierce the gloom. "I think the outlook encouraging but am not prepared to set the day. Wish I could," he wrote Mary about Christmas time. Then, early in 1884, Russell turned his office and the firm's collections over to him and engaged him to sell his property. His income for January through April averaged $50, and June and July brought more than $100 each. He thus had promise of more than he thought necessary to support a family, but sometimes his commissions proved small. Once he sent a bill for collection to a St. Louis lawyer: "Please collect the same if possible and receive as your fee ⅔ of 10 per cent. The fee will not be much for either of us, but we younger legal lights must take anything that comes."[18] And sometimes he could not resist sermonizing. In reply to a debtor who liked his liquor he wrote: "One would imagine from the language of your letter that the saving up of 'whiskey money' was the sole object for which you live. I hope the future has a fortune in store for you, but let me warn you not to spend it for

[16] Letter, July 11, 1883, *ibid.*

[17] Bryan, *Memoirs*, pp. 63–64.

[18] Bryan to Charles W. Holtcamp, March 10, 1884, William Jennings Bryan Papers.

drink: be virtuous, be sober, and be honest and when a lawyer at the request of a client reminds you of a debt don't make an ass out of yourself." [19]

During the summer Bryan gave an oration on "The American Citizen" and thus met the sole requirement for obtaining a master's degree from Illinois College. Then, after a visit to his mother, he returned to Jacksonville with a promise of an advance from his share of the estate, hired an architect, and contracted for the building of a house. He was $750 short, but Dr. Jones took a mortgage. A quirk of fate also made it possible for him to attend the Democratic national convention. He had accepted an invitation to speak on July 4 on condition that only his expenses, about three dollars, be paid. His host pushed a twenty-dollar bill into his hand and Chicago hove into view, for he had a railroad pass and the twenty dollars would pay for a cheap room and enough food to keep him alive. He expressed no preference for a presidential candidate and shouted loudly with the rest when Grover Cleveland was chosen. On October 1, five years after he and Mary had met originally, and four years after their engagement, their marriage took place.

The wedding ceremony was performed in the Baird home before a small group. John Baird was at his amiable best. As expected, Mrs. Baird felt ill and cried. Nevertheless, the wedding went off smoothly, with Bryan slipping onto Mary's finger a ring inscribed with a motto representing the date of their engagement and of their wedding, "Won, 1880—One, 1884." After stowing their letters in a trunk in the Baird attic [20] and exchanging tearful farewells, the newlyweds went to Jacksonville, where they remained overnight at a hotel, then to Salem, where Mariah Bryan gave them a gala reception, and then to St. Louis on a combined honeymoon and shopping trip. Then, because the house was incomplete, Mary proceeded to Perry and Bryan to Jacksonville, where he helped organize clubs and took his turn on the stump. He was attracted to Cleveland because he represented the young Democracy, was unidentified with the old, Civil War issues, and demanded reform in taxation and administration. Into his speeches he adroitly injected references to his being a lawyer. Keenly aware of the

[19] Bryan to W. D. Leadrut, May 31, 1884, *ibid.*

[20] Almost two years earlier Mary had written: "I don't see, dearie, how I can bear to have your letters destroyed after we are married—hadn't we better put them in a little trunk and put them in the attic?" The letters were made available to the author by Mrs. Ruth Bryan Rohde.

value of publicity, he also prepared accounts of his speeches in which he referred to himself as "a promising young lawyer" or as one "likely to go far in the political world" and had them published in the local newspapers. With the election over, Mary decided that she belonged at her husband's side rather than at her father's and went to Jacksonville, where friends put them up until the house was completed. Finally, late in November, the Bryans were "at home."

IV

NOW BRYAN was spurred to great efforts to earn money, for by the end of the year he knew that there would be three mouths to feed instead of two and there was the mortgage to be paid. He applied for the post of Assistant District Attorney for the Southern District of Illinois and was certified as a United States Commissioner. "United States Commissioner" looked good on his new stationery, but fees proved few. Yet he increased his income from $700 in 1884 to $1000 in 1885 and to more than $1500 in 1886, mostly from collection cases.

Once settled in their new home, with the Bairds in a suite of their own, the Bryans decided to undertake only "worthwhile" projects. Mary took an evening course in German at the college and also began to study the same course of law he had taken. The birth of Ruth Baird Bryan on October 2, 1885 only temporarily halted her studies. William participated in almost all the civic organizations of the city. He was chosen president of the Y.M.C.A. and, early in 1887, Chancellor Commander of the Knights of Pythias. No alumnus proved more faithful in Sigma Pi as teacher, speaker, and manager. In season he played baseball on the Morgan County Bar Association team. He attended the monthly meetings of Dr. Jones's philosophical discussion group, the American Académé, and was on duty at the polls on election day and regular in his attendance, with Mary now, at Sunday School, church, and temperance meetings.

The Bryans lived conventional, frugal, and modest lives of bourgeois respectability. They were clean, honest, and hard working, but at the rate he was going he could never earn enough to retire from the law and engage wholly in politics. Yet it is not quite right to say that he spent several clientless years in Jacksonville and then moved because the competition was too keen. In three years he had made a respectable beginning. He admitted, however, that he had overestimated the impression his college career had made upon the people and that his

choice of Jacksonville was a mistake. The city was then and remains
Republican—he had no political future there. Therefore he wanted
to move. He wrote Russell about joining him in Minneapolis but
received no encouragement. He journeyed to Springfield to support
his application for the post of Assistant District Attorney, to no avail.
He applied for highly paid positions in Washington without success.
Finally he decided to leave Kirby and Brown and set up his own
office. He was ready to move in when he talked with Richard Yates, a
college classmate, about a partnership. Yates was city attorney. Well,
said Bryan, he would run against him; win or lose the city attorney
would be with the firm. Yates agreed that the firm would be called
Bryan and Yates, but Bryan's insistence upon the larger share of the
fees—he was earning more than Yates at the time—proved unacceptable and the partnership failed to materialize.[21]

Then occurred a combination of those little incidents that Bryan
felt played such a large part in his life. He was called upon to make
a collection trip to Kansas City for the college, and his father-in-law
wanted him to check on some landholdings in Iowa. Bryan decided to
go via Lincoln, Nebraska, where he would visit his Union Law classmate, Adolphus Talbot. He was so impressed with the possibilities
of Lincoln that he began a removal campaign upon his return. Lincoln
was four times larger than Jacksonville and the capital of a rapidly
growing state. Illinois was comparatively static, Nebraska a frontier
state offering real opportunities. Times were piping; one could earn
10 per cent and more on one's money. Moreover, Lincoln was a college
center whose social and intellectual life paralleled that of Jacksonville.
Finally, Talbot had offered him a partnership.

Were political considerations involved in his move? None, he said,
absolutely none! Ward, city, county, congressional district, and state
were all Republican. "Every argument that impressed me was professional. No thought of politics ever entered my mind." [22] In fact,
he told Mary that the move would end his dream of a political career.
Nebraska was steadfastly Republican, he was a confirmed Democrat,
and neither could be expected to change. Mary said she would go
if he thought the change would be for the better; the Bairds said
they would fit themselves into his plans whatever they might be. Be-

[21] Bryan, *Memoirs*, pp. 72–73; Richard Yates, "Address at the Jacksonville Centennial, October 6, 1925," *Journal of the Illinois State Historical Society*, 18 (October
1925–July 1926), 594.

[22] Bryan, *Memoirs*, p. 74.

lieving that Lincoln could be no worse than Jacksonville and could be
a great deal better, Bryan left in time to arrive in Lincoln on October
1, his third wedding anniversary—another important move on another
important day.[23]

[23] *Ibid.,* pp. 74–75.

CHAPTER 4

The Morning Star of the Reformation

I

ADOLPHUS TALBOT was a Republican, but Bryan felt fortunate in having him as a partner. Following his predilection for the negative, Bryan tried to think as the opposition would while Talbot outlined the positive arguments to be made at court. At the end of each month the one with the greater income gave the other half of the larger amount. Talbot was an attorney for the Missouri Pacific, but Bryan refused to work for railroad corporations and the railroad income was excluded from the accounts. However, as he had in Illinois, Bryan violated consistency and accepted a railroad pass.

Bryan appeared in each of the hierarchy of local and state courts and practiced all branches of law. Of the nine state supreme court cases the firm handled between 1888 and 1891, six involved political disputes, and it was in these that Bryan appeared at his best. Contemporaries like Charles Gates Dawes believed him to be a good jury lawyer who could have built up a successful practice as a pleader.[1]

Once more, as in Jacksonville, Bryan went through the narrows. He tried to avoid the collection business by requesting attorneys from outlying districts to engage him as their Lincoln agent. A few did, but their business also involved mostly collections and tax foreclosures. His income increased year after year, from $800 in 1888 to $2000 in 1890, even though he gave much more of his time to politics than to law. To those who said he was a failure at the bar, Mrs. Bryan retorted that they "should consider that he entered the practice at twenty-three and left it at thirty, and during that period began twice, and twice became more than self-supporting."[2] In Jacksonville Bryan had gotten nowhere politically in four years; in Nebraska he was elected

[1] Charles G. Dawes to the author, September 28, 1948; interview with W. H. Selleck, Lincoln, Nebraska, July 7, 1948.

[2] Bryan Memorandum Book, William Jennings Bryan Papers; William Jennings Bryan, *The First Battle*, p. 48.

33

to Congress at the end of three years, and by 1895 his success in politics warranted giving up his practice.

Bryan soon learned that the political history of Nebraska was distressingly similar to that of Illinois. The Burlington and the Northwestern railroads ruled north of the Platte, the Union Pacific to the south. From the beginning of statehood, in 1867, except for one congressman, the Republican party had won every state and national office. Although the Democrats were split, the situation did not seem hopeless to Bryan because the major problems of Nebraska were the very ones which had beset him and his father in Illinois and which he had debated in college and in two presidential and four congressional campaigns—the tariff, prohibition, railroad regulation, and the currency question. What the Granger and Greenback movements were to Illinois the Farmers' Alliances were to Nebraska, and he felt well prepared to discuss needed reforms.

Bryan carried letters of introduction to J. Sterling Morton and Jefferson H. Broady, the latter a popular Lincoln attorney, and he knew the editor of the Omaha *Daily Herald*. Learning of preparations being made for a tariff reform campaign in 1888, he wrote Morton in November 1887 that "Your efforts in behalf of a reduction of the tariff have made your name well known in Illinois" and expressed his desire to meet him in person.[3] By May 1888 he was corresponding on intimate terms with Morton, who told him that what was needed was enlightenment "as to the diabolism of tariff taxation." This "diabolism" Bryan stood ready to prove.

In his early years, Morton, who led the "slaughterhouse" Democrats against the "packinghouse" Democrats, had published the Nebraska City *News* and begun the agricultural and arboricultural work which obtained him worldwide renown as the founder of Arbor Day. A steadfast defender of the Democracy, he had been nominated for governor three times, in 1880, 1882, and 1884. A conservative, he rarely went beyond his party in demanding reforms; a railroad lobbyist, he nevertheless joined Bryan in denouncing subsidies of any kind and agreed with Bryan in opposing sumptuary legislation.

The "packinghouse" or "administration" Democrats were led by Dr. George L. Miller, a prominent western member of the Tilden machine who had the ear of Daniel Manning in Cleveland's cabinet and of James E. Boyd, the Democratic national committeeman, and thus

---

[3] Letter, November 15, 1887, J. Sterling Morton Papers.

had much to say in regard to patronage, but he was a Randall-type protectionist. Morton was a man of principle who could not reward him, Miller a neo-Republican who could. Bryan hitched his star to Morton.

In his very first speech in Lincoln Bryan likened the tariff to a cow fed by Western farmers and milked by Eastern manufacturers. Within six months he was speaking outside of Lincoln. Within a year Morton noted in his Journal that "Bryan . . . is a remarkably promising young man. He has gifts. He will be, with good habits and right directions, a benefactor to good government." [4] Bryan gained additional recognition in the Lancaster County Democratic convention of April 1888, in which he supported Morton as delegate-at-large to the national convention. Morton won over Boyd and Bryan himself was elected a representative to the state convention to follow. There he gave a "spirited address" on the tariff in which he declared that victory could be won if Cleveland's tariff message of December 1887 were made the basis of a vigorous campaign among Nebraska's farmers. According to all reports, the delegates "went wild," [5] and the state central committee invited him to stump the state for Cleveland and tariff reform.[6]

Upon his return from Jacksonville in the spring of 1888 with his family, Bryan stopped at Nebraska City and finally met Morton. "He came, we liked him. Pleasant day," Morton recorded in his journal.[7] Leaving his family with the Bairds in a new house built with money furnished by Mr. Baird, later repaid with interest, Bryan attended the Democratic national convention held in St. Louis. He was pleased with the renomination of Cleveland and supported him and tariff reform in a stumping tour of Nebraska that covered twenty-four counties. Speaking often for two hours at a stretch, he placed his facts "in a clear and forcible way, dispensing with the usual stump oratory, but illuminating his address by apt stories and bright quotations." [8] At a Saturday night rally, after Morton had already spoken for an hour and a half, he answered demands for additional "entertainment" with a speech in

[4] Arbor Lodge Journal, Morton Papers.
[5] Omaha *Daily Herald*, May 2, 3, 1888.
[6] Euclid Martin to Bryan, September 26, 1888, Bryan Papers.
[7] Entry of May 30, 1888.
[8] Omaha *Daily Herald*, August 15, 1888. The speech was delivered on July 20 but was not reported until August 15, evidence that Bryan wrote up his experiences on the road and handed them to the press upon his return from tour.

which he so "captivated his hearers that they hung upon his words for over an hour and when [he] wished to stop they would not have it so." [9] Soon he was rated the equal of any Nebraska Republican orator. Morton took an almost paternal interest in him and pushed him forward, and Democrats from all parts of the state demanded to hear him. "I wish you would go," said Morton, referring to a particular meeting. "It will do you and tariff reform good." [10]

Bryan's evocative rhetoric captivated audiences wherever he went. He was called "Bryan the Invincible." Upon his return from a short absence, a man named Thomas Colfer heard that the Democrats had become enthralled with a new man. "I am delighted with the laudations given by every one I met, even Republicans," he wrote Bryan after hearing him speak. "By your personal magnetism you won all hearts and by the force of your Eloquence and the irresistible character of your logic you *vanquished* the Enemy." [11] No man had risen so high in Democratic estimation as rapidly as had Bryan. Audiences "fairly exploded" when he spoke, particularly when he showed how the protective tariff entailed the "robbery" of the farmer.[12] The new "darling of the Democrats," he was liked, and often loved, because he spoke in words his hearers understood and addressed men as equals, not as their superior. He appeared the embodiment of honesty and sincerity, of undying faith in the righteousness of his causes. Demanding nothing for himself, he freely gave of his talents in order to improve the lot of the dirt farmer, the underdog in the national economy. Above all, he was capable of articulating and giving emotional impact to the sentiments of those who lacked words to express themselves.

In the fall of 1888 Bryan learned that he had exceptional power over an audience. While in Chadron on legal business he spoke at a rally. His torrential swirl of words quickly stilled the noisy crowd; soon even much older men nodded approval at what he said. He held them enthralled for two hours with tariff talk, and when he finished they barely let him go in time to catch his train. Upon reaching home at daybreak he awakened his wife and told her about the effect of his speech. "Mary," he said, "I have had a strange experience. Last night I found I had power over the audience. I could move them as I chose. I have

[9] Omaha *World-Herald*, August 6, 1888.

[10] Letter of August 10, 1888, Morton Papers.

[11] Thomas Colfer to Bryan, October 8, 1888, Bryan Papers.

[12] Omaha *World-Herald*, August 25, 1888.

more than unusual power as a speaker. I know it." Then he bowed his head and prayed, "God grant I may use it wisely." [13]

At the state convention of 1888 Bryan declined nominations for lieutenant governor and attorney general, saying that he could not afford a campaign and that he would be defeated if he ran. A state office did not really appeal to him, and he would bide his time until bigger game came into view.[14]

After Morton was nominated for Congress for the third time, Bryan spoke in his support in twenty-five counties. Many Republicans confessed that he shed light on darkness and that they would now "cast their votes . . . for their interest instead of being guided by partisan blindness." [15] Evidently not enough light was shed on tariff reform, for both Morton and Cleveland were defeated. "I don't regret it," said Cleveland. "It is better to be defeated battling for an honest principle than to win by cowardly subterfuge." [16] Bryan wrote Cleveland that "we would rather fall with you fighting on and for a principal [sic] than to succeed with the party representing nothing but an organized appetite. Your position was so wisely and bravely taken that I believe the party will look back to you in after years with gratitude and not with reproach." If he would move to Nebraska and run in 1892, suggested Bryan, he could be elected. "As a Western man with friends you have in the East, we can elect you. Why not come to Omaha or Lincoln?" [17] No evidence exists that Cleveland replied. At any rate, Bryan gained a statewide reputation for his efforts of 1888. He had been mentioned for state offices and was also backed by Morton for a post on the state railroad commission as "a representative of the cleanest and most advanced economic thought in the party," but the Republicans naturally rejected him in favor of their own man.[18]

During the two years between important elections Bryan returned to his practice, prepared for the next congressional campaign, and with Mary devoted himself to the social, intellectual, and religious life of

[13] Interview with J. C. Dahlman by Jesse F. Boell, reported in Boell, "The Career of William Jennings Bryan to 1896" (unpublished M.A. thesis, University of Nebraska, 1929), p. 49; William Jennings Bryan and Mary Baird Bryan, *The Memoirs of William Jennings Bryan,* pp. 248–249; Fred Carey, *Mayor Jim: The Life of James C. Dahlman,* pp. 57–60.

[14] Omaha *World-Herald,* August 26, 30, 1888.

[15] *Ibid.,* October 5, 1888.

[16] Allan Nevins, *Grover Cleveland: A Study in Courage,* p. 439.

[17] *Ibid.,* p. 440.

[18] Omaha *World-Herald,* January 11, 1889; Lincoln *Daily Call,* April 1, 1889.

Lincoln. Soon after William Jennings Bryan, Jr. was born, on June 24, 1889, Bryan directed several Democratic friends and Talbot in organizing the Round Table Club. When other Republicans like Dawes and Dr. J. H. Canfield, chancellor of the University of Nebraska, were admitted, the club became nonpartisan. One evening, when the group met at his home, Dawes informally served doughnuts and sweet cider. At the next meeting "light refreshments" were served, and within two years the meetings began with a banquet and ended with oratory.[19] Meantime Mary joined Mrs. Andrew J. Sawyer, wife of Lincoln's mayor, 1886–1887, in founding the Lincoln Sorosis, the feminine counterpart of the Round Table Club. Both clubs provided a type of lyceum of civic worth and may have proved of political value to the Bryans although they were not so designed. Moreover, after two and a half years of study Mary Bryan passed the bar examination. She had studied law, she explained sweetly, simply in order to be able to help her husband in his work.[20]

In the Bryan circle at the time were John J. Pershing, commandant of the cadet corps at the university; Dawes, who hung his shingle in the Burr Block simultaneously with Bryan; and William E. "Pussyfoot" Johnson, lifelong temperance worker. On slack days the three would visit and talk, usually in Bryan's office and usually on the tariff. The Bryans and the Daweses became intimate. The Bryans, sporting a one-horse surrey, would take the Daweses riding, and the Daweses were one of the couples invited by the Bryans on the occasion of their fifth wedding anniversary, when they renewed their marriage vows. While there was no political rivalry between Bryan and Dawes, Dawes won the only jury case Bryan lost in Lincoln.[21]

In 1889 Bryan was invited to help determine party policy. Morton was writing the tariff, prohibition, and pension planks for the state convention, but he thought that Bryan, in the capital, could "best assault state abuses," and he asked him to write a plank against all special legislation.[22] Bryan agreed with Morton that a protective tariff was detrimental to an agricultural state, but he objected to Morton's plank on prohibition. They both opposed prohibition, but because the

[19] Mrs. Thomas S. Allen, Scrapbook; *Nebraska State Journal*, December 30, 1906; Charles G. Dawes, *A Journal of the McKinley Years, 1893–1913*, pp. 6, 10–11, 17, 19, 27.

[20] Thomas S. Allen to Mrs. Ruth Bryan Rohde, February 16, 1944, Mrs. Ruth Bryan Rohde Papers.

[21] Charles G. Dawes to the author, September 28, 1948.

[22] Morton to Bryan, October 11, 1889, Bryan Papers.

Republicans took no stand on the issue Bryan thought that a mere declaration against sumptuary legislation would suffice.[23] Yet he did not agree with various influential Democrats who wanted to say nothing at all. As finally written, the plank favored a well-regulated high-license system. Press reports of the convention spoke highly of the "glowing speech" Bryan made for his favored candidates, and he may have warmed himself with hope as he walked through a chilling rain to vote, but the returns showed that although the Democrats had carried Douglas County, which contained Omaha, the Republicans had won the rest of the state.

II

BRYAN's beginnings in Western politics coincided with the Populist revolt. Kansas, the Dakotas, and Nebraska specialized in corn and wheat, the price for which, fixed in the world market, had fallen steadily since the beginning of the depression of 1873. Nebraska corn which sold for 63 cents a bushel in 1881 sold for 26 cents in 1890; wheat which sold for $1.19 in 1881 sold for 49 cents in 1890; land which sold for $7 and $8 an acre in 1870 and for $25 or $30 an acre at the peak of the end-of-the-frontier land boom now sold for $5 or less. About 40 per cent of the farms of Wisconsin, Michigan, Minnesota, Iowa, and Nebraska were encumbered with mortgages representing values inflated by the land boom, and as Bryan knew as a lawyer, annual farm foreclosures in Nebraska alone ran into the thousands. When it proved cheaper to burn corn than coal as fuel and to kill hogs rather than feed them, the sod-house farmer either "busted" and turned eastward or did the best he could and asked for governmental intervention in his behalf.

The disappearance of the frontier promised the dominance of an industrial economy, but Bryan refused to admit this fact. The Western farmer was in a sad plight, he believed, because he had expressed confidence in the future. He had borrowed in order to establish a farm and extend civilization onto the Great Plains. In seeking to keep his farm he also protected the agrarian way of life. He had worked hard and long. Then the weather had turned against him, with little rain and much cattle-killing snow falling for several years. The decline in land values and the fall in the price of corn and wheat had not been

---

[23] Bryan to Morton, October 11, 1889, in Victor Rosewater, "Life and Times of Edward Rosewater" (Mss., Nebraska State Historical Society, n.d.), pp. 171–172.

matched by compensatory reductions in mortgage debt, interest payments, railroad rates, or taxes.

Bryan found more culprits in the East than in the West to blame for the Western farmers' predicament. In the East were the owners of the railroads, the manufacturers of the industrial products needed by the farmer, and the banks and money-lending institutions that were now foreclosing on Western farms. There was Washington, where laws such as those on the tariff were made to protect industry but not the farmer, whose laws sanctioned banking and currency practices that favored the manufacturer and left the farmer with insufficient currency and inadequate sources of farm credit. No wonder that the ancient Greenback song that had once thrilled Illinois possessed new charm, this time telling of the benefits obtainable through an increased supply of money per capita and free silver, for the Western farmer suffered from a crushing burden of debt that could be relieved only by a more equitable distribution of the national wealth. An agrarian himself, Bryan wished to retain a simple agricultural society as the ultimate source of social values. To do so he must break the economic and political control which the East held over the West and South, and keep the Mississippi Valley, as Walt Whitman put it, "the real genuine America." He fully sympathized with the psychology of the Western farmer, who believed that

> There are ninety and nine who live and die
> In want, hunger, and cold,
> That one may live in luxury,
> And be wrapped in silken folds;
> The ninety and nine in hovels bare,
> The one in a palace with riches rare.[24]

Bryan's reform program was so similar to that of the Populists that he has often been mistaken for a Populist, but he remained a stanch Democrat throughout the Populist period. He was not above joining forces, however, to advance his own political fortunes. He appeared a socialist to some and a visionary to others because he prophesied the income tax, the direct election of senators, and governmental control of railroads, corporations, banking, and currency. Conservatives opposed him because he sought to revitalize the Democracy by the admission of progressive ideologies and to make it a vital reform agency.

---

[24] Quoted in Frieda C. Kuester, "The Farmers' Alliance in Nebraska" (unpublished M.A. thesis, University of Nebraska, 1927), p. 63.

By so doing he became one of the fathers of the Progressive movement which swept the nation during the first two decades of the twentieth century and earned being called "the embodied spirit of Jefferson," [25] "the Jefferson of the new dispensation," [26] "the last great democratic liberal of the school of Jefferson," [27] and simply "the last Jeffersonian." [28] Arthur F. Mullen once said that he set out to break the combination of plutocrats and politicians who throttled the proletariat and that he and his followers came as near doing it as any reformers between the French and the Russian revolutions.[29]

A Jeffersonian in policies and principles, Bryan was nevertheless a Jacksonian in temper and tactics. With characteristic bias he said that "The Democratic party has always claimed to represent the mass of the people. The Republican party has long since ceased to do so. It stands nearer to the corporations and to the special interests than the Democratic party could ever get if it wished to, and when we desert the cause of the people we have nowhere to go but to the grave." [30] As if to emphasize his point, in 1890 the Republicans named a railroad man for governor and renominated for the First Congressional District its incumbent, a tariff protectionist named William J. Connell.

Hoping to obtain the balance of power, the Alliancemen organized the People's Independent Party on July 29, 1890 and went far beyond the older parties in their demands for relief from economic distress. The leading contender for the nomination from the First Congressional District was Charles H. Van Wyck, former state and national senator. Bryan might beat Connell, but could he beat the candidate of a reform party who was himself an experienced reformer?

In February 1890 the Democratic state managers told Bryan that he could have the nomination in the First District. Bryan accepted conditionally. If he were the choice of both the Democratic and Independent parties he would be elected; if not, a three-cornered race would result in Republican victory. He believed that he could gain by a kindly disposition toward the Independents and secretly scouted the prospects of their naming him through Constantine J. Smyth, of Omaha, who negotiated with Joseph A. Edgerton, a leading Nebraska

[25] Merrill D. Peterson, *The Jefferson Image in the American Mind*, p. 260.
[26] Samuel Eliot Morison and Henry Steele Commager, *The Growth of the American Republic*, II, 240.
[27] Charles M. Wiltse, *The Jeffersonian Tradition in American Democracy*, p. 235.
[28] Peterson, *Jefferson Image*, p. 260.
[29] Arthur Mullen, *Western Democrat*, p. 63.
[30] Bryan to A. B. Farquar, October 3, 1891, Bryan Papers.

Independent. As soon as Bryan's nomination by the Democrats appeared probable, Smyth would inform Edgerton because, as Smyth told Bryan, he would not want to accept the Independent nomination until certain of the Democratic, and it so happened that the Independent preceded the Democratic convention by one day. Smyth also told Bryan that he would be opposed by such Democratic conservatives as George L. Miller, Andrew J. Sawyer, and Albert Watkins.[31]

Bryan's leading Democratic opponent was Charles W. Brown of Omaha. When Bryan appeared to have the edge because he was favored by the Democratic progressives, was not too closely identified with either of the old Democratic factions, and commanded the larger popular following in Omaha, Brown wrote Bryan that he did not want the nomination and that he would help Bryan obtain it.[32]

In the preamble of his platform Bryan reaffirmed his faith in Democratic principles and invited all those who believed in "free citizens, just laws, and economical government" to support his standard. He arraigned the Republicans for the "reckless extravagance" of the Fifty-first Congress and for their tyrannical rule and efforts to retain supremacy by fraud and force. Four planks dealt with the tariff and five with other economic questions. He condemned subsidies and bounties, favored liberal pensions, demanded that trusts be prevented and suppressed, and that Congress prohibit the holding of land by nonresidents. Also, "We demand the free coinage of silver on equal terms with gold, and denounce the efforts of Wall Street as against the rights of the people." Four additional planks concerned changes in governmental processes. The first demanded the direct election of senators; the second denounced caucus dictation; the third castigated the federal election bill; and the last denounced the Reed rules of the House.[33] He stressed the tariff more and the money question less than did the Independents, and did not second their demand for the government ownership of railroads and telegraphs. Otherwise his platform appealed as greatly to Independents as to Democrats.

It has been said that Bryan never changed his views as expressed in this platform, but he did refine his interpretation of some of them. In the light of subsequent events the plank most subject to misinterpretation is that on silver. In 1890 Bryan thought that the exactions of the

[31] Letter, Smyth to Bryan, July 25, 1890, *ibid.*
[32] Letter, July 8, 1890, *ibid.*
[33] Typed copy of the platform, *ibid.*

Eastern money lenders, high railroad, warehouse, and elevator charges, and a banking system of little value as a source of credit to farmers were the primary factors which, added to low agricultural prices and an appreciating currency, accounted for the West's burden of debt. The inability of debtors to free themselves, he thought, was due mostly to the appreciation in the value of money. He was working hard to maintain a family and pay off a mortgage and he felt this appreciation keenly, for like his farm neighbors he had to pay back more than he originally borrowed and interest payments further decreased his purchasing power. But in this first known statement on silver he demanded only "equality" for gold and silver because he did not know exactly how "free" silver should be. Since Connell favored silver, they would not debate it. Most important, the people of his district wanted silver, and he wanted what they did. He would look up the arguments later! Not until late 1891, after a year of study, did he decide upon the ratio of 16 to 1.

After his platform was adopted unanimously, Bryan received a majority of 86 votes on the first ballot, with 73 votes scattering among four opponents. Switches changed the vote to 137 to 23, and his nomination was made unanimous. He was ready, he told the delegates, "to meet in joint debate, in every county in my district, the champion of high taxes, whoever he may be, and I shall go forth to the conflict as David went to meet the giant of the Philistines, not relying upon my own strength but trusting to the righteousness of my cause." [34]

Many letters of congratulations contained advice. "Speak everywhere —kiss all the babies—you can do it—you have mouth enough for both," said one.[35] Another hoped that "among the sturdy bullrushes of Democratic faith a Moses had been discovered to lead the chosen people out of their bondage to trusts, tariff abuses, and irrational taxation." [36] The most interesting letter came from an Illinoisan who had recently left Lincoln:

In the great tidal wave we can hear approaching . . . I hope Nebraska will also wheel into line. . . .

I believe it to be her interest to shake off the enormous burdens she has hitherto carried, and which have adhered to her as closely as the fabled "Old Man of the Sea." It appears to me that the dawn is approaching and

[34] Omaha *Bee,* July 31, 1890; Lincoln *Herald,* August 2, 1890.
[35] Edward L. McDonald to Bryan, August 5, 1890, Bryan Papers.
[36] Eli H. Doud to Bryan, July 31, 1890, *ibid.*

that you are the morning star of the reformation which is moving fast upon your State.[37]

III

IN LATER LIFE Bryan said that he entered politics by accident and remained by design. He was nominated for Congress because no one thought it possible for a Democrat to win, but he had not deemed his fight altogether hopeless. The major objections to his candidacy were his youth—he was only thirty years of age—and the shortness of his residence in Nebraska. But the largest cities of the state, Lincoln and Omaha, lay in his district and should return large Democratic majorities.[38] He was campaigning on a platform which denounced every sort of special privilege and which should attract the downtrodden. In an agricultural state like Nebraska, moreover, tariff reform should have great appeal. Bryan delivered more than eighty tariff speeches in this campaign in addition to attacking the trusts and the money power. The Democratic and Independent press gave him good coverage, and reports of his efforts spread into the states of both the Mississippi and the Ohio valleys.

In the Democratic state convention in August Bryan renewed his challenge to debate any Republican and thundered that the mass of the Republicans were as earnest in seeking tariff reform as the Democrats: "They have deluded themselves with the belief that the Republican party was only flirting with organized wealth, but the marriage between the grand old party and monopoly has been consummated, and 'what God has joined together let no man put asunder.' " [39] The major issue of the convention, the liquor question, was settled by the acceptance of a plank favoring high licenses and local option. But by opposing a proposed prohibition amendment to the state constitution the Democrats were open to the charge that they were bidding for the wet vote, a charge apparently corroborated by the nomination of a wet, James E. Boyd, for governor.[40]

In mid-September, with the campaign half gone, Van Wyck declined the Independent nomination. The much weaker candidate substituted

[37] J. J. Kelley to Bryan, August 29, 1890, *ibid.*

[38] At that time the First District included the counties of Cass, Douglas, Gage, Johnson, Lancaster, Nemaha, Otoe, Pawnee, Richardson, Sarpy, and Saunders, with a voting population estimated at about seventy thousand.

[39] *Nebraska State Journal*, August 15, 1890.

[40] Mullen, *Western Democrat*, p. 65.

for him eased the burden for Bryan on the Independent side, but Republican editors had already begun poking fun at "the young Mr. Bryan." Charles H. Gere, of the *Nebraska State Journal,* often went beyond the bounds of decency in criticizing him, and Edward Rosewater, of the Omaha *Bee,* at first disturbed, became angered. When the latter asked Bryan to define "in a manly way his prohibition proclivities and his aristocratic tendencies," Bryan retorted by deploring the silence of some Republicans, especially of the gubernatorial candidate, on the prohibition question. His attacks upon the purveyors of patronage and the pampered monopolies and his defense of the common man won him the support of Gilbert M. Hitchcock, of the Omaha *World-Herald,* who had been favoring the Independents.

The outstanding event of the campaign was the series of tariff debates between Bryan and Connell. In the first debate, in Lincoln, Bryan suffered from stage fright and nausea, but he quickly won control of himself and swept away Connell's conclusions. When the audience insisted upon applauding him he told them to applaud Connell—he wanted his time to convince them that the tariff was a tax.[41]

Dismayed by Bryan's progress, Republican editors resorted to sneers and innuendoes. "Mr. Bryan went to church, leaving his mouth in the back yard practising on a new tariff speech," said Gere. Talbot *and* Bryan, it was said, were attorneys for the railroads. The Republicans also made political capital out of the one good case they had against Bryan. On October 18 he had stated that "I am tired of hearing about laws made for the benefit of the men who work in shops." Said Gere: "Well, there are several thousand men who work in shops in this district who are very tired of Mr. Bryan." Bryan may have made the statement to put himself "in solid" with the farmers who composed the bulk of his constituents, but the harm had been done, and the Knights of Labor were advised to vote for Connell. Bryan further erred by waiting two weeks before explaining. He then admitted that he had meant to say he opposed class legislation.[42] He could have put it better by saying that he was tired of hearing of the protective tariff as a benefit to labor.

Thousands were turned away from the halls in which the last debates were held. With Bryan way out front, the Republicans boldly attacked his stand on prohibition, accused him of having used a railroad pass,

[41] Omaha *World-Herald,* September 25, 1890; *Nebraska State Journal,* October 14, 1890; Omaha *Bee,* October 16, 18, 1890.
[42] Omaha *Bee,* October 31, 1890.

and called him a "calamity howler" who was "effervescent as a bottle of soda pop." The leaders of the Republican party were men who had fought the Civil War, they said, while the Democracy was being led by a man only thirty years old. As Dr. Jekyll, Bryan ran a Sunday School in Lincoln, preached in various churches, and lectured on morality at the Y.M.C.A., but as Mr. Hyde he favored anything that would bring him votes, including frequenting saloons with "the boys" and being "hail fellow well met" with Omaha's ward heelers. Bryan replied that he was frequently with those who drank but that he never touched liquor and that he opposed prohibition because it meant legislation on a moral rather than a political question. He also denied that he was either antilabor or a member of the A.P.A.,[43] and he said that he had given up his railroad pass as soon as he had been nominated. Evidently a lawyer could have one but a politician could not!

The year 1890 was the year of the big drought and the big farmers' uprisings in the West. Their crops utterly burned, Nebraska's farmers organized numerous political picnics and schoolhouse debates. Meetings of from five to ten thousand persons were not unusual, and orators frequently expounded such texts as "boycott the monopoly press" and "let the railroad ticket furnish the means for its own funeral." While the country press sponsored the agrarian cause, the city press emphasized the liquor question. The latter aroused a tremendous amount of bitter feeling and possibly played a larger part in Bryan's election than did the agrarian crusade. The refusal of the Republican gubernatorial candidate, L. D. Richards, to commit himself lost him the support of the Omaha *Bee* and caused defections from both wet and dry Republicans. On the other hand Connell tried to get the wet vote, and in Omaha the Nebraska liquor interests sought to defeat the prohibition amendment by garnering votes for him and for Boyd.[44] The Prohibitionists did not stand a chance, but they let Bryan know that "a Prohibitionist could do no better than to vote for an honest Christian man" and that he would receive their votes.[45]

Connell had defeated Morton in 1888 by 3400 votes. Bryan won over Connell by 6713 votes, 8000 short of a majority but a sufficiently large

---

[43] The American Protective Association was founded in 1887 for the purpose of uniting the American people against the "ever-oppressive hierarchy of Rome" and its influence over public institutions in America. In Nebraska it generally threw its strength to the Republican party.

[44] William E. Johnson to Bryan, October 16, 1890, Bryan Papers.

[45] *Ibid.*

plurality in a Republican district to earn him widespread favorable publicity. Discounting fraudulent Douglas County returns, where the ballot boxes were systematically stuffed to give votes to Boyd, the plurality was nearer 2500,[46] yet the bald conclusion that "what saved Bryan was the saloon" [47] deserves qualification. The Omaha Bankers' and Business Men's Association levied an assessment of $1200 on Connell, who refused to pay. Boyd, wealthy, offered the amount in exchange for association support. Such an agreement can hardly be proved, yet it smacks enough of reality to be given credence. According to Victor Rosewater, son of Edward, Bryan owed his election not to oratory but to the drift of the antiprohibition vote to Boyd. His father's work against prohibition, Edward claimed, opened the door of Congress to Bryan.[48] At any rate, wet Republicans scratched Richards, wrote in Boyd, and voted the rest of the ticket straight, with the result that the Republicans won all of the state offices except the governorship. But they also lost their majority in the legislature to the Independents and failed to elect half the number of congressmen. Of the three new representatives, one was an Independent sodbuster burdened with a $1500 mortgage and the second a fusion Democratic-Independent candidate. Bryan alone claimed to be a straight Democrat.

Republicans asserted that Bryan's election resulted from the fact that thirteen thousand votes were cast for his Independent rather than his Republican opponent, but other reasons suggest themselves. Bryan's youthfulness was as much hindrance as help, but he was better educated than most of his constituents, he was personally presentable, and he possessed a marvelous speaking voice, an ingratiating personality, a winning smile, and humility enough to work without asking for reward. He spoke with a sincerity akin to religious fervor and had a rare ability to dramatize his causes and to popularize himself. Chosen when few believed he had a chance to win, he undauntedly fought an uphill battle. He concentrated on issues of "paramount" importance, and he possessed abundant physical strength for campaigning and debating. Rather than trying to lead the people into new paths he

[46] The vote stood Bryan, 32,376; Connell, 25,663; Root (Independent), 13,066. Details of the election and of the ballot box stuffing are discussed in Boell, "The Career of William Jennings Bryan to 1896," pp. 63–84; J. Sterling Morton and Albert Watkins, *Illustrated History of Nebraska*, III, 230–231; Addison E. Sheldon, *Nebraska: The Land and the People*, I, 685; and James C. Olson, *History of Nebraska*, pp. 235–236.

[47] Paxton Hibben, *The Peerless Leader: William Jennings Bryan*, p. 125.

[48] Rosewater, "Edward Rosewater," p. 171.

joined them along the road they had chosen, giving eloquent expression to the complaints or sufferings they lacked words to describe. It was not statesmanship but it proved to be good politics. His victory came from hard work, a popular stand on the prohibition and tariff issues, support from Morton and various local Democratic leaders, and his appeal to many Independents. In part, too, he was carried along by the general Democratic sweep of the midterm elections.[49]

Bryan was the second Democratic congressman ever elected in Nebraska, and Democratic joy over his victory was ecstatic. Dr. George L. Miller, who earlier had wanted to know "who the hell is Bryan," telegraphed his congratulations. Others wrote about "their boy congressman" and "the Henry Clay of Nebraska, defender of the people's right." Even Rosewater conceded that "Mr. Bryan is not nearly as tired as he might be." Said Morton: "The fruit was ripe. You have wisely gathered it and because of Tariff Reform as well as because of my regard for you personally I rejoice and congratulate," [50] and Hitchcock, now a close personal friend of the Bryan family, congratulated Nebraska for having elected a man possessed of physical and mental qualities that would make him a remarkable man in the history of the nation.[51]

Bryan had told his wife in strictest confidence two years earlier that he would be nominated and elected in 1890. Since the district was Republican he could easily get the nomination, and the growth of Independent strength would split the Republican forces and make his election possible. She had doubted his wisdom and opposed his acceptance of any nomination until he could afford to retire from practice. Now, with his prophecy realized, she believed him a keen reader of the trend of political opinion.[52] Yet time would prove to him that, regardless of provocation, strict partisanship does not pay great dividends, that oratory alone does not win votes, that elections do not turn on "paramount" issues alone, and that his defense of special agrarian and sectional interests would not appeal to the nation as a whole.

---

[49] According to his Memorandum Book, Bryan Papers, Bryan spent $33.85 to win the election. T. S. Allen, later his brother-in-law, estimated his expenses at $200, while Wayne C. Williams, *William Jennings Bryan*, p. 73, put them at $3385.46!

[50] Morton to Bryan, November 3, 1890, Bryan Papers.

[51] Omaha *World-Herald*, October 16, 1890.

[52] Bryan, *Memoirs*, pp. 299–300; Williams, *Bryan*, p. 57.

CHAPTER 5

Congressman: Tariff Reform and the Income Tax

I

BRYAN arrived in Washington, D.C., in late November 1891. When he finally found an apartment, early in 1892, he was joined by Mrs. Bryan and the now three children, Grace Dexter having been born on February 17, 1891. Since there were no House or Senate office buildings as yet, he used a room in his apartment as an office. Instead of hiring just one secretary he spread his clerk-hire among "deserving Democrats," that is, he brought a number of young Nebraskans to Washington for periods of from four to six weeks.

Bryan was uninterested in the polite and literary society of the capital, then dominated by Henry Adams, Whitelaw Reid, William C. Whitney, Don Cameron, and Theodore Roosevelt, then Civil Service Commissioner; and Mrs. Bryan declined invitations to join the Congressional Women's Club, saying she knew nothing but domestic science. But she hired girls to help with her housework and children and devoted as much time as she could to her husband's career. She rarely missed hearing him speak in the House, for she knew that her presence stimulated him to great effort. She read widely and collated material which proved helpful to him, and her analytical mind helped clarify certain topics for him. Some newspaper reporters even believed they could see her influence in his speeches.

Bryan made it a point to meet every member of the House and as many senators as possible. Congressman William Springer, for whom he had stumped while he was still in college, provided him with some publicity, and Richard L. Metcalfe, now the Washington correspondent of the Omaha *World-Herald*, gave him extremely favorable reports. Originally judged "one more of those hayseed Congressmen" because he wore striped trousers, an old-fashioned string tie, slouch hat, and Western boots, his handsome features and organ-like voice soon earned him attention. He himself felt right at home; his presence was pre-

49

destined. "I am just as certain that I would come to Congress as that I am here now," he told a reporter.[1]

There were three major aspirants for the speakership of the House in the Fifty-second Congress—Roger Q. Mills, Charles F. Crisp, and Springer—and two minor hopefuls, Benton McMillin and William S. Holman. When a tie developed between Mills and Crisp and another between McMillin and Holman, Springer held the balance of power. Bryan supported Springer. When Mills refused to bargain, Springer offered his votes to Crisp in return for the chairmanship of the Ways and Means Committee and a reward for Bryan. When Crisp demurred at Bryan's youth and total lack of legislative experience, Springer told him that the appointment would pay in full the demands of Illinois and the other Middle Western states. Once elected, Crisp upheld his bargain and appointed Bryan to the Ways and Means Committee.

Bryan sought as much to please his constituents as to fight for his ideals. Two of his bills providing for verdicts by only three fourths of a jury in federal civil cases failed to see the light because the subject was not an issue before the people and it had no private interests behind it. The Congress passed his bill which divided Nebraska into two judicial districts and his amendment which obtained for Lincoln an extra fall term of court; but it refused to take up his bill to revoke a patent after a hundred thousand dollars had been realized from it. One of the last bills signed by President Benjamin Harrison was Bryan's bill regulating the manner in which federal court judgments could become liens upon real estate. Now nonresident capitalists who used the federal courts for the foreclosure of land mortgages must publish their foreclosure notices in the county in which the land was located, thus giving warning to all against loan sharks. By his efforts the Crop and Weather Bureau was moved from Omaha to Lincoln, where it could work more conveniently with the agricultural experimental station located at the university. However, three bills requesting appropriations for public buildings in Lincoln, South Omaha, and Plattsmouth, and one asking for the establishment of a branch mint at Lincoln, never reached the floor. He obtained more pensions for his constituents than all his predecessors put together, but this was made possible because the Dependent Pension bill of 1890 almost doubled the pension rolls.[2]

[1] Clipping, Washington *Post*, W. J. Bryan Scrapbook No. 3, Nebraska State Historical Society.

[2] *Congressional Record*, 53 Congress, 1 Sess., 23:133, 206; 2 Sess., 26:136–137.

In all matters Bryan proved himself a Jeffersonian Democrat. He fought the Reed rules and the autocracy they represented; protested the procedure by which one Congress contracted obligations to be met by another; opposed the expansion of the Navy and appropriations for special groups; demanded justice in taxation; and favored an investigation of the Pinkertons in the Homestead strike. When private individuals and hired detectives had to execute the laws he stood ready to acknowledge government a failure. While no corporation should have to protect its own property, neither should the safety and lives of citizens be imperiled by a private and irresponsible soldiery. Public order must be preserved by public authority.[3] He favored federal aid to Western states for irrigation, the stricter enforcement of laws regulating trusts, and amendments strengthening the powers of the Interstate Commerce Commission. His bill to place all articles of commerce upon which a duty was levied upon the free list by presidential order if a United States Circuit Court found that a trust or monopoly had been formed for the purpose of controlling trade in that article was clearly designed to break up the trusts by admitting competitive imports free of duty. The bill aroused much public discussion but was deemed "radical" and "experimental" and died in committee. Bryan also demanded the physical valuation of railroads as a basis for determining rates, the prohibition of speculation on stock exchanges, a national bankruptcy law that would be fair to debtor as well as creditor, rural free mail delivery and lower postal rates on educational publications, the public requirement of automatic couplers and other safety devices on trains, and the removal of the duty on such medicines as diphtheria antitoxins. In addition, as "a stickler for local self-government," he did not believe "the general Government should take charge of those local matters which the State can better attend to." He also resented the arrangements whereby an incoming President could request legislation from a short-session Congress dominated by the opposition party, and he supported the reform finally consummated in the Twentieth Amendment.[4]

Bryan maintained quite an independent attitude both inside and outside Congress. In a contested election, he voted against seating the Democrat because he believed the Republican fairly elected. To Nebraskans petitioning for a bounty for the sugar beet industry he re-

[3] *Ibid.*, 23:4225; Omaha *World-Herald*, May 13, 1892.

[4] *Congressional Record*, 52 Congress, 1 Sess., 23:160–161; Omaha *World-Herald*, May 16, 1892, *Nebraska State Journal*, May 17, 1892.

plied that he opposed bounties and would not support special legislation. He would raise taxes only in the amount needed to support government. If the sugar-beet people could not profit, they had best transfer their investment to other enterprises! [5] When the House debated the use of government funds merely to defray the costs of transporting relief supplies to drought-stricken Russia early in 1892, he donated to a private relief fund but objected to the appropriation. If it was unconstitutional to use the tax power to relieve American farmers suffering because of Republican folly, it was clearly unconstitutional to use this power to relieve foreigners suffering at the hands of the Almighty, he said.[6]

Thus Bryan tenaciously and consistently pursued what he considered historic Democratic doctrine. No major legislation bears his name, yet the bills he introduced and the speeches he made show that he followed in the spirit of Jefferson and Jackson. With energy, eloquence, and sincerity he sought laws that would operate equally upon all, give special privilege to none, and make the government more immediately responsive to the will of the people.

II

IN 1891 the House of Representatives contained 235 Democrats, 14 Alliancemen, and only 86 Republicans, so that the Democrats had almost a three-to-one majority. Although the Democrats were divided on tariff reform and the direct election of senators, Bryan made his most extended remarks on these subjects. His direct election bill differed from many others by giving the states the option of electing their senators by their legislatures or by direct popular vote. To those who objected to changing the "sacred" Constitution he replied that it provided for its own amendment and that it had already been changed fifteen times, that it was time to recognize new conditions rather than to worship something just because it was old; but he argued twenty years too soon.

The issues of greatest concern to the Democrats of the Fifty-second Congress were tariff and currency reform. Bryan believed tariff reform paramount. But could a divided Democracy defeat Republicans sin-

[5] Omaha *Bee*, December 19, 1891, Omaha *World-Herald*, December 24, 1891. The attitude of the Lincoln *Daily Call* toward Bryan is revealed by its saying, "Give us that new post office and we'll forgive you your eccentricities."

[6] Omaha *World-Herald*, December 17, 26, 1891, January 10, 30, 1892.

gularly attached to the "American System"? In the Ways and Means Committee were Chairman Springer, William L. Wilson, Bourke Cockran, Benton McMillin, and five lesser lights with whom Bryan formed the majority. Ex-Speaker Thomas B. Reed led the protectionist minority. Since an all-out offensive would fail so long as the Republicans controlled the Senate and the Presidency, Bryan supported Springer's strategy of reducing duties only upon specified articles. The majority members would introduce the bills, the committee would report them favorably, and their authors would lead the debate on the floor. Bryan would handle the lumber, binding twine, barbed wire, iron fence posts, and salt bills. The battle started when McMillin reported the wool and woolens bill, Bryan the binding twine bill, and George Turner the bills dealing with cotton bagging and ties, of special interest to the South, which was fighting the "jute trust."

Quickly overcoming a touch of stage fright, Bryan began his first hour-long speech in the House, on the wool bill, on March 16, 1892, with a penetrating attack on the protective theory. Should the American people leave vested interests alone, as the Republicans and certain Democratic irreconcilables wished, or reduce rates in the interest of the farmer, the worker, and the general consumer? He would unmask those Republicans hiding behind a general tariff revision. As for Nelson Dingley's claim that the Republicans were helping the farmer by aiding wool, he said it was "absurd"; what Dingley feared was an attack on the wool tariff, "the keystone of the protective arch," the base of a system held together by "the coercive power of plunder." He insisted that raw materials be placed on the free list because the incidence of any tax placed upon them fell upon the consumer, because no favoritism should be shown one manufacturer over another, and because "I consider it as false in economy and vicious in policy to attempt to raise at a high price in this country that which we can purchase abroad at a low price in exchange for the products of our toil." Free raw materials and free machinery were all the encouragement a democracy could legitimately give industry.

As Bryan's fine baritone voice filled the House, senators came in numbers to see what the "commoners" were doing, and the galleries filled. Since 80 per cent of customs went into the pockets of the protected industries and only 20 per cent to the Treasury, he denied that a protective tariff could be defended as a revenue-raising measure. Moreover, wool was neither an important nor an infant industry. Then why should it be protected? And why should infant industries that once

free trader Bryan discredits tariff as spur to human progress!

got along with 10 per cent, then 20 per cent, then 30, now be given from 40 to 47 per cent by the McKinley tariff?

His time running short, Bryan turned to his own binding twine bill. The McKinley tariff rate of seven-tenths of 1 per cent, which the Republicans deemed "trifling," had added $700,000 to the price of imported twine, he said. Since no revenue came to the government from this source, it was plainly a tax on the people. Dividing the $700,000 by the thirty-five twine factories in the United States—controlled, incidentally, by the cordage trust—meant that each received $20,000 a year. And no benefit would accrue to the farmer if the "infamous" tariff were abolished, but trusts were permitted to gouge him.

It was the arch-protectionist Julius Burrows who asked unanimous consent for Bryan to proceed. Consent granted, for two more hours he attacked the system "conceived in greed and fashioned in iniquity," slowly drifting from logical exposition to emotional oratory. He would collect part of the revenues from customs, but with raw materials on the free list and the highest duties on luxuries and the lowest on necessities of life. Then he would collect another part by a graduated income tax upon the wealth of the country (loud applause on the Democratic side). The American worker received higher wages than foreign workers, he said, because his output was about once and a half again as high; price reduction resulted from the application of science to industry, not from tariff protection. He charged that the manufacturer pleaded for protection so that he might pay high wages, then pocketed the bonus, and "when the employee asks for the high wages promised him . . . you find Pinkerton detectives stationed to keep him off and foreigners brought in to supply his place," a direct reference to the Homestead strike. These capitalists "are the ones that build their stately palaces, who give their banquets, which rival in magnificence the banquets of ancient times. These are the men who can gather around a banquet board . . . to celebrate 'home industries' at ten dollars a plate when within a stone's throw of their banquet hall were people to whom a ten-cent meal would be a luxury. . . . I am not surprised that a man like Mr. Carnegie is willing to write articles . . . to show what a great benefit a protective system is."

Some day, Bryan concluded, those who lobbied for private interests would find their occupation gone, and some day members of Congress would pass laws for the benefit of "all the people." He wanted to protect the homes of the people, the foundations of national wealth and

security. He wished to remove the 47 per cent tax provided by the McKinley tariff for those who lived in palaces, to prevent it from falling upon the lumber, nails, putty, knives, forks, spoons, glasses, tin pails, and clothing needed to establish a little home. The American worker must not be degraded, for he was the one who produced wealth in time of peace and bared his breast to hostile fire in defense of the flag. A free country could not depend for security on a great navy, a great army, or coastal fortifications—the best defense of a nation lay in contented people willing to die to transmit freedom to their posterity.[7]

Congress had not heard a comparable speech in years. Democratic newspapers called it "dramatic," "logical and practical," "an oratorical firecracker," "wonderfully brilliant." The speech brought Bryan into national prominence as the best tariff speaker in a decade, justified his appointment to the Ways and Means Committee, caused him to be selected as one of the leaders of the tariff struggle of the next Congress, and confounded those who charged him with being a man of shallow intellect. None of his ideas was original, but modern tariff reform studies fail to reveal any important arguments against protection that he did not use.[8] Above all, the speech revealed that he conscientiously, if naïvely, believed with Jefferson that the wisdom and righteousness of the average American would provide solutions for all his political and economic ills. It brought inquiries as to whether he were old enough to be nominated for President—and it made him a marked man in the Republican camp.

After five weeks of debate in which the Republicans took his speech as their main point for rebuttal, five of the "popgun" reform bills, including his twine bill, passed by large majorities, but as he had predicted, the Republican Senate proved the nemesis of tariff reform.[9]

[7] *Congressional Record,* 52 Congress, 1 Sess., 23:2124–36. The allusion to Blaine's Delmonico dinner is evident. The Carnegie articles referred to are the first ones in Carnegie's *The Gospel of Wealth and Other Timely Essays* (New York, 1900).

[8] See Herbert F. Fraser, "Popular Tariff Fallacies," *Annals of the Academy of Political and Social Science,* 141 (January 1929), 53–61; Edward R. Lewis, *A History of American Political Thought From the Civil War to the World War,* pp. 243–248.

[9] *Congressional Record,* 52 Congress, 1 Sess., 23:2667–2675, 3057, 3141, 3840–3843, 5906, 5907; Edward Stanwood, *American Tariff Controversies in the Nineteenth Century,* II, 308–311. Bryan was the first Nebraska congressman since Senator Charles H. Van Wyck to look at tariff reform from the point of view of the consumer. Norbert R. Mahnken, "The Nebraska Congressional Delegation and Tariff Legislation, 1880–1900" (unpublished M.A. thesis, University of Nebraska, 1939), pp. 84, 87–89.

III

RE-ELECTED to Congress in 1892, Bryan plunged wholeheartedly into the tariff reform struggle of the Fifty-third Congress. The panic of 1893 proved the McKinley law incapable of providing needed revenues and upheld his contention that tariff revision was mandatory. Writing in the *North American Review*,[10] he and McMillin together with John Dalzell supported President Cleveland's demand for a tariff for revenue only. It soon became apparent, however, that the loss of revenue caused by lowered duties could be offset only by an income tax which would collect about one hundred millions annually. William L. Wilson, the scholarly new chairman of the Ways and Means Committee, led its majority members in revising the customs rates and chose Bryan to draft an income tax provision and McMillin to head an internal revenue subcommittee.

Bryan regarded Wilson's tariff work as sound. It deleted the duty on wool, increased the free list, and abolished the McKinley law bounty on sugar. While it gave the manufacturer some protection from foreign competition, it relieved the consumer from taxation. Republicans predicted that its operation would cause a devastating revolution in the American economic system and said that the "new" Bryan, now the "eminent Populist Congressman," would fail to get his income tax into it. Wilson, too, wished to leave the income tax out of the customs bill because he feared that it would antagonize certain Senate Democrats if not Cleveland himself and thus hamper the success of tariff reform.

Early in January 1894 the Ways and Means Committee took up the income tax. While noncommittal on a personal tax, Cleveland hesitated to antagonize those who had supported the repeal of the Sherman Silver Purchase Act and his gold bond sales policy, and Bourke Cockran and several others sided with Wilson against Bryan and McMillin, saying they would "expose" a "rascally scheme" of the "wildcat South" and "bankrupt West" to victimize the honest and frugal millionaires of the Eastern cities. Bryan argued vehemently that the tax was vital to the success of the proposed revenue and customs laws, and his demand to add the tax to the Wilson bill was respected. He wanted a graduated tax that began with incomes of $2500 and would affect only between 50,000 and 80,000 people, but the committee directed him to provide

[10] Benton McMillin, John Dalzell, and W. J. Bryan, "The Coming Tariff Legislation," *North American Review*, 157 (October 1893), 493–506.

for a straight 2 per cent tax on personal and net corporate incomes of over $4000. Bryan then went immediately to ask Nebraska's Populist senator, William V. Allen, to line up Senate support for the tax.[11]

Wilson started the debate on the tariff bill on January 8. On the next day Bryan submitted his income tax report, which filled fifteen columns of the *Congressional Record* with data on the income tax laws of foreign nations and the various American states.[12] In his defense of the Wilson tariff on the evening of January 13 he raked over the home market, higher wages, and other arguments advanced by the McKinley school and called them false. Of the many speeches made on the bill, Bryan's was acknowledged as second to none except the one by Cockran.[13]

On January 11 the Ways and Means Committee debated whether to add the income tax to Wilson's bill or to introduce it as a separate measure. Since separating it might send it to its death, Bryan and six other committee members demanded the calling of a caucus to decide the matter. Bryan also pointed out that the Republicans would try to make up the $75,000,000 deficit anticipated from the Wilson bill by raising its rates, thereby defeating tariff reform. Seeing the point, the committee authorized McMillin to add the income tax to his internal revenue bill, but to introduce the latter independently of the Wilson bill. On January 25, a Democratic caucus hopeful of winning the Populist as well as the Southern and Western Democratic vote joined the internal revenue and tariff bills and extended debate until February 1.[14]

On January 25 an exciting fight developed when Cockran, speaking for the East and perhaps at the instigation of Cleveland, opposed adding the income tax to the Wilson bill, and his New York colleagues undertook to filibuster until time to adjourn. On January 29 McMillin moved the amendment of the Wilson bill by adding the income tax

[11] Omaha *World-Herald*, January 3, 6, 9, 1894; Omaha *Bee*, January 4, 1894; Festus P. Summers, *William L. Wilson and Tariff Reform*, pp. 172–174.

[12] *Congressional Record*, 53 Congress, 2 Sess., 26:584–591; Omaha *World-Herald*, January 10, 1894; *Nebraska State Journal*, January 11, 1894.

[13] *Congressional Record*, 53 Congress, 2 Sess., 29: Appendix I, 462–469.

[14] Contemporary studies of the distribution of wealth and income support Bryan's contentions. Thomas G. Shearman, "The Owners of the United States," *Forum*, 18 (November 1889), 262–273, said that indirect taxes took 3% to 10% of the annual savings of the rich and 70% to 90% of those of the poor. George F. Holmes, "The Concentration of Wealth," *Political Science Quarterly*, 8 (December 1893), 589–600, concluded that 91% of the families owned 2% of the national wealth; 8.9% owned 51%; and .03%, the millionaires, owned 20%.

and spoke eloquently in support of the tax. The great debate, between Cockran and Bryan, occurred next day.

Cockran's voice probably equaled Bryan's in power, but Bryan could modulate his along a wider scale of shadings and emotions. Cockran denied the need of the tax as a revenue measure and doubted its democracy, contending that democratic government would collapse if those who enjoyed it were not called upon equally to support it, and he charged that the tax was being offered as a sop to the discontented and that its proponents were being swept away by the rising tide of socialism.[15]

After prolonged plaudits for Cockran died away, Bryan came forward "clad," he said, "in the armor of a righteous cause," the same words he later used in his Cross of Gold speech, to deliver his last speech in the House, considered by many as his best. He acknowledged Cockran's eloquence but believed that the David pebbles of truth would be more effective than the Goliath javelins of error, even when hurled by the giant of the Philistines. He outmatched Cockran in both logic and rhetoric. Cockran spoke for the monopolists and millionaires, he said, while he himself spoke for the sixty million common people. The Supreme Court had upheld the Civil War income tax, which was collected for ten years. Did the tax threaten the participation of the poor in government? "If taxation is a badge of free men the poor people of this country are covered all over with the insignia of free men." Bryan said that the income tax was the most just of all taxes because based upon ability to pay, that it was not socialistic merely because so many escaped from its provisions. It would collect only a small portion of the government's revenues; the customs and internal revenue taxes would still extract more from the poor than from the rich. "They call that man a statesman whose ear is attuned to the slightest pulsation of the pocket book, and they describe as a demagogue anyone who dares to listen to the heartbeat of humanity," he declaimed.

What did Ward McAllister, the leader of New York's "Four Hundred," mean by saying that the adoption of the income tax would "compel many of the best people of New York" to live abroad where living costs were cheaper? asked Bryan. Would they fly to England, where the tax was more than 2 per cent? To Prussia, where the tax was 4 per cent? Or perhaps to Switzerland, Italy, or Austria, where the tax was 8, 12, and 20 per cent, respectively? God pity those whose patriotism was only 2 per cent deep! We were well rid of those who would

[15] *Congressional Record*, 53 Congress, 2 Sess., 26:1655–1658.

expatriate themselves and live under a monarchy without an income tax rather than support a republic! [16]

Cries of "Vote, vote" mingled with the cheers that followed Bryan's speech, and members rushed over desks and chairs to congratulate him. On the next day, after Wilson came out strongly in support of the tax, the House voted down two Populist amendments providing for a graduated tax but added Bryan's clause to McMillin's internal revenue bill. The latter passed, 182 to 48, and on February 1 the Wilson bill itself passed, 204 to 140, and Bryan, Henry George St. Tucker of Virginia, and John Sharp Williams of Mississippi lifted Wilson to their shoulders and paraded with him about the House. Bryan's advocacy of the income tax added to his popularity with the progressive Democrats and with the Populists, and he correctly predicted that the Wilson bill would be passed by the Senate and that the income tax would remain part of it,[17] but he never suspected the terrible mockery which the Senate would make of the Wilson bill.[18]

Angered at Cleveland over the repeal of the Sherman Silver Purchase Act, and for other reasons, the senators longed to rebuff him. More important, a large number of protectionist Democrats led by the Big Four—Arthur Pue Gorman, David Bennett Hill, Calvin S. Brice, and Edward Murphy—opposed both the free list and the income tax.[19] And Cleveland did not insist on the tax. After the Finance Committee tore the bill to shreds, the Senate itself raised many of its rates in 634 amendments. Strangely enough, the income tax was one of the most popular features of the Senate bill. William V. Allen, the "intellectual giant of Populism" who in great part owed his election to Bryan, made a speech in its defense which for fire and ability surpassed that made by Bryan. In contrast Cleveland wrote Wilson on July 2: "You know how much I deprecate the incorporation in the proposed bill of the income tax feature. In matters of this kind, however, which do not vitiate a fixed and recognized Democratic doctrine, we are willing to

[16] *Ibid.*, 26:1730, 1739, 1795–1797, Appendix I, 203–205, 601–614.

[17] *Nebraska State Journal,* February 1, 3, 6, 1894; Omaha *Bee,* February 8, 1894; Omaha *World-Herald,* February 6, 15, 1894; Allan Nevins, *Grover Cleveland: A Study in Courage,* pp. 564–567; Summers, *William L. Wilson and Tariff Reform,* pp. 175–186.

[18] Stanwood, *American Tariff Controversies,* II, 326, 356; Summers, *William L. Wilson and Tariff Reform,* pp. 182–186.

[19] Independent, "Political Career of David B. Hill," *Forum,* 18 (November 1894), 257–269; Everett P. Wheeler, *Sixty Years of American Life: Taylor to Roosevelt, 1850–1910,* pp. 213–214.

defer to the majority of our Democratic brethren." [20] The Wilson-Gorman tariff passed by the narrow margin of 39 to 34.

A poll of the House showed that only two Democrats favored the Senate version. The Democratic caucus opposed yielding anything, and Bryan spurred the Ways and Means Committee behind a resolution of nonconcurrence which was upheld by the House. Cleveland thereupon appealed to Wilson to agree on the ground of maintaining "the party's honor." Prodded by Cleveland and faced with Gorman's ultimatum that the Senate would not accept even a change in punctuation, the House leaders surrendered. Bryan voted for it in order to save his income tax and what was left of the free list. The House had "to meet a condition, not a theory," he said—it could either capitulate on Gorman's terms or reject them and leave the McKinley tariff in operation. Why not get the best one could in conference and then seek to improve the new law by amending it? As Cleveland pondered the new measure, he and others introduced a new series of "popgun" bills extending the free list. His barbed wire bill and three others that passed had no other effect than to record House opposition to the monstrosity the Senate called reform.[21] Defeated by what Carl Schurz called the "capitalistic Democrats," Cleveland let the bill become law without his signature, thereby acknowledging defeat for the agrarian interests of America and for tariff reformers like Bryan. The only survivors of importance in the campaign for free raw materials were wool and lumber, for which Bryan had fought most strenuously;[22] and the income tax had no sooner become law than suits were instituted to have it declared unconstitutional.

In his appointment to the Ways and Means Committee Bryan had established several "firsts": he was the youngest member ever to go on the committee; of its fifteen members he was one of the two from west of the Mississippi River; and only he and one other were new members. His masterful oratory and parliamentary skill helped both Springer and Wilson, and he provided the data upon which the income tax provision of the Wilson-Gorman tariff bill was based and the oratory that defended it against its traducers. Although he disagreed

[20] Grover Cleveland Papers.

[21] *Congressional Record*, 53 Congress, 2 Sess., 26:8468–8497.

[22] Claude M. Fuess, *Carl Schurz, Reformer*, p. 329. Brand Whitlock, *Forty Years of It*, p. 88, said of the defeat of tariff reform: "I suppose no greater moral wrong was ever committed in America."

violently with Cleveland on currency reform, he agreed with him on tariff reform and in this matter gave his unstinting support. Unfortunately, tariff reform during the depression beginning in 1893 appealed to relatively few, for it would reduce the amount of customs collections and make new forms of taxation like the income tax inevitable, and it was opposed by mighty vested interests. Bryan's arguments in favor of reducing burdens on consumers carried little weight in either the Fifty-second or the Fifty-third Congresses, for no organized interest group represented the common people, and his refusal to support home industries and industrial labor lost him votes in Nebraska. The internecine tariff fight widened the gulf between the Western and Southern agrarians and the Eastern city wings of the party largely caused by differing views on currency reform. Opposition over the income tax further broadened the split.

Much as he despised Cleveland's financial policies, Bryan had to defend the President in order to defend his own record on tariff reform. In place of righteous indignation at the iniquities of the conservatives and protectionists he had to substitute mild accents of apology and explanation. While he bravely flouted the Nebraska Republicans and told them that they should close their sugar beet and twine factories if they could not operate them profitably without government subsidy, he overlooked the fact that Nebraska's farmers, mostly Republican by tradition and interest, looked upon these factories as prime purchasers of their crops. Loss of support because of his tariff reform activities was a major reason for Bryan's refusal to run for the House in 1894. The Democrats took a terrible drubbing in the elections of 1894, and Bryan found Nebraska's tolerance for tariff reformers totally exhausted when he competed with a Republican protectionist for election to the United States Senate in the legislature of 1894–1895.

CHAPTER 6

Congressman: Currency Reform

I

DIVISION of sentiment over silver was at least a dozen years old before Bryan demanded equality for silver in his first congressional platform. The ratio between gold and silver in the world's commercial markets had refused to respect that of 15 to 1 established by the basic American law, of April 2, 1792, but changes in the American ratio had fitted commercial realities so well that the mint and market values had remained relatively constant, and in 1874 they were equal.

Bryan had grown to maturity during the paper phase of the war of finance that began with the Civil War and wracked the nation until the end of the nineteenth century. While at college, the greenback and resumption of specie payments questions had provided him topics for debate. At that time Western Democrats had generally favored the "rag baby" while Eastern Democrats and the Republicans had desired the deflation promised by resumption. The depression beginning in 1873 inflamed the farmers against the national banking system and against President Ulysses S. Grant, who vetoed the issue of additional greenbacks. With the failure of Western Democrats to repeal the Resumption Act of 1875 (effective 1879), popular interest in currency reform shifted largely to silver.

With the great silver strikes in Colorado, Nevada, and Utah, silver production increased from $2,000,000 in 1861 to $40,000,000 in 1878. The bullion value of silver dropped from $1.03 in 1861 to $.93 in 1878, and the ratio of silver to gold from 15.5 to 1 to 17.12 to 1. When the miners took silver to the mint, however, they learned that a law of 1873 had demonetized it. Despite vociferous charges that silver was dropped from the coinage by fraud and collusion in which the British loomed large, impartial students of the act have been unable to reveal intention of deceit. The Congress had debated revision cursorily for two years, and the facts that silver was worth 3 per cent more than gold in 1873 and that gold was favored by those who desired a greater volume of money contributed to the ease with which silver was demonetized.[1] However, demonetization occurred at the same time that the nations of Europe, old and new, swung to gold. After the first international monetary conference in 1867, those nations not already on a gold standard followed Britain's example and adopted it. By the close of the seventies, the suspension of silver coinage by every important country in Europe and the simultaneous increased production of silver in the United States caused a great fall in the commercial value of silver. Thus all the materials for "a conspiracy international in extent," as Bryan later put it, were at hand. Europe had "connived" to end bimetallism and dump its silver on the United States. Moreover, many persons, with Bryan in the lead, believed that the fall in the value of silver accounted for the fall in agricultural prices and spoke accordingly.

America's silver miners used the general agrarian demand for inflation as a shield from behind which to ask Congress to "do something" for silver. Others disliked the setting of the price of silver by the bullion market in London and wished for the day when, as Bryan often said, the United States would declare its financial as well as its political independence from Great Britain. Another touch of nationalism was evident in the preference for greenbacks to bank money, for the greenbacks were government money and not susceptible to control by domestic or foreign banking interests. Failure to stop the resumption of specie payments drove government paper money advocates to a second line of defense, a silver coin maintained at parity with gold. The issue provided meat for legislative debate for a generation, captured the imagination of the major political parties, induced dissenters to form third parties, and provoked class, sectional, and philosophical schisms. The opposition of debtor to creditor, the popular hatred of the "money power" and of the bondholders, and idealists seeking panaceas in utopian schemes further confused an already complicated picture.

Congress "did something" for silver in the Bland-Allison Act of 1878 and in the Sherman Silver Purchase Act of 1890. The first made silver a legal tender for obligations public and private "except where otherwise expressly stipulated in the contract" and limited the purchase of silver for coinage purposes to not less than two nor more than four

[1] Davis R. Dewey, *Financial History of the United States*, p. 403; Alonzo B. Hepburn, *History of Coinage and Currency in the United States and the Perennial Contest for Sound Money* (New York, 1903), pp. 278–279; *Annual Report of the Director of the Mint* [1876], pp. 9–10.

million dollars a month. Immensely popular with men of all parties and no threat either to parity or to the government's credit, President Rutherford B. Hayes nevertheless called it a "grave breach of the public faith" which violated "sacred obligations" and vetoed it. Congress promptly passed it over his veto, and one month later Hayes approved a bill leaving about $346,000,000 in greenbacks in circulation.[2]

Nothing more was done for silver during the administrations of James A. Garfield and Chester A. Arthur. Grover Cleveland defeated all attempts to "provide more money" during his first term but failed to overthrow the Bland-Allison Act, and in 1888 the Republicans won the national election on a platform that denounced his opposition to silver. Bryan had supported Cleveland since 1884, but no evidence exists that he took special note at the time of his stand on the money question.

Stimulated perhaps by the resolutions of the First National Silver Convention,[3] which met in St. Louis in November 1889, the Fifty-first Congress "did something" for silver through bargains and compromises. In 1889 and 1890 six Western states were admitted to the Union, all Republican and all silverite. If the silverites in both houses voted together, they could pass a free coinage bill, and the silver Democrats threatened to vote against tariff revision upward unless they got their way on silver. The Senate rejected an administration (Windom) currency reform plan by almost two to one and substituted therefor a free coinage bill. In the House, Chairman William McKinley of the Ways and Means Committee, who had favored silver from his entrance into the House in 1876 and who had helped pass the Bland-Allison bill over Hayes's veto, led the Republicans to favor silver lest the silverites oppose his tariff bill; when Speaker Thomas B. Reed tried to bury the Senate bill in committee, McKinley forced it to light and marshaled the Republican vote. The House disagreed and the bill went into conference. Now Republican Senator John Sherman of Ohio played the part of the great compromiser. He remodeled the bill by staving off free coinage but permitting more liberal silver purchases and succeeded in getting it passed. Not a Democrat voted for it, not a Republican against it. The full responsibility for the act, therefore, lay with the Republicans.

In addition to the trading of votes between Western Republicans

---

[2] David S. Muzzey, *James G. Blaine: A Political Idol of Other Days*, pp. 137–138; Charles R. Williams, *The Life of Rutherford Birchard Hayes*, II, 119–126.

[3] *Proceedings of the First National Silver Convention* (St. Louis, 1889).

who favored silver but objected to tariff protection and Eastern Republicans who opposed silver but demanded protection, another compromise was reached when Southern senators opposed to the Lodge force bill were mollified enough to permit a vote to be taken on the McKinley tariff.[4]

The Sherman Silver Purchase Act authorized the Secretary of the Treasury to purchase monthly four and a half million ounces of silver bullion for coinage. In payment therefor, Treasury certificates of full legal tender would be issued. The price paid for 371.25 grains of pure silver was not to exceed one dollar ($1.2929 per ounce); after July 1, 1891, standard dollars would be coined only when needed for the redemption of notes. The act reiterated the government's purpose to maintain gold and silver at parity and guarded against the depreciation of silver by permitting the redemption of the Treasury notes in either gold or silver.

The amount of silver added to the circulation between 1878 and 1890, about $378,000,000, had not proved excessive in a country growing as rapidly as the United States, and it had answered the demands not only of the silver mine owners but of the community in general for enough money to carry on increasingly larger trade and business transactions.[5] Nevertheless, objections to the Sherman Act were voiced simultaneously with its passage. Sherman himself said that "the day it became law I was ready to repeal it, if repeal could be had without substituting in its place absolutely free coinage." [6] The East objected because it involved the "dangerous" principle of bimetallism, and the West because it did not provide for free and unlimited silver coinage. The West did not believe that the act would provide more money than the nation could absorb and said that silver might stimulate a needed rise in the general price level; the East said that silver would drive gold out of circulation, thereby reducing the amount of circulation and causing deflation and a financial crash. When the British house of Baring collapsed in 1890, British holders of American securities sold them and caused American gold to flow abroad. With seven eighths of

[4] Dewey, *Financial History*, p. 226; James Ford Rhodes, *History of the United States from the Compromise of 1850*, VIII, 351–356, 361–362; William A. Robinson, *Thomas B. Reed, Parliamentarian*, pp. 242–245; Edward Stanwood, *A History of the Presidency*, p. 490; *Annual Report of the Director of the Mint* [1890], p. 12; H. Wayne Morgan, *Western Silver and the Tariff of 1890* (privately printed, 1959).

[5] Frank W. Taussig, *The Silver Situation in the United States*, pp. 10, 50.

[6] John Sherman, *Recollections of Forty Years in the House, Senate and Cabinet*, II, 1070.

its customs duties paid in silver certificates and only one eighth in gold, the government found itself short of gold, and those who had predicted a crash pointed to silver as its major cause. As though in rebuttal, the Senate passed a free silver bill in January 1891. Cleveland, the most likely Democratic presidential candidate for 1892, countered with a demand for the repeal of the Sherman Act. His warning of "the gravest peril" and of "disaster" if, "in the present situation, we enter upon the dangerous and reckless experiment of free, unlimited, and independent free coinage," had its effect and the bill died in the House.

II

BRYAN spent much of his year as congressman-elect studying American and European texts on the precious metals and the currency question as well as that mine of information on American currency legislation and argument, the *Congressional Record*. He was also much influenced by the Populist bible on the greenback, *Kellogg on Money*.[7] His studies rapidly convinced him that there was much to be said in favor of silver. The delegates at the First Western States Commercial Congress, held in Kansas City in April 1891, adopted his resolution that "all legal money of the United States should be made full legal tender for all debts, public and private, any condition in the contract notwithstanding, provided that this should not affect contracts already in existence." Were the Congress to follow him, then anyone with an ounce of silver, worth about seventy-five cents, could count it as a dollar in payment of debt. Four thousand delegates cheered as he cried, "We simply say to the East—take your hands out of our pockets and keep them out." While he received laudatory letters from such nationally known silverites as A. J. Warner, both J. Sterling Morton and Gilbert M. Hitchcock warned him against silver. Hitchcock stated that he would like "to see Bryan fight for free silver coinage against the Eastern gold bug advocates and at the same time resist the demands of the wealthy mine owners who seek to get a bonus of 25% out of the American people," [8] and for a time Bryan kept quiet. He wrote to the Treasury for information, bought more books on the currency ques-

[7] William Jennings Bryan, *The First Battle*, p. 71; bills for books purchased, in William Jennings Bryan Papers.

[8] Omaha *World-Herald*, April 23, 1891; J. Sterling Morton, Arbor Lodge Journal, May 21, June 7, 1891, J. Sterling Morton Papers.

tion, and then entered into a public debate with a Nebraska national bank president.[9] He insisted that he was merely a student of the money question and not a master of it, but when friends warned him against silver he stated that he had advocated tariff reform when in the minority and would advocate silver because he preferred to be right with the minority rather than wrong with the majority. For every man who labeled him a "heretic" for sponsoring silver, two told him they were glad that his name would appear "on the side of the people." Among others, Senator William M. Stewart, the ardent Nevada silverite, read his newspaper debate and urged him on, saying that no gold man could meet the main issue: "Is there enough gold for money?"

By the end of July 1891 Bryan concluded that the correct solution of the money question lay in the free and unlimited coinage of silver at 16 to 1. He believed that the quantitative theory of money answered all questions about the amount of money needed in circulation. Since there was not enough gold to serve the world, silver must be used. The United States must have a currency that increased in proportion to the population and volume of trade and also be equally just to debtor and creditor. He was not seeking merely an inflated currency, however, for he objected both to C. W. Macune's subtreasury scheme and to the plan of Senator Leland Stanford, of California, to have the government loan money at 2 per cent interest on farm crops. Nor was silver as yet the paramount issue. In stumping in the fall of 1891 he spoke on tariff reform first, income tax second, and silver last. Yet he had already begun to translate the economic principles involved in the money question into moral principles, from political issues that could be compromised in the ballot box into moral issues to which there was only one possible answer, right or wrong.

In his stumping Bryan supported Horace Boies, who was running for re-election as governor of Iowa on a free silver platform, and he was so anxious to "combat McKinleyism on its native heath" that he wrangled an invitation from Governor James A. Campbell to stump Ohio. "I take McKinley to task on the coinage as well as on the tariff," he wrote a friend upon his return to Nebraska.[10]

By the end of September Bryan was sure that silver was the coming

[9] A. P. Hopkins to Bryan, May 26, 1891, Bryan Papers. The Bryan-Hopkins debate appeared in the Omaha *World-Herald* from May to July 1891.

[10] Bryan to Campbell, July 27, 1891, Bryan to J. E. Neal, September 11, 1891, Bryan to John Tomlinson, October 21, 1891, Bryan Papers.

issue. At least he saw political sunshine in it. In a letter written shortly before the convening of the Fifty-second Congress he said: "I think the country has suffered enough by the fact that Democratic representatives from [tariff] protected states insist on the policy of robbery simply because their people get the benefit of it and I am sorry if the same thing is going to be attempted on the money question. I cannot tell what the result of this Congress will be, but if the Democratic party allows itself to be frightened away from the support of free coinage, I have little hope of our immediate success." [11]

In keeping with his belief, Bryan supported a silver plank in the Nebraska Democratic state convention of September 1891. Frequently referred to by young Democrats and many Independents as "the future leader of the Nebraska Democracy," he finally earned the distinction. Both Dr. George L. Miller and J. Sterling Morton advised against a "cheap and nasty" dollar and proposed the adoption of "a bold and broad declaration for honest money," but as chairman of the Committee on Resolutions he urged the adoption of a free silver plank. The gold men would take free but not unlimited coinage, and he accepted the compromise.[12]

Morton, for one, refused to stump on a silver platform and warned Bryan that "Free coinage beckons Democracy to disaster in 1892." [13] Bryan had to decide whether to rescind his stand or break with the conservatives who controlled the state organization and depend upon the silver Democrats and Independents. He chose the latter course, telling Morton that he no longer needed his advice or support. Then, when his candidate for the post of state supreme court judge declined the nomination, he argued at a meeting of the state Central Committee in favor of leaving the place vacant and endorsing the Independent candidate. A Democratic nomination insured Republican victory, he said. Except for the Independents' "vicious" subtreasury scheme, the Democratic and Independent platforms were "twin sisters," and there was much to be gained from an alliance with the Independents. He won by the close vote of nine to seven,[14] but his advocacy of fusion gave Bourbon Democrats another reason for opposing him. Republican victory in the state election was irrelevant compared to the importance of the revelation that the Nebraska Democracy had been split into an

---

[11] Bryan to A. B. Farquar, October 3, 1891, *ibid.*

[12] Omaha *Bee*, September 15, 1891; *Nebraska State Journal*, Lincoln *Daily Call*, Omaha *World-Herald*, September 18, 1891.

[13] Letter of September 28, 1891, Bryan Papers.

[14] Omaha *Bee*, October 6, 1891.

aggressive, progressive, silver, fusion, Bryan wing and a defensive, conservative, gold, "straight" wing led by Morton, Miller, Albert Watkins, and others. Division over the speaker for the new House of Representatives revealed a similar and nationwide split in the Democracy.

III

BOTH major aspirants for the speakership, Roger Q. Mills and Charles F. Crisp, supported tariff reform, but Mills favored gold and Crisp silver. Mills was the choice of an Eastern group that endorsed Grover Cleveland for President in 1892. Crisp was the choice of the Western and Southern wing of the party and of a small group of Easterners that preferred Senator David Bennett Hill of New York, a true bimetallist, to Cleveland. Crisp had the support of the silver Democrats and Alliancemen, and his success portended the overthrow of Cleveland on the money question. His appointment of Richard Parks Bland as chairman of the Committee on Coinage at least created an atmosphere favorable for the passage of a free silver measure.

In his annual message for 1891, President Benjamin Harrison asserted that silver purchases by the government under the Sherman Act had not raised the price of silver to one dollar in terms of gold. "That the increased volume of currency . . . was needed and that beneficial results upon trade and prices have followed, I think must be clear to everyone," he added, and he recommended that the law be given a "full trial," yet he reminded the silverites that "the Government is now buying and putting out of the market what is equivalent to the entire product of our mines," and he declared that full use of silver could not be made without international agreement.[15]

The time had come, said Bryan, to use both gold and silver as they had been used before 1873, and on February 16, 1892, the very day Cleveland announced his willingness to accept a third nomination, he persuaded the Committee on Rules to set aside the days March 22–25 for debate on a Bland silver bill. Although Crisp proved his friendship by voting against a motion to table the bill when it received a tie vote, action on the bill was postponed indefinitely. Bryan long remembered the night of March 24 as "the night free silver was killed." A vote could still be forced by cloture, and he and others circulated the necessary petition, but they fell short by ten signatures.[16]

[15] *Congressional Record*, 52 Congress, 1 Sess., 23:13–14.
[16] *Ibid.*, 23:656; Festus P. Summers, *William L. Wilson and Tariff Reform*, pp. 127–129.

Upon the death of the Bland bill, Cleveland reiterated his objection to silver and predicted that tariff reform would be the leading issue of the national campaign. Bryan countered with a demand for naming Horace Boies for President and was pleased to learn that the silver senators meant to introduce a silver bill and thereby force every senator to go on record before the meeting of the national convention,[17] but Harrison forestalled the move by announcing the holding of an international monetary conference and asking that domestic action on the currency await its conclusion. Believing that the conference would fail to reach agreement, as it did, Bryan tried to revive interest in domestic silver legislation. His chance came early in June, when he spoke against a bill providing for the repeal of the 10 per cent tax on state bank notes.

Bryan bolted the party line because he opposed "wildcat banking," the issue of notes not legal tender, and the federal government's surrendering of its sovereignty over the coinage into the hands of private corporations like the national banks. He demanded "honest money," "the gold and silver money of the Constitution," and "paper money . . . issued by the national government alone, and convertible into coin on demand." The House applauded him and defeated the bill.[18]

IV

ALTHOUGH Bryan opposed the renomination of Cleveland, countered him in Congress on the currency issue, and also attempted to wrest control of the Nebraska Democracy from his supporters, Bourbon leaders in the state convention of April 13–14, 1892, sought to chastise him rather than drum him out of the party, for he was in general agreement with them on most issues and had admirable vote-getting qualities. Writing in later years, Morton and Watkins, at least, confessed that they had not fully gauged his audacity. Yet Bryan was also in an embarrassing position: if he ran on a silver platform he would

[17] Under date of February 22, 1892, Charles S. Hamlin concluded from a visit to Washington "That the [David Bennett] Hill men did not wish to have the silver question settled directly in the House; they wished to drag the question along, keeping it before the public as a means of defeating Cleveland." Diary, Charles S. Hamlin Papers.

[18] H. M. Boydston to Bryan, February 8, 1892; Bryan Papers; Omaha *World-Herald*, March 3, 7, 9–10, 13, 22, 27, 29, 1892; J. Sterling Morton and Albert Watkins, *Illustrated History of Nebraska*, III, 240–241.

be opposed by the state organization; if he failed to run on a silver platform, silver Democrats and Independents would defect.

Bryan refused to be chosen delegate-at-large to a national convention that favored Cleveland. When he found the state platform unfriendly to silver he submitted a minority report in one short sentence—"We declare ourselves in favor of the free coinage of silver"—and roared that it was ignoble to dodge such an important issue. James E. Boyd, Nebraska's only Democratic governor, had been elected on a free silver platform, and Bryan argued that the platform should not be changed until another governor was chosen on an anti-silver plank.

Amidst deafening noise the vote taken on Bryan's minority report was recorded as 267 for and 237 against—and he had won. Differences among various tallies forced a recount. Fearful of being victimized, the silverites became a howling mob; they called the chairman a liar and threatened him with personal violence. The recount showed 247 for and 257 against—and Bryan had lost. An observer remarked that "Bryan's livid face, compressed lips, and defiant eyes were a vivid reminder of Edwin Booth in his most dramatic moments." But Bryan was not robbed. He lost all hope of winning, however, because so many of his supporters, convinced that they had been cheated, left the hall before another count could be taken. The delegates remaining then paradoxically adopted a resolution endorsing him for renomination to Congress.

Nebraska had been pledged to Cleveland, but the Bourbons had won their last fight against Bryan. Young men had led the fight on both the gold and silver sides. None matched Bryan for his fervid, earnest, and even passionate determination to fight for what he considered "right." The oldsters did not give up without a good fight, however. Governor Boyd was to have been elected chairman of the state delegation and Judge Joseph Ogden, a Bryanite, was to have replaced Tobias Castor, a gold and Cleveland supporter, as national committeeman. Instead William H. Thompson, silverite, was elected chairman of the state delegation and Castor remained the committeeman. As such, Castor had four years in which to counter Bryan's ambition to win control of the Nebraska Democracy.[19]

On June 20 Bryan was renominated unanimously on a platform that called for a reversal from a double monetary standard "so clan-

[19] Details and conclusions follow the author's "The Nebraska Democratic State Convention of April 13–14, 1892," *Nebraska History,* 39 (December 1958), 317–333.

destinely accomplished by congress in 1873" and for the free coinage of gold and silver at a just ratio. Two days later Cleveland was named for President by a convention organized by the proponents of gold, none of whom would listen to Bryan's pleas to name Boies. Upon his return to Washington Bryan joined the silver hosts in trying to pass a silver bill before the end of the session, but the nearness of the elections drove partisans into line with the presidential candidates, and the majority in the House that had favored silver at the beginning of the session had now evaporated. Yet the Senate passed a silver bill and sent it to the House, where Bland demanded a showdown. When the bill failed, silver went back to the calendar for the rest of the session and Bland's popularity suffered a hard blow. Now the turn of the gold men, Senator Sherman introduced a bill calling for the unconditional repeal of his own Silver Purchase Act, but the Congress adjourned without acting on it.

Cleveland, said Bryan, had been furnished capitalistic spectacles by Wall Street men and would not sympathize with the farmers and industrial workers stimulated to radical discontent by conservative leadership and financial depression.[20] He was the choice of the gold men of the East, not of the farmers of the plains and deltas for whom Bryan himself spoke, and Bryan refused to lift even a little finger for Cleveland during the campaign. Instead he spoke for James B. Weaver, the Populist presidential candidate, hoping thereby to win the large number of Populist votes he himself needed to be re-elected.

As reorganized after the census of 1890, the First Nebraska District excluded Omaha and forced Bryan to depend heavily upon the farmers of his new district. Moreover, the Republicans chose as his opponent Lincoln's Allen W. Field, a forty-year-old district judge and former state legislator backed by both the Lincoln and Omaha Republican press. As national committeeman and a director of the Republicans' Western headquarters, Edward Rosewater strove mightily to defeat Bryan. Recently, too, William McKinley had repaid Bryan for his visit to Ohio in 1891 by telling large audiences in Beatrice, Lincoln, and Omaha that Bryan was wrong on tariff protection.

No sooner had Charles H. Van Wyck been chosen the Populist gubernatorial candidate than allegations were made that he and Bryan

[20] Bryan referred to the fact that after his first term Cleveland had associated with the Wall Street firm of Bangs, Stetson, Tracy, and McVeagh, and that he included among his associates financiers like William C. Whitney, E. C. Benedict, Thomas Fortune Ryan, Oliver H. Payne, and Oscar Straus.

had arranged to trade votes in the First District. That fusion was not in the cards was proved on August 11, when Jerome Shamp received sixty votes and Bryan only twelve in the Populist convention. Field emphasized his confidence of beating Bryan by resigning from the bench the next day. Since the First District contained 13,000 Republicans, 10,000 Democrats, and 8000 Populists, Bryan's reasons for countenancing fusion are self-evident, particularly since all indications pointed to a greater Populist vote in 1892 than in 1890.

Bryan sent his campaign manager, Jefferson H. Broady, into the silver states to collect money, a fact unrevealed until December 1893, when the *Nebraska State Journal* "spilled the beans" about the "passing of the corn popper." The $4000 collected Bryan viewed as made with no ulterior motive, such as that of influencing legislation, although he deemed immoral the contributions made by protected industries to the Republican party. Yet his failure to publicize the source of his contributions reveals that he realized that he might have been defeated had the news become known.[21]

Fearing that Bryan would speak on silver, demand fusion, or even compete with Morton for the gubernatorial nomination, Euclid Martin, the new state chairman, and Castor played upon Bryan's obsession with McKinley and invited him to deliver a tariff speech in the state convention. After Morton was chosen to oppose the "radical" Van Wyck, resolutions endorsing Cleveland but not silver were adopted. Then the delegates cheered a resolution reading "That we endorse the course of Hon. W. J. Bryan in congress and point with pride to him as a resolute and brilliant champion of the masses against the classes." [22] Bryan had been fooled by the state leaders, who secretly applauded their having escaped a silver speech. The uninitiated thrilled to see Morton and Bryan, the old and the young, the conservative and the progressive, cooperate in the convention, but there was no foundation for real accord. While neither favored Cleveland, Bryan defended and Morton opposed silver; Morton appealed to conservatives and Bryan sought Populist votes by saying, "I was born a Democrat but have strong Alliance tendencies." [23]

[21] Lon V. Stephens to Jesse F. Boell, January 25, 1925, Bryan Papers; Charles S. Thomas to Paxton Hibben, July 16, 1928, Paxton Hibben, *The Peerless Leader: William Jennings Bryan*, p. 146.

[22] *Nebraska State Journal*, Omaha *Bee*, Omaha *World-Herald*, August 31, 1892.

[23] Omaha *World-Herald*, September 29, 1892; Jesse F. Boell, "The Career of William Jennings Bryan to 1896" (unpublished M.A. thesis, University of Nebraska, 1929), p. 104.

The outstanding event of the Nebraska elections of 1892 was the series of eleven Bryan-Field debates held between September 12 and October 15. Bryan was so far superior to Field as a debater that the Democratic press spoke of "the walkaway of the hero of tariff reform with the pigmy of bogus protection." [24] Field nevertheless delivered some telling blows, as when he asked Bryan how he could support both silver and Cleveland as the Democratic presidential candidate. "Whatever may be the view of other Democrats," Bryan replied, "I propose to give my every endeavor and my earnest effort to the passage of a free coinage law. Though I should be left alone . . . I would not be turned from my course by the attitude of any other man in my party." [25] When Field asked if he would vote for Weaver or Cleveland if the election went into the House he answered directly: he preferred Weaver, but he had been elected a Democrat and he would vote for Cleveland whether he himself were re-elected or not.[26]

Field then attacked Bryan on moral and religious matters, charging that he was prohibitionist, a Roman Catholic (because Irish!), and a nativist. He also said that Bryan was receiving a boodle fund and that he was being aided surreptitiously by both Morton and Shamp, and Rosewater stated that money raised in the Second District would be used by Bryan to carry the saloon element and the purchaseable vote in the First, especially in Lincoln, where Field was strongest. Evidence indicates rather that Field's managers played the whisky vote by ordering Lincoln's saloon keepers to work against Bryan or be refused license renewals,[27] and the Omaha *World-Herald* revealed that Field had been given $20,000 by the Republicans of the East and that he would receive up to $80,000 more if needed to defeat Bryan.[28] The unconfirmed rumors that Bryan was knifing Morton persisted until the latter became convinced that the silver Democrats were working against him and were his worst enemies. "They are thickest among Bryan's friends and seek to trade me off for Van Wyck to get in exchange votes for Bryan," he wrote a sister.[29]

Bryan presented no learned arguments on the money issue. When

[24] Omaha *World-Herald*, September 21, 1892.

[25] *Ibid.*, September 23, 1892.

[26] *Ibid.*, October 23, November 4, 1892; Omaha *Bee*, November 2, 1892; *Nebraska State Journal*, July 18, September 13, 1892.

[27] Omaha *World-Herald*, October 30, November 4, 1892; Omaha *Bee*, September 8, October 25, November 7, 1892.

[28] Omaha *World-Herald*, October 24, 1892.

[29] Letter to Emma Morton, October 6, 1892, in James C. Olson, *J. Sterling Morton*, p. 344.

questioned, he would say, "I don't know anything about free silver. The people of Nebraska are for free silver and I am for free silver. I will look up the arguments later." [30] While his admission of ignorance won over many farmers, it led Morton to state that "Bryan is so self-adjusting that—in his fine flexibility—he can agree with a greater number of persons who hold different views on the same question than any pinfeathered economist I have ever met." [31] Yet he behaved queerly by unqualifiedly supporting Bryan for re-election and at the same time opposing silver. Did he think that his support for gold might secure him a cabinet post if Cleveland were elected? "There are going to be some very cross-eyed Democrats in the First district who are endeavoring to believe Morton and vote for Bryan," commented Rosewater.[32] The dilemma was well phrased by E. R. Tingley, a gold Democrat and a director of a savings bank in Lincoln, who wrote Cleveland: "The question that confronts me is this; shall I vote for Bryan, free trade, and the obnoxious free silver or for Fields, a safe monetary system, and the obnoxious high protective tariff?" [33]

There is no doubt that Field and Shamp were in collusion against Bryan. Shamp's attempt to lie out of his predicament after his own committee admitted receipt of Republican money proved him a prevaricator unworthy of any man's vote, and his death blow was delivered by a secret "Gideon's Band" which let it be known that he was merely a stool pigeon set up to attract votes from Field and so help Bryan.[34]

Bryan made no attempt to hide his kinship with Populists, and nationally known Populists came to his aid. Mrs. Mary E. Lease, of "let 'em raise less corn and more hell" fame, spoke at Omaha on November 1, and on November 2 she and Weaver spoke in Lincoln, countering the visits of McKinley in August, of Republican Senator Joseph Foraker of Ohio, and of McKinley again in October. Both Democrats and Populists paraded for Bryan on the night before the election, and many a G.O.P. leader confessed that his party was "hanging by its eyebrows in Nebraska." [35]

While the Republicans won the electoral vote, the state offices, and

[30] Omaha *World-Herald*, September 23, 1892.

[31] Letter to Michael D. Harter, January 9, 1893, in Olson, *Morton*, p. 344.

[32] Omaha *Bee*, November 4, 1892.

[33] Letter of August 25, 1892, Grover Cleveland Papers.

[34] Omaha *World-Herald*, October 21, 30, 1892; *Nebraska State Journal*, November 10, 1892.

[35] Omaha *Bee*, October 19, 1892; Omaha *World-Herald*, October 10, 25, 27, November 2, 3, 8, 1892.

three of the now six congressmen, and the Populists took two congressional seats, the vote in the First District was so close that it was not until three days after the election that Bryan was declared the victor over Field by a mere 140 votes.[36] He was again the only Democratic congressman from Nebraska, and his election from a Republican district over the efforts of McKinley added substantially to his national fame. In contrast, Morton suffered his worst defeat in thirty-eight years of political life.

V

BRYAN's defeat in his first senatorial race, in 1893, taught him the power of the Populists and strengthened his conviction that senators should be elected directly by the people. The Nebraska legislature contained 53 Populists, 53 Republicans, and only 17 Democrats, one of whom died before the end of the session and five of whom were irrevocably committed to gold. Success depended upon fusion of either the Republicans or the Democrats with the Populists; all parties were split on candidates. On the Democratic side, Morton, Boyd, and Bryan fought each other. Bryan told the Populists that he alone could be elected by fusion, but he refused either to share control of the patronage in return for their aid or to support a Populist candidate. On February 3 his hopes were crushed when the Populists dropped John Holbrook Powers, leader of the State Alliance, and supported William V. Allen. Bryan urged the election of his friend Allen as the way to keep Nebraska out of the railroads' power, and on February 7 the Democrats and the Populists finally merged and elected Allen. Bryan's influence with the eleven Democrats who voted consistently for Allen was largely responsible for his victory, and he and Allen agreed to cooperate on both state and national matters.[37]

Cleveland rewarded the gold Democrats who had opposed Bryan

[36] In 1888 the total vote cast in the seven counties of Bryan's new district was 32,256; in 1892, 31,042. In 1888 the Democrats in the district had polled 29,055 votes, the Republicans 16,817, minor parties 2307. In 1892 the figures were: Democrats, 4132; Republicans, 15,071; minor parties, 1090; Populist party, 11,084; revealing that in the four year interval the Democrats had lost 6995 votes, the Republicans 2746, and minor parties 1237, while the Populists gained 10,865. Adapted from W. Dean Burnham, *Presidential Ballots, 1836–1892*, pp. 600–617.

[37] The account of the Senate contest is condensed from the author's "William Jennings Bryan and the Nebraska Senatorial Election of 1893," *Nebraska History*, 31 (September 1950), 183–203.

by tendering Morton the post of Secretary of Agriculture. Morton turned the state patronage over to Castor, Martin, and Boyd, who gave conservatives 99 per cent and Bryanites 1 per cent of it. But Bryan already looked forward to 1895, when he could be elected senator in either of two ways—by Democratic-Populist fusion or by election as governor with a Populist lieutenant governor. In the latter case he would go to the Senate and give the Populists the governorship. It was clear, however, that to succeed he must overcome the Populist middle-of-the-roaders and gold Democrats by joining silver Democrats to the Populist fusionists. If he failed he could not convince the nation at large that he rather than Cleveland represented the aspirations of the American people.

VI

IN THE short session of the Fifty-second Congress (December 5, 1892 to March 4, 1893), two propositions split the House Democrats. The Andrews-Cate bill would repeal the Sherman Act and permit the national banks to increase their circulation. Another bill would repeal both the act and the tax on state bank note issues. Stoutly opposing the repeal of the Sherman Act unless a substitute could be secured that would prevent contraction of the currency without augmenting the powers of either the national or state banks, Bryan demanded the substitution of the free coinage of silver for the act and consistently opposed increasing the powers of the banks. At Christmas time, 1892, President-elect Cleveland put the pressure on Crisp: he would not object to his election as Speaker of the Fifty-third Congress if he would reorganize the Ways and Means, Appropriations, Coinage, and Banking committees with majorities favoring the gold standard and a low tariff. Because of his "violent free silver tendencies" Bryan must go,[38] and he warned that he would use the patronage club against men like Bryan and that if repeal of the Sherman Act were not accomplished by March 4, 1893 he might call Congress into extraordinary session to do so.[39] On February 3, 1893, the Senate defied him by refusing to pass Sherman's repeal bill.

[38] Omaha *Bee*, December 29, 1892.

[39] Cleveland to John G. Carlisle, January 22, 1893, James A. Barnes, *John G. Carlisle, Financial Statesman*, pp. 252–253; Omaha *World-Herald*, April 11, 1892; Horace S. Merrill, *Bourbon Leader: Grover Cleveland and the Democratic Party*, pp. 172–176; Allan Nevins, *Grover Cleveland: A Study in Courage*, pp. 523–524.

On February 8 Bryan castigated the Andrews-Cate bill as the first attempt by the Cleveland forces to obtain the repeal of the Sherman Act. Instead of reducing taxes upon the people it would relieve the national banks of an annual tax of half a million dollars by permitting the issue of notes at par of bonds held instead of at 90 per cent. Moreover, it would, by repealing that "cowardly makeshift," the Sherman Act, end government purchases of silver and contract the currency. The price of silver and of agricultural commodities would fall, the debts of millions would increase, and a great obstacle would be raised to obtaining bimetallism. Buttressed by Bland, he prevented passage of the bill. The closeness of the vote, 153 to 142,[40] showed that repeal and anti-repeal strength was as equally divided in the House as in the Senate. Repeal could be prevented for the moment, but so could any legislation favorable to silver.

Bryan also opposed a gold bond bill the Senate sent to the House, for it would cancel the greenbacks when they were redeemed, contract the currency, and substitute an interest-bearing for a non-interest-bearing debt—no way to bring permanent relief to the people! There was no need for the $100,000,000 redemption fund of 1879, which was established when the nation resumed specie payments and feared a great drain on its gold reserves. Now thirty or forty millions would do. Furthermore, the obligations of the United States, be they bonds, greenbacks, or Treasury notes, called for redemption in "coin," which meant either gold or silver, not gold alone.[41] Of what advantage was it to issue bonds for gold if the gold were obtained by the presentation of greenbacks for redemption? Why issue bonds to buy gold when silver lay in the Treasury? This bond bill was "the second skirmish in the great battle of the standards" which, he hoped, would end in victory for "the gold and silver coinage of the Constitution." The House upheld him and killed the bond proposition by the overwhelming vote of 209 to 14.[42]

[40] Congressional Record, 52 Congress, 2 Sess., 24:1377–1382; Omaha World-Herald, February 10, 11, 14, 1893; Bryan, First Battle, pp. 76–77; Robinson, Reed, pp. 278–280.

[41] The Treasury was required to redeem greenbacks in gold when they were presented and to reissue them. The Treasury notes issued under the Sherman Act were redeemable in "coin," either gold or silver, but Carlisle ruled that they should be redeemed in gold. Thus the greenbacks and Treasury notes acted as buckets on an endless chain that scooped gold out of the Treasury.

[42] Omaha World-Herald, February 12–14, March 2, 1893; Congressional Record, 52 Congress, 2 Sess., 24:2121–2185, 2208, 2235–2239.

Cleveland carefully analyzed his strength in the new House, elected in 1892, to ascertain how many members could be induced to vote for the repeal of the Sherman Act. If William F. Harrity, chairman of the Democratic National Committee, failed to whip enough men into line, he would convene the Fifty-third Congress into extraordinary session. In his inaugural address he declared that he meant to use his full power to avert debasement of the currency and disaster to the nation's finances and economy. Bryan read into the message Cleveland's determination to ride roughshod over the silver Democrats until they favored the unconditional repeal of the Sherman Act. Moreover, most of Cleveland's cabinet upheld him on the currency question. The appointment of J. Sterling Morton as Secretary of Agriculture could be interpreted as a step in Cleveland's war to punish Bryan, for Morton rather than Bryan would control the Nebraska patronage. When Morton's recommendations were sent to the Senate and his were held up, Bryan knew that Cleveland was using the appointing power to obtain votes for the repeal of the Sherman Act.

Cleveland knew of Bryan's oratorical power and of the good work he had done for tariff reform, but it was apparent, he said, that "the idea that appealed to his imagination was free silver," and he feared him as an apostle who could make Populism a direct threat to the Democracy. He felt justified in denying him patronage because "Bryan's mind, training, and imagination all combine to make him a Populist, pure and simple. He has not even the remotest notion of the principles of Democracy." None, he added, was more active in seeking patronage than Bryan, and "I discovered . . . that a goodly proportion of those were Populists in reality if not in name." [43]

Both Bryan and Cleveland were rugged Presbyterians and conscientious Democrats, but Bryan would follow where the people led while Cleveland would drive them in the path he wished them to go. Cleveland would relieve the financial embarrassment of the government while Bryan believed government to be made for the convenience of the people, a point which he said Cleveland failed to realize. Would the people choose Cleveland, the President, who represented men of money, resisted experimentation, and demanded stability; or Bryan, a mere congressman, a prophet of the poor who would risk experimentation and demanded change? Bryan's was the bolder approach, for he would risk change. Above all he would try something.

[43] E. R. Tingley to Cleveland, August 25, 1892, Cleveland Papers; George F. Parker, *Recollections of Grover Cleveland*, pp. 208–209, 213–215.

The year 1893, year of the panic, of depression, and of the great fight over the repeal of the Sherman Act, marked the beginning of a three-and-a-half year struggle by Bryan to win the leadership of the Democratic party from Cleveland.

On the stump in the Middle West and South during the spring of 1893, Bryan denounced Cleveland's stand on the currency issue and demanded an alliance of silver Democrats, Republicans, and Populists which would overmatch the hard-shell Democrats and Republicans despite the lashings of Cleveland's patronage whip. He was cheered at the Trans-Mississippi Congress which met in Ogden, Utah, on April 24, where he first met William H. Harvey, and in the South, where he was hailed as a fit leader to oppose Cleveland. He further expounded the silver cause in correspondence with a large number of silverites both in the United States and in Great Britain, in articles for the Omaha *World-Herald* and St. Louis *Republic,* and in working as a member of the Nebraska State Council of the American Bimetallic League.

In April 1893 the gold reserve dropped below the $100,000,000 mark. The psychological effect was overwhelming, for the mark had been held sacred by the gold men as an index by which to measure the maintenance of the gold standard. When the international monetary conference called in 1891 failed to reach agreement, on April 25, 1893,[44] it became obvious that the solution to the money problem must be a domestic one, and on the next day Cleveland and his Secretary of the Treasury, John G. Carlisle, went to New York to seek a $50,000,000 loan. On May 4, amid the festivities marking the opening of the World Columbian Exposition, the failure of the National Cordage Company, accompanied by a sharp drop in the stock market, ushered in the panic of 1893. To climax the cataclysm, Western farmers suffered a partial crop failure. When the price of silver fell by the astounding amount of twenty cents because of the demonetization of silver by India in June, the American farmer believed he saw another link in the chain being fashioned by the gold men to bind to earth the debtor classes of the world.[45] As the great panic rolled on toward the bottom of the business cycle and Cleveland refused to utilize the great opportunity to become a popular hero, the masses sought another who would ride

[44] Omaha *World-Herald,* April 24, 1894; Charles Foster, "The Brussels Conference Reviewed," *North American Review,* 156 (April 1893), 493–500.

[45] See Newton L. Bunnell, "A Farmer's View of Free Coinage," *ibid.,* 156 (June 1893), 753–755.

the whirlwind, give direction to the storm, and lead them through perplexing times. The panic as such had run its course by October, but the depression that followed lasted until 1897 and provided a marvellous setting for the battle of the standards.

Bryan denied that the government's silver purchases caused the depression, for the depression was worldwide and affected gold standard nations as well as the United States. It had been caused by European investors who sold their securities in the United States, thereby draining its gold reserves, and by "the monied sharks of Wall Street trying to frighten Congress into issuing bonds. . . . But you can't legislate a scare out of the people. We must restore public confidence." [46] He charged that the banks had ruined many sound businesses by refusing them ordinary credits. The solvency of the banks had then been questioned, and the government had done absolutely nothing to extend them credit. Thus all counts pointed to the evils of an inflexible banking and currency system.

Bryan urged the people to put their money back into the banks, for only then could loans be made and business revive. He also warned against the "honest dollar" about which the gold men spoke. There never would be a dollar which would buy today, tomorrow, and the day after tomorrow the same amount of goods. The currency problem, moreover, could not be settled only in chambers of commerce: "It is a battle between plutocracy and democracy and democracy will win. . . . If you want a single gold standard the best way to get it is to repeal the Sherman law." He ridiculed the assertion that the United States was powerless to act unless England acted with her, saying, "There is a hardy race of people between the Rockies and the Alleghenies who will legislate for themselves and declare the financial independence of the country." The Sherman Act should not be repealed; indeed, by adding currency to the circulation it was mitigating rather than increasing the severity of the depression.[47]

While not as bellicose as several senators who advocated war with England in the interest of silver, Bryan used the depression to stir the embers of patriotism against the "aristocratic land-grabbers," "tight-fisted creditors," and "bribe givers" whose gold had made the United States forsake silver, and gleefully twisted the British lion's tail. He repeatedly stressed that the government, not the banks, should issue money; warned against being led astray by the metropolitan press,

[46] *Nebraska State Journal,* July 18, 1893; Omaha *World-Herald,* July 22, 1893.
[47] Omaha *World-Herald,* May 5, 6, July 23, 27, 30, 1893.

"which notoriously favored a gold standard"; and severely criticized Cleveland and Carlisle for failing to aid the country effectively. He challenged Carlisle to debate. Carlisle refused,[48] and many Westerners and Southerners who talked loosely about "impeaching" the Secretary who dared suspend silver purchases put their faith in Bryan. Proof of his contention that silver was not to blame for the depression lies in the circumstance that economic conditions did not improve materially for more than four years after the repeal of the Sherman Act.

The depression enhanced Bryan's rise to power, for it offered him the opportunity to sponsor national bimetallism as an immediate remedy. He had no stake in silver as such and represented a wholly agricultural constituency. Therefore his demand for justice must be impersonal, and those who heard him saw him as the hero of the poor and oppressed.

During the two weeks prior to the convening of the special session of Congress Cleveland called for August 7, the silverites made final arrangements to ward off the repeal of the Sherman Act. An American Bimetallic League convention in Chicago drew the largest assembly of its kind in history. It ruled politics out of order, but demands for a third party were made nonetheless. James B. Weaver urged all free silverites to embrace the Populists' Omaha platform of 1892, for it contained all of the silverites' demands, and like Bryan objected to the creation of a distinctly new national silver party. When certain delegates characterized the demonetization of silver as a "revolution" to be cured only by another revolution, Bryan assured them that every evil could be remedied at the ballot box. The platform he helped write reflected his attitude. There would be no compromise. All legislation unfavorable to silver must be expunged. The financial policy of the United States must remain free from dependence upon that of any other nation. The only remedy for current conditions lay in the coinage of free silver at a ratio of 16 to 1. Repeal of the Sherman Act should be favored only if provision was made for free coinage. When he declared himself ready to launch a moral crusade in which the masses would be awakened and their demand for silver made so strong that "the voice of the people will be stronger than the voice of gold," he was cheered and elected to the Ways and Means Committee of the League, which would disseminate silver literature and direct the silver lobby in Washington during the repeal fight and as long thereafter as necessary. Then, in a House caucus on August 5, he demanded that Cleveland's call for the repeal of the Sherman Act be thwarted.

[48] Barnes, *Carlisle*, pp. 452–453.

Since 1873 the silverites had formed the aggressive element; now the gold men took the offensive. History is replete with instances in which rulers gained popularity by wiping out debts by the simple expedient of devaluing the currency. Cleveland reversed the popular current and presented an adamant stand for stabilization, overlooking the fact that stability made the rich richer and the poor poorer. The battle over the Sherman Act would also decide whether Bland, still recognized as the outstanding silver leader, would defeat Cleveland and enhance his opportunity to win the presidential nomination in 1896 or give way to Bryan.

In his short message to Congress Cleveland blamed the financial distress on the Sherman Act. Bryan revealed his determination to oppose repeal until he obtained an acceptable substitute for the act by saying that "We do not generally cancel the mortgage until after the notes are paid," and in a House caucus of silverites held on August 9 he opposed abandoning 16 to 1 in order to obtain a compromise ratio that would maintain parity. However, Bland said that half a loaf was better than none, and he selected Bryan as one of seven silverites who would join seven gold men to work out the details of the debate. As agreed, the vote would take place first on Bland's silver bills on 16 to 1, 17 to 1, and on up to 20 to 1. If these failed, a vote would be taken on returning to the Bland-Allison Act. If that also failed, a vote would be taken on Wilson's unconditional repeal bill. Provision was made for eleven days of debate, with three additional days under the five minute rule. On August 9 Wilson introduced his bill and argued strenuously for it. Cleveland then made it clear that no appointments would be made until it passed.

Bland made the best speech of the first week of debate. As the time for him to speak neared on August 16, Bryan told his wife that he had never felt more deeply the gravity of a question and that he had prayed that he might be "an instrument in the hands of Providence of doing some good for my country." [49] As he arose, the doors of the House were kept open by members rushing in. Almost all of the senators were there; the galleries were jammed and murmuring expectantly. Confident of his ability to present a subject on which he felt he had history and God on his side, he turned his printed speech over and never referred to it.

He possessed no language, Bryan began, with which to describe the weal or woe to all mankind that depended upon the action of the House. With his second breath he directed his appeal over the Presi-

[49] Letter of August 16, 1893, Bryan Papers.

dent's head to the constituency whose rights he had sworn to defend. He believed Cleveland honest, courageous, and sincere, but so were the Indian mothers who threw their children into the Ganges! Cleveland was being deceived, for the demand for repeal did not come from the people's representatives but from the "middlemen, [and] the business interests." Cleveland could no more judge popular sentiment from the expressions of the latter than "measure the ocean's silent depths by the foam upon its waves."

He then gave a closely reasoned exposition of his principles. First, there was not enough gold in the world to permit all nations to go on a gold standard. Second, the adoption of the gold standard by the United States would result in the creation of a dishonest dollar. A government could fix the legal tender qualities of money but not its purchasing power, which depended upon the law of supply and demand. By controlling the amount of money in circulation, however, the government could affect prices. By creating dishonest dollars, then, the government could cause the appreciation of the value of debt. Third, a gold standard promised a vicious contraction of the currency which would idle labor, still enterprise, and force agrarian debtors to become tenants upon their former estates.

The use of two metals would result in a more stable money than one alone. If we established bimetallism, and silver drove gold to Europe, then Europe would have the gold with which to buy our goods; if we adopted gold we lessened Europe's ability to buy from us, for we would have to get the gold from Europe. Also, the sale of bonds for gold in order to support a gold standard would constrict the circulation and increase the stringency of the money market. If these bonds were sold abroad, Americans would have to pay higher taxes and eventually find the gold to send abroad in repayment. On the other hand, the adoption of a silver standard would make the United States the trading center of those nations that used silver, and these contained more than half of the world's population. Trade would be stimulated, and our own mines would furnish the silver we would need.

Bryan's hour was up, but the House readily granted him unanimous consent to proceed.

Rather than force Europe to adopt silver in order to trade with us, Bryan continued, we should adopt bimetallism and trade with both gold and silver countries. The international bimetallists were no closer to agreement now than in 1867. Britain had always provided the stumbling block, and he believed it high time to demand independence from Britain. Were we unable to make our own laws? Were we an independent people or a British colony? If gold alone would make us slaves, then let us use both gold and silver and be free!

The major question facing independent bimetallists, Bryan averred, was to secure that ratio that promised the greatest public advantage with the least injustice. Any change in the ratio, however, should benefit the debtor rather than the creditor. The cupidity of the silver mine owner about which the East perennially complained was the same as that of the gold mine owner, of any businessman who demanded special legislation, of the farmer who desired higher prices for his products, and of the laborer who wanted higher wages. The silver miners merely asked for "the restoration of the money of the Fathers," for the right to receive a price equal to that they had received prior to 1873.

After presenting a bill of grievances against the administration, Bryan suggested some innovations that would restore confidence. First, guarantee bank deposits. Then compel bank stockholders to put up security for their double rather than a simple liability and increase the penalty for stockholders and officers who wrecked banks and profited at the expense of the depositors. A law was needed to limit the liabilities which a bank might assume upon a given amount of capital, so that there would be enough margin left to protect its creditors. Finally, bank embezzlers should receive greater punishment than at present. Let anyone propose real relief, he said, and the House would gladly cooperate.

Above all, Bryan demanded that unconditional repeal should not occur without a substitute that would outline the financial policy of the future. The silverites, not the gold men, he asserted, were the ones to grant terms. A century of history, the pledges of all parties, and the most sacred interests of humanity itself demanded the surrender of the principle of gold monometallism. "Just as long as there are people here who would chain this country to a single gold standard there is war—eternal war; and it might as well be known now!" he declaimed.

Bryan complimented Cleveland as a warrior who had restored fidelity to the public service and who by taking up the banner of tariff reform had converted Democratic hope to reality. Let him now call the party hosts to arms in the greater fight "for the gold and silver coinage of the Constitution."

We have come to the parting of the ways. On the one hand stand the imperious and compassionless corporate interests and moneyed institutions of the country, which demand that the Democratic party become their agent and execute their merciless decrees; on the other stand the masses for whom the party would speak, work-worn and dust-begrimed, suffering from the inequitable distribution of wealth, unable to purchase necessities, beating in vain for relief against the outer walls of legislatures. To the Democracy, standing between these two forces, came the cry, "Choose you this day whom ye shall serve." What will the answer be? Will the party turn its face to the rising or the setting sun, choose blessings or curses, life or death—which, which? [50]

Bryan's speech was the greatest made on his side of the question, and the nation's press acknowledged him rather than Bland the commander of the anti-Cleveland forces. Clevelandites said he was a demagogue, a brilliant word painter who pleaded for a section and a special interest, an "infant phenomenon" who attacked the President because of an insolence nurtured by egotism, but from Missouri to the Rockies he was a hero who had immortalized himself and deserved the presidential nomination on "a people's platform that opposed gold bugs, monopolists, English, Rothschild's manipulation and . . . Eastern despotism," as the *Rocky Mountain News* put it.[51]

Cleveland swung back hard by appointing Morton as Bryan's executioner and denying a single committee chairmanship in the House to anyone from west of the Missouri River. Only because Crisp interceded for him in behalf of impending tariff reform did Cleveland permit Bryan to remain on the Ways and Means Committee.

The highest number of votes cast for any ratio, 123 as against 225, was cast for silver at 16 to 1. Restoration of the Bland-Allison law failed by 136 to 213, and unconditional repeal then passed by 239 to 108. Bryan voted for 16 to 1 and opposed the other ratios. The Northeastern, Middle Atlantic, and Middle Western states had favored, and the Western and Southern states had opposed, repeal. While four fifths of the Republicans had voted aye, the Democrats had divided, 138 aye and 78 nay. Since only two thirds of the Democrats stood by Cleveland, he had won only because of Republican support.

While the Senate studied the repeal bill, the House silverites overrode Speaker Crisp and the Committee on Rules by taking up and referring a seigniorage bill to the Ways and Means Committee, and Bryan introduced bills implementing the suggestions he had made in

[50] *Congressional Record*, 53 Congress, 1 Sess., 25:400–411.

[51] Press notices in Omaha *Bee*, August 17, 21, 23, 1893 and Omaha *World-Herald*, August 17, 23, 1893.

his speech of August 16. However, he would authorize the Treasury to issue greenbacks to an amount equal to the sum collected to guarantee bank deposits, and also to increase the amount of money in circulation by having the Treasury redeem the $35,364,500 outstanding in 2 per cent government bonds. The Ways and Means Committee reported his bank guaranty bill favorably, but it died on the calendar. The Judiciary Committee favored his embezzlement bill, and it passed the Senate in slightly amended form. While the country generally favored bank deposit insurance, Bryan's other propositions were considered undesirable because they would inflate the currency.

VII

IN THE PRIMARIES for the state convention of October 4, 1893, Bryan won his own county and also Morton's, but bolts by gold men in Castor's county and in others resulted in the sending of numerous contested delegations to the convention. Bryan underestimated the effectiveness of administration leaders who were incensed with his treatment of them, who were determined to teach him that it was political suicide to call the President a fool, and who were not above using patronage deals and rigged admissions to gain their objective. All applicants for federal posts had to go to Omaha for a briefing on how to act in the convention, and tickets of admission were denied to Bryanites. As punishment for his "insults" to Cleveland in his August 16 speech against the repeal of the Sherman Act, Bryan could have only one man on the Committee on Credentials and one other on the Committee on Resolutions. He must learn to sneeze when Grover took snuff! He failed to substitute a silverite for the gold man named for chairman, to win election to the Committee on Resolutions, or to prevent the adoption of a platform which endorsed Cleveland and the repeal of the Sherman Act. In support of a minority report favoring silver, however, he delivered a hot speech against the gold men.

Quivering with indignation at his defeat, Bryan lashed at the Cleveland men with fiery impetuosity. It did not matter a snap of his fingers —and he snapped his fingers at the delegates—whether the minority report were voted up or down. He was "right," and it made no difference whether they supported him or not. If the convention endorsed the gold demanded by Wall Street "I will go out and serve my party and my God under some other name than as a Democrat. . . ." He arraigned Cleveland as "absolutely wrong" on the money question and was cheered by many when he declared that he would not support for President in 1896 an advocate of the gold standard.[52] Stating that they would rather sacrifice him than principle, the gold men crushed his minority report by almost four to one and named a gold man, Frank Irvine, for state supreme court judge.

Conservative Democrats declined to crawl blindly into the Populist pit at Bryan's prodding and suggested that it would be good for both him and his constituents if he were retired and left to accumulate a stock of wisdom with the passing years. Morton gave federal offices to two of the convention leaders and declared that Bryan "ought to take a tumble to himself," [53] and Cleveland was greatly pleased with the outcome of the convention.[54] Thomas E. Watson told Bryan that he must abandon either his principles or the Democracy, and the House Populists welcomed him into their ranks by telegram.[55] It was Joseph A. Edgerton, a Populist, who first pointed out that Bryan's minority report was the same as the currency plank in the Democratic national platform and that in voting it down because Bryan favored it the gold men had repudiated their own platform.[56]

Bryan intended neither to leave his party nor accept his rebuff as a matter of course. Taking to the stump against the gold nominees on the state ticket before returning to Washington to hear the closing Senate debates on the repeal of the Sherman Act, he stated that the Democratic masses would not endorse the action of the convention and that he had documentary proof that he had been undone by the "federal pie counter brigade." Moreover, the nomination of Irvine would help the Republicans. Irvine was among his first friends in Nebraska, yet he opposed him because, he wrote in answer to Hitchcock's plea for an endorsement, "I know you do not want me to alienate the friends I have left by apologizing for that convention." [57] However, his attempt to ride two horses at the same time placed him in an awkward position. If he were still a Democrat his overtures to the Populists must

[52] Ibid., Omaha Bee, Nebraska State Journal, October 5, 1893; Bryan, First Battle, pp. 122–124; Morton and Watkins, History of Nebraska, III, 254–255; Addison E. Sheldon, Nebraska: The Land and the People, I, 735–736.

[53] Letter of October 5, 1893, in Olson, Morton, p. 391; Omaha Bee, Omaha World-Herald, October 6–23, 1893.

[54] Morton to John B. Sheehan, October 7, 1893, in Olson, Morton, p. 381.

[55] Watson to Bryan, October 13, 1893, in C. Vann Woodward, Tom Watson, Agrarian Rebel, p. 196.

[56] Omaha World-Herald, October 7, 9, 1893.

[57] Bryan to Gilbert M. Hitchcock, October 12, 1893, Bryan Papers.

be insincere, and the Populists distrusted him because he would not admit being one of them. He stood to be defeated for re-election in 1894 no matter which side of the fence he came down on.

Morton interfered directly for the first and only time with party action by writing the chairman of every Democratic county committee to work against fusion and for Irvine, and for the only time in his life he also appealed to the railroads for aid.[58] Paradoxically, Bryan won when the Democrats lost the November elections to Populists and Republicans. Clevelandites charged him with Irvine's defeat by encouraging Populism and contributing to Democratic disunity. But the election showed that the rank and file preferred Bryan to the administration. Morton contributed much to Democratic disunity by calling for help from the railroads against Bryan and by his attitude toward the farmer. The farmer's most insidious and destructive enemies were not natural ones but the "professional farmers" who "farmed the farmers," he said. The leaders of the National Grange were "the Plowboys of Pennsylvania Avenue"; the farmer's worst enemy was his own ignorance.[59] To farmers suckled on the doctrines of Grange and Alliance and now strangled by one of the worst depressions in history, Morton epitomized the hostility of the Cleveland administration to agriculture.

VIII

From August to October, for eighty days, free silver senators conducted the longest filibuster then on record. Bryan offered a compromise plan in which a seigniorage tax of between 20 and 30 per cent would be charged for the coinage of silver, thus fixing the ratio at about 22 to 1. Rumor had it that Carlisle favored such a compromise, but Cleveland held out firmly for unconditional repeal, and on October 20 the repeal bill passed, 48 to 27, with the Democrats dividing equally, 22 to 22. Almost all of the nays came from the South, and all but one of the dozen Republican votes cast against the bill came from the representatives of silver producing states.[60]

On October 31, when Wilson sought unanimous consent to con-

[58] Olson, *Morton*, pp. 382–383.

[59] *Ibid.*, pp. 367–369; see also Morton's "Farmers, Fallacies, and Furrows," *Forum*, 17 (June 1894), 385–395.

[60] David B. Hill to Clark Howell, July 13, 1893, George S. Bixby Papers; Jeannette P. Nichols, "The Politics and Personalities of Silver Repeal in the United States Senate," *American Historical Review*, 41 (October 1935), 26–53.

sider the Senate bill, Bryan, Bland, and others objected and the bill was held over. On November 1, before an excited House, Bryan tried to forestall if not thwart the culmination of Cleveland's hopes. He jammed the proceedings, but the House refused to support his demand for a roll call. His hour-long filibuster ended, the speaker ordered the question. Fifteen minutes of debate were permitted each side. Bland gave Bryan time enough to say that he realized that it was too late to change the course of events but to ask those who favored repeal whether they really understood that they were perverting the Democratic platform and voting for a Republican measure. They would repeal the Sherman Act but not obtain bimetallism. They had listened to "business men" but not to farmers and laborers, thereby overlooking the fact that the laborers and farmers were as much businessmen and contributed as much to the national wealth as any industrialists. Repeal, he concluded, was the "crime of 1893." It would bury Cleveland and the Democracy in the next election. He considered presenting dilatory motions prior to the taking of the final vote, but he jumped to his feet seconds too late. However, he obtained time to leave the repealers with a prophecy. The cause of bimetallism had not been buried. No tomb was ever made strong enough to imprison a righteous cause, and silver would yet lay aside its shroud and rise to bless mankind. The House then concurred with the Senate, 194 to 94, and sent the bill to Cleveland for his signature.[61]

Bryan believed that Cleveland's victory was a Pyrrhic one, for repeal neither restored prosperity nor allowed him to have his way in financial legislation. Agricultural prices dropped, unemployment spread, and farm foreclosures increased during the winter of 1893–1894. If currency reform could not be obtained in the next Congress, Bryan said, then free silver would be the principal issue in the campaign of 1896.[62] His efforts in the repeal fight apotheosized him in the eyes of the common man, gave him status superior to that of Bland, and put him in position to strike for the leadership of the silver wing of the party. The seigniorage and bond fights that followed further improved his opportunity.

Bryan felt personally vindicated by Cleveland's defeat in Nebraska in 1893. While the party in power usually gets blamed for hard times, he pointed to the repeal of the Sherman Act as the specific cause of Cleveland's defeat. Moreover, unnumbered thousands turned from

[61] *Congressional Record*, 53 Congress, 1 Sess., 25:3058–3063.
[62] *Nebraska State Journal*, November 6, 1893.

Cleveland because he was unable or unwilling to solve the problems of agricultural depression.

Bryan's political technique was well perfected by 1893. For convention officials chosen by the state organization and for majority reports upholding the administration he substituted his own men and planks and forced the fight onto the floor, among those who most closely represented the people. Unable to overcome the Bourbons by himself, he called Populists and silver Republicans to his side. This was the technique he would use in the national convention and campaign of 1896.

IX

CLEVELAND had demanded the issue of gold bonds even before the repeal of the Sherman Act was accomplished. Bryan countered with a demand for the coinage of the seigniorage, and as chairman of the Ways and Means subcommittee on the public debt he pigeonholed all of Cleveland's demands. Losing patience one day in January 1894, Cleveland brought a ham-like fist down on a table in cabinet meeting and stated that bonds must be issued whether Congress liked it or not.[63] Carlisle thereupon authorized the issue of "coin" bonds. Bryan said that he violated the Resumption Act of 1875 and demanded that he meet his obligations in silver dollars. Whether he provoked Senator Allen to do so is unknown, but Allen instituted suit to enjoin the issue of bonds. Carlisle obtained judicial sanction and ensured their sale by persuading various New York bankers to buy them. Defeated, Bryan executed a flank attack and demanded the coinage of the seigniorage.

Seigniorage represents the gain which the government enjoys when it purchases bullion at a price lower than the value stamped on the metal. If the 164,000,000 ounces of silver in the Treasury had been coined at 16 to 1 early in 1894, when the ratio to gold was 32.5 to 1, the government would have profited by $55,156,681.[64] This idea, not overlooked later by the New Deal, was denounced by the gold men as a tricky subterfuge that would hinder the maintenance of parity and provide no benefit to the silver mine owners. Bryan countered that the profit would make bonds unnecessary, and when the House took up Bland's seigniorage bill he launched into a defense of silver similar to that of the previous August. "You may make fun of the West and

[63] Barnes, *Carlisle,* p. 310; Nevins, *Cleveland,* p. 597; Richard Watson Gilder, *Grover Cleveland, a Record of Friendship* (New York, 1920), p. 127.

[64] *Congressional Record,* 53 Congress, 2 Sess., 26:3352.

South if you like," he told the Eastern members. "You may say that their people are not financiers . . . but these people have just as much right to express their ideas and to guard their interests as you have to guard yours, and their ideas are as much entitled to consideration as yours." He then introduced a bill giving the Secretary of the Treasury rather than the holder of a government obligation the option of redeeming it in gold or silver. His bill never emerged from committee, but the House passed the seigniorage bill, on March 1, and the Senate concurred.[65]

The pressure on Cleveland to sign the bill and thereby heal the split in the party created by the repeal of the Sherman Act was almost overwhelming. Cleveland sought advice from Eastern bankers and decided to "drive" the West and South to "sound money." When Bryan called personally to urge approval of the bill he found him unflinchingly resolved not to sign it. His veto spoke of a "dangerous" bill which would destroy confidence in "our sound financial tendencies" and make more difficult the preservation of parity and of a "sensible bimetallism." He then asked Congress for power for the Secretary of the Treasury to issue bonds whenever he needed them to protect the gold reserve.[66]

On April 1 Bland moved to pass the seigniorage bill over Cleveland's veto. On April 4, when the silverites failed by a mere thirteen votes to override the veto, the government was out of the silver business altogether for the first time since 1878. Bryan immediately asserted that the veto would boomerang against Cleveland, for he had revealed the power the moneyed classes had over legislation. Since Cleveland had joined the East and the Republicans, the South and West should join "to restore the gold and silver coinage of the Constitution." "The fight is on and the West and South will win," he predicted.[67]

Silverites henceforth blocked all of Cleveland's demands for financial legislation. When another bill to repeal the state bank note tax was reported, Bryan countered with a demand that the federal government alone issue paper money. The deflation of agricultural prices following 1873 stemmed from the "crime of demonetization," he said, and it was his duty to himself, to his family, to his country, and to his

[65] *Ibid.*, 2463–2465, 2482–2484, 2510–2514, 2981; Omaha *World-Herald*, January 30, February 24, 26, March 7, 12, 1894.

[66] Cleveland to Don M. Dickinson, March 18, 1894, Cleveland Papers; *Congressional Record*, 53 Congress, 2 Sess., 26:3352–3353; Omaha *World-Herald*, March 20, 1894; Bryan, *First Battle*, p. 128.

[67] *Congressional Record*, 53 Congress, 2 Sess., 26:3473; Omaha *World-Herald*, April 27, 1894.

God that caused him to cry out "against the consummation of that conspiracy" that sought to bind the masses to earth. "And we do it, not to help the silver miners—we do it for Humanity!" He demanded that the government adopt a "managed currency" system similar to that now in use throughout the world. In direct opposition to his oft-repeated demands for a government that governs least, he then said that the government could put its paper money into circulation by using it to pay for public works of both civic and military character. While such pump priming would help spark the economy out of depression, he went beyond this to ask for "complete justice" in the form of sufficient inflation to bring back into balance those prices which had fallen since 1873. He would make all government money legal tender and prohibit, as the New Deal later did, the writing of contracts calling for payment in gold or any particular kind of money. As rings were put in the noses of hogs to prevent them from destroying more than they were worth while rooting, so he would put rings in the noses of hoggish creditors to prevent them from rooting into the equal rights of others. Finally, he presented a constructive plan later mirrored in part in the Federal Reserve Act, in which banking reserves would be kept in leading banks in each state rather than in Eastern banks alone.[68]

X

COMPLAINING that "only God knows the way of relief," Cleveland "bridged over" with another issue of bonds in November 1894. He found it least troublesome and most profitable to award the entire issue to J. P. Morgan and Company. The gold reserve was raised to $110,000,000, and the government profited by almost $11,000,000 while the syndicate lost money. But Bryan disbelieved that the syndicate lost, and he ascertained from Carlisle that $48,000,000 of the $58,000,-000 in gold paid for the bonds had been withdrawn from the Treasury.

In its annual convention of 1894 the American Federation of Labor demanded 16 to 1. Supported by the governors of many Western states, Bryan got the Fifth Trans-Mississippi Congress to adopt his plank reading "16 to 1 without waiting for the consent of any other nation." The resolutions of an American Bimetallic League convention paralleled Bryan's ideas, as did a declaration of principles written by Lyman Trumbull for the Populists. In addition to Nebraska, ten Western

[68] *Congressional Record*, 53 Congress, 2 Sess., 26:5808–5815.

and Southern Democratic state conventions adopted Bryan's silver plank.

Following the Democratic defeat in the elections of 1894, Cleveland offered a banking and currency reform plan that would divorce the government from banking and let the banks provide whatever currency they deemed adequate. This ideal diametrically opposed Bryan's demand for government money and government control of banking, and on December 22, 1894, as the "orator laureate" [69] of the silverites, he pounded Cleveland unmercifully for asking the lame duck Congress to "revolutionize" the nation's banking and currency system before the people had a chance to study his plan. "Oh, if in the White House we had an Andrew Jackson," he cried. "If gold be your god, follow it," he told administration supporters. He would not purchase harmony at the cost of principle. Cleveland had consistently opposed bimetallism and also objected to the income tax. Again and again he had joined with the East against the South and West. The responsibility for the division in the party was thus his. In closing he said, ". . . the money centers present this insolent demand for further legislation in favor of a universal gold standard. I, for one, will not yield to that demand. I will not help to crucify mankind upon a cross of gold. I will not aid them to press down upon the bleeding brow of labor this crown of thorns." [70]

The bond issue of January 1894 had lasted ten months, that of November 1894 less than ten weeks. Had Cleveland granted the option of paying the government's obligations in either gold or silver to the Treasury, said Bryan, he would not now have to issue bonds.[71] With the gold reserve down to a new low of $42,000,000 on February 2, 1895, however, Cleveland turned once more to Morgan and his American and European associates, including the Rothschilds, and prepared to sell him his entire third bond issue. He thereby added color to Bryan's charge that a cursed plutocracy had seized control of the government, for he could have sold the bonds by popular subscription.[72] When the House defeated all bond bills presented, Bryan called the defeat of the "monstrous" Cleveland plan "glorious news." The "voice of the people . . . therefore the voice of God," had triumphed over the national

[69] The phrase is from Barnes, *Carlisle*, p. 370.

[70] *Congressional Record*, 53 Congress, 2 Sess., 27:785–789; Omaha *World-Herald*, January 7, 10, 1895.

[71] Omaha *World-Herald*, February 23, 1895.

[72] *Ibid.*; see also Grover Cleveland, *Presidential Problems*, pp. 147–148.

banks and gold after a struggle of twenty years. Within eighteen hours, however, Cleveland boldly directed Morgan to draw up his bond contract and then sent Congress a curt message in which he explained not a plan but his action. If, he said, Congress would substitute gold bonds for coin bonds within ten days, as specified in Morgan's contract, the government could save $16,000,000 in interest charges. Bryan met with the Ways and Means Committee, which proposed nothing because the majority felt as he did about the bonds. When Carlisle appeared to explain the terms of the Morgan contract, Bryan told him that bonds would not be needed if the government exercised its option to pay in silver and that Cleveland should stop discriminating against silver and get rid of the endless bucket. Morgan's terms were "harsh" and "imperious," and Morgan was merely an instrument in Britain's vile attempt to "purchase a change in the financial policy of the United States for a given sum of gold." [73]

On February 14, when William L. Wilson presented another bond bill, Bryan dramatized his opposition to Cleveland by saying that he would willingly lay down his life to defeat his policies. The question before the House involved not merely $16,000,000 but the welfare of all mankind. If the Eastern Democrats and Republicans maintained their offensive alliance, then the rest of the country would be driven to unity in defense of home and welfare. "If this is sectionalism, the East has set the example." [74] The East enjoyed an unearned increment provided by an appreciating currency, the debtors of the South and West resented providing it. With the President and a third of the Congress, the East could stop every demand for reform from being passed over the President's veto. Bryan therefore demanded a Western President and the political union of the South and West; but in the light of the vituperative anger against Cleveland in these sections which made armed revolution far from impossible,[75] his attachment to the principle of majority rule characterized him as a moderate rather than a radical.

Cleveland's supporters characterized the loss of the $16,000,000 as "the price of William Jennings Bryan's first victory over Grover Cleveland," but while Bryan believed the way cleared for a return of

[73] Omaha *World-Herald*, February 12, 13, 1895.

[74] *Congressional Record*, 53 Congress, 2 Sess., 27:2182–2183; Bryan, *First Battle*, pp. 135–146.

[75] Nevins, *Cleveland*, pp. 665–666; C. Vann Woodward, *Origins of the New South, 1877–1913*, pp. 251–252, 266–269, 282–284; Eric Goldman, *Rendezvous with Destiny: A History of Modern American Reform*, p. 34.

free coinage, Cleveland went ahead with the Morgan contract. The bonds sold in twenty-two minutes and netted the syndicate a profit of at least $5,000,000. Bryan pointed out that Cleveland could have prevented the extortion of additional taxes from the people had he not issued the bonds.[76] Since Cleveland's attempt to chain the country to the gold standard caused a rapid rise in the power of the silver Democrats and Populists in the South and West, Bryan concluded that "There is no question now that the campaign of 1896 will be fought on the money question . . . between the capitalists of the Northeast and the rest of the people of the country." [77]

XI

ON FEBRUARY 22, 1895 the Populist leaders asked that all, regardless of party, join them in demanding the free coinage of silver at 16 to 1. Bryan marked their pronouncement as the transition from educational work to true political effort in behalf of silver, and his connections with Populist and silver Republican leaders lend force to the suspicion that he approved of a fusion campaign aimed at making free coinage the sole issue in 1896. Upon emerging from a conference of Western and Southern silverite congressmen held in Washington also on February 22, he refused to say whether the Populist call would result in the formation of a new reform party, but he despaired of shaking the Democracy clear of Eastern influence. In the meeting he had argued as a Westerner for the fusion of all who desired silver to the extent of obliterating party lines. Joseph Bailey and others objected because the South preferred state bank note issues to silver and because Southerners would not train with Republicans, who might revive the race issue. On March 1, as the result of a Bryan-Bailey compromise, the friends of silver in Congress issued an appeal to the Democrats of the United States to subordinate division between the West and South and to take control of the party from the gold men of the East. If the national convention declared for anything short of free silver at 16 to 1 or named anyone but a free silver Democrat, there would be a bolt. Republicans and Populists who joined must enroll under the Democratic flag. There would be no fusion. The money question would be the paramount issue in 1896 and as long thereafter as necessary for the

---

[76] Barnes, *Carlisle*, pp. 392–398; James W. Barrett, *Joseph Pulitzer and His "World,"* pp. 167–171; Lewis Corey, *The House of Morgan*, pp. 188–190.

[77] Omaha *World-Herald*, February 17, 1895.

people to settle it intelligently and patriotically. All Democrats who favored silver at 16 to 1 without waiting for the consent of any other nation were asked to impress their views upon their party leaders, and all Democratic editors were asked to demand the restoration of bimetallism. The construction of the manifesto shows that Bryan wrote it. First to sign was Bland. Equally conspicuous, yet not brashly forward, was the signature of "W. J. Bryan" at the top of the second column of names.[78] Thus occurred the first move by the Democratic silver forces for the campaign of 1896.

Notice of another impending international monetary conference provoked Bryan's last speech in Congress, on the very last day of the session. He favored holding the conference, he said, but he believed it would accomplish nothing. In correspondence with Sir William Harcourt and other British bimetallists he had learned of European despair of any good coming from the conference, and he therefore declared that the United States should undertake free coinage independently, not waiting for any other nation, not even for an hour, to achieve this goal.

Bryan's four years in Congress revealed him ardent in obtaining justice for the people he represented. These were mostly men who tilled the soil and lived in agrarian surroundings not too far removed from those of the days of Jefferson and Jackson. For their benefit he sought to get rid of the protective tariff and to obtain an income tax based on capacity to pay and an equitable banking and currency system. For their benefit he sought to prohibit speculation in grain futures and strengthen the powers of the Interstate Commerce Commission. To increase their voice in government he sponsored the direct election of senators. Cleveland had accepted the Wilson-Gorman tariff and opposed effective banking and currency reform, and the Supreme Court would no doubt destroy the income tax, but Bryan's interest in these reforms was heightened by their defeat. His fight for silver lost him the friendship of powerful men like Morton, and he had no prestige with the administration, yet he deemed his fights against Cleveland the most important of his life, for his opposition to Cleveland had won him support from silver Democrats, silver Republicans, and Populists.

There had been little to indicate that the silver issue would split

[78] *Ibid.*, February 7, 10, 26, March 2-5, 1895; New York *Tribune*, March 2, 3, 1895; Bryan, *First Battle*, pp. 155-158.

the Democracy when Bryan was elected to Congress. That such division occurred resulted largely from the triumph of the Democrats in the elections of 1892 and the irreconcilability of Cleveland and Bryan. To Cleveland bimetallism appeared an indirect way of debasing the currency; to Bryan bimetallism was a method of relieving debtors from distress and of stimulating the recovery of the nation's economy. Lacking sufficient imagination to perceive the honesty of those who supported silver, Cleveland cast his weight to those with vested interests to protect. Far removed from the people, he took advice from Wall Street friends and refused government aid to the people. By selling bonds he saved the gold standard, but he saddled a debt of about $262,000,000 upon the nation, from which bankers profited. And by failing to restore public confidence in the American economy he shattered Bourbon control of his party.[79]

Neither Cleveland nor Bryan was wholly right,,for neither envisaged currency plans based upon the nation's wealth in goods other than gold or silver, although Bryan's demand for irredeemable paper money was vaguely based upon the government's ability to pay. Free silver would not have provided the just and flexible currency Bryan demanded, but he at least wanted the federal government to take the lead in the solution of problems national in scope and to do something, even if in the nature of experimentation, to relieve the nation's distress. If he did not actually foment the discontent of the masses with his opposition to Cleveland he certainly forged that discontent into a weapon for obtaining reform legislation. Beaten by Cleveland, he must now appeal directly to the national electorate.

[79] Bryan to Edgar Howard, in Barnes, *Carlisle,* p. 433; Merrill, *Bourbon Leader,* pp. 183–186; see also Dewey W. Grantham, Jr., *Hoke Smith and the Politics of the New South,* pp. 63, 93–106.

CHAPTER 7

Road to the Nomination

I

ON MAY 17, 1894, Bryan declined to run again for the House. "If I am foot-loose I can help make combinations, and I might stand a good chance for senator," he had written Gilbert M. Hitchcock in April.[1] He preferred retirement to confinement to a single district. His future political affiliation depended on the outcome of the contest within the Democracy; he would join that wing that promised most for reform. He blasted the Cleveland wing but had kind words and advice for the Populists. If the latter preferred defeat by remaining in the middle of the road to victory by fusion, he would support the best man, regardless of party, who had a chance to win. He trusted his future career to that degree of cooperation between the silver Democrats and fusion Populists sufficient to enable him to take control of the whole of the Nebraska Democracy away from Cleveland.[2]

Liberals applauded Bryan's stand. Grover Cleveland and J. Sterling Morton represented *laissez faire,* a gold standard, interest-bearing bonds, and the East; Bryan stood for progressive reforms, bimentallism, governmental economy without borrowing, and the plain people of the South and West. He should be permitted to retire from the House only if he meant to run for the Senate.[3]

On June 21 about three hundred leading Nebraska politicians, judges, editors, businessmen, and civic leaders met by prearrangement in Omaha. The press of the Middle West made much of the fact that, while unofficial, their meeting represented an organized movement by silverites to win control of the official party machinery. "The Talk of All Nebraska" and a topic headlined in the press of the West and South, the convention formed the Nebraska Democratic Free Coinage League, complete from Executive Commitee to precinct captains. The

[1] Letter of April 14, 1894, William Jennings Bryan Papers, Nebraska State Historical Society.
[2] Omaha *World-Herald,* May 18, 1894.
[3] *Ibid.,* May 24–26, 1894; *Nebraska State Journal,* May 18–20, 22, 23, 1894.

delegates cheered Bryan's proposal "for the free and unlimited coinage of silver without waiting for any other nation on earth" and his exhortation to launch a "new crusade" against Cleveland and his gold cohorts, and there appeared little doubt that the official state convention would be forced to adopt silver, that Bryan would be named for senator, and that the Populists would be asked to endorse him.[4]

On August 4 Bryan issued a platform that reflected the series of crises of the year 1894. The twelvemonth following July 1 witnessed Coxey's army, which Bryan had seen enter Washington; the Pullman strike, which he had predicted while he attended law school; the failure of the Wilson tariff bill, including the striking down of his income tax provision; and the sale of gold bonds. During this year of calamities, disintegration, and revolution, each crisis aided Bryan because it caused division within his party and permitted him to contest for its mastery as it slipped from Cleveland's fingers. The labor injunction, industrial unionism, and social reorganization became practical political issues. By adding these to his earlier demands Bryan foreshadowed the national Democratic platform of 1896. Conservatives branded him a "radical" and feared him as a leader of those who supported progressive tendencies in both the Democratic and Populist parties. He could depend upon his effectiveness as an orator, his attractiveness to progressives in all parties, and the support of the Nebraska Free Coinage League. He must overcome the Republicans, the Cleveland administration, the Democratic state machine, the middle-of-the-road Populists, the state's corporate power, and the various "honest money" leagues. Success lay only in fusion.

On September 1, when Bryan opened his campaign, he also began work as editor of the *World-Herald*. To bolster his chances for the Senate, he had suggested that he be made editor of the weekly issue of the Omaha *World-Herald*, which circulated chiefly in rural areas. Gilbert M. Hitchcock, badly needing money, said that he could be editor in chief of the daily issue if he would invest $25,000. Unable to raise more, $9000 was all Bryan ever gave Hitchcock. Of that sum he himself provided $2000 and his father-in-law and friends the rest.[5] That the silver mine owners contributed the rest, although frequently

---

[4] Omaha *World-Herald*, June 21–24, 27, 1894; William Jennings Bryan, *The First Battle*, pp. 149–150.

[5] Robert F. Patterson, "Gilbert M. Hitchcock and William Jennings Bryan," Bryan Papers, Nebraska State Historical Society.

adverted to, is apparently a myth.[6] Now he was able to advocate his issues on the national scene, to reach the farmers of Iowa, Colorado, and Kansas as well as of Nebraska, and to foster his ambition for the presidential nomination. The comment that "he can't smile on paper" well expresses his weakness as a journalist, for his editorials are written orations lacking spontaneity and color, but few ever dealt better with texts from the Bible and from the writings of Jefferson. Henceforth the *World-Herald* trumpeted his demands, among others, for the arbitration of labor disputes, free silver at 16 to 1, the income tax as a "just principle," the direct election of senators, tariff reform, the regulation of corporations "for the benefit of the people," and a single term for President. He constantly urged fusion and also talked with James B. Weaver about how to pump fusion sense into the Nebraska Populists. On the stump, moreover, he delivered at least two speeches a day, Sundays excepted, during the three weeks prior to the primaries. When he won Douglas County, which contained Omaha, in addition to the rural counties, he insured that silverites would outnumber gold men by almost three to one in the state convention and stood on the threshold of taking Nebraska away from Cleveland.

The gold men put up a terrific fight. They packed the galleries with gold shouters, denied tickets of admission to Bryanites, provided free railroad transportation only to gold men, and named the state chairman, Euclid Martin, for temporary chairman.[7] No sooner was Martin presented, however, than Bryan substituted the name of a silverite. Lashing the gold men in a fiery speech he humiliated them with the election of his man, rushed his silver platform to adoption by three to one, and took the party away from Cleveland. He then took the audacious step of delivering his party to the Populists.

The Populists had asked Bryan to support their choice for governor, Silas A. Holcomb, but had offered him nothing in return. Meantime he learned that the Cleveland Democrats planned to support not a Democrat but the Republican lieutenant governor, the Burlington railroad's own Thomas Majors, thereby forcing him to bolt to the Populists. Bryan explained these circumstances to the Democratic convention and nominated Holcomb. He himself was named unanimously

[6] Dan V. Stephens to J. F. Boell, January 25, 1929, Bryan Papers, Nebraska State Historical Society; E. Ross Toole, Director, Montana State Historical Society, to the author, June 11, 16, 1953.

[7] Omaha *World-Herald*, August 15, September 15, 27, 1894.

for the Senate, but unanimity was made possible only because the gold men bolted and set about entering a full ticket of "straight Democrats" that supported Cleveland and Morton. A loophole in the election laws permitted them to use the word "straight" before "Democratic" on the ticket and also enabled them to send a contesting delegation to the national convention.[8]

In the more than eighty speeches he delivered between September 28 and November 6, Bryan called all fusionists to his side. He spoke for Weaver in Iowa and Weaver spoke for him in Nebraska. "Synthesis, not division, is the order of God and of common sense. . . . We must have *two gold bug* tickets in 1896, and only *one* reform ticket," Weaver told him,[9] but he was attacked from many quarters and weakened by defections. The American Protective Association opposed him again. The treasury of the Free Coinage League went dry by mid-October, and all efforts to tap the resources of neighboring states failed.[10] Advertising himself as the "Advance Agent of Prosperity," William McKinley returned to Nebraska to flail Democratic tariff reform and hard times; again, as in 1892, he refused to debate with Bryan. John M. Thurston, the leading Republican senatorial contender, also refused until embarrassed by Bryan's insistence. He finally agreed to debate twice, once in Lincoln and once in Omaha, on October 16 and 17. Five thousand listened to the "Battle of the Giants" on the money question in Lincoln, and fifteen thousand to the tariff debate in Omaha. Bryan revealed himself a superb debater, but again he learned that elections are not won by oratory alone.

The railroads used all their power to defeat Bryan, and banks and loan companies frightened their borrowers into voting Republican by threatening the immediate collection of loans. Many Bryan Democrats did not know better and voted for the "straight" Democrats; others copied a bogus ballot printed by the gold men on which Bryan's name had been forged. Bryan, the rural areas, and the Free Coinage League saved Holcomb, but the Republicans won all the other state offices, a majority of the legislature, and five of the six congressional districts,

[8] H. M. Boydston to Bryan, August 30, 1894, E. M. Harrington to Bryan, September 1, 1894, William Jennings Bryan Papers; Omaha *World-Herald*, Omaha *Bee*, September 30, 1894, *Nebraska State Journal*, October 20, 1894.

[9] Letters of September 1, 30, 1894, Bryan Papers.

[10] F. I. Illick to Bryan, October 13, 1894, J. L. Cleaver to Bryan, October 13, 1894, C. J. Smyth to Bryan, October 13, 1894, *ibid*.

the last going to a Populist. The Democrats were completely shut out. With Bryan out of the race the First District reverted to Republicanism and confusion—it took 1246 ballots to choose his successor.[11]

Perhaps in keeping with a bargain made with Bryan, the Populists named no one for senator. Bryan insisted upon the use of a permissive preference ballot unused for eight years. He received 75 per cent of the votes and Thurston 2 per cent, proving his contention that he could have been elected had direct elections been provided for. Since the preference vote carried no mandate to the legislature, Thurston was sure of election. Bryan would still attend the lame duck session of the Fifty-third Congress, but he was in effect retired from public life. However, by holding almost all the Democratic votes and getting in addition the votes of those Democrats who had gone Populist, he had definitely assumed the leadership of the Nebraska Democracy.[12]

Bryan rejoiced in defeat because he had beaten Cleveland and because Cleveland was thoroughly repudiated in the national elections. He also rejoiced at the Populist gain of 42 per cent over 1892. Since the Republicans would win so long as the Democrats and Populists remained apart, he placed his hope in an alliance in which Populists held him the only Democrat deserving of their support in 1896. He would appeal to the nation at large to adopt his principles.[13] Indeed, the silvery tones of a "Bryan for President" movement tickled his ears. Willis J. Abbot told him that his fight for right would not be forgotten in 1896, and Weaver asked him to "help shape things properly when a new order of things is precipitated." [14] Demands for him to speak came from silver leaders in all parties. Finally, the groundwork was being laid in his own state by James Dahlman, who wrote him, ". . . I have begun to talk you for president—and I mean it. . . . No gift in the hands of the people is too high for you." [15]

[11] Thomas H. Gillan to Bryan, November 10, 1894, *ibid.;* Omaha *World-Herald,* September 20, 21, October 26, November 7–17, 1894. Holcomb was the only Populist governor in the United States.

[12] Omaha *World-Herald,* October 17, 18, 1894; analysis of the official state vote, Chicago *Times-Herald* clipping, Bryan Scrapbook No. 2, Nebraska State Historical Society; Morton to a son, Carl, November 7, 1894, in Kenneth E. McIntyre, "The Morton-Bryan Controversy" (unpublished M.A. thesis, University of Nebraska, 1943), p. 22.

[13] Omaha *World-Herald,* November 5, 9–11, 1894; see Joseph W. Babcock, "The Meanings of the Election," *North American Review,* 159 (December 1894), 742–754.

[14] Letter of November 9, 1894, Bryan Papers.

[15] Letter of November 15, 1894, *ibid.*

II

HIS CONGRESSIONAL career ended, on March 4, 1895, Bryan spent two weeks lecturing on "bimetallism" before returning home on his thirty-fifth birthday. He was now old enough to be President, but he categorically denied presidential aspirations. Mrs. Bryan suggested that he renew his law practice and devote himself to his growing children. However, arrangements were being made by the silverites to win control of the Democratic national convention, the Populists were planning a mighty contest for 1896, and he felt it his "duty" to "save the people" from the consequences of a conservative victory in 1896.[16] Within a month of his return to Lincoln he took to the lecture platform and the stump.

The risk Bryan took in earning a living by lecturing paid off well. For speaking under the auspices of various bureaus he received $50, then $100 for a speech, later more. He was not, as frequently charged, on the payroll of the Western Silver Miners' Association, and there is no record that he associated with any similar organization.[17] Preaching and crusading were the employments most congenial to him and those for which he was best suited. He was now free to attend the many silver conferences scheduled for the fifteen months before the national

[16] Interview with Mrs. Thomas S. Allen, Lincoln, June 29, 1948; Bryan in *Rocky Mountain News,* July 11, 1896; Bryan, *First Battle,* p. 63; William Jennings Bryan and Mary Baird Bryan, *The Memoirs of William Jennings Bryan,* p. 102; Wayne C. Williams, *William Jennings Bryan,* p. 57.

[17] For charges by contemporaries, see Senator Manderson in New York *Times,* July 15, 1896, and Edward Rosewater in Omaha *Bee,* July 17, 1896. Albert Shaw, "William Jennings Bryan," *American Review of Reviews,* 72 (September 1925), 262, said that Bryan was on the payroll of a Western Silver Miners' Association. Paxton Hibben, *The Peerless Leader: William Jennings Bryan,* p. 168, referenced Shaw and popularized his unverified information. There is no record of this particular association in the archives of the Secretary of State of Colorado, in Denver's City Directories, in Denver's newspapers, or in the memory of experts on Colorado's mining history. Letter of June 6, 1958 to the author from John D. Morrison, Assistant State Historian of Colorado. In 1894, A. J. Warner, the president of the American Bimetallic League, stated explicitly that "Mr. Bryan is not now and never has been in the employ of our league. He has contributed to the league, but has never received a dollar from it directly or indirectly" (Omaha *World-Herald,* July 18, 1894). In the biographical sketch of Bryan that Mrs. Bryan prepared for *The First Battle,* p. 63, she stated categorically that "Never at any time was he under the direction of, or in the pay of, any silver league or association of persons pecuniarily interested in silver."

convention, and he spoke and debated on silver in every state of the South and West. He was but one of many silver leaders, yet he was one of the most active and ambitious of them; he proved doubly effective because he combined superb oratorical power with skill in political organization. To the inarticulate and poor he appeared a savior because he sponsored their causes against privilege and plutocracy and asked nothing for himself. Nevertheless, during his travels he met every Western and Southern politician of note and, more important, talked with the leaders of five distinct groups that could feed his ambition: the Populist fusionists, the silver Democrats, the American Bimetallic League, the National Bimetallic Union, and the silver Republicans. While he wrote for the silver press, he depended more upon his magnetic touch with an audience than upon his pen, and few did more in 1895 and 1896 to counter the "sound money" movement launched in the larger cities of the East, South, and Middle West.[18] He also had a hand in establishing various state silver leagues in which the silverites perfected their organization for 1896.

Bryan's repertoire of injustices in 1895 included the income tax and Sugar Trust decisions and the remanding of Eugene V. Debs to jail for contempt of court in the Pullman strike case. The income tax decision loomed large in the Democratic national platform and in the campaign of 1896 partly because Bryan persistently demanded that it be changed either by placing upon the Supreme Court men whose sympathies lay with the people rather than with wealth or by adopting a constitutional amendment specifically authorizing the tax.

The fact that the Supreme Court decided that "manufacturing" was not "commerce" and dismissed a suit against a "Sugar Trust" that controlled 98 per cent of the nation's sugar refining capacity enabled Bryan to assert that the anti-trust laws were not being enforced and that plutocracy was firmly entrenched in the judicial as well as the executive and the legislative branches. The remission of Debs to jail proved to him that the Supreme Court protected big business against the efforts of the small businessmen, farmers, and workers to defend their rights and further their welfare, and he spoke much about the development of a new principle, that of government by injunction or

---

[18] This very vigorous movement included the New York Reform Club, then under the leadership of Cleveland's counselor, Charles S. Fairchild; city leagues like the Chicago Honest Money League; state leagues like the Nebraska Sound Money League, Morton's child; and the National Sound Money League, directed largely by Morton, Henry Villard, George Peabody, and Horace White.

ukase, and of the need for an anti-injunction plank in the national platform.[19]

With the approach of the spring primaries in 1895, Cleveland directed that the Democracy be buttressed in the South, where a loyal front had been held against the Populists in 1892. Various cabinet members responded to his call. When John G. Carlisle spoke at a "sound money" convention in Memphis, Tennessee, on May 23, Bryan accepted an invitation from the state's silverites to reply to him. "How are the mighty fallen," he lamented, as David had for Saul. He objected not to Carlisle's change of mind but to his "change of heart." Once the Moses of the common people, Carlisle was now "the commander-in-chief of Pharaoh's army," he said,[20] and it was on the theme that the silver crusade represented the demands for justice by the farmers, businessmen, and workers rather than by the silver miners that he spoke at two important conventions in June, in Springfield, Illinois, and in Memphis.

Following the Nebraska pattern, Governor John Peter Altgeld of Illinois and his secretary of state, William H. "Buck" Hinrichsen, the latter Bryan's college classmate, called an unofficial silver conference for June 5, a month earlier than the regular state convention. It was high time, Altgeld thought, that the East be stopped from manipulating national conventions at its pleasure.[21] Cleveland marked his call as the beginning of the fight for control of the national convention and asserted that "the line of battle is drawn between the forces of safe currency and those of silver monometallism." [22] Bryan found Cleveland's views "contemptible" and told him he could find "plain English" on the currency question in *Coin's Financial School*.[23] When Cleveland spoke about "sound currency," he declared, "the Almighty himself couldn't tell you what he means by it." [24]

[19] Omaha *World-Herald*, April 9, 10, 21, May 21, June 3, 1895.

[20] *Ibid.*, May 3, 25, 1895; Bryan, *Memoirs*, p. 102; Bryan, *First Battle*, pp. 161–162.

[21] Altgeld to Tillman, June 20, 1895, quoted in Harvey Wish, "John P. Altgeld and the Background of the Election of 1896," *Mississippi Valley Historical Review*, 24 (March 1938), 516; Altgeld, "Letter to Governor Stone on the Position of the Democratic Party on the Money Question," in *Live Questions*, pp. 486–488.

[22] Cleveland to Henry S. Robbins, April 13, 1895, quoted in Bryan, *First Battle*, pp. 158–160.

[23] Omaha *World-Herald*, April 16, 1895; "Open Letter to President Cleveland," April 18, 1895, Bryan, *First Battle*, pp. 160–161; Allan Nevins, *Grover Cleveland: A Study in Courage*, p. 675. See also Jeannette P. Nichols, "Bryan's Benefactor: Coin Harvey and His World," *The Ohio Historical Quarterly*, 67 (October 1958), 299–325.

[24] Omaha *World-Herald*, April 16, 1895. The New York *Times* of April 19, 1895

The Springfield convention proved a great success for both silver and Bryan. It endorsed free silver at a ratio of 16 to 1 and declared that the failure of the Democratic National Committee to call a national convention on silver before August would result in a program of concurrent action between Illinois and other states. Populist demands for fusion on the state level were rejected. Bryan enthralled the delegates on the theme that "We are confronted with a conspiracy greater than that attacked by Jackson, one international in extent and destined in its consummation to produce more misery than war, pestilence and famine," and called the convention "the Sumter of the great contest for the restoration of the coinage of the Constitution." Illinois proved that the demand for 16 to 1 was not limited to the silver mining states and had sounded the signal gun for the battle of 1896.[25] Texas, Mississippi, and Missouri soon held similar special conventions which noted the echoes of "Bryan for President" that boomed from the Illinois convention.

On June 12–13, more than 2200 delegates, nine out of ten of whom were Democrats, attended an American Bimetallic League convention in Memphis. Bryan was elected a vice president of the league and also a member of the convention's Committee on Resolutions. When Joseph Sibley, favored by a minority as the presidential candidate of an independent silver ticket, demagogically presented a choice between "repudiation or revolution" in 1896, Bryan cried him down and obtained a resolution calling merely for independent free coinage at 16 to 1. The delegates then appointed a National Silver Committee to disseminate silver literature.[26] Deeming nonpartisan action ineffective, however, Democratic Senators Isham G. Harris, James K. Jones, and David Turpie, of the committee, issued a letter in which they asserted

alluded to Bryan's comment as made by a Nebraska "has been" and evaluated it "about on a par with some of [his] performances in Congress."

[25] Omaha *World-Herald*, June 6, 1895; Chicago *Tribune*, June 2–7, 1895.

[26] This committee is not to be confused with one of the same name created by the National Bimetallic Coinage Association, a merger of the Colorado Silver Alliance and Nevada Silver Association, in 1890. The leader of the association was the silver-rich Republican Senator John P. Jones of Nevada; the moving spirit of the original National Silver Committee, a propaganda and lobbying agency, was Adoniram J. Warner of Ohio. During 1890–1892, the committee spent only $22,000, most of this amount being furnished by Nevada and Montana, but in seeking to enlarge its sphere of action it created the American Bimetallic League in the Second National Silver Convention which met in Washington in May 1892. Its executive committee included Francis G. Newlands of Nevada, John H. Reagan of Texas, Thomas Watson of Georgia, and John W. Daniel of Virginia.

that success in 1896 lay in the advocacy of 16 to 1 by the Democrats alone and asked that delegates be sent to a convention in Washington in August, when plans would be drawn for controlling the national convention. Bryan was chosen to organize Nebraska.[27]

During the fall and winter of 1895–1896 Bryan toured the Western and Southern states speaking on bimetallism and on the income tax decision. Although railroads owing the *World-Herald* for advertising occasionally paid their debts by furnishing him transportation, there is no evidence that the silver miners subsidized him; and he frequently paid his own expenses because he would not permit the collection of an admission charge from those who could not pay to hear him.[28]

In mid-August 1895 Bryan returned to Nebraska for a bitter fight. The Populist administration had granted no recognition to his Democratic followers, who insisted that fusion was impossible and that great reforms could come only through his leadership of the Democracy.[29] In his absence, moreover, the Nebraska gold men organized a sound money league and called a state convention to select delegates to the national convention. If the gold men controlled the latter, their men would be seated in the national convention regardless of the merits of the silver men's case.

In this off-year election popular interest centered wholly upon the resolutions to be adopted by the two Democratic conventions. As chairman of the Committee on Resolutions of the regular convention, Bryan wrote the currency plank and led the silverites on the committee to victory by the lopsided vote of 500 to 5 over a minority plank that reaffirmed the national platform of 1892.[30] While Bryan resumed

[27] Omaha *World-Herald*, June 13–15, 22, 1895; Bryan, *First Battle*, p. 162; John D. Hicks, *The Populist Revolt: A History of the Farmers' Alliance and the People's Party*, p. 343; C. Vann Woodward, *Origins of the New South, 1877–1913*, pp. 280–281; Philip F. Buckner, "Silver Mining Interests in Silver Politics, 1876–1896," (unpublished M.A. thesis, Columbia University, 1953), pp. 52–60. Speaking in Jackson, Mississippi, following the convention, Bryan was pressed on whether he would support a gold platform. He replied: "I am as certain the Democratic convention will adopt a double-standard platform as that I am standing here, but, if it does not, if the single gold-standard is adopted, I would die in my tracks before I would vote the ticket" (New York *Times*, June 13, 1895).

[28] From May 1892 until it disappeared into the American Bimetallic Union in January 1896, the American Bimetallic League used funds raised from membership fees. Silver mine interests may have contributed to it, but during the depression beginning in 1893, "few mine owners were prepared to throw good money after bad." Buckner, "Silver Mining Interests," p. 50.

[29] C. J. Smyth to Bryan, May 2, 1895, Bryan Papers.

[30] Omaha *World-Herald*, August 22, 23, 1895.

his Western tour, Morton and his friends reaffirmed the national platform of 1892 and in addition demanded the retirement of the greenbacks. They then appealed to the courts to certify them as the "Simonpure, unadulterated, original, and everlasting organization of the Democracy." A Bryanite attorney protested to the Secretary of State against the filing of the bolters' certificates of nomination, but the time established for the filing of protests had elapsed and the bolters could not be enjoined from using the word "Democrat" on their ticket. Bryan rushed back from the West Coast and obtained a court order restraining the gold men from using the word "straight." The court then said it lacked jurisdiction in political matters and rescinded its action. The Secretary of State thereupon certified both the gold and silver nominees and left the choice to the voters. Since candidates for supreme court judge were listed alphabetically, the name of Thomas J. Mahoney, "straight" Democrat, preceded that of Charles J. Phelps, "Democrat." Bryan tried hard to popularize Phelps as the silver man and asked the Populists for aid. He had helped elect Holcomb governor, he reminded them, and they could return the favor by making no nominations at this time. The Populists paid no attention and named their own man. Had they followed his advice a fusion candidate would have won. Since, however, Mahoney's vote was double that of Phelps, the gold Democrats believed that their delegation would be admitted to the national convention instead of Bryan's, and when Bryan suggested that the silver question be submitted to a state primary they laughed him away.[31]

The myth that Bryan was an unknown until he made his "Cross of Gold" speech is readily exploded by the national attention he had earned in his many Nebraska fights, as a tariff and silver orator in Congress and on the stump, and by the large number of letters and editorials which demanded him for President after June 1895. Because of the Nebraska state convention Bryan did not attend the convention called in Washington in August by the National Silver Committee of the American Bimetallic League. However, John W. Tomlinson, a newspaper man from Alabama, wrote that he had talked with many of the delegates "and nearly everyone I talked with was in favor of nominating you for president." [32] By November Bryan had con-

---

[31] *Ibid.*, September 8, 19, 22, October 12, 16–19, 24, 1895.

[32] Tomlinson to Bryan, August 26, 1895, Bryan Papers. See also W. J. Stone to Bryan, August 26, 1895; Josephus Daniels to Bryan; June 1, 1895; and William J. Johnson to Bryan, June 3, 1895, *ibid.*

cluded that the "logic of the situation" made his nomination inevitable. Confiding in a Texas friend, Dr. Charles M. Rosser, he said that he would be chosen if silver controlled the national convention. Richard Parks Bland was the most deserving, but neither he nor Horace Boise could make the kind of campaign needed to win. What about Benjamin Tillman? asked Rosser, for South Carolina had endorsed Tillman as its presidential candidate. Tillman was a great man, replied Bryan, but he would not be nominated. If he himself were named and elected he would make Tillman his Secretary of the Treasury, for he would not ask Wall Street how to run his department. "If he caught them conspiring against the nation's credit," he concluded, "he would have them locked up like common criminals." A visit to Tillman by Rosser confirmed Bryan's estimate of the man.[33]

Democratic defeats in the elections of 1895 failed to budge Bryan's conclusion that he would be named, because Republican victories occurred either in safe Eastern territory or in states in which the gold-silver split in the Democracy had enabled them to win. No elections had been held in the important silver states, and from his tours of the last nine months he knew that silver would control the Democratic national convention. As insurance, however, he continued to organize silver clubs for the National Silver Committee, to editorialize on silver, and to castigate Cleveland on the lecture platform. He was welcomed by the masses as "almost a second Messiah," to use the words of Sidney Brooks, the British journalist. The Trans-Mississippi Commercial Congress of 1895 adopted his 16 to 1 resolution at his behest,[34] and he was pleased with the merging, in January 1896, of the American Bimetallic League, the National Bimetallic Union, and the National Silver Committee, the last an independent Western silver organization launched in May 1895, into a new American Bimetallic Union, A. J. Warner president. The A.B.U. would remain an educational organization. Pressure for an independent, nonpartisan political organization was so great, however, that two weeks later there was created the National Silver Party, which would hold its national convention simultaneously with the Populists on July 22.

In the Fifty-fourth Congress, which met in December 1895, party designations were blurred with respect to the currency question. Sen-

---

[33] Rosser to Bryan, November 23, 1895, *ibid.;* Charles M. Rosser, *The Crusading Commoner,* pp. 19–24.

[34] Omaha *World-Herald,* December 21–24, 1895.

ator Henry M. Teller of Colorado, for example, would leave the Republican party if it did not declare for silver, would not discuss the financial question unless free coinage were considered also, and said he would try to defeat appropriation bills if Cleveland sought to issue more bonds.[35]

When Cleveland, in his annual message of December 2, 1895, suggested that bonds be sold to the national banks and that the banks issue notes with which to retire the greenbacks and Sherman Act notes, silverites of all parties deemed him repugnant, stupid, vacillating, and futile.[36] The country needed more than "a combination of brains, belly, and brass," cried Joseph Sibley in the House [37] while Tillman lambasted him as a "besotted tyrant" and asked to be re-elected so that he could "tickle Cleveland's fat ribs with [a] pitchfork." [38] In an open letter, Bryan asked if Cleveland were "ignorant or dishonest." "Stupidity," he said, reigned in Washington, and he asserted that the President was wrong in both his premises and his conclusions, that all government obligations should be paid in silver, that Cleveland's was a "monstrous scheme" which should be defeated by "the voice of the people, and therefore of God," and that the American people would tolerate another bond issue only to defray the costs of a demonstration to prove that the United States must remain free of British domination.[39]

Here Bryan referred to Cleveland's Venezuelan message of December 17, 1895, which pleased him immensely, as did Cleveland's demand for an appropriation to survey the Venezuela–British Guiana boundary line and of his support for the Monroe Doctrine. He opposed Britain both as a Democrat and as a democrat. Jefferson had written the Declaration of Independence against the British; Jackson had fought the British; the United States had always resented foreign interference in its internal affairs; and he followed Jefferson in opposing the extension of empire by force. He saw Britain as the leader of the conspiracy to induce the United States to adopt the gold standard and as an effete

[35] *Ibid.*, December 3, 1895, January 31, 1896.

[36] *Ibid.*, December 4, 7, 1895.

[37] Nevins, *Cleveland*, p. 675.

[38] *Congressional Record*, 54 Congress, 1 Sess., 1072–1080; Omaha *World-Herald*, January 30, 1896; Francis B. Simkins, *Pitchfork Ben Tillman, South Carolinian*, pp. 315, 322.

[39] Omaha *World-Herald*, December 4, 5, 1895, January 28, 31, February 8, 13, 23, 1896.

aristocracy that sent over its "broken-down lords with one eyeglass and one lung to ensnare, if possible, some of our foolish daughters who have come to believe that an empty title is preferable to a real man." [40]

When the Republican-controlled Congress undertook tariff revision upward rather than currency and banking reform, Bryan charged that the Republicans sought to make the tariff rather than the money question the major issue in 1896 and predicted defeat if they ran on a platform of "prosperity through protection." Western and Southern opposition stalled all tariff and bond bills for months. The Dingley tariff passed the House, but Western senators like Teller would not vote for any tariff bill that did not contain a free silver provision. Asked whether that was an ultimatum, he replied that it was.[41] Bryan then suggested a compromise similar to that of 1890 in which the silverites would vote for protection and protectionists for silver, and a bill to that effect was backed by Senator William V. Allen and reached the calendar. When Easterners sought to demonstrate their power to defend the gold standard by passing a gold bond bill, the Senate substituted a free coinage bill for it. In the House, the representatives of twenty-three states favored silver and those of twenty-two opposed. Bryan rushed to Washington from the Far West to bolster the silverites against bonds and to urge them to bolt their national conventions if they chose gold. Both houses rejected free silver, yet both refused Cleveland the authority to issue bonds. The fate of silver now rested with the party conventions. Cleveland's last bonds were issued on his own authority. In two years, in one of the most remarkable experiments in American financial history, and at the cost of saddling a debt of $262,000,000 upon the people, he had saved the gold standard.[42]

III

THE SILVERITES won several victories in the Democratic National Committee meeting held in December 1895. The date set for the national convention, July 7, permitted them a long preconvention campaign, and compromise on Chicago rather than St. Louis gave them the advantage over the East as to site. The adoption of the unit rule proved the key to success, for dissenting gold elements must bow to the will

---

[40] *Ibid.*, December 18, 21, 23, 25, 1895.

[41] Elmer Ellis, *Henry Moore Teller*, p. 244.

[42] *Harper's Weekly*, January 18, 1896; James A. Barnes, *John G. Carlisle, Financial Statesman*, pp. 299–424; Grover Cleveland, *Presidential Problems*, pp. 159–171.

of the silver majorities in state primaries. In the Populist National Committee, the fusionists who won over the middle-of-the-road men decided to hold their national convention late, in order that, as Weaver put it, they could easily gather up silverites who bolted the major party conventions, ousted Socialist elements from the Eastern cities, and left free silver as almost the sole principle to survive the Omaha platform.

During the early months of 1896 Bryan spoke mainly about his right to bolt and of the need of a fusion campaign. He repudiated Eastern control and demanded "the same liberty, the same independence, the same political rights for the Democrats of the South and West that our Eastern brethren have at all times enjoyed." [43] ". . . we do not want any candidate who is satisfactory to the eastern democrats," he told James Hogg of Texas, and he wrote Weaver, Davis Waite, Marion Butler, Ignatius Donnelly, William V. Allen, Clarence Darrow, and Tillman, at least, that he looked for a bolt from the Democratic national convention and wanted to know how much cooperation he could expect. Weaver promised aid; no conclusions would be reached in the Populist convention until consultations had been held with kindred interests. The wily Butler asked for more information and Waite stuck to the "Omaha party," but Tillman volunteered the information that Bryan had "evoluted" in the last six months and that the leaders of the Democracy were veering steadily toward fusion. When Donnelly said that all parties should support the Democratic nominee if he were a silver man, Bryan felt sure that fusion would become a reality.[44]

Roughly ten states held their primaries in April, ten in May, and twenty in June. Bryan influenced them by writing for silver newspapers and the American Bimetallic Union, debating gold advocates, and undertaking a personal campaign unique in American history. He wrote the chairman of every Democratic state committee of the importance of scoring silver victories early and asked for the names and addresses of all probable delegates to the national convention. To those elected he sent a copy of his silver plank and suggestions on the conduct of the campaign in which he adroitly injected references to his avail-

[43] Bryan's letter to George A. Carden, Omaha *World-Herald,* February 24, 1896; editorial, "The Philosophy of Bolting," *ibid.,* February 26, 1896; Bryan to Hogg, February 24, 1896, cited in Woodward, *Origins of the New South,* p. 284.

[44] Davis Waite to Bryan, November 26, 1895; James Weaver to Bryan, December 31, 1895; Benjamin Tillman to Bryan, December 7, 1895; Marion Butler to Bryan, January 8, 1896, Bryan Papers. See also Charles M. Rosser to Bryan, May 6, 1896, *ibid.,* and Robert C. Cotner, *James Stephen Hogg, A Biography,* pp. 464–469.

ability as presidential candidate. He also stressed the need of sending uninstructed delegations to the convention. For instance, he sent ex-Senator Charles S. Thomas a copy of his silver plank and asked him to have it adopted. Thomas said he would try and intimated that Bryan would need strong support to overcome the contesting Nebraska delegation and win admission to the convention. When Colorado adopted his plank and chose Thomas to head the delegation, he wrote Thomas: "I don't suppose your delegation is committed to any candidate. If we succeed in getting a 16 to 1 plank in Chicago, our own delegation may present my name. Whether it goes further than a compliment will depend upon the feeling in other states. I am not saying this in public, but write you this in confidence. The state would instruct for me, but I prefer to be a delegate, so that I can help to secure the right kind of platform." [45]

Bryan's ambition and superlative assurance jolted Thomas. "Here was a young man barely thirty-six, living in a comparatively unimportant Republican state west of the Mississippi River, audaciously announcing his probable candidacy for the presidential nomination. The very seriousness of the suggestion emphasized its absurdity." He wrote Bryan that he should consider "the expediency of a nomination of some one whose long public service might give him a stronger hold upon the general conservatism of the people than a man west of the Missouri River would be able to develop." [46] In contrast, many delegates from the South and West wrote him that they considered him the only man who could unite all the silver forces against the money power.

Bryan won a sweeping victory in the Nebraska convention. His silver plank was accepted verbatim, and resolutions were adopted which favored the direct election of senators, an income tax, a tariff for revenue only, and the initiative and referendum. After he was elected a delegate at large, he "permitted" James Dahlman to move that the delegation be instructed for him for President. In keeping with his strategy to play on the motto of putting principles before personalities, however, he had Dahlman withdraw his motion. He was subtle enough to realize that no other state would endorse him at this early date. To add proof to his putting of principle before personal honors he declared that he preferred to attend the national convention as a fighter rather than a figurehead.[47] When the gold men elected a contesting delegation, he

[45] Letter of April 16, 1896, Bryan Papers.
[46] Letter of April 18, 1896, ibid.; Thomas in Harper's Weekly, October 11, 1913.
[47] Omaha World-Herald, April 23, 1896.

prepared a brief on the Nebraska quarrel and sent it to a Kansas friend, John H. Atwood, who would be on the Credentials Committee of the national convention.[48]

Since his only chance for the nomination lay in winning the unpledged delegates, Bryan tried to get as many states as possible not to instruct. He wrote every delegate of his faith in the admittance of his as "the regular" delegation, of the need to adopt a platform that was "all right" prior to nominating candidates, and of the possibility of fusion in the various states. Some delegates replied that they favored him for President. Men like Clark Howell, editor of the Atlanta *Constitution,* and John Daniel and Claude Swanson of Virginia saw the wisdom of not instructing and were "agreed on the necessity of having a Western man and for free silver warmly without a doubt." [49] James B. Weaver again let him know that he favored him.

Of the twenty conventions held by the end of May, thirteen favored silver and seven gold. Of the 338 delegates, 172 favored silver and 166 gold, but with victories in Wyoming and Kentucky silver had a majority in the convention, and Bryan's chances improved.

The silver whisper of April and May became a gale in June, and many silver leaders wrote Bryan of the demand for him for President. He alone had "every quality that goes to make up my ideal of a silver candidate," wrote Atwood, who added that Bryan's nomination on a silver platform would bring both the Populist and National Silver parties to his support.[50] After Virginia adopted silver on June 5, silver was on its way to the two thirds needed to nominate. Eastern goldbug newspapers criticized the silverites for seeking a Populist rather than a Democratic candidate, but of the eight most probable candidates they listed Bryan last.[51]

Bryan continued to propagandize on "Principles First," stating that Nebraska at least was "first for an unequivocal declaration for silver at 16 to 1 and after that for the most available man who fits the platform." No one should conduct a campaign for any particular man in such a way as to injure the candidate finally selected. Since such a course would leave the road open for a dark horse, he 'was criticized

[48] Thomas Maloney to Bryan, May 22, 1896, Bryan to John H. Atwood, May 27, 1896, Bryan Papers.
[49] Letters, Swanson to Bryan, May 12, 1896, Howell to Bryan, May 23, 1896, *ibid.*
[50] Letter, June 8, 1896, *ibid.*
[51] Chicago *Record,* July 1–3, 1896; New York *Times,* May 22, June 1, 8, 9, July 2–4, 1896; New York *Tribune,* July 3, 1896; New York *World,* July 2–4, 1896; Omaha *World-Herald,* July 2, 1896; Salt Lake *Tribune,* July 5, 1896.

by those who backed favorite sons, and he was asked particularly by Bland supporters to drop his attitude of neutrality and advocate the nomination of the Missourian.[52] "Principles First" can be interpreted in two ways: as a desire on Bryan's part that no rancor deprive the victor of the support of the vanquished; but also as a device to insure that no one approached a two-thirds majority on the first ballot.

Of the twenty-three states that held conventions in June, eighteen declared for silver. The only hope for conservatives lay in William C. Whitney's assumption, at Cleveland's request, of the management of the gold forces at Chicago. With a great burst of energy Whitney set about organizing the gold campaign, directing, however, that there be no bolt from the convention and no third ticket, for the latter would play directly into the hands of the silverites. Meantime Senator James K. Jones, who headed the Arkansas delegation to the Chicago convention, invited each silver delegation to send a representative to Chicago on June 30, a week prior to the assembling of the convention. Selected by his state, Bryan promised Jones that he would be in Chicago on June 30 to help him convince the regular Democratic National Committee to take no steps adverse to silver.[53]

The last state conventions preferred silver to gold by four to one, and Bryan received additional evidence of support as a presidential candidate. In Texas, where the tariff rather than silver was the major issue, ex-Governor James Hogg "rounded up" the silverites for him, and Rosser helped by circulating a letter in which Tillman said he wanted Bryan on the ticket.[54] "I believe you ought to be nominated," a former congressional colleague wrote Bryan,[55] and Josephus Daniels

[52] J. W. Farris to Bryan, June 3, 1896, George Allen to Bryan, June 5, 1896, Bryan Papers. An excellent illustration of "principles first" is in Bryan's writing James Hogg that "I believe that you have all the qualifications necessary for president and there is no man whom I would rather support than yourself. Whether you secure the nomination or not remains to be seen, and whether you could be elected if nominated is still another matter. I write to you frankly because I know that your interest in democratic principles is greater than your ambition to be president, and therefore you would not stand in the way of the success of any more available candidate if at the convention you found that you could not be nominated. . . ." Hogg of course saw through the transparent bid for his support. Cotner, *Hogg*, p. 465. See also Rosser to Bryan, February 27, 1896, and Hogg to Bryan, May 2, 1896, Bryan Papers.

[53] John W. Tomlinson to Bryan, June 8, 1896, Bryan to James K. Jones, June 23, 1896, Bryan Papers; Omaha *World-Herald*, June 17, 1896.

[54] Rosser to Bryan, May 6, 1896, Bryan Papers.

[55] Clinton Babbit to Bryan, April 23, 1896, *ibid.*

said that North Carolina would support him if he were named. When Bryan suggested putting "principles before personalities," Daniels answered: "I think you are right in saying we ought not to go to Chicago thinking about men, but of the platform, but you will have many friends who will want you on the ticket." [56]

Both sides were vitally interested in Illinois, whose forty-eight votes might prove decisive. The administration forces therein were well organized: all of Chicago's newspapers favored gold. But Illinois was Bryan's home state. He knew most of the delegates to the state convention and was well aware that Governor John Peter Altgeld hated Cleveland because of his intervention in the Pullman strike and his attachment to gold, and that he himself was widely regarded as the most powerful silver leader in the nation.[57] Richard Parks Bland, Horace Boies, and Henry M. Teller also attended the Illinois state convention in order to obtain the governor's support, but none wooed him more assiduously than Bryan. He sent a college classmate, Millard F. Dunlap, to ask Altgeld and William H. Hinrichsen to support him for member of the Committee on Resolutions of the national convention and to sound them out on their candidate. Dunlap reported that Altgeld stood by Bland and that he thought Bryan a good speaker but too young and too new politically to deserve the nomination. Continued importunity by Bryan resulted in Altgeld's telegraphing him that he had "canvassed the presidential situation. Find everywhere great admiration for you but an almost unanimous sentiment that you are not available for president this time. All feel you should be in new cabinet if we succeed. . . ." [58]

Altgeld questioned Bryan's qualities as a thinker. He told Clarence Darrow, for one, that Bryan never comprehended the fundamentals of the money question.[59] On his part Bryan overlooked the fact that Altgeld could be as much hindrance as help. Known as the "Anarchist of Illinois," he would be a cross for Bryan to bear, for he was evaluated

[56] Daniels to Bryan, April 30, May 9, 1896, *ibid.*

[57] The temper of the times, and of Republicans, is well illustrated in Theodore Roosevelt's charge that the delegates to the Illinois convention were "murderers, horse thieves, burglars, libertines, crooks of all kinds—men who have been convicted of crimes ranging from pick-pocketing to arson." Quoted in Ellis, *Teller,* p. 288.

[58] Altgeld to Bryan, telegram, June 12, 1896, Bryan Papers.

[59] Interview by Harvey Wish with Clarence Darrow, April 16, 1935, Wish, "John P. Altgeld and the Background of the Election of 1896," p. 515. The sentiment is supported in William Sulzer to W. R. Browne, January 16, 1923, John Peter Altgeld Collection.

by conservatives as another Waite or Tillman. His presence in the national convention would discredit the opposition and shame delegations "into coming over to decency," Don Dickinson wrote Cleveland.[60]

The primary contests gave 585 to silver and 344 to gold. Gold hopes lay only in the maintenance of the two-thirds rule. The Democratic voters had spoken, said Bryan; the national convention need only record the verdict. He arrived in Chicago on June 29, as did the other members of the Bimetallic Democratic National Committee, to devise the strategy for defeating Cleveland and gold.

Bryan had attended the Republican national convention as a special correspondent of the Omaha *World-Herald*. Since the delegates of only ten states favored silver, the gold leaders could have ignored them altogether had they wished. Bryan noted that the leading presidential contender, William McKinley, had championed silver between 1877 and 1891 and thereafter had shuffled. Now he was being subjected to the powerful pressure of influential friends, including Mark Hanna, to make him declare for gold. Hanna waited until the delegates made their gold views known and thus made it appear to McKinley that he was forced to adopt gold by irresistible party sentiment.[61]

Beaten on a minority report on silver in the Committee on Resolutions, Henry M. Teller stood ready to bolt. Bryan expected "memorable action." Just how much influence he exerted in the convention is difficult to say. He was in close touch with Teller, Frederick T. Dubois, Frank J. Cannon, Richard F. Pettigrew, and other silverites during the struggle over the platform. He later confessed that he was there to encourage the silverites to bolt and that "The convention turned out as I expected and the looked-for bolt took place." [62] Rather than stultifying themselves by joining the Democracy, however, the silver Republicans organized independently and tried to get the Democratic nomination for Teller. If they also succeeded in obtaining the endorsement of the Populist and National Silver parties, they would have formed a union of all the free silver forces without destroying any of the political organizations involved.

[60] Letter of June 12, 1896, Grover Cleveland Papers.

[61] Omaha *World-Herald*, May 18, 1896; New York *World*, June 2–6, 1896; numerous press clippings on the Republican convention in Bryan Scrapbook No. 2, Nebraska State Historical Society; Charles S. Olcott, *The Life of William McKinley*, I, 311–315.

[62] Omaha *World-Herald*, June 18, 1896; Bryan, *Memoirs*, pp. 99–100.

When McKinley asked that a pledge to promote international agreement on free coinage be added to the money plank, he executed the master stroke that most authorities believe saved the Republicans in the election. Bryan called it a lie, for the money plank called for the maintenance of the gold standard until international agreement could be reached, and Teller said he must leave his party. Refusing to inflame the convention by histrionics, and too weak physically to make a real oratorical effort, he delivered a brief, sincere, and temperate valedictory. With tears streaming down his cheeks he started for the door, delegates from Colorado, Idaho, and Utah behind him. Bryan became so excited that he leaped from desk to desk to reach the door. A smile of satisfaction wreathed his face as the silverites departed. Cries of "Go to Chicago!" and "Take the Democratic train!" aimed at Teller caused his eyes to twinkle with delight. "Did he have any vision of what was to happen three weeks later?" asked Arthur Dunn, on whose desk Bryan finally stood, and who watched his face closely.[63] Bryan believed that Republican acceptance of the currency issue as the major one for November would have a "large influence" at Chicago and that it would be to his benefit.[64]

It may seem fantastic that Teller should have received serious consideration as the Democratic nominee, but such was the case. His stand on silver, the income tax, and railroad domination endeared him not only to Democrats but to many Populists as well. However, some Populist leaders considered Bryan to be more "available" than Teller, and Bryan believed it was too much to expect that the Democratic rank and file would split their party by choosing a man who had so recently bolted another and that partisanship would intervene when silver Republicans and Populists in the West demanded that the minority Democrats hand over their state organizations. By persistently demeaning himself, moreover, Teller played right into Bryan's hand and added weight to the idea of "principles first." Nevertheless, Bryan's persistence in advertising his conclusion that McKinley's nomination made his own inevitable provoked excited incredulity in many quarters and comments about his "presumption" and "foolishness." When Charles Gates Dawes told Hanna and McKinley that for the first time

[63] Bryan, *First Battle*, pp. 168–177; Ellis, *Teller*, pp. 247, 255–260; Arthur W. Dunn, *From Harrison to Harding: A Personal Narrative, Covering a Third of a Century, 1888–1921*, I, 181.

[64] Bryan letter to Josephus Daniels, published in Raleigh *News and Observer*, June 19, 1896.

the two parties would nominate men with the same first names—so long as Bryan somehow got to address his convention—he received some good-natured jeers and the reply that Dick Bland was sure to be named.[65]

IV

ON JUNE 27 Bryan attended the funeral of his old mentor, Lyman Trumbull, in Chicago. On June 30 he buried his mother, in Salem. Leaving his own family in Salem he returned to Chicago and took a moderately priced suite of rooms at the Clifton House, across the street from the Palmer House. Mary Bryan would follow in time for the convention itself. Already in Chicago, representatives of all the partisan and nonpartisan silver organizations demanded a silver platform, a silver candidate, and a fusion campaign. Bryan's correspondence with British silverites shows that the hopes of British as well as American bimetallists were pinned on Chicago.

The big meeting of June 30 was that of the 60 state committeemen of the Bimetallic Democratic National Committee, a strictly partisan silver group which sought to win control of the national party organization. On the issue of how to force the regular National Committee to reflect the demands of the silver majority of the convention, Bryan argued that the silverites had the *right* to know the mind of the National Committee. A committee of five appointed to confer with the executive committee of the latter on July 1 reported to a silver men's caucus on July 3 that the Executive Committee would recommend that the National Committee follow precedent and name the temporary chairman. The silver caucus thereupon decided to substitute a silverite for the man it named and constituted the Committee of Five as the steering committee for the convention. Senator James K. Jones, named chairman, was its driving force. However, all attempts at this time to unite upon a presidential candidate failed.

Eastern newspapers like the New York *Sun* and the New York *Times* talked about the way "scruboak and sagebrush politicians" fanatically and impudently planned to deny the gold men a hearing, about the resemblance of the silver men to the "half-crazed French Revolutionists" whose "frenzied suspicions made them fancy that everything was a plot against them," and about the creation of new tests, invidious

[65] Charles G. Dawes, *A Journal of the McKinley Years, 1893–1913*, pp. 88, 89; Bascom Timmons, *Portrait of an American: Charles G. Dawes*, p. 48.

distinctions, and undemocratic methods being used by them to limit the eligibility for temporary chairman to a silverite. They feared mostly Altgeld, the "Populist of Socialist sympathies," a "genuine European 'Red,'" and an astute, unscrupulous politician who would "boss" the convention.[66]

The lack of meticulous organization for a particular candidate made preconvention sparring undignified. The rich newspaper owner from Ohio, John R. McLean, Senator Joseph C. S. Blackburn of Kentucky, Governor Sylvester Pennoyer of Oregon, Governor Horace Boies of Iowa, Senator John Daniel of Virginia, ex-Vice President Adlai E. Stevenson of Illinois, Governor Claude Matthews of Indiana, and Henry M. Teller as well as Richard Parks Bland were being boomed, and the number of dark horses passed all precedent. The silverites were invincible but could not unite on a candidate.[67] Never had a national administration been so completely ignored. Probably no more than a third of the delegates knew whom they would support. Excitement over the candidate was equaled by the expectancy over the transfer of control from old and long accepted hands to untried and revolutionary leadership.

Although frequently mentioned as the silver men's choice for temporary chairman, the chance that he might not be seated in the convention told against Bryan, who then looked forward to becoming permanent chairman. He worked on the speech he would deliver in that capacity as he traveled from Chicago to Crete, Nebraska, and back after debating the currency question on July 4. On the return trip he added one new item, the definition of the "business man" he regarded the most powerful argument it contained.

On the evening of July 4, the Chicago *Times-Herald* pictured "Young Mr. Bryan" as a dark horse possibility, and the Raleigh *News and Observer* printed a large picture of him over the caption "May Be the Next Democratic Nominee for President." But it was still a Donnybrook Fair as far as candidates were concerned. Upon his return to Chicago Bryan attended a silver-men's caucus. Bland was the favorite, but as such he faced the combined opposition of the Iowans (Boies),

[66] New York *Sun*, July 1, 2, 1896; New York *Times*, July 1, 2, 1896; New York *World*, July 2–4, 1896.

[67] Chicago *Record*, July 7, 1896; New York *Sun, Times, World*, July 7, 1896. Until July 4, the most popular badge sported in Chicago was one reading, "I want free coinage at 16 to 1." That afternoon an enterprising huckster sent a number of fakirs into the favorite haunts of the delegates and in two and a half hours had sold five thousand buttons reading, "I want a girl 16 to 28."

Kentuckians (Blackburn), and Ohioans (McLean), and if he were not named on the first or second ballot a prolonged contest might follow in which a dark horse could be selected. Teller's boom collapsed on July 5—to consider anyone but a Democrat was "treason"—as did McLean's, although his money might still attach him to the ticket.

Polls released on July 5 placed Bland in the lead, Boies second, and Bryan the last of seven possible candidates, with his own delegation split six for Bland, six for Boies, and four for him. Although given serious mention by the New York *World* on July 5 and by the Washington *Post* on July 6, the latter called him a protégé of Altgeld, a curious idea that has persisted despite Altgeld's utter devotion to Bland. Only two newspapers, the Chicago *Times-Herald* and the Omaha *World-Herald,* asserted emphatically that he would be the most prominent dark horse if the radicals won control of the convention.

Meantime, on July 5, the silver forces tried to dissuade David Bennett Hill from accepting the temporary chairmanship and agree to a silver substitute. Among others, Senators, Francis M. Cockrell, Stephen White, and John Daniel talked with him, to no avail. Then Constantine J. Smyth and William H. Thompson of the Nebraska silver delegation failed to impress upon him Bryan's "perfect title" to be seated in the convention, and ex-Governor James E. Boyd had no better success. Hill, originally a free coinage bimetallist, now supported gold. He had no use for Cleveland, but as a "regular organization man" he would support Thomas J. Mahoney's gold delegation.

Early on July 6, Senators Jones and Turpie, for the silver Steering Committee, issued an ultimatum: if the National Committee's majority report named Hill, they would oppose and substitute Daniel, who had been promised 552 votes in a silver caucus on July 5. Using "regularity" as their guide, the National Committee seated four contested silver delegates from various states and then the entire gold delegation from South Dakota and enough gold men from Michigan to insure its twenty-eight votes for gold. C. J. Smyth then argued against Mahoney in Bryan's behalf, but the committee upheld Mahoney by a majority of four. Bryan could be seated only by action within the convention. The committee also voted 27 to 23 for Hill for temporary chairman.

The gold members of the National Committee knew that their work would be undone by the convention. Nevertheless, they wrote a strong minority report for Hill to present to the Committee on Resolutions. The great debate would come upon this report, for Hill would support it with the keynote speech he had prepared. Hill refused to get excited. "Senator Hill, why don't you ever smile and look pleasant?" asked an admirer. "I never smile and look pleasant at a funeral," Hill replied.[68]

Meanwhile the various delegations completed their organization. Illinois stood forty-seven out of forty-eight for Bland. Texas was for Bland, and while ex-Senator John H. Reagan and Hogg favored Bryan for temporary chairman, Joseph Bailey blasted him for flirting with Populism, failing to follow the national platform of 1892, and for threatening to bolt if a silverite were not named for President. North Carolina also announced for Bland, but as soon as Josephus Daniels arrived in Chicago he arranged for a committee to call on Bryan. Bryan captivated it but asked it to wait until the older candidates had measured their strength and not bring him out at an inopportune moment. They understood; they would do nothing until he had been seated.[69] The Nebraska silver delegation revealed its faith in being seated by organizing and choosing Bryan as its member for the Committee on Resolutions. While Bland boomers shouted "Bland, Bimetallism, or Bust," four hundred Nebraskans, using the college style of cheering for the first time at a national convention, invaded the lobby of the gold citadel, the Palmer House, and yelled:

> Rah–rah–rah
> Ne–bras–kee
> Rah–rah–rah
> O–ma–ha
> Will–yum–J.–Bryan
> Hoo–rah!

Bryan later told Rosser that the National Committee had unsuspectedly helped him by seating Mahoney's men. Had he been seated during the first day, elected temporary chairman, and made the keynote speech, he would have been deprived of the greater opportunity of debating the platform.[70] Nevertheless, the possibility of his being a candidate aroused so much opposition from the friends of favorite sons that he failed of election as chairman of the Committee on Resolutions. He was before the Committee on Credentials when the choice

[68] New York *World*, July 12, 1896.
[69] New York *Times*, July 7, 1896; Josephus Daniels, *Editor in Politics*, pp. 159–161.
[70] Omaha *Bee*, July 7, 1896; Rosser, *Crusading Commoner*, p. 32.

of chairman was made and thus could not fight for the post, and when he learned that Senator Jones wanted it he immediately deferred to him. He was laughed at by the gold men during the first day of the convention because he and his delegation had to scramble for visitors' tickets in order to enter the hall.

Bryan's success depended upon lack of agreement on a candidate. On the evening of July 5, when visited by a delegation of Coloradoans seeking his support for Teller, he replied that the "logic of the situation" indicated that he rather than Teller would be named. The delegation quickly apologized—they did not know he was a candidate. Bryan said he was prevented from voting for Teller because it was easier to bring "disappointed Republicans" over to the Democracy than "victorious Democrats" over to the Republican party. When asked what support he had, he said he had half of Nebraska's vote and half that of Indian Territory on the second ballot. Someone interrupted at this point and the Teller men left, smiling incredulously at his calculating on the nomination with such poor support. The incident reveals that the Teller men believed Bryan important enough to win over, that he had conducted his canvass so quietly that many of those who should have done so failed to recognize him as a potential candidate. Had he not been interrupted, he would have added that his hope had a substantial foundation in the "logic of the situation" and on the "rule of elimination." By the latter he discarded Pennoyer, Blackburn, and Matthews, who were state rather than national figures or had unsatisfactory records on silver. McLean, Stevenson, and Tillman he regarded as merely possible compromise candidates.[71] This left only Bland and Boies, both of whom had followed his policy of subordinating personalities to principles and now fairly well balanced each other.

The avowed disinterestedness of Bryan's crusade paid handsome dividends. Since the silver manifesto of March 1, 1895 his insistence upon principle had earned him much publicity and invited comment that such selfless seeking should be rewarded. Once the primaries revealed a victory for principle, however, he began work on behalf of his own nomination. If he had not thought about himself as a potential

[71] Bryan, *Memoirs*, pp. 105–106; Williams, *Bryan*, pp. 136–137. Although Tillman's barbed tongue made him practically impossible, he provided a potent symbol. In his lapel he wore his famous "pitchfork" emblem—a silver pitchfork with three prongs impaling three goldbugs, Cleveland, Carlisle, and Sherman.

candidate all along he certainly blundered upon a fortunate course of action.[72] By rejecting a favorite son endorsement from his own state, finally, he remained unencumbered in pursuit of uninstructed delegates.

The maneuver that paid Bryan highest dividends was his fifteen months of missionary work in behalf of silver and cultivation of the Chicago delegates. He knew personally more delegates than did any other candidate; he had the ability to transfer enthusiasm engendered by the "logic of the situation" and "rule of elimination" to a number of important, trustworthy friends; and he was on the ground to superintend his strategy. When he spoke of himself as the nominee, some reacted as Willis J. Abbot did and doubted his mental capacity. How could a boy in appearance, one not yet admitted to the convention, without a single state behind him, dare claim the nomination? The answer was simple, Bryan told Abbot—he had prepared a speech that would stampede the convention. The silver men needed Nebraska's vote—*ergo* his delegation would be seated. Then all he needed was a chance to speak. Would Abbot find out if Altgeld would support him if he were named? Questioning the solidity of Bryan's mind, Abbot nevertheless asked Altgeld and returned with a message: "Tell Bryan he's young enough to wait a few years. Dick Bland has earned this nomination and shall have it if I can influence the convention." Abbot also asked if Bryan would get a chance to speak. Altgeld did not know —the agenda was pretty full.[73]

Bryan depended heavily upon the efficacy of past tactics. For eight years he had carried audiences with him, and a good speech should carry a national as well as a state convention. So sure were they of his ability as a speaker that his Nebraskans ordered a barrel full of Bryan buttons and a number of "Bryan for President" badges. Bryan also stressed his "availability." He had cooperated with groups as disparate as partisan Populists and nonpartisan National Silver Party men and urged fusion to the extent of bolting old party lines, and he was the most "available" progressive in parties other than the Democratic. Nationally known Populists like Weaver and Nebraska's Julius Burrows played into his hand by desiring that the Democratic nomination be "advisory simply and not final." Thus a way would be open "for

[72] Marian Silveus, "The Antecedents of the Campaign of 1896" (unpublished Ph.D. thesis, University of Wisconsin, 1932), p. 187.

[73] Willis J. Abbot, *Watching the World Go By*, pp. 157–159.

a consultation between the Democrats and Populists . . . to bring about a consolidation of forces," as Weaver put it.[74] Bryan's "availability" to the minor parties undoubtedly proved an excellent qualification to those in Chicago who believed that fusion was necessary to defeat the Republicans.

[74] Copy of letter by Julius Burrows to Weaver, Bryan Papers; Weaver to Bryan, June 3, 1896, *ibid.*

CHAPTER 8

The "Cross of Gold" and the Triple Alliance

I

EARLY in the morning of July 7 large crowds converged on the Chicago Coliseum, then the largest permanent exhibition building in the world. While Mary Bryan found a seat in the galleries, Benjamin Tillman, down front, glowered like a medieval chieftain, Joseph Bailey amused the silverites by displaying a silver dollar as a collar button, and even Henry George looked happy because, said a critic, his "silver eggs, long since laid, now give evidence of an early hatchment." [1]

National Chairman William F. Harrity called the convention to order. Immediately after the prayer, the irrepressible antagonism between the gold and the silver forces flamed fiercely in three hours of debate over the majority report of the National Committee, which named David Bennett Hill for temporary chairman. When applause from Eastern delegates subsided, Henry D. Clayton of Alabama offered John Daniel as a substitute and loosed the enthusiasm of the silver men. Not satisfied with merely cheering and shouting, they stomped their feet on the wooden floor and caused a sound like that of a rush of wild steers over a bridge.

William C. Whitney selected brilliant orators to defend Hill, but their appeals fell upon deaf ears. The result was a rout—Daniel 556 and Hill 349—and silver was just forty-eight short of a two-thirds majority. The gold men stared silently as three jubilant silverites escorted Daniel to the chair to the tune of "Britons Shall Never Be Slaves." The scepter of power in the Democracy, according to conservatives, had passed "from the strong, certain hands of the East, to the feverish, headstrong mob of the West and South, from Cleveland to Tillman, from Hill to Altgeld." [2] Although Bryan lost the temporary chairmanship, Daniel's victory prevented the slippery Hill from controlling the convention and placing the party in the hands of vested interests rather than in those of the people, and Bryan said the gold men could have

[1] New York *Sun,* New York *World,* San Francisco *Chronicle,* July 7, 1896.
[2] New York *Sun,* July 7, 1896.

avoided humiliation by recognizing the right of the majority to rule. Daniel reinforced this point by devoting his keynote address to the all-inclusiveness of the silver movement.

Although Nebraska's gold delegates were assigned to committees, Bryan depended upon John H. Atwood, chairman of the Credentials Committee, to "right the wrong" he had suffered.[3] Meantime he and Senators Isham G. Harris of Tennessee and Stephen White of California were considered for permanent chairman. To avoid having two Southerners acting as chairmen in the convention, Harris was dropped. Fearing that his chances for the nomination might be hurt if he were selected, Bryan's friends voted against him and helped select White. White was then chosen over Hill by the Committee on Permanent Organization by the vote of 33 to 6.

A vigorous fight was proceeding simultaneously in the Committee on Resolutions, which met at the Palmer House. When Charles S. Thomas of Colorado moved that a subcommittee of nine be appointed to draft the platform, the gold men tried to amend the motion to read "write all but the financial plank," which they wished written by the gold-controlled full committee. After debate as bitter as any in the convention, the amendment lost and three gold men were sent to face six silverites on the subcommittee. The gold delegates then decided to sit in the convention without participating, but that upon returning home they would report to Senator George Gray of Delaware with a view to naming a separate gold Democratic ticket. In a speech to a crowd gathered before the Sherman House near midnight, Bryan spoke again about the need of putting principles before personalities, saying that the issue was whether the United States could free itself from British control—it was the campaign of 1776 all over again.[4]

On July 8 the Nebraska silver delegation arrived early but sparked only a short and hesitant Bryan boom. Of various speakers, only Joseph C. S. Blackburn set the convention aflame for a moment when he said that "Christ drove with a lash from the temple a better set of men than those who for twenty years have had control of the finances of the country." [5] The crowd wanted bigger game and called for John Peter Altgeld, Hill, and Bryan. Altgeld declined, Hill was not in the hall, and Bryan was then delivering his closing arguments in a snarling

[3] Bryan to Victor Rosewater, Omaha *Bee,* July 7, 1897; Omaha *World-Herald,* July 7, 1896.

[4] Omaha *World-Herald,* July 8, 1896.

[5] New York *Tribune,* July 9, 1896.

fight before the Credentials Committee, but the mention of his name by Chairman White provoked a demonstration at least equal to that given Blackburn. Altgeld finally succumbed. Pale, thoughtful, disdaining the arts of oratory, a semi-invalid capable of sustained physical exertion only by the force of a tremendous will, he sounded the keynote—no compromise on the silver issue!

Meantime the subcommittee on platform threw out the financial plank offered by the gold minority. Hill thereupon declared that he would make a minority report directly to the convention—he would not waste breath on the committee. Tillman then asked for an hour in which to reply to Hill and to introduce a resolution censuring Cleveland's financial policy. Senator Jones, in charge of debate, said that such a long speech would tire the delegates. Tillman exploded: "I'll have an hour or nothing. No crowd ever gets tired when I'm talking." [6] Jones capitulated and gave him 50 minutes. At this moment Bryan entered the room.

When the Credentials Committee recommended seating Bryan's rather than Thomas J. Mahoney's delegation, ex-Governor William E. Russell of Massachusetts demanded a roll call of the committee. Atwood declared his committee unanimous, and Russell desisted. Mahoney thereupon sarcastically thanked Chairman White and retired while Bryan received one of the few real demonstrations yet granted. Bryan's seating was a stinging rebuke to both the old National Committee and to the gold men who pretended to represent Nebraska. To be seated with the other silver delegations would have been one thing, said Bryan, but "to walk down the aisle and put the gold standard delegation on the tip of my toe is another." [7]

Proceeding to the Committee on Resolutions, Bryan forced out the Nebraska gold member and read the platform. His money plank remained just as he had written it several weeks earlier for Charles H. Jones, editor of the St. Louis *Post-Dispatch*, who compiled the original draft:

We demand the free and unlimited coinage of both silver and gold at the present legal ratio of 16 to 1, without waiting for the aid or consent of any other nation. We demand that the standard silver dollar shall be a full legal tender, equally with gold, for all debts, public and private, and we favor such legislation as will prevent for the future the demonetization of any kind of legal-tender money by private contract.

[6] Daniel C. Roper, *Fifty Years of Public Life*, p. 84.
[7] Charles M. Rosser, *The Crusading Commoner*, p. 33.

Other paragraphs reserved the option of redemption in gold or silver to the government, opposed the issue of interest-bearing bonds in times of peace, denounced the issue of notes by banks, and demanded that all paper money be issued by the government and that it be redeemable in coin.

The tariff and income tax planks were closely joined. While the tariff should be "for-revenue-only," the Wilson-Gorman tariff should not be changed until the currency question was settled unless to meet the deficit in revenue caused by the adverse decision on the income tax law. The plank on the tax itself was immediately called a "court packing" plan by its opponents because it said: "We declare that it is the duty of the Congress to use all the Constitutional power which remains after that decision, or which may come from its reversal by the court as it may hereafter be constituted, so that the burdens of taxation may be equally and impartially laid. . . ."

Other planks destined to arouse intense antagonism were those which denounced arbitrary interference by federal authorities in local affairs, a reflection of Altgeld's opposition to Cleveland's sending of troops into Illinois in 1894; called for the arbitration of labor disputes; demanded the strengthening of the Interstate Commerce Commission against railroad consolidations and pools and trusts of all kinds; and suggested the abolition of life tenure in the civil service.

Then followed the customary pronouncements on the protection of American labor by prohibiting the importation of foreign labor; economy in government; pensions for veterans; and improvement of internal waterways. The platform also favored the early admission of the territories of New Mexico, Arizona, and Oklahoma as states; supported the Monroe Doctrine; and opposed a presidential third term. Although these issues did not play a great part in the debate on the platform or in the campaign, they were opposed by the East because they would admit three more states favoring silver, the Monroe Doctrine plank appeared an insult to Britain, and the no presidential third term was a direct slap to Cleveland. Bryan was directly responsible for only the planks on money, arbitration, and the Monroe Doctrine, although the whole was similar to his congressional platforms. The finished product was adopted in committee by 33 to 15.

While awaiting the report on the Michigan delegation, Tillman looked at Hill and said, "There's going to be hell tonight. Hill's got his white face on. I have seen it in the Senate. He means business, and by God, so do I. He wants us to indorse Cleveland in the platform.

But if Hill tries to put a white robe on the sinner tonight we'll pull it off." Everyone looked to a clash between him and Hill, but Hill remained silent and the fight was postponed to the morrow.[8] The old National Committee had given Michigan to gold by 49 to 1. Atwood's final report gave it to silver, and the crowd cheered for eighteen minutes. When Chairman White announced that silver now had two-thirds of the votes, the crowd cheered for twenty minutes more. Another outburst came on the roll call, which the silver men won by a vote of 558 to 368, and for another twenty minutes there was whooping and shouting. The course of history might have been changed if the decision had gone against the Michigan and Nebraska silverites, for in winning a two-thirds majority the silver men had by coincidence offered Bryan his opportunity to win the nomination.

For two days silver had triumphed at every point. "In the enthusiasm and fierceness of debate, the convention is as a highly seasoned tamale to a peanut compared to the St. Louis affair," commented the *Rocky Mountain News*.[9] The most popular of all slogans was "without regard to the action of any other nation." Every time it was uttered there was a "wow wow," said the New York *Sun*.[10] The next day would be the day of great speeches and of great hopes, for the platform would be debated by the ablest speakers of both sides, and if time permitted nominations would begin.

At home, Richard Parks Bland asked his doctor for something to quiet his nerves. "Do you think you will be nominated, Mr. Bland?" asked the doctor. "Yes, I am sure of it. I do not want it but it seems to be coming my way," replied Bland.[11] But Bryan's chances had improved with the spread of the knowledge that he had written the money plank and would debate in defense of the platform, and with his launching of an aggressive campaign on the floor of the convention. His Nebraskans were canvassing mightily, as were a large number of the North Carolina delegates. Friends were offering him as bait to the Populists, who would soon meet at St. Louis, and National Silver Party men were veering toward him as a running mate for Joseph Sibley. All he needed now was the chance to address the convention.

[8] New York *World, Rocky Mountain News*, July 9, 1896.
[9] July 9, 1896.
[10] July 9, 1896.
[11] William Vincent Byars (ed.), *An American Commoner: The Life and Times of Richard Parks Bland; a Study of the Last Quarter of the Nineteenth Century*, pp. 234, 296.

Not long after Bryan was seated, Senator James K. Jones asked him to take charge of the debate on the platform. Having been denied the positions of temporary chairman, permanent chairman, and chairman of the Committee on Resolutions, Bryan finally was given his chance. Afterward Bryan asked Jones why he had selected him "to close such a debate [that] has never come to any other person during this generation." Jones said he was the only prominent speaker who had not addressed the convention. Moreover, he deserved the honor because he had taken such a long and active part in the silver crusade. Finally, Jones had a sore throat and could not make himself heard. Bryan knew that he would be more effective in a brief closing speech than in a long opening speech. By speaking first he would utter propositions for others to demolish; by speaking last he could make an apparently extemporaneous reply and an emotional appeal. But how to get Tillman to switch?

Bryan saw Hill and arranged for an hour and fifteen minutes of debate for each side. Then he asked Tillman whether he wished to open or close. Tillman said he had fifty minutes to close. Bryan suggested that Hill would oppose such a long closing speech, and Hill did object, telling Tillman that he should use his time to open. Thereupon Tillman agreed to let Bryan close. Bryan spoke later about "circumstances" that favored him, but without mentioning that he had importuned every member of the Committee on Resolutions to get Jones to let him close the debate, and that Hill's dislike for Tillman was a contributing factor in his success.[12]

As agreed, Hill, Senator William F. Vilas of Wisconsin, and Russell would speak for gold, and Tillman and Bryan for silver. Recalling his ability to snatch victory from defeat with a speech, his friends had high hopes that Bryan would make the most memorable address of the convention. On the morrow it would be Bryan against Hill, Nebraska against New York, the West against the East, progressivism against conservatism, men against money.

That evening, while dining with Mary Bryan and Dr. Charles M. Rosser, Bryan smiled upon the noisy Bland and Boies rooters on parade and said confidently, "These people don't know it, but they will be cheering for me just this way tomorrow night. I will make the

[12] William Jennings Bryan and Mary Baird Bryan, *The Memoirs of William Jennings Bryan*, pp. 109–111; W. J. Bryan, *The First Battle*, p. 615; Rosser, *Crusading Commoner*, pp. 35–37; Mark Sullivan, *Our Times: The United States, 1900–1925*, I, 123.

greatest speech of my life tomorrow in reply to Senator Hill. Hill is at heart a bimetallist; he will not be talking his sentiments, but the sentiments of New York and that section of the country. I wrote the main features of the platform and I believe in the soundness of every sentence. I will be at my best. Hill is the brains of the opposition, and when I have answered him it will dawn on the convention that I am a pretty good man to lead the fight."

Mrs. Bryan turned to Rosser. "Don't you think that Mr. Bryan has a good chance to be nominated?"

Rosser had failed to impress the Texas delegation with Bryan, and several newspaper men had told him that he was "looking on Bryan as a tin god" or that Bryan was a political adventurer, or that Rosser had a distorted imagination. Before he could reply, Bryan interposed: "So that you may both sleep well tonight, I am going to tell you something. I am the only man who can be nominated. I am what they call the 'logic of the situation.' " [13]

II

EASTERN delegates viewed the impending battle as one "between the Democracy of the Atlantic States and the so-called Democracy sprung from the schisms and enmities of Populism, fanaticism, and socialism of the restless and reckless South and West." [14] Westerners and Southerners retorted that the East was demanding policies designed to favor a comparatively small class, that it had controlled the party by encouraging a fictitious sectionalism between the two producing sections. They were as thoroughly American by birth and blood as any Easterners, and as nationalistic in their thinking, and it was high time that the division by which the East ruled was ended and that it bend to the will of the majority of the people.[15]

On July 9 Chairman White opened the convention in an air charged with the electricity of excitement. While Senator Jones read the plat-

[13] Omaha *World-Herald*, July 9, 1896; Rosser, *Crusading Commoner*, pp. 37–38. Tammany's McClellan met Benton McMillin in the lobby of the Auditorium and asked him who the candidate would be. "Mac," he replied, "I am afraid that it is going to be that little whelp, Bill Bryan of Nebraska. . . . There are a lot of men here who are going to try to slip him over, but how they are going to do it I can't find out." Harold C. Syrett (ed.), *The Gentleman and the Tiger: The Autobiography of George Brinton McClellan, Jr.*, p. 112.

[14] New York *World*, July 9, 1896.

[15] New Orleans *Times-Democrat*, July 6, 1896.

form, Francis E. Leupp, a reporter for the New York *Evening Post*, wired his paper that "William J. Bryan, of Nebraska, is looming up as a candidate." Henry George and the veteran reporter John Russell Young happened to see what Leupp wrote and looked at him quizzically. Who was this Bryan? Young asked. Leupp pointed to "a youngish man with a smooth face, high forehead, and pronounced jaw. . . . He has on a short alpaca coat, and is sucking a lemon." "Why pick him for a winner?" continued Young. Leupp replied that since Bryan was sucking a lemon to clear his throat it was evident that he was going to speak. The convention was deadlocked, feeling was running high, and the silver delegates were looking for a Moses. "If Bryan gets before them while they're in this condition," he said, "they're gone." George said that Bryan had not stirred the House greatly. Leupp pointed out that in Congress Bryan had addressed shrewd debaters in an unemotional atmosphere; now he faced mostly farmers and village oracles, men of little book learning who plowed on weekdays and listened to an exhorter on Sundays. Their libraries consisted of a family Bible, a history of the United States, and some farm publications. With his voice and his genius for gesture Bryan would make them imagine they saw whatever he wanted them to see.

Unable to convince his friends, Leupp said he would talk with Bryan. Proceeding to the Nebraska delegation he told Bryan that he had reported him to New York as "the coming man of the Convention." Bryan's smile revealed that the possibility had crossed his mind, but he made a deprecatory gesture, as if waving away such an idea. "You're premature, you're premature," he protested.

"It may be," Leupp replied, "but I'm right nevertheless."

"What makes you think so?"

"You are going to make a set speech. . . ."

"Yes, Senator Jones was slated to speak in support of the resolutions, but he has a sore throat, and has asked me to take his place."

"And that will settle it. If you talk a half-hour to this Convention in the condition in which it is now, nothing less than a miracle can prevent your nomination."

With a slightly broader smile and a wag of the head demure rather than negative, Bryan dismissed Leupp by bending forward to listen as Jones finished reading the platform.[16] As usual with him before making an important speech, Bryan felt a weakness in the pit of his

[16] Francis E. Leupp, "Dark Horse Convention," *The Outlook*, 101 (June 8, 1912), 297–302.

stomach. He wanted to lie down. This being impossible, he went to the lobby and returned to his seat with a sandwich and a cup of coffee.

Upon completing his reading, Jones explained the procedure to follow. First there would be a minority report; then two amendments to the majority report would be offered by Hill. The first of these commended the Cleveland administration. The second stated that any change in the monetary standard should not apply to existing contracts and that the free coinage of silver should be suspended if at the end of one year it failed to bring gold and silver to parity. Then the majority report would be debated.

Now Tillman came forward as the first supporter of the majority report. Dark face suffused with blood, hair unkempt, collar wilted, necktie askew, jacket wrinkled, his pitchfork emblem on one lapel and a Cuban flag on the other, and a strange gleam in his one eye, he glanced from right to left, placed one hand on his hip, rocked on his heels, and threw his head back. To the gold men he appeared vengeful and defiant. Sensing the prejudice against him, he boomed out that he would introduce himself, stating, "I come from a State which is the home of secession." The South and West were in bondage to the East, he declared, the hewers of wood and drawers of water; as a result of the financial system and Republican legislation their sustenance was being drained by the East. "Some of my friends . . . have said that this is not a sectional issue. I say it is a sectional issue."

Cries of "Time" and "Oh, boil it down," made Tillman angry. He became personal and vituperative. To endorse Cleveland would be to make "asses and liars" out of the delegates. Cleveland had overriden the Constitution, which made both gold and silver the money of the country, and he had been "faithful . . . unto the death of the Democratic party." And there stood Hill, his sponsor and apologist. When the audience hissed his use of the words "secession," "disruption," and "sectional," he retorted that only three things hissed—serpents, geese, and men. His earlier diagnosis that "We'll have a —— of a time in Chicago" proved right.[17]

That he said what needed saying was beside the point, for all sought to drown the monster of sectionalism in waves of patriotic platitudes. He concluded that the South and West had burned their bridges

[17] Atlanta *Constitution*, New York *Sun*, New York *Times*, Omaha *World-Herald*, San Francisco *Chronicle*, July 10, 1896; *Harper's Weekly*, April 11, 1896; *The Nation*, February 6, 1896; Francis B. Simkins, *Pitchfork Ben Tillman, South Carolinian*, pp. 4, 17–18.

behind them and then offered a resolution arraigning Cleveland. He had been allowed to make the longest address of the convention in favor of a platform approved by a large majority, but he had mistaken his audience and overshot the mark, and both Jones and Hill repudiated his charges of sectionalism. Bryan said he had made the only kind of speech he knew how to make, but he also realized that Tillman's blunder placed the entire burden of defending the platform upon his own shoulders.[18]

As Hill moved forward, Clark Howell sent Bryan a note. "You have now the opportunity of your life in concluding the argument for the majority report. Make a big, broad, patriotic speech that will leave no taste of sectionalism in the mouth and which will give a sentiment that will touch a responsive chord in the heart of the whole country. You can make the hit of your life." Bryan replied: "You will not be disappointed. . . . I will speak the sentiment of my heart and I think you will be satisfied." [19]

Waves of cheers enveloped Hill as he ascended the platform. In great contrast to Tillman, he was calm and impeccably attired. Knowing of his past treacheries, many expected him to cut Russell out, desert sound money, and stampede the convention for himself. But Hill kept the faith. "In reply to Senator Tillman I would state that I am a Democrat and not a revolutionist," he began. "I am utterly opposed to most of the planks in this unnecessary, ridiculous, and foolish platform." With badgerlike ferocity he gave a bravura performance and a superb defense of Cleveland. He defended international cooperation on the money question, said that the platform should have asked for the remonetization of silver rather than for free silver, thought it unwise to make the income tax a test of Democratic faith, believed the condemnation of Cleveland's bonds "foolish," and refused to join in the demand for the reconstruction of the Supreme Court. He received the largest demonstration yet granted, and Bryan acknowledged that he had made a "very strong speech." [20] Like Tillman, however, he had overshot the mark—in the opposite direction. His clear, reasoned, logical exposition lacked sufficient emotion to make it a truly moving speech.

[18] Atlanta *Constitution,* New York *Tribune,* New York *World,* July 10, 1896; Bryan, *Memoirs,* p. 112; Simkins, *Tillman,* pp. 335–336.

[19] Atlanta *Constitution,* July 11, 1896.

[20] Bryan, *Memoirs,* p. 112.

Senator Vilas then "pounded the advocates of free coinage without mercy," to use Bryan's words.[21] But he was dull, and after his voice broke he received scant courtesy, particularly when he ate into Russell's time. Fearing that he would be cut out, Russell protested to Hill. Bryan overheard, stepped across the aisle, and suggested to Hill that time on both sides be extended ten minutes. Hill agreed; Russell was grateful; and Bryan had another "unexpected bit of good fortune" in gaining ten additional minutes for his speech.[22]

Quaintly impressive because of apparent physical weakness—he died shortly thereafter at the age of forty years—Russell directed his attack against the financial plank alone, warning that disaster and dishonor would follow if the silverites under radical leadership demanded a new policy on the grounds of expediency.

From his seat in the gallery it appeared to Edgar Lee Masters that Bryan "sprang" from his seat and hurried to the platform with athletic agility. Those who sat along the aisle bid him Godspeed. He jumped the platform steps two at a time and walked rapidly to the speakers' rostrum. Amidst a terrific din, those in the galleries stood up while crowds at the doors pushed forward to see him. Slim, tall, raven-haired, beaked of nose, for a full minute he maintained a statuesque pose—head thrown back, foot thrust forward, left hand on the lecturn, right arm extended over his head toward the delegates in an appeal for silence. As he surveyed the acres of people the thought flashed through his mind that he was to be the voice of the triumphant majority in as perfect a setting for a speech as one would ever find. Tillman had been sectional and vituperative; Vilas had been verbose and dull; Russell had not been heard; Hill had been cold, deliberate. His speech, while not extemporaneous, would appear to be so; he needed only to add references to those who had preceded him.

"Wait until you hear Bryan," the silver delegates whispered expectantly. His appearance pleased them, for he dressed as a plain Westerner in a black sack suit of alpaca, a low-cut vest, and trousers that bagged at the knees. Under the guidance of his outstretched hand the crowd finally fell silent. He took a step forward. The smile on his mobile face melted away as he lowered his arm to his side and uttered his first words.

"It would be presumptuous indeed," he began modestly, "to present

[21] *Ibid.*

[22] *Ibid.*, pp. 112–113.

myself against the distinguished gentlemen to whom you have listened if this were a mere measuring of abilities; but this is not a contest between persons. The humblest citizen in all the land, when clad in the armor of a righteous cause, is stronger than all the hosts of error. I come to speak to you in defense of a cause as holy as the cause of liberty—the cause of humanity." At the end of the debate, he added, he would move to lay on the table both the Hill and Tillman resolutions on Cleveland because he objected to having a contest over principle degenerate into one over persons.

The monetary issue was the greatest issue ever contested in the history of American politics, Bryan continued. With the Democratic Congressional Manifesto of March 1895 the silver men had begun to contend for a silver declaration in the national platform. "With a zeal approaching the zeal of Peter the Hermit, our silver Democrats went forth from victory unto victory until they are now assembled, not to discuss, not to debate, but to enter up the judgment rendered by the plain people of this country."

In this contest father had been arrayed against son and brother against brother; old leaders who refused to express the desires of their followers had been brushed aside by new ones who would "give direction to the cause of truth." He reiterated his belief that the contest was impersonal. He, for one, did not expect Senator Hill—toward whom he turned—to speak against the wishes of his state. Neither did he wish Russell to believe that he had any hostility for the great state of Massachusetts. Yet, he insisted, "we stand here representing people who are equals, before the law, of the greatest citizen of Massachusetts. "When you [turning toward the gold men] come before us and tell us that we are about to disturb your business interests, we reply that you have disturbed our business interests by your course."

The audience was with Bryan from the first. For a time nothing could be heard except his voice, which carried clearly to the very doors of the hall, and the applause that greeted his remarks. The audience would rise, shout its endorsement of each comment, and sit down again as one man and be silent when he began anew. The instantaneous response to almost every point he made caused him to think of a trained choir. His words, his thoughts, his manner, and his earnestness held the thousands in bonds mightier than steel. His was a power incomparably greater than that of any other speaker.

Easterners had too limited a definition of the businessman, he said, and he gave his classic definition:

The man who is employed for wages is as much a business man as his employer; the attorney in a country town is as much a business man as the corporation counsel in a great metropolis; the merchant at the crossroads store is as much a business man as the merchant of New York; the farmer who goes forth in the morning and toils all day—who begins in the spring and toils all summer—and who by the application of brain and muscle to the natural resources of the country creates wealth, is as much a business man as the man who goes upon the board of trade and bets upon the price of grain. . . .

The crowd cut him off with cheer after cheer, and the number of handkerchiefs waved made the galleries appear a sea of white. Shortly before he was to speak, Rosser heard one farmer-spectator say to another: "I think I'll go because I do not care to stay to hear that crazy Populist, Bill Bryan of Nebrasky." After Bryan's definition of the businessman the farmer sailed his hat without thought of its destination, violently thrashed the vacant seat before him with his coat, and exclaimed, "My God! My God! My God!" When to his definition Bryan added "the miners who go down a thousand feet" he provoked a new uproar which prevented him from proceeding for several minutes.

Bryan refused to say a word against those who lived along the Atlantic, but he was certain that the pioneers [he pointed toward the West]—those who had braved the dangers of the wilderness and made the plains bloom with the institutions of civilization—were just as deserving of the consideration of the Democracy as any people in the nation. "It is for those we speak," he said with a note of challenge in his voice. "We do not come as aggressors. Ours is not a war of conquest; we are fighting in the defense of our homes, our families, and posterity. We have petitioned, and our petitions have been scorned; we have entreated, and our entreaties have been disregarded; we have begged, and they have mocked when our calamity came. We beg no longer; we entreat no more; we petition no more. We defy them!" The audience greeted his note of defiance with another set of cheers that rolled from floor to gallery, back and forth, and back and forth again.

While Senator Vilas might fear the rise of a Robespierre, Bryan said he sought an Andrew Jackson "to stand . . . against the encroachments of organized wealth." Cheers followed his declaring that the Democracy, its eternal principles unchanging, must be made to meet new conditions as they arose; that the income tax, one of the new conditions, was constitutional when passed as a law and would be paid gladly by those worthy to enjoy good government; and that he supported the platform demand that only the government issue paper money and that the banks get out of the governing business. He threw the burden of proving that silver and gold could not be maintained at parity by the adoption of bimetallism squarely back to Hill, who with his fellows had for twenty years sought an international agreement and for twenty years had failed. Then he moved on to the "paramount issue":

If they ask us why it is that we say more on the money question than we say upon the tariff question, I reply that, if [tariff] protection has slain its thousands, the gold standard has slain its tens of thousands. If they ask us why we do not embody in our platform all the things that we believe in we reply that when we have restored the money of the Constitution all other necessary reforms will be possible but that until this is done there is no other reform that can be accomplished.

"We go forth confident that we shall win," said Bryan as he laid down the line of battle. "If the gold standard is a good thing, we ought to declare in favor of its retention and not in favor of abandoning it; and if the gold standard is a bad thing why should we wait until other nations are willing to help us to let go? . . . We care not upon which issue they force the fight; we are prepared to meet them on either issue or both."

After quoting from Carlisle's speech of 1878 to show that Carlisle once favored the masses rather than capital, Bryan contrasted two ideas of government, the latter very suggestive of New Deal Democracy: "There are those who believe that, if you will only legislate to make the well-to-do prosperous, their prosperity will leak through on those below. The Democratic idea, however, has been that if you legislate to make the masses prosperous, their prosperity will find its way up through every class which rests upon them." Then came his peroration:

You [turning to the gold men] tell us that the great cities are in favor of the gold standard; we reply that the great cities rest upon our broad and fertile prairies. Burn down your cities and leave our farms, and your cities will spring up again as if by magic; but destroy our farms and the grass will grow in the streets of every city in the country.

My friends, we declare that the nation is able to legislate for its own people on every question, without waiting for the aid or consent of any other nation on earth; and upon that issue we expect to carry every State in the Union. . . . It is the issue of 1776 over again. . . . [W]e care not upon what lines the battle is fought. If they say bimetallism is good, but that we cannot have it until other nations help us, we reply that, instead of having a gold standard because England has, we will restore bimetallism, and then let England have bimetallism because the United States has it. If they dare to come out in the open field and defend the gold standard as a good thing, we will fight them to the uttermost. Having behind us the producing masses of this nation . . . we will answer their demands for a gold standard by saying to them: "You shall not press down upon the brow of labor this crown of thorns, you shall not crucify mankind on a cross of gold."

When he voiced the first metaphor his two hands, raised to the sides of his head, the fingers spread inward, moved slowly down and close to his temples, so that the spectators were almost hypnotized into seeing the thorns piercing the brow and the blood trickling from the wounds. "You shall not crucify mankind upon a cross of gold." Here his hands left his head and followed his arms out at right angles to the body. There he stood, the crucified man in the flesh! He retained his position for about five seconds. Then he placed his arms at his side and took a step backwards. The delegates sat as if transfixed, and he started toward his seat in a silence he found "really painful." It was not until he had almost reached the floor that the spell broke.[23]

Indian yells from the Georgia delegation signaled the loosing of all the noise-making machinery in the world while several sturdy delegates carried Bryan about the hall on their shoulders. Twenty thousand persons shouted, waved their arms, threw about everything harmless, marched, danced, sang, cried. Hanna's spies ripped a path through the herd gone mad to report on the success of "an incarnate drum," [24] while some delegates screamed "Down with gold! Down with the hook-nosed Shylocks of Wall Street! Down with the Christ-killing gold bugs," thereby alienating the Jewish vote, which was convinced that Democratic as well as Populist leaders were anti-Semitic.[25] After about ten minutes Bryan was landed in his seat, where he could hardly breathe for the press of friends old and new who in congratulating him sat in his lap, hung about his neck, wrung his hands, shouted in his ears, and danced on his feet.

Like buoys floating from their places in a river to a whirlpool the banners of all but twelve of the states converged upon the Nebraska reservation. Early in the demonstration Altgeld said, "That is the

[23] New York Sun, New York Times, New York World, July 10, 11, 1896; Bryan, First Battle, pp. 199–206; Bryan, Memoirs, pp. 114–116; Rosser, Crusading Commoner, pp. 48–49.
[24] Thomas Beer, Mauve Decade, pp. 64–65.
[25] New York Sun, September 16, 1896.

greatest speech I ever listened to. I don't know but its effect will be to nominate him," but he kept the Illinois standard anchored for Bland. Suddenly he saw it start toward Bryan in the hands of a Nebraska delegate. He peremptorily demanded its return. Then he saw the Missouri banner go by. "Now you can take it. Missouri is in line, and I guess we can all afford to join," he said. Turning to those about him he asserted that he would rather be able to make a speech like Bryan's than be President.[26]

Introducing a novelty, Southern delegates held their banners aloft and marched down the main aisle to the music of one of Sousa's triumphal marches. Behind them came the banners of 20 states and territories. Bland's thirty years went down before the assault of thirty minutes. When the silver "yawpers," as the New York *Times* called them, threatened to subside, the Nebraska delegation called for another outburst, and for five minutes more the walls resounded to a fresh Niagara of sound. A fresh sensation came in the form of the rumor that George Fred Williams of Massachusetts was going into the Alabama delegation as a substitute to place Bryan in nomination. News of the Bryan stampede reached the outside, and the crowds in the street began snake-dancing and cheering him frantically. "Through the nerves of the telegraph that speech thrilled a continent, and for a day a nation was in a state of mental and moral catalepsy," wrote William Allen White.[27] Finally, after those on the floor had asked, "What's the matter with Bryan for President?" and the galleries had answered, "He's all right!" the demonstration died of sheer exhaustion half an hour after it began.

At some time during the tumult Charles S. Thomas asked Bryan if the time had come for Colorado to present his name. Yes, said Bryan, the time had come, but he meant to retire to his hotel as soon as the convention adjourned and wait there until notified of his nomination. Thomas said he would wait in vain. Bryan asked rather angrily why he thought so. Thomas reminded him of James G. Blaine at Cincinnati in 1876, a perfect analogy. "No," said Bryan, "you are mistaken. I shall be the nominee. It is as certain as any human event can be." When Thomas called at the Clifton House next day, Bryan's face broke into a grin as he delivered a horrible pun: "Are you still a doubting Thomas?" Thomas replied that his faith was now as firm as the mountains.[28]

[26] New Orleans *Times-Democrat,* New York *Tribune,* Omaha *Bee,* July 10, 1896.
[27] Quoted in M. R. Werner, *Bryan,* p. 76.
[28] *Harper's Weekly,* October 11, 1913.

At the conclusion of the demonstration, Jones sent Bryan a note: "You can be nominated on the first ballot. Shall the voting begin?" Bryan wrote back: "If my boom won't last overnight, it won't last until November." To those who importuned him to strike in the white heat of the moment he replied in the negative and then instructed his own delegation to take no part in preventing an adjournment.[29]

Since his own nomination William McKinley had spoken only on the tariff, as though ignoring the silver issue would make it vanish. When Murat Halstead telephoned him and told him that Bryan would be named, he was incredulous. "That is rot," he said as he hung up the phone.[30]

When quiet was restored to the Coliseum, Hill moved the adoption of his minority report and was defeated by a vote of 330 to 626. He did not desire a roll call on his two amendments but demanded one on his resolution commending the Cleveland administration. This lost also, by 357 to 564. Deeming its failure equivalent to a vote of censure, Tillman withdrew his own motion of censure. The roll call on the majority report, taken in almost perfect silence, was 628 aye and 301 nay, but none had the energy to demonstrate over a platform Bryan had ensured of adoption. The revised Democracy was now ratified and sealed. While a Western reporter gleefully noted that "The solemn, tearful Easterners have about as much influence on this convention as an over-patient hen might have on a porcelain egg," [31] Easterners felt that Cleveland had lost his party "to an ugly little Anarchist from Illinois." [32]

When the proceedings were recessed until evening, the managers of leading candidates hurriedly called strategy meetings on how to head Bryan off. Needless to say, a change had come over the convention. Bryan was the man. He conferred with his Nebraskans in the short time they had before returning to the hall but declined to influence the convention by a personal appearance and remained behind.

In anticipation of the nomination, more than twenty thousand people packed into the brilliantly lighted and stifling Coliseum, with perhaps ten thousand more massed outside. At 8:30 P.M. Jones moved that nominations begin. Alabama refused George Fred Williams the right to name Bryan and gave way to Missouri. Its Senator George G.

[29] Bryan to George Darby, January 3, 1921, William Jennings Bryan Papers; Willis J. Abbot, *Watching the World Go By*, p. 166.

[30] Chicago *Record*, Chicago *Times-Herald*, July 10, 1896.

[31] San Francisco *Chronicle*, July 10, 1896.

[32] New York *Sun*, July 10, 1896.

Vest spoke without heart, but his rhyme that "Silver Dick would make McKinley sick" in November sparked a twelve-minute demonstration for Bland. Then an unknown Georgia delegate, Judge Henry T. Lewis, came forward, and it was thought that he would second him. Lewis caught the crowd with his first sentence. He did not intend to make a speech, he said. He wished only to present a man, a "sterling Democrat . . . a soul come to lead the Israelites to battle." Then he hurled the words "William Jennings Bryan" as though from a catapult. Seeing the "explosive" result, he wisely stopped, having won his case without argument.[33] Bryan, half asleep in his rooms, received the news of his nomination with "pleasant surprise"—surprise only in the sense that Georgia had jumped in ahead of Nebraska. Altgeld had predicted that by the morrow his boom would be "dead as a door nail," but it took Chairman White fifteen minutes to restore order from bedlam. The nomination of Claude Matthews elicited slight enthusiasm. Although his managers said that Bryan's speech had not hurt Boies's chances, Boies himself admitted that his strength had fallen away and that Bland's was also going to Bryan. The naming of Blackburn, McLean, Pennoyer, and Robert E. Pattison of Pennsylvania completed the nominations, for Massachusetts, New York, and Wisconsin refused to name anyone on a silver platform. At 12:55 A.M. on July 10 an adjournment was forced to 10 A.M. by those who feared that the convention might be stampeded for Bryan were the balloting to begin. Caucuses held during the early morning hours proved Bryan gaining at Bland's expense. Illinois, for example, now listed thirty-one out of forty-eight for Bryan, and Southern states deserted Bland for him so quickly that he soon approached complete control of the section. Altgeld conceded the loss of a Southern state or two but none of the Western. Since enthusiasm for Bryan came from the galleries and since his boom lacked formal organization, he concluded that Bland was impregnable.[34]

Bryan remained at the Clifton, but he sent his delegation final instructions: "There must be no pledging, no promising, no trading on any subject with anybody. No delegation must be permitted to violate instructions given by a state convention. Our delegation should not be too prominent in applause. Treat all candidates fairly." [35] On the first roll call Alabama voted for Boies, Arkansas for Bland, and Califor-

[33] New York *Times*, New York *World*, July 10, 1896; Bryan, *First Battle*, pp. 210–213.

[34] New York *World*, July 10, 1896.

[35] Fred Carey, *Mayor Jim: The Life of James C. Dahlman*, p. 79.

nia split, giving nine votes to Blackburn and one to Bryan. After Florida divided, with one vote for Bryan, Georgia cast its entire twenty-six votes for him, thereby detracting from Bland's vaunted control of the South. When Louisiana, Mississippi, and North Carolina voted for him, the myth of Bland's control disappeared. Ten states from New York northward refused to vote. Bryan then won Nebraska and twenty-nine scattered votes from other states. At the end of the first ballot, although Bland had 233, Bryan came second, with 103, having already overtaken Boies, who had 86.

Bland gained forty-eight votes on the second ballot but Bryan gained ninety-two. Nebraskans and North Carolinians went about warning others that it was going against fate to stand by favorite sons. The third ballot was a locking of horns, but when Bland picked up only ten to Bryan's twenty-two the Bryan trend became apparent. The break came on the fourth ballot when Alabama and Kansas switched from Bland and Colorado from Teller and gave Bryan a majority. Bryan boosters sought to stampede the convention by sparking a demonstration that almost matched that following the "Cross of Gold" speech. While Tillman shouted for "that matchless knight of the West, the emancipator of the white slaves, William Jennings Bryan," Carter Glass fought in the Virginia delegation against Walter Addison for control of the state's standard until he discovered that both were trying to tug in Bryan's direction.[36] When James Hogg of Texas tried to take New York's standard, George Brinton McClellan, Jr. hit him on the jaw and knocked him down. Still shouting "Bryan, Bryan, Bryan, Bryan," Hogg arose and went his way.[37] Twenty minutes elapsed before quiet was restored and the balloting proceeded. Then the question was raised as to whether a two-thirds vote of all the delegates or of those voting was needed. Chairman White ruled that two thirds of those voting would suffice and made Bryan's nomination possible on the next ballot.

When the fifth roll call began Bryan really competed only with Bland. When Arkansas and California voted solidly for him, however, all knew that the game was up. Altgeld had stood by Bland, but his impatient delegation forced him to agree to a caucus. He turned his weary smile to Darrow and said, "I have been thinking over Bryan's speech. What did he say anyhow?" [38] Although Bryan had sapped his

[36] Rixey Smith and Norman Beasley, *Carter Glass: A Biography*, p. 44.
[37] Syrett, *Gentleman and the Tiger*, pp. 113–114.
[38] Clarence Darrow, *The Story of My Life*, p. 92.

control, Altgeld held out until he sensed a crisis. With his face as white as death he finally directed that the state's vote be cast for Bryan. Only he and one other stuck by Bland, and he lost control of the delegation.[39] Thereupon William J. Stone read a letter in which Bland authorized the withdrawal of his name whenever a silver candidate had a majority. Stone lowered the standard of "the son of Missouri" and raised "the sun-tipped banner of Nebraska," withdrew Bland, and cast Missouri's thirty-four votes for Bryan. The remaining states joined the bandwagon and made Bryan's nomination unanimous. The feeling of Cleveland supporters was well expressed by the New York *World:* "Lunacy having dictated the platform, it was perhaps natural that hysteria should evolve the candidate." [40]

When told of his nomination, Bryan wrote out a message to the American people. In order that he might have no ambition but to discharge faithfully the duties of the office of President, he would, if elected, under no circumstances seek a second term.[41] When Willis J. Abbot rushed in, he honored him with an audience in his favorite place for confidential interviews, the bathroom, and with him worded a long telegram to William Randolph Hearst. Hearst opposed silver and was on friendly terms with William C. Whitney, but he wanted to build up circulation for his New York *Journal.* After additional prodding by Abbot, Hearst overrode the advice of all business heads and made the *Journal* the only important newspaper in the East to support Bryan throughout the campaign.[42]

At about four o'clock, when the Bryans finally had a chance to eat, they read some of the thousands of telegrams that cascaded upon them. Pennoyer wired the "young giant of the West" that the story of David and Goliath would be repeated. "The reform forces of the country must support you," said Senator James H. Kyle, the South Dakota Populist. All the defeated candidates promised support, and to cries of "traitor" leveled at Bryan, Bland replied that there had been no treachery. Teller declared himself satisfied with the "especially strong" nomination and gloried in the thought that he had proved the John the Baptist

    [39] Carter H. Harrison, *Stormy Years: The Autobiography of Carter H. Harrison, Five Times Mayor of Chicago,* p. 167.

    [40] New York *World,* July 11, 1896.

    [41] *Ibid.*

    [42] New York *Journal,* July 1, 1912; Abbot, *Watching the World Go By,* pp. 168–169; John K. Winkler, *W. R. Hearst, An American Phenomenon,* pp. 21–22, 26–27, 96–98, 122–123; W. A. Swanberg, *Citizen Hearst: A Biography of William Randolph Hearst,* pp. 81, 84–86.

for Bryan. He became the prime mover in the endorsement of Bryan by the silver Republicans, wrote many letters to Populist leaders asking that they nominate him, collected money for his campaign, and spoke for him to the limits of his physical capacity.[43]

During his meal Bryan wrote a telegram to the New York *World*, the largest Democratic newspaper of the East, to object to its description of the faith of the silver men as a "craze." The restoration of silver to its ancient place by the side of gold would restore parity and permit the return of general prosperity, he wrote. The *World* had done effective work in behalf of an income tax; it would find a still larger field of usefulness in supporting "the gold and silver coinage of the Constitution." Then, after a twenty-minute nap during which his door remained open and visitors passed in and out, seemingly satisfied with a glimpse of their slumbering hero, Bryan took to handshaking. "I seem to have plenty of friends now, but I remember when they were very few," he said to Rosser. Early in the evening he made the first speech of the campaign from the balcony of the Clifton House to a vast crowd gathered outside. As he returned to his rooms he recalled that George Carden of Texas had been one of the first to declare for him for President. "I wonder if George Carden can survive this dispensation of Providence?" he asked Rosser.[44]

III

CRITICS called Bryan's nomination an accident resulting from emotion or clever manipulation. Some said he had captured the delegates by appeals to sentiment rather than by logical reasoning; others spoke of "put-up schemes" and considered as ingredients for an indictment his association with the Populists, his intimacy with the bolters from the Republican convention, and his wide solicitation of support from the Chicago delegates.[45] Nevertheless, in every presidential year since 1896 feature writers have retold the story of his triumph and deemed his speech the most famous one ever made in any American party convention and one of the world's great orations.

[43] Letters and telegrams of July 10–11, 1896, Bryan Papers; Washington *Evening Star*, July 11, 1896; Byars, *Bland*, p. 233; Elmer Ellis, *Henry Moore Teller*, pp. 273–284.

[44] Rosser, *Crusading Commoner*, p. 57.

[45] New York *Sun*, New York *Times*, New York *Tribune*, Omaha *Bee*, July 11, 1896; Ellis, *Teller*, p. 273; G. W. Steevens, *Land of the Dollar*, pp. 134–137; Perry Belmont, *American Democrat, The Recollections of Perry Belmont*, pp. 419–422.

Bryan had won men's hearts, diverted their passions and preferences, obscured every other presidential aspirant, and wrecked the plans of skillful managers by interpreting the delegates to themselves, by articulating their sufferings and desires in memorable words. He changed men's lives. Edgar Lee Masters, for one, marked the speech as "the beginning of a changed America," dropped his study of classical economists and English writers, and threw himself into a new cause which concerned itself with humanity rather than with the tariff and Civil War issues. Bryan appeared a Jefferson redivivus, a Jackson reborn to sweep the country in a mighty crusade against privilege. He would reclaim the country from the banks and syndicates that had robbed the people since 1861 and made it impossible for young men to get ahead in the world save in alliance with financial oligarchs.[46]

Bryan never declared his speech original. Nor was he conscious of the subtlety and skill he employed. "While I regarded the nomination as possible," he later wrote Mark Sullivan, "I regarded it only as a possibility and counted on the logic of the situation rather than my speech. I had not thought of my speech having the effect it did. I was fighting for a principle and found, as Jefferson once expressed it, that 'firm allegiance to a principle is the best handmaiden to ambition.' " Sullivan commented that Bryan did not recall how much assistance he had given the "logic of the situation." [47]

Bryan's nomination was received enthusiastically by the workingmen of the East and by men of all classes and parties in the West, especially in Nebraska and the silver mining states. Republican newspapers like the Salt Lake *Tribune* and Populist papers like the *Rocky Mountain News* immediately endorsed him. The children of America fell in love with him; the aged saw America as a land of opportunity illustrated by a common man who had the courage, talent, and will to achieve the heights. But could he, like Jackson, Douglas, and Lincoln, rationalize the divergent interests of all sections and classes into a common pattern of thought? Could he combine, as the others had done, businessmen, farmers, and workers into a single following? Would his definition of the "business man" prove the common denominator? He reflected

[46] Edgar Lee Masters, *Across Spoon River: An Autobiography*, pp. 208–210; see Thomas C. Cochran, *The American Business System: A Historical Perspective, 1900–1955*, pp. 1–10, and Eric Goldman, *Rendezvous with Destiny: A History of Modern American Reform*, pp. 50–51.

[47] Bryan to Sullivan, March 6, 1925, Bryan Papers; Sullivan, *Our Times*, I, 123–131.

primarily the unhappiness of the West and South in being economic and political colonies of the Northeast. Could he make real the reformers' dream of a *national* union of the discontented? Whether the American people, after four months of deliberation, would entrust their destinies to his untried hands was a moot point, but there was no doubt that he appeared the most dramatic product of American national politics, the most sensational and picturesque creation of his age.

IV

ONCE the crowd drifted away from the Clifton House at about eleven o'clock on the evening of July 10, Bryan joined a group at the Sherman House and listened with concentrated interest to talk about his running mate, who would be selected on the morrow. Among those mentioned were Bland, Boies, Daniel, McLean, and Matthews. One school favored a poor man, since the campaign would be one against privilege; another wanted an angel with a barrel. A group of senators tried to impress Bryan with McLean, for he had received Ohio's vote for President, promised to start a free silver paper in Chicago if nominated, and could give the money needed to win the campaign. Easterners offered George Fred Williams of Massachusetts and especially Arthur Sewall of Maine. Williams had caused a great stir by his conversion to silver just before the convention. The sixty-one-year-old Sewall had a good Civil War record, was one of the greatest shipbuilders of his generation, ran a fleet of ships, and was a director of many enterprises, including the Maine Central Railroad and the Bath Bank. He was as convinced of the justice of free silver as Bryan and one of the relatively few businessmen who believed that an inflation of the currency would stimulate depression-bound industry from the doldrums.

Josephus Daniels noted how Bryan's face tensed when the talk turned to McLean and suggested to Senator Jones that Bryan be consulted. When Jones asked his opinion, Bryan's jaws clamped and his lips spread tightly in a straight line. He had not given the matter much thought, he said, and believed the delegates could make a better selection than he. It was supremely important, however, that the ticket be harmonious, that both nominees represented the same principles and convictions. He did not reveal that he had already refused a deal Rosser had arranged with the Ohio delegation whereby the Ohio vote would fall to him in return for his support of McLean for Vice President, nor that McLean had sent Melville Stone to him with a similar proposition,[48] but he flatly declared that he would decline his own nomination if McLean were named. McLean was an immoral man who preached free silver but whose convictions and interests were with those who exploited the public, and his nomination would give the lie to the professions of the Democracy. "We would be selling the Party's birthright for his campaign money. We cannot win this election by appealing to men who stand for privilege." McLean's supporters gasped. Bryan was magnificent but he was not waging war. "You cannot drive off everybody who isn't one hundred per cent virtuous," exclaimed Blackburn. But Bryan had spoken, and there was no appeal. It was not war, but Daniels felt elevated in spirit by the dawn of a new day, with "a man . . . come into leadership who truly incarnated the principles of Jefferson with the virtues and courage of a Savonarola." [49] The meeting broke up at 2:30 A.M. without agreement, although Bryan's suggestion that it would be wise to name an Easterner probably selected Sewall.

Ten hours later the delegates assembled for the last time. Sixteen men were named, but serious consideration was granted only to Bland, McLean, Sibley, and Sewall. When Bland withdrew, his votes went to Sewall, who came within forty votes of McLean on the fourth ballot. Then McLean withdrew and the swing to Sewall came on the fifth, with 250 gold delegates either absent or not voting.

The nomination of Sewall came as a greater surprise to the country than that of Bryan, for he was politically unknown. Yet his nomination appeared to be an excellent one. Age was joined to youth, business to the law; and the ticket was relieved of the charge of being sectional. It recognized the free silver sentiment of the East and it emphasized the fact that a leading New England businessman worth five to six millions was a worker in the silver cause.

V

BRYAN was to have the full support of no political party. As expected, Democrats like Bourke Cockran, John G. Carlisle, and David Bennett Hill bolted him. Some, like Miles Poindexter, turned Republican because "the old Democracy was swallowed up in Populism, free silver,

---

[48] Rosser, *Crusading Commoner*, pp. 54–55; Melville E. Stone, *Fifty Years a Journalist*, pp. 222–223.

[49] Josephus Daniels, *Editor in Politics*, pp. 168–169.

single tax, and fusion."[50] Dazed by his repudiation, Grover Cleveland nevertheless felt that he could not advise his followers to bolt to the Republicans and counseled caution to those who would organize a separate party. The gold Democrats were divided. Could they repudiate their official nominee and support William McKinley, whose tariff they held largely responsible for the nation's plight?[51] Must they allow their desire to defeat Bryanism to destroy their party so that no seeds remained for the future? Certain irreconcilables called for a new convention as early as July 11. The sound money leagues added to the clamor, and all gold Democratic national committeemen met in Indianapolis on August 7 to arrange for a national convention.

Bryan's nomination stunned the Republicans. They had not expected the money question to be made the paramount issue and could not predict the results of a strenuous personal campaign made by Bryan. Some wanted to await his assault before devising a strategy of counterattack, but McKinley laid down the line of battle in his first speech following Bryan's nomination. The Civil War had been a struggle to preserve the government; the present war was to preserve the government's financial honor. The earlier contest had arrayed section against section; now men of all sections must unite to rebuke the repudiation of obligations and debasement of the currency.[52] He thus accepted the money question as the paramount issue.

William C. Whitney's hopes for cooperation between the Republicans and his gold Democrats disappeared when partisanship intruded. Mark Hanna damned all Democrats indiscriminately, and Republican speakers and editors adopted a similarly hostile tone.[53] Theodore Roosevelt, for example, said he would refuse to shake hands with John Peter Altgeld because he might momentarily be called to face him sword to sword in battle, and he charged the leaders of the new

---

[50] Poindexter to J. W. Sullivan, September 23, 1910, in Howard W. Allen, "Miles Poindexter and the Progressive Movement," *Pacific Northwest Quarterly*, 53 (July 1962), 115.

[51] Cleveland to Richard Olney, July 15, 1896, Cleveland to Lamont, July 15, 1896, Grover Cleveland Papers; Robert McElroy, *Grover Cleveland, the Man and Statesman*, II, 225. William L. Wilson explained to W. C. P. Breckinridge that he was "resolved . . . not [to] fall into the mire of protectionism, and . . . not leap into the foul pit of repudiation, socialism, anarchy, *et. cetera*, temporarily . . . miscalled the grand old name Democracy." Quoted in James A. Barnes, *John G. Carlisle, Financial Statesman*, p. 466.

[52] Omaha *World-Herald*, July 11, 1896.

[53] Mark D. Hirsch, *William C. Whitney, Modern Warwick*, p. 506.

Democracy with plotting a social revolution and the subversion of the Republic. Whitelaw Reid made his New York *Tribune* a vehicle for virulent and vituperative attacks on Bryan as an unknown and untried leader of dubious party record and affiliations and the creation of a chance emotional upheaval. Others said that Bryan would soon talk himself out and that the Democrats had done well to make free silver the issue, for, as Roosevelt asserted, "there is not a crook or criminal in the entire country who ought not to support them." [54] The foreign-born, especially the Germans, would have none of him. Since he would find support in the Far West and South but not in the East, the contest need be made only in the states of the upper Mississippi Valley. The bolt of the gold Democrats also detracted from his power.

Upon checking out of the Clifton House, Bryan figured that his expenses in obtaining the nomination were less than one hundred dollars. When a representative of one of the large railroads offered him a private Pullman for his homeward trip, Willis J. Abbot objected. "Mr. Bryan, you should not accept this offer. You are the great Commoner, the people's candidate, and it would not do to accept favors from the great railroad corporations." Bryan agreed. The title "Great Commoner" remained his for life.[55]

Using a regular day coach, Bryan stopped often en route to Lincoln to advise the people to study the money question, the greatest issue before them. "Talk not to me about crises through which we cannot pass; tell me not of dangers that will overcome us, or of obstacles too great to overcome; we know none such," he declared. Excited and enthusiastic crowds proved their idolatry in various ways. At one place a woman rushed up with a baby she had named William Jennings Bryan Jones or something. Men pushed forward saying "God bless you," and women struggled to touch his hand or offer him flowers. Banners inscribed with the words "McKinley and John Bull *vs.* Bryan and the Common People" and the like appeared in profusion. Twenty thousand persons paraded in the rain and heard him give a non-political address in Lincoln, where he promised that when he died he would mingle his ashes with the Nebraska earth—a promise that was not kept—and thanked the people in his wife's name as well as in his own, for she had shared his struggles and now shared his glory. During the next three weeks he answered every one of the five thousand letters and telegrams received since his nomination, listened to telephoned

---

[54] Roosevelt to Lodge, July 14, 1896, in Henry Cabot Lodge, *Selections from the Correspondence of Theodore Roosevelt and Henry Cabot Lodge, 1884–1918*, I, 224.

[55] Wayne C. Williams, *William Jennings Bryan*, p. 157.

reports of the Populist and National Silver party conventions, and prepared his acceptance speech. He wrote the latter with great care and determined to read it rather than to extemporize, for he had decided to deliver it in Madison Square Garden, New York, and feared that unfair reports of it would be made in the Eastern press.[56]

VI

THE "SIAMESE TWINS," as the Populist and National Silver party conventions which met on July 22 were called, were held during the excitement over Bryan's nomination. The Nebraska delegation to the Populist convention was headed by Bryan's good friend William V. Allen, contained Silas A. Holcomb, the only Populist governor, and was expected to wield great influence. Because the delegates were chosen in proportion to the votes cast in 1892, Western men predominated.

Bryan left the Populists the Hobson's choice of joining him or of finding new issues and followers only three months before the elections. The Populists themselves were split into a conservative wing that favored a broad program rather than the endorsement of silver alone, supported the poorer farmers, advocated certain socialistic reforms, and followed Thomas E. Watson, Eugene V. Debs, and Henry D. Lloyd in the middle-of-the-road position; and a progressive wing that demanded silver as a one-plank platform, mirrored the demands of the silver mine owners and wealthier farmers, opposed Socialism, and followed James B. Weaver, Julius Burrows, William A. Peffer, and Henry E. Taubeneck in demanding fusion with the Bryan Democrats.

Western fusionists like Thomas M. Patterson, editor of the *Rocky Mountain News,* said that the Chicago platform was a slightly revised Omaha platform, that only a "very extreme" Populist convention would declare for more radical remedial legislation, and that "fair" deference had been paid the Populists in the naming of Bryan. Jerry Simpson added, "I care not for party names. It is the substance we are after, and we have it in William J. Bryan." So too thought James B. Weaver, William V. Allen, L. D. Lewelling, R. F. Kolb, Davis Waite, and a host of lesser Populist lights. Teller, for the Silver Republicans, also urged the Populists to endorse him.[57]

[56] New York *Times,* July 14, 1896; Omaha *World-Herald,* July 12–18, 1896; Bryan, *First Battle,* pp. 233–237.

[57] *Rocky Mountain News,* July 11, 1896; Teller to Bryan, July 15, 18, 1896, Bryan Papers; John D. Hicks, *The Populist Revolt: A History of the Farmers' Alliance and*

The middle-of-the-road group "boiled." As Lloyd put it: "If we fuse, we are sunk; if we don't fuse, all the silver men we have will leave us for the more powerful Democrats." [58] Watson, leader of the Southern Populists, advised them to "avoid fusion as they would the devil." If the silver Republicans would not support Teller, said Marion Butler, he wanted every true friend of silver "to fight the Democratic party to the bitter death." [59] Other irreconcilables, like Paul Vandeervoort of Nebraska, Lemuel H. "Calamity" Weller, and Clarence Darrow wanted Jacob S. Coxey and Eugene V. Debs to head the Populist ticket on the full reform program provided in the now broadened Omaha platform. They believed that National Chairman Taubeneck had been "flim-flammed" into believing that silver was the supreme issue and viewed the Democracy as a bourne from which no reform elements ever returned. Southern Populists also opposed Bryan because Democrats had ostracized them, insulted them, physically injured them, and cheated them out of winning state elections. Like their Northern brethren, they resented the rewriting of the subtreasury, government ownership, fiat money Omaha platform to read free silver alone. Watson had seen the Democracy disintegrate, flare in revolt, undergo realignment, and metamorphose itself with Bryan's coup; but he trusted Bryan no more than Marion Butler, who was seeking to line up Populists and silver Republicans, and refused to attend the convention. [60]

Three demands arose in the Populist convention: the endorsement of the entire Chicago ticket, the endorsement of Bryan but the naming of a Populist for Vice President, and a straight Populist ticket. The last had little support, and the fight was made between the fusionists and the mid-roaders. Bryan was embarrassed because the majority wanted him but not Sewall. [61] He may not have been privy to all the arrangements made for fusion on electors and state tickets by Senator James K. Jones, the new chairman of the Democratic National Committee, but Jones reflected his insistence that both Sewall and he be

the People's Party, pp. 355-357; Alex M. Arnett, The Populist Movement in Georgia, pp. 185-190; Martin Ridge, Ignatius Donnelly, The Portrait of a Politician, pp. 348-350.

[58] Arnett, Populist Movement in Georgia, p. 190; Caro Lloyd, Henry Demarest Lloyd, I, 259-260.

[59] Butler to William M. Stewart, July 6, 1896, Ellis, Teller, p. 275.

[60] Omaha World-Herald, July 20, 1896; Omaha Bee, July 21, 1896; C. Vann Woodward, Tom Watson, Agrarian Rebel, pp. 279-291.

[61] Omaha Bee, July 19, 1896; Bryan, First Battle, pp. 296-297.

named if the Populists insisted upon endorsing the Chicago nominees.

The East characterized the Populist delegates as a "mongrel crowd" of "queer people" who could be called "business men" only by Bryan's definition. Compared with the bewhiskered Peffer, "Cyclone" Davis, "Calamity" Weller, and "Jumpin' Jim" Weaver, Jerry Simpson appeared the sanest of them all. Grown white-headed in previous independent party movements, acquainted with the difficulties of fusion, and accustomed to being traded out of existence, the majority revealed their demand for Bryan by singing:

> No crown of thorns to its brow shall press,
> Never again, say we, no cross of gold mankind distress;
> Never again say we. We'll loosen all the cords that bind;
> Give equal chance to all mankind, and here a new Redeemer find,
> Leading to victory.[62]

Temporary chairman Marion Butler castigated the major parties for bringing the country to the verge of ruin. A month earlier the Republicans had gone over bag and baggage to the money kings of Wall Street and Europe. Two weeks earlier the Democrats had stolen the Populist platform. He demanded that the Omaha platform be saved and that the party not become an "annex" to the Democracy. When he asked, "What shall we do?" a voice cried out, "Nominate Bryan!" Governor William J. Stone of Missouri was long suspected as the man who turned the lights out during the evening session to create confusion, break up the convention, and prevent the nomination of a Populist for Vice President, but a severe rain and electrical storm was more likely the true culprit.[63]

Next day the fusionists won a great victory by electing William V. Allen permanent chairman. Asked to comment on Allen's election, Bryan declined to be interviewed about anything going on at St.

[62] Henry D. Lloyd, "The Populists at St. Louis," *American Review of Reviews,* 14 (September 1896), 298–303; Robert W. Smith, "Comedy at St. Louis: A Footnote to Nineteenth Century Political Oratory," *Southern Speech Journal* (Winter 1957), 122–123; C. Vann Woodward, *Origins of the New South, 1877–1913,* pp. 245–246, 287–288.

[63] Omaha *World-Herald,* July 22, 23, 1896; New York *Times,* July 23, 1896; Carl Snyder, "Marion Butler," *American Review of Reviews,* 14 (October 1896), 429–431; Bryan, *First Battle,* pp. 259–264; Addison E. Sheldon, *Nebraska: The Land and the People,* I, 763; Ridge, *Donnelly,* p. 355; Robert F. Durden, "The 'Cow Bird' Grounded: The Populist Nomination of Bryan and Tom Watson in 1896," *Mississippi Valley Historical Review,* 50 (December 1963), 415–416.

Louis.[64] Allen said he was not advocating Bryan's nomination, yet he outlined the choice as between taking him or facing defeat on a separate ticket. When Democratic "intruders" like Jones and Stone insisted that both Bryan and Sewall be named, the mid-roaders threatened to bolt, saying that Sewall would foul every plank of the Omaha platform. Butler sought to compromise on Bryan for first and Watson for second place. Lulled by Jones's promise that he would withdraw Sewall if Bryan were named, the mid-roaders capitulated, but they used the immense undercurrent against Sewall to obtain the selection of a Vice President first, thereby preventing enthusiasm for Bryan, had he been named, from overflowing to his running mate. Jones wired Bryan: "If it is not Sewall, what shall we do? I favor declination in that event. Answer quick." Bryan wired his ultimatum: "I agree with you fully. If Sewall is not nominated, have my name withdrawn." Bryan wired a similar message to Allen but asked him not to make it public until authorized to do so by Jones.[65] Jones and Allen kept their messages from the convention for five hours while it nominated Watson and received the news that the National Silver party had endorsed Bryan and Sewall, and Allen ever afterwards denied that he had received any message. In the following morning's newspapers the delegates read with amazement the telegram Bryan had sent Jones [66] and also a letter in which Jones denied that he had ever committed himself to withdraw Sewall. Bryan refused to answer questions. Bryanites vouched for his sympathy with Populist principles, but that was all the satisfaction the mid-roaders ever obtained.

As chairman of the Committee on Resolutions, Weaver ensured that the platform followed Bryan's closely. It made silver the paramount issue, but it also contained most of the strongest demands as defined in the Omaha platform. Allen cynically told those who would write a more radical document that he would never let them speak, and the platform was adopted without debate. Weaver then nominated Bryan, saying that the Populists were not being asked to abandon their party but to join Bryan in assaulting the confederate gold power. Whether the Populists captured Bryan or Bryan captured Populism was a moot point, but Weaver insisted that the Populists could not refuse the three

[64] Omaha World-Herald, July 23, 24, 1896; New York Times, July 23, 25, 1896.

[65] New York Times, July 25, 1896; Omaha Bee, July 26, 1896.

[66] "See Senator Jones at once. Have wired him that I will not be a candidate before the Populist convention unless Sewall is nominated. Do not give this out until Jones authorizes it." Bryan to Allen, telegram, New York Times, July 25, 1896.

million Democratic and one million silver Republican votes needed to
elect "that matchless champion of the people, that intrepid foe of
corporate greed, that splendid young statesman—William J. Bryan." [67]
A twenty-minute demonstration for Bryan and silver ensued in the
same hall in which McKinley and gold had been cheered a month
earlier.

Even though he had the pledged support of a third of the 1300
delegates, Debs declined to be named.[68] Fearing that his nomination
would disrupt the Populist party, he instructed his followers to endorse
Bryan. He later wrote Bryan that "under your administration the rule
of the money power will be broken and the gold barons of Europe will
no longer run the American government," [69] and he actively stumped
for him.

Debs's refusal to assume leadership gave a great blow to the radical
wing of the Populist party. However, many delegates agreed with
Lloyd that "the question of social control of privileged social power
. . . is the question of the times." [70] Determined to force the "social
issue" to the front, the mid-roaders re-formed their lines and countered
Bryan by naming Colonel S. F. Norton. Allen meantime wired Bryan
to retract his objection to being named without Sewall. Bryan did not
reply. On the only ballot taken Bryan received 1042 votes and Norton
321. The fusionists thus named Bryan over his protests, ditched Sewall,
and left a tangled mess to be straightened out. A New Yorker wired
Allen: "Wall Street bankers and McKinley managers wild with delight
over convention's action. . . . They felt crushed at prospect of silver
forces being combined. Today they bet 10 to 1 on McKinley and
gold." [71]

Bryan's managers should have done more to impress his will upon
the Populist leaders, yet the major responsibility for naming him rests
with Allen and his fusionists. Fearful of missing a unique opportunity
to unite the reform forces, they had overcome their academic differences of economic doctrine and all their old political prejudices and
nominated him without assurance that he would be their candidate.

[67] *Ibid.*, July 26, 1896; New York *World*, July 26, 1896.

[68] H. Wayne Morgan, *Eugene V. Debs: Socialist for President,* p. 12; Caro Lloyd,
Lloyd, II, 261.

[69] Debs to Bryan, July 27, 1896, Bryan Papers.

[70] Lloyd, "Populists at St. Louis," p. 300.

[71] New York *Sun,* New York *Times,* New York *World,* July 26, 1896; Hicks,
Populist Revolt, pp. 265–266; Arnett, *Populist Movement in Georgia,* pp. 197–201.

Stating that they knew his position before they named him, Bryan made his acceptance dependent "upon the conditions that are attached to it." The Populists had endorsed some policies he could not approve and had failed to name Sewall. Bryan would do nothing to endanger the cause of bimetallism; neither would he do anything unfair to Sewall.[72]

VII

Do NOW what he might, Bryan was definitely identified as a Populist. The New York *Times* thought it fitting that the "freaky Coxeyites" at St. Louis voted for "an irresponsible, unregulated, ignorant, preju-diced, pathetically honest and enthusiastic crank" for President,[73] and the New York *Sun* predicted "repudiation, revolution, and national dishonor" if he won.[74] Many Populists were also displeased. Irrecon-cilables complained that their party had been reduced to guerrilla forces fighting outside of the regular ranks and that the fruits of victory, if won, would be appropriated by a general who would not recognize them.[75] Westerners happy with Bryan decried the blow dealt Sewall and wondered how Bryan would operate a ticket with two tails. Southerners praised Watson and demanded that Sewall be "taken down." The Populists had expected both major parties to write staid platforms and name conservatives, leaving them to round up all ad-vocates of reform, but Bryan had spoiled their strategy. If they now insisted on their own candidate they would split the reform vote and assure the defeat of Bryan and the election of McKinley. By naming Bryan they surrendered their leadership to him and sacrificed the broad Omaha platform for a program placing undue emphasis upon silver. In permeating the Democracy with silver they reached the greatest heights ever attained by a third party, but at the same time they lost their identity as a party. Yet in Bryan they found for the first time since the Civil War a leader upon whom almost all progres-sive forces could converge, give the demand for reform a national setting, and demand respect from the Republicans. The few like Lloyd, Debs, and Darrow who veered toward Socialism did so not because they loved Bryan less but because he deviated from the demands for

[72] Omaha *World-Herald*, July 26, 1896.
[73] New York *Times*, July 26, 1896.
[74] New York *Sun*, quoted in Omaha *Bee*, July 31, 1896.
[75] Lloyd, "Populists at St. Louis," p. 302.

government ownership, antimonopoly, and labor reforms and stressed silver too much.[76]

Subsequent discussions between Bryan and Populist leaders proved bitter. Watson "reluctantly" accepted his nomination because he was convinced that he alone could harmonize all factions and save his party from extinction.[77] Bryan noted that his own nomination by the Populists had come despite his objections, and Jones brusquely declared that Sewall would remain on the Democratic ticket. Butler, the new Populist national chairman, said that Watson was in to stay and that the unity needed to beat the gold men could be obtained only by Sewall's declination. Bryan talked with many leading Populists and said he would act with deliberation and do nothing to hinder the success of bimetallism. Since Populist custom did not include a ceremony of notification, he suggested to Allen that he be notified my mail, which Allen did, on September 14. However, he consistently maintained the attitude that since the Populists had named him after the Democrats did that they could neither ask him to go beyond the Democratic platform nor to drop Sewall. After the election he said that it was better to have had two vice presidential candidates than to have caused embarrassment by forcing the withdrawal of either.[78]

The National Silver party had had plain sailing. Those who addressed the convention talked about the money question alone, to which the entire platform was devoted. Senator Jones was received with an ovation, but the mere mention of Cleveland provoked a delegate to comment: "Oh God, give us cyclones, if they must come, war, famine, and pests, but oh, God, in mercy, save us from another four years of Grover Cleveland." Described as one who "shall bid the golden sun and the silver moon stand still while he fights the battle for human freedom" and one worthy to stand with Demosthenes, Brutus, Hampden, and Mirabeau, Bryan was endorsed by acclamation, as was Sewall, but the conference committee that met with a Populist committee on July 24 failed to achieve fusion because of the silverites' nomination of Sewall.[79]

[76] Chester M. Destler, *American Radicalism, 1865–1901: Essays and Documents,* p. 30; Caro Lloyd, *Lloyd,* I, 263–265, 267; Morgan, *Debs,* p. 13.

[77] Woodward, *Watson,* pp. 303–305; Arnett, *Populist Movement in Georgia,* p. 200.

[78] Bryan, *First Battle,* p. 298.

[79] New York *Sun,* New York *Times,* New York *World,* July 23–26, 1896; Bryan, *First Battle,* pp. 238–258.

Thus Bryan led a Triple Alliance. He looked upon his nominations not as personal compliments but as incontrovertible evidence that the people meant to make bimetallism the paramount issue of the campaign. With three national and several minor parties behind him he felt that he could not fail, particularly when all these parties, including Edward Bellamy's Nationalists, Henry George's Single Taxers, and the Reverend W. D. P. Bliss's Christian Socialists, believed the major issue to be that "between men and money" and felt that they could not afford to side with money against men.[80]

[80] Bryan was also supported by the "broad gaugers," who broke away from the "narrow gauge" Prohibitionists, held a convention of their own, adopted silver, and endorsed him. For the eight national platforms, see Kirk H. Porter and Donald B. Johnson, *National Party Platforms, 1840–1956*, pp. 97–111.

CHAPTER 9

The Hero of a Lost Cause

I

ON AUGUST 7 the gold Democrats decided to convene in Indianapolis on September 2 and establish a party in opposition to Bryan. That same day Bryan started his march "from Nebraska to the sea" in a train containing James B. Weaver, Horace Boies, other supporters, and many newspaper reporters. He had chosen to be notified in New York, he said, "in order that our cause might be presented first in the heart of what now seems to be the enemy's country, but which we hope to be our country before this campaign is over." [1] The East tore the phrase "enemy's country" from context and threw it back at him for the rest of the campaign.

In every state along his route, despite a heat wave that killed ten persons in New York alone on August 9 and 25 on August 10, large crowds gathered to hear Bryan. In Canton, where Richard Parks Bland joined him, he yielded to a sudden impulse and called with the Missourian upon a very surprised William McKinley. "My dear," said McKinley to his wife, "this is Mr. Bland whom Mr. Bryan defeated for the Democratic nomination for president." Turning to Bland he said, "Bland, you should have been nominated; you were the logical candidate and the strongest man your party had." Bland replied: "I am satisfied if my party is." [2]

Bryan avoided extensive discussion of political questions on his trip, but he made his first mention of the fact that the laborer was being coerced to vote against him, and his stated objective of "capturing and holding the common man" frightened conservatives. He was "a complacent soul who pandered to ignorance and appealed boldly to mob unrest and passion with his cry of 16 to 1 in order to counter the loss of those with business, professional, and law abiding sense,"

[1] Omaha *Bee,* August 8, 1896; William J. Bryan, *The First Battle,* p. 300.

[2] New York *Times,* Omaha *World-Herald,* August 6–9, 1896; William V. Byars (ed.), *An American Commoner: The Life and Times of Richard Parks Bland; a Study of the Last Quarter of the Nineteenth Century,* p. 298.

said *The Nation,* the most influential Democratic journal of opinion.[3] ". . . while there is nothing [at Republican national headquarters] like the dread of defeat, there is a clear comprehension that the blatant wild ass of the prairie will get the votes of a good many others of his kind, and it will require more work than we thought was necessary to beat him," John Hay confided to Henry White. To Henry Adams he wrote: "Mr. Bryan has much to answer for driving so many great and good people into the support of Anti-Christ. On the other hand, whisper it soft and low, a good many worthy Republicans are scared blue, along of the Baby Orator of the Platte." [4] And Mark Hanna complained that "the situation . . . is quite alarming as business is going all to pieces and idle men will multiply rapidly. With this communistic spirit abroad the cry of 'free silver' will be catching." [5] Meantime he kept McKinley at home to conduct a front porch campaign.

According to the East, any attempt Bryan made to disclaim his "economic vagaries," allay the fears of capital, or appease the discontent of old-fashioned Democrats would be "bad politics," for he could not risk losing the West to win the East. A howling, naked Nebraska Populist could not escape detection in New York, and those who would go to hear the Boy Orator would be propelled mainly by curiosity. To arouse fear of the "avant courier of panic and crash," Eastern journals asserted that if he were elected he would be accompanied to Washington by a cabinet composed of John Peter Altgeld, Benjamin Tillman, Thomas E. Watson, James B. Weaver, Jacob S. Coxey, and Eugene V. Debs "and the horde of political and socialistic tramps who have been for years past waking the echoes of the country with their demands that the government should make their circumstances easy, and that without labor or forethought on their part." [6]

The absence of gold Democrats and administration personnel was as conspicuous in Madison Square Garden on the evening of August 12 as the presence of the leaders of organized labor and of Tammany. Fifteen thousand persons outside sought to enter a stifling Garden already jammed with twelve thousand. Bryan walked in with James K.

---

[3] *The Nation,* August 13, 1896.

[4] Letters of August 4, 5, 1896, respectively, William Roscoe Thayer, *The Life and Letters of John Hay,* II, 150.

[5] New York *Times,* Omaha *Bee,* August 12, 1896.

[6] New York *Times,* August 1, 10, 12, 1896; New York *World,* August 11, 1896; Chicago *Chronicle,* August 10, 1896; *Harper's Weekly,* August 8, 1896; *The Nation,* August 13, 1896.

Jones, William J. Stone, Bland, and Elliott Danforth, the national committeeman from New York, and stepped quickly to the platform while a huge American flag was lowered behind him. Danforth, who had agreed to preside after David Bennett Hill had absolutely refused to do so,[7] gave a short greeting; Stone excoriated Grover Cleveland and the McKinley Republicans before reading the letter of notification. The temperature stood at ninety-seven degrees. Bryan received a spirited welcome as he came forward, his face pale, his lips taut. As he held up his hand for silence he regained his color and composure. In a low voice that quickly grew in volume and filled the remotest corner of the hall, he assured his hearers that his platform did not menace private property, public safety, the social order, or national honor. He would not reconstruct society by leveling but by ensuring that all would stand equal before the law. He was particularly careful to explain that he did not dispute the authority of the Supreme Court but that the court had erred in the income tax case and that he hoped it would reverse itself. He then gave a long and closely reasoned exposition of both the national and international aspects of the money question. His peroration was a plea that the East cooperate with the West and South in building a prosperous and independent nation. Did the East prefer seeing the Statue of Liberty bound hand and foot facing Europe or standing erect facing America? [8]

In moderate language, Bryan had appealed to noble rather than to base sentiments in a sober, analytical, and comprehensive presentation of the issues. "Distinctly creditable and dignified," declared the Chicago *Record*. "Unanswerable," asserted the New York *Journal*. According to a Southern newspaper he had proved himself more than "a puff from the prairie," [9] and even *Harper's Weekly* admitted that his language had been "decent enough." [10] However, his excellent lecture made a poor speech. He gained nothing by trading his most precious talent, evocative oratory, for a manuscript; his reading did not, as he had hoped, convince the East that he was a man of sound judgment; and he was overly suspicious in feeling that the Eastern press would misrepresent him unless he furnished a printed document.[11] The

[7] New York *Times*, August 8, 1896; *American Review of Reviews*, 14 (September 1896), 260.

[8] New York *Times*, August 13, 1896; Bryan, *First Battle*, pp. 307–337.

[9] Clipping, Bryan Scrapbook No. 2, Nebraska State Historical Society.

[10] *Harper's Weekly*, September 12, 1896.

[11] Clipping, Bryan Scrapbook No. 2, Nebraska State Historical Society; Charles M. Rosser, *The Crusading Commoner*, pp. 68–69.

merely curious left early, for they could read the speech in the next day's newspapers, and Republicans planted in the audience stomped out noisily in groups, with the result that at the end of his overlong speech of an hour and forty minutes he had lost half his audience. He was now characterized as the "Boy Reader of the Platte." Publicized as a man of fire who would give a cyclonic performance, he had fallen flat as a Professor Dryasdust economist reading an endless essay on the curreny.[12] Theodore Roosevelt wrote Henry Cabot Lodge that Bryan "fell perfectly flat" and told a sister that "Bryan fell with a bang," [13] and a New York *World* cartoon showed Father Knickerbocker taking home an unused fire extinguisher.[14]

Bryan could have been notified in Nebraska and lived up to his reputation as an orator with an extemporaneous speech in New York. Even better, he should have spoken on the income tax or on government by injunction, the two issues which appealed most to the workingmen of the East. Moreover, he had dwelt at greatest length on the money question, which most observers deemed the least important issue in the campaign, the most difficult to explain to ordinary men, and the one most misinterpreted because it was consonant with the selfish interests of the silver kings. E. L. Godkin ranked him in the "booby class in business" and knew of few who displayed "crasser ignorance" of economics,[15] while Hanna immediately realized that he had picked the wrong weapon. "He's talking silver all the time and that's where we've got him," he exclaimed.[16] As Joseph B. Foraker put it, "Mr. Bryan made himself by one speech, and now he has unmade himself by one speech." [17]

Despite his "failure," Bryan had proved so attractive that representatives of banking, commercial, and manufacturing interests gave serious thought to saving their skins by appealing to the very masses they

---

[12] New York *Commercial Advertiser,* New York *Evening Post,* New York *Sun,* August 13, 1896.

[13] Roosevelt to Anna Cowles, August 15, 1896, Anna Roosevelt Cowles, *Letters from Theodore Roosevelt to Anna Roosevelt Cowles, 1870–1918,* p. 191; Roosevelt to Lodge, August 13, 1896, Henry Cabot Lodge, *Selections from the Correspondence of Theodore Roosevelt and Henry Cabot Lodge, 1884–1918,* I, 230.

[14] New York *World,* August 13, 1896.

[15] *The Nation,* August 20, 1896.

[16] Frank P. Stockbridge, "Bryan, the Great Commoner," *Current History,* 22 (September 1925), 867; Thomas Beer, *Hanna,* p. 155; Thomas Beer, *Mauve Decade,* p. 517; Matthew Josephson, *The Politicos, 1865–1896,* p. 696.

[17] Joseph Benson Foraker, *Notes of a Busy Life,* I, 494.

despised. During several days in Chicago, Hanna had astounded that city's businessmen with talk of raising an unheard-of three millions to defeat Bryan and succeeded in getting P. D. Armour and other Republican employers of labor to subscribe liberally.[18] On August 15, in New York, he and James J. Hill went uptown and downtown to all the major railroad offices, banks, and financial houses, pointed to the reality of the dangers Bryan threatened, and collected money to meet a "real emergency." William Rockefeller and Cornelius Bliss were similarly active. A number of solid citizens were so frightened of Bryan that they declared that if Bryan were elected they would sell everything they had and move to Canada or Europe.[19]

Because of the poor reception granted the Garden speech, the group of national committeemen who met with Bryan on August 13 vetoed an extended Eastern tour and suggested that he stump only the Middle West and South, thereby admitting that he had lost the East.[20] James K. Jones suggested Washington for national headquarters, but Bryan's better judgment was followed in the selection of Chicago. Hanna, who had already established headquarters in New York, thereupon also opened offices in Chicago.

Bryan spent the last two weeks of August in New York state. In Upper Red Hook, in the home of some friends, he completed his letter of acceptance. In good voice, and with an earnestness reminiscent of the "Cross of Gold" speech, he then delivered the first speech of the campaign, in Madalin, New York, on August 22. He attacked rather than defended. He knew that his platform offended some people but he said it was "right." Since businessmen used politics to their advantage, he urged the "toiling masses" to make politics their business "this once" and demand equal rights in protecting their homes and families. "The great political questions are in their final analysis great moral questions," he added, "and it requires no extended experience in the handling of money to enable a man to tell right from wrong." He greatly oversimplified the issue by asserting that one need understand merely the law of supply and demand in order to comprehend the money question.[21]

---

[18] Omaha *World-Herald*, August 12, 1896.

[19] Henry Adams to Mrs. Charlton Paul, August 13, 1896, Worthington C. Ford (ed.), *Letters of Henry Adams*, II, 150; Beer, *Hanna*, p. 157; Beer, *Mauve Decade*, p. 517.

[20] Omaha *World-Herald*, August 14, 1896; *The Nation*, August 20, 1896.

[21] New York *Times*, August 23, 24, 1896; Bryan, *First Battle*, pp. 342–349.

Bryan called on David Bennett Hill at his summer place near Albany, but neither he nor Hill would comment on what they discussed. Nor did Hill accompany Bryan to Albany, where he told ten thousand people that while he endorsed every syllable of the Chicago platform he did not expect every Democrat to support every plank. A platform was written by the majority; the minority had the choice of accepting it or leaving the party, else the minority would rule. Moreover, each campaign had a paramount question which determined allegiance to the ticket, and he asked those who believed the money question the outstanding one to join in exterminating the gold standard. "We ask no quarter; we give no quarter. We shall prosecute our warfare until there is not an American citizen who dares to advocate the gold standard," he declaimed. He would not be satisfied with the Presidency alone—he wanted a Congress favorable to reform legislation. He also demanded that no man be sent to the forthcoming state conventions unless he made it known that he stood with the people for silver.[22] He moved his hearers to great excitement, and as he crossed from New York into Pennsylvania and then Ohio he said that he would tell the people of the West that he had received a hearty reception everywhere in the East except in Wall Street.[23] As for McKinley's letter of acceptance, issued on August 26, he overlooked its placing of silver in the first place and dismissed it as merely a diatribe against free coinage, as "the golden text of the Republican lesson." [24]

Gold Democratic leaders selected Bourke Cockran, probably the most eloquent Democrat opposed to Bryan, to break the charm the Nebraskan had cast over at least the rural East. Cockran stated that the Chicago platform was "a singular combination of lunacy and villainy" that contained "monstrous" propositions and tended to provoke civil strife. He now supported McKinley in order to obtain "sound money." [25] On August 18 he replied to the Madison Square Garden speech in an address entitled "In Opposition to Repudiation." Most of his hearers were Democrats who were supporting McKinley. He admitted Bryan's personal honesty but doubted that he understood the nature of his faith. Were he to understand it, "his own hands would

[22] Bryan to George S. Bixby, May 16, 1920, George S. Bixby Papers; New York *Times*, August 17–29, 1896; Omaha *World-Herald*, August 26–29, 1896; *The Nation*, September 3, 1896; Bryan, *First Battle*, pp. 349–353, 367–368.

[23] New York *Times*, August 30, September 1, 1896.

[24] Omaha *World-Herald*, August 28, 1896; Charles S. Olcott, *The Life of William McKinley*, I, 324.

[25] Omaha *World-Herald*, August 3, 1896; Omaha *Bee*, August 3, 4, 1896.

be the first to tear down the platform on which he stands." Americans were not ready to change institutions which had stood the test of a century for those based upon "the fantastic dream of Populist agitators" or "consent to substitute for the Republic of Washington, Jefferson, and Jackson the Republic of Altgeld, Tillman, and Bryan." He concluded that "Bryanism is a conspiracy between professional farmers who want to pay low wages and unreconciled slaveholders who would like to pay no wages." [26] Roosevelt wrote Lodge, "The meeting to hear Bourke Cockran was a phenomenon," [27] and Thomas B. Reed wrote Cockran, "What an awful drubbing you gave the Boy Orator of Marengo!" [28]

Bryan said he would answer Cockran but not debate with him. He would debate with only one man—McKinley. Hanna retorted that the Chicago platform contained anarchistic doctrines and that the Democrats had erred in naming Bryan. They should have chosen Coxey, for then they could have won all the Populist following.[29] Moreover, he correctly asserted that McKinley appreciated too highly the dignity of the position he sought to use "catch-penny schemes" to gain publicity.[30] Bryan replied that he preferred to have it said that he lacked dignity than backbone to meet the enemies of the public.[31] It was not generally known that Hanna had once secretly journeyed to Canton and entered McKinley's house through the back door. "Things are going against us, William," he said. "You've got to stump or we'll be defeated." McKinley leaned forward in his chair and replied, "You know I have the greatest respect for your wishes, Mark, but I cannot take the stump against that man." [32] Charles Gates Dawes quoted McKinley as saying: "I will not try to compete with Bryan. I am going to stay here [in Canton] and do what campaigning there is to be done. If I took a whole train, Bryan would take a sleeper; if I took a sleeper, Bryan would take a chair car; if I took a chair car, he would ride a freight train. I can't outdo him, and I am not going to try." [33]

[26] New York *Sun*, New York *Times*, August 19, 1896; James McGurrin, *Bourke Cockran: A Free Lance in American Politics*, p. 151; Bascom Timmons, *Portrait of an American: Charles G. Dawes*, pp. 57–58.

[27] Roosevelt to Lodge, August 19, 1896, Lodge, *Correspondence*, I, 230.

[28] McGurrin, *Cockran*, pp. 159–160.

[29] Atlanta *Constitution*, July 11, 1896; New York *World*, July 11, 1896.

[30] Omaha *World-Herald*, September 12, 1896; Olcott, *McKinley*, I, 318.

[31] Bryan, *First Battle*, p. 477.

[32] Charles Cooper, corresponding secretary to McKinley as governor of Ohio, clipping, Miami (Fla.) *Daily News*, William Jennings Bryan Papers.

[33] Timmons, *Dawes*, p. 56.

II

WITH good political sense Bryan devoted most of the campaign to the Ohio and Mississippi valleys. Of his two hundred and fifty major stops, he made one hundred and sixty in the states of Illinois, Ohio, Iowa, Wisconsin, Michigan, Kentucky, and West Virginia. He found his largest crowds in the Ohio Valley and came closest to winning those states to which he devoted most effort. When he proved bitter in criticizing the "bolting Democrats" who would meet on September 2, saying that the sound money Democrats were an army of generals without soldiers,[34] the East accused him of "getting reckless again." He was in poor voice, he told crowds of 50,000 in Columbus, 10,000 in Springfield, and 30,000 to 40,000 in Toledo, because he had left part of it along his line of travel "calling sinners to repentance." Satan's stealing of the livery of Heaven was no worse than a goldbug's wearing of the principles of Andrew Jackson. Those who had failed to use the Democratic party for private gain were now trying to elect McKinley by nominating a Democratic gold standard ticket. The people who lived west of the Alleghenies should take the government into their hands and administer it for themselves, not for foreign syndicates.[35]

Impressed by the heavy blows Bryan delivered in Ohio, McKinley sent for Chauncey Depew and had him trace Bryan's route and speak in the same places Bryan had spoken from Cleveland to Cincinnati.[36]

After consultations with the National Committee in Chicago, Bryan went to Milwaukee to deliver a major address on the financial policy of the administration and to assert that the gold men were coercing and intimidating voters. On August 24, for example, the Sargent and Greenleaf Company of Rochester, New York, one of the largest firms engaged in the manufacture of locks, received an order for $4000 worth of goods "conditioned on the outcome of the election. If Bryan wins the order is not to be filled." [37] And on September 5 the McCormick Machine Company, among other "great trusts," notified employees that they must shut down if Bryan won.[38]

In a nonpartisan Labor Day speech in Chicago, when forty thousand

---

[34] *American Review of Reviews*, 14 (September 1896), 260.
[35] Omaha *World-Herald*, September 2, 3, 1896.
[36] Chauncey M. Depew, *My Memories of Eighty Years*, pp. 152–153.
[37] New York *Times*, August 25, 1896.
[38] Omaha *World-Herald*, September 6, 1896.

workers paraded in his honor, Bryan praised men who earned their bread by the sweat of the brow. He extolled Jefferson's dictums that all men should stand equal before the law, that government should show no partiality toward individuals or classes, and that all men had the right to complain about abuses in government, for such complaints led to progress—discontent voiced in the ballot box spelled reform. He praised labor unions, demanded the arbitration of labor disputes, suggested that the current unemployment could be traced to "vicious legislation," and begged the worker to vote as his conscience, not his employer, dictated. The debtor, too, should vote freely and not at the behest of his creditor.[39] Within a week Eugene V. Debs threw his American Labor Union to him, John McBride of the United Mine Workers and the American Federation of Labor agreed to head a national labor bureau in Chicago under Democratic auspices, and James R. Sovereign opened an office for the Knights of Labor in his name.[40]

However, the position of labor toward Bryan was ambivalent; its loyalties were divided between Sovereign's Knights of Labor and Samuel Gompers's AFL and between remaining aloof from or joining the Farmers' Alliance and Populist movements. Bryan too was caught between supporting the "employing farmers" who made up the bulk of the farmers' movement and the farm laborers who had nothing in common with their employers yet hesitated to ally themselves with the mechanics and laborers of the industrial centers. He naturally applauded the adoption of free silver by the Knights of Labor beginning in 1890 and by each AFL convention from 1893 down to that of 1898, but possibly because it proceeded under Populist auspices, he failed to endorse the labor-Populist alliance consummated in Illinois in 1894. Although spread to numerous other states by men like Henry D. Lloyd, Eugene V. Debs, Ignatius Donnelly, and Lyman Trumbull, the alliance never grew into a national movement. Therefore he had no labor *party* to call to his side.[41]

Industrial workers naturally object to inflated agricultural prices, for they must pay more for food and clothes. During a depression, how-

[39] *Ibid.*, September 3, 10, 1896.

[40] John R. Commons and Associates, *History of Labour in the United States*, pp. 509–514; Philip S. Foner, *History of the Labor Movement in the United States*, II, 287–312; Selig Perlman, *A History of Trade Unionism in the United States*, pp. 139–141; Philip Taft, *The A.F.L. in the Time of Gompers*, p. 130.

[41] Chester M. Destler, "The Labor-Populist Alliance in Illinois, 1894," *Mississippi Valley Historical Review*, 27 (March 1941), 589–602; Foner, *Labor Movement*, II, 315–332.

ever, jobs are more important than the prices of the goods they purchase, and in 1896 the unemployed grasped readily at silver because
they believed that inflation would help revive business and restore
prosperity, because Debs said that Bryan's election would "blunt the
fangs of the money power," and because Gompers asserted that free
coinage would "make money cheaper, mankind dearer." [42] More important in causing labor to support Bryan was his advocacy of the income tax and the conviction that McKinley epitomized the antilabor
monopolist forces and that the attack by conservatives on Bryan
centered on the anti-injunction plank rather than on free silver.[43] Since
the Knights of Labor and various members of the Executive Committee
of the AFL supported Bryan, Gompers remained the only major labor
leader who did not do so. Instead he fought desperately to keep unionism out of politics. At a banquet in Chicago, with Gompers present,
Bryan announced that if elected he would appoint him to the cabinet.
Gompers declined. Bryan expressed regret and said he hoped Gompers
would change his mind. Gompers thereafter spoke in favor of free
silver but not for any party, thereby earning the odium of both gold
and silver advocates in all parties.[44]

Gold Democrats used Bryan's earlier demand that silverites bolt the
nomination of a gold man as justification for their bolting him and
elected to their Indianapolis convention men who had earned national
reputations for their stanch support of the Democracy for a long generation.[45] Senator John M. Palmer of Illinois spoke for those who
would preserve the integrity of Democratic principles, forgive the trans-
gressions of Bryan's followers, and welcome back with open arms those
who returned to "the party of your fathers." But Senator Donelson
Caffery of Louisiana voiced the hatred of many for Bryan by saying
that "We propose to make a funeral pyre of the cadavers of populism

[42] Debs quoted in Foner, *Labor Movement*, II, 336. A similar sentiment is found in
a letter to Bryan of July 27, 1896, Bryan Papers, also printed in H. Wayne Morgan,
Eugene V. Debs: Socialist for President, p. 12. Gompers's comment is in Irving
Bernstein (ed.), "Samuel Gompers and Free Silver," *Mississippi Valley Historical
Review*, 29 (December 1942), 398.

[43] *American Review of Reviews*, 14 (September 1896), 262–263; Foner, *Labor
Movement*, II, 336.

[44] Omaha *Bee*, September 10, 1896; Bernstein, "Gompers and Free Silver," 398;
Samuel Gompers, *Seventy Years of Life and Labor: an Autobiography*, II, 76, 87–
88.

[45] New York *Times*, August 20, 1896.

and anarchy. We propose to drag behind our triumphant chariot wheels . . . around the National Capital, the dead Frankensteins, personifying their pernicious creed and their turbulent fanaticism." When urged to accept the presidential nomination, Cleveland replied that he was "unalterably opposed" to such a step.[46] Overriding those like Euclid Martin, who would instruct gold Democrats to vote for McKinley, a majority chose Palmer and Simon Bolivar Buckner of Kentucky to head a National Democratic ticket, yoking rival generals of the blue and gray who had fought each other at Chickamauga in a bid for a solid nationalism in opposition to Bryan's "sectionalism."[47] While Bryan refused to be interviewed about the nomination of Palmer and Buckner, Cleveland thanked God that "the glorious principles of the party have found defenders who will not permit them to be polluted by impure hands,"[48] Morton damned all those who would "deliver the safety of this nation into the hands of socialism, zealotry, fanaticism and dishonesty,"[49] Henry Watterson applauded the building of a "bridge to McKinley" which insured the latter's election,[50] and the New York *Times* called the new party "the culmination of the revolt of all that is soundest and best in the great organization which was prostituted to Populism at Chicago."[51] Calling the Bryan party the "Popocratic" party or the "Bryanarchy," administration leaders put pressure on officeholders who supported Bryan, with the result that many who wished Bryan well kept quiet or supported the Palmer-Buckner ticket. In turn, Bryanites called the National Democratic Party "an annex of the Republican party." To them, Cleveland supporters were "boltocrats," "cuckoos," "goldbugs," and "yellowbellies," and they tossed them out of state or local party positions.[52]

[46] Telegrams, D. B. Griffin to Cleveland, Cleveland to Griffin, September 2, 1896, Grover Cleveland Papers.

[47] New York *Times*, September 2–6, 1896; Omaha *World-Herald*, September 2–6, 1896; Bryan, *First Battle*, pp. 388–390; John M. Palmer, *Personal Recollections: The Story of an Earnest Life*, pp. 275–278, 595–600; *Proceedings of the Convention of the National Democratic Party;* Elbridge Gerry Dunnell, "The Rise of the 'National Democracy': The Movement for Sound Money and the Indianapolis Convention," *American Review of Reviews*, 14 (October 1896), 434–445.

[48] Cleveland to William Vilas, September 5, 1896, Cleveland Papers.

[49] Omaha *World-Herald*, September 4, 1896.

[50] Arthur Krock (ed.). *The Editorials of Henry Watterson*, pp. 75–87.

[51] New York *Times*, September 5, 1896.

[52] Because of "open and active opposition to the regular nominee," the Omaha Jacksonian Club threw out, among others, John P. Irish, John A. McShane, Albert Watkins, Euclid Martin, T. J. Mahoney, Tobias Castor, and A. L. Sawyer. John P.

A favorite theme of Bryan's detractors was his "degeneration." The only support he would have, said Godkin in *The Nation*, would be that of the "Populist and Anarchist groups," [53] and Adolph Ochs of the New York *Times* said that Bryan was trying "to stir up hatred, envy, and malice between Americans and foreigners, between classes, and between sections." [54] Carl Schurz, in answering Bryan's Madison Square Garden speech in Chicago on September 5, intimated that Bryan did not know what free coinage meant even though he was its most ardent apostle.[55] Senator Lodge wrote to Moreton Frewen, the British bimetallist who supported Bryan: "We must win heavily and decisively in order to crush out the revolutionary resolutions put forth by the Democratic party, which has passed completely into the hands of the Populists." [56] This from one who had lately supported silver, had favored more silver in return for more tariff protection, and was a leading Anglophobe. A Philadelphian wrote Bryan that "The people here think that if a man talks Bryan *he is nutty*." [57]

The East, in general, could no more see the heroic aspect of Bryan than the West, a generation later, could feel the magnetism of Al Smith. Yet many Eastern Democrats of intelligence, like Josiah Quincy, were torn between gold and McKinley and Bryan and silver. Others objected less to Bryan than to the company he kept. "I like Bryan, always have liked him, he is as honest as daylight," George L. Wendling wrote William B. Morrison, "but being honest, he will pay his debts to Altgeld, Tillman, Stone, Peffer, Cyclone Davis, and that crowd and that will bankrupt him and the country, therefore I will not vote for him." [58]

Deeply hurt by the rejection of his leadership by the gold Demo-

---

Hopkins and Ben T. Cable, among others, either resigned or were expelled from the Illinois Democratic State Executive Committee, and the Virginia Democratic Association in Washington, D.C., expelled Governor Charles T. O'Ferrall of Virginia because he bolted Bryan and campaigned for McKinley. Omaha *World-Herald*, August 4, November 14, 1896; Allan Moger, "The Rift in the Virginia Democracy in 1896," *Journal of Southern History*, 4 (August 1938), 308.

[53] *The Nation*, September 17, 1896.
[54] New York *Times*, September 5, 1896.
[55] Omaha *Bee*, September 6, 1896; *The Nation*, September 10, 1896.
[56] Letter of September 4, 1896, Moreton Frewen Papers.
[57] W. M. Carroll to Bryan, August 6, 1896, Bryan Papers.
[58] Quoted in James A. Barnes, "Illinois and the Gold-Silver Controversy, 1890–1896," *Transactions of the Illinois State Historical Society, 1931* (Springfield, 1932), p. 55.

crats, Bryan referred to them in increasingly critical tones, particularly when he learned that they were scuttling him by naming weak candidates for state and federal positions; and after the election he asserted that they "sought to use the party name for purposes of deception." [59] He could have been elected with their support. He never forgot or forgave.

On September 1, Vermont's Republicans won their largest plurality in twenty-four years. Edward Rosewater's asserting that Vermont told "the story of the doom of Bryanism" [60] was correct. Although the silverites had conceded the state, only about a fifth of its Democrats had been loyal to Bryan, and their most eminent state leaders had denounced him and emphatically declared for McKinley. Two weeks later, Maine bore out the prediction that "Bryan would stand no more chance in Maine than a paper man in hell" [61] by rolling up the largest Republican majorities in its history, and the New York stock market began to grow stronger. While Cleveland's friend Richard Watson Gilder concluded that the September elections had "settled Bryan's hash," [62] the Nebraska silver Democrats held a harmonious state convention, endorsed the Populist state ticket, and sang a new campaign song:

> Tramp, tramp, tramp, the boys are marching;
> Marching on to victory;
> And we'll vote for Billy Bryan,
> And we'll show the British lion
> That they'd better keep their goldbugs o'er the sea.[63]

However, the gold men had held a state convention following the Indianapolis meeting and now appealed to the secretary of state for a place on the ticket. The secretary decided that their convention was "a delegate convention and regularly held." Therefore they would appear on the Nebraska ballots as "Democrats" while the Bryanites had to use "People's Democrats" or "Independent Democrats" and again undertake a vigorous campaign of voter education.[64] In November,

[59] New York *Journal*, New York *Times*, September 5, 1896; Bryan, *First Battle*, pp. 390–391.

[60] Omaha *Bee*, September 4, 1896.

[61] G. W. Steevens, *Land of the Dollar*, p. 55.

[62] R. W. Gilder to Helen Gilder, September [?], 1896, Henry Steele Commager Papers.

[63] Omaha *World-Herald*, September 5, 1896.

[64] *Ibid.*, September 5, October 18–22, 1896.

many voters anxious to help Bryan marked everything labeled "Democratic" and thereby spoiled their votes.

Railroads which had granted half-fare rates to the Indianapolis convention refused to cut fares for the fifty thousand persons who traveled to Lincoln to hear Bryan accept the National Silver party nomination on September 8.[65] The next day he accepted the Democratic nomination, and on October 13 he mailed his acceptance of the Populist nomination. His first trip, from Chicago to Lincoln, was 830 miles long. His second trip, from Nebraska to the sea and return, totaled 3898 miles. John Hay gave his impression of the campaign to Henry Adams: "What a dull and serious campaign we are having! The Boy Orator makes only one speech—but he makes it twice a day. . . . He has succeeded in scaring the Goldbugs out of their five wits."[66] Theodore Roosevelt, however, was more sanguine. From a visit to Republican headquarters in Chicago he admitted that affairs were "demoralized" in some states of the Middle West but that the East and Far West were "safe" and that, despite "the savage hatred of the prosperous for the unprosperous . . . the wage-earners are drifting our way and the revolt among the farmers is shrinking and . . . we shall win."[67]

III

BY NOW Bryan had mastered the science of electioneering by train. "Mr. Bryan has a damnable habit of going to bed at 12 o'clock and getting up at 1:30 for work," complained Richard Oulahan of the United Press.[68] He made as many as thirty-six speeches a day and averaged eighty thousand words a day, Sundays excepted. His endurance astounded the world. Only once, near the end of the campaign, was he too exhausted to meet his engagements. He never could have stood the strain had he not been physically strong and able to fall asleep in a matter of seconds, either in his chair or stretched out on the floor of his car. Seconds after he was awakened he would be ready to speak. He never got his sleep at one stretch, but he got more than the newspaper men did. Another saving factor was his capacity for food. A big

---

[65] *Ibid.*, September 1, 9, 1896.

[66] Letter of September 8, 1896, Thayer, *Hay*, II, 151.

[67] Roosevelt to Anna Cowles, September 13, 1896, Cowles, *Letters of Theodore Roosevelt*, p. 192; Roosevelt to Lodge, September 14, 1896, Lodge, *Correspondence*, I, 232–234.

[68] Omaha *World-Herald*, November 4, 1896.

man, he said, especially one who worked hard, needed food, and it was not unusual for him to eat six meals a day, each sufficient for several men. His magnificent vocal equipment also stood him in good stead. At the end of the campaign, except for a huskiness that eventually wore off, his voice quickly returned to normal. Few speakers have been able, as he was, to make themselves heard to fifty thousand persons. It was reported that he solved his laundry and bathing problems by taking his clothes off between stops and rubbing himself with gin to eradicate the odor of perspiration, and that he occasionally appeared for a speech "smelling like a wrecked distillery." [69] At night, on his knees, he prayed to the clicking of the wheels.

Bryan's caravan was followed with great interest by the foreign as well as the domestic press. He became "the best advertised man the country has produced since the days of P. T. Barnum." [70] Farm men and women traveled as much as a hundred miles by foot, bicycle, horseback, or carriage, sometimes waiting for hours huddled in blankets sodden with rain or blowing in the cold winds of night in order to hear him and try to shake his hand or touch the hem of his coat. Babies by the hundreds were named William or Jennings, or William Jennings, or William Jennings Bryan something or other; twins would be named William and Jennings, and triplets William, Jennings, and Bryan. Hundreds of babies were brought to him that he might bless them. He also captivated the newspaper men who accompanied him, among them the seasoned James Creelman, Julian Hawthorne, Alfred Henry Lewis, and Richard Oulahan. Hawthorne, at first suspicious, was now reminded of the embattled farmers during the American Revolution. "These men were actuated by the same spirit and acted in support of the same principles as did the old Concord farmers of 1776," he said of those who came to hear Bryan.[71]

In rural areas, Bryan's reception was often colored by a holiday mood, pageantry, and democratic simplicity. He would be met by wagonloads of maidens dressed in white, or sixteen girls in white riding white horses and a young man dressed in gold on a yellow horse. Dead "goldbugs" were carried on stretchers and attended by pallbearers; others appeared on pitchforks. By him paraded wagons loaded with huge boxes marked "Hanna's Money" or "Millions for Votes" and monstrous fat men with false faces resembling Hanna's. Street fakirs

[69] M. R. Werner, *Bryan*, p. 96.

[70] *Nebraska State Journal* (Lincoln), October 1, 1896.

[71] Clipping, Bryan Scrapbook No. 2, Nebraska State Historical Society.

did a thriving business in gold canes with the head of Bryan in silver, and in Bryan pins, badges, horns, hats, and caps. When he left his coach to eat he would proceed rapidly to the nearest restaurant, usually to the tune of his favorite march, "El Capitan," played by a local band, eat in full view of a crowd peering at him through windows, and march back again. Very often he surprised men he had not seen for years by calling them by name. If people called to him while he was in his car he would stick his head out of the window and smile and wave a hand. It made no difference if he were in his undershirt and shaving—he would smile through the lather.

The upper South, to which Bryan addressed himself after only three days of rest in Lincoln, received him gladly. Twenty thousand horsemen paraded in his honor in Lexington, Kentucky. To seventy thousand persons in Louisville he appealed not on the ground that he was the "regular" nominee but on the higher ground of conscience.[72] He released from support those who believed that the success of the Chicago ticket imperiled the nation. No one must put fealty to party above love of country. He threw Carlisle's words of 1878 into his teeth and thanked God that the Democracy had driven from its ranks those who would rivet upon the industrial classes shackles prepared by syndicates. Such was his reception that he believed Kentucky "safe beyond peradventure." [73]

In North Carolina Bryan had his way lighted from Asheville to Raleigh by burning tar barrels. Asked whether he did not get tired of traveling and of having people pull him about, he quoted the idol of the state, the late Senator Zebulon Vance—"Yes, it does nearly kill me, but if they did not do it, it would entirely kill me." As for those who deserted the Democracy when it fought for the common people, he told large audiences, "they must come back in sack cloth and ashes . . . [and] bring forth works meet for repentance." [74]

The reception in Asheville was typical. Long before he was due a surging mass of plain, well-behaved, and sober farmers filled the courthouse square. After resting and eating at a hotel, Bryan uncomplainingly swallowed dust in a carriage drawn by four white horses preceded by a bodyguard of a hundred or so citizens. He looked like a Western country lawyer or preacher, heavy of jaw, broad of chin, strong of mouth, but he was so tired that his complexion was sallow. His eyes

[72] Omaha *World-Herald*, September 15, 1896.
[73] *Ibid.*, September 15, 16, 1896; Bryan, *First Battle*, pp. 446–449.
[74] Bryan, *First Battle*, p. 452; Josephus Daniels, *Editor in Politics*, pp. 189–191.

were dull and he looked older than he was. Although carrying far, his voice grated as his larynx revolted against abuse. His gestures were more adapted to the pulpit than to the forum. He threw out both arms at right angles to the body, or above his head, rarely moving one arm singly; when coming to a climax he lifted himself on his toes and came down with a thump on the last word of the sentence. He uttered words but his features did not speak, yet his speech, devoted to the single topic of silver, received continuous applause, for Asheville was a silver town. His reception in North Carolina was greater than that granted Henry Clay when he was a presidential candidate.[75]

Although he believed campaigning in Virginia unnecessary, Bryan spoke in Richmond and other cities on his way to Washington, D.C., where he spoke on the hundredth anniversary of Washington's Farewell Address. Eighteen thousand persons waving American flags screamed deafeningly as a band signaled his approach with "See the Conquering Hero Comes." He accepted a rose from a little girl dressed in silver and then slowly, like St. Paul, reached forth his hand and made passes—one, two, three—toward the crowd. The din abated as his voice, low but plain, hoarse but still rich, reached for the horizon. Rain began to fall. Someone held an umbrella over his head. When the wind of a rising storm blew it inside out he jammed his black Stetson on his head, turned up his coat collar, and spoke to a forest of cheering umbrellas. His demand for "real civil service reform," the rotating office type advocated by Andrew Jackson, was one of the serious breaks of his campaign and received little applause, but he was cheered for his attack on Carlisle's conduct of the Treasury Department. He would rather see the Army in the hands of a foreign general and the Navy in the hands of a foreign admiral, he said, than see a Secretary running the Treasury on the Rothschild plan. Cleveland and Carlisle had no more right to betray the United States into the hands of British financiers than Benedict Arnold had to betray the American colonies to British soldiers. Washington's Farewell Address gave him his cue for closing—"foreign influence is one of the most baneful woes of American government." [76]

After his Washington speech Bryan finally acknowledged the opposition to him voiced by certain ministers. The Reverend Dr. Charles

[75] Letter of W. T., of Asheville, in *The Nation*, September 24, 1896; Bryan, *First Battle*, pp. 449–451.

[76] Omaha *World-Herald*, September 17, 19, 20, 1896; Daniels, *Editor in Politics*, pp. 189–191; Steevens, *Land of the Dollar*, pp. 80–86.

Parkhurst of New York charged him with a deliberate attempt to destroy the credit of the nation, saying, "I dare, in God's pulpit, to brand such attempts as accursed and treasonable." Others called him "a very commonplace sort of citizen" and "the enemy of the toiling masses who would pay for their labor in depreciated coin." Still others said he championed "a doctrine that leads to anarchy" on a "platform made in hell." The Reverend Thomas Dixon, Jr., who later wrote the novel upon which "The Birth of a Nation" was based and who ended his life in shame, referred to him as "a mouthing, slobbering demagogue, whose patriotism was all in his jaw bone." [77] Although Dwight Moody characterized his crusade as the greatest since that of Peter the Hermit and wished he were a religious rather than political evangelist, it rankled Bryan to be criticized by the ministry. He wondered from where his detractors received their religion and said that those who did not come into actual contact with the poor could not really appreciate their sufferings. Some no doubt sought notoriety in attacking him; others were influenced by Hanna's letter to all churches charging that free silver would harm those engaged in church work. He took courage in the thought that city ministers were exceptions to the larger number in the countryside who supported him. So acrimonious was the debate within the Roman Catholic church that the pope finally advised against injecting religion into the campaign, to the displeasure of the Eastern and Southern Irish, most of whom were supporting Bryan.[78]

Bryan received his greatest affront when John Boyd Thacher, the Democratic gubernatorial nominee of New York, refused to run except on a gold platform. Hill had refused to attend the state convention, as had most eminent Democrats. The logical candidate appeared to be William Sulzer, leader of the rural Democracy, but Tammany's John C. Sheehan had chosen Thacher, who he knew opposed silver, in order to balance the silver platform (or because he had been bribed by the Republicans, it was whispered) and thus please both wings of the party. Highly indignant, Bryan directed state chairman Danforth to remove Thacher from the ticket and find a man who would stand on the Chicago platform or he would cancel his engagements in New York. Tammany soon found a more tractable candidate.[79]

[77] Bryan, *First Battle*, p. 474.

[78] Omaha *World-Herald*, August 16, 22, 1896; *The Nation*, October 15, 1896; Bryan, *First Battle*, pp. 469–475.

[79] James K. Jones to David B. Hill, September 3, 1896, Hosea H. Rockell to Hill, September 21, 1896, Robert Titus to Hill, September 23, 1896, Bixby Papers; Omaha

WILLIAM JENNINGS BRYAN

Political Evangelist, 1860-1908

All illustrations courtesy of the Nebraska State Historical Society unless otherwise credited.

Silas L. Bryan   Mariah Elizabeth Bryan   William Jennings Bryan

Birthplace of Bryan
in Salem, Ill.

Bryan farm near
Salem, Ill.

Courtesy of Illinois College

Mary Elizabeth Baird as a student in Jacksonville Female Academy in 1880 when she first met Bryan.

Bryan, aged 20, as a student at Illinois College in Jacksonville.

An intercollegiate debate contest in 1880 at which Bryan (fourth from left standing) represented Illinois College.

Courtesy of Illinois College

Members of the "Yale Band" at Illinois College who influenced Bryan included (left to right) Henry E. Storrs, Julian M. Sturtevant, and Edward A. Tanner.

Lyman Trumbull,
Bryan's benefactor in
Chicago.

The bearded Bryan as a young lawyer of
Jacksonville, Ill. (1883–1887), and of Lincoln, Nebr. after October, 1887.

The Bryan home on D Street in Lincoln, Nebraska.

Bryan campaigning in the fall of 1890. He was elected to Congress from Nebraska's Second District.

Floral tribute given Bryan at the conclusion of his successful campaign to win re-election to Congress in the fall of 1892.

As Bryan began his political career, two of his closest associates were his law partner, A. R. Talbot (left), and James C. Dahlman, Omaha.

In the spring of 1896 the Bryan family posed before their home in Lincoln's D Street. Shown, left to right (above), are Ruth, Mrs. Bryan holding Grace, Bryan, and William Jennings, Jr. Bryan and his wife are shown below in his study.

In the summer of 1896, Bryan delivered his famous "Cross of Gold" speech (above) and the resulting demonstration (below) helped him win the nomination for the presidency.

Courtesy Nicollet County (Minn.) Historical Society

Bryan campaigned indefatigably; no crowd was too large or too small for him to address. Residents of St. Peter, Minn. gather in the street (above), and a crowd turns out to hear the Commoner in Rochester.

A popular campaign photograph of Bryan in the 1896 election.

"YOU SHALL NOT PRESS DOWN UPON THE BROW OF LABOR THIS CROWN"

Harper's Weekly bitterly attacked Bryan and his campaign associates.

LEADER ALTGELD AND HIS MASK.

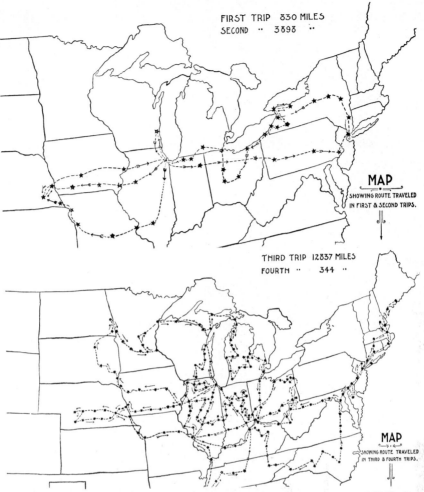

FIRST TRIP 830 MILES
SECOND " 3898 "

MAP
SHOWING ROUTE TRAVELED
IN FIRST & SECOND TRIPS.

THIRD TRIP 12837 MILES
FOURTH " 344 "

MAP
SHOWING ROUTE TRAVELED
IN THIRD & FOURTH TRIPS.

Bryan traveled 18,000 miles by train in four campaign trips. While he
lost to McKinley, he received more votes than any previous candidate
for the presidency.

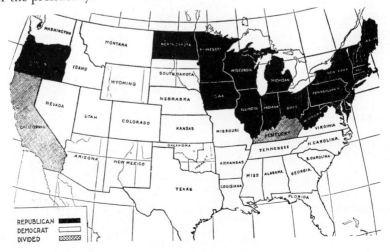

REPUBLICAN
DEMOCRAT
DIVIDED

Bryan volunteered for the war with Spain. Above, he rides at the head of his regiment of Nebraska volunteers at the Trans-Mississippi Exposition in Omaha in the summer of 1898. Below, he is seen in camp in Florida with General Fitzhugh Lee.

William McKinley

Theodore Roosevelt

William Jennings Bryan

Adlai E. Stevenson

Wharton Parker

Ignatius Donnelly

The candidates in the 1900 presidential campaign for (top to bottom) the Republicans, Democrats, and Populists.

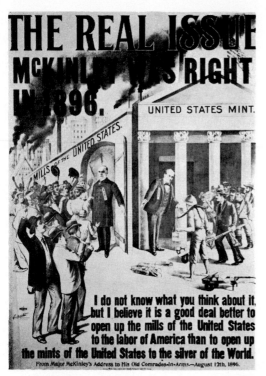

Courtesy Chicago Historical Society

Courtesy Chicago Historical Society

Broadsides widely distributed in the 1900 campaign.

A TOO-CONTINUOUS PERFORMANCE

Harper's Weekly

IF BRYAN WERE PRESIDENT.

CROKER: "That's proper, William; don't forget to feed
the tiger."—From the *Inquirer* (Philadelphia).

American Review of Reviews

Silver and Tammany provided material for anti-Bryan cartoons.

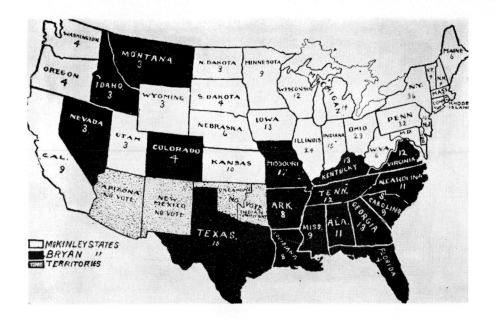

The vote and Bryan's acknowledgment of a second defeat.

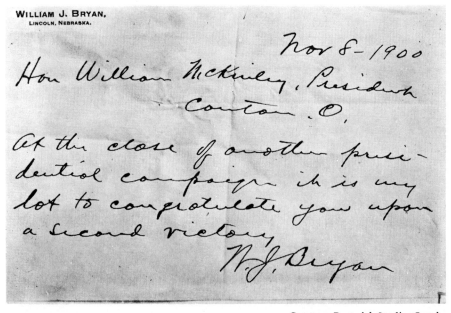

Courtesy Bostwick Studio, Omaha

Back home in Lincoln, in 1906 Bryan founded *The Commoner* to carry on the battle for his kind of Democracy.

"ECONOMY OF PRODUCTION"--HOW THE PROCEEDS ARE DIVIDED.

The Commoner enjoyed a small but influential circulation. Cartoons are typical of Bryan's anti-trust campaign.

"A hand in everything."

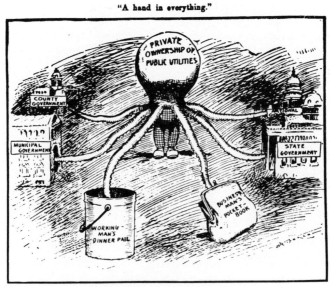

The greatest octopus of them all.

AUNTIE BRYAN: "You know, Alton, this pains me as much as it does you!"
From the *North American* (Philadelphia).

Bryan's backstage role in the 1904 campaign as portrayed by cartoonists.

WHEN MR. BRYAN SPEAKS FOR PARKER.
From the *Mail* (New York).

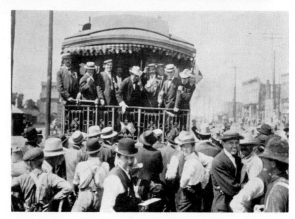

All photos courtesy Bostwick Studio, Omaha

Bryanism was given new life when the Great Commoner returned to America from a world cruise in August, 1906. Enthusiastic throngs met him at the pier (top photo), in New York City (center photo), and at innumerable whistle stops enroute home to Lincoln (bottom photo).

ROPED.
From the *Spokesman-Review* (Spokane).

Cartoons of the 1908 campaign.

THE SILENT BELL—WHY IT NEVER RINGS.
From the *Brooklyn Eagle* (New York).

Friends gather at Fairview, Bryan's new Lincoln home, following ceremonies held at the state capitol officially notifying him that he was, for
a third time, the presidential nominee of the Democratic party. At
right, the principal campaign broadside of the Bryan-Kern ticket.

FOR PRESIDENT
WILLIAM
JENNINGS
BRYAN

FOR VICE-PRESIDENT
JOHN
W.
KERN

Bryan, the "silver-tongued orator" in action.

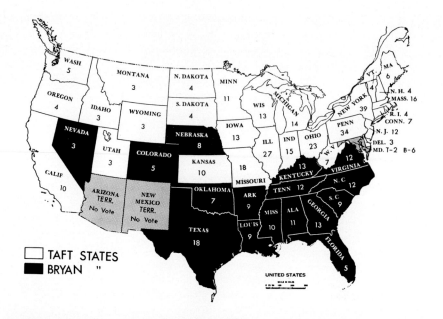

TAFT STATES
BRYAN   "

The thrice-nominated and thrice-defeated Bryan in his study in
November, 1908.

After two weeks in the upper South Bryan again tackled the heart of the "enemy's country" with speeches in Pennsylvania, New Jersey, and New York as well as in New England. He thereby flouted the advice of most silver leaders, who discounted the East, and overlooked Hanna's announced objective of concentrating upon the Middle West, where the "battle royal" must be fought.[80] "Probably the only passage in the Bible read by some financiers is that about the wise men of the East," Bryan declared. "They seem to think that wise men have been coming from that direction ever since." When the children of Israel made a calf of gold and worshipped it, it displeased God, and he ground it into powder, he reminded the East.[81] But in New York City he avoided repeating the Madison Square Garden fiasco and stuck to the income tax and injunction planks of his platform.

A vivid instance of the reign of terror Bryan faced in New England was that at Yale University. Hecklers made it difficult for him to begin; then applause, shouts, catcalls, and cheers for McKinley interrupted him so much that he refused to proceed. "I have been so used to talking to young men who earn their own living that I hardly know what language to use to address myself to those who desire to be known, not as the creators of wealth, but as the distributors of wealth which somebody else created," he snapped, knowing that at Yale there were the sons of the Rockefellers, Whitneys, Wadsworths, Harknesses, and Jelkes. In general, public opinion condemned the students, and references were made even in the opposition press, except for the irreconcilable New York *Sun*, to "un-American and cowardly" actions in interfering with the freedom of speech.[82]

In the New England states Bryan criticized the gold standard because it created a "balloon dollar" which transferred the bread one man earned to men who did not earn it, silently decreased the value of property and added to the value of the dollar, and made the rich richer

---

World-Herald, September 22–27, 1896; Omaha *Bee*, September 22–26, 1896; *The Nation*, September 24, October 22, 1896; *American Review of Reviews*, 14 (October 1896), 389–390 and 14 (November 1896), 520–521; Denis Tilden Lynch, *Grover Cleveland: A Man Four Square*, pp. 484–486; Steevens, *Land of the Dollar*, pp. 63–70.

[80] Omaha *World-Herald*, October 3, 1896. "It was decided before we came here, that it would be useless to expend money for the cause in the states east of the Allegheny Mountains, or north of the Potomac River. . . ." Edwin B. Light, Secretary, National Bimetallic Union, Chicago, to Bryan, October 22, 1896, Bryan Papers.

[81] Omaha *World-Herald*, September 23, 1896; Bryan, *First Battle*, p. 478.

[82] New York *Sun*, September 27, 1896; Omaha *World-Herald*, September 25–29, 1896; Omaha *Bee*, September 25–26, 1896; Manchester (Conn.) *Union*, September 26, 1896; Bryan, *First Battle*, pp. 484–488.

and the poor poorer. "And when the poor complain, those who are benefited by the system turn upon them, call them a mob, dispute their intelligence, and even question their right to participate in the government of the country." [83] While he was speaking in Worcester to a crowd covering six to eight acres, someone unfurled an enormous red flag from a building opposite him. He paused temporarily, blushed slightly, turned away, and proceeded without referring to it.[84]

Many Connecticut and Massachusetts firms bore large placards reading "This factory will be closed on the morning after the November election if Bryan is elected. If McKinley is elected, employment will go on as usual." [85] Fear of labor spies kept many workers from applauding him, but the fact that his audiences averaged fifteen thousand threw a scare into Hanna. Bryan gave high praise to the former Republican lawyer, George Fred Williams, who was running for governor and doing yeoman work for him, while the gold press referred constantly to the fact that support for Bryan and Williams came only from the "nondescript element" which had elected Greenbacker General Benjamin F. Butler governor a dozen years earlier, or from those who sought to build a new Democratic organization with untried and inferior men, for all the good men were gold men.[86] On Boston Common Bryan addressed another fifty thousand. Proper Bostonians who expected a Western hellraiser and ignoramus heard him quote Wendell Phillips, Emerson, Whittier, and ex-President E. Benjamin Andrews of Brown University. Andrews had written a book, *Honest Money*, which favored independent bimetallism, and thus displeased the Board of Fellows, or trustees, which favored gold. John D. Rockefeller, Jr. was a student at Brown, and Richard Olney sat on its board. When Andrews invited Bryan to address the students, the board fired him.

Leading New Englanders like David A. Wells and Edward Atkinson characterized Bryan as a daring adventurer and a political fakir, the latter speaking of Bryan as "leading the army of the half-witted." With evident symbolism Henry Cabot Lodge referred to the "Boy Orator of the Platte" and then quipped that "The Platte is a stream 1,250 miles long, with an average depth of six inches and a wide mouth." [87] Bryan

[83] *The Nation*, October 8, 1896; Bryan, *First Battle*, p. 489.

[84] New York *Times*, September 26, 1896.

[85] Omaha *Bee*, October 1, 1896.

[86] *Harper's Weekly*, October 10, 1896; Bryan, *First Battle*, pp. 493, 497–498.

[87] Omaha *World-Herald*, October 13, 1896; John A. Garraty, *Henry Cabot Lodge, A Biography*, p. 174.

made no public rejoinder, but made the extremely interesting comment, to an Illinois College classmate, that "in his attacks upon plutocracy . . . he was speaking . . . not so much for those who were hearing him . . . as for publication in the western journals." [88]

One of the greatest demonstrations of the campaign was granted Bryan upon his entry into Tammany Hall on September 29, where he replied to an extremely critical attack made earlier by ex-President Benjamin Harrison.[89] When Josephus Daniels commented on the ardor that greeted him, he replied, "If you think you have seen enthusiastic people you should go with me to Ohio, Indiana, and Kansas. These people have given us a great welcome in the East, but the West is on fire." Daniels recalled that it was, "at that time." [90] But this was before the Republican campaign of intimidation was in full swing, although New York itself proceeded as though the Republican ticket was the only one in the field.

Both the September states had gone Republican. Although state elections in Alabama, Arkansas, South Carolina, Georgia, and Florida gave solid Democratic majorities, the combined Democratic-Populist vote ran as much as 20 per cent less than in 1892, indicating that Bryan encountered greater opposition than expected in the South, even though free silver had been a party creed there for several decades.[91] Republicans had a fighting chance in the border states, particularly in Kentucky and Tennessee, but the contest would be decided in the upper Mississippi Valley, to which Bryan decided to devote the rest of the campaign.

IV

THE AMERICAN PEOPLE talked about little except the campaign during October, when Bryan undertook his last stumping tour. Josephus Daniels, who had accompanied him throughout New England, dropped off in Washington and was replaced by Benton McMillin, who would

[88] Julian Wadsworth, "William Jennings Bryan, '81—College Days," *Illinois College Alumni Quarterly*, 15 (1939), 13.

[89] Omaha *World-Herald*, September 30, 1896; Omaha *Bee*, October 1, 1896; Mary Lord Harrison (comp.), *Views of an Ex-President*, pp. 430–432, 439–451; Bryan to William R. Hearst, September 30, 1896, Bryan Scrapbook No. 2, Nebraska State Historical Society.

[90] Daniels, *Editor in Politics*, p. 197.

[91] *The Nation*, September 24, October 15, 1896.

take Bryan's place should weariness overtake him.[92] As his train chafed over the topmost levels of the Alleghenies, with the rain beating a tattoo against the cars, Bryan heard wild shouts and saw torches waving, indicating that bands of loyal Democrats who could not hope to see him nevertheless gathered to cheer him on his way.[93]

At Keyser, West Virginia, Bryan was introduced by ex-Senator Henry Gassaway Davis. A rich man, and speaking as a businessman, Davis said he feared no evil results from Bryan's election. Bryan voiced his pleasure that a rich businessman with legislative experience should support him. He compared the silver McKinley of 1876–1896 to the gold man of the moment and pointed to the fact that the National Democrats were in close touch, for financial reasons, with Hanna's treasure collectors, while Cleveland had perhaps two hundred thousand government officers, postmasters, and contractors working against him.[94] In Ohio and Indiana he spoke early and late to overcome an admitted lack of newspaper support and of funds for campaign literature. After stumping Illinois for the third time he crossed the Mississippi to St. Louis, where a number of banks were circulating announcements that they could not furnish their customers with gold but that they could do so a few days after a "correct settlement" of the money question was made.[95]

In St. Louis on October 5, as his twentieth speech of the day, Bryan used a meeting of thirty thousand members of the National Association of Democratic Clubs to reply to Cockran's speech of August 18. Taking Jefferson as his theme, he spoke in favor of "equal and exact justice to all," the avoidance of favoritism as a major political sin, "entangling alliances with none," states' rights but a solid nationalism, local self-government, acquiescence in the rule of the majority, and the advancement of agriculture and education. "If you ask me what is my highest ambition, I reply that above all offices that human hands can give, above all honors which confidence and esteem can bestow . . . I would have history say of me: He did what he could to make the Government what Jefferson desired it to be." As the nominee of the Triple Alliance he promised that if elected he would, "so help me God . . . carry out the Chicago platform to the letter." "Be not terrified by abuse, nor discouraged by epithets," he advised. "I believe, that as surely as to-

---

[92] Daniels, *Editor in Politics*, pp. 187–196.

[93] Clipping, Bryan Scrapbook No. 2, Nebraska State Historical Society.

[94] Omaha *World-Herald*, October 1, 1896.

[95] *Ibid.*, October 3–6, 1896; Bryan, *First Battle*, p. 443.

morrow morning's sun shall arise, the day will come when bimetallism shall be restored . . . when the money of the Constitution will again be ours." [96]

Senator Jones oozed confidence and gave Bryan 36 of the 45 states and 334 electoral votes. On October 4 the New York *Herald* gave him 237 electoral votes, 13 more than he needed; and Hanna and William Bynum, chairman of the National Democratic National Committee, were quoted as saying their chances were "exceedingly doubtful." Alarmed, Hanna told his workers to "Quit blowing and saw wood," for he had only a month in which to win.[97]

Bryan made a wide sweep of the border South on his way to Chicago. In Nashville he spoke to forty thousand, and to fifteen thousand in Memphis, where John W. Tomlinson relieved an exhausted McMillin as his chief assistant. For two days in Indiana, before sixty thousand in Indianapolis and smaller crowds in various cities all the way to Hammond, he castigated the National Democrats as being engaged in a "transparent fraud" in seeking to elect a Republican President.[98]

Now in *The Idler,* a most inappropriately named private car, Bryan devoted the last three weeks of the campaign to the upper Mississippi Valley. In Iowa he compared the "silver McKinley" to the "goldbug McKinley." In South Dakota, Senator Richard F. Pettigrew took him in tow. Men and women of Sioux Falls rendered homage by pulling his carriage through the muddy streets. Thousands at three meetings at Aberdeen listened to him between 1:30 and 2:30 in the morning after having listened for six hours to William A. Peffer, James H. Kyle, and others. A huge meeting was held at Fargo, North Dakota. Congressman Charles A. Towne made excellent arrangements for Minnesota, where Bryan delivered seven major addresses, three in St. Paul and four in Minneapolis, on October 10. Bryan said that those who had deserted the Democracy would find him girded for a long battle and that those who returned to the true Democracy would find no fatted calf but would have to saw wood a long time before being served dinner. In Minneapolis, too, Bryan was pleased to be the first presidential candidate to address an all-woman audience.[99]

Under the stewardship of Daniel J. Campau, Bryan devoted four

---

[96] Omaha *World-Herald,* October 7, 1896; Bryan, *First Battle,* pp. 443, 518–524.

[97] Omaha *World-Herald,* October 7, 9, 1896; Fred E. Haynes, *Third Party Movements Since the Civil War with Special Reference to Iowa,* pp. 369–370.

[98] Omaha *World-Herald,* October 5–8, 1896; Bryan, *First Battle,* pp. 525–533.

[99] Omaha *World-Herald,* October 8–13, 1896; Bryan, *First Battle,* pp. 536–554.

days to Michigan. He paid special attention to Grand Rapids, Flint, Bay City, and Detroit, and to the men who worked in Hanna's Iron Mountain Mine, although he made no direct reference to Hanna himself. On the first day he traveled 200 miles and made 13 speeches; on the second he traveled 400 miles and made 12 speeches; on the third he spoke 16 times and on the fourth 25 times. In Ohio on October 19 and 20 he averaged 15 speeches a day and spoke in almost every congressional district. He repeated this performance in Indiana, where he charged that the Republicans had nominated the wrong man—they should have named Hanna instead of McKinley. "If you want to know who is going to be prosperous if the Republicans win, I beg you to find out where the money comes from. Then you will know who the men are who contribute the money and expect to be prosperous for four years and get back more money from the people than they spent to corrupt them," he asserted.[100]

After sending greetings to Altgeld, who was on his way to speak in Cooper Union, New York, Bryan returned to Illinois, which had just been stumped by such Republican Civil War generals as Daniel Edgar Sickles, O. O. Howard, and Russell A. Alger—at Hanna's expense. In Danville he took the hide off Uncle Joe Cannon. In Springfield he complimented the state for its leadership in the silver cause. In Peoria he condemned the egging of Carlisle in Covington, Kentucky.

Despite the increasing number of gold ribbons worn by those in his audiences, Bryan suffered no disorder throughout the campaign except at Yale and once in New York, when some boys egged him. Talk about "revolution" came from gold men rather than from silverites as election day approached. Men in New York stated that "We will not abide by that decision" if Bryan were elected. Over wine tables in Chicago, millionaires boasted that if coercion, bribery, and violence at the polls did not carry the election they would appeal to force of arms.[101] Editorials

[100] Omaha *World-Herald*, October 22, 23, 1896; Bryan, *First Battle*, p. 569. According to Richard P. Bland, "Hanna's fat-frying tactics show that moneyed men are behind McKinley, and heads of trusts and combines. Those who bolted the Chicago platform include notorious beneficiaries of trusts including Standard Oil and those who raise beef prices and degrade labor, and who benefited from bond sales" ("Duty of the Hour," *North American Review*, 163 [September 1896], 369–370). According to Republican Senator William E. Chandler, ". . . it is beginning to be believed that the McKinley movement is to be a boodle canvass from start to finish. . . . McKinley has placed himself in the hands of managers who . . . will own him and make merchandise of him if elected." Washington *Post*, March 16, 1896, quoted in Omaha *World-Herald*, October 4, 1896.

[101] Omaha *World-Herald*, October 20, 1896.

in the Chicago *Inter-Ocean* and Chicago *Evening Post* brazenly encouraged coercion. Professor Edward A. Ross, of Stanford University, charged that college professors were coerced to talk for the gold standard.[102] There were also tales of the purchase of Democratic election judges and of the hiring of sluggers for the polls. As the Omaha *World-Herald* put it, "The McKinley-Hanna combine" was guilty of "coercion, bulldozing, intimidation, false representation, suppression of facts, debauchery of purchaseable votes and forced ballots." [103] A man in St. Louis peremptorily fired twelve of his workers because they intended to vote for Bryan. Palmer and Buckner, "Hanna's decoys," spoke in Omaha on October 26. On the stump, Judge Allen W. Field asserted that Bryan was "an immoral man advocating immoral principles." [104] According to D. E. Thompson, Lincoln's political boss in general, Bryan's followers were "of the riff-raff order. I mean by this that there is scarcely a fellow whom one would call reputable who belongs to that side of the deal." [105] No secret was made of the fact that ex-Senator William E. Mason of Illinois was paid to trail him and speak in the same halls to the crowds he had gathered.[106] Even Godkin slipped a moral peg when he stated that it was all right for businessmen to influence labor by placing orders to be filled only in the event of McKinley's election but that it would be "bribery" for Democratic employers to offer higher wages if Bryan were elected.[107] *Harper's Weekly* went absolutely purple. "The Truth About Mr. Bryan," it declared, was that while he appeared to some as "the second Son of Man" his mission was to invite anarchy and murder. "Beyond his feeble and ignorant presentation of his money heresy lies the deep abyss of socialism, into which . . . he is inviting the American people to plunge." [108] According to a poll of Sing Sing, said the New York *Dispatch,* most of its inmates favored Bryan.[109] Actually more violence occurred in the South between Democrats and Populists than between silver and gold Democrats.[110]

[102] Letter to James D. Richardson, September 23, 1896, *ibid.,* September 30, 1896.
[103] *Ibid.,* September 29, 1896.
[104] *Ibid.,* October 27, 1896.
[105] *Ibid.,* October 31, 1896.
[106] *Ibid.,* October 20, 1896.
[107] "The Week," *The Nation,* 63 (October 29, 1896), 319.
[108] *Harper's Weekly,* October 24, 1896.
[109] New York *Dispatch,* August 8, 1896.
[110] *The Nation,* October 29, 1896; James A. Barnes, *John G. Carlisle, Financial Statesman,* pp. 483–485.

Knowing the value of Chicago, Bryan gave it three of his last days. He believed its enthusiasm provoked by devotion to the principle of bimetallism, not from regard for him personally. The only thing he contributed, he said, was confidence that he would be true to his principles if elected. His opponents feared him because they knew he would enforce the law. If elected, he would not let the little criminals wear striped clothing and let the big ones escape to run the government; nor would the trusts be permitted to select the Attorney General.[111]

Bryan's reception in Wisconsin was at first as chilly as the weather. Having avoided the land boom bubble and burst of the late eighties, with the mortgage paid off and crops good, and a fairly diversified economy, the Wisconsin farmer could breast a depression much better than farmers farther west and south, particularly those dependent upon staple crops. Moreover, the grain growing and free labor Northern farmer had long since affiliated with the Republican party. Aware of the favorable position of the Northern as compared with the Western and Southern farmer, Bryan stressed the even greater difficulties of the laboring man who, with rent to pay and food to buy, would suffer much more than the farmer during a depression.

Another factor accounting for the cool reception Bryan received in the upper Mississippi Valley was the large number of foreign-born persons in the area, mostly Scandinavians and Germans, who by tradition supported gold. Nevertheless, perhaps because he finally acknowledged the various canards directed at him, his audiences "warmed up." He sought to set at rest rumors about patronage promises, his employment by the silver barons, his once having acted in the theater, and his harboring of religious prejudices. He was neither insane nor a degenerate, as letters in the New York *Times* insinuated; nor did he suffer from "paranoia querulenta" or "oratorical monomania." Over and over he asserted that his election promised no threat to law and order, the form of government, or the welfare of society. He was weary, but he was still strong enough to stand between the people and the Wall Street syndicates.[112]

With evident reference to Republican methods and objectives and the Declaration of Independence, Bryan declared that the nation was

[111] Bryan, *First Battle*, pp. 580–589.

[112] New York *Times*, October 15–30, 1896; clipping, October 30, 1896, Bryan Scrapbook No. 2, Nebraska State Historical Society; Bryan, *First Battle*, pp. 592–593, 595.

passing through a crisis made possible by the neglect of civic duties by the common man. In times of quiet, abuses sprang up. "The people suffer until suffering ceases to be a virtue; they are patient until patience is exhausted and then they arouse themselves and take the reins of government back upon its old foundation." Moreover:

> Our opponents have accused us of arraying class against class, yet to them belongs the discredit of making more appeals to class and sectional prejudice than any other party ever made. They have tried to array the money loaner against the man who borrows money; they have tried to array the financiers against the rest of the people; they have tried to array the soldiers against their country. There is not a class to which they have not appealed. Aye, they have even gone into religion and have appealed to missionary societies and to church boards, and have told them that the free coinage of silver would lessen the value of their investments.[113]

Despite his request that silverites not abuse gold men, anti-gold demonstrations occurred with increasing frequency at the end of the campaign. None was serious, but more than one gold man living in a silver area feared for his life, and the throwing of rotten eggs, pieces of bricks, cigar stubs, and other missiles at Carlisle on October 22 cut down his exceedingly narrow margin in Kentucky. These demonstrations were made to appear as proof of his encouragement of anarchy and frightened the Republicans. "Most of my friends think Bryan will be elected and we shall all be hanged to the lampions of Euclid Avenue," John Hay wrote Henry Adams. A week later he wrote that "the last week of the campaign is getting on everybody's nerves. There is a vague uneasiness among Republicans. . . . I do not believe defeat to be possible, though it is evident that this last month of Bryan, roaring out his desperate appeals to hate and envy, is having its effect on the dangerous classes. . . . The canvass is all right—the betting also. But nobody knows what Jack Cade may do." [114] Bryan meantime remained buoyant in spirit and unmindful of personal inconvenience, discomfort, and criticism, and his supporters asked whether the people wanted to legislate for themselves or let Britain write their laws, to work for trusts or for men, to vote for one who was wax in the hands of another or for one whom no man owned or controlled.[115]

[113] Bryan, *First Battle*, pp. 594–596.

[114] Letters to Henry Adams, October 20, 1896, and to an unnamed correspondent, October 27, 1896, in James Ford Rhodes, *The McKinley and Roosevelt Administrations, 1897–1909*, p. 143.

[115] Omaha *World-Herald*, October 31, 1896.

Bryan's return to Lincoln on November 1 ended his longest trip of the campaign—12,837 miles. "The gold syndicates and the trusts are fighting for existence and we must be prepared to meet them at every point," he wired Jones in Chicago, and he asked him to have silverites stand guard at the polls and educate those confused by the two Democratic tickets.[116]

Bryan's mail contained hundreds of letters that expressed appreciation for his great fight. Some were reminded of Paul, the great apostle who brought words of comfort to the poor, or of a new Lincoln, one who sought to free the wage slaves. The prayer of many was that he would drive out the money power and place the country back into the hands of the people. Whether he won or lost he had a crown awaiting for his strenuous efforts in the people's cause. Dr. Charles M. Rosser wrote him from Texas: "I want to say that no matter what may be the result . . . you will be greater than any other man since Christ," [117] and Willis J. Abbot sagely remarked: "And, Bryan, my dear fellow, I think that if defeat should be our lot you will find almost as many supporters and admirers, will receive almost as many messages of Godspeed, as if you were elected." [118] He never imagined that Bryan would receive 186,000 letters and telegrams. "We love you, Bryan, brave and true," was the theme of many letters, and thousands quoted his "Be of good cheer, truth crushed to earth will rise again." Hamlin Garland would vote for him rather than for the "silver idea." "You have become the oracle of the producer against the parasite and as such you have my heartiest hand-clasp. . . . This battle for human rights will not end tomorrow," he predicted.[119]

On Monday, November 2, while Bryan made a 344-mile tour of Nebraska for the benefit of the Democratic congressional ticket that ran his total to 18,009 miles, gold Democrats made a round of speeches against "repudiation, national dishonor, and anarchy" and Hanna made his final appeal to "unfurl your flags, show your colors, and vote for the protection of your family." Bryan closed the campaign with seven speeches to packed halls in Omaha in the early minutes of election day, bringing his grand total of speeches to three thousand. Betting

[116] Telegram, Bryan to Jones, November 1, 1896, Bryan Papers, Nebraska State Historical Society; Bryan, *First Battle*, pp. 602–603.

[117] Letter of November 2, 1896, Bryan Papers.

[118] Letter of no date but on the eve of election, *ibid.*

[119] *Ibid.*

in Chicago and New York closed at almost three to one in favor of McKinley.[120]

Late in the morning of November 3 Bryan voted in Lincoln. He had lost only ten pounds during his three months of strenuous exertion, but with the sudden release of pressure he almost collapsed and at 6:30 in the evening he went to bed, saying, "After two days' rest I will be as sound and as strong as when I began, and able to begin again." "If they elect McKinley," he added, "I will feel a great burden lifted off my shoulders," and promptly fell asleep.[121]

V

Bryan most likely would have won had the election been held before the gold Democrats put their ticket into the field and before the businessmen of the East gave Hanna their millions and Hanna effected his superb organization of intimidation and misrepresentation. While his managers insisted that the South and West would elect him, the returns pointed to McKinley from the first. By 11 o'clock most Bryan Democrats had conceded, and Mrs. Bryan's face betrayed the purport of the bulletins she carried to her husband's bedroom. He realized that while "the returns from the country" might change the result, the success of McKinley was "more than probable." Rather than being downcast, however, he sighed with relief and promptly went to sleep again.[122]

Late on the morning of November 5 Senator Jones put the Middle West and West Virginia in the Republican column and conceded defeat. Bitter, he telegraphed Bryan that the result was brought about "by every kind of coercion and intimidation on the part of the money

[120] Charles M. Pepper, *The Life and Times of Henry Gassaway Davis*, p. 148.

[121] Dan Bride Memorandum, Commager Papers.

[122] James B. Cox, among others, has attested that his defeat brought a great sense of relief to Bryan, who was honest enough to admit that he had no administrative experience and viewed the Presidency with no pleasurable anticipation (James B. Cox, *Journey Through My Years*, p. 285). In 1915, his host at dinner, Louis F. Post, stated that he had felt beaten when Bryan was defeated in 1896. Bryan replied: "A great many of my friends doubtless felt the same, but to me the news of my defeat was a relief. Before the news came I literally and sincerely prayed, 'O, Lord, let this responsibility be averted; nevertheless, not my will but thine be done.' When the news came, I went to bed happy." Post to Marietta Stevenson, April 18, 1926, Louis F. Post Papers.

power, including threats of lockouts and dismissals and impending starvation, by the employment of the largest corruption fund ever used in this country, and by the subordination of a large portion of the American press." A newspaper man said to Bryan: "I think it is better so, Mr. Bryan; it must be a great relief to you." James Creelman noted that Bryan's eyes flashed as his lips formed a determined smile. "Yes," he said slowly, "I regard it in some respects as fortunate that I was not elected, considering the fact that for four years I would have been confronted by a gold congress. No free silver bill would have been passed. My hands would have been tied." Then he wrote the first message of congratulations a presidential candidate ever sent his victorious opponent: "Senator Jones has just informed me that the returns indicate your election, and I hasten to extend my congratulations. We have submitted the issues to the American people and their will is law." A reporter asked, "Will this defeat hurt the cause of bimetallism?" Clenching his fist tightly and bringing it down softly on his desk, Bryan replied, "The fight has just begun. That is all I have to say tonight. Tomorrow I will issue a statement to the bimetallists of the United States." [123] McKinley wired Bryan: "I acknowledge the receipt of your courteous message of congratulations and thanks, and beg you will receive my best wishes for your health and happiness," but at the same time he wired Hanna the thoughts uppermost in his mind:

The people in their majesty, ignoring party lines, have declared their detestation of repudiation and dishonor in whatever specious guise they may be presented. They have . . . affirmed their devotion to law and order and their undeviating respect for justice and the courts . . . [and their] unfaltering determination to support and uphold the constituted authorities of the country. . . .[124]

A great swath of 21 states from North Dakota to Maine, and Oregon and California, gave McKinley 271 electoral votes. With 26 states and territories, Bryan won only 176 electoral votes, although the popular vote was fairly close—7,107,822 to 6,511,073, or 50.88 per cent for McKinley and 46.77 per cent for Bryan. Bryan had polled only 84,212 votes less than the combined Democratic-Populist vote of 1892 and a million more votes than Cleveland had received that year, with the vote of 1896 two million greater than that of 1892. Even in the states

[123] Omaha *World-Herald*, New York *World*, November 6, 1896.
[124] Omaha *World-Herald*, November 6, 1896.

McKinley carried, Bryan ran 56,000 ahead of Cleveland and only 215,000 behind the Cleveland-Weaver vote of 1892.

Bryan's failure to carry a single industrial state or the Solid South plainly revealed the sectional and economic lines along which the battle was fought. For the first time in twenty years the South did not vote solid, with Delaware, Maryland, West Virginia, and Kentucky going Republican, as did the industrial cities of the South. A revolution also occurred in the proverbially Democratic state of New Jersey, and Tammany proved to be the only obstacle to a clear Republican sweep of New York City. Bryan had explained late in the campaign that in denouncing the Rothschilds he and his friends were "not attacking a race; we are attacking greed and avarice which knows no race or religion." [125] His vote in New York City, especially among the Socialist Jews, would have been greater had he not been unjustly identified with anti-Semitism.[126] Nebraska gave Bryan a plurality of merely 13,000, but the re-election of Holcomb as governor by 21,000, the continued Democratic-Populist control of the legislature, and the saving of four of the state's six congressmen indicated a victory for fusion as well as for Bryan personally. Although he failed to carry his old First District, Bryan gave the Republicans their first complete defeat in Nebraska's history.

Although McKinley won most of the large cities and all of the industrialized states, Northern city workers supported Bryan better than did farmers. In every Southern state but Virginia the rural voter supported Bryan better than the urban voter, but the cities of Maryland, Delaware, and Kentucky overbalanced the farm votes in these states. Rural Oregon was for Bryan; Portland gave the state to McKinley. In general, also, Bryan received the vote of rural areas in which tenancy was widespread, and McKinley the vote of farmers who owned their land. The Irish and Eastern Europeans of the Atlantic coast cities voted for Bryan, but the urban foreign-born of predominantly rural states, especially those of the upper Mississippi Valley, voted for McKinley.[127]

[125] Bryan, *First Battle*, p. 581.

[126] Edward Flower, "Anti-Semitism in the Free Silver and Populist Movement and the Election of 1896" (unpublished M.A. thesis, Columbia University, 1952); Richard Hofstadter, *The Age of Reform, From Bryan to F.D.R.*, pp. 77–81; Norman Pollack, "The Myth of Populist Anti-Semitism," *American Historical Review*, 68 (October 1962), 76–80.

[127] Henry White to Gompers, November 4, 1896, cited in Foner, *Labor Movement*, II, 342; William Diamond, "Urban and Rural Voting in 1896," *American Historical Review*, 46 (January 1941), 281–303; V. O. Key, "A Theory of Critical Elections,"

Although they won only 133,148 votes, the gold Democrats diverted enough votes from Bryan in the critical states—particularly Kentucky, Michigan, and Indiana—to ensure McKinley's victory therein. With their votes Bryan would have carried these states, and with them and 1040 he would have won Oregon. McKinley credited Palmer for having aided "materially" in his election,[128] and the gold Democrats unabashedly admitted honeymooning with the Republicans during the campaign. Of them Hanna said after the election, "I have a rather soft feeling for them, I know that they consulted our wishes at every step." [129] Bryan figured that a change of 962 votes would have given him the nine votes of California instead of one, and that changes of 1069 in Oregon, 142 in Kentucky, 9002 in Indiana, 2826 in North Dakota, and 5445 in West Virginia would have won him those states. A total of 19,446 votes distributed in this manner would have given him 48 additional votes, a total of 224, and a majority of 1.

Hanna's money had flowed freely to anyone who could inject enthusiasm for McKinley into the people. With his great advantage over Bryan in the matter of money, Hanna succeeded in increasing the average vote from one in five to one in four in the hard-fought states of the Middle West. Could he help it if a few floaters got in? [130] Stanch Republicans like Chauncey Depew stated that "There was no corrup-

---

Journal of Politics, 17 (1955), 1–18; Duncan MacRae, Jr. and Charles E. Gilbert, "Critical Elections in Illinois, 1888–1958," *The American Political Science Review,* 59 (September 1960), 679–683. Unfortunately for Bryan, the middle and lower class reformers who soon after the election busied themselves in the Progressive movement had not yet begun their attempts to right the wrongs of their urban society. Joseph Huthmacher, "Urban Liberalism and the Age of Reform," *Mississippi Valley Historical Review,* 59 (September 1962), 231–241. Huthmacher suggests that the urban middle class reformers were moved in part by the "pocket-pinching price inflation that got under way in 1897. . . ." *Ibid.,* p. 232.

[128] Palmer, *Recollections,* p. 618; George T. Palmer, *A Conscientious Turncoat: The Story of John M. Palmer,* p. 278.

[129] New York *Times,* November 14, 1896. See also New York *Tribune,* July 31, 1896; Chicago *Tribune,* August 3, 1896; James J. Hill to David B. Hill, September 11, 1896, Bixby Papers; Calvin Tomkins to William D. Bynum, July 17, 1896, Bynum Papers; Abram S. Hewitt to Don Dickinson, October 6, 1896, Dickinson Papers; Allan Nevins, *Abram S. Hewitt, With Some Account of Peter Cooper,* pp. 562–567.

[130] Arthur W. Dunn, *From Harrison to Harding: A Personal Narrative, Covering a Third of a Century, 1888–1921,* I, 194–195; Sidney Ratner, *American Taxation: Its History as a Social Force in Democracy,* p. 217.

tion or purchase of votes in Mr. Hanna's management. It was publicity and again publicity. . . ." [131] However, post-election accounts by Republican editors and politicians point to widespread corrupt practices in McKinley's behalf which have never been refuted. Money was used to purchase some of the foreign and Negro vote; tricks were used to get men to vote for McKinley rather than for Bryan; and in some cases Bryan ballots were counted for McKinley. Kentucky, West Virginia, Illinois, Indiana, Ohio, and Michigan contained areas that cast more ballots than there were people. Persons ineligible to vote because not registered, because they lived on federal reservations, or because they were in jail were permitted to vote—for McKinley.[132] Weaver described the vote in Iowa as "absurd and dishonest." [133] Bryan's loss of Minnesota may be ascribed in large degree to fraud. In Louisville, Chicago, Philadelphia, Baltimore, and New York, at least, Hanna's money paid managers who imported Negroes and some whites to vote for McKinley, or to vote as many as sixteen times for him at $5.00 a vote.[134] In a Philadelphia district numbering 30,000 people, 48,000 ballots were cast, and Carter Harrison estimated that more than 60,000 phantom citizens voted in Chicago. Honest returns would have given Bryan at least Maryland, West Virginia, California, Kentucky, Indiana, and Ohio—and he would have won. Altgeld declared that fraud was so prevalent in various states that Bryan was actually the winner,[135] and Bryan's papers contain many letters showing how fraud and corruption lost him badly needed votes in the East and Middle West. Josephus Daniels stated that Bryan never doubted that he was elected but that

[131] Depew, *Eighty Years*, p. 150.

[132] Randolph W. Hill to Josephus Daniels, September 3, 1913, Daniels Papers; Dr. G. R. Jenkins to Bryan, November 13, 1896, T. T. Hudson to Bryan, November 23, 1896, Mrs. Minnie Kraft to Bryan, November 20, 1896, Joseph Sibley to Bryan, November 19, 1896, Elisha H. Bearse to Bryan, January 17, 1897, Bryan Papers; Jasper B. Shannon, with Ruth McQuown, *Presidential Politics in Kentucky, 1896–1948*, pp. 71–73; letter to the author from Bennett H. Wall, September 22, 1959; Louise Overacker, *Money in Elections*, p. 45.

[133] Letter, November 7, 1896, Bryan Papers.

[134] Joseph Sibley to Bryan, November 11, 1896, Frank Stephenson to Bryan, November 5, 1896, *ibid.*

[135] Arthur Kitson, "William Jennings Bryan," *Fortnightly Review*, 706, New Series (October 1925), 565; Altgeld, "Address at Tremont House, January 8, 1897," in *Live Questions*, pp. 693–699; Harold C. Syrett (ed.), *The Gentleman and the Tiger: The Autobiography of George Brinton McClellan, Jr.*, pp. 114–116; Clarence Darrow, *The Story of My Life*, p. 92.

Bryan refused to contest the election because he feared a civil war might follow.[136]

VI

THOUGHTFUL men in all parties realized that Bryan's central theme throughout the campaign was his demand for general social reform, but the East proved irreconcilable. It made much of the victory of "decency" over "indecency." McKinley's carrying of the eighteen states north of the Ohio and Potomac and east of the Missouri, an area that contained 56 per cent of the population, 64 per cent of the estimated wealth, and "the most intelligent people of the land," was proof to E. L. Godkin of *The Nation* of the victory of "the great civilizing forces of the republic, as against the still surviving barbarism bred by slavery in the South and the reckless spirit of adventure in the mining-camps of the Far West." [137] Men like Theodore Roosevelt, John Hay, Whitelaw Reid, and Carl Schurz deemed the contest of 1896 more critical than that of 1861–1865. In the latter the question had been whether a democratic government could maintain itself against armed insurrection; in the former the question was whether the people could use the suffrage with an intelligent understanding of the public interest and just regard for the rights of all.

Bryan was particularly blamed for having waged a "nightmare campaign" of emotion and passion that stirred the unthinking masses into a frenzy not witnessed since the witchcraft craze of colonial Massachusetts. He had attracted the ignorant, discouraged, and discontented with his dreams of a magic wampum that would relieve them of debt. Throughout the campaign Roosevelt's letters teemed with references to "Bryanism" as "ugly," "criminal," "vicious," "a genuine and dangerous fanaticism." Bryanism was "a semi-socialistic, agrarian movement," he asserted, ". . . a revolt aimed foolishly at those who are better off, merely because they *are* better off; it is the blind man blinding the one-eyed." According to John Hay, "All that is left of the [Democratic] party is rank Populist. Its unquestioned leaders are the Altgelds, the Tillmans, the Debses, the moral dynamiters, whose lawlessness stops just short of the criminal courts." To Hay, Bryan was "a halfbaked glib little briefless jack-leg lawyer . . . grasping with anxiety to col-

[136] Daniels, *Editor in Politics*, pp. 198–199.

[137] "Significance of the Verdict," *The Nation*, 63 (November 12, 1896), 358. See also *Harper's Weekly*, October 31, November 14, 1896.

lar that $50,000 salary, promising the millennium to everybody with a hole in his pants and destruction to everybody with a clean shirt." [138]

Hot words were exchanged. Andrew Carnegie called Bryan a "conjurer." Hay wished to feel the "phrenological bumps" of the "glib-tongued adventurer" who promised "fairy money" for votes from the "lunatic factions." Several Chicago millionaires were quoted as saying they would use force to prevent Bryan from controlling the government were he elected. "We wouldn't be such damned fools as the South was in '61. We wouldn't walk out of Washington and turn it over to that crowd!" When his conversation with a Kansas Populist turned to Bryan's chances of winning, Hanna exploded with a blood-curdling threat: "Do you think that we'd let that damned lunatic get into the White House? Never! You know you can hire half of the people of the United States to shoot down the other half if necessary, and we've got the money to hire them." He was probably letting off steam somewhat recklessly, but his feelings represented those of many of Bryan's opponents.[139]

Various Bryanites also breathed fire and swore vengeance. An Ohioan wrote him that "We have guns and powder and I promise to stand to our Party as long as I live," and appended the names of several hundred workingmen who felt the same way.[140] *"If the common people cannot win in a fair contest, then the financial question must, and will be, adjudicated by the sword!"* wrote an Illinoisan,[141] while an Alabaman declared: "We of the South, as you know, are 'natural born rebels.' We did manage to take the oath of allegiance in '65, but I register a most solemn vow never to swear allegiance to Clevelandism or McKinleyism

[138] Roosevelt to Anna Roosevelt Cowles, September 27, August 2, October 4, 1896, Cowles, *Letters from Theodore Roosevelt*, pp. 89, 194, 195; Roosevelt to Lodge, November 26, 1896, Lodge, *Correspondence*, I, 240; Hay to Whitelaw Reid, August 31, September 23, 1896, Reid Papers; editorial, New York *Tribune*, November 5, 1896; John Hay, *The Platform of Anarchy: An Address to the Students of Western Reserve University, October 6, 1896* (Cleveland: 1896); Rhodes, *McKinley and Roosevelt Administrations*, pp. 22, 27–28. All important British newspapers had fiercely opposed Bryan. Their sighs of relief at the end of the campaign were incomplete, however, because they predicted that McKinley would raise the tariff rates in the near future. Moreton Frewen to Bryan, July 16, 1896, Bryan Papers; "Money and the Masses in America," *Quarterly Review*, 184 (October 1896), 567–584; clippings from British newspapers in Bryan Scrapbook No. 2, Nebraska State Historical Society.

[139] Horace A. Keefer, "The Experiences of an Unsuccessful Legislator," Mss., Commager Papers; Washington *Evening Star*, October 23, 1932.

[140] Frank Dietrich to Bryan, November 16, 1896, Bryan Papers.

[141] Robert A. Mills to Bryan, November 11, 1896, *ibid.*

or any other damnable ism emanating from the foul hotbed of corruption and plunder." [142] Bryan's soothing of these men reflected his pacifism; the reluctance of the American people to resort to arms in the most bitter campaign in their history revealed the solidity of their democratic institutions.

Although fulsome praise for the courage, ability, and sincerity of the "evangel of the workers and producers of the country" came from various gold Democrats, the most perceptive tribute to Bryan is found in a letter from Mrs. Henry Cabot Lodge, whose husband opposed Bryan, to Sir Cecil Spring-Rice, the British ambassador:

The great fight is won and a fight conducted by trained and experienced and organized forces, with both hands full of money, with the full power of the press—and of prestige—on the one side; on the other, a disorganized mob at first, out of which there burst into sight, hearing, and force—one man, but such a man! Alone, penniless, without backing, without money, with scarce a paper, without speakers, that man fought such a fight that even those in the East can call him a Crusader, an inspired fanatic—a prophet! It has been marvelous. Hampered by such a following, such a platform—and even the men whose names were our greatest weapon against him, deserted him and left him to fight alone—he almost won. We acknowledged to seven millions campaign fund, against his $500,000. We had during the last week of the campaign 18,000 speakers on the stump. He alone spoke for his party, but speeches which spoke to the intelligence and hearts of the people, with a capital P.[143]

Bryan had set a new record for campaigning. Others have covered more miles in comfortable trains and reached more people by radio and television, but none has matched his physical endurance or has been able to address larger audiences. The reporters who accompanied him were impressed with his unaffected humanity, his decency, his wit, his lack of pose, his refusal to compromise with the truth as he saw it, his belief in the infallible "rightness" of the common people.[144] Thousands wrote to him for advice in solving myriads of personal problems, hundreds sent him unsolicited gifts which overflowed his home. "Sixteen to one" came in the form of a potato with 16 sprouts, a vase with 16

[142] J. G. Heaton to Bryan, November 11, 1896, *ibid.*

[143] Stephen Gwynn, *The Letters and Friendships of Sir Cecil Spring-Rice: A Record*, II, 197–198.

[144] "Rules of the Road" adopted by the journalists who accompanied Bryan, copy in Bryan Papers; Stockbridge, "Bryan, the Great Commoner," p. 868.

handles, and other ingenious ways.[145] Daughter Ruth collected 700 letters between midsummer 1896 and the end of the year that indicated that babies had been named after her father.

Thousands of letters show that Bryan won particularly the love of America's youth and aged poor. "P.S. No cross of gold, no crown of thorns," was added to many a letter, and persons of religious bent thanked God for "an able, wise, just, patriotic, Christian Hero." His trials were compared to those of Jesus. Both had been baffled, despised, and crucified, one at the hands of silver, one by gold. Bryan told Mark Sullivan that he knew of a family that thought of him as the second Christ and that it was common to compare him with Paul.[146] Letters of praise also came from the organized bimetallists of England and Australia as well as America, and hundreds of veteran Prohibitionists, Populists, and Republicans wrote him that they had deserted their own parties to vote for him, that he was "the Greatest American living," "a new Moses in the form of a Populist Yankee," "a volunteer St. George battling against the dragon of organized greed." He was "the Peerless Leader of the People," the "Wellington of the silver forces."

VII

BRYAN summed up the cause of his defeat by saying "I have borne the sins of Grover Cleveland." [147] To a degree he was right, for millions impoverished by the "Cleveland depression" snapped eagerly at Mc-Kinley's "prosperity" argument. Without the depression, the tariff might have been the paramount issue; because of it Bryan was fated to engage in controversy over the financial system in the first national campaign in which it was the prime issue. Moreover, since Bourbon leaders deserted him, his organization was new and directed in many instances by men lacking political experience or talent or by partisans interested only in patronage, with the result that it failed adequately to discipline its farm and labor components, the very "producers of wealth" Bryan had depended upon to provide the common denominator that would have spelled his success.

Bryan was defeated by Hanna rather than by McKinley. The best

[145] William Jennings Bryan and Mary Baird Bryan, *The Memoirs of William Jennings Bryan*, pp. 264–267.

[146] Mark Sullivan, *Our Times: The United States, 1900–1925*, I, 112 n.

[147] Robert McElroy, *Grover Cleveland, the Man and Statesman*, II, 37.

estimate of Bryan's war chest is $300,000, which expenditures by local committees may have swelled to $600,000.[148] Until mid-September Hanna admitted that Bryan was sweeping all before him. Then he settled down to elect the man he had nominated and in a month completed his work. He gathered about him a committee of forty-five whose wealth ranged from a low of $2,000,000 to a high of $125,000,000. Their contributions, those by corporate interests, and sums shaken out of bankers, businessmen, life insurance companies, public utilities, and other employers of labor amounted to about $7,000,000, while total national and local expenditures may have approached $16,000,000.[149]

[148] The silver states contributed about a fifth of Bryan's campaign chest, giving the lie to stories of boodle funds provided by English as well as American silver interests. Even if the mine owners did give the highest estimate noted, $228,000, by Paxton Hibben in *The Peerless Leader: William Jennings Bryan,* p. 193, this amounts to only three cents per vote polled. Bryan had no direct connections with the silver mine owners after his second congressional campaign. A mine owner, Marcus A. Daly, made the single largest contribution to his campaign fund, of $50,000, but Bryan's Papers reveal that he declined to give the additional $300,000 requested of him by James K. Jones and Arthur Pue Gorman. Such silver mine owners as Eben Smith, Simon Guggenheim, and S. A. Josephi denied the existence of any organization of silver miners that sought to foster Bryan, and diligent research has discovered none. From research in the State Historical Society of Colorado, Nevada State Historical Society, and Library of the University of California, H. Wayne Morgan concluded that there is "no evidence whatever in these places indicating that Bryan was in the pay of the Western silverites." He cogently added that any such evidence would probably have been destroyed long ago (letter to the author, August 22, 1958). Distressed by Senator Thurston's charge that he was in the pay of the silver barons—for which charge Senator Teller and ex-Senator William Stewart called Thurston a liar and won a retraction—Bryan published his account book, which showed that since leaving Congress he had received only $150 a month while with the Omaha *World-Herald,* some income from his law partnership, and pay for speeches arranged by lecture bureaus, and challenged the Republican National Committee to make an official charge so that he could prove his innocence. Public appeals for funds issued by Jones and various newspapers brought in only small amounts. The New York *Journal* raised the largest public subscription, $40,000, toward which Hearst himself gave $15,000. See New York *Times,* August 17–19, 1896; Omaha *Bee,* August 8, 10, 1896; Omaha *World-Herald,* August 15, 19–21, 1896.

[149] Omaha *World-Herald,* September 7, 1896; John Hay to William McKinley, August 3, 1896, McKinley Papers; *The Commoner* (Lincoln, Nebraska), April 27, May 4, 1906; Herbert Croly, *Marcus Alonzo Hanna,* pp. 206, 217–221; Overacker, *Money in Elections,* pp. 1, 21–28, 107–108. E. H. Harriman gave $35,000; Marshall Field $10,000; Standard Oil $250,000; the Beef Trust $400,000; John Wanamaker his "customary" $10,000; and John Hay contributed $1000 a month from August to

Thus he systematized and nationalized the fat-frying tactics of Corporal James Tanner and Senator Matthew S. Quay and capped the alliance between politics and big business which had flourished since the Civil War and remained undisturbed until Bryan challenged it. Bryan eloquently preached the rights of the poor, dreamed of equality, and refused to employ the forces of political corruption that strove for his patronage and might have elected him. Hanna, who frankly championed plutocracy, pitted cold cash against him and won. Theodore Roosevelt later asserted that Bryan frightened capital too much, that those who feared him threw themselves into the arms of those who opposed him.[150]

Hanna defeated Bryan in every detail of campaign management. In a campaign peculiarly one of education, Bryan distributed about 10,000,000 copies of speeches on silver by himself and others; Hanna issued 120,000,000 copies of 275 pamphlets and speeches. Lithographs, cartoons, and posters advertised McKinley as the "Advance Agent of Prosperity," or, as in the cartoons of W. A. Rogers in *Harper's Weekly*, depicted Bryan as an unrestrained Populist, anarchist, blasphemer, and Anti-Christ. The Democrats provided some "boiler plate" for both the weekly and the daily press. Hanna furnished so many of these patent insides that each week 5,000,000 families received 13,000 newspapers containing material unfavorable to Bryan.

While Bryan shouldered the greatest part of the Democratic speaking campaign, Hanna paid "colporteurs" to do missionary work among the farmers of the Middle West and provided an "Old Soldiers' Touring Special" to enable Union generals Alger, Howard, Stewart, and Sickles to declaim on the theme of "strength in the Union and the hell with the Democrats." McKinley, a veteran, had the advantage over Bryan in the North, especially with the then 350,000 members of the G.A.R. Hanna also made special appeals to teachers and clergymen to popularize the threat to their professions posed by free silver. While more evidence is needed to prove the point, it is probable that the

---

November. In the course of the life insurance investigations of a decade later, the directors of the New York Life, Mutual, and Equitable insurance companies confessed that they had given of their policy holders' funds to defeat free silver. New York State Legislature. Joint Committee on Investigation of Life Insurance. *Armstrong Committee. Testimony, Exhibits and Report, 1905*. (7 vols., Albany. J. B. Lyon Co., 1906), I, 639, III, 2062; Overacker, *Money in Elections*, pp. 107, 180–181.

[150] *Autobiography*, pp. 273–274.

Roman Catholic vote shifted from the Democratic to the Republican party.[151] Hanna had ten good speakers for one of Bryan's, and Bryan's did not always help him. Tillman, whom the East called "a filthy baboon," spoke in thirty states but lent color to the Republican charge that lawlessness was the ruling element in the Democratic party and helped defeat Bryan. Nor did Altgeld help, for the East regarded him, too, as one of Bryan's "evangels of Anarchism." [152] The most eloquent Democratic speakers, Bryan excepted, were Cockran and Schurz, both of whom opposed Bryan, and Hill refused to stump for him.[153]

Bryan was like a private citizen waging war on a daily newspaper. About half the Democratic and Independent press opposed him.[154] He had no friendly newspaper in Chicago, and James J. Hill bought the St. Paul *Globe,* the only Democratic newspaper in the upper Mississippi Valley, and made it a gold organ. Teller failed to bring the Scripps-McRae league over to Bryan, and the publications of the educational silver organizations, like the *National Bimetallist,* were smothered by gold Democratic papers and Hanna's subsidized sheets. Gustav Schwab estimated that 503 of the 581 German-language newspapers opposed Bryan.[155]

Bryan went to the people. Hanna brought the people to McKinley, expenses paid. Obdurately refusing to allow extemporaneous addresses in his presence, McKinley would stand on his front porch and face a field of leaping yellow ribbons. The head of each delegation would

[151] C. Vann Woodward, *Tom Watson, Agrarian Rebel,* p. 422.

[152] Francis B. Simkins, *Pitchfork Ben Tillman, South Carolinian,* pp. 338–339. Altgeld, Stone of Missouri, Tillman, Weaver, Bland, Teller, Towne, George F. Williams, Homer S. Cummings, and Edward Carmack were Bryan's major stump speakers. Others who helped were Shively, Turpie, and Matthews in Indiana; Blackburn in Kentucky; Hogg and Reagan in Texas; Vest in Missouri; Tom Johnson in Ohio; John W. Daniel and Carter Glass in Virginia; Adlai E. Stevenson and Clarence Darrow in Illinois; Henry G. Davis in West Virginia; and William E. Borah, Republican, of Idaho.

[153] Hill to Judge Hamilton Ward, September 12, 1896, Bixby Papers.

[154] Except for Hearst's New York *Journal* and McLean's Cincinnati *Enquirer,* Bryan had little support north of Mason and Dixon's line and east of the Mississippi. Hearst in California, Thomas M. Patterson in Denver, Charles H. Jones in St. Louis, and the Salt Lake *Tribune* provided most of his Western support, and the New Orleans *Times-Democrat* and the Atlanta *Constitution* his Southern. The Atlanta *Journal,* owned by Hoke Smith, who had resigned from Cleveland's cabinet in September, supported him as the party's nominee but rejected his platform.

[155] Schwab cited in "A Notable Bolt of Newspapers," *American Review of Reviews,* 14 (August 1896), 142.

read a carefully prepared speech that had been submitted beforehand, revised, and returned. Then McKinley would reply from a manuscript, not without a stumble or two, but always dignified, always commonplace and dull but proper, safe, sober, and always, says Herbert Croly, "with a high respect for the proprieties of political life." [156]

Bryan put on a one-man steeplechase. Hanna provided the populace with circuses bigger and better than those of Blaine's "plumed knights." On Chicago Day, October 9, 100,000 men with golden badges, hats, caps, and shoes marched in honor of "sound money" for five hours before a crowd of half a million. In the evening came a counter demonstration of only 40,000 workingmen.[157] In New York, on the Saturday before election, 110,000 men marched for gold in the largest demonstration since the disbanding of the veterans in Washington in 1865. Employers either "suggested" that their men march or plainly told them to march or lose their jobs. All day long New York resounded to the singing of "We'll hang Billy Bryan on a sour apple tree as we go marching on," while below their breath the workers sang:

> You ask me why 'tis thus
> That I make this outward show,
> Because my millionaire employer
> Says "Bryan men must go."
> And I have got a wife at home
> With little ones to feed,
> And must appear to think and vote
> To suit the goldbugs' greed.[158]

The most effective tactic used to defeat Bryan was the coercion of productive labor. Orders labeled "Cancel if Bryan Wins" and "Double this Order if McKinley Wins" or made "contingent" upon McKinley's election directly affected industrialists and workers alike. Hundreds of workers wrote Bryan that their employers warned them that they would close their shops if he were elected or that Bryan men need not return to work if Bryan were elected. Some workers who favored Bryan were fired and blacklisted; others were forced to contribute money to the Republican campaign fund. Particularly bitter complaints reached Bryan about detectives assigned to "work on the workers" on the rail-

---

[156] Croly, *Hanna*, p. 215. See also Olcott, *McKinley*, I, 318, 321.

[157] Omaha *World-Herald*, October 10, 1896; Steevens, *Land of the Dollar*, pp. 186–192.

[158] New York *Journal*, New York *Times*, November 1, 1896.

roads.[159] "The brutality of the methods is almost incredible," said Professor Edward A. Ross.[160]

Political blackmail was probably a more potent argument with workers than all the benefits gold men set forth for an "honest" currency. "Our defeat is due to the fact that hungry stomachs know no law," a factory hand wrote Bryan.[161] "For daring to speak, and write, one letter in the [Philadelphia] *Evening Telegraph* alone, made a difference in my business of at least 25 per cent. Many old friends and acquaintances remaining away and still doing so," reported a grocer,[162] revealing that support for Bryan could result in social ostracism as well as reduced profits.

Farmers were subjected to similar pressures, and Bryan declared that "the coercion practiced by large financiers upon the small ones, and by the small ones upon borrowers, was far reaching in its extent." [163] Banks and loan companies blackmailed their borrowers by refusing to extend credit or to renew loans that fell due or by demanding the immediate collection of debts held by those who favored silver. Banks that held the notes of the industrial and commercial firms of a town dictated to both employer and employee by threatening to call in loans, declining to discount even the best commercial paper, and refusing ordinary accommodations.[164] Champ Clark was once denied the right to cash a personal check because he supported Bryan.[165] The Eastern insurance companies, which held many Western mortgages, also sent agents to contact every borrower and to offer a five year extension of loans at low interest rates if McKinley were elected. Tens of thousands found the temptation too great to resist.[166] Even stocks were quoted "cum McKinley." One exchange, for example, quoted Postal Telegraph

[159] New York *Times*, August 2, 1896; Omaha *World-Herald*, November 15, 1896; Foner, *Labor Movement*, II, 341.

[160] San Francisco *Examiner*, September 27, 1896.

[161] M. J. Pareneau to Bryan, November 7, 1896, Bryan Papers.

[162] R. W. Jennings to Bryan, November 11, 1896, *ibid.*

[163] Bryan, *First Battle*, p. 617.

[164] Wilson Hutchins to Bryan, November 11, 1896, J. W. Hemsted to Bryan, November 11, 1896, George W. Bird to Bryan, November 11, 1896, P. Burton to Bryan, November 24, 1896, Bryan Papers; Omaha *World-Herald*, July 24, 30, August 1, 1896.

[165] Werner, *Bryan*, p. 142.

[166] For example, see George L. Kinney to Bryan, November 11, 1896, George W. Bird to Bryan, November 11, 1896, and James V. Bouvier to Bryan, December 15, 1896, Bryan Papers.

shares at 80½ "regular" and 83 "cum McKinley." [167] Only three members of the New York Stock Exchange favored Bryan.[168]

In every presidential election except that of 1932 in which the Democrats staked their case on hard times, something happened about August to raise prices, satisfy the farmers, and still the revolt of rural Republicans. The price of wheat rose from 47 cents a bushel in 1894 to 53 cents in August 1896 and to a three-year high of 84 cents in December. The reason lay with crop failures abroad, but the price of wheat had been used since the Civil War as a barometer of agricultural discontent, and Bryan had assiduously cultivated its intimate connection with the price of silver. The failure of the price of silver to follow that of wheat in the fall of 1896 effectively burst his contention. Many farmers thought the rise in the price of wheat presaged a general upturn in prices and voted accordingly.[169] Of the wheat-growing states, Bryan won only three—Nebraska, South Dakota, and Kansas—and he lost the corn-producing states of the Middle West.

Bryan made other egregious mistakes in his canvass. The nomination of Sewall was a mistake, for Sewall failed to hold the East and irked Watson. Bryan probably should have declined to run with Watson, who hurt him by reaffirming the important Populist principles omitted from the Chicago platform and by appealing for a sectional alliance between the South and West.[170] Moreover, Bryan could not make fusion work. In the South, Marion Butler ditched the Democracy and fused with the Republicans. In the West, Teller complained of unfair Democratic treatment of the silver Republicans, and fusion arrangements finally made in twenty-six states involved various legal battles and fierce fights over local patronage which in the end detracted from

---

[167] *The Nation*, November 5, 1896.

[168] James V. Bouvier to Bryan, December 15, 1896, Bryan Papers.

[169] *Thirty-ninth Annual Report of Trade and Commerce of Chicago, for the Year Ending December 31, 1896*, pp. 9, 12; Wilfred E. Binkley, *American Political Parties, Their Natural History*, pp. 315–316; Alexander Dana Noyes, *Forty Years of American Finance, 1865–1907*, pp. 264–265; James A. Barnes, "Myths of the Bryan Campaign," *Mississippi Valley Historical Review*, 34 (December 1947), 392–394. See also Edward Atkinson, "Our Grain Farmers the Creditors of the World," *Harper's Weekly*, September 12, 1896, and the penetrating analysis by Gilbert C. Fite, "Republican Strategy and the Farm Vote in the Presidential Campaign of 1896," *American Historical Review*, 65 (July 1960), 787–806.

[170] Watson rebuffed all offers of reconciliation, including a purported cabinet post tendered by Tillman, if he retired. Sewall to Bryan, July 25, August 31, 1896, Bryan Papers; John D. Hicks, *The Populist Revolt: A History of the Farmers' Alliance and the People's Party*, pp. 368–369; Woodward, *Watson*, pp. 316–325.

Bryan's strength.[171] Since Bryan would have gained votes where he needed them by dropping Sewall and taking Watson, he did not act out of mere expediency; yet he persistently ignored Watson. He did not acknowledge his aid in stumping the West and he disagreed with his methods. It was not until 1907 that he thanked him and offered a weak apology for the discourteous and possibly dishonest treatment of him by Jones in 1896.[172]

Bryan erred in permitting Jones to head the Democratic National Committee. Jones had no unusual facility for touching the hearts of the poor or the pockets of the rich, was from a safely Democratic state, did nothing to bring out the vote, and failed to reject the endorsement of Bryan by such organizations as Tammany, whose leaders should have been jailed for their criminal activities. He bungled badly both in permitting the naming of Sewall and in his dealings with the Populists at St. Louis, and his treatment of the Populists, rather than Bryan's, made complete fusion impossible. A rabid Southerner, he let it slip that he hated the very thought of Watson, that the Populists of the South were "a bad lot, a discreditable class out for nothing but the spoils," and that they should "go to the Negroes, where they belong." [173] Despite additional violations of party discipline, Bryan refused to dismiss him. On the other hand, Bryan rejected Jones's sage advice to concentrate on the Middle West and the doubtful states and went "skylarking" in the East, which Jones believed already lost.

Aware of his extraordinary effectiveness as a speaker, Bryan adopted the normally futile experiment of electioneering from rear platforms. He was heard by perhaps three million persons, but he failed to take into account the curiosity that moves men, and his touring did not disprove the principle that elections are won not by oratory but largely by effective organization of a sufficient number of minority groups into a majority. In a Western state a stranger approached him, saying, "I have ridden fifty miles to hear you speak tonight. I have always read

[171] Omaha *Bee*, August 10, September 3, 1896; Bryan to James K. Jones, February 21, 1898, Bryan Papers; Daniels, *Editor in Politics*, pp. 171–178; Elmer Ellis, *Henry Moore Teller*, pp. 277–280, 285–286, 303; Hicks, *Populist Revolt*, pp. 357–359; Alex M. Arnett, *Populist Movement in Georgia*, pp. 202–204, 209–210.

[172] Bryan to Watson, January 24, 1907, Woodward, *Watson*, p. 323; Bryan, *First Battle*, pp. 622–623; Eugene H. Roseboom, *A History of Presidential Elections*, pp. 316–317.

[173] New York *Times*, August 4, 8, 1896; Omaha *Bee*, August 7, 30, 1896, *The Nation*, August 6, 1896; W. J. Bryan, "Memorandum on James K. Jones," Bryan Papers; Willis J. Abbot, *Watching the World Go By*, p. 179.

every speech of yours that I could get hold of. I would ride a hundred miles to hear you make a speech. And, by gum, if I wasn't a Republican I'd vote for you." [174] Bryan often retold this incident in accounting for his success and failure—he attracted people but not votes. His "heart to heart" appeal won a number of undying friendships. What he lacked was the group diplomacy needed to win the minds of millions.

Bryan's understanding of the money question was imperfect, and in taking free silver as his paramount issue he campaigned on too narrow a front. He erred in saying that the supply of silver had not exceeded that of gold between 1870 and 1896, and he overlooked the reduction in the price of silver caused by mechanical and chemical advances. His belief that the remonetization of silver would bring prices and values back to where they had been in 1873 was based on the quantitative theory of money alone—he disregarded credit and the velocity of circulation and the fact that in 1896 at least 80 per cent of our international trade was transacted with gold standard countries. The restoration of bimetallism would have worked some injustice, for the debtor and creditor of 1873 and 1896 were not necessarily the same, and it would have benefited the holders of long-term rather than of short-term loans. Moreover, how could both farmers and workers be aided by free silver? Until his mortgage is paid off, and annually until the harvest is garnered, the farmer tends to be a debtor, whereas the laborer, paid weekly or monthly, need not be a debtor and is less affected than the farmer by the long-term appreciation of the currency. Nevertheless, Bryan was basically right; in the 70 per cent decline in the price level that occurred between 1865 and 1896 he had an excellent base for an economic reform program, and he clearly saw that depressions were inherent in the price system rather than in the economic system as such; yet to many of his opponents silver was not the issue at all—the issue was "Altgeld's policies of free riot, free spoils, and free injustice." It is quite likely that Bryan was defeated more because he reflected Altgeld's attack upon the executive and judicial power than because he sponsored silver, a single practical issue which did not give full expression to the reformation of *principles* demanded by Democratic and Populist liberals.

Bryan was right in demanding economic justice in the name of the millions harmed by a grossly inequitable banking and currency system, the appreciation of gold,[175] and the concentration of wealth in the

---

[174] Daniel C. Roper, *Fifty Years of Public Life*, p. 87.

[175] The decline in the gold price of silver is better expressed by saying that the

hands of a few, but he was wrong in method. He used free silver as a text for sermons on discontent designed to create a popular demand for reform via a revitalized Democracy, yet he failed signally to sponsor the more effective remedies he had proposed in his speech of August 16, 1893, in which he had at least hinted at a managed currency, a federal reserve system of banking, and the insurance of bank deposits. Free silver without further changes in the banking and currency systems such as occurred under Woodrow Wilson and Franklin D. Roosevelt would not have been a miraculous contrivance to relieve debtors of their burdens and restore the nation to prosperity. Indeed, inflation of the currency alone, by encouraging production, would have aggravated the problem of too many farmers already producing too much. Moreover, the mere anticipation of the relief of financial stringency by the influx of gold discovered in 1896 in Alaska, Australia, and South Africa worked against him, as did the trend toward a favorable balance of international trade.[176]

As an extreme nationalist and "little American," Bryan held Britain largely responsible for America's troubles and believed the unfounded story so widely promulgated in Populist and silver Democratic literature that an international gold conspiracy had bribed American congressmen to demonetize silver so that they could keep gold at a premium and use their wealth to buy up productive enterprise during times of depression.[177] His belief, said some, was on a par with that of thousands of less well educated men who thought "16 to 1" meant that their silver dollars would somehow multiply by sixteen when he was elected. As a young engineer named Herbert Hoover put it, Bryan's

---

gold dollar of 1873 had become a two-dollar dollar in 1893 than by saying that the silver dollar of 1873 had become a 50-cent dollar. Taking the gold dollar of 1873 as 100 in its purchasing power over wholesale goods, the 1893 dollar was a 140-cent dollar and that of 1896 a 164-cent dollar. Alonzo B. Hepburn, *History of the Currency of the United States*, p. 433; J. G. Hodgson (comp.), *Stabilization of Money*, pp. 56–64; Edwin Walter Kemmerer, *Money*, pp. 361–364, 368.

[176] Cecil Spring-Rice to Henry Adams, August 24, 1896, Gwynn, *Spring-Rice*, I, 209–210; Joseph Sibley to Bryan, November 11, 1897, Bryan Papers. The per capita circulation fell from $24.28 in 1894 to $21.10 in 1896. Four years later it had increased to $25.75 because of the new gold influx, which exceeded the rate of population growth. If the year 1899 is considered 100, the value of farm products rose to 106.4 in 1900 and to 133 in 1905. Theodore Saloutos and John D. Hicks, *Agricultural Discontent in the Middle West, 1900–1939*, p. 21. Generally good industrial times marked the years 1897 to 1907.

[177] Hofstadter, *Age of Reform*, pp. 74–76; Henry Nash Smith, *Virgin Land: The American West as Symbol and Myth*, esp. pp. 126–298.

16 to 1 was his "first shock at intellectual dishonesty as a foundation for economics." [178] There is no direct evidence that Bryan was intellectually dishonest, but his conclusions on the money question, his suspiciousness of Eastern, metropolitan, and British ideas and actions, and the reasons he adduced for the depressed status of the American farmer point to his having eschewed the treatises of scholarly economists and read instead such books as William A. Peffer's *The Farmer's Side*, Ignatius Donnelly's *Caesar's Column*, Hamlin Garland's *Main Travelled Roads* and essays such as "Under the Lion's Paw," James B. Weaver's *A Call to Action*, and especially Mrs. S. E. V. Emery's *Seven Financial Conspiracies Which Have Enslaved the American People*, all written by Middle Westerners and all published between 1888 and 1892.[179]

VIII

BRYAN was capable of concentrated study, and he had a retentive memory, but he was not a widely read man. He immersed himself in the Bible, the writings of Jefferson, and the history of the Democratic party. His speeches on the tariff and the income tax remain classic appeals to the intellect; those on the money question reveal imperfect knowledge of the business, mercantile, and financial world. Had he wished, he could have mastered areas in science, philosophy, literature, or language, but he was "too busy" to study them, and he had no training in the appreciation of the fine arts. But he had three qualities that marked him for leadership—love for people as individuals, power to interpret popular demands, and unique capacity to give voice to popular passion. He mirrored the mind of the average man, particularly of the provincial and isolationist farmers of the Middle West and South who had sought reform via Grange, Greenback party, Alliance, and Populism. Without greater intellectual insight than they, he also reflected the suspiciousness and hostility of the "producing classes" to forces and movements they feared because they did not understand. By nature he was more a preacher and exhorter than a politician and statesman; he was a missionary who sought to change men, a political

[178] *The Memoirs of Herbert Hoover: I. Years of Adventure, 1874-1920*, p. 28.

[179] Mrs. Emery's conspiracies included the "exception clause" of 1862, the National Bank Act of 1863, the retirement of the greenbacks, the Credit Strengthening Act of 1869, the refunding of the national debt in 1870, the "Crime of 1873," and the abolition of fractional paper money in 1875.

evangelist. He threw himself wholeheartedly and with consuming passion into "causes." He refused to dodge issues. He made a sentimental appeal because of his fight for the little fellow and because there was no such thing as an "off year" in his fight against special privilege. He appealed, too, because of his grace of person, unimpeachable moral character, courage, sincerity, honesty, forcible imagery in speech, pure and mellifluous language, and his professing of Christianity. Yet friend and foe alike agreed that he sought "yes" and "no" answers to complicated questions, that he deduced conclusions before his argument was complete yet held them sacred, that he was so sure of the correctness of his methods that he was not susceptible to argument. He was a purist without a redeeming vice except a voracious appetite. Above all he was profoundly Western and agrarian. No one owned or controlled him. More commonplace than original in conception, he reflected the thoughts that animated the millions and uncannily identified himself with the mass sense of need, with the common man's hopes and fears. He would curb the power of great corporations, divest the industrial system of the abuses of monopoly capitalism, sunder the proved alliance between big business and reactionary politicians, apportion the national income so that the agricultural community would no longer feel a sense of blighting frustration before the financial and political power in the East, and restore the moral and civic virtues he believed embodied in a simple rural economy.

In this sense Bryan could be called a liberal and a progressive. He resented predatory wealth, not wealth itself. In another sense, however, he was the rankest of conservatives, for he resented industrialism and urbanism and perpetuated the myth of Protestant-Yankee agrarianism. He sought to avoid for the American farmer the ills the Industrial Revolution visited upon the English and European peasant. To him, the man who tilled the soil or engaged in otherwise "honest" labor was the most important of America's producers of wealth. The family farm was the "Gibraltar of security" that furnished the nucleus of democratic and egalitarian society. Rather than noting their conflicts, he believed that the farmer, laborer, and small businessman were blood brothers in economic interest, and he insisted upon vigorous government action to restore not only political democracy but the equality of opportunity, or economic democracy, without which political democracy cannot truly exist. In the long run, his demand for an interventionist government was the major reason for objection to him on the part of the devotees of the laissez faire policy of the day.

When it is said that Bryan "spoke as if he had just had a spiritual visitation from Jefferson," [180] the import is upon his looking upon Jefferson as an eloquent exponent of democracy as the American political ideal. Both were sincere and enthusiastic believers in the rights of humanity. Both advocated the maximum of personal liberty, opposed the concentration of industry, disliked urban life, and eschewed the trappings of aristocracy and riches. Both confused liberty and equality and believed that the latter could be obtained simply by the destruction of special privilege.

As his followers looked upon him as a reincarnated Jefferson, so Bryan looked upon Jefferson's political principles as a code that was fundamental and unchangeable. Herein lay his tragedy, for in leading the third great revolt against plutocracy, or monopoly capitalism, he proved himself to be a political fundamentalist when the times called for change. He overlooked the fact that subsistence farming had shifted largely to commercial farming. The farmer whom he had apotheosized in his "Cross of Gold" speech and for whom he would rebuild Jefferson's Arcadia had made possible large-scale industry and the rise of the city, but he farmed for money rather than just to make a living; he was now a farmer-businessman who produced too much and was caught in the mechanism of distribution in a world market controlled by the law of supply and demand. By 1896 the value of industrial exports alone exceeded that of America's farms, and between a third and a half of America's people lived in cities—in sum, Bryan fell short in seeking largely to redress the grievances of the agrarian minority in an industrialized nation.

Like Jefferson's, Bryan's objectives were more important than the methods each used; [181] like Jefferson's, Bryan's influence was "on the spirit of the people and their attitude toward their institutions rather than on the formation of the institutions themselves." [182] Popular sovereignty had ended in the rule of the political machine. Bryan's cure was more popular sovereignty, enough to control the machine. Individualism had ended in the tyranny of the corporation. His cure was more individualism, enough to permit representative government to protect the rights of man rather than of money. Progress, he said, "is measured not so much by the discovery of new principles as by the

[180] Merrill D. Peterson, *The Jefferson Image in the American Mind*, p. 230.
[181] Carl Becker, "What Is Still Living in the Political Philosophy of Thomas Jefferson?" *American Historical Review*, 48 (July 1943), 691–706.
[182] David S. Muzzey, *Thomas Jefferson*, p. 70.

more perfect assimilation of old principles." Thus like Jefferson, Bryan believed that the greatness of America lay not in the strength of government but in the government's release of the individual talents and energies of its people, and in the right of the ability of the people to govern themselves.[183] As has been suggested, however, he stood the Jefferson of the Kentucky Resolutions and the Jackson of the Maysville Road veto and hard money "on their heads" by shaking his party clear of its fear of the national government and advocating that it become interventionist, that it serve the people rather than merely govern them.[184]

Although only thirty-six years old in 1896, Bryan had captured the leadership of a great political party. He found it demoralized; he reorganized it and gave it new life. He drew heretofore incoherent reform forces into a national progressive movement. He infused these forces with a new spirit, a consciousness of power, and a hope of victory to challenge the control of the businessman and his political henchman who had ruled the country since the Civil War. In defending the tenets of a frontier already living on borrowed time he provoked a social revolt so savage that it appeared to threaten a civil war over a new balance of class power. He failed because he ran on a new issue, and no new party in America ever succeeded in winning the Presidency in its first campaign. The dynamics of the era gave much greater leverage to the directors of corporations than to individual entrepreneurs. Rather than use the ballot box to demand paternalism or interventionism, the people decided to retain laissez faire. Rather than create a welfare state in which the government would redistribute the national wealth on an equitable basis, the voters determined to keep the Hamiltonian system as better fitted to an industrial rather than agricultural economy.

Though defeated, Bryan's crusade for social justice was not wasted. The adoption of income and inheritance taxes, abolition of government by injunction, approval of the labor boycott, sharp reduction in the tariff, strict control of banks, railroads, and industrial corporations attempting or exercising monopoly control, changes in the currency and banking system that benefited the agrarian community, sweeping

[183] Merrill D. Peterson, "Thomas Jefferson and the National Purpose," *Proceedings of the American Philosophical Society*, 105 (December 1961), 517.

[184] Carl N. Degler, *Out of Our Past: The Forces That Shaped Modern America*, pp. 336–337.

changes in the order and procedure of the House of Representatives, the direct election of senators, direct primaries and direct legislation, and modifications of the Supreme Court's powers were all accomplished within a generation of 1896. All that was reasonable in Bryanism—and in Populism—was eventually granted.

The significance of the election of 1896 lay not in the temporary defeat of the New Democracy but in the breaking of the backbone of the agrarian resurgence. Tangential effects included the death of the labor-Populist alliance and the withdrawal of organized labor from political action for more than a decade. So long as the New England, Middle Atlantic, Central, and North Central sections united in supporting the Republican party, they would control the electoral college and thereby the Presidency. The influence of the small farmers and pioneers of the West and South, which had elected Jefferson and Jackson, would henceforth pale before the combined power of the more prosperous rural interests and the commercial and industrial interests of the town and city. America's farmers and wage workers would receive little help from government until they formed strong self-interest blocs in Congress and forced recognition of their demands. Thomas E. Watson was one of the few perceptive men who tasted the irony of Bryan's phrase "The First Battle," for the election of 1896 was the last battle, the "last aggressive stand of agrarian provincialism against capitalist industrialism." [185] Henceforth the business-minded farmer sought government aid in the form of parity, export debentures, equalization fees, and crop allotments rather than by repeating Jeffersonian rhetoric.

In his statement of November 6 to the bimetallists of the United States, Bryan revealed himself still insufficiently aware of the impact upon the country of the agricultural, commercial, and industrial revolutions of the nineteenth century. He retained his faith in the eventual righting of their wrongs by "the people." Bimetallism had been overcome, not vanquished, by small pluralities and was now stronger than ever. Let the roll call be sounded for the next engagement! Let all bimetallists renew their allegiance to the cause! Right shall yet triumph! Agitation of the truth must result in the remedying of abuses! The election meant that the people wanted to continue the experiment of the gold standard for four years more—but as sovereigns they could make a change in 1900. To his followers nothing was more certain than that he would run again in 1900. "The fight has just begun. We have

[185] Woodward, *Watson*, p. 330.

enlisted for the war. We look for you to blaze the way," Josephus Daniels wired him, and John Clark Ridpath noted that Jefferson marked the first stage of historic Democracy, Jackson the second, and Bryan the third.[186]

[186] Daniels to Bryan, telegram, November 4, 1896, Bryan Papers; John Clark Ridpath, "Three Epochs of Democracy and Three Men," *The Arena,* 19 (May 1898), 543–563.

CHAPTER 10

Cuba Libre and America's Mission

I

"IF I COULD only feel that the defeat was a personal one," Bryan wrote William V. Allen on November 9, 1896, "it would be very easy to find someone else to carry out our ideas, but if the Republicans can frighten the people against our ideas, no matter who honestly stands for them, it is going to be a more difficult matter, and yet in the end we must triumph." [1] A week later, in Denver, he launched his campaign for 1900, saying, "Those who fought in the battle will continue in the ranks until bimetallism is restored." [2]

Upon his return from Denver, Bryan collected photographs of Richard Parks Bland, James B. Weaver, and Henry M. Teller, to whom he dedicated his book *The First Battle*, and of many other silver leaders.[3] The prime objectives of his work, which is a hurried compilation of speeches and documents rather than a narrative, were to thank and praise those who had aided him, to provoke continued interest and work in behalf of fusion and free silver for the campaign of 1900, and to leave at least a partial record of the official documents and addresses delivered in the battle of the standards that would prove useful to campaign workers if not to posterity.[4] As revealed subsequently, the venture was also undertaken to raise some money for the silver cause.

Issued early in 1897, *The First Battle* sold at the rate of a thousand copies a day for the first two months of 1897, to a total of about two hundred thousand copies. Bryan received $35,643.60 for sales through August 31, 1897. When Marion Butler and William V. Allen refused to serve on a nonpartisan commission that would distribute half this

---

[1] Letter of November 9, 1896, William Jennings Bryan Papers.

[2] Omaha *World-Herald*, November 16, 1896.

[3] Watson refused the use of his photograph, biography, and speeches, saying he had given up politics and would not let it be thought that he looked forward to any political future. Letters to Bryan of November 25, December 9, 1896, Bryan Papers.

[4] William J. Bryan, *The First Battle*, pp. 621–629.

sum, he gave the money directly to the silver organizations in proportion to votes cast for him in the election.[5]

The First Battle is a history of the silver movement from 1889 through the campaign of 1896. Mark Sullivan labeled it "a weird hodgepodge of autobiography, Bryanesque philosophy, and propaganda—but nevertheless with attractions for those who can see reality in unconventional forms." [6] Bryan emphasized political mechanics too much. Although he said he was "fully aware of the magnitude of the issues involved," he paid too little attention to the profound social implications of the campaign.[7] While it does not do justice to the Populists it remains the best history of the currency movement of the period, and it is the fullest repository of Bryan's campaign speeches.

A silver Republican-Democratic bloc in Congress rejected President William McKinley's request for support for a bill authorizing the sending of delegates to the international monetary conference of 1897. Moreton Frewen's writing Bryan that "All eyes are turned on you" revealed that English as well as American hopes for bimetallism rested upon him rather than upon McKinley. Bryan replied that the Republicans' pledge on international bimetallism was made to deceive the voters and that their inability to implement it strengthened the Democratic cause. One wonders whether their success would not have given his aspirations a jolt. Nevertheless, McKinley promised Cleveland at his inauguration that he would stand fast against silver.[8] Because he needed gold Democratic support in the Senate, McKinley originally chose Bourke Cockran his Secretary of the Treasury. Cockran declined, saying that his acceptance would throw suspicion on the motives of gold Democrats, and advised him to run a responsible government that

[5] Bryan to Teller, March 22, 1897, Henry Moore Teller Papers.

[6] Mark Sullivan, *Our Times: The United States, 1900–1925,* I, 304–305.

[7] Bryan, *First Battle,* pp. 625–626; James A. Barnes, "Myths of the Bryan Campaign," *Mississippi Valley Historical Review,* 34 (December 1947), 386.

[8] Frewen kept Bryan informed of the hopes of bimetallists in the British Empire as well as those of Europe. See Altgeld to Frewen, February 18, May 20, 1897, James K. Jones to Frewen, February 23, 1897, Moreton Frewen Papers; Frewen to Bryan, August 24, October 22, November 4, 1897, Bryan Papers. McKinley supported gold even though he knew that Cleveland had used the income from his bond sales to meet ordinary government deficiencies. Frank A. Vanderlip to George B. Cortelyou, November 23, 1897, William McKinley Papers; *American Review of Reviews,* 15 (January 1897), 15; Denis Tilden Lynch, *Grover Cleveland: A Man Four Square,* p. 493; Robert McElroy, *Grover Cleveland, the Man and Statesman,* II, 254.

could be judged by its own fruits. McKinley then chose Lyman J. Gage, a gold Democrat Chicago banker.[9]

Bryan had little use for the McKinley administration. To the complaint of scarcity of money and credit McKinley responded by reaffirming the gold standard. To agrarian protests at the high cost of industrial products in relation to the price of grains he raised the protective schedules to new heights, and he cleared the way for an epoch of gigantic industrial and financial consolidations that made competition ever more difficult for the small entrepreneur. His Attorney General was disinclined to assail the trusts, which boomed to a climax in 1901, while Mark Hanna frankly asserted that the Sherman Anti-Trust Act was unwise and the Interstate Commerce Commission a nuisance.[10] Labor's demands for collective bargaining, an eight-hour day, a living wage, and the end of injunctions ran up against a Supreme Court and Constitution proclaimed sacred and unchangeable; deaf ears were turned to all demands that nominations and elections be made more directly responsible to the popular will; and civil service reform took a step backwards.

Instead of calling for free raw materials and an income tax, Bryan urged the speedy passage of the Dingley tariff bill in the hope that McKinley would fall into a hole. His supporters in the House obeyed. Nelson W. Aldrich, William B. Allison, O. H. Platt, and John C. Spooner, the "Big Four" who ran the Senate for the next decade, permitted 872 amendments and also had their way with the Conference Committee. McKinley's signing of the bill, on July 24, 1897, raised the general duty level from 47 to 57 per cent. Bryan's objective of embarrassing McKinley had backfired. However, because the following decade was relatively prosperous the tariff ceased to be a lively public issue.

II

As THOUGH he had learned nothing from his defeat in 1896, Bryan spent most of 1897 speaking on bimetallism. However, knowing that reforms that fail in Congress may succeed by state action, he addressed

[9] Whitelaw Reid to William McKinley, December 5, 1896, McKinley Papers; Charles G. Dawes, *A Journal of the McKinley Years, 1893–1913*, pp. 112–114.

[10] Matthew Josephson, *The President Makers: The Culture of Politics and Leadership in an Age of Enlightenment, 1896–1919*, p. 617.

various state legislatures on the need of railroad regulation, trust control, direct elections, the prohibition of contributions by corporations to campaign funds, and the reform of state constitutions along progressive lines. He also made his last appearance as a member of the bar, as an unpaid associate counsel before the United States Supreme Court in the famous Nebraska maximum rate case, *Smyth* v. *Ames* (171 U.S. 163). Bryan argued that reproduction costs, not original investment, should be the basis of rate-making. Although it decided against him, the court for the first time proposed a method of appraising the property of public utilities.[11]

Many gold Democrats looked upon the Dingley tariff as an act of treachery and became increasingly irritated with the McKinley administration, yet they had less use than ever for Bryan. Cleveland spoke of Bryan's "bogus Democracy" and cheered plans to oust Bryanites from control of the party in the various states. The gold Democratic upsurge, which Bryan labeled the "reorganizer movement," soon spread to all important cities and states. To smooth over the discordant Democratic elements should have been his great task; instead he took the extreme position of making the Chicago platform the sole test of faith, saying, "There is no room for two Republican parties in this country. The gold Democrats cannot come back to the party and run it on Republican ideas. They left because of the platform, called me a Populist long before the Chicago convention, and unless they have changed their views must stay with the Republicans. The Democratic party is committed to silver, and will continue to fight for it." [12]

Those who opposed him learned that Bryan would go to great lengths to overcome them. Such was the case in his fight against William F. Harrity of Pennsylvania, the chairman of the Democratic National Committee from 1892 to 1896, who had not supported him in the campaign. The contest came to have immense proportions and national significance, and it occupies considerable space in Bryan's personal papers.[13] In the end, although the National Committee would not meet until January 1900, Harrity was thrown out in August 1897,

[11] James Hogg to Bryan, March 20, 1897, Bryan Papers; Omaha *World-Herald*, April 15, 1897; Arthur Mullen, *Western Democrat*, pp. 92–94.

[12] Omaha *World-Herald*, November 17, 1897; William Jennings Bryan, "Has the Election Settled the Money Question?" *North American Review*, 163 (December 1896), 703–710.

[13] See, for example, letters to Bryan from Chauncey F. Black, April 2, 1897, W. H. Thompson, April 29, 1897, Joseph Sibley, May 4, 1897, James Kerr, May 13, 1897, and C. S. Thomas, May 18, 1897, Bryan Papers.

when his state committee declared his post vacant. Rather than leaving the door open for gold Democrats to return, as he often said, Bryan opened it to kick them out, and his fight against Harrity appeared to be one of revenge.

Another who learned that only the faithful and pure in heart could remain in the ranks was Boss Richard Croker. When he invited "Bryant," as he always called Bryan, to speak before Tammany but to avoid the money question, Bryan accepted on condition that he not be restricted. He would not be a guest where the Chicago platform was denied a hearing; he did not want the New York vote Croker promised if it meant soft-pedaling silver. The Boss got the point when Bryan concluded that "Tammany needs the Democracy of the nation as much as the national party needs Tammany, and Tammany should recognize that fact." [14]

Bryan kicked off the Nebraska primaries of 1897 on the theme of fusion and then was off again "to preach the gospel to every creature" in a countrywide stumping tour on the topics of bimetallism, the encroachment of the trusts and money power on the rights of the people, and the evils of a protective tariff and of government by injunction. He also took part in a National Irrigation Congress held in Lincoln, repeating a thought he frequently expressed in Western states, that the terms and conditions under which water was furnished should not be left to large corporations.[15]

As in former years, three anti-Republican conventions met simultaneously in Lincoln, with three thousand Democrats, Populists, and silver Republicans soon in entire accord. Bryan and William V. Allen moved from convention to convention in the interest of silver. By prearrangement, the third party agreed to the candidate selected by the other two, and Bryan was presented a fusion victory. Bryan then entered other states. For a full week in Ohio he spoke against Hanna for senator, strongly attacking him and his "connections." Hanna squeaked

---

[14] Bryan to Willis J. Abbot, March 16, 1897, *ibid.;* Willis J. Abbot, *Watching the World Go By*, pp. 204–205. At the New York state convention, a platform presumably written by Hill leaned toward free silver and proved acceptable to the gold men until McClellan objected. Although Hill characterized his demand for a gold plank "not only inopportune but very dangerous," McClellan won. Hill made the best of the situation and henceforth helped lead the Democracy "from the free silver heresy." (Harold C. Syrett [ed.], *The Gentleman and the Tiger: The Autobiography of George Brinton McClellan, Jr.,* pp. 116–117.)

[15] Omaha *World-Herald*, October 1, 1897; *American Review of Reviews*, 14 (October 1897), 130.

by with a majority of one vote which, according to General A. J. Warner, he was able to obtain "only by shameless corruption." [16] Strangely enough, he gave only tacit support to Henry George, the choice of the Bryan Democrats and of other progressive groups, in New York City's sizzling mayoralty contest, and the Democratic convention fell completely under Croker's control and named a nonentity, Judge Robert Van Wyck, for mayor. Bryan thereupon wished George godspeed in putting Croker in the penitentiary, but George died before the election. When Van Wyck won, Tammany snake dancers sang, "Well! Well! Well! Reform has gone to hell!" Croker was the Master of Manhattan. Yet all the Democratic candidates were careful to assure Bryan of their personal loyalty, and Croker knew exactly where he stood. [17]

While he said he was satisfied with the elections, which were held only in twelve states and turned largely upon whether improvement in the nation's economic condition would continue, Bryan's contention that the electorate was unhappy with Republican rule is difficult to uphold, even though the National Democrats polled such a small vote that he was left in practically undisputed sway in Democratic councils. He remained strong in the South and West but weaker than ever in the East; yet he refused to drop any of the planks of the Chicago platform or to admit new ones. Of matters not covered in that platform, popular interest centered upon the initiative and referendum and the government ownership of railroads and of other natural monopolies. He was often told that the rapidly growing demand for these issues doomed any candidate in 1900 who did not espouse them. Could he not add them to his platform without belittling silver? He replied that these "extrinsic" issues should not be pushed "at this time." Events might force a change in emphasis or issues, but he preferred to fight for reforms that could be obtained "now," while the people were ready to support them, rather than admit the issues of 1896 "wrong." [18] He constantly denied that any other

[16] A. J. Warner to Moreton Frewen, January 16, 1898, Frewen Papers.

[17] Frank Campbell to Bryan, October 4, 1897, George Fred Williams to Bryan, November 10, 1897, Willis J. Abbot to Bryan, November 20, 1897, Bryan Papers; Alfred Henry Lewis, *Richard Croker* (New York, 1901), pp. 341–343; Lothrop Stoddard, *Master of Manhattan: The Life of Richard Croker*, pp. 178–186; Syrett, *Gentleman and the Tiger*, p. 156.

[18] Willis J. Abbot to Bryan, July 15, September 2, 1897, Altgeld to Bryan, September 20, 1897, Frederick Upham Adams to Bryan, November 12, 1897, George F. Washburn to Bryan, January 11, 1898, Bryan Papers; Bryan to F. U. Adams, November 27, 1897, Omaha *World-Herald*, March 23, 1899.

issue would seriously contend with silver for public favor in 1900. There were more people killed in the United States by the gold standard each year than there were Cubans killed by Spaniards, he declared late in the year. Yet the Cuban issue gradually forced itself upon him. "I would not want you to commit me publicly until I have time to discuss the entire situation with you," he wrote Senator Allen with reference to providing arms for the Cubans prior to the recognition of their belligerency,[19] and so long as the Senate resolution on belligerency lay dormant in the House he concentrated on free silver.

In a comprehensive Jackson Day address in Chicago on January 8, 1898 Bryan reiterated his faith in silver, excoriated the money changers, and asserted that "Since the election [of 1896] . . . events in rapid succession have been vindicating the position taken by the bimetallic forces. . . . The Republicans, too, intoxicated by success, have been disclosing their schemes, which were carefully concealed during the contest. We may, therefore, expect continuous accessions to our ranks. . . ."[20] The Republicans' "schemes" were the Dingley tariff and Lyman J. Gage's new currency reform plan, which Bryan found an undisguised effort to retire the greenbacks and other government paper money by the issue of national bank notes and the fastening of the hated national banking system on the American people.

In response to his call the leaders of the reform parties agreed to maintain a solid fusion front in 1898, thereby raising Bryan's popularity to a new high. The Democratic masses still enthusiastically endorsed him. Organized labor, strongly opposed to Gage's currency plan, leaned more heavily toward him.[21] Irked by McKinley's "treason" in raising the tariff, Bourke Cockran spoke for many gold Democrats when he said that no conspicuous supporter had abandoned Bryan or suggested that his principles be changed, whereas McKinley was losing his hold upon public esteem.[22]

When Republicans and gold Democrats counseled McKinley to make sound money the rallying cry for 1900 and to ensure his success by cementing the Republican–gold Democratic association of 1896,

[19] Undated letter, Henry Steele Commager Papers.

[20] Omaha *World-Herald*, January 9, 1898.

[21] Bryan to Gompers, January 24, 1898, Rowland Hill Harvey, *Samuel Gompers*, p. 87; Gompers to Bryan, January 28, 1898, Bryan Papers; copies of a heated Gompers-Gage correspondence in the McKinley Papers and in the *National Bimetallist*, January 15, 1898.

[22] Letter to Frewen, January 25, 1898, Frewen Papers.

Bryan retorted that reform could come only through the continued cooperation of the reform parties and listed nine items on which they held common beliefs. They unalterably opposed gold monometallism and favored the immediate restoration of bimetallism at a ratio of 16 to 1 by independent action. They opposed the retirement of the greenbacks, the issue of paper money by national banks, the issue of interest-bearing bonds in time of peace, trusts, and government by injunction. They favored an income tax and the settlement of labor disputes by arbitration. These issues had been submitted to the people in 1896 but had not been settled, "and will not be settled until they are settled right." Yet he insisted that until the right of the people to legislate on the money question was secured the discussion of other questions availed nothing.[23]

On February 15 the leaders of the three reform parties issued a call for a renewed charge that would sweep them to victory in 1900. The Democrats, Populists, silver Republicans, and National Silverites in the Congress heartily endorsed the call. A few hours later came the news that the *Maine* had been sunk in Havana harbor.

III

THE CUBAN crisis forced Bryan to shift his attention from domestic reforms to foreign affairs. Opposed in principle to war, yet deeply moved by Cuba's trials, Bryan, like McKinley, demanded discretion while the sinking of the *Maine* was being investigated and the avoidance of haste while international questions were being deliberated. But there was a strong war party in Congress that resented his and McKinley's restraining hands. Hearst printed the sort of sensational news that earns money; the New York *World* and other newspapers rapidly succumbed to yellow journalism; and the Cuban junta in New York fanned the flames of intervention.

Meantime the fight over the money question raged unabated. If war came, Secretary Gage wanted to issue gold bonds. Cleveland spurred the gold Democrats to support Gage while Bryan insisted that no emergency, however great, should force the government to deal with Wall Street syndicates. He deplored the fact that the income tax had been declared unconstitutional, thereby making it necessary to place tax burdens upon those least able to bear them while leaving

[23] Omaha *World-Herald*, February 5, 14, 1898; M. E. Ingalls to McKinley, January 11, 1898, A. B. Farquar to McKinley, February 12, 1898, McKinley Papers.

untouched the swollen incomes of the rich and creating millionaires out of war. All the vigorous attempts by the silverites to defeat Gage failed, but it was not until mid-June, with the war six weeks old, that the Congress passed his $400,000,000 gold bond issue bill. The $200,-000,000 in bonds offered at popular loan was promptly oversubscribed, and it was clear that the national emergency could not be used as a device for "doing something for silver," [24] yet Bryan continued to insist that the silver issue would be paramount in 1900. His refusal to discuss Cuba until a report was made on the *Maine* confounded Republican editors, for they had expected him to criticize McKinley, not to side with him. As for Hanna, who with McKinley was drifting toward intervention, Bryan continued anathema. To a group of senators gathered in the Marble Room he said, "Look out for Mr. Bryan. Everything that goes wrong'll be in the Democratic platform in 1900. You can be damn sure of that!" "But," asked Henry Cabot Lodge, "will not the Democrats hesitate before offering Mr. Bryan the nomination?" "Hesitate," Hanna growled. "Does a dog hesitate for a marriage license?" [25]

Late in February Bryan asked an excited people to stand behind McKinley's efforts to avoid war. But on March 9 he approved of a defense appropriation, saying that it would "show the world that Congress and the American people, without regard to political differences, are ready to support the Administration in any action necessary for the protection of the honor and welfare of the nation." Convinced that the United States must defend Cuba, he aroused tremendous enthusiasm on lecture platforms by waving a small American flag in his right hand and a Cuban flag in his left. Editors who opposed him politically now paid tribute to his qualities as a patriot. When it came to the defense of America there was for him no "enemy's country." He was no longer Bryan of Nebraska but Bryan of America. However, party lines shattered: silver Republicans like Teller supported his going to war; gold Democrats like Cleveland, Cockran, E. L. Godkin, and Carl Schurz, and the pacifist Populist, Thomas E. Watson, opposed

[24] Omaha *World-Herald*, April 5–June 11, 1898. Senator Richard Pettigrew, for one, was stirring his colleagues to insurgency. "The island [of Cuba] would not be worth anything to us unless it was sunk for 24 hours to get rid of its present population, but I want a war with Spain, because I believe it will put us on a silver basis," he said (Arthur W. Dunn, *From Harrison to Harding: A Personal Narrative, Covering a Third of a Century, 1888–1921*, I, 231–232).

[25] Thomas Beer, *Mauve Decade*, p. 552.

war; and the stalwart Republican, Andrew Carnegie, sided with him in an uneasy yoke.

While McKinley sought by diplomatic discussions with Spain to obtain peace for Cuba, Bryan stated that "Humanity demands that we shall act." "War is a terrible thing, and cannot be defended except as a means to an end," he declared, but war was the only means left when counsel and persuasion failed and reason and diplomacy proved of no avail. However, Democrats as well as Republicans had voted for the war appropriations, and the Republicans must not revive the issues of the Civil War and use them for political purposes, he said, revealing a terrifying naïveté in believing that the Republicans, at his request, would not seek to make political capital out of the war.[26]

McKinley knew that his failure to rise to the expectations of the people might lead to a war for Cuban liberty that would be the crown of thorns with which the free silver Democrats and Populists would cap him in the fall elections. With that sign held aloft and proclaimed by magnetic orators like Bryan they would sweep the country like a cyclone. McKinley was committed to peace, but if he opposed war his political power would be crushed. Why not be the hero of a popular war?

A careful reading of McKinley's war message would have showed Bryan that McKinley had not exhausted all means to prevent war. Spain had either yielded to every demand made or agreed to arbitrate, and McKinley in effect suppressed a crucial message of April 5 from our minister to Spain which announced Spain's capitulation. A nation lashed to fury over the de Lome letter and the *Maine* and to frenzy beyond logic over "Cuba Libre" by the yellow press gave his request that Spain's capitulation be given "just and careful attention" no attention at all, and Bryan let himself be swept away with the rest.[27] After four days of debate Congress passed a resolution tantamount to a declaration of war and accepted the self-denying Teller amendment —the United States disclaimed any intention to annex Cuba. McKinley then issued an ultimatum which Spain must answer in three days. On April 23, 1898, when he deemed the Spanish reply unsatisfactory, he issued a call for 125,000 volunteers, of which Nebraska would furnish 2114. On April 25 Congress declared war.

[26] Omaha *World-Herald*, March 31, 1898; Sam Hanna Acheson, *Joe Bailey, the Last Democrat*, pp. 97–100.

[27] Letters of congratulation to McKinley on his war message outnumber those of criticism by more than nine to one. Letters between April 11 and 18, 1898, McKinley Papers.

IV

BRYAN's offering of his services, on April 25,[28] must have presented McKinley as much trouble as Roosevelt did to Wilson during the First World War. It was not until May 7 that he acknowledged Bryan's offer, and then only to ask for what branch of service Bryan deemed himself best qualified.[29]

Meantime a host of arguments for his not going to war fell upon Bryan. Senator James K. Jones feared that the war might provide a military hero to take Bryan's place as party leader and raise new issues which would lessen public interest in the old ones.[30] His leadership could not be duplicated:[31] there were many generals to lead the army but only one supreme commander upon whom the defenders of the ancient faith could unite in 1900.[32] McKinley would enjoy getting him out of the country and exposing him to Spanish bullets and the great danger of yellow fever.[33] Both Democratic and Populist congressional leaders objected to his enlisting.[34] No one doubted his devotion and loyalty; there was no need to prove himself.[35] But Bryan was determined to serve and leaned toward those who urged him to accept a state regiment.[36]

The First and Second Nebraska regiments were mustered into service on May 12. On May 16 the First left Lincoln for Manila. On May 19 the Second left for training camp and Bryan enlisted as a private in the Nebraska National Guard for a three-year term "unless sooner discharged by proper authority." On May 20 Governor Holcomb authorized the recruiting of twelve companies for the Third Regiment, of which it was understood that Bryan would be elected colonel. When the War Department ordered companies in the field under the first call for volunteers to increase their enlistment, a plan that would make

[28] William Jennings Bryan and Mary Baird Bryan, *The Memoirs of William Jennings Bryan*, p. 119.

[29] McKinley to Bryan, May 7, 1898, McKinley Papers.

[30] James K. Jones to Bryan, May 11, 1898, Bryan Papers.

[31] Thomas C. McClellan to J. K. Jones, May 24, 1896, *ibid.*

[32] William V. Allen to Bryan, May 18, 1896, Charles S. Thomas to Bryan, May 18, 1898, *ibid.*

[33] General Joseph Wheeler to Bryan, May 14, 1898, *ibid.*

[34] Representative W. L. Greene to Bryan, May 18, 1898, Representative J. D. Botkin to Bryan, May 18, 1898, *ibid.*

[35] William S. Jennings to Bryan, May 26, 1898, *ibid.*

[36] Joseph Sibley to Bryan, May 16, 1898, *ibid.;* Richard L. Metcalfe (comp.), *The Real Bryan*, pp. 21–22.

a third Nebraska regiment unnecessary, General Joseph Wheeler and Governor Silas A. Holcomb objected, and Governor Lon V. Stephens jumped into the breach by offering Bryan command of a Missouri regiment, a tender Bryan declined with thanks, saying he owed his service to Nebraska. Thereupon Secretary of War Russell A. Alger disregarded the new order and accepted the entire regiment.[37]

On June 11 Bryan and his staff moved to Fort Omaha, on the northern outskirts of Omaha. The Republicans were critical. Bryan's physical endurance and love of fight had been proved in the campaign of 1896. Now, his last tour in behalf of bimetallism having fallen flat, he was wise to trim his sails to the changing breeze and go to war, particularly since a great deal of military ardor should mark the campaign of 1900 and the American people were never hostile to military heroes as Presidents. His supporters retorted that 6,500,000 men had expressed belief in his ability to be commander-in-chief of all the nation's armed forces. Critics might call his command the "Silver Legion" or "Willie's Wonders" if they liked, but they should keep quiet at least until he made mistakes.

The charge has often been made that McKinley deliberately barred Bryan from engaging the Spaniards so that he could gain no glory that would help him politically.[38] Bryan really did not care where he was sent and would brook no interference in his behalf. "If the War Department asks my wishes I expect to leave matter entirely with my superior officers and go wherever they see fit to send me," he told Senator Allen.[39] The Republicans had scored only one victory over him thus far: so long as he was in uniform he could not criticize them. When Willis J. Abbot asked him to comment on some matter for the New York *Journal,* he wired: "I would not feel justified in expressing an opinion unless the Government was about to make an important departure in its general policy." [40]

Soon afterwards there occurred an important departure that caused Bryan to deliver a long speech on "Imperialism" in which he set forth the policies that should be followed in foreign affairs. He prayed for the day promised in Holy Writ when swords would be beaten into

[37] Omaha *World-Herald,* May 21, 24, 28, 29, June 2–5, 1898; Lon V. Stephens to Bryan, May 31, 1898, Bryan to Lon V. Stephens, May 31, 1898, Bryan Papers.
[38] See Abbot, *Watching the World Go By,* p. 225; Josephus Daniels, *Editor in Politics,* p. 279; Walter Millis, *The Martial Spirit,* p. 219.
[39] Telegram, June 6, 1898, Bryan Papers.
[40] Telegrams, Abbot to Bryan, May 20, 1898, Bryan to Abbot, May 21, 1898, *ibid.*

plowshares, but he believed that the United States had exhausted diplomacy in its efforts to secure a peaceable solution of the Cuban question and had taken up arms only when compelled to choose between war and a vile acquiescence in cruelties which were a disgrace to barbarism. History would vindicate America's position, but he demanded that the principles involved in the inauguration of the war be observed in its prosecution and conclusion. It would be joining hypocrisy to greed if a contest for the sake of humanity degenerated into a war of conquest. Was our national character so weak that we could not withstand the temptation to appropriate the first piece of land that came within our reach? Our guns had destroyed the Spanish fleet at Manila; could they destroy the self-evident truth that government derives its just powers from the consent of the governed and not from superior force? Should we abandon a just resistance to European encroachment on the Western Hemisphere in order to mingle in the controversies of Europe and Asia? Others might succumb to the psychology of "National Destiny"—a phrase synonymous with land-covetousness—but he believed that the people would insist upon good faith in the making of peace. Others might dream of the splendors of a heterogeneous empire around the globe; he would remain content to bring enduring happiness to a homogeneous people consecrated to the purpose of maintaining a free and democratic government.[41]

Bryan had broached a new issue, one that might overshadow all others in 1900. He was supported by many newspapers in the East that had opposed him in 1896, and he received more support from the East, the headquarters of the anti-imperialist movement, than from the West. However, his plan to withdraw from the volunteers whenever they were ordered to extend the possessions of the United States beyond its boundaries was criticized as an early announcement of "anti-imperialism" as an issue upon which he would campaign in 1900.

While doubt existed as to Bryan's objectives, none existed about Republican intentions to obtain political advantages from aggrandizement. Henry Cabot Lodge, major exponent of the "large policy," wrote Theodore Roosevelt ten days after Bryan's speech: "[Secretary of State] Day tells me . . . [that] the feeling of the country is overwhelming against giving the Philippines back to Spain. . . . Bryan has announced that he is against colonization. . . . We shall sweep the country on that issue in my judgment. Republican conventions are all declaring that where the flag once goes up it must never come

[41] The speech was printed in all major newspapers on June 15, 1898.

down." [42] Lodge was right. The people were thrilled with visions of a New Destiny. Of no avail were Bryan's warnings that the annexation of Hawaii would be the precursor of a period of imperialism involving huge standing armies, constant turmoil, and political corruption. Few Democrats opposed the Hawaiian joint resolution, which McKinley signed on July 7. The indefatigable "jingo bacillus" having completed its work, Congress adjourned and left McKinley uninterrupted in running the "splendid little war."

On July 13 the Third was mustered in, Bryan was commissioned, and the regiment passed in review before Governor Holcomb. Bryan was well pleased with what had been accomplished in just fourteen working days. On July 18 the Third entrained for Camp Cuba Libre, along the St. Johns River in a heavily wooded area five miles north of Jacksonville, Florida, and set up its floorless tents. The thermometer averaged 110 degrees and the sulphurous water was hardly fit to drink, but there was at first no typhoid fever. Flies, mosquitoes, spiders, lizards, scorpions, centipedes, and snakes made life miserable, and the first big wind promised to blow away the tents, for the stakes would not hold in the sandy soil.

Bryan listened to his officers and then acted on his own best judgment in reaching command decisions. No regiment possessed a colonel with greater personal regard for the welfare of each man. He inspected quarters frequently, tested the quality of the food at each mess, enforced sanitary regulations, spent long hours in individual counseling, and helped manage two Y.M.C.A. tents. Letters of appreciation came from even such bitter political enemies as Albert Watkins, who had a son in the Third. Bryan asked for little for himself. He shared his tent with Dan Bride, who had attached himself to the Bryan family since 1891, slept on a regulation cot, and used a rough wooden table as a desk in the small white tent—the "White House"—that served as his office. He cared nothing for military etiquette, blithely cut red tape, and could see no difference between officer and enlisted man. The man inside the uniform, not the uniform, was the important thing. As a soldier he was thus a flat failure and a grand success. Pitifully awkward in the field, none matched his perseverance in championing the privileges of his men. Compared with his lieutenant

[42] Letter of May 24, 1898, in Henry Cabot Lodge, *Selections from the Correspondence of Theodore Roosevelt and Henry Cabot Lodge, 1884–1918*, I, 313. See also Roosevelt to Lodge, May 25, and Lodge to Roosevelt, May 31, 1898, *ibid.*, I, 300–302.

colonel, Victor Vifquain, a fifty-five-year-old hero of the Civil War, he was sloppy. Rather than learning the commands from the manual he read them from slips of paper.[43] As an administrator, however, he made his camp a model followed by others. He refused to enter the social life of the military, avoided if he could gatherings where liquor was served, remained in camp more than his men, and complained privately, in letters to his wife. He was justifiably proud of the health of his regiment. "We have been here two weeks and not a case of serious illness yet. If *no one* out of 1,300 is seriously ill you need not fear for me—the most robust of them all," he wrote her on August 7. And he lived up to his declaration that politics was adjourned for the duration. Nearly every one of his officers was a Republican, but no word ever indicated that he thought any less of them. He declined to be named for governor of Nebraska, turned deaf ears to requests for advice on the writing of state platforms even though support for his nomination in 1900 was offered as bait, and rejected invitations to deliver political speeches.[44]

V

ON AUGUST 7, after Spain agreed to discuss peace terms, Bryan wrote his wife he had "no idea what they will do with us." On August 13 Dewey took Manila, which surrendered *after* the peace protocol was signed, and McKinley decided to muster out between 75,000 and 100,000 volunteers. Bryan had so many doubts as to what to do that he urged Mrs. Bryan to come to Florida for a consultation. He enclosed a message for Governor Holcomb: "I do not want him to ask to have us sent to Cuba nor do I want him to ask to have us mustered out. I prefer to leave the matter *entirely in the hands of the war department.* Read this part of the letter to Governor Holcomb and then destroy this letter." [45] He had 21 men in the hospital and 30 sick in

[43] Albert Watkins, Jr., "Bryan as a Soldier," Omaha *World-Herald,* September 10, 1900. When the *Army and Navy Journal* printed an exchange to the effect that discipline was "free and easy" in the Third, that, for instance, the corporal of the guard would remove his pipe from his mouth and say "Hello, Billy," when Bryan passed, Nebraska's Adjutant General P. H. Barry wrote the *Journal* that the statements were "entirely false" and that the *Journal* was prejudiced against Bryan. *Army and Navy Journal,* July 30, August 13, 1898.

[44] Omaha *World-Herald,* July 23, August 2, 7, 23, 1898; telegrams, Bryan to O. V. Humphrey, August 1, 1898, James M. Cox to Bryan, August 17, 1898, Bryan Papers.

[45] Letters to Mrs. Bryan of August 21, 23, 1898, Bryan Papers.

quarters on August 21, and 24 and 63 respectively on August 26, and protested in the name of humanity at the fatal bungling of the army's quartermaster, commissary, and medical services. Every day Mrs. Bryan saw men carried to the hospital on stretchers, and she grieved with him as he packed the belongings of the dead and shipped them home with a personal note of sympathy to their families.[46]

At the end of August famine and disease caused the Second Nebraska Regiment to return home. On September 3 Adjutant General Henry C. Corbin ruled that the First would remain in the Philippines and the Third in Florida. On September 5, when Bryan had 60 men in the hospital and 97 sick in quarters, Governor Holcomb asked the War Department to muster out the Third. In a confidential telegram to Secretary Alger, Senator Allen stated that "It is being suggested that the retention of the Third is for the purpose of keeping Colonel Bryan from participating in campaign [for the fall elections] or forcing him to resign that administration press may criticize him." Alger replied that he had "never heard the motive you suggest spoken of at headquarters" and forwarded the telegram to McKinley, who remained mute.[47] "It may be," Bryan wrote Mrs. Bryan, "that the Republicans are not anxious to have this particular regiment go home." If he resigned, the Republicans could send his regiment into active service and then charge him with cowardice.

Pablo Beach, the new campsite to which Bryan moved on September 8, was no more healthful than Cuba Libre. Although he was unwell, on September 22 Bryan left for Washington to confer with Holcomb and Congressman William L. Stark and to call on General Corbin. When he requested the discharge of those who wanted to go home, Corbin told him to go through channels. Bryan, Holcomb, and Stark then called on McKinley. After discussing details of demobilizing the Third, McKinley said, "Colonel Bryan has expressed no wish in the premise whatever." Bryan hinted that he had expressed no wish out of consideration for him. McKinley did not understand. "If I expressed a wish in the matter and you did not think it right to grant it, you might, in view of all the circumstances, find yourself much embarrassed in refusing, even if you felt it your duty to do so," Bryan retorted. McKinley did not see it that way. If Bryan made a request that should be granted, he said, he would grant it; if he made one that should not

[46] Mary Bryan Journal, December 1, 1898, Mrs. Ruth Bryan Rohde Papers.

[47] Telegrams, Alger to Allen, September 12, 1898, Alger to McKinley, September 12, 1898, McKinley Papers.

be granted, he would not be embarrassed in refusing it. Bryan thereupon stated that his men felt they had a *right* to be mustered out because the issues of the war had changed. "They volunteered to attempt to break the yoke of Spain in Cuba, and for nothing else. They did not volunteer to attempt to subjugate other peoples, or establish United States sovereignty elsewhere," he said. McKinley took his plea under advisement.[48]

The following morning Bryan had a fever and was put under a doctor's care. Mrs. Bryan rushed to Washington and was relieved to find him sitting up part of the time and talking about returning south "in a day or two." Meantime Holcomb had jarred McKinley by protesting against Nebraska's being compelled to furnish more than its quota for garrison duty. McKinley passed the buck—let the governor select the regiment to be mustered out. Holcomb then wired Bryan. "The right thing to do," said Bryan, was to consult both regiments, but the First had won distinguished battle honors in the Philippines and should receive preferment. He would learn the wishes of his own men as soon as he could. No sooner had he reached Hot Springs, Virginia, where he intended to take several days' convalescent rest, than the War Department ordered him to join his regiment immediately. On October 5 he polled his men and reported that he and his officers had no choice—they were at the disposal of the government—but that 87 per cent of his men wanted to go home. Holcomb told McKinley that the retirement of one regiment would work hardship on many in the other; if McKinley wanted to retain a whole regiment *he* must decide which one. Crossed, McKinley let the matter lie while Bryan's men died. On October 8, with 154 men in the hospital, 29 in sick quarters, and one additional death, the Third was alerted for garrison duty in Cuba. Bryan thereupon wired Mrs. Bryan to have Holcomb meet him in Washington on October 20, that he had a plan he could not trust to paper, and that she should return to Florida. "The one question which I am considering is whether I can be more useful in the army or out of it," he wrote on October 26, for he had been studying the political situation closely:

As soon as Congress convenes there will be a demand from all the parents for the muster out of all the volunteers and before January 1 a new army will be in the process of recruiting for garrison duty. Thus we may not leave here

[48] McKinley asked Lyman Gage to remain in the Cabinet Room while he talked with Bryan. The conversation is based on "Lyman Gage Memorandum, September 26, 1898," *ibid.*

at all. Amid this uncertainty I have scarcely known what to do. Added to this is the uncertainty in regard to the President's policy in the Philippines. . . . The Philippine question would probably not be determined for 10 days. . . . Come *at once*. . . .[49]

VI

TWENTY-FIVE pounds lighter, pale, and weak as a result of his bout with typhoid, Bryan reached home on a thirty-day furlough in time to vote on November 8. Fusion won in Nebraska and in several other states, but the national elections favored the Republicans so heavily that President McKinley had both houses with him. The Republicans had despaired of winning because of their mismanagement of the war, but as in '96 Hanna raised the money needed to win. "I milked the country," he confessed.[50] Knowing of the disfavor of the East with McKinley, he had concentrated on the West, with the result that the West, which had supported Bryan in 1896, now saved McKinley.[51]

Bryan expressed amazement at Republican partisanship on the issue of "imperialism." According to them, a vote cast against a Republican candidate was a vote in favor of Spain and against the government of the United States. But, he said, "everybody," not just Republicans, had fought the war. The Republicans were using the issue of imperialism to overcome public indignation with Algerism, collusion in war contracts, and other scandals. Their loss of 43 of their majority in the House was equivalent to a moral defeat. They should have done better because they were bringing to conclusion a successful war. Had the election turned on the management of the war, McKinley would have been defeated, but Republicans who otherwise would have voted him down supported him in order not to embarrass him while his commissioners were drafting the peace treaty. The people had not surrendered to the trusts or given up to the money power. They had merely postponed reform to fight the war. The Chicago platform still lived and would be reaffirmed in 1900. Nor were the elections a mandate on imperialism. Until the peace terms were published the people

[49] Bryan to Mrs. Bryan, October 26, 1898, Bryan Papers.

[50] Hanna to Senator Thomas Carter, October 14, 1898, in Herbert Croly, *Marcus Alonzo Hanna: His Life and Works*, pp. 292-293.

[51] Hanna to McKinley, November 10, 1898, McKinley Papers; Omaha *World-Herald*, November 12, 1898; Croly, *Hanna*, pp. 291-294; Elmer Ellis, *Henry Moore Teller*, pp. 300-305.

could not pass judgment on them. "Whether the war will raise any question of sufficient importance to turn public attention away from domestic problems remains to be seen." [52]

In mid-October McKinley had declared that if silver were repudiated in the elections he would call the Congress into special session to pass a gold standard law. His supporters had immediately tried to force an administration bill through the House. When the Democrats killed it, the Republicans swore that the issue would be the great issue in the elections and that if they won the new House they would pass it. Despite these declarations and occurrences, McKinley asserted that the elections were an endorsement of the gold standard. Thereupon silverites of all complexions renewed their promises to Bryan to fight on for silver and to support him for President in 1900, although some suggested that he agree to the ratio of 22 to 1, the current market ratio, instead of 16 to 1. With the House Republican, the Senate opposed to 16 to 1, Moreton Frewen saying that 22 to 1 was the only ratio that had a chance, Hearst weak on 16 to 1 but willing to support a ratio that would result in the adoption of bimetallism, and Chairman Jones and most Democratic and Populist leaders agreeable to giving 22 to 1 fair consideration, Bryan should at least study its merits. Bryan replied "No!" with an ardor that appeared insolent to some correspondents. Great Britain and the nations of Europe would not agree to international bimetallism, he replied, and the Republicans were unwilling to force the issue. The adoption of any ratio except 16 to 1 would violate the Chicago platform and displease the Democratic masses.[53]

McKinley's political sense was better than Byran's in detecting that imperialism held greater promise for victory in 1900 than silver. Bryan refused to admit that the war had introduced new issues, had an almost superstitious belief in the paramountcy of silver and of domestic over foreign policy issues, and constantly feared the evil effects foreign influences would have upon America's institutions.[54] When he finally

[52] Bryan interview, Omaha *World-Herald*, November 16, 1898.

[53] Letters to Bryan from Weaver, November 14, 1898, Marion Butler, November 23, 1898, C. S. Thomas, November 20, 1898, William Sulzer, November 23, 1898, George Fred Williams, November 26, 1898, Bryan Papers; letters to Moreton Frewen from James K. Jones, July 19, December 12, 1898, C. A. Towne, August 3, 1898, George Fred Williams, September 21, 1898, A. J. Warner, November 17, 1898, H. M. Teller, December 23, 1898, Frewen Papers.

[54] William Jennings Bryan, "Foreign Influence in American Politics," *The Arena*, 19 (April 1898), 433–438.

admitted imperialism an important issue he grasped it on the side defended by a minority, and so long as he remained in uniform and could not speak freely he proved ineffective.

When Spain announced that it would yield the entire Philippine archipelago for the $20,000,000 offered by the United States, the Filipinos prepared to resist annexation by force. While Bryan wrote out the anti-expansionist speech he would deliver as soon as he quit the Army, McKinley, tortured by indecision with respect to the Philippines, worked on his forthcoming message to Congress. When Madrid finally agreed to the American demands, the peace commissioners began to draft the terms of the treaty of peace.

Upon his return to his regiment, which was now at Savannah, Georgia, Bryan read McKinley's long message to the Fifty-sixth Congress. On the two matters of greatest public concern, expansion and currency reform, McKinley said nothing or was extremely vague. Bryan disapproved his suggestion to keep the volunteer army in existence until the standing army could be enlarged, denied his right to hold volunteers after the peace treaty was signed, considered him incorrect in saying the people endorsed the gold standard, and thought it singular that he utterly ignored the question of the government of the Philippines. He agreed that Cuba should be given independence but disagreed with McKinley's assertion that the elections of 1898 constituted an endorsement of imperialism.[55]

Bryan refused to speak on public issues while he prepared his regiment for transfer to Cuba. His imminent departure for Cuba and eagerness to affect the outcome of the peace treaty hastened his decision to resign. On December 10, the day the treaty was signed, he tendered his resignation. The war was over, and he believed he could be more useful to his country as a civilian than as a soldier, he asserted. After writing his wife that "I believe our country is in more danger now than Cuba was when I enlisted,"[56] he received his discharge papers and rushed to catch the first train for Washington, for "the Treaty was in danger."

His "lockjaw" cured, Bryan quipped that "I had five months of peace in the army and resigned to take part in a fight,"[57] and then with great seriousness delivered his long-rehearsed speech in opposi-

[55] Omaha *World-Herald,* December 6, 1898.

[56] Bryan to Mrs. Bryan, December 10, 1898, Bryan Papers.

[57] J. R. Johnson, "Imperialism in Nebraska, 1898–1904," *Nebraska History,* 44 (September 1963), 145.

tion to imperialism. With the war ended, the nation could resume discussion of domestic problems and of the new questions arising out of the war. "Our people defended Cuba against foreign arms, now they must defend themselves and their country against foreign ideas—the colonial idea of European nations. Heretofore greed has perverted the government and used its instrumental interference for private gain; but now the very foundation principle of our government is being assaulted." The imperialistic idea was antagonistic to ideas and ideals cherished since the writing of the Declaration of Independence. We must refrain from entering upon a colonial policy or abandon the doctrine that governments receive their just powers from the consent of the governed. He borrowed a Bible quotation, "A house divided against itself cannot stand," and paraphrased Lincoln's declaration, "This nation cannot endure half-republic and half-colony—half free and half vassal." He distinguished between the type of expansion approved by Jefferson, into contiguous territory usable for future settlement by kindred peoples, and the type that would involve the United States in the quarrels of Europe and Asia and wars for the subjugation of alien races. He would end hostilities now, sign the treaty, thereby freeing the nation of international complications, and let Congress resolve what the policy of the nation should be on expansion. We should reserve harbor and coaling stations in Puerto Rico and the Philippines as the price for services rendered, and could also ask Cuba for various concessions. Indeed, he would interpose no objection to the annexation of Puerto Rico if its people agreed, but the Philippines were too far away and their people too different from ours to be annexed even if they desired annexation, which they did not.

Newspaper headlines of the following morning told about "Mr. Bryan's Return to Politics." [58]

VII

REPUBLICANS in general favored expansion. Those opposed, like Andrew Carnegie and Senators George F. Hoar and William E. Mason, would either defeat the treaty or amend it to prohibit the acquisition of the Philippines. Democrats in general, and southern Democrats in particular, also favored expansion. Bryan led a minority that would

[58] *Ibid.*, December 14, 1898. As he promised his men he would, Bryan asked McKinley on January 24, 1899, to muster out the Third, which was finally discharged on April 19, 1899.

ratify the treaty in order to end bloodshed, detach the Philippines from Spain, and then grant the Filipinos independence by congressional resolution.[59] But how could he avoid expansion by supporting a treaty that provided for the acquisition of the Philippines? What appears a dichotomy in his thinking becomes clear if it is understood that the ratification of the treaty would accomplish the first part of his purpose—to push Spain out of the picture and leave the United States in control of Filipino destiny—and that he would then have the United States take the islands only long enough to enable the Congress to resolve that they were free. He explained this strategy to a number of senators on December 14. On December 16, after consulting with Carnegie, who saw him a formidable candidate in 1900 if he would drop free silver and campaign only on anti-expansion, he returned from New York to Washington for extended talks with leading anti-expansionists. On December 18 the American peace commissioners left Paris. George Gray, the only Democrat, had opposed annexation; all the others favored it.

The formal debate on the Treaty of Paris, which lasted from January 4 to February 6, 1899, proceeded in profound ignorance of conditions in the Philippines and was complicated by McKinley's sudden proclamation of American sovereignty over the islands on the basis of military conquest and his ordering of American troops from Luzon to other islands.

Bryan failed to see the incongruity of being on McKinley's side and argued that the treaty was a solemn obligation that must be enforced. He hoped that the question of imperialism would be settled quickly, so that he could campaign in 1900 on the money and trust issues. "Just now I am talking against imperialism not because I have changed my mind on the other questions but because this attack of the imperialists must be met now or never," he wrote Carnegie, and when McKinley requested senatorial approval of the treaty he began to tour the country on the theme that the mission of the United States was to liberate those in bondage, not to place shackles upon those struggling for freedom. He denied that we must govern the Philippines for their own good, that we needed the profits obtainable from trading with them, and that McKinley's "religious duty" argument was sound. He de-

[59] The rest of this chapter follows the author's "Bryan, McKinley, and the Treaty of Paris," *Pacific Historical Review*, 26 (May 1957), 131–146. See also Leon Wolff, *Little Brown Brother*, and Emilio Aguinaldo and Albano Pacis, *A Second Look at America*.

clined Carnegie's request to ask his followers in the Senate to vote against the treaty and held out for both the treaty and Philippine independence. Finally, on January 24, Augustus O. Bacon of Georgia introduced a resolution which would prevent the impending rebellion and implement his policy. Whenever the Filipinos organized a stable and independent government worthy of recognition, said Bacon, the United States would transfer sovereignty of the islands to them.

Leaks invalidated the secrecy surrounding the executive session on the treaty that began on January 12, and various senators went on record as to how they would vote. Lodge estimated that all the Democrats but two would vote against the treaty, but he wrote Roosevelt that the proponents of the treaty were quietly gathering in votes behind the scenes. As ringleader against Bryan, Arthur Pue Gorman had aligned all but five or six Democrats against ratification while the Republicans talked about preventing rejection of the treaty either by postponing the vote until the new Senate met or by having McKinley withdraw the treaty and then resubmit it. Teller wrote Bryan that he could not influence the situation, and Bryan realized that he could exercise little real control. Jones of Arkansas, for example, told him that the Republicans would help him ratify the treaty and then laugh at him when he asked for Philippine independence. On January 25, two days after Emilio Aguinaldo proclaimed the Philippine Republic, the Foreign Relations Committee set the date for the vote on the treaty for February 6.

Aguinaldo rejected the "large share" in the Philippine government McKinley had promised and insisted upon complete independence. During the night of February 4 an exchange of shots between sentries of the First Nebraska—ironically—and a Filipino patrol developed into an engagement that took both American and Filipino lives. Some believed that Aguinaldo had resorted to hostilities in order to prevent approval of the treaty and charged Bryan with applauding him, which was not the case, for Bryan insisted that until the nation's Philippine policy was determined American soldiers must defend American interests.

The Filipino revolt forced wavering senators to make up their minds. The vote on the treaty was 57 to 27, just one more vote than the necessary two thirds. Bryan has been denounced as responsible for ratification, for fastening upon the nation the imperialism he opposed by provoking the Filipino revolt, and for proceeding "secretly" and "stealthily" to achieve his objective. Although disagreement exists on the exact number of senators he was supposed to have influenced, it was Lodge rather than he who convinced three of the four doubtfuls on the Saturday before the vote. Of the ten Democrats he supposedly influenced, eight were already on record as favoring the treaty. The two doubtfuls, Samuel D. McEnery and John L. McLaurin, were won over by Republican promises of patronage and of support for their resolutions calling for the eventual independence of the Philippines. Of the Populists, silver Republicans, and the lone Silverite who voted yea, Bryan may have influenced William V. Allen and John P. Jones but not the others. Benjamin Tillman said that many senators had yielded to "pressure" rather than voting freely, and Richard F. Pettigrew utterly discounted Bryan's influence on the vote. Lodge himself modestly gave credit to Nelson W. Aldrich, William E. Chandler, Mark Hanna, Stephen B. Elkins, Henry C. Hansbrough, and Thomas H. Carter, not to Bryan, and no major metropolitan newspaper gave Bryan credit for ratification. Politics played a part, for defeating the treaty meant repudiating McKinley and throwing the Philippines back into the uncertainties of international diplomacy. McKinley himself played an important part, not only in selecting important senators as peace commissioners but in impressing his views upon the country with tours of the Middle West and South late in 1898.

Bryan let his desire to do the "right" thing and his love of peace place him in an embarrassing position. He crowned McKinley's success, yet he remained convinced that his own stand was correct. The fate of the Filipinos had been taken out of the hands of diplomats and placed in the hands of Congress, which must answer the people's demand for Philippine independence.

The Senate and McKinley decreed otherwise. When Republicans stalled debate on resolutions seeking to define Philippine policy for two weeks after the ratification of the treaty, Tillman said that some sort of pledge had been made to McEnery and McLaurin prior to the vote on the treaty. Gorman hinted at "peculiar circumstances" in a letter to Carnegie; Mason wrote the steel king that "The trade was made for four votes and on an absolute agreement to pass the McEnery resolution"; and Hanna's correspondence with McKinley reveals that he was engaged in heading off senators who demanded Philippine independence. When a tie occurred on the vote to add Augustus O. Bacon's resolution to McEnery's, Vice President Garret A. Hobart broke it by voting in the negative. The Democrats favored Bacon's plan, which would have established Bryan's policy, but the Republicans put over the McEnery resolution, which was merely a pious hope expressed by twenty-six senators. Since it never reached a vote in the House, Philippine annexation was not accompanied by a formal declaration of policy. Bryan continued in vain to call for a speedy declaration of policy. Then, on February 22, in a terse and epigrammatic speech entitled "America's Mission," he condemned the immorality of imperialism and asserted that imperialism would be an issue in 1900 unless settled before then.

Bryan had blessed America's going to war in the name of self-determination for an underdog. However, he had unequivocally declared his opposition to imperialism at a very early date; he would have opposed ratification of the Treaty of Paris if he believed it would impel the nation upon a career of expansion. He could have prevented ratification and the acquisition of the Philippines; had he been a mere politician he should have opposed ratification because McKinley approved. He wanted to avoid entering the campaign of 1900 with his party divided on a popular issue and fervently prayed that ratification would settle forever the question of imperialism and leave him free to campaign in 1900 on the issues left unsettled since 1896. He defied Democrats who demanded that he make expansion the major issue, and it was not until the Kansas City convention that he agreed to make it "paramount" and silver subsidiary.

Toward the end of his life Bryan wrote that he had "never regretted the position taken; on the contrary, I never showed more statesmanship than I did when I insisted upon the termination of the war and the making of the promise embodied in the Bacon resolution." He agitated for another sixteen years before his demand for a return to fundamental principles was in part answered by the Jones bill of the Wilson administration. Not until he was a decade in his grave, however, did the nation, once more under Democratic leadership, finally promise a full return to the basic democratic mission of the United States as he had defined it in 1898.

CHAPTER 11

Kansas City

I

THE WAR stimulated industrial and agricultural production, the increase in the gold supply raised prices and strengthened the gold reserve, and McKinley's popularity reached new heights, particularly when many silver Republicans rejoined the fold after the elections of 1898. Meantime Bryan's refusal to subordinate silver to the new trust, imperialism, and militarism issues lost him many friends. The reorganizers were active in various cities and states, especially in New York, without which he could hardly expect to win the election of 1900, and in Chicago. He had no patronage to offer his heterogeneous following, Cleveland and his kind still bitterly opposed him, and those who had seen fusion fail preferred not to fuse again.

Bryan also lost by demanding absolute obedience from his followers and continued attachment to his principles. For example, he rejected Perry Belmont's invitation to attend a $10-a-plate Jefferson Day banquet of the Democratic Club of New York because Belmont had openly repudiated the Chicago platform and had not publicly announced his conversion to it. Bryan had paid eloquent tribute to Jefferson before the Jefferson Club of Lincoln in 1895. By expounding Jefferson's First Inaugural line by line during the campaign of 1896 and in subsequent speeches he had done more than any other public figure to revitalize the image of the Sage of Monticello in the Jeffersonian revival that rolled on from 1880 to its climax in 1900.[1] "Just as a good Christian would revolt at having the sacraments administered by an infidel, so a good Democrat objects to a Jeffersonian banquet presided over by Perry Belmont," Bryan therefore wrote Belmont. Democracy, he added, was defined in the Chicago platform. Since 6,500,000 voters had supported it and only 133,000 had voted for Palmer and Buckner, it was

---

[1] Merrill D. Peterson, *The Jefferson Image in the American Mind*, pp. 251, 253, 259–260.

clear that the people preferred his definition to that of the reorganizers. Changes could be made only by those who had supported it in 1896, not by those responsible for its defeat.[2]

Bryan heightened the division within his party by consistently refusing to attend "reorganizer" banquets and speaking instead at a large number of "Jefferson dollar dinners"—Chicago platform affairs from beginning to end, with celery rather than flowers gracing the tables and coffee supplanting wine.[3] He was not trying to drive professed believers out of the party, he said; he was attempting to impress upon *all* Democrats the importance of the triumph of Democratic principles. He did not want to be President, he added, "unless those who think as I do believe that I can do more for the principles of the party already adopted than anyone else. If the Democratic party wants somebody to lead a retreat they must find someone accustomed to walking backwards." [4]

No marked change occurred in Bryan's understanding of the currency question. Continued increases in gold production were undermining his defense of bimetallism, yet he sought refuge in the quantitative theory of money. The new gold supply was not a serious factor in shaping monetary policy, he said with a straight face.

During the eighteen months prior to the meeting of the Democratic national convention Bryan stumped the country with speeches on expansion, silver, and trusts, and engaged in various state campaigns of 1899 and in the primary battles of the spring of 1900. He made his most perceptive contribution in the field of "trust busting." The economic benefits promised by "monopoly" did not outweigh the social and political evils wrought in their train, he asserted. Trusts paid lower prices for raw materials, decreased wages and reduced their labor forces, and then sold a poor product at an exorbitant price. Their prime purpose was to avoid competition. By destroying individual motivation and independence they tended to create an aristocracy of wealth in the land of the free.[5]

[2] The complete exchange of letters may be found in the Omaha *World-Herald*, March 15, 21, 23, 25, April 10, 21, 1899, and in Perry Belmont, *An American Democrat: The Recollections of Perry Belmont*, pp. 434–453.

[3] Homer S. Cummings to the author, interview, Washington, D.C., July 16, 1955.

[4] *The Nation*, April 20, 1899; *Public Opinion*, April 20, 27, 1899.

[5] Bryan's good friend in St. Louis, Colonel Moses C. Wetmore, was associated with the Liggett and Myers Tobacco Company for twenty-five years. Starting in 1897, in negotiations conducted in part by Bernard Baruch, the "tobacco trust" bought out Wetmore's associates and finally forced him out too. Wetmore gave

As things now stood, said Bryan, trusts enjoyed life in the shadowy area between federal and state jurisdiction. Should not the hand that created the corporation also regulate it? Congress, for instance, could limit the income from a patent to $100,000 or $200,000 and make the Sherman Anti-Trust Law effective by providing it with adequate penalties. The Supreme Court might change its mind on the distinction between "commerce" and "manufacturing" under a strengthened interstate commerce law. Better still would be a constitutional amendment specifically conferring upon the federal government the right to suppress any monopoly extending beyond the confines of a state. Federal inaction, however, should not delay state action. A state could compel a new corporation to furnish evidence that it was chartered only for legitimate purposes, or it could place a limit upon the capital stock of a corporation. In the long run, however, reform could come only if the Attorney General in Washington wanted to enforce current law and recommended new legislation and constitutional amendments to Congress.[6]

In the four-day Chicago Anti-Trust Conference of September 1899, Bryan, Bourke Cockran, and John Bates Clark outlined three possible approaches to the trust problem. Cockran argued that as long as trusts allowed the consumer to share in the economies of large-scale production they were both legitimate and desirable outcomes of the competitive struggle, but he would punish directors of corporations who mismanaged them and injured both stockholders and the public. His remedy lay in publicity extending to the point where any customer could find out how another, even a competitor, was treated. He was interrupted by applause several times, especially when he referred to the "monopoly on excellence" held by Bryan and to Bryan's "monopoly on the Democratic hearts of the country," which Bryan blushingly acknowledged.[7]

John Bates Clark, the contemporary economist whose ideas on monopoly and economic law Bryan's most closely paralleled, made a sharp distinction between combinations and complete monopoly. He would preserve "potential competition" by preventing abuses and by abolish-

---

Bryan all the details. Omaha *World-Herald*, January 21, 1898; Mark D. Hirsch, *William C. Whitney, Modern Warwick*, pp. 544–546.

[6] Bryan to F. D. Butler, June 5, 1900, William Jennings Bryan Papers; Omaha *World-Herald*, April 30, 1899, June 15, July 6, 1900.

[7] Omaha *World-Herald*, September 16–17, 1899; Chicago Civic Federation, *Conference on Trusts*, pp. 462–494, 586–598.

ing all rebates and discriminations. Thus he and Cockran would allow trusts to exist under regulation.[8] But Bryan found monopoly indefensible. He took the ground that trusts were conceived in sin, were born in iniquity, and lived by crime. He would kill extant ones and prevent the birth of others, saying, "Whenever you put capital upon an equal footing with labor, or above labor in the structure of the government you are on the road toward a government that rests not upon reason but upon force." Drawing upon his farm experiences, he said he would put rings into the noses of monopolistic hogs to keep them from rooting out the freedoms of the people. He demanded a federal law prohibiting a corporation from doing business outside of the parent state until it received from some body created by Congress a license authorizing it to engage in interstate commerce, and which would grant licenses only under conditions that would proscribe the watering of stock, prevent monopoly in any branch of business, and provide for publicity for the transactions of corporations. If such a law were unconstitutional, the Constitution should be amended.[9]

The Chicago conference aroused public opinion and gave a large boost to the anti-trust movement. Eastern advisers told Bryan he could carry the East on the trust question and win in 1900 if he gave assurance that he would not again demand 16 to 1. This assurance he refused to give.

Democratic victories in the elections of 1899 are traceable largely to Bryan's efforts. The addition of planks on militarism and expansion to those of the Chicago platform by the Nebraska Democratic state convention of 1899 foreshadowed the importance of these issues in the national platform in 1900, and his endorsement by Nebraska and various other Middle Western and Southern states pointed to an easy road toward his renomination. His intervention in favor of McLean, whom he had deemed an immoral man in 1896, as gubernatorial candidate, probably saved Ohio from the reorganizers,[10] but he gave long and earnest consideration to the local situation before entering Kentucky.

[8] Omaha *World-Herald*, September 16, 1899; *American Review of Reviews*, 20 (October 1899), 399.

[9] Bryan to C. H. Ingersoll, December 30, 1899, Bryan Papers; Omaha *World-Herald*, September 16–17, 1899; Chicago Civic Federation, *Conference on Trusts*, pp. 495–512, 582–586; Editorial, "Bryan *versus* Labor Men on Trusts," *Gunton's Magazine*, 17 (November 1899), 377–384.

[10] James A. Rice to Bryan, September 7, 1899, Allan Thurman to Bryan, September 9, 1899, A. J. Warner to Bryan, September 19, 1899, Bryan Papers.

Bryan had received letters from both the William Goebel group, which held a convention late in June, and the John Young Brown faction, which met in August and charged Goebel with receiving support from gold men. Both groups supported the Chicago platform, opposed imperialism, endorsed Bryan for President, and wanted him to speak for them. Bryan believed Goebel loyal and demanded harmony, for a Republican victory in Kentucky would make his own canvass more difficult and endanger the return of a silver senator from the state. Finally, despite John Peter Altgeld's stating that Goebel was an enemy of the Chicago platform, Bryan hammered for three days on the theme that Kentucky was the skirmish line for 1900 and that Goebel deserved election as governor.[11]

When Brown presented his case and explained the intricacies of the Goebel election law,[12] Bryan replied that he would neither sit in judgment nor discuss law. It was not a question between Goebel and Brown but between Goebel and a Republican. To Altgeld he made an extremely interesting observation: *"There is no doubt that the Republicans stole the electoral vote of Kentucky* in '96 and the Goebel [election] law was passed to prevent the recurrence of this." Moreover, he saw no way of re-electing Joseph C. S. Blackburn to the Senate other than by supporting Goebel, for Brown had senatorial aspirations.[13] Confused by conflicting testimony and standing to lose the support of either Goebel or Brown, Bryan deplored the situation but provided no satisfactory solution. The only pleasant result of his efforts in Kentucky was the recantation of both William B. Haldeman, general manager, and of Henry Watterson, editor, of the Louisville *Courier-Journal*. While neither completely agreed with him, particularly on silver, each promised to support him henceforth. With respect to Watterson, the "henceforth" meant as long as no one with a better chance than Bryan came along.

[11] Omaha *World-Herald,* October 15–17, 20, 22, 1899; Altgeld to Bryan, August 7, 1899, John Peter Altgeld Collection; Herbert Croly, *Marcus Alonzo Hanna: His Life and Work,* p. 296; Robert W. Woolley, "Politics Is Hell," mss., Woolley Papers.

[12] The Goebel law of 1898 put the election machinery in the hands of three state commissioners chosen by the state legislature. The commissioners would appoint all county election boards, and the latter would appoint the local and precinct election officers. Whoever could manipulate the choice of the three commissioners could thereby control any state election. Goebel said the law was necessary to prevent the Republicans from stealing the election of 1899 from Bryan, as they had done in 1896.

[13] Bryan to Altgeld, August 18, 1899, Altgeld Collection (italics added).

Except for Kentucky and New York, Bryan's renomination was apparently assured. In June, James Creelman of the New York *World*, who had just spoken with Richard Croker, went to Nebraska. He asked Bryan why he did not compromise with Croker, who said that the East was opposed to silver, by agreeing to a simple declaration in favor of the remonetization of silver, leaving the ratio to be determined by Congress. Would not that be expedient? Would that not instantly reunite the Democracy? With a thunderous "NO!" Bryan repudiated the suggestion. Public questions could not be decided on the basis of expediency. They must be decided on the basis of what is "right." Creelman concluded that Bryan was "the most stubbornly sincere and convincingly convinced" political leader he had ever met.[14]

Meantime a number of Bryan's friends put pressure on Croker, who intended to control the New York Democracy and form a national organization hostile to Bryan. At Tammany's July Fourth celebration, designed to launch an experimental presidential boom for Judge Robert Van Wyck, James Hogg stampeded the crowd for Bryan and Croker decided he had better bring his Tigers into line. At the next state committee meeting he "bottled up" David Bennett Hill and informed Bryan that Tammany would give him its "heartiest support." Since he failed to mention silver, however, Altgeld and others warned Bryan that Croker "misinterpreted" his views and that he had declared for him only because he had seen the way to self-preservation. Yet with New York "safe," Bryan's Eastern friends believed that "what remains now for the national convention is a matter of detail, and the platform and candidate are no longer problematic." [15]

Stating that the Nebraska election had been fought on the national issues, Bryan took the re-election of Holcomb by 20,000 to mean a protest against the McKinley administration. His candidates, running on his platform, had won the first fight on imperialism. Moreover, his missionary work afield had helped reduce the Republican pluralities in Ohio and New York, squeeze Goebel by in Kentucky,[16] and recover Maryland from the Republicans.

[14] Omaha *World-Herald*, August 27, 1899.

[15] George Fred Williams to Moreton Frewen, October 5, 1899, Frewen Papers; John H. Girdner to Bryan, September 20, 1899, Philo S. Bennett to Bryan, September 22, 1899, James K. Jones to Bryan, October 17, 1899, C. J. Smyth to Bryan, December 22, 1899, Bryan Papers; Omaha *World-Herald*, September 4, 5, October 9, November 28, 1899; *American Review of Reviews*, 20 (August 1899), 140.

[16] On January 17, 1900, the Republican governor called two regiments of militia to Frankfort to prevent the meeting of the state legislature. On January 30, after

Although Bryan said the Democratic gains of 1899 were provoked by principle alone, they really represented a personal victory. His winning of Nebraska, said Charles Gates Dawes, "was due to Bryan's personality," [17] and Allan Thurman wrote: "To talk about separating your personality from the campaign of 1900 is to my mind simply lunacy." [18] Arthur Pue Gorman analyzed the returns and dropped from the race, and John R. McLean decided to keep hands off. There was no one else who could put the national contest on a plane over and above state differences, and Theodore Roosevelt was but one of many who believed him stronger in 1899 than in 1896. Yet it was generally agreed that William McKinley would have little trouble in beating him again. At the year's end the New York *World* put the electoral vote of 1900 at 285 for McKinley and 162 for Bryan. Bryan had fought the good fight for three years; election year would appear but the completion of a process much too long in its consummation. However popular Bryan might be personally, his chosen issue was waning. When he said that with respect to silver "I stand just where I stood three years ago," a New York editor commented, "Sit down, Mr. Bryan. You must be awfully tired, *too.*" [19]

II

BRYAN disappeared from public view while moving his family to Texas for the winter in an attempt to improve the health of his younger daughter, but he used the rented home merely as headquarters from which to continue the making of converts. Taking as his theme Matthew IV:13, "I'm armed with more than complete steel, the justice of my quarrel," he was back on the stump within ten days of the elections of 1899.

---

an electoral canvassing board found Goebel truly elected, Goebel was shot by an assassin from the governor's home town. Goebel was sworn in even as Governor Taylor dismissed the militia, but he died on February 2. Taylor asked McKinley for help, but McKinley could find no way to do so and advised him to give up. The Democratic lieutenant governor, J. C. W. Beckham, was sworn in on February 2. When the United States Supreme Court upheld the decision of the Kentucky Court of Appeals on May 21, Kentucky finally obtained a Democratic governor. The L.&N. Railroad spent half a million, and would have spent another million, to defeat Goebel. Omaha *World-Herald,* January 17–May 21, 1900; Woolley, "Politics Is Hell."

[17] Charles G. Dawes, *A Journal of the McKinley Years, 1893–1913,* p. 204.
[18] Letter, September 9, 1899, Bryan Papers.
[19] Mark Sullivan, *Our Times: The United States, 1900–1925,* I, 305–306.

Late in November 1899 the Democratic National Committee announced itself unanimously in favor of silver as the main issue for 1900 but also eager for an anti-trust crusade. To give up on silver, agreed Bryan, would be "ignorant or cowardly." The outlook was good, he insisted, and Democratic strength in 1900 would be increased by the labor vote and the anti-trust movement. Thereupon the silver Republicans declared their adherence to Democratic principles as he defined them, endorsed him as their nominee, and asked the anti-imperialists of the East to join them in a nationwide silver and anti-expansion organization. Since most anti-expansionists were reorganizers, they declined.[20]

A National Anti-Trust Conference held in Chicago in February 1900 adopted a platform that included many of Bryan's demands, particularly the placing on the free list of all trust-made goods, and control over patents lest they lead to the creation of trusts. However, when middle-of-the-road Populists tried to pledge the delegates to vote for no party that did not demand government ownership and direct legislation, Bryan's friends blocked the move and also an attempt to create a national anti-trust party.[21] The failure of the anti-trust leagues to join the Populists rendered them "as impotent," said Ignatius Donnelly, "as last year's bird nests." This factor, plus Bryan's refusal to subordinate silver to the anti-trust movement, prevented the anti-trust issue from becoming the paramount one in 1900.

In conference in New York City early in 1900, anti-imperialist leaders discussed the possibility of forming a third party which would force the major parties to agree to Philippine independence. But they lacked a nationally recognized leader. Many of them believed that there were "even worse things than silver and Tammany," and Bryan was assured "confidentially" that he would be nominated for President by an anti-imperialist convention to be held in August if he dropped silver,[22] but he knew that he could expect little support from the anti-expansionists. David Starr Jordan wrote him that his holding to silver would not gain him 5 per cent of those who had voted for McKinley in 1896, for the Republicans could easily hold the line against silver in the East, "where the votes are."[23] George F. Hoar wrote him that

[20] Omaha *World-Herald*, November 11–14, 19, 21, 29, December 1, 1899.

[21] *Ibid.*, February 12–15, 1900; M. L. Lockwood to Bryan, January 13, 19, 1900, Bryan Papers; *Official Report of the National Anti-Trust Conference Held February 12, 13, 14, 1900.*

[22] Elwood S. Corser to Bryan, March 8, 1900, Bryan Papers.

[23] Jordan to Bryan, March 7, April 13, 1900, *ibid.*

he held him responsible second to McKinley for the ratification of the Treaty of Paris and for its lamentable consequences and refused to support him.[24] To all anti-expansionists who demanded that he drop silver Bryan replied that he would not desert principle just to win an election. To Cockran and his fellow reorganizers, even though they supported him on the issue of anti-imperialism, he retorted that they must not dictate terms. If, he said, Cockran believed that "imperialism is a government thirteen inches in diameter, round, and fired out of a cannon," then the only way to fight imperialism was to remain loyal.[25]

In mid-February 1900, when a boom was launched for Admiral George Dewey, Bryan said he was gratified to find one question he need not discuss. He refused to take the admiral seriously, and Republicans like Roosevelt found him politically contemptible. Knowing that Bryan was "in" for 1900, reorganizers like Whitney looked ahead to 1904 and sought to avoid any intervening intraparty strife. Bryan knew how his followers felt from letters such as the one by Kentucky's Ollie James: "Judas Iscariot would have as much right to have been clamering [sic] over the hill of Calvary after his Master's crucifixion to re-organize the believers, as Grover Cleveland or Don Dickinson have to rush forth to reorganize the party they betrayed." [26]

Bryan characterized McKinley's message of December 1899 as a plea for gold and empire, but it was evident that he was singing silver's swan song. With the war ended, the time had come for the Republicans to redeem their prewar pledges of currency reform, and a gold standard bill written by bankers rather than by congressmen was introduced.[27] When the "Hanna party" sought to pass it in the House, on December 18, 1899, silver senators called for fight and introduced free silver bills. Democratic and Populist members charged the Re-

[24] Letter, May 15, 1900, ibid.

[25] Omaha World-Herald, January 28, 30, 1900; Harper's Weekly, March 17, 1900.

[26] Ollie James to Bryan, June 30, 1900, Bryan Papers. See also W. D. Mann to Bryan, October 2, 1899, C. S. Thomas to Bryan, April 10, 1899, ibid.; Omaha World-Herald, April 4-6, 1900; Charles S. Hamlin Diary, pp. 245–246, Hamlin Papers.

[27] Letters to McKinley from Joseph Medill, October 28, 1898, Seth Low, November 21, 1898, Charles G. Dawes, December 21, 1898, H. H. Kohlsaat, n.d. but late 1898, and Spencer Borden, January 3, 1899, William McKinley Papers; Henry Parker Willis, The Federal Reserve System: Legislation, Organization and Operation, pp. 9, 10, 14; Charles A. Conant, "Plans for Currency Reform," American Review of Reviews, 17 (January 1898), 43–52; Frederick Albert Cleveland, "The Final Report of the Monetary Commission," Annals of the American Academy, 13 (1899), 31–56.

publicans with the unblushing repudiation of legislative obligations, and Republican William E. Chandler of New Hampshire fought strongly to break the power of the gold men; but nothing could prevent the "Crime of 1900." On February 15 the bill passed by a strict party vote, with all the Republicans except Chandler "responding to the lash of the Goldocracy," and the House accepted the compromise bill. McKinley approved on March 14 and the gold standard was the law of the land.[28] Bryan had demanded governmentally directed inflation via bimetallism, really through silver. The Republicans provided governmentally directed inflation via gold. Nonetheless the money question was relegated to secondary importance by those who believed that the new law would not be affected by the election of 1900 and that it would outlive the McKinley administration. In fact bimetallism had been debated seriously for the last time in Bryan's generation.

The Republicans then defeated Bryan on the Puerto Rican tariff bill. The immediate question was whether the Constitution's provision for the equality of impost and excise taxes extended to the island; the vital issue at stake was the determination of the future status and government of the overseas possessions. When the Republicans proposed a tariff of 15 per cent for two years, Bryan charged that pressure from commercial interests swayed Congress, and his supporters opposed the bill. He also argued that all taxes must be uniform, that the Puerto Ricans could not be taxed without their consent, and that they should enjoy free trade.[29] The bill passed nonetheless. The Constitution did *not* follow the flag, said the Republicans, and the Supreme Court upheld them in 1901.

In addition to failing to stop the gold standard and Puerto Rican tariff laws, Bryan lost prestige from his interference in the Nebraska senatorship contest of 1900. When Monroe Leland Hayward, the

[28] New York *Times*, March 15, 1900; Charles S. Olcott, *The Life of William McKinley*, I, 357–361; Leon Burr Richardson, *William E. Chandler, Republican*, pp. 593–596. The act provided that gold would be the standard of value, that all other money issued would be kept at parity with this standard, and that the Treasury notes issued under the Sherman Act would be redeemed from a reserve gold fund. Silver would be used only for subsidiary coins. But no satisfactory provision was made for maintaining the gold standard. Willis, *Federal Reserve System*, p. 14; Roland P. Falkner, "The Currency Law of 1900," *Annals of the American Academy*, 16 (1900), 33–55.

[29] Omaha *World-Herald*, February 19, 20, 1900; Bryan in the New York *Journal*, reprinted in Omaha *World-Herald*, February 25, 1900.

junior senator, died on December 5, 1899, the appointment of his successor fell to the Populist governor, William A. Poynter, who asked
Bryan's advice. Bryan said that "good faith" required the appointment
of ex-Senator William V. Allen, Populist, and that the two other
leading aspirants, Gilbert M. Hitchcock and William H. Thompson,
both Democrats, would be rewarded "if we win the presidential contest." Hitchcock had strongly supported Bryan since 1890 and had
been defeated as a fusionist candidate for Congress in 1898. Incensed,
he wired Bryan that "If you insist on sacrificing me we part company
forever." He felt that Bryan's saying that "good faith demands the
appointment of Allen" branded him as unfaithful and nullified his
influence for the future, and the "sting of ingratitude" letter he published upon the appointment of Allen marked a break in his friendship
with Bryan which did not heal. Soon he would be leading one Nebraska Democratic faction and Bryan another, thus hastening the day
of the Republican redemption of the state.[30]

In mid-March 1900, at the Nebraska Democratic state convention,
Bryan asserted that the three most important issues were silver, trusts,
and imperialism. In speeches to the Populist and silver Republican
conventions he pushed fusion and excoriated McKinley for his position
on trusts, the Philippines, and the Puerto Rican tariff. In their endorsement of the Chicago platform and of several new issues the
fusionists foreshadowed the Kansas City platform: they favored direct
legislation and the public ownership of municipal franchises; condemned the Republicans for their failure to regulate trusts and their
Puerto Rican tariff; opposed militarism and sympathized with the
Boers; and favored an immediate declaration of the nation's purpose
to give the Filipinos a stable form of government, independence, and
protection from outside interference. The "corpse of Bryanism" so
oft interred in the opposition press had risen again.

With Congressman John J. Lentz of Ohio at his side, and Altgeld,
James Hogg, Tom L. Johnson, George Fred Williams, and O. H. P.
Belmont frequently in company, Bryan spent a month in kicking off
the Eastern primaries. Reports of his progress varied between ecstatic
praise and criticism to the effect that vast crowds cheered him when
he attacked Mark Hanna, suffered when he demanded an income tax,
cringed when he discussed silver, and were exhausted by his long ex-

[30] This account is an abridgement of the author's "A Tempest in a Teapot?—
Governor Poynter's Appointment of William V. Allen to the United States Senate
in 1899," *Nebraska History*, 38 (June 1957), 155–163.

hortations against imperialism. Since he was wildly acclaimed, the gold Democrats believed his welcome represented Eastern devotion to silver, and Bryan was convinced that the East was no longer "the enemy's country" and that New York state, which had enough power to tip the election either way, must fight the rest of the country in November. As in 1896, however, he suffered various indignities. The trustees of Brown University refused him permission to address the school's debating society, and gold men killed a move to invite him to address the Maryland legislature. Also important was his failure to get Arthur Brisbane to swing William Randolph Hearst over to anti-imperialism. There were 70,000,000 dissatisfied Americans anxious for someone to suggest measures as useful to them as McKinley was useful to the trusts and millionaires, Brisbane told Bryan: "I hope you will be able to suggest such measures as will get their votes. I don't think that interest in Aguinaldo or any metallic ratio will move them." [31] Still destructive to his hopes, too, was his characterization in the Eastern press as an airy, voluble, and self-confident Bohemian who confounded politics with opera bouffe, one who had made more capital out of fewer resources of statesmanship than any other capering compound of hortation and histrionism in modern times, and a victim of his own vocabulary who never fluttered in his fluency and yet whose smooth sentences would break should they strike the rough edge of a thought.[32]

In 1896, in accordance with the "logic of the situation," Bryan had fought to have the delegates to the national convention uninstructed; now he stated that delegates should be instructed so that the nominee would be chosen by men "acting for the people." In 1896 he had talked about silver everywhere; now he adjusted his demands to local geography, saying little about silver in the East, subordinating it and the income tax in the South and West, and hitting hardest everywhere on trusts and imperialism. However, his personal influence resulted in the election of delegates friendly to his silver views to the Populist and silver Republican national conventions as well as to the Democratic.

III

AT SIOUX FALLS, South Dakota, early in May 1900, the Populists adopted a Bryanite platform, named Bryan for President by acclama-

[31] Letter, February 6, 1900, Bryan Papers.
[32] Clipping, February 20, 1900, Bryan Papers, Nebraska State Historical Society·
Omaha *World-Herald*, April 12, 15, 1900.

tion, declined to consult with Democrats and silver Republicans, nominated Charles A. Towne for Vice President against the advice of Bryan and of James K. Jones, and then vowed that nothing would hinder fusion or deny Bryan Populist support.[33] However, there seemed to be a general understanding that Towne would withdraw in favor of a Democratic vice presidential nominee if he were not endorsed at Kansas City, thereby preventing the repetition of the "Tom Watson mistake." [34] Towne regretted any embarrassment he might cause Bryan but believed his candidacy should lose him none of the votes he had won in 1896. Nevertheless, the Populists had nominated the presidential candidate for the Democratic party, dictated its platform, and further alienated the middle-of-the-road men and the Democratic reorganizers. As for the silver Republicans, who would meet in Kansas City simultaneously with the Democrats, they were left to ponder the choice of rejoining the Republican party or of joining the Democratic.[35]

During May and June Bryan worked on his newly purchased farm near Lincoln, absorbed political counsel from about 200 letters a day, and wrote Chairman Jones long letters of advice, particularly with respect to influencing the Congress to adopt laws that would provide reform or embarrass the Republicans.[36] By early June, 24 Democratic state conventions had met. Of these, 22 favored him, and he controlled 436 out of the total of 930 votes. By mid-June enough states had instructed for him to give him two thirds, but the stormy fight in the key state of New York still remained to be settled.

Some of Bryan's friends were so sure that he would be nominated that they did not intend to have the New York delegation instructed, but John H. Girdner wrote Bryan that New York hinged on Bryan him-

[33] James K. Jones to Bryan, April 26, 1900, Bryan Papers; Omaha *World-Herald*, May 1–12, 1900.

[34] W. V. Allen to Bryan, April 8, 1900, Pettigrew to Bryan, April 9, 1900, T. T. Hudson to Bryan, May 16, 1900, Willis J. Abbot to Bryan, May 12, 1900, Bryan Papers.

[35] Favoring direct government issue of paper money over free silver, the middle-of-the-road Populists held their own convention and named Wharton Barker for President and Ignatius Donnelly for Vice President. Barker called personally on McKinley and told him he was seeking to detract from Bryan's Populist support and thereby help him win re-election. Omaha *World-Herald*, May 18, 1900; *Harper's Weekly*, May 19, 1900; Martin Ridge, *Ignatius Donnelly: The Portrait of a Politician*, pp. 397–398.

[36] Jones to Bryan, April 26, 27, 1900, Bryan Papers; Bryan, "Memorandum on Senator James K. Jones," *ibid*.

self, "the right man from this state," and "a platform that reaffirmed in a few lines the platform of 1896 and then came out strongly for the newer issues." [37] The "right man" was David Bennett Hill, but Girdner's plan to have Bryan run on a conservative platform and support Hill for Vice President in return for Hill's support for Bryan for President was developed without Bryan's knowledge. It was probably conceived after Chairman Jones, without consulting Bryan, assured Hill that "we'd reaffirm [not reiterate] the Chicago platform and declare against Imperialism and Trusts," and Bryan may have been confused by Jones's reporting to him that Hill was "all right." Hill was satisfied that Bryan could be elected if he would reaffirm the Chicago platform in three or four lines and thereby avoid the folly of alienating the conservative voter.[38] "Hill will make a hard fight for you when the campaign opens. I am satisfied of that. But he is distinctly not your friend," Creelman warned Bryan.[39]

When Jones told Bryan that Hearst now was "all right" but that Joseph Pulitzer would support him only if he kept quiet on silver east of the Blue Ridge Mountains,[40] Bryan outlined his position at length to Bradford Merrill of the New York *World*. "I want the Filipinos to have a chance to celebrate the Fourth of July and I want every private monopoly destroyed, but I also want silver restored at the ratio of 16 to 1 and I want the national banks deprived of the power to issue paper money. I also want the Constitution amended so as to authorize an income tax and the election of senators by the people. In addition to these I want to see the system known as government by injunction abolished and arbitration between labor and capital established." He still placed principles before personalities, saying that he would not purchase the nomination by sacrificing what he believed to be "right." If his principles were as unpopular as the gold Democrats said they were, why not nominate a gold man? He would fight for a complete restatement of the Chicago platform.[41]

Creelman then interviewed Democratic leaders from all sections of New York and reported to Bryan that they opposed the specific reaffirmation of silver in either their state or the national platform. The national platform should be a new creed to fit the new issues. "If they

[37] Girdner to Bryan, April 23, May 21, 1900, *ibid.*
[38] James K. Jones to Bryan, April 21, 1900, *ibid.*
[39] Creelman to Bryan, April 22, 1900, *ibid.*
[40] D. L. Baumgartner to Bryan, May 3, 1900, *ibid.*
[41] Letter, April 26, 1900, *ibid.*

say anything else to you they lie," he wrote. As for Hearst, he was saying, "we cannot, cannot, cannot, and will not, will not, take up 16 to 1 in the East." Simply "reaffirm," Creelman advised Bryan, and New York would be his.[42] But Bryan would not budge and banked on Croker to defeat Hill as state leader. Croker won the first round by stating that the vice presidential candidate should not come from New York.

Since 1896 Bryan had won adherents in the South and West by telling of his fight against the Eastern reorganizers and Tammany. In the spring of 1900 the ice trust disclosures gave Tammany its most disastrous blow since the days of Tweed, yet when it instructed its delegates to the state convention to vote for him, he did not spurn its support.

In the state convention Hill proposed a compromise platform in return for tacit acknowledgment that he, not Croker, bossed the state organization. The money plank was a wobble which demanded parity for gold and silver. Hill dominated the convention but Croker took his revenge by electing Augustus Van Wyck to the Committee on Resolutions of the national convention.[43] Had Hill either tied the delegation by the unit rule or been elected to this committee, he might have blocked Bryan's demand for free silver in the national platform.

On June 22 the Republicans renominated McKinley. Largely an assembly of businessmen, the convention was perfectly disciplined. As Chauncey Depew had predicted, the issues were to be "gold and glory—gold, the standard which . . . had given us the first rank among commercial nations, and the glory of our arms, which has made us a world power. . . ."[44] The delegates properly "went mad" with a stampede carefully arranged by skillful leaders and applauded a platform Bryan characterized as the most thoroughly hypocritical document ever submitted to the American people.[45] Stating that they had followed promise by performance, the Republicans took high ground: they had established the gold standard, restored confidence in the nation's financial system, disproved Bryan's charges that the gold standard meant economic disaster, and brought prosperity to the nation.

[42] Letter, June 2, 1900, *ibid.*

[43] New York *Times,* New York *World,* June 6, 1900; D. A. S. Alexander, *Four Famous New Yorkers: The Political Careers of Cleveland, Platt, Hill, and Roosevelt,* pp. 339–344.

[44] "Remarkable Party Harmony," *American Review of Reviews,* 21 (January 1900), 7.

[45] Omaha *World-Herald,* June 23, 1900.

Did the people want "four years more" of Republican prosperity? They said little about the bloody suppression of the Filipino revolt and implied that independence would be inconsistent both with the welfare of the Filipinos and the responsibilities of the United States. Hanna himself wrote the trust plank.[46] In countering the Democratic demand for reform he borrowed a slogan from the poker player, one that soon became synonymous with orthodox Republicanism: "I say, Stand Pat!" [47] The vice presidential nomination went to Theodore Roosevelt by default, yet the "hero" of the Cuban War decidedly strengthened the ticket. Popular, strong, imaginative, and capable, he rather than McKinley would lead the campaign against Bryan.

Forecasts on the eve of the Democratic convention generally agreed that McKinley, aided by the gold Democrats, would win easily. In McKinley's papers is a study of July 1 by Henry C. Payne. Of 447 votes, with 224 necessary for election, 206 were safely Republican and 64 probable. Bryan was given ten states in the South, with North Carolina questionable, and Utah was listed as "probably Democratic." The "doubtful" states of Delaware, Idaho, Kentucky, Maryland and Nevada had a total of only 30 votes. The Republicans were extremely confident. "I get good letters from all about. They say we are going to make an end of Bryanism this time for good and all," John Hay wrote McKinley.[48] Bryan himself judged the Far West "generally safe," the Middle West uncertain, and the East lost.

In the lead article of the June issue of the *North American Review* Bryan wrote a thoroughgoing exposition of his beliefs. The Republican position on each of the three great issues for 1900 represented the "plutocratic" attitude and the Democratic the "democratic" viewpoint. The gold standard law was but another Republican attempt "to deceive the public." Sixteen to one was the only ratio with a "positive, earnest and active force" behind it. "When the money question is fully understood, the struggling masses and those who sympathize

[46] *Ibid.*, June 18–23, 1900; *Harper's Weekly*, June 23, 30, 1900.

[47] Dawes, *Journal of the McKinley Years*, pp. 230–232; Croly, *Hanna*, pp. 303–304, 307; Matthew Josephson, *The President Makers: The Culture of Politics and Leadership in an Age of Enlightenment, 1896–1919*, pp. 106–111.

[48] Letter, July 2, 1900, McKinley Papers. H. C. Payne attended a meeting of the Executive Committee of the Indianapolis Sound Money League. He found that half of the members were "Sound Money Democrats" who intended to support the nominee of the Republican party and who sent McKinley a copy of their money plank for possible inclusion in the Republican national platform. Letter, June 1, 1900, *ibid.*

with them will support the double standard, and the money-owning and bond-holding classes and those who sympathize with them will favor the gold standard."

The trust question was another phase of the struggle between plutocracy and democracy. ". . . as on the money question, the line is drawn between those who believe that money is the only thing to be considered and those who believe that the people have rights which should be respected. . . . A line must be drawn at some point where the corporation seeks to establish a monopoly and deprive individuals or smaller corporations of the right to compete." As on the money question, "the sympathies of those who control the policies of the Republican party are entirely with organized wealth in its contest with the masses."

Nor did the Republicans have an acceptable foreign policy. Their treatment of Filipinos as subjects rather than as citizens and their Puerto Rican dealings violated every principle in the Declaration of Independence. Those who said an imperial policy would pay must be prepared to place a cash value on the lives of Americans lost in the Philippines. Moreover, "We cannot set a high and honorable example for the emulation of mankind while we roam the world like beasts of prey seeking whom we may devour."

The "issue" for 1900, then, was "the issue between plutocracy and democracy," for "All the questions . . . will, in their last analysis, disclose the conflict between the dollar and the man."

Surely the rapid development of plutocracy during the last few years will arouse the people to the dangers which threaten our Republic. . . . No nation has ever traveled so far, in the same space of time, from democracy to plutocracy as has this nation during the last ten years. . . . Foreign influence . . . has been felt as never before. Fortunes have been made more suddenly than ever before. Wealth has been concentrated in the hands of a few more rapidly than ever before. Corporate capital exerts an influence over government more potent than ever before. Money is more freely used than ever before to corrupt elections.

The great need of the hour was "to end the bondage of the American people and bring deliverance from the Pharaohs who are enthroning Mammon and debasing mankind." [49]

The article made a deep impression. Tom L. Johnson rejected free silver yet supported Bryan "because I believed that the free silver fight

[49] William Jennings Bryan, "The Issue for 1900," *North American Review,* 170 (June 1900), 753–771.

was the first great protest of the American people against monopoly—
the first great struggle of the masses of our country against the privileged classes. It was not free silver that frightened the plutocratic
leaders. What they feared then, what they fear now, is free men." [50]

Bryan's renomination was assured, but he faced a herculean struggle
against men like David Bennett Hill, who would reaffirm rather than
specifically restate the Chicago platform. In a sense the campaign of
1900 included two referendums. The first, on Bryan's principles in the
convention, was the decisive one, for it would determine whether the
Democratic rank and file would follow him. The election itself would
ratify decisions made in Kansas City in a nationwide referendum.

IV

"MY FRIENDS who suppose that I have any personal ambition for the
Presidency are mistaken. I regard myself as a Moses rather than an
Aaron," Bryan once said.[51] To illustrate his point he declined to attend
the Kansas City convention, although he kept in touch with it by
telephone and telegraph. He refused to indicate which issue, if any,
should be paramount, yet he molded the platform by approving or
carefully revising the wording of each plank and causing several
changes to be made in the sequence of planks.[52]

The drafting of the money plank provided the greatest difficulty.
In opposing Bryan's demand for a complete restatement of the money
planks of the Chicago platform, William J. Stone well phrased the
attitude of many of Bryan's friends:

The question in my mind is whether it is best to make a general declaration
that we indorse the Chicago platform . . . and stop with that, or whether
we should go further and renew in specific terms a demand to especially
restate and emphasize the 16 to 1 issue. . . . If a concession by us to our
friends in New York, Indiana, or Illinois, so immaterial as this, would
strengthen their hands and increase their chances, then what ought we to
do? . . . We must carry New York to win. . . .[53]

Bryan replied that "If it were not for the fight that has been made
against the silver plank for the last four years it would not now be so
necessary to restate it." However, the Republicans had made the gold

[50] Tom L. Johnson, *My Story*, p. 109.

[51] Louis F. Post to Marietta Stevenson, April 18, 1928, Post Papers.

[52] James K. Jones to John G. Johnson, May 3, 30, 1900, Charles H. Jones to Bryan,
June 26, 1900, Bryan to W. J. Stone, May 30, 1900, Bryan Papers.

[53] Stone to Bryan, June 25, 1900, *ibid.*

standard "the only positive plank in their platform. . . . It is true that when you reaffirm the platform, you cannot fairly be accused of deserting it. But we are not dealing with fair enemies." He would not run on a platform which merely reaffirmed the silver issue.[54]

On July 1 Stone, James K. Jones, John G. Johnson, James M. Guffey, and Daniel J. Campau wrote Bryan a joint letter. They believed that a large majority of the delegates and nine tenths of "the most thoughtful and conservative" Democrats preferred a general reaffirmation of the Chicago platform to a specific restatement of 16 to 1 and that it would be enough to say: "We reaffirm and endorse, in whole or in part, in letter and in spirit, the platform adopted . . . in 1896." If, upon "mature reflection," he concurred with these views, the writers would assume responsibility for having pushed them upon him. If he did concur, thousands of gold Democrats from all sections, not just the East, would rejoin him.[55]

Bryan replied immediately. He knew that the writers were loyal to "every line and syllable" of the Chicago platform, that they desired success as much as he did, that they were older men who had greater political experience than he, and that "the presumption of right is with you five as against me." But a mere reaffirmation of the Chicago platform would be regarded as an evasion of the money question, and a reiteration of all planks except that on silver would be regarded as an attempt to evade the problem of ratio. Perhaps a platform along these lines with a candidate in harmony with it would enable the party to win. Only the convention could decide this question. He had considered it for "months"; his conclusion thus was not a hasty one. It pained him to state that "as I believe you ought to follow your judgment, so I believe that I should follow mine." Distressed by difference of opinion, he assured his friends of his "great love and respect," but he preferred to fight rather than accept "a simple reaffirmation." [56]

[54] Bryan to Stone, June 30, *ibid.* Bryan had Hill come to Lincoln, where for three and a half hours they discussed "whether the silver plank of 1896 should be reaffirmed with the rest of the platform or be specifically restated," as Bryan recalled. Bryan to George S. Bixby, May 16, 1920, Bixby Papers. The conclusion may be gauged from Hill's comment upon his return to Kansas City: "I have a reputation for being somewhat cold at times myself, but I am not an iceberg." Telegrams, Hill to Bryan, June 29, July 1, 1900, *ibid.;* Henry Steele Commager interview with Millard F. Dunlap, n.d., Commager Papers; Omaha *World-Herald,* July 2, 1900; New York *World,* July 1, 2, 1900.

[55] Joint letter to Bryan, July 1, 1900, Bryan Papers.

[56] Letter to James K. Jones, July 2, 1900, *ibid.*

Bryan's forces at Kansas City were led by Altgeld, George Fred Williams, Charles S. Thomas, and Richard L. Metcalfe of the Omaha *World-Herald*, the last his personal representative and Nebraska's member of the Committee on Resolutions. Hill led the opposition to Bryan's "radicalism." He would "reorganize the party and make success assured" by selecting "careful, conservative, long-headed men" for the Committee on Resolutions.[57] His asking Norman Mack if it had occurred to him that Bryan "had to make a sort of sham battle" revealed that he misunderstood the arrangement with Girdner in which he, not Bryan, was to have made the "sham battle" against silver.[58] However, many delegates believed that he had Bryan's blessing as the vice presidential candidate, and Bryanites had to exert superhuman efforts to convince them that his nomination would either force Bryan from the ticket or compel the convention to disavow the Chicago platform.

To bolster Bryan, the Nebraska delegation resolved in favor of a separate 16 to 1 plank, Teller stated categorically that failure to stand by silver meant defeat in November, and Altgeld prevented Carter Harrison, who opposed 16 to 1, from replacing Thomas, who favored it, as keynoter.[59] During the night prior to the opening of the convention Bryan spoke by phone with every prominent leader in Kansas City. All found him a rock in holding his principles more important than party success. Meantime a special train stood by in Lincoln. If it appeared that 16 to 1 would be defeated, he would be whisked to Kansas City to make a fight for silver from the convention floor.

The convention opened at noon on July 4. The first item on the agenda, the unveiling of a huge sculptured bust of Bryan, provoked a pronounced demonstration among the 2000 delegates and 20,000 spectators. According to a critic, the man who turned the bust around so that everyone could see it was the only man who ever "moved" Bryan.[60] Equally unmoved, however, was Hill to cries for him for Vice President. Keynoter Thomas was forceful, eloquent, and unexpectedly conservative, and permanent chairman James B. Richardson gave sixteen reasons why McKinley should be condemned, but neither

[57] Omaha *World-Herald*, July 3, 1900.

[58] E. E. Crandall to Bryan, July 14, 1900, Bryan Papers.

[59] Carter H. Harrison, *Stormy Years: The Autobiography of Carter H. Harrison, Five Times Mayor of Chicago*, p. 202; Harry Barnard, *"Eagle Forgotten": The Life of John Peter Altgeld*, pp. 422–424.

[60] *Harper's Weekly*, July 28, 1900.

speaker mentioned 16 to 1 or the Chicago platform. The forty-minute ovation that followed Richardson's mention of Bryan, during which Hill maintained a sphinxlike posture, proved stillborn the hope that the platform would be as moderate as the speeches.

In the Committee on Resolutions, which met at 4:00 P.M., Metcalfe presented a specific 16 to 1 plank and precipitated a bitter fight that lasted for twenty-four hours. Bryan followed the proceedings by telephone and telegraph with a sense of expectancy somewhat diminished by a touch of ennui, for he could have written the history of the convention before it assembled. When Towne, George Fred Williams, Josephus Daniels, and others called upon him on July 8 to congratulate him personally, he took them out to his farm. "I must cut these oats in a few days," he said. "In fact, it is my solicitude for the oats that kept me from going to Kansas City." [61] The greatest pleasure Bryan received on July 4 was to give the signal, "Start the presses," for the first edition of Hearst's Chicago *American*.[62] Two hundred thousand copies containing a full-page colored portrait of Bryan were in the hands of the delegates a few hours later. Never suspecting that Hearst had presidential aspirations, Bryan was very happy with Hearst's asserting that he opposed silver but was nevertheless "anxious to please" and "to be of service."

The subcommittee on platform did not reach agreement until the early morning hours of July 5. Metcalfe presented Bryan's resolutions. Girard of Georgia and Van Wyck of New York proffered platforms identical with Bryan's except on silver. Tillman thunderously asserted that the committee would sit until the difference was settled, and Bryan threatened by telephone not to accept the nomination if a distinct 16 to 1 plank were not accepted. Late that evening Norman Mack, Croker, and others drew up a 16 to 1 majority report for the New York delegation and got Van Wyck to promise not to sign a minority report being prepared by Hill. When Bryan learned of Hill's defeat he said, "It did not come from here," but Hill's bid for the vice presidential nomination had evaporated, Croker reigned supreme in

[61] New York *World*, July 9, 1900.

[62] Hearst proposed to make real Bryan's dream of a Democratic newspaper in Chicago if Bryan gave him credit for it and arranged to have Mayor Harrison's organization back him. Chairman Jones approved, and Creelman got Harrison to promise support and then wrote Bryan, *"The thing is done."* Hearst immediately rushed the establishment of the newspaper he named the Chicago *American*. Hearst to Bryan, May 20, 1899, Creelman to Bryan, June 6, 8, 1900. W. J. Abbot to Bryan, May 29, June 4, 1900, Bryan Papers.

New York politics, and there disappeared any strength that the New York delegation might have exerted had it named for Vice President such well known conservatives as Judge Alton B. Parker or Elliott Danforth.

The decision of the New York delegation not to introduce a minority report greatly influenced the Platform Committee, which then veered toward the idea that an issue other than silver be made paramount. Since more than half the platform dealt with imperialism, militarism, Cuba, the Philippines, and Puerto Rico, those opposed to 16 to 1 said it would be logical to make imperialism the paramount issue. To please Bryan, the Chicago platform was "reaffirmed," but the free silver plank itself remained unchanged. Division of sentiment was so close, however, that the plank carried by a single vote, that cast by a "plump little nigger from Honolulu," as Watterson put it. "Prince Cupid," as the Hawaiian delegate was called, remarked in imperfect English that he had come 5000 miles to attend the convention. "And he did attend to it with that vote," ruefully commented Chairman Jones.

When Hill entered the hall at 3:00 P.M., he was applauded for 27 minutes. "That is my answer to Mr. Croker," he said while frantic friends telephoned Bryan about the demonstration. Unruffled, Bryan replied: "Never mind Hill. He is not running this convention and has no power. He cannot possibly disturb us." [63]

At 4:00 Tillman began reading the platform to the delegates. "We recognize imperialism as the paramount issue of the campaign," he cried, shouting the word "paramount." Cheering lasted but a minute and a half. Chagrined at the lack of response, he sought an answer from men seated on the stage. "Read it again," whispered Chairman Jones. Tillman read it again, pausing between each word. When he came to "paramount" he threw his hands in the air and shook his manuscript at the delegates as an invitation to rise to the occasion. The delegates understood. Three fourths of them arose and shouted in a wild demonstration free of stage management. From apparently nowhere 10,000 flags appeared, on each of which was printed "The flag of the Republic forever; of empire never," and "A republic should have no colonies." The delegates marched about and cheered for 21 minutes in honor of the new issue. When Tillman read the silver plank, however, only about a third of the delegates arose, and their outburst lasted only four and one half minutes.[64]

[63] Wayne C. Williams, *William Jennings Bryan*, p. 221.
[64] New York *Tribune*, New York *World*, July 6, 1900.

After a committee to deal with the Populists and silver Republicans was appointed, the order called for nominations. When Alabama yielded to Nebraska, William B. Oldham glowed, panted, and thundered in a truly impressive and sincere speech of nomination. His long address was tolerated only because all knew that at the end he would say the magic words "William Jennings Bryan." No one was surprised when he uttered them, but everyone acted as though Bryan had overcome obstinate resistance and cheered him for thirty-five minutes, with Croker and Hill both cheering as loudly as they could. Hill then seconded Bryan, stating that he would have New York's loyal support. He was followed by a judicious assortment of Bryanites and reorganizers. After unanimously nominating Bryan, the convention adjourned until the morrow, when the vice presidential nomination would be made.

Upon receiving the news of Bryan's nomination, Adolphus Talbot bounded into Bryan's parlor shouting, "You're nominated, old man! You're nominated!" With an unusual touch of cynicism Bryan said that "if congratulations were based on sound judgment November would be a good time to extend them," and he referred to the seconding speeches by Hill and other gold men as made by "prodigal sons." [65]

Throughout the previous night the Bryans had lived in suspense. Mrs. Bryan had never seen "Will" more distressed, for many on the Committee on Resolutions who opposed him on silver were his best friends and confirmation that silver had won did not arrive until 4:00 A.M. Several hours later, while musing about the actions of his friends at Kansas City, he put an arm around her and said, "Well, I have my wife left anyway." To which she replied, "Yes—and 16 to 1," and their laughter broke the tension.[66]

Bryan wanted a running mate who would be acceptable to each of the reform parties. He believed Towne the man but expressed no preference. His managers at Kansas City at first approved of Towne. On July 6, however, they switched to Adlai E. Stevenson and demanded that Towne be taken off the Populist ticket. Stating that their national committee would wish to name someone else if Towne were withdrawn, the Populists pleaded for a thirty-day delay.

The undercurrent for Stevenson had grown rapidly. As Vice President, he had lived with Cleveland for four years even though he favored silver. Known in the West and South as "a radical from the

[65] Omaha *World-Herald*, July 6, 1900.

[66] Mary Baird Bryan Journal, August 13, 1900, Mrs. Ruth Bryan Rohde Papers.

ground up," he nevertheless was looked upon in the East as a conservative who would mitigate Bryan's extremism toward business interests and altogether an admirable compromise. However, Thomas F. Grady, the Tammany orator, provoked the most dramatic incident of the convention by insolently defying instructions and proposing Hill for Vice President. From the roar of the crowd it appeared that Hill would be named, but when he persisted in objecting a dead silence came over the convention. Since he had refused to endorse the Chicago platform and support Bryan in 1896 he would be humiliated if he were named. Perhaps with his record in mind, the delegates suddenly dropped him. Thus Croker publicly shamed him and had a notable Democrat who favored gold drummed out of the ranks, a warning to all gold Democrats of the fate that awaited them.[67]

Towne received honorable mention but did not have a chance after Stevenson was brought forward. Bryan characterized his selection on the first ballot as "deserved recognition of party service." He had supported the ticket in 1896 and could be depended upon to defend the platform of 1900. He was "more available" than Towne.[68]

Stevenson placated the gold Democrats but lost Bryan votes in the Middle West, including Nebraska, and his election also ended Towne's high political ambitions. Towne's determination to withdraw as the vice presidential candidate of the Populist and silver Republican parties caused dissatisfaction among fusionist elements and weakened the cohesiveness of the reform parties. Perhaps Bryan should have insisted upon an Easterner like Girdner, who had a Southern background, or George Fred Williams, for either might have won the East on imperialism while he won the West and South on silver.

On the same morning that Stevenson was named the silver Republicans completed their platform. Led by Towne, the temporary chairman, and Teller, the permanent chairman, they accepted a platform more radical than Bryan's. After Teller named Bryan for President and Nebraska's state senator Frank T. Ransom seconded him as "the incarnation and personification of Americanism," the delegates chose him unanimously. While Teller, John F. Shafroth, and others tried to convince the delegates to support Towne for Vice President, Towne pleaded for a pooling of forces with the Democrats and the taking of

[67] Pulteney Bigelow, "What I Saw at Kansas City," *Contemporary Review,* 72 (September 1900), 451; *Harper's Weekly,* July 14, 1900; Harrison, *Stormy Years,* pp. 192–201.

[68] Omaha *World-Herald,* July 7, 1900.

Stevenson. Unable to agree, the delegates adjourned without naming a vice presidential candidate and handed the problem to their National Committee, in effect denying that their organization, as an organization, could remain alive. The next day the National Committee named Stevenson, but Bryan was still left with two vice presidential candidates, Stevenson the Democrat and Towne the Populist.

CHAPTER 12

The Solemn Referendum: The Election of 1900

I

BRYAN had been honored singularly, for only twice before had a major party renominated a candidate originally defeated. He was in addition the choice of all the anti-McKinley parties worth mentioning. Without spending a dollar, without the support of largely circulated newspapers, and without guaranteed financial backing, he had kept the leadership of the Democracy. Defeat appeared certain, yet he accepted the nomination out of "duty," he told Charles M. Rosser, because "I can save more senators, congressmen and governors that way than perhaps may be done by any other candidate and the party machinery will be left in better condition." [1]

Had Bryan veered from his dedication to the ratio of 16 to 1 his honesty, sincerity, and candor would have been impugned. "Your heroic stand . . . not only saved our cause but made you the grandest figure in the civilized world. I believe we are going to win. . . . God bless you," John Peter Altgeld wrote.[2] He had to keep faith in order to retain the support of the reform parties, yet his success was taken as a personal as well as political victory. Editor Charles H. Gere of the *Nebraska State Journal,* who bore Bryan no love, attested to his personal magnetism by saying, "Once remove hero worship from the politics [of Nebraska] and Republican control will be permanent," [3] and Judge Edgar Howard told the Omaha Jacksonian Club: "It is time for us to quit saying we are not hero worshippers. Truthfully I confess to you . . . that I am. No man has ever confronted me in public or private life who has exercised such an influence over me. . . . He brightens and betters all those who come into contact with him. Then why not go before the world and preach this man—the personification of purity—as well as his principles?" [4] Said Henry M. Teller: "If there

[1] Charles M. Rosser, *The Crusading Commoner,* p. 86.
[2] Letter, July 7, 1900, William Jennings Bryan Papers.
[3] *Nebraska State Journal,* July 11, 1900.
[4] Omaha *World-Herald,* July 11, 1900.

is a man in the United States today who comes near to Abraham Lincoln, that man is William Jennings Bryan. . . . I say Bryanism is Americanism, and if we could have less Hannaism and more Bryanism we should be better off." [5]

Bryan of course stressed principles rather than personality. "I hated very much to differ from some of our friends, but I felt like the moral prestige of the campaign would be gone if we took a position which could be regarded as ambiguous," he wrote Altgeld.[6] Friends found fault only with his will, which approached inflexibility. Josephus Daniels believed he had erred in pushing 16 to 1 again. "But," he said, "nobody could convince Bryan." [7] Unfriendly critics took his forcing of 16 to 1 upon a reluctant convention as an exhibition of personal power and iron rule not witnessed since the days of Andrew Jackson. However, Bryan now admitted that imperialism was more important than the money question, that trusts should come second and the money question last. After all, he rationalized, an economic evil could be corrected more easily than one that attacked the foundations of the government.[8] Had he admitted this much before the convention, as many had advised him to do, he might have been elected.

Irreconcilable reorganizers were left to ponder the fact that for another four years they could have no influence with the Democracy. J. Sterling Morton, for one, asserted that "There can be no reunited Democracy with either Bryan or 16 to 1," and Cleveland minced no words when he said that he had not yet been "forgiven" by Bryan for lack of support in 1896 and, *"pending his pardon,* have no standing in the new Democracy. . . ." The country would be safe, he added, only with a rehabilitated "old Democratic party" that would repel the excesses of McKinleyism and avoid the "absurdities" an "acrobat" like Bryan and a "sham" Democratic organization would perpetrate. Since he could not support McKinley and would not support Bryan, he must refrain from voting, yet he advised against a third ticket because it would help Bryan.[9] The National Democrats took his advice and killed plans for fusing with the anti-imperialists and for a separate

---

[5] Elmer Ellis, *Henry Moore Teller,* p. 333.

[6] Letter, July 11, 1900, John Peter Altgeld Collection.

[7] Josephus Daniels, *Editor in Politics,* p. 357.

[8] William Jennings Bryan and Mary Baird Bryan, *The Memoirs of William Jennings Bryan,* pp. 123–125.

[9] Letters to Edward M. Shepard, February 7, 1900, and to Judson Harmon, July 17, 1900, Grover Cleveland Papers.

third party.[10] However, various gold Democrats planned to put a separate anti-imperialistic ticket into the field at a convention to be held in August. Since the National Anti-Imperialism League, which favored Bryan, had already called for a Liberty Congress to meet on August 15, there were two rival anti-imperialist groups, one independent, one seeking to endorse Bryan.

Most anti-imperialists were pleased with Bryan. William B. Haldeman would not vote for the Republican party because there was "no honor there." Richard F. Pettigrew sacrificed re-election to the Senate to ensure Bryan's success. Horace White, Patrick Egan, Carter Harrison, and William A. Croffut deemed the Democratic plank on imperialism "admirable beyond question" and estimated that 16 to 1 would not lose Bryan 100,000 votes in the East. Others, like Carl Schurz, supported Bryan by the negative method of striving to defeat McKinley, or, like E. L. Godkin, supported him because unable to stomach the Lodge-Roosevelt type of Republicanism.[11] But the man who provoked the greatest dismay in the Republican and gold Democratic camps by coming out openly for Bryan was Bourke Cockran. Told that imperialism was merely a mask to hide Bryan's Populist principles and charged with inconsistency for opposing Bryan in 1896 and supporting him in 1900, Cockran retorted that his abhorrence of the Chicago platform was undiminished. Yet he cared as little for tariff protection as he did for silver. He had supported McKinley in 1896 on sound money alone. He was not a gold Democrat, silver Democrat, Bryan Democrat, or anti-Bryan Democrat. He was a Democrat "without limitation, qualification or hyphen." A new and overshadowing issue had arisen, and he would uphold Bryan in preventing the Republican party from perverting the fruits of a war for humanity into a cruel, cowardly, and treacherous policy discreditable to Americans and murderous to Filipinos.[12]

Thousands from all the reform parties gathered in Lincoln on July

[10] Charles W. Fairbanks attended the meeting of the Executive Committee, held in Indianapolis, and reported to McKinley: "Our gold Democratic friends feel much encouraged over their meeting; and they have determined to make a vigorous campaign *strictly* for you." Letter, July 27, 1900, William McKinley Papers.

[11] Letters to Bryan from William A. Croffut, July 8, 1900, C. H. Jones, July 18, 1900, Tom L. Johnson, July 10, 1900, Carter Harrison, July 10, 1900, Samuel J. Randall, July 31, 1900, Bryan Papers; interview by the author with Homer S. Cummings, Washington, D.C., June 16, 1955.

[12] James McGurrin, *Bourke Cockran: A Free Lance in American Politics*, pp. 203–204.

6 for a huge ratification meeting on the theme that "We want a change" —a change from trusts, despotic expansionism, war in the Philippines, taxation without representation, and an administration that placed the dollar above the man. Said Bryan: "You cannot have industrial despotism and political independence; and the Republican party stands today for industrial despotism and industrial aristocracy as dangerous to human liberty as the landed estates against which Jefferson contended in the early days of the Republic." With respect to the seething Boxer Rebellion, he cautioned that the United States must act honorably toward China. Other nations might try to "slice the Chinese melon," but the United States must firmly adhere to a policy of justice and fair dealing that would establish an example for other nations to follow as well as provide security for Americans residing in China. He warned American merchants that trade is profitable only when mutually advantageous, and he reminded missionaries that their task was to preach the gospel of love, not to act as forerunners of fleets and armies.[13]

A week later, in notifying William McKinley, Henry Cabot Lodge predicted that his re-election promised not only protection to American industry but the maintenance of the gold standard, "the very cornerstone of our economic and financial welfare." In reply, McKinley eulogized protection, said nothing about the trusts, and devoted more than twice the number of words to silver than to imperialism.[14] With unerring political instinct he seized upon the weakest point in Bryan's platform and made silver the paramount issue.

Bryan conferred with leaders of the three reform parties while preparing his Democratic acceptance speech. He found the cementing of fusion difficult. Since his platform was less radical than that of 1896, he could not win the middle-of-the-road Populists. Thomas E. Watson could not be enticed to stump for him. Sincere (or professional) Populists would not drop Towne in favor of Stevenson, and Butler sold out to the Republicans in North Carolina in return for his re-election to the Senate.[15] In a quandary, Towne visited Bryan. Should he decline

[13] Omaha World-Herald, July 7, 1900.

[14] New York World, July 13, 15, 1900; Charles G. Dawes, A Journal of the McKinley Years, 1893–1913, p. 236; Murat Halstead, The Illustrious Life of William McKinley, pp. 173–175; Charles Henry Grosvenor, "A Republican View of the Presidency," North American Review, 171 (July 1900), 41–54.

[15] Letters to Bryan from Willis J. Abbot, July 12, 1900, Sam P. Davis, July 21, 1900, Josephus Daniels, August 1, 1900, Henry L. Colquitt, July 13, 1900, Bryan Papers; Altgeld to Henry D. Lloyd, August 2, 17, 1900, Henry Steele Commager Papers.

the Populist and silver Republican nominations? If so, when? It was decided that he should drop out after Bryan delivered his speech and that the two minor reform parties could have a month after that to decide what to do.[16]

On August 8, in Military Park, Indianapolis, before fifty thousand persons, Bryan was notified by James D. Richardson. Instead of giving the usual acceptance speech he devoted ten thousand words to the single topic of imperialism. Except to explain that he read his speech because advance copies had already gone to the press, and for his peroration, he never deviated from his manuscript. In a cool manner, his voice completely at his command, he announced that "the contest of 1900 is a contest between Democracy on the one hand and plutocracy on the other." He reviewed his part in the ratification of the Treaty of Paris and the historical difference between Democratic and Republican concepts of geographical expansion, scourged those who would have the United States retain the Philippines in order that it might engage in international politics as a world power, castigated those who demanded expansion for commercial reasons, and chided those who believed that the spread of Christianity would be facilitated by a colonial policy. Above all he lashed out at the army contractors, ship owners, franchise seekers, public officials, and others who would gain pecuniary profit from expansion. He demanded that the Philippines be evacuated and that self-government be extended to them gradually. If elected, he would call Congress into special session to see that this was done. He also accused the Republicans of demanding a large army for reasons inimical to the existence of a republic, "to suppress by force the discontent that ought to be cured by remedial legislation." [17]

Lofty in spirit and captivating to its hearers, the speech gave evidence of intellectual power; it combined ardor without intemperance, argument without abuse, and fire without fanaticism. Its tone was moderate except for the charge that the Army built forts near large cities in order to intimidate the workers therein. Like Cleveland in his famous tariff message of 1887, he had dealt with one subject alone in an eloquent and dignified manner. In 1896 he had been a fiery agitator; now he could be called a statesman. The speech became a major campaign document and won Bryan many friends in the East. Outstanding

[16] Letters to Bryan from Thomas M. Patterson, July 16, 1900, James D. Richardson, July 16, 1900, Charles A. Towne, July 23, 1900, Elwood S. Corser, August 22, 1900, Bryan Papers; Omaha *World-Herald*, July 30, August 1, 1900.

[17] Omaha *World-Herald*, August 9, 1900.

among its converts were Thomas W. Higginson, John P. Hopkins, and Perry Belmont.

The Republicans naturally arraigned Bryan not for what he said but for what he did not say—because he did not mention silver, for example—and charged him with trying to secure political advantage on anti-imperialism when he had advocated expansion by urging the ratification of the Treaty of Paris.[18]

After Stevenson was notified, Towne published his letter of declination as the Populist and silver Republican vice presidential candidate. Rather than endangering the cause of reform by dividing it with his "phantom candidacy," he would give full and cordial support to Bryan and Stevenson. The difference between him and Watson was duly noted. On September 1 the Populist National Committee officially dropped Towne and chose Stevenson in his place. Now all the reform parties supported Bryan and accepted imperialism as the paramount issue.

While Bryan worked in Lincoln on his notification speech for the Populists, four hundred members of the Liberty Congress of the National Anti-Imperialism League assembled in Indianapolis. George S. Boutwell, Moorfield Storey, Edwin Burritt Smith, and William Lloyd Garrison, among others, declared McKinley the willing tool of special interests rather than the helpless instrument of blind fatalism. Unable to find a man of sufficient ability to head a third party, they advised "direct support of Mr. Bryan as the most effective means of crushing imperialism." [19]

Bryan spent the second and third weeks of August in addressing large audiences in Nebraska, concentrating on McKinley's stand on imperialism and bimetallism and his do-nothing attitude toward trusts. Then, in Topeka, Kansas, on August 23, with Jerry Simpson presiding in the absence of the discredited Marion Butler, he was notified by the Populists. In his forty-minute address to the twenty thousand as-

[18] Charles W. Fairbanks to McKinley, August 16, 1900, McKinley Papers; Omaha *World-Herald*, August 13, 27, 1900.

[19] A group of gold Democrats and anti-imperialists met in New York on September 5, organized the National Party, and named Senator Donelson Caffery for President. Caffery declined. Electors appeared in several Eastern states but the party proved unimportant. Wharton Barker planned to run on the anti-fusion People's Party ticket and win votes from Bryan in the Middle West and also the Irish-American vote in the East. He wrote McKinley to direct Hanna to furnish him the necessary money, but McKinley apparently did not succumb to his blackmail. Barker to McKinley, August 11, 1900, McKinley Papers.

sembled he stressed the need for cooperation on silver, trusts, and imperialism. He accepted a platform that called for direct legislation and the governmental control of railroads as well as of trusts, but he guarded his language and qualified his statements so as to give the least offense to conservative citizens. His speech was a skillful one, cautious and reserved in marked degree compared with 1896, furnishing evidence that he was more conservative than the "radical socialist" many Easterners believed him to be.

II

WITH MOST of the official ceremonies completed by late August, the campaign bogged down, as though by mutual consent. Despite good speeches by Bryan and an exciting stump scrap between Towne and "that predestined and incorrigible eccentric," as he called Theodore Roosevelt, the American people could not be aroused by any wrongs being done across the seas. Mark Hanna raised only a third of what he had collected at the same time in 1896, and Roosevelt complained to Henry Cabot Lodge about the situation in New York: "There is not the slightest enthusiasm for Bryan but there is no enthusiasm for us and there seems to be no fear of Bryan. The wage worker is no longer interested in free silver and cannot be frightened by the discussion of it." A week later he predicted a falling off in the Republican vote in the East, an increase in the West, and "very much the same fight in the Middle West that we had in '96 with much the same result." [20] Best Republican estimates in early September gave McKinley 22 states and 249 electoral votes and Bryan 18 states and 145 electoral votes.[21]

Bryan decided to whip up some enthusiasm. While Towne began a complete swing about the circle designed to counter Roosevelt's widespread stumping, he invaded the ten states most suspected of Republican leanings—Illinois, Indiana, Ohio, Wisconsin, Michigan, Minnesota, New York, New Jersey, Maryland, and West Virginia. The Republicans sneered at his "taking to the hippodrome" again. "That slackjaw of his will give him away every time he sets it going," John Hay wrote McKinley,[22] but the Vermont and Maine elections showed Democratic

[20] Roosevelt to Lodge, August 22, 30, 1900, Henry Cabot Lodge, *Selections from the Correspondence of Theodore Roosevelt and Henry Cabot Lodge, 1884–1918*, I, 474, 476.

[21] Youngblood estimate, September 4, 1900, McKinley Papers.

[22] Hay to McKinley, September 3, 1900, *ibid.*

gains of 13 and 23 per cent, respectively, compared with 1896. Most Republicans declared themselves satisfied. In 1896, a year of depression and discontent, they had carried Vermont by 40,000; in 1900, a year of prosperity and of no special excitement, they had won it by 30,000, and also won Maine by 30,000. Democrats noted that if this ratio of Republican "victories" continued, Bryan could yet be elected.[23]

From engagements in Indiana Bryan sped East to seek converts in Maryland. With him went Samuel "Golden Rule" Jones and George Wellington. Wellington, elected to the Senate from Maryland, had recently renounced Republicanism and now supported Bryan, particularly on imperialism. Trailing them came ex-Governor John M. Pattison of Pennsylvania, an ex-gold Democrat now stumping for Bryan. Bryan spoke mainly of his pleasure at the return to the fold of such gold Democrats as William L. Wilson, Hoke Smith, and Richard Olney, all of whom had been in Cleveland's cabinet, and about militarism and imperialism. In West Virginia he luxuriated in a private car furnished by its Democratic national committeeman, John R. McGraw, until he reached the Ohio border. There the railroad managers refused to let it be attached to the regular train going west from Parkersburg, and he proceeded to Chicago in a public car. Suspected of this discourteous gesture was H. H. Rogers, president of the road, head of Standard Oil's interests, and an intimate of Senator Stephen B. Elkins.[24]

Bryan opened the Wisconsin campaign by attacking the Republican full dinner pail argument, saying that the Republicans put the dollar above the man in everything they did. If Republican arguments were valid, how did they explain the impending anthracite coal miners' strike or the average daily miners' wage of 90 cents? He quoted from Dunn's reports and *Iron Age* to show that business failures were increasing, that less iron was being produced, that fewer spindles were busy. Competition, not trusts, he asserted, was the blood of life. On September 12, John Mitchell, of the United Mine Workers, called out 12,000 miners; on September 16, with 134,000 miners out, there was precipitated one of the worst strikes in American history. This naturally redounded to Bryan's political benefit until Hanna adopted his

[23] Joseph H. Manley to McKinley, September 4, 1900, John Barrett to George B. Cortelyou, September 7, 1900, McKinley Papers; New York *World*, September 4–6, 1900; Omaha *World-Herald*, September 5, 1900.

[24] *Ibid.*, September 7, 1900.

demand for the arbitration of labor disputes and threw his weight toward the side of the miners and asked for the arbitration of differences and the raising of wages.

On September 8 McKinley had issued his letter of acceptance, which contained an unequivocal declaration for the single gold standard but did not mention the trusts. Fully two thirds of it was devoted to answering Bryan's Indianapolis speech on imperialism. Republican policy, he said, was to establish a suitable government in the Philippines, to prepare the inhabitants for self-government, and to give them self-government when they were ready for it. Thus far he agreed with Bryan. But he neither defined self-government nor stated when it might be granted, thereby committing himself and his party to nothing.

There were only seven weeks left to election day, with the campaign still fairly apathetic. What appeared to be a boost for Bryan came in mid-September with his endorsement by the New York Democracy. Although Judge Alton B. Parker had some support for governor, David Bennett Hill endorsed Bird S. Coler, a young anti-Tammany Wall Street broker doing a creditable job as comptroller of New York City. Richard Croker baited Hill by sponsoring his former law partner, a machine hack named John B. Stanchfield, of Elmira. Hill buried the hatchet long enough to agree to Stanchfield, endorse the Kansas City platform, and ratify the nomination of Bryan. Nevertheless, out of his desire to satisfy personal revenge, Croker had nominated a dead weight Bryan could not overcome. Had a better man been selected by the Bryan forces, Bryan might have won New York and the election.[25]

In Ohio, Bryan charged McKinley with doing to the Philippines what England was doing to the Boers. On one hand he appealed to the Republican farmer to draw away from the party of big business, on the other he asked McKinley to explain the full dinner pail in the face of the coal miners' strike. By speaking fifteen times a day and putting in seventeen-hour days in Illinois, Missouri, and Kansas he impressed thousands with his opposition to imperialism and trusts. Alerted to his progress, Hanna told his representatives to "Wake UP." New York was not wholly safe, Illinois was not in the best possible condition,

[25] Willis J. Abbot to Bryan, September 18, 1900, Bryan Papers; Joseph Manley to McKinley, October 3, 1900, McKinley Papers; Omaha *World-Herald*, September 13, 1900; D. A. S. Alexander, *Four Famous New Yorkers: The Political Careers of Cleveland, Platt, Hill, and Roosevelt*, pp. 346–353; Lothrop Stoddard, *Master of Manhattan: The Life of Richard Croker*, pp. 223–226.

there was need for a hard fight for Ohio, and Indiana was in positive danger. "Wake UP!" [26]

Bryan returned to Lincoln to accept his nomination by the silver Republicans and to publish his acceptance of the Democratic. In addition to a succinct exposition of each of the Kansas City planks, his letter contained his promise that if elected he would not be a candidate for a second term. He then devoted several days to stumping Nebraska before proceeding to Chicago headquarters to start the last tour of his canvass.

Bryan's last tour matched his most hectic progress of 1896. In one day in Minnesota he delivered four hour-long speeches and shorter talks that added up to six hours of speaking. At an average rate of 175 words a minute, he uttered 63,000 words, enough to fill 52½ columns of a newspaper. In Wisconsin, he spoke a dozen times in fifteen hours on one day and only six times on an "easy" second day. Then he headed for Indianapolis and a huge meeting of the Democratic Clubs at which Stevenson, Cockran, James R. Sovereign, and others declaimed in opposition to McKinley's imperialistic principles. He spoke fourteen times in counties near Indianapolis before crossing over to Ohio on his way to Salem, Illinois, where he rested on Sunday, October 7, prior to stumping his home state. At the time, the prevailing odds were about two to one on McKinley. [27]

With the campaign in the close-fighting stage, Bryan shifted somewhat his base of attack. He asserted that imperialism was the paramount issue, but in the East he hit hardest on the trusts, imperialism, and labor issues and dropped silver; in the Middle West he concentrated on the labor and trust issues; and in the South he fought for silver. But the Republicans shifted too. Dropping imperialism, they talked about the evils of silver and about the prosperity and beneficence Republican rule promised laboring men. The status of American labor thus became a major issue. Also, while Bryan concentrated upon the Middle West and East, the Republicans wrote the East off and concentrated upon the Middle West and Far West. As in the last month of the campaign of 1896, moreover, both sides increased their mudslinging. In numerous speeches to tremendous crowds Bryan charged that the Republicans "will buy every vote than can be bought . . . coerce every vote that can be coerced . . . intimidate every laboring man who

[26] Omaha *World-Herald*, September 18, 1900.

[27] N. B. Scott to George B. Cortelyou, October 9, 1900, McKinley Papers; New York *World*, October 3, 4, 1900.

can be intimidated . . . bribe every election judge who can be bribed
. . . corrupt every court that can be corrupted." [28] His "decline" and
"deterioration," according to the opposition press, was evident in his
sinister agitation to excite class hatred, his appeals to the envy and
passions of the ignorant, and his stirring up of unreasonable discontent
and resentment on the part of the laboring man and the farmer against
the employer and the well-to-do. In 1900, as in 1896, therefore, he was
a foe of the social order, a promoter of dangerous dissension, and an
adroit and slippery demagogue. "What a thorough paced hypocrite
and demagogue he is, and what a small man," Roosevelt wrote Lodge.[29]

A unique feature of the campaign was that the winner of New York
state would probably carry the election. Since New York had given
McKinley a majority of 268,000 in 1896, Bryan must force a remarkable
change in public sentiment to carry it. Croker's arrangements for him
included speeches at Madison Square Garden and Tammany Hall on
October 16 and at Cooper Union on October 17. Heeding advice not
to set the city on fire against him by speaking on silver, he planned to
avoid silver except to point out that the Republicans were using it to
obscure the overshadowing issue of imperialism. His reception in New
York was a happy one, with such former opponents as Edward M.
Shepard, Hugh McLaughlin, and Cockran joining Hearst, O. H. P.
Belmont, and John B. Stanchfield in granting him a demonstration in
great contrast to that received in 1896.

The crowd of fifteen thousand in Madison Square Garden cut short
Shepard's introduction by shouting "Three cheers for our next President," at which Bryan raised his hand in deprecation and came forward
for a two-hour speech. He gave an adroit address, one pitched to the
level of his audience and spiced with humor, satire, and righteous
indignation if not contempt for Republican principles. He compared
the Democratic and Republican platforms to show how one supported
honest wealth and the other predatory wealth. McKinley, Hanna, Roosevelt, and their sort were "trust lovers" who sheltered trusts behind
tariff walls and tried to fool labor with their full dinner pail argument.
The Republicans sought the "splendors of empire"; they liked to hear
the tramp of armies and the beat of the drum; they wanted the glory
of crowned heroes coming home. In contrast, the Democrats "want the
light of liberty to shine so brightly here that it will be seen around the

[28] *Harper's Weekly*, November 3, 1900; Mark Sullivan, *Our Times: The United
States, 1900–1925,* I, 346–347.

[29] Letter, October 14, 1900, Lodge, *Correspondence,* I, 478.

world and everywhere inspire people." He was willing to take responsibility for ratifying the Treaty of Paris if the Republicans would take responsibility for what had happened since. He made it clear that the trust issue was at least as important as the others if not more so, but he reserved his peroration for the administration's policy on expansion.[30] Without a manuscript, in an easygoing manner, and without a single revolutionary phrase he appealed greatly to his hearers as a new Bryan, one chastised by 1896, one grown temperate and more respectful of conservative opinion.

On the next day, at Cooper Union, Bryan lost all his gains. Millions looked to him as the Messiah of their pious hopes for a sanctified land, praised him even as God's vicegerent. He stood in the dingy old hall where Lincoln had proclaimed his faith: it was expected that in Gayest Gotham, the very citadel of sin, he would hurl defiance at the forces of iniquity and oppression. Instead he held his hand over a square-faced man who stared at him unblinkingly and cried, "Great is Tammany, and Croker is its prophet!" Tammany's Tigers howled, and Tammany was his, but he had broken his scepter by aligning himself with a force of evil and paying homage to one of the most infamous figures in American society. He made Crokerism an issue of the campaign and lost support among the moral-minded. Roosevelt waxed sarcastic, saying, "Bryan has just moved into my own state to try to help that apostle of political purity . . . Croker, to get control of the state government and bring it down to the level of infamy to which he has reduced the government of New York City." Carl Schurz, filled with disgust, cried, "Bah! Wasn't it awful!" [31]

In the next four days in New York State Bryan spoke to almost half a million people. His friends naturally insisted that New York was safe for him. Letters promising him support increased in number as election day approached, particularly from old Republicans who said they would vote the true Republican ticket, that of Lincoln, by voting for him. But estimates made in the third week of October listed New York as Republican in all cases. McKinley was given between 273 and

[30] New York *World*, October 17, 1900; Omaha *World-Herald*, October 17–19, 1900.

[31] New York *World*, October 17, 1900; Omaha *World-Herald*, October 17–19, 1900; Schurz to Henry Adams, November 5, 1900, in Carl Schurz, *The Reminiscences of Carl Schurz*, III, 447; William Allen White, *Masks in a Pageant*, pp. 17–18. "Embarrassed" when Bryan volunteered to speak in his district, McClellan suggested imperialism as a safe subject. Bryan discreetly stuck to the topic. Harold C. Syrett (ed.), *The Gentleman and the Tiger: The Autobiography of George Brinton McClellan, Jr.*, pp. 279–280.

311 electoral votes; only five states, with 35 votes, were considered doubtful.[32] Part of the explanation of Bryan's probable loss of New York and the election, in addition to his consorting with Croker, lay within the state's Democratic organization, for the Hill and Croker factions disagreed violently and only professed admiration for him and his principles.[33]

Swinging south, Bryan spoke on trusts at Baltimore, making light of Hanna and of Roosevelt, who said there were no trusts. Such was his reception in Maryland, New Jersey, and Pennsylvania, the "trust ridden states" and heart of the "imperialist country," that his friends spoke happily of the tide that was definitely running for him and of the fact that he was still in perfect physical condition to complete his canvass.[34]

Roosevelt was cheered by a crowd of 100,000 when he arrived to speak in New York on October 26. New Yorkers gave an even more impressive demonstration at "The Second Coming of Bryan," when an estimated 150,000 greeted him on October 27. Fourteen thousand heard him in Madison Square Garden and thousands more in Cooper Union and in various outdoor meetings on a theme from Proverbs: "Remove not the ancient land marks which thy fathers have set." "The Democratic party," he asserted, "is the conservative party of today; the Republican is the revolutionary party." Deciding at last to meet the Republican challenge that he dodged free silver in the East, he declared in Cooper Union to a primarily German group that he stood where he stood in 1896 on the Chicago platform and did not attempt to conceal that fact, but that imperialism was now the paramount issue. "'Tis a gr-reat rayciption they do be givin' Bryan down in New York State," said Mr. Hennessy. "A fine rayciption f'r a State," said Mr. Dooley, "is that he's not dangerously wounded. Anything short iv death is regarded as a friendly an' inthrested rayciption. . . . All ye can say about Willum Jennings Bryan's rayciption is that he got by Wall Sthreet without bein' stoned to death with nuggets fr'm th' goold resarve." [35]

The campaign was now at fever heat. Apathy disappeared as election day neared, with voter interest attested by registrations 25 to 30 per cent higher than in 1896. Yet the odds were lengthening, with bets

[32] Revised Youngblood estimate, October 18, 1900, McKinley Papers; New York *Tribune*, October 23, 1900.

[33] Willis J. Abbot to Bryan, October 25, 1900, Bryan Papers.

[34] Omaha *World-Herald*, October 24, 25, 27, 1900.

[35] *Ibid.*, October 26–28, 1900.

made of four to one and even five to one on McKinley. The fight was hottest in New York, Ohio, Indiana, Illinois, and Nebraska. Bryan stepped his pace up to 20 speeches in New York on October 29 and to a new record of 32 on October 30. He had delivered a total of 110 speeches in the state and believed he had an even chance of carrying it. Then he devoted one day to Ohio, where 100,000 persons heard him. Said John Hay of his progress on October 31:

> I do not believe defeat to be possible, though it is evident that this last month of Bryan, roaring out his desperate appeals to hate and envy, is having its effect on the dangerous classes. Nothing so monstrous has as yet been seen in our history. He starts with the Solid South where he does not need to spend a postage stamp; he has Tammany with its vast vote and big corruption fund; and every walking delegate in the country; and of course adds to that all the regular Democratic vote of the North. We have an awful handicap to overcome.[36]

The fight in Nebraska was one for existence for both Bryan and Allen. The Republicans circulated the rumor that since his chances of winning the national election were none too good, Bryan would hedge—he would save Nebraska in order to get himself elected to the Senate. Two Senate seats were at stake, and they saw ways of winning both. If they could beat Bryan for President and senator, he would suffer political extinction; if elected to the Senate, he would go as a Democrat, knock out Allen, and practically wipe Populism from Congress. These rumors jarred Democratic senatorial aspirants like Gilbert M. Hitchcock and William H. Thompson and those Populists who wished their party kept alive. To Hitchcock's demand that he declare publicly that he would not accept the senatorship "under any circumstances," Bryan obliged by stating that he would not, even if defeated for the Presidency, accept a senatorship "under any circumstances." Thereupon Hitchcock promised Bryan full support for the rest of the campaign.[37]

While Bryan campaigned in the East, the Republicans burned his bridges behind him. By early September, Postmaster General Charles Emory Smith and Senators Joseph B. Foraker, William P. Frye, Julius C. Burrows, William M. Stewart, John C. Spooner, Charles W. Fairbanks, Albert J. Beveridge, Edward O. Wolcott, and Jonathan P. Dol-

[36] Letter to Samuel Mather, October 31, 1900, William Roscoe Thayer, *The Life and Letters of John Hay*, II, 256.

[37] Bryan to Hitchcock, June 7, 1900, Hitchcock to Bryan, June 16, July 5, 1900, Bryan Papers.

liver had agreed to speak against him in Nebraska, with Roosevelt, Hanna, John P. Irish, J. G. Schurman, General O. O. Howard, and Mary Ellen Lease, now a Republican, slated to follow. Great interest was aroused by five joint debates on the issues by Hitchcock and Edward Rosewater, while Hanna provided a slush fund that flowed like rain in some counties. Hanna found Rosewater a "cuss," and Henry C. Payne spoke of "undesirable gentlemen" who wished to go to the Senate, yet Rosewater exerted great pressure through his powerful Omaha *Bee* and took steps both legitimate and illegitimate to win a legislature that would send him to the Senate.[38]

During the last six weeks of his tour Bryan traveled 9000 miles and spoke in 14 states. His "visits" to five other states ran his totals to 19,000 miles and about 550 speeches. He had concentrated upon New York and Illinois, and had only infrequently gone west of Nebraska or south of Mason and Dixon's line. Although imperialism was the paramount issue, he spoke more against trusts than on any other subject.

In a three-day cyclone canvass of Chicago Bryan asserted that he was a conservative campaigning on the major issue of democracy versus plutocracy, that if elected he would make the Declaration of Independence the law of the land, and that the issue of imperialism made the present contest a more important one than that of 1860. Upon his return to Nebraska on November 5 he declared that the fight had been made and won. Money and coercion had robbed him of victory in 1896, but he believed they were powerless to change the result "this time." Wherever attempted, intimidation had angered rather than coerced the voter. Yet betting closed at four and a half to one in favor of McKinley.

III

As IN 1896, those who shouted approval at Bryan's words did not vote for him. McKinley received 292 electoral votes, Bryan 155; the popular vote was 7,219,530 to 6,359,061. In 1896 McKinley received 61 per cent of the electoral vote and 51 per cent of the popular vote; in 1900 he received 65 per cent and 52 per cent, respectively, with a popular plurality of 886,000. The Republicans immediately translated his small

[38] Omaha *World-Herald*, September 8–November 3, 1900; letters to McKinley from C. S. Smith, October 12, 1900, J. G. Schurman, October 25, 1900, John P. Irish, October 4, 1900, Mark Hanna, October 14, 1900, H. C. Payne, October 16, 1900, McKinley Papers.

increase over 1896 into a "popular landslide." Actually he gained little over 100,000 votes in excess of 1896, while Bryan lost but 150,000. Bryan carried every Southern state and the silver states of Colorado, Nevada, Idaho, and Montana. He lost his own state, city, and precinct, and the Republicans took Nebraska's senators and two of the six congressmen, raising the question whether Populism paid or fusion fused. Populism was doomed, and there was no further need for silver Republicans, most of whom turned Democrat. Bryan won his greatest pluralities in the deep South and Colorado. While he won New York City by about 30,000 votes, McKinley won the state by about 145,000 and the Republicans won the governorship by about 95,000. McKinley won all the states he had carried in 1896 except Kentucky and six that had gone to Bryan. Having received the highest electoral vote given a Republican since 1872, he asserted that "I can no longer be called the President of a Party. I am the President of the whole people." [39] The Congress also went Republican, with 53 Republican senators to face only 37 opponents still possibly inclined toward silver, and a working Republican majority in the House.

It had been a peaceful battle, one in which the crowds had been orderly and in which Roosevelt received more heckling than Bryan. There was a generally quick and good-natured acceptance of the inevitable by those disappointed; again congratulations and acknowledgments were exchanged between Bryan and McKinley. And with his second defeat some opponents were charitable enough to try to understand Bryan's objectives. Since the Spanish-American War, agricultural prices and rural land values had risen and the austerity of farm life had been softened by various technological and social innovations. The farmer was a "hayseed" rather than an "anarchistic Populist," "crank," "fanatic," or "communist." Most pertinent was the retraction of the charge that he was a socialist, a term frequently launched at him in the heat of partisan discussion and which was tantamount in 1900 to a mid-twentieth-century communist. As one of his neighbors, a gold Democrat, explained, Bryan's "radicalism" on free silver stemmed from his representing agrarian American rather than the silver states. To "get even" with those benefited by tariff and transportation tribute and monopoly, to overcome obstacles to competition and individualism, farmers would pay their creditors with a cheapened dollar. Albeit shortsighted and economically impractical, the silver scheme was never-

[39] Charles S. Olcott, *The Life of William McKinley*, II, 296.

theless thoroughly human, and the desire to prohibit railroad, banking, and industrial corporations from gaining at the popular expense was not socialism.[40]

Bryan lost in part because his political organization was heterogeneous. The South voted Democratic irrespective of issues, but the strength of the Southern Democracy had been vitiated in its fight against Populism, and fusion won him only four states. His increased vote in the East was cast against McKinley rather than for him, and he lacked the full support of a single party: in 1900 the splinter parties that had supported him in 1896 dropped off and named their own candidates; for every gold Democrat like Cockran, Watterson, and Olney who joined him in 1900, ten like Cleveland and Lyman J. Gage stayed away or, like Joseph Sibley, went Republican. Leader of a great party which was itself an amalgam of Democracy and Populism, he was not practical enough to master both parties. Again, as in 1896, he had mistakenly assumed that the interests of rural and industrial labor were the same, that their enemies were identical.

If Bryan's failure to heed the widespread demand for civil service reform lost him some support from the small but powerful Eastern group that advocated it, "too much Croker" proved fatal. Hanna said that Bryan had promised to let Croker name one or two cabinet positions and intimated that Croker might fill one himself. Others charged that he would reward Croker by turning the national patronage over to Tammany. Bryan never admitted that he was wrong in allying himself with Croker. Were it not for Tammany he could not win New York or the election. With a great deal of moral obtuseness he therefore relied upon Croker without considering that anyone who conspired with him would be deemed unworthy to aspire to the Presidency.[41]

Bryan simply could not hide the currency question from the people. Had he not insisted, the Jonah of 16 to 1 would have been omitted from his platform, the reorganizers and the foreign-born would have been

[40] Albert Watkins, "Is Socialism an Element of Bryanism?" *The Arena*, 24 (September 1900), 225–235. The persistence of the railroad regulation issue in the South is well illustrated in Alex Mathews Arnett, *The Populist Movement in Georgia*, pp. 68–72, 218–220; in the West by Russel B. Nye, *Midwestern Progressive Politics; A Historical Study of Its Origins and Development, 1870–1950*, pp. 31, 35. See also *ibid.*, pp. 102 f.

[41] *Harper's Weekly*, July 21, 28, September 9, October 6, 13, 1900; New York *Times*, New York *World*, November 4, 1900; Bryan to Ben Scherer, December 17, 1907, Bryan Papers.

won over, and the Republicans would have been denied their major weapon against him. Fear of the disturbance of business was a more powerful cause of his defeat than in 1896, for silver was a hard luck issue, and by 1900 Cleveland soup kitchens had given way to McKinley's "full dinner pail," which in reality was not full. Yet with the reaffirmation of the Chicago platform he was again pictured as the agent of repudiation, dishonor, and anarchy; because of his stand he was again criticized as being "opposed to everything science, experience and the best statesmanship of the world sustains." [42] Were he to drop silver *now*, friends suggested, he could be elected in 1904, but he must face the fact that the gold standard had come to stay.[43]

Bryan's attack on the trusts merely put money into the Republican campaign chest and left him open to the charge that he entertained no recognition of modern business conditions, that his hostility to corporations extended to capital itself and to thrift as such, and that he stirred up class hatred on the trust issue in order to ride into power as the governor of an unhappy and discordant people. As for his attack on the protective tariff, the Republicans said that it had aided in bringing on the current era of prosperity and that he was biting the hand that fed labor. Increased gold production and the stimulus of the war had pushed the economy into an upward swing, and his citing of statistics to the contrary simply did not fit the facts. Chairman Jones wrote him that friends in Arkansas voted Republican because they did not want "any more five cent cotton." [44] Champ Clark was speaking to a farm audience on imperialism when an old farmer called out, "Well, I guess we can stand it so long as hogs are 20 cents a hundred." That argument carried the Mississippi Valley for McKinley, said Clark.[45] Again and again the Republicans played on the theme that the foundation of prosperity lay in confidence that the future would warrant the expansion of capital investment and that only the re-election of McKinley promised that confidence. Could Bryan not see that prosperity had replaced depression, that wages had increased and employment multiplied, that general optimism had taken the place of universal pessimism? He had not sounded a new idea or rejected an old heresy since 1896. Therefore he was not a constructive leader. Rather he was an

[42] Editorial, "Mr. Bryan's Proclamation," *Gunton's Magazine*, 19 (July 1900), 27.
[43] Moreton Frewen to Bryan, November 7, 1900, Philo S. Bennett to Bryan, December 1, 1900, Bryan Papers.
[44] James K. Jones to Bryan, December 1, 1900, *ibid.*
[45] Wayne C. Williams, *William Jennings Bryan*, p. 236.

eloquent scolder, at his best when describing calamity, at his worst in suggesting constructive policy.[46]

Bryan was again outclassed in every aspect of campaign management. As in 1896 the largest donors were the silver mine owners, but the Democratic campaign fund failed to reach half a million dollars. Hanna and Cornelius Bliss raised between two and one half and five millions. Since contributions came out of principal in 1896 but out of profits in 1900, John Hay commented that those who made but gave not "deserved to be robbed to the enamel of their teeth." [47] Ample funds enabled Perry Heath to distribute between forty and fifty million copies of McKinley's acceptance speech alone, and his newspaper work was more intensive than Hanna's in 1896. He issued sixty documents on the various issues of the campaign, only one of which, however, dealt with the trusts. No major foreign-language newspaper supported Bryan this time, while money poured into the propaganda activities of such opposing interests as those represented by the American Protective Association.[48] In contrast, Willis J. Abbot, head of the Democratic Literary Bureau, had to scrimp and scrape. His largest circulation, of eight million copies, went to Bryan's Indianapolis speech. Except for Hearst's Chicago *American,* moreover, Bryan had no newspaper support in the entire upper Mississippi Valley, and most independent newspapers opposed him because of 16 to 1.[49]

The Republicans again played heavily on the soldier vote. When search of Bryan's war record availed them nothing, they attempted to vilify that record with a whispering campaign, and Hanna got the G.A.R. to his side by promising a Pension Court of Appeals, better pensions, and preferential treatment for dishonorably discharged veterans. As in 1896, General O. O. Howard headed a group of veterans who toured various states, including Nebraska, in McKinley's name.

As in 1896, Bryan carried the burden of the speaking campaign. Altgeld repeated his earlier performance, and Towne gave invaluable aid, but the Republicans had a larger number of good speakers than they had in 1896. Toward the end of the campaign Republicans de-

[46] "Mr. Bryan's Proclamation," pp. 27–28.

[47] Hay to Horace Porter, October 2, 1900, Thayer, *Hay,* II, 255.

[48] Perry Heath to George B. Cortelyou, August 20, 1900, McKinley Papers; William L. Strong to John Hay, December 2, 1900, Hay Papers.

[49] Omaha *World-Herald,* August 30, October 1, 1900; Willis J. Abbot, "The Management of the Democratic Campaign," *American Review of Reviews,* 22 (November 1900), 556–582; Willis J. Abbot, *Watching the World Go By,* p. 237.

livered 7000 speeches a day and Democrats only 2500. Roosevelt barn-stormed even more vigorously than Bryan. Bryan traveled 19,000 miles in 18 states, visited 493 towns and cities, and delivered 546 speeches to 2,500,000 people. Roosevelt traveled 21,000 miles, visited 567 towns and cities, and delivered 673 speeches to 3,000,000 people. Bryan lacked Roosevelt's inexhaustible vocabulary of vilification, and Roosevelt attracted thousands who wanted to see "Teddy of San Juan Hill," the man who had been "alone in Cuba" and "single-handed whipped Spain to a frazzle." [50] Strangely enough, Hanna was rated the third best speaker of the campaign. When McKinley tried to discourage him from stumping, he said that God hates cowards and went off to attend to Bryan, Pettigrew, and the West in general. He showed the people he was not the ogre he had been made out to be and did not wear clothes covered with dollar signs, as Homer Davenport had portrayed him. He branded Bryan's charges of Republican corruption "false as hell" and kept his promise to call him a liar and a demagogue in his home town. Similar tactics in South Dakota helped defeat Pettigrew for the Senate and to make Hanna personally popular.[51]

The Republicans and gold Democrats also conducted an effective smear campaign. Bryanism was not a faith but a disease, a nervous prostration that could be cured only by the lapse of time and the exercise of willpower. Bryan was a demagogue; a sophist who wore a colonel's uniform in Aguinaldo's army; "Lord Paramount" who was running on a "crazy-quilt-Populist-patchwork" platform resembling Joseph's coat; one who made a bold and a bad appeal; one who had a lawyerlike quickness in repartee but never convinced one honest searcher for light; a dishonest fakir, a pitiable blatherskite, a Janus-faced trickster, a quack nostrum doctor, and an impractical man who was the head anarchist in the United States. He was the choice of those who would evade responsibility either in the face of a creditor or in the face of a rebellion against the authority of the United States.

[50] William C. Beer to McKinley, September 24, 1900, McKinley Papers; Omaha World-Herald, September 30, 1900; Harper's Weekly, August 11, 1900; Harry Barnard, "Eagle Forgotten": The Life of John Peter Altgeld, p. 424; Matthew Josephson, The President Makers: The Culture of Politics and Leadership in an Age of Enlightenment, 1896–1919, pp. 112–113.

[51] George P. Waldorf to McKinley, October 13, 1900, McKinley Papers; New York World, August 1, November 3, 1900; Omaha World-Herald, September 25, 27, 30, October 8, 1900; Theodore Roosevelt, Autobiography, p. 127; Thomas Beer, Hanna, pp. 228–232; Herbert Croly, Marcus Alonzo Hanna: His Life and Work, pp. 332–340; Arthur W. Dunn, From Harrison to Harding: A Personal Narrative, Covering a Quarter of a Century, 1888–1921, I, 345–346.

"Not an appeal, from beginning to end, to the higher motives. The yelp and snarl of a cur from start to finish," asserted Hay.[52] Said Elihu Root: "When I see so many Americans running after him, I feel very much as I do when a really lovely woman falls in love with a cad." [53]

Bryan may have erred in championing too many issues. On one day he was an anti-imperialist, the next a silverite, on the third a trust-buster, the fourth a friend of labor, the fifth an Anglophobe working for the German and Irish vote, the sixth an advocate of the income tax. Only on the seventh day did he rest! A paragon of statesmanship with special adaptability for the mimetic art, he was heralded as the highest authority on monetary science, the application of the Constitution to the newly acquired territories, the control of trusts, the management of the Army and Navy, national taxation, and international relations and foreign policy in general. The wonder is that he did so well with such a heavy load.

As in 1896, slush funds, coercion, and intimidation helped defeat Bryan. Maryland might have made a good showing for him had it not been flooded with enough Republican money to obtain the purchasable vote. Some contracts were made contingent upon McKinley's election, and some workers were promised jobs only if McKinley won.[54] Later, when Nebraska's Senator Charles H. Dietrich took newly elected Congressman George W. Norris to meet President Theodore Roosevelt, Edward Rosewater, also present, told how he had printed a large number of ballots apparently Democratic but actually Republican that had been voted and counted. Roosevelt declared the trick disgusting, dishonorable, and disgraceful.[55] John J. Lentz of Ohio was defeated by eight votes for re-election to Congress and wrote Bryan that "Bribery ran riot in every ward and township in the district." [56] Altgeld said that "The enemy simply bought the ground from under us. They had carried this election by crime," [57] and Teller asserted that the Republicans had "plenty of money for purposes legitimate and illegitimate." [58]

[52] Letter to McKinley, September 19, 1900, McKinley Papers.
[53] Philip Jessup, *Elihu Root,* I, 236.
[54] John F. Osborne to Bryan, December 7, 1900, Bryan Papers; Baltimore *Sun,* October 26, 28, 29, 1900; Omaha *World-Herald,* October 17, 1900; *Harper's Weekly,* October 10, 1900; John R. Lambert, *Arthur Pue Gorman,* p. 283.
[55] George W. Norris, *Fighting Liberal: The Autobiography of George W. Norris,* p. 145.
[56] Lentz to Bryan, November 10, 1900, Bryan Papers.
[57] Altgeld to Bryan, November 7, 1900, *ibid.*
[58] Teller to Bryan, December 17, 1900, *ibid.*

Bryan's issue of imperialism did not "click" in a "khaki" election. Roosevelt rather than he aroused enthusiasm. Many were convinced that he had driven unwilling senators to vote for the Treaty of Paris so that the Philippines would be acquired and he could paint McKinley a new Caesar, and charges were made that he had met with certain insurgent leaders and promised them independence if he were elected.[59] He was kept well advised of the atrocities committed by American troops in the islands, yet he made no use of the information, possibly because he was embarrassed, for he knew the Filipinos were almost defeated yet fought on in the hope that his election might gratify their dreams of freedom. He could not convince the voters that his plan for the Philippines was better than McKinley's. His impassioned plea for abstract principles was applauded; his solution of the problem was deemed impractical, for it divorced responsibility from authority. Could we give the Filipinos a free hand and yet be responsible for their acts? American businessmen, among them cotton merchants of the South, desired new markets which he would deny them. He also countered the praiseworthy American mission of expanding the area of liberty and freedom to benighted peoples. He and McKinley presented a choice between evils to men like Henry D. Lloyd, David Starr Jordan, and J. Sterling Morton. Schurz voted for him and afterward said that "To vote for him was the most distasteful thing I ever did," while Jordan reluctantly voted for McKinley.[60]

In an article in the December issue of the *North American Review,* Bryan spoke of three major causes for his defeat—Republican money, the Spanish War, and "better times." Their large campaign fund had permitted the Republicans to undertake all the legitimate work of a campaign but also to secure the transportation of voters who were away from home, like college students; pay for political effort; and purchase votes directly. Second, they gained from the argument not to swap horses in midstream. Specifically, voters had answered their plea that the war in the Philippines must be ended *before* adopting

[59] Dean C. Worcester and Ralston Hayden, *The Philippines, Past and Present,* pp. 248–252.

[60] Letters, Jones Lee Jameson to Bryan, April and May, 1900, James K. Jones to Bryan, September 8, 1900, Bryan Papers; Joseph Manley to George B. Cortelyou, October 3, 1900, Abram Hewitt to James F. Scovel, October 2, 1900, McKinley Papers; Morton to Cleveland, November 2, 1900, Cleveland Papers; Claude M. Fuess, *Carl Schurz, Reformer,* p. 365; E. M. Burns, *David Starr Jordan: Prophet of Freedom,* p. 35; Jessup, *Root,* I, Chapter XVI.

a Philippine policy. Their most potent argument, however, was whether the voters wished to return to the depression times of Cleveland or enjoy Republican prosperity.

Asserting that the Republicans had received much of their money from large corporations, Bryan demanded that the public be protected against the improper use of money in elections by laws similar to the Hatch Acts of later years. He would make it a penal offense for officers of a corporation to contribute to campaign funds, limit the amount of money a candidate or a committee could spend, and publish the names of contributors and the amounts contributed.

The slogan "Destiny, Divinity, and Dollars" had helped elect McKinley. The destiny argument was a subterfuge, for the destiny of the American people was determined by the people, not by accident. The Divinity argument was merely the old theory of the divine right of kings, and Bryan saw no need for a carpetbag government in the Philippines. The Republican party was not a missionary society but a trust-ridden party attempting to force the nation into land-grabbing for the profit that was in it. He predicted that the expansion policy would be dropped when the voter came to see that it violated the principles of the Founding Fathers and predicated a large and expensive military establishment and increased taxes. Nor had the election settled the money question, and he correctly predicted that "When prosperity fails, the gold standard will lose its charm." [61]

IV

TEN YEARS of intensive political activity had apparently taken little toll on Bryan's physical vitality. He looked his forty years when viewed from the front, for his hairline was receding rapidly, yet he carried his two hundred pounds well and could do a good day's work on his farm. That his lecturing and writing paid well was true. Denounced as an enemy of property in 1896, in 1900 he was denounced in some quarters as a plutocrat because he was supposed to be the richest man in Lincoln. This was untrue. Moreover, he gave away $17,000 from his receipts from *The First Battle,* and his contributions to churches and charities were large, so that he was probably worth $20,000, mostly in real estate.

Many who disagreed with Bryan in 1900 nevertheless admired him

[61] William Jennings Bryan, "The Election of 1900," *North American Review,* 171 (December 1900), 788–801.

for his resilience and good spirit even in defeat. He consciously avoided humor on the stump lest he be taken as a mere entertainer, but he could be amusing. His humor was clean, never salacious, and rarely sharp. "The watering of stock has become so common that somebody has defined a syndicate to be a body of men entirely surrounded by water," he once declared. Again: "I am sometimes encouraged by the fact that while the Republicans have on their side the people with large fortunes, we have on our side the people with large families and we may grow into a majority." He was also capable of telling a story on himself: "I heard it said that President McKinley had no Philippine policy until he made the Omaha trip. He resolved to feel the pulse of the people and gather public sentiment from the rear end of a railroad train. If he had only asked me I could have told him how unreliable is public sentiment gathered from the rear of a railway train. I gathered some myself in '96." [62]

Except for an excessive partisanship that caused such aberrations as his lauding of Croker in 1900, Bryan's public and private life were ruled by moral passion. To be with him was like walking in the sunlight, for there were no secrets in his life, said James Creelman.[63] He was earnest, indifferent to abuse, intensely and peculiarly patriotic, deeply religious, and temperance incarnate. Impelled by an inner drive to seek the betterment of fellow men by engaging in political life, his second defeat did not diminish his belief that the people could obtain economic as well as political equality by the democratic process in the ballot box. He was a rare idealist who firmly believed in the eventual triumph of right and had the physical strength of an ox with which to seek it. "Stiff necked beyond precedent," an "unbending character," a man who "won't recant," said Champ Clark in admiration.[64] He was a man of simple tastes who preferred the trout stream to the theater, the farm to the city, the small church to the cathedral. He appeared somewhat provincial, but in a Lincolnesque way—careless of his clothes but careful of his morals.

The depressed and disordered 1890's have been portrayed as an "angry decade," "the watershed of American history," or "The Heartbreaking Nineties" that were "mauve" only to those who enjoyed comfort and privilege, not to the millions of workers and farmers.

[62] Omaha *World-Herald*, October 22, 1899, February 2, 18, 1900.
[63] New York *Journal*, May 13, 1900.
[64] Omaha *World-Herald*, October 19, 1899.

The problems of an industrial and urban society could not be solved by Bryan's essentially agrarian reforms. Not a single one of his predictions made in 1896 came wholly true by 1900, but the domestic issues with which he dealt—the tariff, money and banking, railroads and trusts, direct elections and nominations, the malicious influence of wealth upon politics, the maldistribution of wealth, and a conservative Supreme Court—were not completely resolved despite Square Deal, New Freedom, New Deal, and Fair Deal. Nor could the problems of a world power be resolved by traditional institutions. In foreign policy, Bryan failed in the short run but was right in the long run with respect to the Philippines and the whole "colonial question." Unrealistic, perhaps, in his doctrine that morality, love, and the brotherhood of man would solve international problems, he certainly represented the Middle West's belief that becoming involved in power politics meant becoming involved in problems characteristic of a decadent Old World and that the Monroe Doctrine should continue to ensure against both European intervention in the United States and American intervention abroad.

Behind all the perplexing questions of the 1890's Bryan saw a deep and lasting struggle between human rights and human greed, between acquisitive and humanitarian societies. Without the religious training of Walter Rauschenbusch or Washington Gladden, the economics of Richard T. Ely, John R. Commons, or Thorstein Veblen, or the sociology of Lester Ward and Edward A. Ross—some of whom never joined a political party—he gave political voice to their demands, as well as those of the masses, that morality keep pace with the changing American environment—that conservatism and capitalism be made responsive to demands for social betterment and that they should invoke ideals higher than those of the cash register. If this meant a welfare state, then he agreed with state leaders like Robert La Follette, Hiram Johnson, John Lind, Altgeld, and Tillman, and also with such later conservatives-turned-liberals as Theodore Roosevelt and Woodrow Wilson. At the turn to the twentieth century he was closer to Roosevelt than to Wilson, for he used essentially the negative voice, yet he pioneered in the advocacy of more important legislation than any other politician of his generation.

The major criticism of Bryan in 1900 was that he lacked the scientific habit of mind—he distrusted the expert, lacked pragmatism, was a romantic who appealed to the heart rather than to the mind. For instance, "he managed to penetrate to the nature, though not to the solution of the economic problems that harassed his followers." [65] However, if he lacked critical acumen "he had nevertheless a firm grasp on political realities . . . [and] was the first major political figure to give articulate expression to the rumblings of discontent that were sweeping the nation, the first to understand that the problems of politics were primarily economic, the first to formulate a broad program designed to translate the hopes of the nineteenth-century democracy into policies relevant to the practical needs of the twentieth." [66] Again, "It is a thorough misconception of Bryan to consider him a demagogue, a mere exhorter who appealed to the gullible masses. Bryan was a shrewd, realistic politician who stole two parties, welded them into one, and dominated that one for almost fifteen years." [67]

Bryan's defeats in 1896 and 1900 were symbolic of the growing pains necessarily connected with progressive democracy, for he was a symbol rather than the leader of reform, a diagnostician rather than a curer of social ills. He stirred people up, made them angry and inquisitive; he educated them to see the alliance between politics and business that kept men economically and politically subdued and unable to realize the promises of American democracy. A tireless physical machine fired by a burning faith, he was the "outward symptom of an internal irritation," a herald who never warmed his throne, a rhetorical voice crying before the Progressives and the New Dealers.

Bryan retained the title Great Commoner because of the Jeffersonian democracy of his manner, his teaching by example as well as by precept, his courage and aggressiveness, his being so full of agrarian America's prejudices and confidence, his sincere belief in the inevitable triumph of justice. He appeared revolutionary because he championed reforms conceived intuitively, by a sort of emotional vision, reforms anathema to those who had achieved economic and social status. Cleveland had been unwilling to tackle special privilege: he

[65] Added Henry D. Lloyd: "Nothing can be expected from Bryan but incorruptibility and an old Jeffersonianism. [He] has absolutely no comprehension of the modern spirit that is seeking transition through political action." Letter to Dr. Henry Fay, March 10, 1898, Commager Papers.

[66] Henry Steele Commager, *The American Mind: An Interpretation of American Thought and Character Since the 1880's*, p. 346.

[67] Nye, *Midwestern Progressive Politics*, p. 113. See also C. Vann Woodward, "The Populist Heritage and the Intellectual," *The American Scholar*, 29 (Winter 1959–1960), 55–72.

sided with capital against labor, corporations against consumers, bankers against borrowers, entrenched political and judicial power against the common man. Although some glimmerings of liberalism may have marked McKinley's last days,[68] he was even more conservative than Cleveland. "With him," wrote Edward A. Ross, "reaction was in the saddle and rode like a drunken bully." [69] He switched from silver to gold in 1896; he refused to lower the tariff, prosecute industrial trusts, regulate railroads, or do anything specific for the submerged farm and industrial worker; and he projected the United States from a century of self-imposed isolation into the world of international politics.

Few noted a significant development in the Bryan of 1900—his devotion to the idea that love was the only truly uplifting force in the world, as necessary in public relations and international affairs as in private life, and that virtue would inevitably triumph. Based on his home training, religious tenets, and experiences in the Spanish War, the idea cropped out in his attitude toward the Filipinos, Puerto Ricans, Chinese, and Boers as well as in his championing of the ordinary American farmer and worker. While it did not play an important part in the campaign of 1900, it eventually blossomed into an advocacy of arbitration, "cooling off" treaties, and neutralism if not pacifism in international affairs.

In 1900 Bryan enjoyed international acclaim as a progressive political evangelist, the foremost representative of the reform spirit that moved the masses at the beginning of the new century. The loss of such a few votes in 1900 compared with 1896 hid the fact that he had reached the height of his political pulling power in 1896. In the years ahead he lost control of the Democracy to the reorganizers, then regained control and ran for the Presidency for a third time. Although defeated again, he proved of inestimable value to President Wilson in getting New Freedom legislation through the Congress, thereby proving his long-lived political vitality. But during these years and those following he became more and more effective as a political Puritan crusading for such causes as business morality, peace, prohibition, and fundamentalist religion than as a purely evangelistic politician.

[68] Wilfred E. Binkley, "The Man in the White House," Ms.
[69] Edward A. Ross, *Seventy Years of It: An Autobiography*, p. 62.

CHAPTER 13

Low Ebb: 1901-1904

I

AFTER the election of 1900 Bryan refused various offers in the field of journalism and declined to run for the Senate, saying, "I made my fight for the presidency and lost. I am not going to take other men's positions away from them." He continued to lecture and to write. He also brought to fruition an idea he had harbored since 1895, a small weekly journal of opinion that would sell for only five cents a copy or a dollar a year, and that would provide him with a permanent and profitable business that would multiply his political influence by reaching thousands of people every week. There was no doubt, therefore, that he meant to continue in agitation the issues left unsettled since 1896.[1]

Knowing that he could not both manage and edit *The Commoner*, as he named his journal, Bryan engaged his brother, Charles Wayland Bryan, as business manager, J. R. Farris as superintendent of publication, and Richard L. Metcalfe as his associate editor, the last at double his Omaha *World-Herald* pay. He and Metcalfe saw eye to eye; it is difficult to tell whether an editorial is written by Bryan or Metcalfe or, for that matter, by Charles Wayland Bryan or by Mary Bryan, who contributed frequently. Bryan was rarely in *The Commoner* offices, in downtown Lincoln, but he made them a model by providing good working conditions, paying 50 per cent over prevailing wage rates, and having his workers observe an eight-hour day. He wrote his editorials at home or mailed or telegraphed them to Charles if he were away. With press work hired out, he had to invest nothing in plant and ma-

[1] Each of the three weeklies furnished to party workers, the *National Democrat, National Watchman,* and *Working Democracy,* was in financial straits in 1900. Abbot, Jones, and Johnson, of the National Committee, and Bryan could not agree on a merger, and each eventually disappeared, *The Commoner* taking over the *National Watchman.* Abbot to Bryan, November 11, 1900, December 30, 1901, Blair Lee to Bryan, January 10, 1901, J. K. Jones to Bryan, November 12, 1901, William Jennings Bryan Papers; *Commoner,* February 3, September 6, 1901.

chinery, and the 17,000 subscriptions received before the presses rolled more than returned his original investment. He secured good discounts by paying cash and gave preference as local agents for *The Commoner* to Democratic precinct captains; these could keep 20 cents for each dollar subscription obtained.[2]

The first issue of *The Commoner*, 175,000 copies, appeared on January 23, 1901. It ran eight pages on $10\frac{1}{2}$ by $13\frac{1}{2}$ paper. It would not seek to rival the regular dailies or weeklies as a news organ, "but as an exponent of Democratic sentiment and as a defender of Jeffersonian principles it hopes to make itself useful." Its purpose was "to aid the common people in the protection of their rights, the advancement of their interests, and the realization of their aspirations." The term "common people" included "the rich man who has honestly acquired his wealth and is not afraid to entrust its care to laws made by his fellows" but excluded the poor man "if he fawns before a plutocrat and has no higher ambition than to be a courtier or a sycophant." The common people are those "who form the industrious, intelligent and patriotic element of our population; they produce the nation's wealth in time of peace and fight the nation's battles in time of war. They are self-reliant and independent; they ask of government nothing but justice and will not be satisfied with less."

Like the newspapers of Ignatius Donnelly, Thomas E. Watson, and Robert La Follette, *The Commoner* was a wholly personal journal supported by the devotion of its readers. Numerous exchanges and clubbing arrangements enabled Bryan to reach the entire country. He was frequently quoted by the metropolitan press, particularly when he launched into a new crusade, but he was no muckraker. He was rather an essayist in progressivism, and his brief, pointed, and often humorous paragraphs on the activities of Congress and state governments came to be feared, for he discussed men and measures in no uncertain terms.

The first issue of *The Commoner* was too heavily political, quite dull, and obviously partisan. To those who advised him to "lighten it up a little," to put more "snap and ring" and "sensationalism" in it, Bryan replied that he would be satisfied if enough would be interested who were "on our side of public questions" to give it a fair circulation. He rejected William Randolph Hearst's advice to move the paper to New York or Washington, D.C., where the newspaper

[2] Interviews of J. R. Farris, Lincoln, Nebraska, July 5 and August 3, 1952, by the author; *Nebraska State Journal*, July 25, 1925.

money market was, and insisted upon dealing with principles rather than with personalities. Nevertheless he rapidly improved the paper. In April 1901 he enlarged it from eight to twelve pages, including two pages of unpaid advertisements, enlivened it with a "home department," garnished it with "witty sayings," and added writings on religious and patriotic themes. A year later the journal grew to sixteen pages and included additional departments, frequent reruns of Bryan's speeches, and an occasional cartoon. Increased costs were finally met by the acceptance of paid advertising, but Bryan steadfastly refused to accept money he held "tainted." He would not advertise tobacco, liquor, or goods made or controlled by a trust, or anything he considered "unfit for a family newspaper," thereby rejecting a competence of perhaps $200,000 a year in favor of a mere $5000; but in keeping with the times he advertised a host of patent medicines.

Many of the costs of publishing *The Commoner*, of constructing Fairview, the new house Bryan built in 1901, and of running the Bryan farm were met from advertising, and the large number of books sent him built him a wonderful library. Unfortunately, he read few books and preferred to editorialize about those he read than to review a larger number. He paid out of his own pocket for thousands of subscriptions to *The Commoner* and broadcast copies freely to members of Congress and others. When someone complained to the Post Office Department about having to receive the paper, the rumor spread that the department would investigate his circulation methods. Bryan blazed forth about "political persecution" and the department quieted down.[3]

For twenty-two years *The Commoner* mirrored the issues that divided men and parties in the first quarter of the twentieth century. It is a major repository of Bryan's political speeches, addresses at commencements and banquets, talks on religious topics, travel reports, and of the two long articles on "The Democratic Party" and "Bimetallism" he wrote for the *Encyclopedia Americana;* and it reveals the gradual extension of Bryan's interest from political to moral reforms.

Between 1900 and 1904 Bryan propounded many reforms and demanded that progressive Democrats support them. He wanted a single term for President, the popular election of senators, and the end of

[3] Alexander Del Mar to Bryan, July 27, October 2, 1901, Bryan Papers; New York *World*, July 4, 1904; Willis J. Abbot, *Watching the World Go By*, p. 242; Bascom Timmons, *Portrait of an American: Charles G. Dawes*, p. 113.

lame duck sessions. He castigated the lack of popular government in the House of Representatives, cheered on the coalition of Democrats and Republican progressives (Insurgents) that sought to curtail the "one man power" of the speaker, and continued his crusade to prohibit corporations from contributing to campaign funds. He would end speculation in stocks and guard against monopoly by putting a limit on the profits to be obtained from new patents. In addition to renewed demands for railroad regulation and for good roads he favored the initiative and referendum, the direct primary rather than the convention system, the recall of judges, and the municipal ownership of public utilities. He supported the idea of a postal bank, the reformation as well as the punishment of criminals, and pure food laws. He praised the National Reclamation (Newlands) Act of 1902 and the investigation into the "embalmed beef" scandals of the Spanish War, and he cried out against the exploitation of child labor. As a nationalist he would aid American labor by prohibiting Chinese and other Asiatic "coolie" immigration. He mentioned the currency question in *The Commoner* only four times in 1901 and only six times in 1902, but he consistently opposed laws providing for asset currency and until at least 1906 had a stock answer for those who insisted that the influx of gold had killed the silver question—that they admitted the correctness of the quantitative theory of money.[4]

Ever since he had moved to Nebraska Bryan had been so immersed in converting men to his political beliefs that he had not taken time to win them to Christianity, or at least to his concept of Christian ethics. Freed of crucial political pressure, he now confessed that he had been slack in serving God and began to try to influence skeptical young men who avoided the church. To this end he prepared "The Prince of Peace," his most widely published and most often delivered lecture, and inserted a defense of the Christian religion into other lectures, as in "The Value of an Ideal." College students and others have gladly admitted that hearing him determined them to go into full-time Christian work.[5] He spoke to all who would listen, be they

[4] *Commoner,* February 13, March 1, April 12, 26, May 21, June 21, July 26, August 16, 1901; April 18, May 9, 23, November 21, 1902; February 12, 26, September 5, 19, 1903; April 22, 1904.

[5] Dr. Joseph Sizoo to the author, interview August 25, 1952, Washington, D.C.; Reverend John Ironside to Bryan, March 16, 1922, William Jennings Bryan University Archives.

nonsectarian, Epworth League, Christian Endeavor, Roman Catholic, Jewish, or Protestant. The Y.M.C.A. in Canada as well as in the United States owes much to the thousands of speeches he delivered during organizational drives, and he spoke often at the laying of cornerstones, the dedication of new churches, and in church fundraising campaigns. He approved of, but did not join, the "Americanization" work undertaken in the settlement houses by Jane Addams and others, and confessed himself impotent in mission work.[6] He joined the Westminster Presbyterian Church of Lincoln by letter in 1902 and served it as an elder until he moved to Florida in 1921, although the family attended the Methodist church at Normal, near Fairview, most of the time. It made little difference to him what church he attended while traveling—the nearest one to his hotel would do.

Bryan's opposition to "tainted money" again illustrated his demand that men live by high moral standards. His arguments paralleled closely those of Walter Rauschenbusch, the young George D. Herron, and Washington Gladden,[7] and directly contradicted those of the Andrew Carnegies, Daniel Drews, and Russell Conwells, who argued that money making, although ignoble in itself, was holy because the money could be spent for good causes. He had no objection to the honest accumulation of wealth or to inherited wealth, but the amassing of riches through private monopolies was "a menace to government and civilization." The rich were merely the stewards of their wealth and should use it for social purposes. If they disregarded the claims of the needy they were selfish and self-centered. If they flouted their wealth before the poor they were vain, inconsiderate, and lacking in human sympathy. There was no place in the United States for "idle rich" but there was a great need for rich men who would devote themselves to public affairs and to works of charity.

Why this debauching of the moral spirit? "The commercial spirit that puts a price on everything and resolves every question into 'will it pay?' " he replied, and the theory which popularized the idea that special governmental privileges could be given a few special interests.

---

[6] William Jennings Bryan and Mary Baird Bryan, *The Memoirs of William Jennings Bryan*, pp. 454–456.

[7] See Walter Rauschenbusch, *Christianity and the Social Crisis*, esp. pp. 380, 387–388; Eric Goldman, *Rendezvous with Destiny: A History of Modern American Reform*, pp. 83–85; Russel B. Nye, *Midwestern Progressive Politics: A Historical Study of Its Origins and Development, 1870–1950*, pp. 162–172.

But, he insisted, money given directly was obtained indirectly from the pockets of the taxpayers. "We see the theory in operation on every side. The protective tariff schedules illustrate it; our financial system rests upon it; the trusts hide themselves behind it, and the imperialists are substituting this theory for the Constitution." It was no wonder, then, that money was being used to carry elections, that certain party managers turned to favored corporations for campaign contributions, that public officials high and low were using the government as if it were a private asset, and that ordinary individuals "yielded to the temptation to sell the only political influence they have, namely—the ballot." What was the remedy? There was but one remedy—"an appeal to the moral sense of the country; an awakening of the public conscience." [8] In a widely publicized speech in Madison Square Garden in January 1904 he said: "When I tell you that the first and most important object of government is not money-making or the extension of commerce or even the care of property, but rather the protection of human rights, I am not asserting an original proposition, I am not promulgating a western theory; I am simply giving expression to a fundamental truth. . . ." [9]

Bryan's favorite target as the immoral businessman was John D. Rockefeller. The recipients of gifts from illegally or immorally acquired sources, as from the Standard Oil trust, he insisted, would suffer a "silencing influence." They would be restrained from denouncing the misconduct of the benefactor and his disregard of human rights in the acquisition of wealth. Rockefeller, said Bryan, "has in acquiring his fortune resorted to every evil practice known to the trusts. If but a few of the facts set forth in [Henry D. Lloyd's] *Wealth vs. Commonwealth* were correct, no criminal now incarcerated . . . for larceny has shown more indifference to human rights and property rights than this same Rockefeller. Does it lessen his sins that he has given liberally to churches and colleges? Nay, it exaggerates them, for he attempts to make others share with him the odium that his conduct merits." He concluded that "a Christian has been too well defined to enable a man like Rockefeller to be mistaken for one." [10]

Bryan judged politicians as well as educators and businessmen by

[8] *Commoner,* January 29, 1904.

[9] *Ibid.,* February 12, 1904.

[10] *Ibid.,* November 21, 1902; June 5, October 23, 1903; January 29, February 12, May 13, 27, June 10, 1904.

moral standards. In the South Carolina senatorship contest of 1901 he preferred Benjamin Tillman to John L. McLaurin because "Tillman represents the man and McLaurin the dollar." In Ohio he opposed John R. McLean for senator because he was silent on the principles of the Kansas City platform, and he opposed both Nebraska senators because they represented, respectively, the Burlington and Union Pacific railroads rather than the people and because no crusade for the reduction of the rate of interest, the lowering of railroad rates, the establishment of government savings banks, or the extermination of the trusts would be demanded by them.[11] Finally, former Populist and gold Democrat leaders who were being appointed to office by McKinley proved that "there was secret fusion between the Republicans and the middle-of-the-road Populists" in 1896 and 1900, and "a secret understanding between the Republicans and those who were in charge of the Palmer and Buckner movement." [12]

Thus Bryan offered more than mere political leadership. If, as millions believed, the government was slipping away from them into the hands of powerful commercial interests, if imperialism was a costly crusade for political and financial spoil, if the tariff was the mother of trusts, if commercialism debauched municipal, state, and national governments and tainted money corrupted education, then Bryan peculiarly represented the forces that sought to overthrow those who were turning government into a commercial asset. His broadened political interests, his emphasis upon principle, and his appearance as teacher and preacher rather than as perennial candidate led to his characterization as a moral philosopher. As an editor and speaker he had a poor place from which to seek another presidential nomination. But as an editor and speaker, particularly on the Chautauqua circuit, he was in an excellent position to publicize needed reforms and to name candidates.

II

ON SEPTEMBER 6, 1901 McKinley delivered a speech at the Pan American Exposition at Buffalo in which he frankly confessed that he was outgrowing his old doctrine of an exclusive tariff. Reciprocity treaties were in harmony with the spirit of the times, measures of retaliation were not. "If perchance some of our tariffs are no longer

[11] *Ibid.*, March 8, May 31, July 26, 1901; May 23, 1902.
[12] *Ibid.*, August 9, 1901.

needed for revenue and to encourage and foster our industries at home, why should they not be employed to extend and promote our markets abroad?" he asked,[13] thus indicating that an era of American history had ended. The address had an important bearing on the future tariff policy of the Republican party, and for the rest of his life Bryan quoted McKinley in rebuttal to protectionist arguments.

Leon Czolgosz's bullet opened the Roosevelt era, an era of profound change for the Presidency, for the United States, and for Bryan. Bryan expressed sincere admiration for McKinley as a man. "He was gentle in spirit, and kind in word and deed," he said as he fulminated against the use of violence, especially in a democracy.[14] He attended the services held for McKinley in Lincoln and delivered a tender memorial address for the man he had fought so bitterly in two campaigns.[15]

Theodore Roosevelt was a far cry from both McKinley and Bryan. Roosevelt was the Patrician Reformer; Bryan the Commoner. Both men sought to bring disinterested honesty of purpose into public life; both were ambitious; both were magnetic figures. But Bryan was an Atomist and Roosevelt a Regulationist, Bryan a purist and Roosevelt a compromiser. Bryan would smash all business combinations he believed monopolies; Roosevelt would regulate the former and when necessary forbid the latter, following a distinction between "good" and "bad" trusts. Bryan was a Jeffersonian using Jacksonian tactics, Roosevelt a Hamiltonian with a social conscience. Roosevelt sought to close the breach between capital and labor by dealing justly with each; Bryan favored the small businessman over the corporation. Roosevelt and Bryan disagreed over the degree of conformity required by the principle of the separation of powers. Bryan wanted the Supreme Court to reflect the convictions of the people; Roosevelt wanted it to reflect, as far as possible, the convictions of the President. Roosevelt wanted judges who knew the law; Bryan wanted judges who understood the failings of men. Bryan would have the Congress an equal in the legislative process; Roosevelt would prevent the Congress from disintegrating into its sectional elements and foundering

[13] Kansas City *Star*, October 8, 1901; Chicago *Daily News*, October 9, 1901; *Commoner*, September 27, 1901; Charles S. Olcott, *The Life of William McKinley*, II, 311–332, 377–384.

[14] *Commoner*, September 13, 1901.

[15] *Ibid.*, September 20, 1901; Murat Halstead, *The Illustrious Life of William McKinley*, pp. 265–267.

in a bog of contrary purposes by making the Presidency a place for real rather than negative leadership.

Roosevelt avoided really controversial questions like tariff revision and banking reform, yet he dramatized his issues and asked the right questions even if he did not find the right answers; and it is generally agreed that the significance of the election of 1896 became fully apparent with his incumbency. Bryan demanded reform "now" and dared Roosevelt to be a progressive. Both were at a disadvantage, however. Bryan had the reorganizers against him and could not speak for a united party. Moreover, if Roosevelt became a reformer, he himself would have to become increasingly radical, perhaps to the point of acceding to Lloyd's demand to "get up and produce the sentiment" for the ultra-Populists' and Socialists' dreams of the public ownership of utilities and direct legislation. Bryan later complained that the new St. George stole the lance with which he had twice campaigned, and Vachel Lindsay declared that Roosevelt "cursed Bryan and then aped his ways." It is paradoxical that Bryan, who had gone twice to defeat leading a liberal Democratic-Populist coalition, should find his reforms implemented by a conservative turned progressive.[16]

Before Roosevelt could become a reformer, however, he had to undergo a remarkable personal conversion, as Woodrow Wilson later did, for his social philosophy in 1901 lagged behind even that of Mark Hanna, or of McKinley. During his early years as President, moreover, he was caught between a group of Republican reform governors and mayors and the Republican Insurgents in Congress on the one hand and the Old Guard on the other. Bryan was a theorist powerless officially to institute his program of reform. Roosevelt was a conservative busy with means rather than ends, but he had the practical problems of nationalizing the reforms demanded by the Midwestern agrarians and of certain Easterners and of administering the government in such a way that dissident elements within his party would not

[16] George Fred Williams to H. D. Lloyd, February 18, 1903, Lloyd to Williams, March 1, 1903, Henry Steele Commager Papers; Theodore Roosevelt to John St. Loe Strachey, March 8, 1901, in Elting E. Morison and John M. Blum (eds.), *The Letters of Theodore Roosevelt*, III, 8–9; Roosevelt to Lodge, June 19, 1901, Henry Cabot Lodge, *Selections from the Correspondence of Theodore Roosevelt and Henry Cabot Lodge, 1884–1918*, I, 493–494; John Morton Blum, *The Republican Roosevelt*, p. 61; Caro Lloyd, *Henry Demarest Lloyd*, II, 239, 254, 272; Frederick A. Ogg, *National Progress 1907–1917*, p. 217; George E. Mowry, *The Era of Theodore Roosevelt, 1900–1912*, pp. 38–58.

be offended and, above all, would support him for a full term. "Political expediency," he once said, "draws the line." Bryan demanded a graphic program; Roosevelt sold the voters the idea that he would be fair, would give them a "square deal." [17] Had Roosevelt been more the progressive and less the politician, he might have provided national leadership, as Bryan had for the Granger-Greenback-Populist-liberal Democratic alliance, to the sectionally potent but nationally impotent Progressive movement.

In foreign affairs Bryan was an isolationist. As an anti-imperialist, anti-monarchist, and silverite, he disliked Britain. A martial chauvinist and an imperialist, Roosevelt liked Britain and undertook a vigorous foreign policy that advanced the United States to a position of world prominence. Roosevelt respected military power perhaps unduly; [18] Bryan put increasing emphasis upon the power of love as an agent for maintaining world peace. Roosevelt would keep the United States strong and thus able to avoid threats to world peace; Bryan would let the United States live such an exemplary life that its example would be followed by other nations.

Never has a twice-defeated candidate of a party so ably and conscientiously performed the task of leader of the opposition as did Bryan. He said that he would test Roosevelt on merit—he had no disposition to prejudge. Being more a Southern than a Northern Democrat and a firm believer in white supremacy, in his next breath he said that Roosevelt's inviting of Booker T. Washington to dine at the White House was "unfortunate," for it would "give depth and acrimony to a race feeling already strained to the uttermost." [19] Within two weeks of Roosevelt's taking of the oath he began to offer

[17] George E. Mowry, *Theodore Roosevelt and the Progressive Movement,* pp. 10–16; Blum, *Roosevelt,* pp. 1–36.

[18] "How dangerous Roosevelt is few of us have the imagination to foresee. . . . He can't see a cowboy on a bucking horse without talking War. He is a degenerate —Caesar come again. . . . He is a mad dog. I don't detect a single trait or purpose in Roosevelt sympathetic to anything sane and good." Henry D. Lloyd to Samuel Bowles, June 23, 1903, Commager Papers.

[19] B. T. Washington to Bryan, October 26, November 14, 1901, Bryan Papers; *Commoner,* September 20, November 1, 1901; Roosevelt to Washington, Morison and Blum (eds.), *Letters of Roosevelt,* III, 181 n. See W. J. Bryan, *Under Other Flags,* pp. 263–264, and Edward McNeil Burns, *The American Idea of Mission,* pp. 20, 24, 55–58, 188–189. That Bryan supported education for Negroes is revealed in his contributing money to the Tuskegee Normal and Industrial Institute. B. T. Washington to Bryan, February 25, 1890, Bryan Papers.

advice. Roosevelt had three and a half years to prove himself. Would he spend his efforts in official duties or in trying to capture the next Republican convention? Rather than seek election he should renounce his candidacy in 1904. Thus he could devote his "strenuous life" to making his administration honest and efficient rather than to fighting the Republican party's bosses or surrendering to them. If he ran he would antagonize the great corporations whose contributions were so helpful in campaigns and also have to placate the financiers who insisted upon controlling the financial policy of his administration. Roosevelt had to decide between himself and the people. Which road would he take? [20]

Roosevelt took an "on the one hand this and on the other hand that" attitude in his first message on matters of greatest concern to Bryan. Organized labor was entitled to protection but must not be allowed to abuse its privileges. Perhaps the tariff should be lowered, but not at the expense of industry. The granting of rebates by railroads must be halted, but instead of real trust control he recommended the creation of a Department of Commerce and Labor that would merely investigate corporate earnings. Bryan was dissatisfied. The President was "badly scared," he said, "and had borrowed the epithets of the trust magnates" in speaking of corporation control.[21]

Bryan's major criticisms for the rest of Roosevelt's term dealt largely with Roosevelt's cabinet changes; his lack of progress in trust control, tariff reform, and currency reform; his bellicose foreign policy; his dealing with only the superficial aspects of the coal strike of 1902; and his activities in seeking the presidential nomination.

Roosevelt had said he would keep McKinley's cabinet and follow his policies. Within three months, however, Postmaster General Charles Emory Smith resigned and was replaced by a "shrewd wire-puller," Henry C. Payne, and Secretary of the Treasury Gage was replaced by ex-Governor Leslie M. Shaw of Iowa, an "ultra-gold man," said Bryan, and "an ultra-advocate of the doctrine that the Treasury Department should be run according to the wishes of Wall Street." By early 1904 only John Hay and James Wilson remained of McKin-

[20] *Commoner*, September 27, 1901.

[21] *Ibid.*, December 13, 1901. See Roosevelt to Knox, November 10, December 19, 1904, Philander C. Knox Papers; Benjamin Parke De Witt, *The Progressive Movement: A Non-partisan, Comprehensive Discussion of Current Tendencies in American Politics*, pp. 49, 113–123; Arthur M. Johnson, "Theodore Roosevelt and the Bureau of Corporations," *Mississippi Valley Historical Review*, 45 (March 1959), 571–590.

ley's original cabinet. Moreover, for personal political ends, Roosevelt appointed to office some men, like James C. Clarkson, whom he had declared unfit for public service while he was Civil Service Commissioner.

In *The Commoner,* in articles in such magazines as *The Independent* and *Collier's,* and on the stump, Bryan waged incessant war on Roosevelt's attitude toward trusts and the tariff. By appointing Shaw, retaining Philander C. Knox, a former trust attorney, as Attorney General, and by his messages to Congress, it was evident to Bryan that Roosevelt preferred to control rather than abolish trusts. He challenged Roosevelt to destroy the "indefensible and insufferable" United States Steel Company, the first billion dollar corporation, alleging that it would provoke grave social and political consequences. Apprised by John Moody of the continuation of industrial and financial mergers and amalgamations, he frequently complained about the "Morganization of America"; he complimented governors like Robert La Follette of Wisconsin for their efforts to regulate corporations but was not silenced even by Roosevelt's suit against the Northern Securities Company, saying that the President should broaden the scope of his suits to include other trusts, especially the beef trust (which Roosevelt soon did), and institute criminal as well as civil proceedings against them. Since Roosevelt "talked" against the trusts but did nothing to "hurt" them, he concluded that he was insincere, that perhaps the rumor was true that a senate cabal had offered him a free hand in everything else if he would leave economic and financial policy to Nelson W. Aldrich. The rumor was substantiated, in part, by the fact that the Elkins law, which forbade rebating, was framed with the consent of the railroad operators; that the investigations of the Bureau of Corporations, so feared by business, would not begin until after the elections of 1904; and that Roosevelt retained the personal friendship of the trust magnates. But Roosevelt was not so naïve as to institute criminal proceedings against corporation directors with the Republican national convention in the offing. Despite Bryan's assertion that all he had done was to approve laws that provided "publicity, publicity, publicity," [22] Roosevelt waited until after the election of 1904 to take real action against the trusts. It was the forty-four suits instituted in his seven years, mostly in 1906 and 1907, that earned him the name "trust buster." Later he came

[22] *Commoner,* January 4, February 5, March 11, 18, 25, 1904; Arthur M. Johnson, "The Anti-Trust Law, 1901–1909" (unpublished Ms.).

to agree with Bryan that effective action against the trusts could come only through "Federal control over all combinations engaged in inter-state commerce, instead of relying upon the foolish anti-trust law. . . ." [23]

Bryan also was disgusted with Roosevelt's straddling on the tariff. In 1902 Albert B. Cummins's "Iowa Idea" of abolishing tariffs on trust-made goods and Republican-sponsored bills placing on the free list all iron and steel goods produced by trusts put the Republican reformers where Bryan had been a decade earlier. Hanna became frightened while Roosevelt, fearing the power of Middle Western congressmen, sought delay via an investigatory congressional commission. "Only Congress can revise the tariff," said Bryan, "and the sooner it begins the better." But with convention time approaching Roosevelt beat a strategic retreat from a question which he knew contained dynamite. The year before the presidential election would be "a most unwise one in which to enter upon a general upsetting of the tariff," he wrote Henry Cabot Lodge on April 22, 1903.[24] He submitted prepared speeches on the trusts and the tariff to Aldrich for advice and approval, saying, "I want to be sure to get what I say on these two subjects along lines upon which all of us can agree." With these safe speeches in hand he then toured the farm belt, gathering popular strength in the West by castigating the "wicked trusts" and "labor extremists." [25]

Nor was Bryan satisfied with Roosevelt's handling of the coal strike of 1902. When Roosevelt appointed a commission to investigate the dispute and hinted that he would use troops to seize and work the mines, Bryan stated bluntly that "arbitration is the remedy." Roosevelt could help settle the strike less by taking part in it than by urging the passage of five laws—one providing for arbitration by a national board at the request of either party in all cases in which a corporation engaged in interstate commerce had a difference with its employees; one protecting miners from "government by injunction"; one discriminating between natural man and the corporate giant and bottling the latter up in its state of origin; one taking the tariff off coal; and one prohibiting railroads engaged in interstate

[23] Roosevelt to Joseph B. Bishop, February 17, 1903, in Mowry, *Era of Theodore Roosevelt*, p. 134.

[24] Lodge, *Correspondence*, II, 6.

[25] Matthew Josephson, *The President Makers: The Culture of Politics and Leadership in an Age of Enlightenment, 1896–1919*, p. 149.

commerce from operating coal mines except to supply fuel to their engines.[26] Roosevelt intervened and the strike was settled by arbitration. Bryan's demand for a special session of Congress to enact his program went unheeded, but his first, second, and fifth points eventually became law. More immediately, Knox's six-point program of 1903, which closely paralleled Bryan's, resulted in the Elkins rebate law and in the creation of the Department of Commerce and Labor.[27]

Roosevelt's attitude on currency reform was marked by extreme circumspection rather than mere caution. He wrote Cleveland that "now we have definitely won out on the free-silver business and therefore I think you are entitled to thanks and congratulations." [28] When Aldrich proposed that the Secretary of the Treasury be empowered to accept as security for the safekeeping of public money bonds other than those of the national government, Bryan jumped upon his plan less for its faults than on the grounds that it was class legislation, a device to benefit the rich, a provision for asset currency.[29] Aldrich lacked faith in that mysterious "elastic currency" which Roosevelt believed attainable and knew him to be indisposed to obtain real monetary reform. A sharp stock market decline occurred in 1903. Roosevelt found the situation "ugly" but said he could do nothing. He called Aldrich, John C. Spooner, William B. Allison, and O. H. Platt to Oyster Bay to discuss financial legislation and also sounded out Speaker Joseph G. Cannon. Cannon, a gold standard man, cor-

[26] *Commoner*, October 3, 10, 1902.

[27] *Ibid.*, October 3, 10, 17, 24, 1902; George F. Baer to Elihu Root, October 1, 1902, Root Papers; George B. Cortelyou to Knox, January 3, 1903, John J. Jenkins to Cortelyou, January 6, 1903, Knox to Roosevelt, March 30, 1903, Roosevelt to Knox, October 21, 1904, Knox Papers; Roosevelt to Winthrop Murray Crane, October 22, 1902, in Morison and Blum (eds.), *Letters of Roosevelt*, III, 356–366; Mowry, *Roosevelt and the Progressive Movement*, p. 18; Henry F. Pringle, *Theodore Roosevelt: A Biography*, pp. 264–278; Lloyd, *Lloyd*, II, 187–208; Irving Stone, *Clarence Darrow for the Defense*, pp. 127–157. In 1903, the president of the National Association of Manufacturers reported that in 1902 the association had been influential in defeating both the federal eight-hour work bill and a bill limiting the issuance of labor injunctions by federal courts. Mowry, *Era of Theodore Roosevelt*, p. 12.

[28] Letter of November 22, 1900, Grover Cleveland Papers.

[29] Bryan objected to asset currency because he thought the banks would profit thereby. If bank assets were good enough for currency, why not have the nation issue greenbacks based upon the nation's assets? he asked. Further, if the government must guarantee a bank note, why not let the government issue the note? *Commoner*, February 21, April 18, May 30, October 3, 1902; April 29, 1904. The currency reform bills of Charles N. Fowler and of Ebenezer J. Hill, which provided for the asset currency to which Bryan objected, never reached a vote in the House.

rectly predicted that no financial legislation could pass Congress. The pale issue of finance, including a demand for another international monetary conference, vanished ghostlike into the babble of popular interest aroused over Cuba and the treaty with the new Republic of Panama.

During these years Bryan was a persistent thorn in Roosevelt's side in foreign affairs. He had much to say against our "giving in" to the British in the Hay-Pauncefote treaties, Republican Philippine policy, the jamming of the Platt Amendment down the throats of the Cubans, the Insular Cases, and Roosevelt's "Big Stick" and constant demand for "expansion." In 1901 he suggested that administration favor was being given the Panama over the Nicaraguan canal route because of railroad influence. After Roosevelt "took" Panama he marked the difference between the Roosevelt-Hay interest in the integrity of China and indifference toward the integrity of Colombia. When Civil Governor W. H. Taft declared that the Filipinos were rapidly acquiescing to American control, Bryan asserted that he took the silence of dead men for consent—dead American soldiers returned from the islands were "mute protests against a war of conquest." Was it not curious that the Declaration of Independence was barred from the Philippines on the ground that it was "an incendiary document"? How could we preach free government here and practice imperialism elsewhere? [30] Publication in 1901 of the correspondence between McKinley and his Paris commissioners convinced him that McKinley was solely responsible for the acquisition of the islands, and he predicted that the Philippine question would be one of the most important issues in 1904. Roosevelt deemed the Republican program practical and stood pat. By and large, however, the American public was beginning to regard the Philippines as an embarrassing liability, and Roosevelt himself soon came to see them as indefensible against Japan.

Nothing could be more alive than Roosevelt when it came to his campaign for re-election. In 1902 he engaged in one of the most

[30] Fortunately for the Republicans, he did not know, and the public was never told, that a committee composed of Carl Schurz, Edwin Burritt Smith, Herbert Welsh, and Andrew Carnegie found evidence that American troops in the Philippines were guilty of kidnapping and murder under circumstances of aggravated brutality; robbery; torture, both of men and women, and rape of the latter; and the infliction of death on parties on the strength of evidence elicited through torture. Statement dated July 23, 1902, William Howard Taft Papers.

ambitious stumping tours ever undertaken by a President; in 1903 and early 1904 he made similar excursions. By July 1903, having routed Hanna's organization by the astute use of patronage, he had pledged to his support more delegates than he needed to secure his nomination. The only task he left the national convention was to name him and endorse his choice for vice presidential candidate, Charles W. Fairbanks.

III

THE YEARS 1901–1904 constitute a low point in Bryan's influence in the Democratic party. He was a leader without a machine, for machines feed only on victories, and predictions were freely made that he could not prevent the reorganizers from molding the party along conservative lines and that he would never again be a nominee for President.

Bryan had announced immediately after the election of 1900 that he would not be a candidate in 1904. He wanted other aspirants to know that the field was clear and said again that he looked upon himself as an Aaron rather than a Moses, that time might prove his mission one to advocate rather than execute. He was never more squarely in the right, yet no one personally competed with him for leadership of the Democracy. His personal popularity with the masses undiminished, he was as if in a somnolent state, ready to unleash his political power whenever the demand arose for a revived progressive leadership. Altgeld, Blair Lee, James Creelman, Charles A. Towne, "Golden Rule" Jones, Champ Clark, Richard F. Pettigrew, and the aging J. C. S. Blackburn, among many others, wrote him of their love and of their willingness to help at any time in any service. Others said that he was a stronger and better man because of his two defeats. He was still young—he would be forty-one years of age in March 1901—and he could well retire for a period of study and reflection.[31]

Bryan replied that he had made his fights for principles he believed American and that "we must continue to do our duty as we see it, regardless of temporary reverses." The contest between plutocracy and democracy could not end until one or the other triumphed.

[31] Sidney Brooks, "Bryanism," *Contemporary Review,* 78 (November 1900), 633–642; *Harper's Weekly,* November 10, 1900.

He himself was only an incident.[32] To Dr. H. K. Jones he wrote: "What distresses me most is that so many people seem incapable of considering moral questions or fundamental principles." He was distressed but not embittered, and he retained his sense of humor and his perspective. "He bore his defeat with the utmost composure. I never heard a sigh or the slightest expression of bitterness from him —which is more than can be said of his wife," recorded Mrs. Bryan.[33] He also made it amply clear that he was in politics only to serve the American people. In a letter to the Reverend Dr. W. M. Hindman of Kenton, Ohio, he wrote:

I do not know what my real work in life is, and I have often been impressed with our scant knowledge of the future—even of our own lives. I feel that I have been able to do something to raise political ideals and if my life is spared, I hope to do much more. My great concern has for years been, and still is, to throw whatever influence I may have, be it small or great, upon the right side of each question, to the end that human rights may be sacredly defended and public interests advanced. While I have been a candidate for office, this has been merely incidental and no part of my general plan. I do not want to hold office except as it may assist in realizing the plans that I have laid for the advancement of the interests of the common people. In fact I shall feel relieved if I am permitted to work as a private citizen and can leave the cares and responsibilities of office to others. My life is now an ideal one. With a happy home to which I can retire when weary and from which I can go refreshed; with a sufficient income for my modest needs and with nothing upon my mind and heart but the work in which I am engaged, what more could I ask? If I have been defeated in my political aspirations the defeats weigh like dust in the balance against the blessings that I have received and that I now enjoy. . . .[34]

Bryan was keenly aware of his disadvantages in the fight against the reorganizers. He had led the progressives twice and lost, and the conservatives were promising victory if they were put at the helm. As he put it, Grover Cleveland, William C. Whitney, Don Dickinson,

[32] Bryan frequently said that the principles of the parties were not understood by the people and that "Therefore it is the duty of Democrats to go on teaching the public as to their real character." Editorial, "Political Topics," *The Independent,* 54 (January 16, 1902), 123. In the *Commoner* for January 31, 1902 he said, "Both writing and speaking furnish such agreeable occupation that one does not notice the loss of a little thing like the presidency." That he was incurably naïve is revealed by his saying that success in politics depended upon three things—honesty, industry, and ability. *Ibid.,* May 29, 1902.

[33] Mary Bryan Journal, December 18, 1902, Mrs. Ruth Bryan Rohde Papers.

[34] Josephson, *President Makers,* pp. 393-394.

Abram S. Hewitt, and their kind were "scheming" to conquer the Democracy. With Charles S. Hamlin in Massachusetts, David Bennett Hill, Alton B. Parker, and James K. McGuire in New York, Arthur Pue Gorman in Maryland, Carter Harrison, John R. Walsh, John P. Hopkins, and Robert E. Burke in Illinois, John G. Carlisle and Henry Watterson in Kentucky, J. Sterling Morton, his son Paul, and Albert Watkins in Nebraska, and Rolla Wells, A. M. Dockery, and David R. Francis in Missouri they planned to take over the management and reorganize the party. These men, he said, hankered after the fleshpots; they would not support their party unless they could rule it; and they caused so much division that agreement on principles was impossible. In great contrast were his six million unbought followers, the "regenerated" Democracy. For these, on December 9, 1900, he provided a creed—nothing more than the eternal principles of the Kansas City platform—and demanded the continued cooperation of progressive Democrats and fusionist Populists.

Within two weeks following the elections of 1900 the anti-Bryan forces began to organize for control of the party in 1904. In New York City on December 22, Hill, Parker, Carlisle, and Watterson, among others, launched the fight in the East. Three hundred Bryanites countered with a meeting in Lincoln on December 26 to cheer Bryan. But once the party organization of a city or state fell to the reorganizers the Bryanites had the unpleasant choice of fighting the "regulars" or of joining them, and Bryan was asked to intervene in various city and state contests. He opposed the nomination of reorganizer Rolla Wells as mayor of St. Louis, for he viewed his candidacy as part of the reorganizers' plan "to capture the organization by stealth and then make the Democratic so much like the Republican party that there will be little choice between them." Wells won, and the subsequent election of Dockery as governor of Missouri enabled the reorganizers to threaten the entire South.[35] Harrison's defeat of John Peter Altgeld in the selection of a new state central committee chairman indicated a strong comeback for the gold Democrats in Illinois. In Indiana, too, a gold man was elected chairman of the

[35] Bryanites in Missouri in midsummer 1901 organized the Allied Third Party on the basis of a Kansas City–public ownership platform. It was led by Lee Meriwether, who was defeated by Wells for mayor of St. Louis, and designed to gather all Bryan supporters into a new fusion group that would name Bryan for President in 1904. Bryan sympathized with the movement and conferred with its leaders for one entire day, but the venture proved stillborn. Kansas City *Star*, June 18, 19, 1901.

state committee. In fact Bryan received little but bad news throughout 1901. Justin Whiting reported the Michigan Democracy "hopelessly divided." In Ohio the Judson Harmon–John R. McLean forces repudiated the Kansas City platform by 944 to 6. Virginia's Democrats repudiated silver and its governor spoke of "a desperate fight" in his state. In Pennsylvania the Bryanites confined their platform to state issues lest an attempt to endorse the Kansas City platform end in humiliation. The Bryanite and truly progressive Edward M. Shepard was defeated by the Republican, Seth Low, as mayor of New York City. Cleveland criticized Bryan in *Collier's* and advised Charles S. Hamlin not to sacrifice himself in behalf of the Massachusetts Democracy by seeking the governorship. "And perhaps, too," he added, "the rebound might be greater if the party was allowed to play the fool a little longer. . . . Of course the silver craze is done for; but there is a lot of meanness yet, among those who have been shouting for it. . . . This will all be knocked or thrashed out of them sometime and I hope speedily. . . ." [36]

Although the Nebraska Democratic state convention upheld the Kansas City platform and found support in the Populist camp for a fusion ticket, Bryan admitted that the elections of 1901 rebuked the regenerated Democracy. The Republicans obtained five governors to one for the Democrats, won most of the important city elections and, in Nebraska, elected their candidate for supreme court judge. Personal regard for McKinley and Roosevelt, general business prosperity, interest in local rather than national affairs, and Democratic factionalism played a part in the Republican victories.

With an eye to the congressional elections of 1902, Bryan stepped up his crusade against the reorganizers, but with even less success than in 1901. When he charged Cleveland with having been the pliant tool of predatory wealth who had earned the odium that was the main cause of the Democratic defeats of 1896 and 1900,[37] Cleveland hit back. "If we only had a little bit of the old style of Democratic leadership, I believe we might confidently hope to see the disturbance settle our way; but good Heaven! what can we look for under the management of Bryan and Jones and Stone and such haphazard blunderbuss shooters?" he wrote Richard Olney on February 8, 1902.[38] Two weeks

[36] Letter, August 18, 1901, Cleveland Papers; Charles S. Hamlin Diary, pp. 262–268, Hamlin Papers.

[37] *Commoner*, February 7, March 14, 28, 1902.

[38] Letter, Cleveland Papers.

later he gave to the press a letter in which he stated that he believed "that the time is fast approaching when our grand old party will shake off the dreadful dreams that have afflicted it, and fight again, as of old, the glorious battles of 'pure Democracy.' " [39] Bryan retorted that Cleveland was deluded in believing himself "the sole and only embodiment of 'true Democracy.' " It was he who had tried to secure currency legislation desired by Republicans even though he knew he would split his party by so doing; it was he who had refused to enforce the anti-trust laws or to sign the Wilson-Gorman tariff. Presumably opposed to imperialism, he had not spoken a word in support of the Democratic ticket in 1900. Bryan issued a peremptory challenge: "If Mr. Cleveland thinks that the Democratic party is ready to return to the mire into which he led it and in which he left it, let him announce his candidacy on any platform he is willing to write and he cannot secure the delegation from a single state. . . . The party will never go back to the odious and odorous days of 1892–1896." [40]

Throughout 1902 internecine warfare continued to cut deeply into Democratic strength that should have gone into opposing Republicans. Most Democratic state platforms cut loose from Bryan and his Kansas City principles. Most damaging of all was Bryan's loss of Illinois. He was on the verge of reconciling Altgeld and Harrison when Altgeld was stricken during his Joliet speech and died shortly thereafter. Bryan spoke eulogistically of Altgeld at the funeral, saying, "It was fitting that he should die as he lived—pleading the cause of the oppressed," but soon thereafter he conceded that Illinois was lost to the reorganizers. "With Hopkins in control of the party machinery the platform is immaterial," he said, "because he cannot be trusted with the carrying out of a platform embodying the Sermon on the Mount." [41]

At the opening of the new Tilden Club House in New York on June 19 the reorganizers began their drive for the nomination of a conservative presidential candidate. Although Cleveland announced his permanent retirement from active politics, many at the meeting

[39] Letter dated February 26, 1902, addressee not given, quoted in *Commoner*, March 21, 1902.

[40] *Ibid.*, March 21, 1902.

[41] *Ibid.*, March 21, June 26, 1902; Carter H. Harrison, *Stormy Years: The Autobiography of Carter H. Harrison, Five Times Mayor of Chicago*, p. 209. Harrison kept Hopkins from representing his senatorial district on the state Central Committee, but Hopkins was elected at large and later became state chairman. *Ibid.*, p. 211.

looked upon him as their choice for 1904. Bryan had declined an invitation to attend, saying he would not swing incense before the "unrepentant apostate from New Jersey," and renewed his challenge —if Cleveland represented the Democracy, let him accept the nomination! [42] In one of his now rare Eastern appearances, Bryan spoke on Boston Common on "The Basis of Harmony." There were, he said, only two parties, one Democratic, one Aristocratic, divided by an impassable gulf. The basis of harmony lay only in belief in democratic principles as espoused by the regenerated Democracy.[43] As if in reply, Cleveland offered a laissez faire program: tariff reduction, support of the gold standard, strict governmental economy, freedom for the Philippines, and "finding a solution to the trust problem in the common law and the wisdom of state legislatures."

Bryan refused to run for governor of Nebraska but was pleased with the Bryanite platform adopted by the Democrats and the willingness of the Populists to split the ticket, to take the lieutenant governorship and accept his choice, William H. Thompson, for governor. Tom Johnson's defeat of McLean in Ohio helped to balance the loss of Massachusetts by George Fred Williams to Josiah Quincy, but Hill regained control in New York and Tammany's new leader, Charles F. Murphy, was an anti-Bryanite. Wherever Bryanites won in the primaries the Kansas City platform and Bryan were endorsed; wherever the reorganizers won the issues of trusts, tariff reform, and imperialism predominated and the money question was dropped, even in the South.

The elections wiped all Populists and Independents from the map. Based on the vote of 1902, a Republican presidential candidate would have won 322 electoral votes, a Democrat 154. Bryan's loss of Nebraska for the second time proved that Republicanism was returning to its traditionally dominant position in the state. Roosevelt's popularity, industrial prosperity, bumper crops, and the lack of truly important national issues stopped the swing of the pendulum that normally goes against an administration at midterm. While Bryan was not extinct, the elections proved that no man who had actively supported him could hope for the Democratic presidential nomination in 1904. As yet, however, there was none who vied with him for leadership of the regenerated Democracy.

It was during 1902 that Bryan adopted an attitude toward presi-

[42] *Commoner*, June 27, July 4, 11, 1902.
[43] *Ibid.*, July 25, 1902.

dential aspirants that drove his followers to distraction and his opponents to mirth. He said that any reasonably intelligent, honest, and progressive Democrat could fill the Presidency. "I am going to . . . show that we have plenty of material and don't have to go to the reorganizers for material," he wrote Louis F. Post.[44] Among those available were Senators William J. Stone and Francis M. Cockrell, and Louis J. Folk of Missouri; Tennessee's Senator William B. Bate, Governor Benton McMillin, and Nashville's Mayor James H. Head; James R. Williams and Judge Owen P. Thompson of Illinois; Governor L. F. C. Gavin of Rhode Island; ex-Governor John E. Osborne of Wyoming; John W. Bookwalter, silverite publicist of Ohio; and North Carolina's Judge Walter Clark. But he urged the candidacy of no particular "Kansas City Democrat" over another—he would let events determine the question of "availability." [45] The biographies of these men published in *The Commoner* drove the reorganizers to laughter. Stone, Cockrell, and perhaps Folk enjoyed national reputations, but who were the others? When the New York *Evening Post* and the New York *World* twitted him about "The Little Unknowns from Nowhere," Bryan retorted that the reorganizers could not be expected to know the merits of true Democrats. His negative procedure nevertheless also earned him criticism from regenerate Democrats, for it gave him the veto power and freed him to seek the nomination while playing the neutral toward others.

Throughout 1903 and the first half of 1904 Bryan frequently reviewed the un-Democratic actions of the second Cleveland administration and of the "Cleveland element" since 1896 and charged that the reorganizers now sought to bring the entire Democracy into harmony with the principles of a neo-Republican who was anathema to the rank and file of his party. "Cleveland represents as no one else does the plutocratic element of the party," he asserted, "and is the logical candidate if the party returns to its wallow in the mire." [46] In 1893, he said, he had followed blindly the leaders of the Democracy. "Why, it was when my boy was born [1889]—when I was such an admirer of Grover Cleveland and John G. Carlisle that if I had named my child after public men I would have called my boy Cleveland Carlisle Bryan. . . . You can imagine how I would feel now if I had

[44] N.d., Louis F. Post Papers.

[45] *Commoner*, March 28, April 10, 17, 24, May 1, 8, June 5, July 10, 31, August 7, 14, October 2, November 27, 1902.

[46] *Ibid.*, May 8, August 28, 1903.

given him that name!" He would rather meet at a Democratic board "an open Republican enemy than a hypocrite who pretends to be a friend of the party while opposing its principles. . . . I have a right to speak of Grover Cleveland's Democracy, for I have borne his sins in two national campaigns." [47] The reorganizers could not be trusted to bring about a single reform, he warned many audiences. If they regained control of the party they would rewrite its platform to please the commercial and financial interests of the East. Their objective was to crush him in Nebraska and prevent his election to the national convention while they lined up as many delegates as possible for a conservative candidate.[48]

Bryan needed to control only a third of the delegates to veto an unacceptable nominee. A Populist editor who talked with him in August 1903 found that "he thinks and feels sure that Grover Cleveland and his crowd will not have the least showing in the next convention." [49] He said flatly that he would endorse only men who had supported the ticket in 1896 and 1900 and dared the leading reorganizer candidates to state their views on public questions. Most repugnant to the regenerated Democrats was Judge Alton B. Parker, who was being groomed by Hill and boomed by such newspapers as the Brooklyn *Eagle,* New York *Times,* and New York *World,* and being pushed forward by James Gerard.[50]

Despite all his efforts, the year 1903 plunged Bryan to his lowest political depths since 1896. The new Progressives, nurtured in the Populist and Bryanistic faith but seeking a stronger government to cure the ills of an urban as well as a rural society, were mostly Republicans, followers of La Follette and Roosevelt. Democrats drove off in different directions: they adopted anti-Bryan platforms, as in Iowa; fused, as in Nebraska; avoided national issues, as in Pennsylvania; or, in the rare instance of Colorado, endorsed the Kansas City platform. The diners at the New York City Jefferson Banquet hissed Bryan's name when the chairman of the state committee charged him with failing to aid the state in 1902, and Tammany cheered a letter sent by Cleveland and acclaimed him as their choice for 1904. Even Roosevelt picked Cleveland as his probable opponent. Although Bryan would bolt him, Roosevelt believed "the old fellow"—Cleve-

---

[47] *Ibid.,* March 6, 1903.

[48] *Ibid.,* March 13, 20, 27, April 3, 10, 24, 1903.

[49] James N. Ferris to Willis J. Abbot, August 21, 1903, Commager Papers.

[50] *Commoner,* October 16, 1902, February 27, March 6, 1903; James W. Gerard. *My First Eighty Years,* pp. 100–105.

land was approaching seventy years of age—would be "a very formidable candidate." He would have the support of Wall Street, which was angry with the administration, and draw a great many votes "from the honest rich and the fool respectable classes," he wrote Lodge.[51] Replied Lodge: "I wish from the bottom of my heart that Cleveland could be nominated. He would be the easiest man in the country to beat." [52] Even more revealing of Republican thought is Taft's letter to Roosevelt of May 9, 1903, in which he expressed his sincere wish "that the gold Democrats may succeed in nominating a straight out gold Democratic candidate, and that a split may come by which Bryan and his followers shall be relegated to the limbo of populism where they belong. . . ." [53]

The elections of 1903 strengthened the reorganizers despite a vigorous Bryan swing about the circle with special attention to the Middle West. The Republicans won most of the states, including Nebraska. Bryan had actively supported Tom L. Johnson against Myron T. Herrick for governor of Ohio and hoped to elect a Democratic legislature which would retire Mark Hanna from the Senate. With the aid of Standard Oil, Herrick and Hanna won, and Johnson dropped from the height of popularity he enjoyed as mayor of Cleveland and as a potential presidential candidate.[54] In New York City, meantime, the plurality of 60,000 by which George B. McClellan, Jr. beat Seth Low and the general sweep by Tammany of the city offices placed the name of McClellan on the lips of many. While boomlets also raged for several men Bryan mentioned, the most prominent candidates after Cleveland took himself out of the race in November were Richard Olney, George Gray of Delaware, Gorman, Parker, Cockrell, and Hearst. Parker appealed most to the South and East, with Gorman a close second. Bryan charged that reorganizers had won because aided by "the reactionary elements—especially the representatives of the corporations," and denied that the elections indicated any decided trend toward either issues or candidates.[55]

Between 1900 and 1904 Bryan profited financially but lost politically. *The Commoner* was a going instrument through which he kept

[51] Letters of March 4, 23, 1903, Joseph B. Bishop, *Theodore Roosevelt and His Times, Shown in His Own Letters*, I, 241.

[52] Letter, May 21, 1903, Lodge, *Correspondence*, II, 15.

[53] Taft Papers.

[54] *Commoner*, September 4, 1903; Tom L. Johnson, *My Story*, p. 200.

[55] *Commoner*, July 3, November 13, 1903.

his issues alive, and he was a frequent contributor to other newspapers as well as to various magazines. His lecturing paid well, and he had been able to build a large house and to engage in the farming he enjoyed so much. And he had devoted more time than ever to organized church work, to speaking on religious topics, and to the betterment of mankind through subsidizing the education of youngsters. He said in 1903 that he was worth between $15,000 and $20,000, but the New York *World* set the figures at between $50,000 and $75,000.[56] But no such progress was observable in politics, unless it was his continued attachment to progressive politics, including support for more direct methods of expressing the people's will and for the municipal ownership of public utilities. On national and international issues he refused to deviate from those of the Chicago and Kansas City platforms. In his fight with the reorganizers he came out second best, and it was certain that a conservative would be named for President in 1904. Meantime Roosevelt had shown a willingness to undertake reforms in closely prescribed areas. The nation as a whole was pleased with him, and there was little doubt that he would be nominated and elected in his own right.

IV

PHILO SHERMAN BENNETT, a wholesale grocer of New Haven, Connecticut, had begun writing Bryan during 1896 to extol him as the world's great champion of the disinherited. After the campaign he sent him $3000 for his personal use and helped manage his investments. On May 22, 1900, while visiting Lincoln, Bennett dictated his will to Bryan and made him its executor. From an estate of about $300,000 he left $100,000 for Mrs. Bennett and $20,000 to Bryan to help educate

[56] *Ibid.,* February 6, 1903; New York *World,* July 4, 1903. To five acres acquired in 1893 Bryan eventually added 30 more. Fairview was built during the winter of 1901–1902, with the family moving in on Bryan's forty-second birthday, March 19, 1902. He grew corn, wheat, alfalfa, berries, and melons, and had an orchard. To chickens, turkeys, ducks, horses, and pigs he gradually added registered blooded cattle. Here the children grew to maturity. Here Ruth, not quite eighteen, upset her parents by marrying an artist almost his own age whom Bryan had engaged to paint his portrait. Here, after a divorce to which the parents objected on religious grounds, Ruth was happily married to a British army officer. Here, too, Grace was married. Bryan's idealized conception of the value of life on the farm may be followed in his "Farming as an Occupation," *Cosmopolitan,* 36 (January 1904), 369–371, and in his *Commoner,* January 15, 1904.

poor boys and girls. He then made a special bequest—that Mrs. Bennett hold in trust for Bryan $50,000 to be used "for purposes set forth in a sealed letter which will be found with this will" but which should not be made public. Both the will and the letter to "My Dear Wife" which explained the special bequest were placed in a safety deposit box in New York City. In the letter Bennett said that since Bryan's political work prevented him from earning money, he took pleasure in setting aside $50,000 "so that he may be more free to devote himself to his chosen field of labor." If Bryan did not want the money for himself, he was to distribute it among charitable and educational institutions.

After Mr. Bennett died in an accident on August 10, 1903, Mrs. Bennett and her daughter learned about the will for the first time and refused to carry out its provisions, in part because he had left $20,000 to a woman with whom he had lived during business trips to New York. Feeling that he himself had done nothing wrong, Bryan entered suit in the superior court of New Haven, Connecticut. Defeated, he took an appeal to the supreme court of errors. He described fully the relationship that had existed between him and Bennett and won public acclaim by his excellent conduct while under voluntary cross examination. While the court found that he had not exercised undue influence over Bennett, it held that the letter telling Mrs. Bennett how to distribute the $50,000 was not sufficiently identified in the will to warrant its being incorporated into the will by reference. On the latter point Bryan appealed to the supreme court of the state, but the higher court upheld the lower. It is the judgment of lawyers who have studied the case closely that the courts erred.[57] At any rate, Bryan pushed matters by filing a cross-complaint in superior court to have the trust executed. Were this done he promised to keep none of the money but to distribute it among charitable and educational institutions. When the court ruled against him, he appealed again, and again in vain. He took a somber and moral approach in describing the case in *The Commoner,* but the nation's newspapers fed a sensation-hungry public a version that damaged him personally and politically, for he was pilloried as having tried nefarious tricks and underhanded schemes to secure undue influence over Bennett, was seeking to rob the widow, and as an apostle of purity was fighting doggedly for a libertine's $50,000. According to Bryan's daughter Grace, "Perhaps nothing in his life was more distressing to my father

[57] Wayne C. Williams, *William Jennings Bryan,* p. 250.

than this lawsuit," and Mrs. Bennett herself eventually regretted the contest. Nevertheless, reverberations from the incident continued for years, with Woodrow Wilson receiving letters opposing the appointment of Bryan to his cabinet because "[A] man who would rob a widow is not fit for any position." [58]

With the elections of 1903 and the Bennett case both over, Mrs. Bryan's suggestion that he visit Europe grew upon Bryan. *The Commoner,* with a circulation approaching 150,000, was in good hands; the primaries for the national convention were still months away, Hearst was willing to pay handsomely for articles about his travels; and a trip would give the public temper time to cool and also give him time for reflection and observation. He would enjoy the company of his son, now fifteen years of age, and meet new people and absorb new ideas. Mrs. Bryan remained at Fairview because she believed she was with child. "How I miss you, sweetheart," he wrote as the RMS *Majestic* pulled out of New York on November 14. "There is no one else in all the world to whom I can unbosom myself and tell all my plans and ambitions—no one who can be as you are a part of myself." If she had another son, he wrote on November 17, they would name him Baird Bennett; if another daughter, Rose Bennett. They had been married nineteen years, and their elder daughter, Ruth, was already married, but if they had another child "It will be like commencing our married life." [59] As it turned out there was no fourth child.

During his two hectic months in Europe Bryan was granted honors and attentions reserved only for high state officials. Henry White, of the American Embassy in London, had expected him to be a bore. He was pleasantly surprised to find him an extremely good fellow but a better talker than listener, and one better versed in government than in history, art, and letters. At a dinner given him by Ambassador Joseph Choate, who had called him a communist in 1896, Bryan talked with Arthur J. Balfour, the prime minister, and Moreton

[58] F. H. Woodward to Woodrow Wilson, n.d., Woodrow Wilson Papers. Bryan's version of the case is found in the *Commoner,* November 6, 13, 20, 1903, and April 22, 1904. Daughter Grace's comment is in her manuscript, "William Jennings Bryan," I, 114, Bryan Papers. As a *cause célèbre* with respect to the reference of the will and the letter, see David L. Daggett's review of Frederick H. Jackson, *Simeon Eben Baldwin—Lawyer, Social Scientist, and Statesman* (New York, 1955), in *American Bar Association Journal,* 41 (June 1955), 541–542. With Bennett's partner, Alfred P. Sloan, Bryan remained the executor of the Bennett estate until his death.

[59] Letters in Rohde Papers.

Frewen, both leading bimetallists. Interested as ever in good oratory, he traveled far from London to hear Joseph Chamberlain, Lord Asquith, the Duke of Devonshire, and Lord Goschen. Interested in ideas, he listened to speeches on tariff protection, then a leading issue in England, Liberal politics, and labor. In John Burns, the Labourite, he found a kindred spirit. From him and the Sidney Webbs, and from a visit to Scotland he intensified his interest in the public ownership of utilities, a topic which played an increasingly larger role in his political career for the next decade. Leading Irish patriots, including John Dillon and John Redmond, gave him a dinner when he visited Ireland. They cheered his expressed sympathy with the cause of home rule, as did the members who heard him speak at the National Liberal Club in London. The efficacy of the principle of the public ownership of public utilities for combating the "special interests" grew upon him during visits to Switzerland, Holland, Belgium, Denmark, Germany, and Russia. He was particularly interested in the German method of state rather than federal ownership of railway transit. He delivered in London a Thanksgiving Day address, "in good voice, on a high plane," he wrote his wife, on the theme that "love, not hate will control," concluding that he contemplated "with joy the coming of the day when rivalry between nations will not be to see which can injure the other most, but to show which can hold highest the light that guides the pathway of the human race to higher ground." [60] So much was he talked about in Europe that he was characterized as "the man of the month." [61] The opposition press in the United States, however, took notice of him primarily by printing literally hundreds of cartoons lampooning him for rushing about the Continent getting ideas for the next campaign.[62]

While dining with the Henry Whites in London, Bryan had expressed an intense interest in Tolstoy, saying that one of the principal objects of his tour was to visit that great teacher. When Mrs. White asked which of Tolstoy's books had impressed him most, Bryan replied, "Oh, I have not read Tolstoy's works; but I have read a great many articles in the magazines and the Sunday newspapers about him." [63]

Bryan impressed the Czar with his notions of democracy before

[60] Bryan to Mrs. Bryan, November 26, 1903, Bryan Papers.
[61] *American Review of Reviews*, 29 (January 1904), 23.
[62] *Ibid.*
[63] Allan Nevins, *Henry White: Thirty Years of American Diplomacy*, p. 228.

feeling the magnetism of Tolstoy. In Moscow, in full swallow tails, Bryan faced the young Romanoff, Nicholas II, and praised him for the establishment of the International Court of Arbitration at The Hague. Then he dared remind him that edicts granting freedom of speech and measures of self-government to local communities had not been fully implemented. In closing the interview, the like of which he had never before experienced, Nicholas asked Bryan to assure the American people of Russia's friendship and of his interest in the principle of arbitration in international disputes.[64]

A hundred and thirty miles south of Moscow, at Yasnaya Polyana, Bryan spent several days walking, riding, and talking with the seventy-six-year-old Tolstoy, "this intellectual giant of Russia, the moral Titan of Europe, and the world's most conspicuous exponent of the Doctrine of Love." Thoughtful questions about Tolstoy's doctrine of passive resistance proved to Bryan that Tolstoy was a thoroughly confirmed pacifist whose theories paralleled his own Christian beliefs against the use of force. Another decade of concern with religious and idealistic matters would gradually dull Bryan's objections to pacifism on the grounds of impracticality and wed him to Tolstoy's principle that love alone could conquer force and violence. Tolstoy followed Bryan's career until his own death in 1907 and urged him to "help the working people to enjoy the whole fruits of their toil." Bryan's continued concern for the well-being of the common man, his "cooling off treaties," his resignation as Secretary of State, his opposition to war, and his demand for disarmament can be traced in large part to the reinforcement of his own ideas by those of Tolstoy.[65]

Bryan's comportment in Europe earned him added prestige at home and raised his stature to that of a world figure. Among those who greeted him upon his return in New York were Charles F. Murphy, Hearst, Shepard, Cockran, and James B. Weaver, admittedly a curious assortment of politicos. Taking time only to deliver a nonpartisan "thank you, neighbors" speech in Lincoln, Bryan then plunged into the campaign of 1904.

[64] W. J. Bryan, "Russia and Her Czar," *Commoner*, February 5, 1904; Williams, *Bryan*, p. 254.

[65] *Commoner*, October 18, 1901, February 13, 1902; Bryan: *Memoirs*, pp. 460, 461, *Under Other Flags*, pp. 9–126, *The Old World and Its Ways*, p. 561; Count Leo Tolstoy, "Garrison and Non-Resistance," *The Independent*, 56 (April 24, 1904), 882; Merle Curti, "Bryan and World Peace," *Smith College Studies in History* (Northampton, Mass., 1931), pp. 135–137.

CHAPTER 14

Keeping the Faith: 1904

I

"REORGANIZATION means Clevelandism," cried Bryan. "Organize!" he demanded of progressive Democrats. It was no secret, he said, that the trust magnates and financiers believed Roosevelt potentially dangerous and wanted a conservative Democrat to oppose him. They might obtain one, but he predicted that the reorganizers could not write a platform acceptable to the party. Moreover, they were using Cleveland as a "bogie" to force the progressives to accept a compromise candidate who represented his principles yet was less objectionable personally.[1]

Reorganizers retorted by calling Bryan a slanderer of his betters and a promoter of hate, strife, and revolution who prated about morality in order to achieve his selfish purposes. Grover Cleveland sneered at the "Bryan-Hearst outfit" and wrote John G. Carlisle that "Such Democrats as you and I are entitled to make our position understood as distinctly and fightingly opposed to any more Democratic fool business," [2] and Henry Watterson editorialized that "Mr. Bryan is first a socialist, then a Democrat." [3] Bryan's reply to Cleveland was sharp, that to Watterson worthy of Wilson's New Freedom. He would not, as the socialists desired, eliminate competition; he would, however, limit the rate of interest and hours of labor and prohibit the sweat shop and the employment of children. He would seek laws that "will lay the axe at the root of the tree, and by making a private monopoly impossible restore industrial independence, and by a revival of competition, give protection to the consumer and stimulus to the producer." [4]

Late in February Cleveland refused to be named for President and suggested Richard Olney, George Gray, or Alton B. Parker. By April

[1] *Commoner*, March 27, May 6, 1904; New York *American*, July 1, 1904.
[2] Letter of February 18, 1904, Grover Cleveland Papers.
[3] Louisville *Courier-Journal*, quoted in *Commoner*, May 6, 1904.
[4] *Ibid.*, May 6, 27, 1904.

he openly endorsed Parker as the "very best candidate in sight" because he was clean, decent, and conservative and was not seeking the
nomination—rather the nomination was seeking him.[5]

Bryan's objections to Parker mounted as the trend toward him increased. Cleveland's nomination he believed out of the question.
Arthur Pue Gorman's failure to lead the Democratic minority against
Roosevelt's policies struck him from the list. Olney was merely a
stalking horse for Cleveland, and David Bennett Hill was not a possibility because he was managing Parker, with the obvious objective
of becoming the power behind the throne. This left the "interrogation mark," Parker, a man even more dangerous than Hill. Parker
lacked political record, refused to state his convictions on current
public issues, had spent twenty years on the bench but revealed no
qualifications as an executive, and was supported by trusts and corporations, as represented by August Belmont and Hill. "The fact that
Mr. Parker is an enigma ought to remove him from consideration,"
he said a week before the meeting of the New York Democratic state
convention.[6] He failed to see, as Parker did, that by eliminating so
many possible candidates he forced state leaders everywhere to concentrate on the only two he had not eliminated, Parker and William
Randolph Hearst.[7]

Since he had managed Hill's gubernatorial campaign in 1884 Parker had avoided political activity and declined to run for public
office or accept appointment to a nonjudicial post. Except for a rather
liberal attitude in labor cases he was a conservative, yet he had maintained party regularity. He had voted for Bryan in 1896 and 1900.
His remarkable campaign for judge of New York's highest court in
1897 had attracted national attention, and he had acknowledged that
his support of Bryan in 1896 had largely accounted for his victory.
But he was determined to remain a judge. His secret hope was that
he would some day become a justice of the Supreme Court of the
United States. He was well aware, however, of a movement for him
as a presidential candidate. At Hill's suggestion he had taken a long
tour in 1902 to sound out Southern opinion. Various Southern and
Eastern editors, including Joseph Pulitzer of the *World* and St. Claire

[5] Cleveland to Lamont, February 28, 1904, to William B. Hornblower, March 29,
1904, to William F. Vilas, June 24, 1904, Cleveland Papers; Cleveland, "Parker,"
McClure's Magazine, 24 (November 1904), 5.

[6] *Commoner*, April 8, 1904; John R. Lambert, *Arthur Pue Gorman*, pp. 293–309.

[7] Parker to George S. Bixby, March 16, 1904, George S. Bixby Papers.

McKelway of the Brooklyn *Eagle,* demanded his nomination with great vigor. There was no other Democrat with a comparable record who had supported Bryan; many liked him because Tammany opposed him; and it was believed he could carry the important state of New York. Hill himself was persuaded of Parker's chances about six months before the meeting of the national convention.[8]

In the New York convention, at Albany, after Hill had defeated Tammany, interest had turned to the platform, which could foreshadow the St. Louis declaration; but it proved as noncommittal and innocuous, according to Bryan, as any utterance ever made in the history of American political parties. Not a line was written in behalf of the people; not a line could be criticized by Wall Street. "We have had enough protection of property rights," he said, "what we needed was more protection of human rights." Hill's objective, he believed, was to get a conservative candidate who would receive large contributions from corporations and an adroitly prepared platform that would entice the "radical and socialistic" elements of the party. It was Hill who overrode Parker's objections and had the money question absolutely ignored in the Albany platform. Therefore, said Bryan, "The New York platform is a dishonest platform, fit only for a dishonest party. No one but an artful dodger would stand on it. . . ."[9] Meantime Tammany's promise to fight on against Parker raised the question whether Bryan would join Tammany in support of Hearst.[10]

Immediately after the Albany convention Bryan charged that Cleveland, August Belmont, Thomas Fortune Ryan, and other Eastern financiers behind Parker's boom had contributed to the defeat of the Democratic party in 1896 and 1900 and now threatened to defeat it again unless they could control it. Parker was not a "harmony" candidate but the choice of the corporations, trusts, and money power, the "muzzled candidate of Wall Street."[11]

Bryan's continued antipathy to the East was cordially reciprocated. But control of the Democracy had shifted. Tired of providing votes and never winning rewards, the South was seeking to line up with the East rather than with the West. Senator John T. Morgan of Alabama, for instance, meant no disrespect to Bryan but said he "should

[8] Parker to Bixby, March 20, 1904, *ibid.*

[9] *Commoner,* April 22, May 29, 1904.

[10] New York *World* July 20, 1904.

[11] Omaha *World-Herald,* April 22, 1904; *Commoner,* April 22, 1904; *American Review of Reviews,* 29 (May 1904), 516.

recognize that he . . . has had his day in court." Two nominations, like two elections, should be enough. "He will have to subside and the country understands the fact." [12] Out of grace in both East and South, Bryan could at best exercise but a veto power with the West. But the parties themselves were in juxtaposition compared with 1896 and 1900, for the "square dealing" Republicans appeared to be the anti-trust party and the reorganizer Democrats the pro-corporation party. Since current events had killed off Bryan's old issues and the Republicans were united and the Democrats divided, it seemed that the only question for 1904 was whether Roosevelt should be given a vote of confidence. The Democratic reorganizers themselves were caught in the paradox of trying to repudiate Bryan's tariff, trust, and money issues and at the same time making the condemnation of the Roosevelt administration their paramount issue.

The May primaries revealed steady progress but not a stampede for Parker. In the East, although he was regarded as the "most available" candidate to repress "the Wild People," meaning Bryan's followers, Olney, Gorman, and Hearst also won some delegates. In the Middle West, although Hearst men were active, Indiana was made a unit for Parker, and Thomas Taggart was recommended for national chairman. Parker now had New York, New Jersey, Connecticut, and Indiana, the four states the Democrats needed to carry to win in November. Ohio named Judson Harmon, Minnesota and North Dakota supported Parker, and Wisconsin chose Edwin C. Wall as its favorite son. The hottest and dirtiest fight occurred in Illinois, where John P. Hopkins and Roger Sullivan routed both the E. F. Dunne (Hearst) and Harrison forces by methods Bryan considered so "arbitrary, unfair, and unprincipled" that he determined to appeal to the national convention to overturn the "usurpation of power by a conscienceless gang of political pirates." [13]

Bryan retained complete control of the Nebraska convention. His platform promised that the Democracy, if victorious, would rid the country of trusts, militarism, imperialism, and "colonial systems." On the money question he declared that the Democracy would prevent the coinage of legal tender silver dollars into limited legal tender coins, secure to the people a volume of standard money equal to their

[12] John T. Morgan to Alton B. Parker, February 29, 1904, John T. Morgan Papers.

[13] *Commoner*, June 24, 1904; Hamlin to Henry L. Nelson, January 12, 1904, George Perkins to Hamlin, April 2, 1904, Richard Olney to Hamlin, April 22, 1904, Charles S. Hamlin Papers.

needs, and seek to obtain paper money issued by government without the intervention of national banks.[14] He himself was chosen to lead the delegation to St. Louis.

Pulitzer voiced the general Eastern and Southern demand that the gold standard should not be an issue in the campaign and that the Democratic convention "should accept the double verdict of the American people in Bryan's defeat in 1896 and 1900." Bryan retorted that with respect to Kansas City "I was right and my platform was right, and I have no apologies to offer nor a single word to retract." Leaders from all sections who tried to convince him to drop silver were driven to despair by his invincible firmness even if they admired his consistency as a crusader. O. O. Stealey, Washington correspondent for the Louisville *Courier-Journal*, said to him, "The folks down South like you, but they are tired of going into the Post Office and having their mail handed them by a Republican." Bryan replied that his support of silver was a matter of principle.

"That may be decisive with you, Mr. Bryan, but how are you going to enforce your principles if your party doesn't get into office?"

"I think we can win with this issue."

"Not in 1904."

"Well, then, in 1908."

"Not in 1908, and not in twenty-five years."

"Well, then, in seventy-five years." [15]

Bryan fought two wars, one against Roosevelt, one against the reorganizers. His attitude toward both antagonists is well revealed in correspondence with Texas's grand old man, the eighty-five-year-old John H. Reagan. Reagan advised Bryan to subordinate division within their party, agree on a platform, win the election, and settle differences afterwards. Defeat was inevitable if division continued; defeat meant the success of the "dangerous" Roosevelt. Bryan replied that he was well aware of the "dangerous tendency of Republican policies" in all departments of government. As for Roosevelt: "His imperialistic ideas, and his imperialistic methods, his refusal to enforce the law against men of great wealth who conspire against their country and its statutes, his subserviency to Wall Street, and his willingness to mortgage his administration to the great corporations in order to secure a second term—these ought to lead to his defeat in the coming election." As for Reagan's suggestion of postponing the settle-

---

[14] *Commoner*, June 10, 1904.

[15] Charles W. Thompson, *Party Leaders of the Times*, p. 51.

ment of differences until after the election, Bryan was positive that this should not and could not be done. The reorganizers could produce neither a satisfactory statement of principles nor an acceptable candidate. Parker, for example, was known only by the company he kept, namely Hill and August Belmont. "The trust magnates, the great bankers and the railroad attorneys would not be so unanimous in his support if they did not have secret assurances in regard to his position." Furthermore, "The men who deserted the party are really more antagonistic to Democratic principles than the average Republican. I cannot believe that the Democratic party will throw away the great opportunity it now has to make a successful attack on the strongholds of Republicanism—not by trying to win back by fatal concessions corporation-controlled Democrats, but by appealing to the conscience of the country and to the patriotism of the people." "I must," Bryan concluded, "continue to oppose [the reorganizers] in season and out of season. . . ." [16]

As anticipated, the South gave Parker the bulk of his strength. He would have two thirds of the delegates after the first or second ballot, yet his boom lacked popular confidence because he refused to the end to go on record. He would say nothing until the party had acted in convention, he said. While he refused to say whether he would demand that the words "gold standard" be used in the platform, he asserted that he would stand on any platform "conservatives" adopted.[17]

With newspapers in major cities in the East, Middle West, and Far West, Hearst clubs built upon the National Association of Democratic Clubs, of which he had been president for years, and ample funds, Hearst alone competed with Parker. He entered the convention with 104 votes. Had Bryan supported him early and late he could have been named. But Hearst was so radical that he drove conservatives to concentrate. He had supported Bryan in 1896 and 1900 and drew his strength mainly from Bryan country, yet Bryan refused to endorse him or to place him in nomination because he had purchased or intimidated delegates to support him and was not a part of the progressive reform movement. Moreover, his personal life was, according to the New York *Post*, "a sewer laid open." However, because of his personal feud with the Hopkins-Sullivan machine, Bryan went to

---

[16] The correspondence, which occurred in late April and early May, is reproduced in the *Commoner*, May 13, 1904.

[17] Omaha *World-Herald*, July 2, 3, 1904; St. Louis *Globe-Democrat*, July 2, 1904.

Chicago and offered to support his contesting delegation in the national convention. Hearst demurred, saying he did not wish to provoke further disturbance. Bryan insisted that he must do so in order to block the naming of a conservative candidate, although it is not beyond the realm of possibility that he hoped to create a deadlock in which he would be accepted as a compromise candidate. He also admitted making a "probable" mistake in attacking avowed candidates without suggesting others. Would he but name a man, many told him, they would support him. Since he would not, they must select for themselves, and Parker later acknowledged that Bryan's opposition in part made his nomination possible. It was not true, he said, that Hill alone won him the nomination; if it were true he would have given him credit for it. "Bryan, who disliked me, as I dislike him, contributed tremendously toward it, by the elimination of Cleveland, Hill, Gorman, Harmon, and others, by saying he would bolt them. The nomination of Coler [for governor of New York in 1902] at a Convention controlled by Hill followed by his defeat, contributed tremendously toward it. . . . But the fact is, that a chain of circumstances to which Bryan and the Coler nomination contributed, focused attention upon me. The result was, that . . . there were only two names considered at the Convention: W. R. Hearst and myself." [18]

To obtain a platform that would not sacrifice what the party had fought for since 1896 and a candidate who would be endorsed by those who had supported him twice, Bryan engaged in a historic fight for his political life against the same forces that treated him so brutally between 1896 and the Baltimore convention of 1912. By stemming the serious attempt by the conservatives to dominate the progressive Democrats, he "kept the faith."

II

"EVERYTHING according to schedule" and "no damned reformers," said the Republicans who met in Chicago on June 21 to hear keynoter Elihu Root demand "judgment upon the record of effective performance" and then go through the motion of naming Theodore Roosevelt. They praised their party for defending the gold standard but did not mention Grover Cleveland's fight for it. They alone had fought the Spanish War; they alone were the guardians of American

[18] Parker to Bixby, March 16, 1920, Bixby Papers.

prosperity. They charged that Democratic tariff policy would bring disaster and seemed to threaten the South with reduced representation in Congress because of its disfranchisement of Negroes. Charles W. Fairbanks of Indiana was chosen for Vice President because, as Roosevelt said, "who in the name of heaven else is there?" According to Mr. Dooley: "Th' raypublican convention labored, too, like a cash reigister. It listened to three canned speeches, adopted a predigested platform, nommynated a cold storage vice presidint, gave three especially prepared cheers and wint home. Th' convintion's mind was all made up f'r it befure it met. . . ." Roosevelt's platform, Bryan stated, contained only one emphatic plank, the one on the tariff, which rebuked the revisionists. ". . . standing alone and judged by its merits the Roosevelt administration is anything but an antimonopoly administration," he added. Nor did he find any encouragement for the laboring man or the Filipino in the Republican pronouncements. George W. Perkins, P. D. Armour, John Cudahy, Andrew Carnegie, and James Stillman were to Roosevelt what August Belmont and Thomas Fortune Ryan were to Parker, he said, and Roosevelt should reveal no anxiety about Parker's nomination.[19] Roosevelt nevertheless feared that he might fail of re-election and personally requested Nicholas Murray Butler to attend the Democratic convention, observe what was said and done, and report to him in detail as soon as practicable. Butler's report reassured him, and Butler never outlived his vivid memory of Bryan's exhibition of "oratorical power of a very high and impressive type." [20]

Bryan's decision not to run in 1904 greatly influenced the Populists. The Nebraska Populists had decided to support the Democracy if Bryan won at St. Louis but to try to reunite the fusionists and middle-of-the-road men and run an independent ticket if the Cleveland wing triumphed. At a meeting in Denver in August 1903 they issued a call for a separate national convention prior to the Democratic. Bryan tried to block them, arguing that nothing short of a revolution would enable a third party to win a national election. Determined to proceed independently, about two hundred Populists met at Springfield, Illinois, on July 4, 1904, where Arthur F. Mullen represented Bryan and pleaded in vain for a postponement until after the Democrats had met.

[19] *Commoner*, July 1, 1904.
[20] Nicholas Murray Butler, *Across the Busy Years, Recollections and Reflections*, I, 237–238.

Were he in politics, Thomas Watson had said in March, he would support Hearst for the Democratic nomination, for he appeared as an expression of "the radical element in the Jeffersonian tradition," but he declined a lucrative post on Hearst's editorial staff. The prospective victory of the Democratic conservatives caused him and many other Populists to believe that the silverites, if not Bryan himself, would bolt the reorganizers and thereby increase the Populist vote.[21] The middle-of-the-road men in control at Springfield reaffirmed the Omaha principles and called for the government ownership of public utilities and for strict control of corporations engaged in interstate commerce. Watson did not want the nomination, but on July 5 he was named over William V. Allen, and he accepted the honor seriously.

III

Once the idol of roaring multitudes, Bryan entered St. Louis on July 3 without welcome. At first he remained quiet as to plans and purposes. Then, as though silence pained him, he delivered a violent blast against Parker as a creature of Wall Street who could be judged only by his friends, namely "Hill and his financial agent, August Belmont." Benjamin Tillman, for one, supported him, saying, "How can you figure out Parker as a strong candidate when he has to carry the load of Hill and Belmont on the one side and the opposition of Tammany on the other? . . . How could we tell whether we would have a pig or a possum if we nominated him?" [22] Nine out of ten men in St. Louis believed Parker would be named. Bryan insisted that his nomination was "highly improbable if not impossible," but he could not unite the forces opposed to him. Neither Hearst men nor Tammany's Charles F. Murphy would listen to him.

The cry in St. Louis was not "Elect a Democrat" but "Bury Bryan." The major newspapers, the *Globe-Democrat* (Republican) and the *Post-Dispatch* (gold Democrat), the latter now controlled by Joseph Pulitzer, influenced the delegates against him. Reorganizers who had

---

[21] Arthur Brisbane to Thomas Watson, June 23, 1904, Thomas Watson Papers, University of North Carolina, quoted in Commager Papers; New York *Times*, July 5, 1904; C. Vann Woodward, *Tom Watson, Agrarian Rebel*, pp. 355–357; William V. Allen, "A Western Statesman's Reasons for Supporting Hon. Thomas E. Watson," *The Arena*, 32 (October 1904), 395.

[22] New York *Times*, July 5, 1904.

been compelled to bend to his will in 1896 and 1900 now took un-alloyed satisfaction in dictating to him. At Kansas City, Hill had drunk the dregs prepared for him by Croker; now he was in the saddle, riding roughshod and indifferent over all opposition. Said Hopkins: "I am in favor of making a slaughterhouse job of it. . . . The first duty of this convention is to kill Bryanism, root and branch," [23] and Adolph Ochs called the reorganizers rather than the Bryanites the "regenerated party." But Bryan was not, as Ochs charged, "sulking in his tent." [24] Asked whether he would desert his followers, he replied indelicately, "I shall stand here until the last dog is dead." [25]

Bryan had secured a petition from a large majority of the delegates to the Illinois convention demanding the seating of the Hearst men. On the afternoon of July 3 he filed contests in every one of the four-teen Illinois districts; on July 4, when he and Hopkins appeared be-fore the National Committee, he was turned down both on Illinois and on the contesting delegation from Washington, D.C., headed by his friend Cotter T. Bride. Defeated, he claimed victory, for the National Committee, on the question of jurisdiction, ruled that frauds had been practiced in Illinois. He then obtained the proxy of the Nebraska member and prepared to present his case to the Committee on Credentials.

Nor did Bryan gain ground in his attempt to name the presidential candidate. Pennsylvania's delegation came to St. Louis uninstructed. On July 4, after his appearance before the National Committee, Bryan sent for Colonel James Guffey and asked him to bring ex-Governor John M. Pattison out against Parker. Would Guffey do so, he said, he would deliver to him all his following in the convention and Pattison would be named. Guffey looked him straight in the eye and asked him just what his "following" meant. Bryan said the Nebraska delegation would support him. Guffey replied that he doubted the delegation a unit on the nominee. Annoyed, Bryan made no denial. Then he said he had scattered delegates in a number of Western and old silver states. With tongue in cheek Guffey said he could not decide for his delegation but would submit the matter to a caucus. Unbe-knownst to Bryan, Guffey had reached complete agreement with the Parker leaders and now led his state in casting its sixty-eight votes for Parker on the first ballot, thereby settling the question of the nominee.

[23] New York *World*, July 5, 6, 1904; Omaha *World-Herald*, July 7, 1904.
[24] New York *Times*, July 3, 4, 1904.
[25] New York *American*, July 3, 1904.

Bryan was also rebuffed by Ohio, which rejected his importunities to bring out Harmon in opposition to Parker. Among others, William J. Stone of Missouri, Richard F. Pettigrew, and Frederick T. Dubois made the rounds of the delegations but failed to move them against Parker. All Bryan could do was to symbolize his opposition to Parker by causing Nebraska to scatter its votes to Francis M. Cockrell, Harmon, and others, but none for the New Yorker.[26]

By July 5 Bryan's power had dropped to low ebb. His blast against Parker gained him nothing. He had been defeated before the National Committee. A conservative platform appealed to all wings of the party except to him, unless he could be called a wing, and the candidate was all but named. "The platform ought to . . . make an end of Bryan and the false Bryan creed and be done with it forever. The party has been reorganized enough for that," asserted the New York *Times*.[27] Pettigrew and Dubois, among others, declared that they had followed Bryan in defeat for eight years but now realized that the time to change had come; even Tillman preferred compromise to fight. "Mr. Bryan's leadership has come to an end, and a conservative policy animates the party," wrote James Creelman for the New York *World*. Creelman overlooked Dooley's comment that "There's a thousan' red-hot convintions inside iv ivry dimmycratic convintion" [28] and the fact that Bryan would never be still, on this or any other occasion, and that he was no quitter.

The first day of the convention, July 6, was hard on Bryan. For the first time in two campaigns he entered a convention hall unheralded and unnoticed. On July 4, when he had spoken at the World Fair grounds, his voice had not been in good condition. He awoke on July 5 with a fever and pains in his chest. On July 6 a doctor told him to keep his bed and see no one. This he did until noon, when, saying that he would go to the convention if he had to go on a stretcher, he went to the hall. John Sharp Williams's keynote speech contained praise for Cleveland rather than for him, attributed the establishment of the gold standard to Cleveland's repeal of the Sherman Silver Purchase Law rather than to Republican legislation, and advocated the adoption of the Mississippi state platform, which was

[26] Chicago *Record*, July 5, 1904; New York *Times*, July 5, 6, 1904; New York *World*, July 5, 1904; Omaha *World-Herald*, July 5, 1904; St. Louis *Globe-Democrat*, July 5, 1904.

[27] New York *Times*, July 6, 1904.

[28] *Ibid.*, July 6, 1904.

silent on the money question. By stating that the gold standard was destined to remain the standard of the country and that the Democrats would not nominate on "dead issues," Williams elicited cheers for Cleveland so spontaneous and long-lived that it appeared that his ideas again dominated the party.

As soon as the Credentials Committee was formed Bryan went before it and presented his version of the Illinois contest. Defeated, he planned to present a minority report to the convention on the next day. The popular ovation that greeted him at about 4 P.M. on July 7 was ample notice that the Parkerites were not to have things their own way. After a Parker counter demonstration Bryan walked to the stage. The chairman read the majority report, which threw out the Hearst delegates from Illinois and Washington, D.C. Bryan countered with a dreary recital of the details of the Illinois case and then demanded fifteen minutes for debate for each side. He stepped forward. His face was bloodless; his eyes shone. His lower lip trembled distinctly. Burning with fever, he moved his tongue about his cheeks thirstily. He gave a free swinging speech from the shoulder, without notes, full into Hopkins's face, with a savage earnestness in his words that bared his knowledge that he was fighting for existence. He had come to the convention hoping that agreement could be reached on the platform and the candidate and regretted that he was compelled to present a divisive subject. "But, if there is one Democratic principle more fundamental than another, it is that the majority has a right to rule." Applause. The majority had not been allowed to rule in Illinois. Indeed, "The evidence shows that no band of train robbers ever planned a raid upon a train more deliberately or with less conscience than they did." [29] The almost seven thousand spectators applauded him and cheered his denouncing of those who had bolted him in 1896. When charged with exploiting the situation for personal ends, he turned white with anger, laid aside the pitcher of ice water from which he took great gulps while speaking, clenched his fists, and waved them over his head while shouting that he would not be called a liar.[30]

Bryan never made a more direct appeal to the sentiments of his hearers. The galleries cheered everything he said, but the men who had the votes sat stolidly under what the New York *Times* called his

[29] *Official Report of the Proceedings of the Democratic National Convention Held in St. Louis, Missouri, July 6, 7, 8, and 9, 1904,* pp. 103–104.
[30] *Ibid.,* pp. 108–114.

"vituperative eloquence" and then voted him down 647 to 299. Bryan returned to his seat, his thin lips drawn closely together and his forehead puckered in a scowl, and soon left the hall to attend the meeting of the Committee on Resolutions being held at the Southern Hotel.

Although Hearst had spent probably $1,500,000, he and Bryan could barely muster 150 delegates. Hearst was through, and it was widely held that Bryan's eight years as party chief had ended. "Tomorrow's session of the convention will witness the full and complete departure of the Nebraskan from the arena of political power," predicted the New York *Times*.[31] "No other American politician ever arose so quickly from obscurity to great prominence, dominated a great political party so absolutely for a time and then faded so quickly into semi-obscurity as Mr. Bryan," said the New York *World*, adding that since he had no talent for building but only for destroying, in the end he had succeeded in destroying himself.[32] Yet Bryan regarded his defeat as a victory because the spectators had been with him, and their favor strengthened him for the battles that followed. Moreover, he had made it clear that he attended the convention only from a sense of obligation to the millions who had followed him in two campaigns. He must get the best platform he could for them, and "make the convention partly Democratic."

The election of Champ Clark as permanent chairman over Hill's protests was only partly a Bryan victory, for Joseph Bailey and Hill stood guard to see that he remained neutral. But Bryan's appointment by Chairman John Daniel of the Committee on Resolutions to the subcommittee of ten, later twelve, that would draft the platform gave him a position from which to fight.

Until Senator Francis G. Newlands was added to the subcommittee [33] Bryan alone opposed the Parker forces, and only about a quarter of the delegates favored endorsing the Kansas City platform. The first session of the committee, which lasted from eight in the evening to 1:30 A.M. on July 8, considered conservative platforms offered by John Sharp Williams, Charles S. Hamlin, and John Poe of Maryland, and a Bryan interpretation offered by Newlands. The latter included, as Hamlin recorded in his Diary,"planks on national bank notes, against

[31] July 8, 1904.
[32] July 8, 1904.
[33] The men on the committee were Daniel of Virginia, Hill of New York, Williams of Mississippi, Dubois of Idaho, Hamlin of Massachusetts, Cable of Illinois, Poe of Maryland, Shively of Indiana, Davis of West Virginia, and Newlands of Nevada.

melting silver dollars, favoring greenbacks, against Aldrich Committee bills, etc., etc.: Pettigrew offered (of course with Bryan's connivance), planks for public ownership of railroads and telegraphs and others. . . . Bryan also advocated an internal revenue tax on all corporations selling products cheaper abroad than in the United States." [34]

Busy in the convention on the Illinois case, Bryan and Williams returned at about 11 o'clock to find that the subcommittee had completed its work and was prepared to report to the full committee. A gold plank introduced by Hill had been adopted by a vote of 7 to 3. Even if he and Williams had been present and voted against it the result would have been 7 to 5. For sixteen hours, from 8 o'clock in the evening until noon the next day, July 8, the battle raged in the full committee. Each time the Parkerites demanded a conservative plank Bryan moved a substitute for it. In each case he found a majority, with the result that he wrote a good deal more of the platform than he had of the Chicago platform. While he did not get everything he wanted, he kept out everything to which he objected.

Bryan began the fight over the money plank by moving to affirm the Chicago and Kansas City platforms. He was overwhelmingly voted down, but the majority against adopting a gold plank, 35 to 15, was larger than that on any other plank because many Parkerites also opposed it. When Daniel asked whether the members believed such a plank would weaken the party in his state, more than half of them arose, among them some of Parker's stanchest supporters, including Williams, Tillman, Bailey, and Edward Carmack. These men, said Hamlin, "were against us *in spite of Bryan* also opposing. . . . They *despised* Bryan and only regretted their apparent accord with him in this one matter." [35]

During the course of the discussion Bryan asked Hill when he had decided that a gold plank should be adopted. Hill replied that he had decided only a few days prior to the convening of the convention. Bryan shook a finger near Hill's nose and asked what Parker's views were on the money question. Had he talked with Parker about it? Hill said he had not. Yet when Bryan offered to accept a plank that stated that the quantitative theory of money had been established and that the increased volume of money had removed the money question from politics, Hill objected. Hill's plank, supported by Williams,

[34] Hamlin, Diary, p. 340.
[35] *Ibid.*, p. 339.

Hamlin, Carmack, and others, was based on one written by the financial expert, Charles A. Conant, which sugar-coated the gold pill by affirming the quantitative theory, thereby substantially admitting Bryan's contention. The recent discoveries of gold, read the plank, have "contributed to the maintenance of a money standard of value no longer open to question, removing that issue from the field of political contention." Conant had written the plank after consulting such New York financiers as August Belmont, and Hill admitted that its adoption would satisfy Eastern interests. It was therefore obvious to Bryan that Hill wanted a conservative platform to fit Parker, and he told the committee that they could better run Cleveland, whose opinions were known, than Parker, the "interrogation mark." Albeit under Eastern pressure to obtain a gold plank, Hill sensed that further debate would disrupt the party and indicated his readiness to compromise. Seeing that the best he could do was to prevent any expression on the subject, Bryan also conceded that the platform should not mention it. But agreement was reached only after all of his other financial planks were voted down, and he threatened to revive them all in a minority report if the committee tried to revive a demand for a gold plank.[36]

The conservatives pondered hard over whether to submit a minority report. Many of them agreed with Bryan in opposing a gold plank. The defeat of a gold minority report could be taken by the country as a vote against the gold standard and thus lead to the nomination of a radical candidate and certain defeat in November. Furthermore, most of them believed that "in all human probability" Parker would account in his letter of acceptance for the silence on gold in the platform. Since the planks adopted fulfilled the realistic expectations of the gold delegates, and since Bryan would agree to the platform as written, they desisted from further effort.[37]

A majority of the committee, especially the Southern members, upheld Bryan's demand for an income tax, but they opposed an income tax *plank* for fear of appearing "to antagonize the decision of

[36] New York *American*, July 6, 7, 8, 1904; New York *Times*, July 7, 1904; *Commoner*, July 15, 1904; William Jennings Bryan and Mary Baird Bryan, *The Memoirs of William Jennings Bryan*, pp. 149–150. Bryan's cold bothered him so much that at one point he absented himself from the committee room and gave a friend money to buy him some mustard plasters. "What do you want the plasters for?" asked a newspaper man who overheard. "Trying to draw Hill out on what are Parker's views," Bryan quipped with a wink. New York *Times*, July 8, 1904.

[37] Hamlin, Diary, pp. 338–341, 356–360; *Official Proceedings*, pp. 296–299.

the courts." Hill objected to the plank as displeasing to the financial interests of the East, and Daniel baited Bryan in personal terms in arguing against him. "Conditions have changed in the last few years," he said, "and heroic changes demand heroic remedies. We must consider New England, New York, and that section of the country. . . . [Bryan] has reviled every man whom any state has recommended for the Presidency and, so far as I have been able to learn, has as yet presented no candidate of his own." Over cries of "Order! Order!" Bryan shouted that Daniel be permitted to proceed, and it was not until Tillman interceded that the Virginian subsided. Bryan bargained: he would withdraw the income tax if the committee would adopt the anti-trust plank of the Kansas City platform, which was stronger than that being proposed. When a member remarked that the effect of his plank would be "to frighten capital and scare away campaign contributions," Bryan saw his chance and "bellowing like a mad bull he said the party leaders had made a bargain with the trusts and corporations in return for campaign contributions." The committee gave in and Bryan and Hill wrote an anti-trust plank as strong as Bryan believed it would accept. Little opposition was made to his labor planks. Although he failed to get a direct legislation plank, his demands for the direct election of senators and for anti-imperialism were adopted unanimously. The Philippine Independence Commission, turned away by the Republican convention, had its petition granted in a plank that proposed "to set the Filipino people upon their feet, free and independent, to work out their own destiny." [38]

The contest over the tariff plank was one of the most spirited of all. As originally written it smacked of protection, and Bryan was joined by Parkerites like Hamlin and Hearst supporters like Ben Cable in making it more acceptable to tariff reformers. So strong was Southern opposition to protection that Bailey threatened to bring in a minority report if the original proposition were adopted. Despite some heat in arguments between Bryan and various other members, an amended plank that "roared gently" was obtained without arousing ill feeling.

At about noon on Friday, July 8, Bryan and Hill, both smiling,

[38] Hamlin, Diary, pp. 339–340; New York American, July 8, 1904; New York Times, July 9, 1904; Commoner, July 15, 1904; Richard B. Doss, "Democrats in the Doldrums: Virginia and the Democratic National Convention of 1904," Journal of Southern History, 20 (November 1954), 522.

left the committee room and were immediately surrounded by reporters. So husky and hoarse that he could barely speak above a whisper, Bryan said he was "well satisfied" with the platform but that he had made some concessions to obtain what he wanted. "Now boys," he added, "be sure and get Hill's platform right."

With an unusual display of good nature Hill laughed and retorted, "I think that we will have to share the honors on that."

"We are all satisfied," said Bryan.

"I am perfectly satisfied," echoed Hill.

"Will Mr. Parker stand on the platform?" a reporter asked Hill.

"I do not see why not," Hill replied,[39] never dreaming that on the morrow, after he was named, Parker would object to it.

Bryan had won a tremendous personal victory. Refusing to admit that everything was lost before he arrived in St. Louis, without lieutenants to whom he could delegate responsibilities, ill, with little sleep for several days before July 6 and none from July 6 to 8, he had overturned the majority and proved himself to be very much alive politically. He had knocked the cocky Hill to his knees by keeping a gold plank out of the platform, yet he had furnished a platform which both he and Hill could accept without too much grimacing. He had fought with no holds barred, especially against those who had bolted him in 1900. According to Hamlin, "All the leading members . . . begged Bryan almost with tears in their eyes to be reasonable for the sake of the Party, but he was obdurate. He insulted almost everyone and seemed more like an insane man. He insulted Judge Parker— called him a tool of trusts—and even attacked Senator Daniel. He insulted me when I begged him to be moderate, denounced me for not voting for him in 1896, finally called me a tool of monopoly. I arose and was proceeding to express my mind vigorously when Bryan apologized." [40] Parker later wrote: "I have been told more than once by men who sat in that committee, that they doubted whether any man living could have kept his head absolutely level with the insulting speeches of Bryan which he had to meet." [41]

[39] New York *American*, Omaha *World-Herald*, July 9, 1904.

[40] Hamlin, Diary, 346. Bryan's personal relations with Hamlin were good, for he had recently written him: "What about those white guineas that you promised me. . . . I want a pair—I will pay you a reasonable price for them, or name them after you, or do anything else in return for them except advocate the nomination of Grover Cleveland."

[41] Parker to Bixby, March 20, 1920, Bixby Papers.

No inkling of the bitterness in the committee reached the delegates, and when it was announced that it would report itself "unanimously" agreed, the delegates set off an explosion that beat all convention records. The galleries sensed that the platform reflected Bryan's efforts, and the moment the conservatives finished applauding the fact that "harmony" had been achieved they gave their shrill yells of "Hurrah for Bryan." Yet Bryan's greater fight lay on the morrow.

IV

REORGANIZERS complained that Bryan's "unsafe and insane" platform would insure a walkover for Roosevelt, castigated Hill for surrendering to him, and demanded that Parker go on record for gold before nominations occurred.[42] In contrast, Republican newspapers like the St. Louis *Globe-Democrat* spoke of the "cowardly platform" but admitted that "Rarely have eloquence, courage, sincerity and persistence won over brute numbers in any great assemblage as the Nebraskan has just achieved." [43]

During the afternoon recess Daniel asked Chairman Clark if it would be in order to couple the previous question with the motion to adopt the platform. Since the motion on the previous question was undebatable, this tactic would result in the adoption of the platform without debate. Hill then asked Clark the same thing. Clark sent a trustworthy man to ask Bryan how he felt. Bryan said he wished to avoid discussion. At 8 P.M. Daniel read the platform in pantomime, for he could not be heard ten feet away, and whispered his two motions. Clark put them "instanter," and the platform carried with a whoop because both sides wished to avoid debate.[44]

When the nominations began Bryan had not yet indicated his choice. Parker, Hearst, Gray, Cockrell, and several others were named. During the eighteen-minute demonstration that followed the naming of Parker, Bryan and his Nebraskans craned their necks to see what was going on but did not rise. When Hearst was named, Bryan led

[42] New York *Times*, July 9, 1904; New York *World*, July 9, 1904; *The Nation*, 79 (July 14, 1904), 24.

[43] St. Louis *Globe-Democrat*, July 9, 1904.

[44] Champ Clark, *My Quarter Century of American Politics*, II, 140–143. The anti-Roosevelt character of the platform is summed up in its stating that "The existing Republican administration has been spasmodic, erratic, sensational, spectacular, and arbitrary. It has made itself a satire upon the Congress, courts, and upon the settled practices and usages of national and international law."

the volley of cheers that came from the crowd by standing up and waving a small American flag. "It seems to be decreed by fate that the men who scuttled the Democratic ship shall once more be placed in charge," shouted Clarence Darrow as he seconded Hearst. When he mentioned Bryan the crowd cheered, and many of the Hearst enthusiasts who marched about the hall stopped to shake hands with him. He stood up during the early part of the demonstration but sat when wracked by a violent fit of coughing. In seconding Parker, Carmack took an ugly swipe at Bryan, saying, "I have yet to learn that laryngeal activity is the supreme test of statesmanship . . . that the width of a man's mouth is commensurate with the breadth of his understanding or that the length of his tongue measures the depth of his wisdom." In nominating General Cockrell, Clark voiced the general demand of the South for a reward to the section that regularly furnished the bulk of the votes. He was amazed and lost half of his speech when the crowd shouted and demonstrated for half an hour upon his first mention of the Missourian.[45]

As arranged earlier so that he could speak last, Bryan yielded to Wisconsin, which named Wall, so that it was not until almost 4 A.M. that he got to speak. In choosing Cockrell he again revealed his oratorical artistry and parliamentary skill. He believed Cockrell could logically be named as a true Bryanite; second, as an ex-Confederate soldier he might do better in the South than Parker.[46] Parker, however, believed Bryan's reasons were "one, that he might . . . fascinate the Convention, second, in the belief that there would not be mustered for my nomination two-thirds of the Convention, that Hearst would be able to control little more than a third, and that ultimately the Convention would take him, although he was not openly a candidate." [47] The same logic was applied by many conservatives to Bryan's efforts in the Baltimore convention of 1912.

Stating that he could not second Cockrell in the four minutes permitted by the rules, Bryan asked Clark either to extend his time or permit him to name someone else. Two thirds of the delegates were for Parker, yet they gave him unlimited time to speak. Most of them were near collapse from the heat and lack of sleep. Some were eating sandwiches brought in from nearby places. Most had their coats off,

[45] Clark, *Quarter Century*, II, 144–145; New York *World*, July 9, 1904; *Official Proceedings*, pp. 166, 210–213.

[46] Bryan, *Memoirs*, p. 152.

[47] Parker to Bixby, March 20, 1920, Bixby Papers.

and some slept in their chairs despite the perpetual roar of sound made by thousands of hoarse and broken voices. The doorkeepers were letting everyone in, and discipline was at an end.

As dawn broke, about 4:30, Bryan moved down the aisle to a tremendous ovation by both foe and friend, for it was assumed that he would merely second some nomination. When he advanced to the front of the platform he was given a mighty greeting. There was a smile on his face and a look of joy in his full, dark eyes. No one had been able to do anything with the mighty mob of about twenty thousand, and he let the uproar continue for about ten minutes. He then waved his arms for silence, scowled down the shouters, and imperiously motioned for order. The crowd obeyed; the vast audience grew still as he began to speak. Soon the thousands hung on his every word.

"Two nights without sleep and [a] cold make it difficult for me to make myself heard," he rasped, "but I trust that my voice will improve in a moment." Reaching again into his stock of Bible lore, this time to Paul's letter to Timothy, he began by saying: "Eight years ago at Chicago the Democratic National Convention placed in my hand the standard of the party and commissioned me as its candidate. Four years ago at Kansas City that commission was renewed. Tonight I come back to this Democratic National Convention to return that commission and to say to you that you may dispute over whether I have fought a good fight, you may dispute whether I have finished my course, but you cannot deny that I have kept the faith." The phrase "kept the faith" provoked the most tumultuous demonstration of the convention even though two thirds of the delegates sat glumly in their seats. It made the headlines of the nation's press and did much to regain for Bryan a position of leadership in his party, especially with its Western wing. Digging his voice out of his tortured chest by mean force, he then told of his love for his party, attacked Roosevelt as a militarist, and asked the delegates to name a pilot who would lead the party "away from the Scylla of Militarism without wrecking her upon the Charybdis of Commercialism." For a time his voice grew strong. His words clapped through the hall like the ringing of a silver bell, and the crowd sat as though carved in stone. But his voice trembled when he said he asked for nothing for himself. He denied that he had ever been a dictator and pointed a finger directly at Hill as he said so. By his work on the Committee on Resolutions he had helped to bring the party together, and without thought of any particular candidate. Near the end of his speech he almost reeled from exhaustion, and at times he panted for breath as though he had reached the limits of his physical endurance. At the very end he grasped at a straw by seconding Cockrell.[48] The announcement fell flat, for the Missourian did not stand a chance. The unthinking crowd went wild, but Parker had the delegates.

Bryan believed his "Keeping the Faith" speech the high water mark of his oratorical successes "because he converted a convention hostile to him into one that gave him a larger measure of applause than he ever received, before or afterwards." [49] It was devoid of tawdriness, emotionalism, and show and as near to a harmony talk as a man of his pugnacity could make. To hear him pleading in behalf of a minority was in itself dramatic and sensational. Demanding nothing for himself, he asked only that his principles be remembered. He did not even demand the nomination of a Bryanite—he merely opposed anyone who adored the "god of gold." There were many good Democrats whom the delegates could choose, among them Hearst, Wall, and Pattison, he said, but they should not force him to accept Parker, who represented the money power he had been fighting for so long. The speech revealed him at his best, as a fighter who fought to the limit of physical endurance. It is not too much to say that he risked his life that night, as he did later at Dayton, in fighting for his faith.

Men in all walks of life praised Bryan. To Senator Albert J. Beveridge he was "the hero of conscience"; to Walter Wellman his leadership was "the finest thing in American life," for he was a man who moved men. August Belmont, who sat down front and to whom Bryan appeared to speak, said, "Now I understand how that man gets his great following. He is a giant, isn't he?" Even Adolph Ochs admitted that "Had the convention been less steel-rivetted than it was the Cockrell demonstration would have swept it off its feet." [50]

So completely exhausted that he could not even rise to cast Nebraska's vote, Bryan fell to his seat and was half-carried, half-led to a cab and driven to his hotel, where he immediately fell asleep. His doctors said he was threatened with pneumonia and prescribed a month's rest lest his life be endangered; however, this diagnosis was

[48] *Official Proceedings*, pp. 236–245.

[49] Josephus Daniels, *Editor in Politics*, p. 474.

[50] Letter of Clarence Wood, Louisville *Courier-Journal*, January 4, 1932; Charles W. Thompson, "How Bryan Picked His Issues," New York *Times*, August 2, 1925; New York *World*, July 11, 1904.

not permitted to reach convention hall. With Bryan gone the inevitable occurred in the naming of Parker, at 5:45 A.M., on the first ballot. Hearst received 181 votes; Cockrell, with only 42, was the highest of the rest. Belmont was jubilant; Hill alternately laughed and cried. At 6 o'clock the convention adjourned until 2 P.M., when work would begin on naming the vice presidential candidate. In the interim the Parker leaders conferred and agreed on Henry G. Davis; Cockrell and Hearst wired their support for Parker; the Republicans talked about "Roosevelt against an unknown"; and Lodge wrote the President: "I think Parker will be as handy for us to beat as anyone and more so than some. We shall do him up early I believe." [51]

All men named for Vice President, including William A. Harris, Senator George Turner, John W. Kern, John Sharp Williams, and Henry G. Davis, had supported Bryan, but Davis had dropped free silver in 1900. The roll call was proceeding when excited groups of delegates began conferring and passing a piece of paper from one to another. Finally, when the roll call reached Texas, Senator Charles A. Culberson exclaimed: "We want to know, before a candidate for vice president is nominated, who will be the nominee of this convention for President." [52] He referred to rumors that Parker, from his home in Esopus, New York, had telegraphed William F. Sheehan that "The gold standard is irrevocably established by law, and I cannot accept the nomination unless the plank is contained in the platform"; that he had wired Senator Carmack that he would refuse the nomination unless the platform specifically endorsed the gold standard; and that Hill had ordered the suppression of the telegram sent Sheehan, saying that Parker would have sent it directly to the convention had he wished it revealed to the delegates. Tired of waiting for Sheehan to produce the real telegram, some newspaper men had framed the one to Carmack.[53] All eyes turned toward the New York delegation, where Sheehan and Hill were talking excitedly, while Charles A. Towne, Willis J. Abbot, and others rushed to Bryan for a carefully guarded caucus.

Parker had in effect repudiated the platform, and the convention leaders immediately adjourned to 8:30 P.M. Southern delegates par-

[51] Lodge to Roosevelt, July 9, 1904, Henry Cabot Lodge, *Selections From the Correspondence of Theodore Roosevelt and Henry Cabot Lodge, 1884–1918*, II, 87.

[52] *Official Proceedings*, p. 273.

[53] Alton B. Parker to William F. Sheehan, July 9, 1904, New York *Times*, July 10, 1904; Omaha *World-Herald*, July 9, 10, 1904.

ticularly were threatening to withdraw their votes from Parker, saying that he had made victory impossible. The crowd was jeering Parker and cheering Hearst and others, but most of all Bryan, who was being honored as the hero of the convention. Benjamin Tillman towered over Senator Daniel, who had influenced him in favor of Parker, and shouted that he had been "deceived, seduced, maltreated, and horse-woggled." He then shook his clenched right fist in Hill's face and cried, "This may split the party!" Wiping his perspiring forehead nervously, Hill said, "We'll talk it over. . . . Everything will be all right." [54] When Sheehan finally produced the telegram and it looked for a time as if Parker would decline the nomination, Missouri's hope for Cockrell was revived, the Hearst forces took renewed heart, and a lively boom for Bryan began. Daniel intimated that he would move to table any motion to amend the platform and conferred on the floor of the convention with Hill, Sheehan, Daniel J. Campau, John Poe, Tillman, and others, protected from reporters by policemen, and then joined a group at the Southern Hotel which studied Parker's telegram and prepared a reply.

The convention met at 8:30 in a spirit for battle. Disregarding the order of business, Governor James K. Vardaman of Mississippi demanded that the New York delegation furnish the Parker telegram, that it be read to the convention, and that the questions it raised be settled before proceeding with the vice presidential nominations. Williams, Tillman, and Carmack joined him on the stage and tactfully and skillfully handled the situation. Williams obtained the telegram and had it read in full:

I regard the gold standard as firmly and irrevocably established and shall act accordingly if the action of the Convention of today shall be ratified by the people. As the platform is silent on the subject, my view should be made known to the Convention, and if it is proved to be unsatisfactory to the majority I request you to decline the nomination for me at once, so that another may be nominated before adjournment.[55]

The reorganizers were making progress in allaying the fury of the crowd when a new uproar arose at 10:15 when, aided by his brother Charles and Willis J. Abbot, Bryan entered the hall. His face was white and drawn. He had a poultice about his chest and he breathed with difficulty. His forehead was beaded with perspiration. Disregard-

[54] *Ibid.*, July 10, 1904; *Commoner*, July 15, 1904; Clark, *Quarter Century*, II, 150.
[55] *Official Proceedings*, p. 277.

ing doctors' orders and the pleading of family and friends, he had left his bed as soon as he learned of Parker's telegram, for he saw his chance to turn defeat into victory. He had pneumonia in one lung, but he battled the whole night through and almost won.

Tillman read the reply prepared to Parker's telegram:

The platform adopted by this convention is silent on the question of a monetary standard because it is not regarded as a possible issue in this campaign, and only campaign issues were mentioned in the platform. Therefore there is nothing in the views expressed in the telegram just received which would preclude a man entertaining them from accepting a nomination on said platform.

Tillman then asked the delegates to forget their differences and end the dissension which had torn them for the past ten years. The yearning note in his voice melted the crowd, and men sat unashamedly as tears rolled down their cheeks.[56]

At about midnight Bryan made his way to the stage. His face was ghastly white. His lips were compressed in a thin line and his brows were drawn straight. He fanned himself nervously and paid no attention to the hands held out to him as he passed. He reviewed the discussion and vote on the gold plank in the committee. He then read Parker's telegram and told about his talk with Hill with respect to Parker's views on gold. If the convention adopted a gold plank, he would interpose no objection except to vote against it. However, if the delegates insisted upon leaving the gold standard out of the platform "because it is settled," then he insisted that the reply to Parker be amended by asking him whether he favored "the melting up of the silver dollars . . . asset currency . . . national branch banks, and the national bank currency." He thundered, "I want you gentlemen to know that if there is discord in the convention, you cannot lay it at my door. (Applause.) I have been the harmonizer." However, he would not support a candidate "who comes and injects into the platform this question, and makes it not merely a gold standard plank, but . . . an irrevocable gold standard proposition, denying us even the right to oppose it at a future time." He was distressed and embarrassed that this question should have arisen, but he rejected Parker's proposition because "I want us to win in this campaign. (Applause.) I want us to defeat the Republican party."

[56] New York *Times*, July 11, 1904; *Official Proceedings*, pp. 279–285; George C. Osborn, *John Sharp Williams: Planter-Statesman of the Deep South*, pp. 117–118.

He asked the reorganizers to avoid expediency and meet the question candidly, fairly, honestly, for "an open, frank declaration will not lose you any more votes than an attempt to dodge this issue and to ignore it, now that it has been raised." (Applause.) Parker should have spoken sooner. He *must* now go on record on each of the questions he posed in his amendment.[57]

The reorganizers rebuffed Bryan with insults. Williams, for example, spoke bitterly against him, once refused him the right to speak, and charged him with being the only man in the convention who sought to prevent harmony.[58] Moreover, they found Parker's telegram "astounding" and "exhilarating" and the Judge, as Cleveland put it, a man of "unique courage and unequivocal independence." To dispute these arguments, as Bryan did, was to "quibble." [59] In contrast, Bryanites regarded the reply to be sent Parker as an endorsement of the gold standard, said it violated the agreement reached in the Committee on Resolutions, disputed the claim that the delegates knew that Parker was a gold man when they voted for him,[60] and, as Bayard Cutting put it, "looks like a concocted scheme of Hill's to which Parker, with not too nice a sense of honor, lent himself." [61]

It was almost 1:00 A.M. when the delegates decided, by 794 to 191, to send the reply to Parker as written, without Bryan's amendment. Realizing that a recorded vote on his amendment would make Democratic victory impossible, Bryan withdrew it, declared he would vote for New York's candidate for Vice President,[62] and left the hall for his sickbed. Davis was named on the first ballot. He was over eighty years old and worth about forty millions. "Perhaps he is expected to

[57] Memoranda, "First Speech on the Last Night of the Convention," "Second Speech on the Last Night of the Convention," Bryan Papers; *Official Proceedings*, pp. 287–303.

[58] *Official Proceedings*, pp. 309–314; Osborn, *Williams*, p. 118.

[59] Cleveland, "Parker," pp. 3–8.

[60] Roosevelt called the telegram "a bold and skillful move," but, he wrote Lodge, to say that Parker had acted from principles was "nonsense," else he would have inserted a gold plank in the Albany platform. Then he was hunting delegates; now he made "a perfectly safe but spectacular game." Nevertheless, "I think this act gave him all of Cleveland's strength without any of Cleveland's weakness, and made him, on the whole, the most formidable man the Democrats could have nominated." Lodge to Roosevelt, July 12, 1904, Roosevelt to Lodge, July 14, 1904, Lodge, *Correspondence*, II, 88–89.

[61] Memorandum, Bayard Cutting Mss., Commager Papers.

[62] Memorandum, "Third Speech on the Last Night of the Convention," Bryan Papers.

leave his money to the party," said the St. Louis *Globe-Democrat.* Yet he had supported Bryan twice, was acceptable to the East, and it was good politics to name a man from a doubtful state.

What had Bryan accomplished in the convention? To those prejudiced against him he was just what the people wanted—a star, a bullfighter, a chief matador, a hero. He was "The Wrecker," for his single and ignoble ambition since 1896 had been to punish those who had defeated him then and in 1900 and to keep himself conspicuous in political affairs. The unkindest cut of all came from Watson, who charged that he had gone down to his knees, in effect, "To apologize for the abuse [his party] had heaped upon the Republicans for eight years. . . ."[63]

Given the situation that existed prior to the convention, Bryan had exerted a tremendous influence and achieved great results at St. Louis. He was extremely conscious of and sensitive to the loneliness of his position, yet he did not seek to force himself on the convention. None but he could have silenced the impatient, sweltering crowd while he read the long lawyer's brief on the Illinois contest; none but he, once he had thrown his manuscript aside, could mix oratory, pleading, and savage denunciation to whip the crowd to a white frenzy. For three days he had been, as he said, "counsellor for the interest of a united Democracy." Both in committee and on the floor he had advised harmony and proved willing to compromise just this side of outright surrender of principle. Reviled, despised, and trampled underfoot, he had proved an admirable minority leader. For one supposedly singing the swan song, he had come back so strongly that he was the towering figure of the convention. Even if he were wrong in fighting on for silver and for government rather than bank money, there were few who could match his sincerity, persistence, purity of purpose, political zeal, parliamentary skill, and gifts of oratory. His debate had been logical, unemotional, reasoned, and reasonable. Although another was the candidate and he would have no official force in the councils of his party, he had recaptured the popular imagination and gained a position from which he could reassert his leadership under more favorable circumstances.

V

REORGANIZERS cheered the nomination of Parker as the death knell of Bryan and Bryanism. "Such Democrats as you and I ought to be

[63] *Tom Watson's Magazine,* June 1905, p. 390.

pretty well satisfied. Bryan and Bryanism are eliminated as influential factors in Democratic councils, true Democracy has a leader and its time-honored and approved principles again are set before the people of the land without apology or shame-facedness," Cleveland wrote Parker.[64] Democrats could now devote their energy to seeking victory over the Republicans rather than to the "supreme task of beating back the wild hordes of Bryanism." Watterson, Ochs, and Pulitzer worked hard for Parker, and Wall Street figures like Jacob H. Schiff and James J. Hill lauded him, but there was really little enthusiasm for him. Ryan and Belmont backed the ticket strongly, the latter giving $250,000 of the $620,000 campaign fund, but Hill did not stump; Cleveland and Cockran made only a few speeches; and Murphy knifed him in order to avoid creating a place of power for Hill. Disappointed in the gold telegram, the South felt as John Sharp Williams did, that the Democrats had "no more chance of winning the election than a snowball had of staying in the lower regions." [65]

No Democrat, let alone Parker, could have been elected in 1904. The country had "gone Rooseveltian, not Republican." Most Bryan Democrats and Populists, many Socialists and, according to E. L. Godkin, those with "wild notions in their heads," preferred Roosevelt to Parker. Roosevelt was splitting his party by appealing to the masses on the basis of the similarity of his ideas and the "residuum of Bryanism." Rather than aiding Parker split the Republican opposition, Bryan was splitting the Democracy by painting Parker a plutocrat supported by those who had opposed him in 1896 and 1900.

A month passed before Bryan was able to take to the stump, but on July 12, the day he returned home, he stated in a front page article in *The Commoner* that he would support Parker because Roosevelt was injecting the race issue into politics and stood for "the spirit of war," and because the Democratic platform opposed imperialism and favored reducing the standing army. But he would not misrepresent the issues or appeal for votes for the ticket on false grounds. Parker's victory precluded progress on economic matters. Moreover, he had made a "plain and deliberate attempt to deceive the party" on the money question. His nomination was secured "by crooked and indefensible methods, but the Democrat who loves his country has to make his decisions upon conditions as he finds them, not as he would like to have them." Finally, he said he would organize the progressives

[64] Letter of July 14, 1904, Bixby Papers.
[65] Osborn, *Williams*, p. 119.

for 1908 with the object of marshaling the support "of a radical and progressive policy to make the Democratic party an efficient means in the hands of the people for securing relief from the plutocratic element that controls the Republican party, and for the time being is in control of the Democratic party." [66]

As in 1900 Bryan saw other issues more important than those of finance and would have the former settled before tackling the latter. Louis F. Post, who talked with him soon after the convention, wrote Tom L. Johnson: ". . . I am *sure* Bryan really hopes for Parker's election. He thinks it would take the race question and the Philippine question out of politics and leave the way clear for economic questions. My impression is that Bryan would regard Parker's election by small majorities in pivotal States, yet by a smaller popular vote in the whole country, than he himself got in 1896 and 1900, as ideal from the point of view of the future radical Democracy." [67]

On July 21 Bryan furnished his plan of reorganization. Bimetallism was still as sound in theory as ever, but the need for it was no longer apparent. His "radical changes and . . . departure from conservative lines" included the government ownership of railroads and control of telegraphs, the income tax, the election of federal judges by the people, and the public ownership of municipal franchises. These reforms, he said, would have great weight "when the party goes forth, as it must ultimately, to appeal to the masses," and the contest for them must be made "whether the party wins in November or not. A single election is but an incident in the life of a party. . . ." [68] Seeing red, the reorganizers called him a traitor to his party and deemed his new departure socialistic and dangerous. He would deprive the judiciary of independence; his ownership plan would lead to federal centralization. His objective, they said, was "to frighten Eastern Democrats away from the ticket . . . and to hold together the remnants of Bryanites in the West and South as an independent organization equally hostile to the Democrats and to the Republicans." When Roland Morris came away from St. Louis profoundly impressed with Bryan and sought to convert Woodrow Wilson by saying that he "represents the only live part of the Democratic party," Wilson responded: "The trouble is that Bryan has caught the spirit and instincts of the finer aspirations of American life, but Morris, the

[66] *Commoner*, July 12, 1904.
[67] Letter of July 24, Commager Papers.
[68] Omaha *World-Herald*, July 22, 1904; New York *Times*, July 23, 1904.

man has no brains. It is a great pity that a man with his power of leadership should have no mental rudder." [69]

Parker was being advised by the leading reorganizers. Cleveland, for example, wrote him: "Our best campaign matter just now is— YOU. . . . I mean 'you' as you are manifested . . . in the despatch you sent to St. Louis. The spirit and sentiment aroused by this utterance of yours, should be kept alive and stimulated from time to time during the campaign. . . . Bryan is doing the cause much good in his present mood; and I for one hope it will continue." [70] Yet Parker tried to get Bryan on his side. He asked him to call whenever he went East, "for I should like very much to have a talk with you," but Bryan had no intention of going East. His "inconsistency" was already the subject of much comment, and Parker's defeat, if it came, might be attributed to his support. Yet he wrote Parker several letters and gave him a copy of his acceptance speech of August 1900, which was wholly devoted to anti-imperialism, and which Parker acknowledged gratefully and humbly. Yet Parker had his own "inconsistency," his predicament of being a gold man who had voted twice for Bryan, and he stood to lose many votes from those who had supported Bryan. Moreover, his acceptance speech was so crude and amateurish that Hill and Daniel Lamont got Charles S. Hamlin to devote an entire week to rewriting and editing it. [71]

On August 10, when he was notified, Parker elicited most attention and cheers when he spoke against militarism and imperialism, but when he failed to mention the money question and also said he would not be a candidate again Hill said he would drop out of politics at the end of the year. Hill nevertheless sent a feeler in Bryan's direction by writing William V. Allen that "I hope that he will lend his great influence to the support of the ticket." [72] Rather than being in Parker's audience Bryan was attending the Nebraska Democratic and Populist state conventions, which were meeting in separate halls in Lincoln.

The star attraction in the Populist convention, Thomas E. Watson, spoke for two hours. Bryan applauded his strong points, which almost matched those of his own bold new program. He then addressed

[69] Ray Stannard Baker, *Woodrow Wilson: Life and Letters*, III, 202–203.

[70] Letter, July 14, 1904, Allan Nevins (ed.), *Letters of Grover Cleveland, 1850–1908*, pp. 583–584.

[71] Hamlin, Diary, pp. 364–367.

[72] Letter of August 4, 1904, Commager Papers.

both conventions and successfully advocated fusion on state issues, but the Populists would not accept Parker, with the result that each party named its own presidential electors. Gilbert M. Hitchcock, seeking re-election to Congress, cooperated with Bryan, bolstered the move to obtain a legislature that would send Bryan to the United States Senate, and threw his *World-Herald* behind fusion and Bryan's choice for governor, the anti-railroad man George W. Berge. But Progressive Republicanism had not made much headway in Nebraska, and with every corporation up in arms it was freely predicted that the Democrats would be in the "also ran" class on election day. As for Populism in Nebraska and elsewhere, it had "reached the point where it is nothing with fusion and nothing without it." [73]

By mid-August Bryan was fully recovered from his illness and could have taken the stump for Parker. He opened the Missouri campaign for Joseph W. Folk on September 1 but suddenly announced that he would go to Arizona for a month before undertaking active campaign work. Many suspected, and with good reason, that he had willingly submitted to the suggestion of radical colleagues that he "get sick on purpose" in order to deny Parker his help. On the Chautauqua circuit during September he concentrated against Roosevelt's militarism with his speech "A Conquering Nation," and his *Commoner* kept up a rapid-fire attack on Roosevelt, but it said little in support of Parker and Davis.[74]

Meantime Parker was becoming increasingly critical of the sources of Roosevelt's campaign contributions. In his own letter of acceptance, issued on September 12, Roosevelt challenged Parker to be specific in his charges, which were being pushed and improved upon by the Democratic and independent press, particularly by the New York *Times* and *World*. The inference was that George B. Cortelyou, the treasurer of the Republican National Committee, who headed the Department of Commerce and Labor in 1903 and 1904, was raising funds by tapping the railroads and other corporations. Cortelyou knew personally or by report most of the important businessmen of the

[73] Omaha *World-Herald*, July 14, 16, 17, 18, 23, August 11, 12, 28, 1904; *Commoner*, August 19, September 16, 1904; James C. Olson, *History of Nebraska*, p. 249; Addison E. Sheldon, *Nebraska: The Land and the People*, I, 807–808.

[74] *Commoner*, October 7, 1904. If a deal was made between Tibbles and Thomas S. Allen, Bryan's brother-in-law, to the effect that Tibbles would support fusion on the state ticket and Bryan would not speak for Parker, Bryan broke it by speaking for Parker during October. T. H. Tibbles to T. E. Watson, November 16, 1904, Woodward, *Watson*, pp. 361–362.

country, already long tapped by Mark Hanna's organization. He was ambitious and capable, "almost slick," [75] and had at hand a heavy bludgeon in the form of the investigations undertaken by the Bureau of Corporations.

For the first time since 1892 the Democrats, as reorganized under conservative leadership that promised no interference with property rights, did not lack for funds while the Republicans were for the first time hard pressed. Early in October Roosevelt appealed to Edward H. Harriman, railroads, and Henry C. Frick, United States Steel, who agreed with the banker, James Stillman, and Morgan partner George W. Perkins, insurance, that he rather than Parker should be elected. Harriman gave $50,000 and raised $250,000 more. Frick gave $100,000. Roosevelt made no precise pledges, but some sort of agreement with respect to New York politics was made, and subsequent revelations seem to uphold the conclusion that he may have promised big business political immunity. Years later Frick said to Oswald Villard, "He got down on his knees to us. We bought the son of a bitch and then he did not stay bought." [76] When Charles Gates Dawes, in charge of Republican expenditures in the West, met with Roosevelt, Treasurer Cornelius Bliss, and Cortelyou, Roosevelt said he wanted publicity for campaign funds. Bliss told him that he could not get contributions if names of donors were published. Roosevelt replied that he supposed he needed contributions more than publicity.[77]

On October 3, rested and buoyant, with his voice in magnificent condition, Bryan began a week's tour of Nebraska. His large audiences cheered lustily as he castigated Roosevelt for his militant spirit and his negative attitude toward tariff and currency reform. But he supported Parker and Davis in a backhanded way, only because if victorious they would remove from the political arena those questions which blocked economic reforms. He acceded to National Chairman Thomas Taggart's request to speak in Indiana and West Virginia but not elsewhere. Then he reconsidered and devoted one day to Ohio and five days to Illinois. On October 11 he revealed himself in good trim by speaking five times en route and then delivering a long

[75] John Morton Blum, *The Republican Roosevelt*, p. 69.

[76] New York *Sun*, August 11, 1904; New York *Tribune*, February 15, 1906; *Commoner*, April 12, July 12, 1907; Matthew Josephson, *The President Makers: The Culture of Politics and Leadership in an Age of Enlightenment, 1896–1919*, pp. 162–167; Oswald Garrison Villard, *Fighting Years: Memoirs of a Liberal Editor*, pp. 178–183.

[77] Bascom N. Timmons, *Portrait of an American: Charles G. Dawes*, p. 122.

address in St. Louis. In eight days he spoke fifty-two times in Indiana. With great sincerity he said that he would rather surrender his leadership of the Democracy for the current campaign than permit the enemy to win because of division. "We are not willing that the party should die. It has rendered too great service in the past; it is too necessary at present and its future contains too much of love of the human race. It must not die." [78] Pundits wondered whether the great applause he received came from his support for Parker or from those who were pleased with his plans for the future. At any rate, when criticized later for not taking an active part in the campaign, he replied that he had taken an active part. In fact, he added, "The campaign fell so flat toward the close . . . I was about the only speaker who drew any considerable crowd." [79]

On October 23 Daniel Lamont furnished Parker the information that various Wall Street men were underwriting Roosevelt's campaign. On October 24 Parker said he would deliver several speeches between November 1 and 4 on the "Cortelyou scandal." His largely attended meetings in New York, New Jersey, and Connecticut aroused great enthusiasm even though he made no attempt at oratory. He provided the first real excitement in the dullest campaign in the memory of living men, but he provided it too late.

On November 4 Roosevelt fired a terrific blast at Parker. He did not deny that the corporations had given him large sums but he refuted the "monstrous" charge of blackmail, which he declared "unqualifiedly and atrociously false," thereby calling Parker a liar. Next day Parker said that Roosevelt had not answered his questions about the "blackmail" and that his reply was a "confession of wrong doing," thus making the major issue of the campaign a "moral" issue and giving a big boost to demands for laws regulating campaign contributions by corporations. Betting closed at five to one in favor of Roosevelt on election eve, November 7.

Roosevelt won the largest Republican victory since 1872. He considered his three and a half years as a first term and said he would not run again. He had been fortunate, he told Joseph Foraker, in having

[78] Omaha *World-Herald,* October 26, 1904.

[79] Bryan to George Darby, October 2, 1921, Bryan Papers. To similar criticism, Hearst retorted: "I did, as a matter of fact, shut my eyes, hold my nose, and support Parker. . . . But I am not proud of having done so. It is the one act of my political career that I am heartily ashamed of." Edmond D. Coblenz (ed.), *William Randolph Hearst: A Portrait in His Own Words,* p. 37.

had Parker as his opponent, "not because of any lack of ability and character, but because his views were such that a large element in the Democratic party could not very well become his supporters," [80] meaning of course the Bryanites. Of the 476 electoral votes Roosevelt received 336 and Parker 140. Roosevelt won 33 states and 7,623,486 popular votes; Parker won 12 states and 5,077,911 votes, 1,400,000 fewer than Bryan had received in 1896 and 1,300,000 fewer than 1900. In 1900 Bryan had carried four Western states; Parker did not run in the West at all. Parker carried no state outside of the South and lost Missouri, which Bryan had carried in 1900. Of considerable importance, however, was the fact that although the combined Republican majority in Congress was the largest since the Civil War, several states that went for Roosevelt elected Democratic governors. Democrats also supported Robert La Follette in Wisconsin, and in Milwaukee the Socialist vote was larger than the Democratic. Eugene V. Debs's vote, up from 98,000 in 1900 to 400,000 in 1904, measured the protest vote, for Thomas E. Watson received only 117,000 votes. Watson had demanded that Bryan support him rather than Parker. Stating that a vote for him meant a vote for Roosevelt, Bryan denied Watson support and gave the death blow to Populism. He thereby proved that he was not the Populist he had been painted in 1896 and 1900.[81] In Nebraska, Roosevelt received 138,558 votes and Parker 52,291. Hitchcock lost his bid for re-election in the Second District while George W. Norris, a progressive Republican, won in the Fifth.

Those who for eight years had endured ridicule and abuse for supporting Bryan had followed Bryan's advice and repudiated the man he had denounced and opposed before and during the St. Louis convention. Parker was supported by those who voted Democratic regardless, by sound money Democrats, and by those independents who could stomach such of his managers as Thomas Taggart. All admitted that it would have been a miracle for the reorganized Democracy to win after Bryan had offered renewed leadership under a bold new program. But the election also buried the silver question as an issue in American politics too deeply for even Bryan to revive it.

Within twenty-four hours of Parker's defeat Bryan renewed his offer to reorganize the Democracy. He saw in the election a lesson— "Do Not Compromise with Plutocracy." Parker had suggested conservative remedies for conditions that required radical remedies. The

[80] Joseph Benson Foraker, *Notes of a Busy Life*, II, 203.
[81] Woodward, *Watson*, pp. 360-362.

Democracy had nothing to gain by catering to predatory wealth; it must take the side of "the plain, common people" if it hoped to win. Those who favored the corporations should either join the Republicans or denounce the corporations and cooperate with the Democrats of the South and West in making the Democratic party a positive, aggressive, and progressive reform organization. There was no middle ground. The party must be placed on a fighting basis for 1908. It mattered little who the next nominee might be, for "during the next three years circumstances could bring into the arena some man especially fitted to carry the standard." With a prescience respected by Republicans as well as Democrats, he declared that the party could well start its campaign for 1908 by making its attack on the trusts so vehement that no one would suspect it of securing aid from them, and by proving its sincerity by publishing its contributions list. " 'With malice toward none and charity for all,' " he concluded, "let us begin the campaign of 1908; let us appeal to the moral sentiment of the country and arraign the policies of the Republican party before the bar of the public conscience." [82]

The election of 1904 showed that Bryan came closer to representing what the Democracy wanted than did the reorganizers. The gold wing of the party had had its inning and lost. Immediately after the election Parker said that he would never be a candidate again, and there began a widespread demand at the grass roots from both reorganizers and Bryanites that Bryan exercise party leadership. Thus he rather than Parker became the titular chief of the party and the logical candidate for 1908.

Soon after the election Bryan wrote his friend James Dahlman: "The defeat was so overwhelming that we are not likely to hear much more—for some years at least—of the reorganizers. The Democratic party will now have a chance to become a real reform party. I suppose it was necessary to go through all these experiences in order to get into a position to fight." [83]

[82] New York *World,* November 10, 1904; *Commoner,* November 11, 1904. See also Richard B. Scandrett to Philander C. Knox, November 14, 1904, Knox Papers.

[83] Letter of November 1904, quoted in Fred Carey, *Mayor Jim: The Life of James C. Dahlman,* p. 113.

CHAPTER 15

The Return of the Innocent

I

BRYAN began the campaign of 1908 immediately after the election of 1904. Alton B. Parker's saying that he would never run again left him a clear field, and Theodore Roosevelt's stating that he would not seek re-election led him naïvely to believe that he would divorce himself from partisan objectives during his "elective term." He therefore told Roosevelt that he had a "Great Opportunity" to be a real reformer. Excluding tariff and currency reform, the rest of the reforms demanded in his own "bold new program" were within reach. Until the federal government acted on these matters he advocated state action on those within the scope of their powers. The states should also seriously consider the subject of old age annuities and state insurance programs and permit cities by franchise to establish municipal water and power plants.[1]

On December 10, at the request of the *Outlook,* Bryan wrote a creed of more than ordinary interest because of its heavy new emphasis on morality. The Democrats had been defeated in 1904 because the reorganizers had shunned the "fixed principle—equal rights to all and special privileges to none." Every great political question had an economic bearing, every economic question was basically a moral question, he said; and moral questions could be settled only by an appeal to "the moral sense" of the nation. Thus only "necessary" taxes should be collected, the "immoral" and "indefensible" trusts should be abolished, a permanent board of arbitration should be established to settle labor problems, and the Philippines should be freed. He propounded a collectivist rather than individualist philosophy and demanded that the Democracy forsake its traditional policy of governmental noninterference and accept a stronger central government. The Congress should employ its delegated powers to the fullest extent necessary for the protection of human rights and the public welfare. Lest anyone

[1] *Commoner,* November 18, 25, December 9, 1904; January 3, February 17, June 9, August 11, 1905.

think he was advocating socialism, he stressed that the Democrats favored legislation that would restore, not reduce, competition. Finally, it was high time "for the arraignment of the plutocratic tendencies of the Republican party before the bar of public conscience." [2]

Roosevelt's annual message of December 1904 failed to fulfill Bryan's demands except in his observations on the moralities. Yet his demands for workmen's compensation laws, the elimination of child labor abuses, the supervision of insurance companies, and laws against corruption in federal elections hinted at a note of progressivism which might blossom into his Bryanization or, as Herbert Croly and others fortified with hindsight professed to see, "the New Nationalism" or "New Hamiltonianism." Then, on January 5, 1905, Roosevelt startled the businessmen who believed him "safe" and electrified the country with a Bryanesque demand for increasing national power to the point that it could prevent any railroad, industry, or corporation from abusing the interests of the people as a whole. On January 21, when Bryan called, he gave him a gracious welcome, ushered him into his private room, and spoke with him for about ten minutes. To reporters Bryan afterwards said that he had been pleased to commend the President's attitude on some things. "Not on all things, then?" he was asked. "No, of course not," he replied. However, confessing that "In President Roosevelt himself there have been symptoms of reform that I for one had no suspicion of," he then asked the Democracy to "forget itself and to help the President carry out whatever is good." It was not only "right" but also expedient to support Roosevelt, for remedial legislation would benefit the country and redound to the credit of the Democracy.[3]

[2] "The Future of the Democratic Party: A Discussion of Moral Issues in the Pending Questions," *The Outlook*, 78 (December 19, 1904), 919–927. An investigation in 1905 showed that the majorities of the boards of directors of all important railroads east of the Mississippi River could be selected from a group of thirty-five persons. In Nebraska the organization of the legislature of 1905 resulted in Burlington control of the House, and Union Pacific and Elkhorn control of the Senate. *Commoner*, January 13, 1905. Bryan took the building by the federal government of a railroad across the Isthmus of Panama as a vindication of his demand for public ownership and as a potent precedent for future legislation. Moreover, Secretary Taft's ordering of building materials for the Panama Canal in Europe because prices were 50% lower than in the United States was an obvious tariff lesson.

[3] *Commoner*, January 6, 13, February 10, 1905; Washington *Post*, January 22, 25, 1905.

Since Bryan had revealed a cast-iron immobility with respect to the reforms he had sponsored since 1890, the change in attitude that permitted harmony with Roosevelt must therefore have occurred in Roosevelt. If the President had no definite reform program as yet and still shied from tariff and currency reform, he had at least moved toward a stronger governmental authority which would foster rather than prevent the exercise of the popular will. But Bryan meant to test his understanding that Roosevelt tended toward progressivism. Would he have the courage, he asked publicly, to support reform legislation that would divide and thereby jeopardize the success of his party? [4] Roosevelt failed the first test when, in his inaugural address, he rejected Bryan's advice to act independently of the Old Guard and, rather than urging domestic reform, spoke of warlike preparations, as though the country were menaced by the combined navies of Europe. The mountain had labored and brought forth a mouse, Bryan declared. Evidently the President had taken heed of warnings by conservatives that attempts to secure radical legislation would split his party.[5]

During the years 1902–1905 the revelation of the excesses of the masters of capital by Thomas W. Lawson, Charles Evans Hughes, Louis D. Brandeis, Albert J. Beveridge, Harvey Washington Wiley, and the muckraking exposés by Ida Minerva Tarbell, Lincoln Steffens, and others helped marshal a Republican reform element behind Roosevelt. By mid-1905 Bryan saw that "the light was breaking" upon the President.[6] He applauded his show of independence from the Old Guard and cheered rather than complained when Roosevelt, in initiating his reforms, stole his thunder. When both he and Roosevelt attended the Gridiron Club in January 1905, the suggestion was made that they debate. "What's the use?" was the retort. "They are both on the same side." Nevertheless, Roosevelt unkindly said that

[4] Bryan, "Has the President the Courage to Be a Reformer?" *Public Opinion,* 39 (April 15, 1905), 557–559.

[5] See the cartoon in the *Commoner* for March 17, 1905.

[6] *Ibid.,* June 2, September 29, October 13, November 17, 1905. Bryan persisted in urging that Roosevelt direct the return of contributions from the insurance companies to the policyholders to whom they belonged. He made much of the "dark lantern methods" used by the "defenders of national honor"—those who had contributed to the Republican party in 1896 "to preserve national honor"—for eighteen of them lied while under investigation, asked that officials who prostituted the premiums of the policyholders be prosecuted, and that the states establish their own insurance programs.

the good things in the Democratic platform were absolutely useless in Bryan's hands because he would never be in position to put them into operation. With good humor, Bryan replied that the Republicans, now entering the Valley of the Shadow of Death, could emerge from it only if they made their party the champion of human rights and popular government rather than the tool of corporate greed and predatory wealth. The popularity of Roosevelt, as of Robert La Follette, Jonathan Dolliver, and Albert Cummins, could be explained only by their espousal of Democratic principles. "When Republicans can build up a following by adopting Democratic ideas," he concluded, "let no Democrat falter in the fight." [7]

Acting as Roosevelt's conscience, Bryan was quick to point out where he faltered or failed. Thus Roosevelt "blundered" in refusing to prosecute trust officials because they did not have *personal* knowledge of their companies' illegal operations; "whitewashed" Paul Morton, his Secretary of the Navy and a trust vice president; and "erred" in moving Elihu Root from the War to the State department because "his brains have been for hire to any corporation that could offer to pay the price demanded." Meantime he persisted in urging that the Democracy remain pure in the faith. A favorite lecture of his for 1905 was one in capital letters—"TO COMMAND THE CONFIDENCE OF THE PEOPLE THE DEMOCRATIC PARTY MUST BE PROGRESSIVE." The party will win, he said, "when it shows the collar galls of progress instead of the breeching strap scars of so-called conservatives" like Parker or of immoral men like John R. McLean.[8]

II

BRYAN was increasingly aware, particularly from his contacts with Professor Edward A. Ross, now of the University of Nebraska, of the character of social sin—not that of the assault and battery type but that which was committed without coming into close contact with its victims, as in adulterated foods and drugs; stock swindling; failure to use safety appliances in mines, industry, and railroading; the employment of young children; and the Supreme Court decision, by five to four, which found a New York ten-hour law unconstitutional because it denied the laborer his freedom of contract! "Too often," he said, "educated and cultured men are found increasing their divi-

[7] *Ibid.*, February 3, 10, 1905; Arthur W. Dunn, *Gridiron Nights*, pp. 154–156.
[8] *Commoner*, January 6, April 21, 28, July 14, 1905.

dends by methods that must be called criminal when measured by any moral law," and he was hard on moral offenders large and small. When President Woodrow Wilson of Princeton said that the trusts should be "moralized" rather than abolished, he twitted him, saying, "the danger seems to be that the trusts will immortalize the presidents of our big trust-fed colleges before the moralizing process reaches the trusts." He goaded Roosevelt, too, asserting that the "time for action is at hand; the people have been permitted to suffer too long." [9]

By his support of Roosevelt, his condemnation of conservatives, and his demands for reform legislation Bryan maintained the leadership of the progressive movement he had helped establish. Yet with so many attorneys in the Senate he deemed it unlikely that legislative relief could be provided. Therefore what was needed was "moral courage" in reform. First, each individual owed it to his Creator and to society to fit himself for the largest possible service and efficiency in his work. Second, in keeping with what he called "the law of just rewards," there should be established "the principle that compensation should be commensurate with service, each one drawing from society in proportion as he contributes to the welfare of society." Third, there should be established the doctrine that "government should be for the governed and that communities should do for themselves what they are now permitting individuals or corporations to do." Finally, each individual must employ his influence to place his party upon the "right side" of every question, and name for office only those capable of performing the duties of the office who were known to be in sympathy with the common people. Were the people made aware of the dangers threatening them, they would find the moral courage necessary to reform. "The longer a needed reform is delayed the more radical the remedy is likely to be and the more danger that the spirit of retaliation will make itself manifest," he warned. Concern with moral issues thus played an increasingly larger part in Bryan's life during the banner years of the muckraking era and the early manifestations of the Progressive movement.[10]

Bryan's crusade against "tainted money" and in behalf of the "stewardship" principle enlivened the newspapers and sparked unusually bitter quarrels both in Nebraska and in Illinois. In the Nebraska Democratic state convention of September 20, 1905, he

[9] *Ibid.*, February 3, 10, 17, March 10, April 14, 28, 1905.

[10] *Ibid.*, February 3, March 23, May 26, July 7, 28, August 18, September 8, 22, October 27, 1905.

sponsored a resolution demanding that the members of the legislature and all judges give up their railroad passes, and at his behest the platform bitterly attacked the trusts. He hand-picked the candidates, and when the small group of Populists meeting simultaneously decided to join him rather than nominate for themselves, he gained full control of the fusion organization. Although organized Populism ended in Nebraska, Bryan Democrats and Roosevelt Republicans now competed in issuing radical pronouncements in order to win the still important Populist votes.[11]

Bryan's denouncing of a $66,666 gift to the University of Nebraska stirred up a new furor. In 1903, John D. Rockefeller had offered to meet two thirds of the cost of a building on the campus on condition that friends of the university raise the other third. Now Bryan argued that its accepting of the gift would place the university under capitalistic influences. Instead of making gifts in the name of "an unknown friend," he said, Rockefeller offered them at the foot of the stage, in the floodlights. Churches which accepted his money could hardly condemn his methods; acceptance of his "hush money" thus quieted criticism. "If you have stolen a sheep it will avail you nothing to give the feet to God," he warned. Rockefeller's conscience, he added, was "too seared" to be of service to him. Punctual in his churchgoing, his life nevertheless was a record of "extraordinary moral obliquity," for he could bankrupt a competitor through the rebate system, bribe a college with a donation, or evade a court summons with equal facility. In the field of indefensible and antisocial business methods he had acquired an "odious eminence." [12]

The university nevertheless got its building.

In 1902 Bryan had contributed to relieve the deficit of Illinois College, spoken in its endowment campaign, and accepted membership on the Board of Trustees. To placate him, the college had dis-

[11] *Ibid.*, August 3, October 20, 1905; Addison E. Sheldon, *Nebraska: The Land and the People*, I, 813–814.

[12] *Commoner*, April 7, 14, 21, September 22, November 10, 1905; Ralph H. Gabriel, *The Course of American Democratic Thought: An Intellectual History Since 1815*, pp. 314–315; Allan Nevins, *John D. Rockefeller: The Heroic Age in American Enterprise*, I, 534, 537–539; Harold U. Faulkner, *The Quest for Social Justice, 1898–1914*, pp. 198–201; Bryan, "The Price of a Soul," in *Commoner*, September 22, 1905. Other "ethical" matters that played on Bryan's mind at this time were the decay of patriotism evidenced by the longing of rich American girls to marry impoverished but titled foreigners, and the social, political, and religious implications of Charles Darwin's *The Descent of Man*, which he read early in 1905.

solved a tenuous connection with the Rockefeller-sponsored University of Chicago, and Bryan had expressed willingness, under certain conditions, to raise money by delivering a series of lectures on the science of government.[13] On January 17, 1905 he was elected president of the board. When he declined the presidency of the college itself, Charles H. Rammelkamp was elected. Rammelkamp made no bones about opposing his political, economic, educational, and theological views but gratefully acknowledged his services to the college in its hour of need.[14] On January 31 Bryan promised to pay $500 in each of five annual installments at 5 per cent interest, and when four other members matched him they almost wiped out the deficit. Bryan also established two $1000 scholarship endowments, one from the Bennett fund, one from his own pocket, and promised to make a public appeal for the college through friends and the pages of *The Commoner*.[15]

Meantime Rammelkamp hoped to get some money from Andrew Carnegie, and Frank A. Vanderlip spoke to the philanthropist about the college. Bryan, in the midst of his attacks on predatory wealth, would have "none of it" and offered twice to resign. He was dissuaded, and the board stated that all would be as he wished. On June 7 Bryan presided at a meeting of the board and also delivered the commencement address—dressed in a black alpaca coat because he had a personal prejudice against cap and gown. On September 9, at another board meeting, no action was taken to deal with an increasing deficit. Later, deeming the financial condition of the college critical, Rammelkamp offered a resolution that the college would accept funds from Carnegie and Rockefeller if given under proper conditions. He was supported by a majority of the board, but Judge O. P. Thompson and Millard F. Dunlap, and eventually a third member, resigned in protest, alleging a breach of faith with Bryan. Dunlap cabled the resolution to Bryan, who was on a world tour.[16] From Hong Kong Bryan mailed his resignation, adding:

[13] Bryan to M. F. Dunlap, January 5, 1905, in *Minutes of Board of Trustees, Illinois College.*

[14] Charles H. Rammelkamp, *Illinois College: A Centennial History, 1829–1929,* pp. 457–458.

[15] *Minutes of the Board of Trustees,* January 17, 31, April 1, May 9, 1905.

[16] Dunlap to Bryan, May 1, 1905, *ibid.,* and record of the meetings of September 9 and November 6, 1905; *Illinois College Rambler,* 27 (1905), pp. 98, 113–117, 123, 217; *Commoner,* January 27, 1905; Rammelkamp, *Illinois College,* p. 465.

Our college cannot serve God and Mammon. It cannot be a college for the people and at the same time commend itself to the commercial highwaymen who are now subsidizing the colleges to prevent the teaching of economic truth. It grieves me to have my Alma Mater converted into an ally of plutocracy, but having done what I could to prevent it, I have no other recourse than to withdraw from its management. . . . I regret the action . . . was not taken before I gave my notes, for I regard the money given as worse than wasted, if the college is to be under the shadow of a great monopoly.

He had given $1000. At the board meeting of February 12, 1906 his resignation was accepted. Shortly thereafter Carnegie offered $50,000 conditional upon the raising of $75,000, which condition was met. Then Bryan urged that his notes be canceled and that he be permitted to name another beneficiary. He also asked that his name be taken from a prize he had established in 1903, adding, "If you can drop my name from the list of graduates I shall be still more pleased for I do not want my name connected with the institution." In 1908 he paid the interest due on his remaining notes and again urged their cancellation, but the trustees refused, saying they had no legal authority to do so.[17] Thus Bryan was forced to contribute to a "trust-supported" institution.

III

ON SEPTEMBER 21, 1905, the Bryan family less Ruth left Fairview for San Francisco and, on September 27, boarded ship for Hawaii. Except for a reception by the San Francisco Press Club and half a dozen people at the dock, the Bryans were practically ignored by the public.[18]

The domestic accomplishments of the first year of his new administration failed to fulfill Roosevelt's promises, yet it appeared to Bryan that he had shown some courage to be a reformer, and as he left for his world tour he wrote him a farewell letter of advice and encouragement:

Permit a parting word. You have the contest of your life before you and I desire to render you all the assistance in my power. You have asked Congress

[17] *Minutes of the Board of Trustees*, February 12, March 15, July 14, 1906, June 3, December 15, 1908.

[18] *Commoner*, August 4, October 8, 1905; Mrs. Grace Bryan Hargreaves, "William Jennings Bryan," unpublished Ms., I, 352, William Jennings Bryan Papers. In Salem, Illinois, on September 8, Bryan had broken ground for the Bryan-Bennett Library on the site of the house in which he was born. His contributions and those of friends defrayed more than $3000 in costs.

to enact a law so enlarging the powers of the Interstate Commerce Commission as to permit it to fix and enforce a reasonable freight rate. . . . The railroads will try to persuade you; if they fail in this they will try to scare you; if they fail in this also they will try to defeat your recommendation. It will embarrass you to have strong party leaders against you; you may have been embarrassed by having so many Democrats cooperate with you, but you must reconcile yourself to both. . . .

Pass over the railroads and appeal to the people.

Then, after hinting at the need of reduced tariffs and of a permanent board to settle labor disputes, he concluded:

Stand by your guns! You have developed a reform element in the Republican party; you must lead it or suffer the humiliation of seeing the leadership pass to someone else.

. . . Go forward! You owe it to yourself, you owe it to your party, and more than all, you owe it to your country.[19]

Bryan's world tour was paid for by his selling to Hearst and others a series of articles of a descriptive nature, all later reprinted in *The Commoner*.[20] The articles reveal his concern with contemporary political institutions and religious observances, but he showed such faint interest in history and the fine arts that it is doubtful that his experiences widened his eyes or broadened his mind. Nevertheless, his travels strengthened his opposition to "coolie" immigration and his devotion to peace and to the proscription of war. As in his visit to Europe in 1903 he looked for "new issues" which might profit him politically; and he showed an almost fanatical concern over the presidential nomination of 1908.[21]

Wherever he went, both civilian and military leaders strained to pay Bryan homage. At the reception and banquet given in Tokyo to Admiral Togo, who had helped raise Japan to world eminence by defeating Russia's navy, he used his devotion to temperance as an excuse for not toasting him spirituously. Everyone drank champagne but he, who drank water. Asked why, he replied: "Admiral Togo won his great victory on water, so I drink to him in water. When he wins a great victory on champagne, then I will drink to him in cham-

---

[19] *Commoner*, September 29, 1905.

[20] The series of forty-five articles runs from January 19 to November 23, 1906.

[21] Letters, Bryan to Charles W. Bryan and Mrs. Thomas S. Allen, Silas Bryan Papers; Henry White, "Reminiscences of the Late William Jennings Bryan," Henry Steele Commager Papers; C. W. Thompson, New York *Times*, December 27, 1925.

pagne." The quip pleased the Japanese, who liked him; he in turn liked them and sought their friendship, saying, "Steam has narrowed the Pacific and made us neighbors. Let justice make us friends." Coached by the American minister, Lloyd C. Griscom, he dutifully bowed three times before the emperor and then answered questions put him. Among others who attended a dinner in his honor given by Count Okuma was Marquis Ito, the president of the Japanese Privy Council, with whom he was soon on friendly terms; and at a dinner given him by Huntington Wilson, the secretary of the American legation, he met many other makers of Japan's domestic and foreign policies.[22]

The Bryans also visited the home of Yamashita, fifteen miles from Kagoshima. During the campaign of 1896, fan mail for Bryan included letters from one Yachichiro Yamashita to "My dearest American Parents" indicating that he wished to study at the feet of such a wonderful expositor of world peace and that he would soon call upon his "adopted parents." Mrs. Bryan replied that she had three children of her own and forgot the incident until a letter from San Francisco revealed Yamashita's plight—he needed train fare to Lincoln. Shortly after Bryan had asked friends in San Francisco to explain that he simply could not take him into the family, Yamashita knocked at his door. Permission to stay overnight was extended to "for a little while" and finally to five years, until "Y. Bryan Yamashita" graduated from the University of Nebraska. Now "Yama" met the Bryans in Yokohama, served as their interpreter, introduced them to everyone in his home village, and stood by in sincere admiration as Bryan planted a camphor tree with double trunks symbolizing Japanese-American friendship.[23]

Interested in Japan's "problem" with respect to Korea, Bryan also visited the Hermit Kingdom. He was the last Western visitor received by the royal Korean family, which had reigned for about five hundred years, before the Japanese assumed suzerainty.

From Korea the Bryans entered China, where Mrs. Bryan and Grace were not recognized by Chinese gentlemen callers. Bryan said that China was "the most overrated country in the world." It was what Japan had been forty years earlier and just beginning to wake

[22] *Commoner*, October 27, 1905.

[23] William Jennings Bryan and Mary Baird Bryan, *The Memoirs of William Jennings Bryan*, pp. 308–310; W. J. Bryan, Jr., "My Japanese Brother," *Reader's Digest*, June 1955, pp. 17–21.

up. He could not readily forget the congestion, foul odors, and horrors witnessed in leading Chinese cities—"Worse than Korea for filth"—and when he read the favorable report on China in *The Letters of a Chinese Official*, by the Cambridge don, G. Lowes Dickinson, the Western Puritan in him provoked a published reply, under title of *Letters to a Chinese Official*, in which he defended his Christian faith and the standards and purposes of the American people.[24]

From Hong Kong in late December the Bryans went to the Philippines, where they were provided a military escort by Generals Leonard Wood and Henry C. Corbin. However, Bryan declined to be the guest of Governor General Henry C. Ide, saying he was traveling as a reporter and citizen and would not place himself under obligation to the government. There was no criticism of him when Emilio Aguinaldo showed up at a reception in his honor on Christmas Eve, but on December 27, after his spiking the rumors that he would say something spectacular about Philippine independence by refusing to speak about imperialism, the Manila press grew increasingly unfriendly. His lockjaw would be cured when he left the islands, Bryan promised. Questions that he could raise at home would only encourage endless debate now, he added, and he refused to say a word about the future of the islands. The Manila *American* gave him credit for the anti-trust crusade being undertaken by Roosevelt but concluded that his interest in Philippine independence was influenced "neither by the merits of the case nor the welfare of the Filipinos but merely by the prospect of such a plank in the Democratic platform as a vote getter." "Hot air," it added, "will never build a Filipino nation." [25]

Both Bryan and Mrs. Bryan could see that the Americanization of the Philippines was progressing rapidly, yet he said that most Philippine problems sprang from the fact that "the country is governed by laws made for it, but not binding upon the country which makes the laws." That consummate diarist, General Wood, recorded that "Mrs. Bryan . . . said that whatever his views were in regard to the rest of the Philippines it was evident that the people of the Moro province were not yet ready for self-government. . . . Mrs.

[24] Bryan to C. W. Bryan, December 9, 1905, Silas Bryan Papers; *Commoner*, August 31, 1906; Bryan, *Memoirs*, p. 313; W. J. Bryan, *Letters to a Chinese Official;* G. Lowes Dickinson, "Eastern and Western Ideals: Being a Rejoinder to William Jennings Bryan," *The Century Magazine*, New Series, 51 (December 1906), 313–316; "Bryan as a Defender of Christianity," *Current Literature*, 41 (October 1906), 437–438. Dickinson had written a satire, but Bryan took him seriously.
[25] Manila *American*, December 28, 1905, January 3, 1906.

Bryan is a sensible level-headed appearing woman and I have no doubt has a restraining influence on her husband." [26] Although Bryan wrote his brother Charles that "This trip is wonderfully instructive. I can run for several years on the information I am accumulating," and that "I think I have discussed imperialism in the Philippines without doing injustice to our officials there," [27] he had created the impression of a kindly man caught in an embarrassing situation.

The Bryans spent several weeks seeing the Dutch East Indies, Singapore, Ceylon, Burma, and India. The British in India knew that Bryan opposed them on the currency question, monarchial form of government, and profit-seeking imperialism, yet they placed their blue books and other documents at his disposal. Meantime the natives, in the thick of the agitation led by Gandhi and others after the departure of Lord Curzon, flocked to tell him what conditions were "really" like under the British.

The Bryans devoted the spring months of 1906 to Egypt, Syria, Turkey, and other countries of the eastern Mediterranean, where they were frequently in contact with native reformers seeking to overthrow Turkish rule. In Palestine they spent two and a half days by the Sea of Galilee, where they gathered pebbles and shells as gifts to the members of the little church near Fairview. When he reached Berlin, in mid-June, and learned of the probable dissolving of the first Russian Duma, Bryan rushed to what is now Leningrad, mingled with the members of what he believed the most representative body ever assembled in Russia, and predicted that the Duma would rise again. What impressed the Bryans most in the countries of central and western Europe was the dogged attachment to the institution of monarchy, the dim realization of the true meaning of democracy, the "parlor socialism" being discussed in Germany, and the weakness of the ties that bound the Austrian Empire compared with those of the British. But they were optimistic, for they believed the idea of popular sovereignty definitely growing.[28]

Arriving unannounced in Norway, the Bryans were courteously seated near the throne during the coronation ceremonies for King Haakon VII. When interviewed by newspaper men, Bryan feigned

[26] Diary, entries for May 20, 1902 and January 31, 1908, Leonard Wood Papers.

[27] Letter of January 20, 1906, Silas Bryan Papers; see also *Commoner*, April 13, 20, 27, May 4, 1906.

[28] A Correspondent, *Living Age*, 28 (July 17, 1915), 179. See Bryan, "British Rule in India," in his *Under Other Flags*, pp. 365–378.

surprise that various state conventions had endorsed him for President in 1908 and said that it was simply too early to talk about the nomination. Yet his absence from the United States was proving to be a positive good as far as his political objectives were concerned. The progressive wing of the Democracy was steadily gaining strength. Launched in February 1906, Colonel George Harvey's boom for Woodrow Wilson for President failed to create popular excitement, and Wilson himself asserted that "nothing could be further from my thoughts than the possibility or the desirability of holding high political office." [29] In order to head off the "radical" Hearst, the leaders of the influential Democratic Club of New York announced in April that Bryan might qualify as the candidate if he would acknowledge other issues more important than the ratio of 16 to 1, and he encouraged the conservatives by saying that it was "time to call a halt to Socialism in the United States; the movement has gone far enough!" [30] It was agreed by both Republicans and Democrats that he alone could be the Democratic nominee. Indeed, were Roosevelt to run again, he would be the "radical" and Bryan the "conservative" candidate. As Republican Senator John C. Spooner put it:

Bryan will undoubtedly be the Democratic nominee. He has evidently grown during the last few years. His speech in the Philippines was patriotic, dignified and able. . . . If he comes home, leaving government ownership of railroads out of his programme, standing fairly against centralization and paternalism, respecting the rights of the States under the Constitution, declaring himself so far in favor of conservatism as to prefer the unostentatious and discriminating correction of evils to hysterical agitation, generalization and the blare of trumpets and trombones, partly for the benefit of the people, but largely for self-exploitation, one need not be surprised if he is the next President.[31]

But Bryan played coy about his aspirations. He directed Charles to take no part in the Nebraska primary campaign and declined invitations from political organizations to address them upon his return. When he reached London early in July, however, his anxiety about the nomination was made known to several callers.

[29] Harvey to Wilson, n.d., Woodrow Wilson Papers; Wilson to St. Clair McKelway, n.d., *ibid.;* New York *Times,* February 3, 1906.

[30] W. J. Bryan, "Individualism vs. Socialism," *The Century Magazine,* New Series, 71 (April 1906), 856–859. See the criticism of this in Frank H. Giddings, "Bryan and Our Complex Social Order," *ibid.,* 73 (November 1906), 154–157.

[31] Letter to his son, Willet M., June 11, 1906, John C. Spooner Papers.

Arrangements for Bryan's visit to London were made largely by Ambassador Whitelaw Reid. At a reception given by Reid during the afternoon of July 4, to which anyone who was anybody flocked, including Winston Churchill and the prime minister, Bryan shared the spotlight with Mrs. Nicholas Longworth, President Roosevelt's daughter, and the London press spoke of the "most-talked-of American woman in the world" and "the silver tongued orator . . . who is regarded by many Americans as the next president." Suddenly a friend took him in tow and, walking up to a portly gentleman, said, "Mr. Morgan, this is Mr. Bryan." Here were personified the leading protagonist and antagonist of the monopoly principle. "Bryan? Bryan?" queried Morgan. "The name sounds familiar, but I never had the pleasure of meeting you before." Onlookers laughed, but the principals looked at each other "very narrowly" as their hands met and drifted apart without conversing.[32]

That evening, at a banquet of the American Society of London, Reid and Bryan exchanged sharp but good-natured blows over their political differences. Reid confessed his unalterable opposition to Bryan, asserting that "the country we both love and try to serve has not been ruined by its gold," and then introduced Bryan as a "typical American whose whole life has been lived in the daylight and one whom such a great host of my countrymen have long trusted and honored." Stating that he suppressed a desire to make a political speech—he had made none in ten months—Bryan replied that Reid had fought him well. He rejoiced that he was three thousand miles from home and wished there were more offices abroad "to take all the Republicans out of the country." He then disappointed his large audience by reading his Independence Day address on "The White Man's Burden in the East," a diatribe against imperialism that concluded that "the example of the Christian nations . . . is gradually reforming the world." [33] Bryan had turned the tables on Reid, who had informed Roosevelt that he would use the occasion to make a "keynote" speech that would put him in line for the nomination, and Reid admitted that English public men "are now talking about him as having grown more conservative and as having spoken in a temperate and moderate way" and that there had been a "rather curious desire on the part of most members of the Government here to make

[32] London *Daily Express*, July 5, 1906.
[33] *Commoner*, July 6, 13; Reid to Roosevelt, July 17, 1906, Whitelaw Reid Papers; Alice Roosevelt Longworth, *Crowded Hours*, p. 123.

his acquaintance." When Sir Edward Grey, who was not going out after the tragic death of his wife, asked to meet him, Reid arranged a private session. Grey later told Reid that Bryan "does talk interminably," and Reid was shocked at his ignorance of current affairs when Bryan asked him what post, if any, Grey filled in the Government, even after he had introduced him as the Minister of Foreign Affairs. But Bryan was trying, Reid continued. He was "quite anxious to do the right thing"; he impressed people by his simplicity yet, "like all half-educated people, he dogmatized dangerously on a multitude of topics," including Philippine independence.[34]

Reid hoped that Bryan would not ask to be presented to the King of England, for he probably could not arrange it. However, the king himself asked to see Bryan, although he would appear before him as one of the two principal speakers at the Interparliamentary Union rather than in his individual capacity. "Of course I went and found [the king] a very genial man," Bryan wrote Charles. Actually the king had steered him away from such dangerous topics as the Russian upheaval and in the end he had "appeared well." Months later Reid wrote Roosevelt that the king's private opinion of Bryan was that he was "agreeable and intelligent but a little gaseous, you know," and Henry White concluded that "He was a kindly man, with fewer powers of reason and gifted with an amount of ignorance greater than almost any other man, in a position in any way approaching his, whom I have come across in any country." All in all, Reid concluded, Bryan "has risen decidedly in the estimation of the English and of the diplomatic corps;—but then it must be remembered how low he stood a few years ago. There seems to be a general idea among them that he has a fair chance of being the next president, and of course they are all curious to want to see him and many of them worldly enough to want to establish good relations." [35]

Between sightseeing and speaking, Bryan conferred with several important American political figures. On July 5 he spent two hours with George Harvey, who he knew was sponsoring Wilson for President and who insisted that he discuss matters in general with Thomas Fortune Ryan. Bryan said he would speak privately with Ryan but feared that such a meeting would prove embarrassing, for it could

[34] Reid to Roosevelt, July 17, 1906. Theodore Roosevelt Papers.

[35] Bryan to C. W. Bryan, July (?), 1906, Silas Bryan Papers; White, "Reminiscences"; Reid to Roosevelt, July 27, September 14, 1906, Roosevelt Papers; London *Daily Express*, quoted in *Commoner*, July 24, 1906.

not be hidden from the public. Rumors would spread about a Ryan-Bryan combine, or that Ryan had been Bryanized, or that Bryan had been Ryanized, and generate a vast amount of misapprehension and misunderstanding. Moreover, Ryan was so rich that he could not engage in the fight for popular supremacy "unless he was not only absolutely free from entanglements, but in a position to convince the public that he was free."

Tell Mr. Ryan that he is in a position to do one of the greatest services to his country that any man has ever rendered. He should rid himself of all personal pecuniary interests in, at least, all corporations having to do with public utilities, railroad stocks and bonds, and all such properties, and invest his money in Government bonds. Then he could stand before the people as having but one interest in the world, that of his country. There his money would be, and there his heart would be. Holding that position, he would immediately become probably the most potent individual factor in national life. I, and everyone who believes in what I believe, would not only be in a position but most glad to act with him. To indicate how fully I am convinced of this fact, I say to you in all sincerity that, under these circumstances, I would much rather work to make him President of the United States than to become President myself.

Bryan was apparently in great earnest. Were Ryan to divest himself of his utility investments, they could then fight "shoulder to shoulder" for the common good. Ryan's example would be followed by others and a wave of patriotism would sweep the land. Unlike the young man whom Jesus told to get rid of his property before following him, Ryan would need merely to reinvest in government securities, "thereby making his personal interest unquestionably and irretrievably single. That is the only position that I can conscientiously take. I believe it is correct and there is no getting away from it. . . . I only wish that he could be made to see and act upon it."

As for the Presidency, Bryan reverted to his "principles before personalities." If "circumstances" pointed to him, he would of course respond, but he "honestly hoped" that conditions would make someone else available. He would be remembered fifty years hence because of the principles he advocated rather than because of any official position he filled. At any rate, under no circumstances would he serve more than one term. On bimetallism his views had not changed. Unlike Moreton Frewen and other Britons who would have him revive the discussion of bimetallism in America, he admitted that gold production had "relieved the tension." He favored "ultimate" government ownership of railroads but did not believe its time had yet come. Finally, private monopolies must be eradicated, and interstate corporations should be licensed and controlled by an effective Interstate Commerce Commission.[36]

Bryan also spoke with John Sharp Williams, the minority leader in the House of Representatives, who journeyed to London especially to persuade him to adopt a conservative program in contrast to Roosevelt's "radicalism"; were Bryan to give up his idea of nationalizing the railroads he would be the strongest candidate for the Presidency. Similar advice came from Nathan Straus via Richard Croker. To Hayne Davis, a loyal friend and a press representative to the Interparliamentary Union meeting, he gave his regular "principles before personalities" speech.[37] For George B. McClellan, Jr., however, he played a different tune.

Before leaving the United States Bryan had asked Hearst to have McClellan find out how Cleveland felt about his nomination. McClellan dutifully journeyed to Princeton. "Well," said Cleveland, "I don't feel as bitterly about Bryan as I once did. You can tell him that if you like, in your own words." When McClellan called on Bryan at the Hotel Cecil, he was dictating to Mrs. Bryan. Shooing her out, he inquired eagerly, "Did you see Cleveland, and what did he say about me?" McClellan replied that he seemed to be more sympathetically inclined than he had ever known him to be. "Thank God for that," said Bryan. "Do you think he will back me for the nomination?" McClellan expressed grave doubt but repeated his assurance that Cleveland was less bitter than formerly. Bryan asked him to see Cleveland when he returned and then launched into an hour-long disquisition on national political issues with a reasonableness and conservatism worthy of Cleveland himself. Impressed but not taken in by Bryan's attempt to win Cleveland over through him, McClellan left.[38] Several weeks later Bryan delivered his "radical" address in New York City.

In seeking a new and striking issue, Bryan had become increasingly impressed with government ownership, particularly after long talks

[36] Harvey to T. F. Ryan, July 5, 1906, in W. F. Johnson, *George Harvey, "A Passionate Patriot,"* pp. 120–122. See also Whitelaw Reid to Moreton Frewen, October 31, 1906, Reid Papers, and Frewen, "The Fall in the Value of Gold," in *Commoner*, August 3, 1906.

[37] Croker to Bryan, July 24, 1906, Bryan Papers; Nathaniel Stephenson, *Nelson W. Aldrich*, p. 187; George C. Osborn, *John Sharp Williams: Planter-Statesman of the Deep South*, p. 148; Albert L. Gale and George W. Kline, *Bryan the Man*, p. 68.

[38] Harold C. Syrett, (ed.), *The Gentleman and the Tiger: The Autobiography of George Brinton McClellan, Jr.*, pp. 280–281.

with Professors Frank Parsons of Kansas and Edward Bemis of Chicago. He wrote an editorial for *The Commoner* on it and asked his brother Charles and editor Richard L. Metcalfe to criticize it. On July 5 Charles replied that he and "Met" believed that the people were not ready for government ownership. The best advice he received from correspondents, Charles added, was to avoid the government ownership issue and to defer announcing Bryan's candidacy. All felt, however, that he would win the nomination unanimously.[39]

In mid-July the Bryans began a trip through England, Scotland, and Ireland, with Bryan's interest sharpened by visits to the homes of William E. Gladstone, John Knox, and Robert Burns. While at Lochkatrine, Scotland, on July 17, he struck another blow at Roger Sullivan via Judge Owen P. Thompson, of Jacksonville. In the spring of 1905, correspondence between Millard F. Dunlap and Carter Harrison had led Harrison to believe that Bryan was asking him to head an organization in opposition to Sullivan's. Anxious to fight Sullivan, Harrison nevertheless demanded assurance of Bryan's support. This came from Dunlap, and Bryan himself attended the organizational meeting. However, he had earlier met with Sullivan, and at the Harrison meeting he attempted to salve the wounds inflicted upon the "train robbers" in the St. Louis convention and obtain harmony. Now he directed Thompson to read a first letter to Sullivan. If he resigned from the National Committee, then a second letter should be destroyed without divulging its contents; if he refused to resign, it should be published at once. A third letter declared that forcing Sullivan's resignation was his own idea, not Dunlap's or anyone else's. The jist of his argument was that Sullivan's presence on the committee belied the party's attempt to convince the people of its good intentions; his corporate connections would harm the party far beyond his power to aid it; and he was not actually the choice of the Illinois Democrats but held his position by virtue of fraud, thereby making it impossible for honest Democrats to associate with him. If he did not resign "at once" he should be ejected from the committee. Soon *The Commoner* took up the chant. When Sullivan refused to resign, Bryan vowed to launch a personal campaign against him. For good measure, *The Commoner* also attacked the "immoral" Thomas Taggart, chairman of the Democratic National Committee.[40]

[39] C. W. Bryan to W. J. Bryan, July 5, 1906, Silas Bryan Papers.
[40] Bryan to Thompson, July 17, 1906, *ibid.*; *Commoner*, July 20, August 10, September 14, 1906; Carter H. Harrison, *Stormy Years: The Autobiography of Carter H. Harrison, Five Time Mayor of Chicago*, pp. 256–261.

Upon his return to London, Bryan attended the Interparliamentary Union conference. In the summer of 1904, when he was "too sick" to campaign for Parker, he had spent several days in the Rocky Mountains with a touring Union group and received an invitation to address a meeting. On July 24, as a main speaker, before representatives of twenty-six nations, he emphasized the need for higher moral standards in international as well as national life. He also spoke in favor of a strong disarmament resolution, which was adopted by a large majority. The model arbitration treaty adopted by the conference excluded questions of national sovereignty and honor. By amendment he sought to include these "vital" questions and then suggested the basis of what were later known as his "cooling off" treaties—all controversies, regardless of kind, should be submitted to an international commission of inquiry. While its decision would not have binding effect, publicity, delay, and sober second thought would prevent war. The unanimous acceptance of the amendment was a tribute to the excellence of his suggestion as well as to his forceful oratory. Convinced that men everywhere were brothers, Bryan insisted that love, not force, should provide the basis for international relations.[41]

Crossing the English Channel, Bryan visited Holland, took a trip up the Rhine, and spent several days in Switzerland before entering Italy, France, and Spain. Henry White, who did his best to show him Italy in five days by traveling at night and sightseeing by day, was amazed at his lack of curiosity in historical antiquities. Tiring, Bryan once pointed to the newspaper men who trailed them and said, "I really don't think it is worth while for us to go on any further, as these boys will telegraph all that is necessary to America about what I have seen here." Then he asked White if he were a Democrat. White replied that he was a diplomatist, that no one could well represent the United States abroad if he were a partisan politician. Bryan expressed regret because a change of administration was not improbable and he wished White could remain in the public service—a service he could not perform under a Democratic administration, which would fill its posts abroad only with "loyal Democrats." White recalled that

[41] London *Standard, Daily Mail, Daily Telegraph, Times,* July 25, 1906; London *Daily Mirror, Times,* July 26, 1906; Reid to Secretary of State, July 26, 1906, Reid Papers; *Commoner,* August 3, 17, 1906; Merle Curti, "Bryan and World Peace," *Smith College Studies in History* (Northampton, Mass., 1931), pp. 139–141; W. J. Bryan, "Path to Peace," *Independent,* 61 (August 30, 1906), 483–489.

He said this with apparently real regret and friendship for me . . . It never occurred to him for a moment that the slightest training was necessary, or the interests of our Government should be in any way hampered,—nor indeed that there could be any such real interests abroad, by the substitution of a "good Democrat" possessing no knowledge whatever of the intricacies of European diplomacy for the man who spent many years of his life in close contact with all those questions.[42]

After speeding through France and Spain, the Bryans were joined by the Edgar Lee Masterses and Millard F. Dunlaps and embarked for home from Gibraltar on August 20, with Bryan planning to write aboard a speech which, he wrote Charles, "I think will not disappoint you." [43]

Through his *Commoner* and interviews, Bryan had continued to blast a progressive path even as he toured the world. By the fall of 1905 the battle against city and state bossism was in full swing. The muckrakers and Insurgents were beginning to unnerve Roosevelt, who early in 1906 confessed that there "had been an era of over-confidence and speculation. . . . Sooner or later we shall undoubtedly have . . . reaction." [44] He now realized that many of the reforms Bryan had long demanded had large popular backing, yet he refused to admit spiritual kinship with him and never acknowledged that he had "borrowed" his corrective ideas or thanked him for the Democratic support in Congress without which he could not have effected much of his program. In turn, Bryan predicted that he was too arbitrary to get along with Congress and that Insurgent opposition to him would grow until it split his party. In mid-March Roosevelt complained to William Howard Taft that "I do not like the social conditions at present. The dull, purblind folly of the very rich men; their greed and arrogance . . . and the corruption in business and politics, have tended to produce a very unhealthy condition of excitement in the popular mind, which shows itself in the socialistic propaganda." [45] In April he spoke about "fortunes swollen beyond all healthy limits" and hinted at the need for an inheritance tax if not for an income tax. When he sent a special message to Congress criticizing federal Judge J. Otis Humphrey because of a "miscarriage of justice" in his

[42] White, "Reminiscences."
[43] Bryan to Charles W. Bryan, August 12, 1906, Silas Bryan Papers.
[44] Letter to Nicholas Murray Butler, January 10, 1906, Roosevelt Papers.
[45] Letter of March 15, 1906, William Howard Taft Papers.

decision in the Beef Trust cases, Bryan commented that "Little by little, but steadily as man's march to the grave, the Chicago platform is being vindicated," for in language stronger than that of the Chicago platform the President had condemned the very offense for which Republicans in 1896 had poured bitter condemnation upon the head of faithful Democrats and called them and their leaders "anarchists." [46] He criticized the Hepburn bill because the rates fixed by the Interstate Commerce Commission upon complaint of a shipper were made subject to court review. Bills to permit the removal of the tariff from articles needed to meet the emergency caused by the San Francisco earthquake and fire led him to note that the present schedules enabled large corporations to sell their products cheaper abroad than at home. The meat inspection act, too, could have been improved by authorizing the "date on the can" and by charging the packers with the costs of inspection. Furthermore, Roosevelt had done nothing to implement his promise of requiring publicity for campaign contributions or to require an explanation from the Republican national chairman of his acceptance of contributions from insurance companies in 1904. Asked whether it was true that "Roosevelt caught you in swimming and stole your clothes," Bryan replied that Roosevelt had not gotten all of them; moreover, he could not quite fill them. Roosevelt had responded "somewhat" to the popular demand for relief from corporate oppression, but he had faltered at critical moments and compromised on vital features of important reform measures. Finally, some credit for reform was due La Follette, who was now deliberately insulted by his colleagues and derided by Republican editors because he refused to compromise with the enemies of popular government. Could Bryan have his way, the Republican reformer he would like most to see named in 1908 was not Roosevelt but La Follette.[47]

Shortly after leaving Europe Bryan had stated that he could not, as the *Nebraska State Journal* (Lincoln) suggested that he do, "forget the Chicago platform." That platform, he told the New York *Times*, was being vindicated in the court of public opinion and its spirit would be reflected in a "safe and sane" platform in 1908. Moreover, were another Democrat found more available than he at nomination time, he would support him. William Randolph Hearst, Joseph Bailey, and Joseph W. Folk, at least, should be considered.[48] He said

[46] *Commoner*, April 27, May 4, 1906.
[47] *Ibid.*, May 4, 11, 18, June 8, 15, July 13, 20, 1906.
[48] *Ibid.*, July 13, 20, August 10, 1906.

all this of course with tongue in cheek, for he well knew of the definite boom for him: the Progressive movement was in full swing; the Republican Old Guard in the Senate was breathing its last; Roosevelt was aggressively campaigning against the trusts; and during his absence the Democrats recalled their miserable failure in 1904 and were ready to hand him the nomination.

Conservatives like Ryan, Perry Belmont, George F. Baer, and A. J. Cassatt detested Hearst and preferred Roosevelt to Bryan. However, since Roosevelt had compromised too much, they decided to risk a chance with Bryan, whose position was crystal clear. On the other hand, the recrudescence of Bryan's popularity was attested by the support promised by such opponents in 1896 as M. E. Ingalls, who now regarded him as "the foremost American citizen"; ex-Governor Thomas T. Crittenden of Missouri, who predicted he would be the greatest American President; David R. Francis, ex-governor of Missouri and Secretary of the Interior under Cleveland, who now extolled him and Cleveland in the same breath; and William F. Vilas, Joseph Bailey, and Richard Croker. To the rank and file there was no other acceptable candidate than he in either major party. In 1904 his leadership had appeared ended; now he was being cheered with enthusiasm as spontaneous as it was sincere. Much of the recrudescence stemmed from the fact that Roosevelt had taken over his policies. Since the Republicans had no adequate progressive successor to offer, Bryan must be chosen because he was the most logical man to follow in Roosevelt's footsteps.[49] The only strong objector to this logic was Joseph Pulitzer, who did not believe Bryan could be elected. Therefore those who supported him were revealing great devotion but not good sense. Moreover, they were ruining his chances by bringing him out too early. He could understand that Bryan, being human, would accept another nomination. But the party was being foolish. Where was the sagacity, wisdom, foresight, and knowledge needed by leaders to steer them through the current hullaballoo?[50]

And a hullaballoo it was as Bryan approached New York on August 30. Every well-known Democrat in the country had contributed toward the costs of his reception, and almost every prominent Democrat in

[49] B. O. Flower, "Bryan and the Presidency," The Arena, 36 (August 1906), 189–190; J. L. West, "The Recrudescence of Bryan," Forum, 38 (October 1906), 147–152.

[50] Pulitzer to George S. Johns, August 10, 1906, Joseph Pulitzer Personal Papers. See also the criticism in Lyman Abbot, "William Jennings Bryan: A Character Study," The Outlook, 84 (September 8, 1906), 66–68.

the country was in New York to pay him homage in person. Mayors like Tom L. Johnson and James Dahlman mingled with governors like Joseph W. Folk and Robert B. Glenn and other state and city leaders, all with full delegations. Railroad companies gave cut-rate fares from distant points. The 120 men in the Nebraska delegation stocked up well with liquor. Although they knew Bryan did not like "Wild West stuff," about 200 men hired tugs and went to meet his ship. Ship and factory whistles blew as the tugs approached. The unerring aim of Omaha's "Cowboy Mayor" slipped a lariat around broad shoulders, and Dahlman drew Bryan toward him. "Hello Jim! God bless you!" cried Bryan as they hugged in mutual joy. Transferring to millionaire Edward Goltra's yacht, he had several hours of peace before entering the city.[51]

IV

AMONG others who urged Bryan to avoid reference to the railroad question in his speech at Madison Square Garden the next evening were Senators Joseph Bailey and Charles A. Culberson and Congressman John Sharp Williams. Bryan insisted that he must include it. Mrs. Bryan asked him not to read his speech, for he would never win his audience. Bryan said he feared he would be misrepresented. He would be misrepresented anyhow, she replied. But he was determined to read.

Pushing his way through streets packed with humanity Bryan entered a swelteringly hot Garden, scene of his fiasco of 1896. Tom L. Johnson, the presiding officer, asserted that Bryan's charm lay in the sincerity of his eloquence and his great moral courage and pointed to the need for his leadership in a period of national awakening against special privilege. As he faced the huge audience of 12,000, Bryan pressed his thin lips together and blinked his eyes to repress the tears, but he could not, and the crowd cheered and cheered. For more than an hour he outlined the issues for 1908. He was glad to be back in the United States, with love of country strengthened by absence. He brought a message of peace, of anticolonialism, of the need for making

[51] Treasurer's Report, Finance Committee, Bryan Reception, August 29, 1906, Bryan Papers; New York Times, World, Tribune, August 31, 1906; interview by the author with a member of the Nebraska delegation, John A. MacDonald, Omaha, August 4, 1952; Fred Carey, Mayor Jim: The Life of James C. Dahlman, p. 117; Gale and Kline, Bryan the Man, pp. 66–79.

the government more responsive to the will of the people. The cause of international arbitration was close to his heart, and he suggested that peace be furthered by not using the Navy for the collection of debts. By its experiment in colonialism the United States had lost rather than gained prestige abroad, and the Philippines should be freed even though we retained naval and coaling stations.

Having noted that several European governments were more responsive to the will of the people than the American, he suggested improvements in the form of a lame duck amendment and the popular election of senators. Many of the most conservative countries of Europe collected an income tax, and he favored a constitutional amendment that would provide one for the United States. He also demanded the arbitration of labor disputes by a national labor board and an eight-hour day.

Thus far he spoke on what he considered "nonpartisan" objectives. Now he turned to a topic close to the Democratic heart—the "unexpected conditions" which had removed the cause of difference over the money question "and permitted us to present a united front on present issues." In sum, the money issue was dead. Moreover, the results of the insurance investigations of 1905–1906 had revealed the need for prohibiting campaign contributions by corporations, and from what he could gather the anti-trust issue appeared to be the most important one for 1908. He would vigorously follow the principle that "A private monopoly is indefensible and intolerable" and provide laws against the holding company form the trusts were using to avoid regulation, against interlocking directorates, and in favor of the federal licensing of corporations engaged in interstate commerce. Those who argued that there was an economic advantage in private monopoly were aiding Socialism, of which he would have no part.

Tariff reform should accompany trust regulation, for it would limit the extortions of the trusts and the amount of "fat" they gave to the Republicans in return for favorable legislation. Furthermore, by selling cheaper abroad than at home, manufacturers showed ingratitude to those who provided the tariffs, continued to lay a heavy burden upon the consumer, and aroused resentment and provoked retaliation from abroad.

Interwoven with the trust question was the railroad question. He rejoiced that the President was pressing railroad regulation upon Congress. However, he warned against the use of an appointed regulatory commission that might induce the railroad men to select a

President friendly to them. If this happened, "the sentiment in favor of government ownership is likely to increase as rapidly throughout the country as the sentiment in favor of municipal ownership has increased in the cities."

In the light of the tremendous amount of criticism aimed at his comments on government ownership, his exact words bear quoting:

I have already reached the conclusion that railroads partake so much of the nature of a monopoly that they must ultimately become public property and be managed by public officials in the interest of the whole community in accordance with the well defined theory that public ownership is necessary where competition is impossible. I do not know that a majority of my own party favor it, but I believe that an increasing number of the members of all parties see in public ownership the only sure remedy for discrimination between persons and places and for extortionate rates for the carrying of freight and passengers. Believing, however, that the operation of all the railroads by the federal government would so centralize the government as to almost obliterate state lines, I prefer to see only the trunk lines operated by the federal government and the local lines by the several state governments. . . . Investigation in Europe has convinced me that it is entirely practicable. . . . If any of you question the propriety of my mentioning this subject I beg to remind you that the President could not have secured the passage of the [Hepburn] rate bill had he not appealed to the fear of the more radical remedy of government ownership and nothing will so restrain the railroad managers from attempting to capture the Interstate Commerce Commission as the same fear.

In his peroration Bryan lashed out against plutocracy. Plutocracy was abhorrent in a republic, for it was more despotic than monarchy, more heartless than aristocracy, and more selfish than bureaucracy. It was sapping the strength of the nation, vulgarizing social life, and making a mockery out of morals. "The time is ripe for the overthrow of this giant wrong. In the name of the counting rooms, which it has defiled; in the name of business honor, which it has polluted; in the name of the homes which it has despoiled; in the name of religion which it has disgraced; in the name of the people whom it has oppressed, let us make our appeal to the awakened conscience of the nation." [52]

Of the fifty-three paragraphs in the speech, three were introductory, six were devoted to peace and anticolonialism, and thirty-eight dealt

[52] New York *Times*, New York *Tribune*, New York *World*, August 31, September 1, 1906.

with topics that would make the government more responsive to the will of the people. The railroad question occupied only six short paragraphs that took but four minutes to read, but the opposition press acted as though he had spoken on government ownership alone. Next morning's headlines read BRYAN OUT FOR GOVERNMENT OWNERSHIP. Newspapers like the New York *Times* and *World* deliberately misrepresented and twisted his statements. Political leaders of all descriptions also chose to interpret his suggestion of "ultimate" to mean "immediate" government ownership, and with this interpretation fixed in the public mind the impressive political strength with which he entered the Garden oozed away. As with the ratio of 16 to 1 in 1896, he had again split his party. He had built up during his absence the idea that he was a conservative; he had been asked by keen readers of the public pulse not to mention government ownership, which was particularly unpalatable to the state-rights South; yet he had brashly proclaimed an entirely new and radical idea. He was astounded by the roar of fury he had aroused and chagrined to learn that he had smashed the good impression he had made while abroad. He had failed to find a "paramount" issue, and conservative Democrats began seeking another candidate, with some favoring Woodrow Wilson.[53] Even so strong a supporter as George Fred Williams admitted that Bryan faced a solid wall of opposition, especially from Southerners like John Daniel, Isidor Rayner, Thomas S. Martin, Joseph Bailey, John Sharp Williams, and "others of their kind," some of whom he knew to be "under the direct influence of the railroads. . . ." [54] If Cleveland had earlier been "less bitter," he now declared that he disbelieved that "the recent symptoms of Bryan insanity" would infect the party, and Bryan began a tour of explanation in various states, asserting that he wished to force government ownership upon neither his party nor the country. He thought for himself alone and wanted others to have their say; the Democratic platform would be made by the voters, not by a single man or a few leaders. Even Southerners, once they understood his proposition, would not oppose it so violently. He also frequently adverted to Roosevelt's stealing of his issues, saying, "The trouble with the President has been

[53] New York *Times, Tribune, World,* August 31, September 1, 1906; Reid to Roosevelt, September 14, 1906, Reid Papers; Adolphus Talbot to H. S. Commager, January 4, 1936, Commager Papers; Harvey to Wilson, December 17, 1906, Wilson Papers.

[54] Williams to Judge Walter Clark, September 19, 1906, Commager Papers.

that when he tried to do anything, he had to whip the Republican party in line with the Democratic platform instead of the Republican platform. . . . The only way you can stand by the President, if he really wants reform, is to give him a Democratic Congress to back him up instead of a Republican Congress." [55]

Stalwart Republicans like Foraker and Taft lampooned Bryan, and Roosevelt evaluated him as one with "kindly and amiable traits" but a "shallow demagogue." "I drew a sigh of relief after reading Bryan's speech," he wrote Lodge on September 24. "I think he has helped us immensely. Down at bottom Bryan is a cheap soul. He felt that he had to take an attitude that would show that he was really a great deal more radical than I was. He did it. Now he has been inclined to hedge about it, which will merely give an added impression of weakness." [56] When he wrote Reid in the same vein, Reid replied that Bryan's speech had produced "an instant revulsion" in Europe, that Bryan had "dished himself." [57] Then, in a speech at Harrisburg, Pennsylvania, on October 4, Roosevelt took "emphatic ground" about Bryan's government ownership, "the only great issue which he has produced." He would not deal with the lesser figures in Pennsylvania, he had told Lodge, but "Bryan himself is a national issue, and so I could deal with him." Moreover, he wrote Lodge soon afterwards, no man could consistently take Bryan's attitude toward the Filipinos and not fight against the conduct of the Democratic party in the South toward the Negro. Bryan's wholesale denunciation of British rule in India was "not only ignorant, but curiously reckless." [58] The Madison Square Garden speech had "dumped him from the heights,"

[55] *Commoner*, September 7, 14, 21, 1906.

[56] Joseph Benson Foraker, *Notes of a Busy Life*, II, 379, 381–382; Roosevelt to Lodge, September 24, 1906, Henry Cabot Lodge, *Selections from the Correspondence of Theodore Roosevelt and Henry Cabot Lodge, 1884–1918*, II, 223–224

[57] Reid to Roosevelt, September 14, 1906, Roosevelt Papers; see also Roosevelt to Reid, September 25, 1906, *ibid.*

[58] Letter, October 16, 1906, Lodge, *Correspondence*, II, 247–248. Roosevelt's attitude was that "To exercise a constantly increasing and constantly more effective supervision and control over the great common carriers of the country prevents all necessity for seriously considering such a project as the government ownership of railroads—a policy which would be evil in its results from every standpoint. . . . The government ought not to conduct the business of the country; but it ought to regulate it so that it shall be conducted in the interests of the public." For the opposite view, one upholding Bryan, see Benjamin Parke De Witt, *The Progressive Movement: A Non-partisan, Comprehensive Discussion of Current Tendencies in American Politics*, pp. 123–124.

he wrote Reid, "but I don't believe we have heard the last of him. His party is dreadfully hard up for Presidential timber, and in reaction from Hearst may come back to him again." [59]

V

ON SEPTEMBER 5 Bryan concluded his world journeying in Lincoln. Within a few days he was busy with local and national politics. By 1906 the Republicans in Nebraska had progressed to where the Populists had been in 1890, and there was really little difference between the Democratic and Republican state platforms. The occasionally progressive Edward Rosewater had died, and leadership had fallen to liberals like George W. Norris, but these vied with rather than joined Bryan in progressivism. The Democrats and Populists, who fused, were encouraged by the return of Bryan and his undertaking of a vigorous speaking tour, particularly in support of William H. Thompson for United States senator, and by the fact that Bryan's brother-in-law, Thomas S. Allen, now chairman of the Democratic state committee, attended diligently to affairs. [60]

Bryan won his home state but failed to defeat Sullivan. In a speech in Chicago on September 4 he had asserted that there could be no friendship with him or harmony in Illinois until Sullivan resigned as national committeeman. He had depended upon a coalition led by Judge Owen P. Thompson, Millard F. Dunlap, and Congressman Henry T. Rainey to oust Sullivan. In March, Rainey had established the Democratic Majority Rule League as a vehicle for winning the chairmanship of the state convention and also to offset serious Republican and reorganizer-Democratic opposition to his re-election to Congress. But at the state convention he suddenly withdrew in favor of Sullivan's candidate for chairman, possibly because Sullivan threatened to denounce him for his mileage grab vote in the House in 1903, and Sullivan retained control of the party machinery. Yet the delegates endorsed Bryan for President, an endorsement Bryan did not reject. [61]

Bryan   Democrats   and   progressive   Republicans   honeymooned

---

[59] Roosevelt to Reid, October 8, 1906, Reid Papers.

[60] Commoner, September 14, 1906; Victor Rosewater, "Life and Times of Edward Rosewater," pp. 329–331; Sheldon, Nebraska, I, 816–820.

[61] Commoner, September 14, 1906; Kenneth D. Raab, "Henry T. Rainey," unpublished Ms., pp. 73–77; Harrison, Stormy Years, p. 261.

throughout midsummer of 1906. While Bryan complimented such Republican reformers as Governor Cummins of Iowa, Senator Beveridge of Indiana, and La Follette, La Follette confessed his indebtedness to "the Democrats [of Wisconsin] who were patriotic enough to put party behind and join with us in saving the state from corporation rule." [62] Stumping the South and Middle West in September and October, Bryan threw bouquets at the Populists and admonished his Democratic followers to obtain harmony within their party, especially on the anti-trust issue. Since the Bible said that no man could serve two masters, he held that "No man who is financially connected with a corporation that is seeking privilege ought to act as a member of a political organization because he can not represent his corporation and the people at the same time." He was pleased to learn that Henry Watterson would support him for President in 1908 and did not reject honors tendered him by the Virginia followers of Thomas F. Ryan.[63] Thomas E. Watson had lately referred to him as "William Jenkins Blatherskite" and as a "consummate hypocrite," revealed disgust with his sympathy with the Negroes punished by Roosevelt in the Brownsville incident, and openly sought the disruption of the Democracy. Yet Bryan wrote him that he was sorry that he could not return a visit Watson had earlier paid at his home, adding: "It is gratifying to know from what I have learned that we are going to be able to act together in the coming contest. There has been a remarkable change in public sentiment, so that things that were formerly denounced as radical, are now regarded as not only quite reasonable but even necessary." [64]

The Republican vote dropped drastically in Maine's September election. Buoyed with hope, Bryan devoted three weeks to various Middle Western states before stumping Nebraska in the last week of the cam-

[62] *Commoner,* August 24, September 14, November 2, 1906; January 11, 18, 1907. In the spring of 1905 Bryan had delivered a "captivating and effective" speech on progressive issues in Wisconsin. La Follette had it printed and distributed in Democratic districts, where Bryan's influence would be felt. Belle Case La Follette and Fola La Follette, *Robert La Follette,* II, 190.

[63] *Commoner,* September 21, 28, 1906; William E. Dodd to Judge Walter Clark, September 1, 1906, Commager Papers.

[64] *Commoner,* January 13, March 10, 1906; Bryan to Watson, September 22, 1906, quoted in C. Vann Woodward, *Tom Watson, Agrarian Rebel,* p. 396; Dewey W. Grantham, Jr., *Hoke Smith and the Politics of the New South,* pp. 131–179; Emma Lou Thornbrough, "The Brownsville Episode and the Negro Vote," *Mississippi Valley Historical Review,* 44 (December 1957), 469–493.

paign. He excoriated George W. Perkins of the New York Life Insurance Company, the J. P. Morgan Company, and others whose contributions to the Republican party had counted heavily against him. He also indicated whom his followers should support, including Hearst against Charles E. Hughes for governor of New York; R. T. Sutherland, Democratic fusionist, against George W. Norris in Nebraska's Fifth District; and John M. Pattison against Cincinnati's Boss George B. Cox and Ohio's Governor Myron T. Herrick. He even took the unusual step of writing a personal letter to his New York friends in Hearst's behalf, thereby overlooking Hughes's excellent record as a reform governor and brilliance of intellect.[65]

The most singular occurrence of the years 1904–1906 was not the reacceptance of Bryan as the leader of the Democracy but Roosevelt's "committing larceny in the wood-yard where Bryan kept his platform planks." In 1904 Roosevelt would have denied strenuously his affinity to anything Bryanesque. In 1906 he could say that "We want no more Wall Street civilization," and he eventually admitted his indebtedness to the Nebraskan and stopped sneering at his advice on certain matters.[66] At a White House dinner he grossly violated protocol and had Bryan seated next to him. By saying he would support him every time he thought him "right," however, Bryan assumed an anomalous and ambivalent position, for it is the traditional task of the opposition to criticize and to offer alternative proposals, not to support administration policy. He had taken his position on government ownership, he explained, less to make converts than to offer it for further consideration. He then made much of Roosevelt's demand for legislation which would so regulate the railroads as to make public ownership unnecessary, saying that what was needed was "a baptism

[65] *Commoner,* October 5, 19, 26, 1906; Bryan to Bird S. Coler, November 3, 1906, quoted in Sam Hanna Acheson, *Joe Bailey, the Last Democrat,* p. 229; J. P. Barrett, *Joseph Pulitzer and His "World,"* p. 190. Hughes's investigation revealed that the Big Four—New York Life, Mutual, Equitable, and Prudential—had contributed to the Republicans $21,000 in 1896, $80,000 in 1900, and $128,000 in 1904; that contributions made in 1904, as by George Perkins, "to assist in the maintenance of a proper monetary standard," were odd, for the currency was not an issue in 1904; that New York's Senators Platt and Depew, ex-Senator David B. Hill, and various Republican state representatives were on their payrolls; and that the companies sought to corrupt the press, influence public opinion, and kill legislation harmful to them. Mark Sullivan, *Our Times: The United States, 1900–1925,* III, 62–66; Merlo J. Pusey, *Charles Evans Hughes,* I, 140–166.

[66] *The Letters of Archie Butt,* pp. 45–46 (June 22, 1908).

of self-respect, so we can stand erect in the presence of the almighty dollar." But he asserted the right of criticism afforded the leader of the opposition when he spoke bitterly against a bill providing for asset currency, saying that "the man who goes on record in favor of asset currency places upon himself an indelible brand—the brand of Wall Street." Moreover, having praised Roosevelt for mediating the Russo-Japanese War, he now urged him to undertake the writing of "cooling off" treaties. His military exploits would pale before leadership of a successful peace movement, he noted, but Roosevelt did not reply.[67]

In 1900 Roosevelt had carried the oratorical burden of the Republican campaign. In 1906, complaining that "I sometimes wish I was not in the White House and could be on the stump and speak frankly," he let favorites like Taft, Root, and Leonard Wood "set forth the case of the administration." He was particularly anxious that Taft's speeches be well received, for he had chosen him as his successor, and Taft began taking Bryan's measure as his most likely opponent in 1908. "Bryan has great crowds, as he always does," he wrote Roosevelt late in October, "but it is always a doubtful question whether he does not do more good for the major party than the minority by his trips, for if he puts excitement into the campaign at all he is likely to bring out the Republicans." [68] Taft erred, however, in overlooking Bryan's power in the states, as in Oklahoma.

Unable to address in person the Oklahoma constitutional convention, which met on November 20, 1906, Bryan wrote a very long letter of unusual importance as a progressive document since it foreshadowed the Democratic national platform of 1908. The new constitution should have an enlarged bill of rights, permit verdicts by three-fourths of juries in civil cases, the popular election of judges, and local home rule. Costs of elections should be thrown as much as possible upon the community rather than upon candidates or parties; absolutely no contributions should be accepted from corporations, and publicity should be given contributions before elections. He favored direct primaries over nominating conventions, the initiative, referendum, and recall, the creation of boards to control municipal franchises and transportation and other corporations, and laws against monopoly and duplicating directorates. Franchise-holding corporations should

[67] *Commoner*, September 18, 25, 1905, September 21, 28, November 23, 30, 1906.
[68] Roosevelt to Taft, July 29, 1905, November 8, 1906, Taft to Roosevelt, October 31, November 1, 4, 1906, Taft Papers.

be created only for short periods, say twenty or thirty years, and only after a favorable vote of a majority of the people of a city. The state should lease rather than sell coal, iron, and other mineral lands, and cities should be empowered to own and operate whatever municipal plants a majority of their people desired. Industrial, transportation, communication, and elevator corporations should be carefully controlled, and the legislature should be empowered to fix the length of the working day on public projects, regulate child labor, and provide for the arbitration of labor disputes by a permanent board of three to five members. Then he had the temerity to apologize: he had "by no means covered the entire field. . . . And I fear I have given you little that is new." He was too modest, for virtually every item he suggested was incorporated into the new constitution, the most progressive in the nation. Moreover, his four stumping tours contributed greatly to Democratic victory in the new state.[69]

Bryan had predicted that the elections of 1906 would indicate a trend in favor of the Democrats. If they revealed anything, however, the returns showed a trend toward progressivism in both major parties. Hughes defeated Hearst by a narrow margin, but the Southern states generally elected progressive governors. Oklahoma went resoundingly Democratic. In Georgia, Hoke Smith, backed by Thomas E. Watson, defeated the "corporation representative," Clark Howell, and soon put through a large part of the Bryan-Populist program. Fusion again failed to win Nebraska, but Governor George Sheldon was a self-confessed reformer and had a progressive Republican legislature which in 1907 enacted the most complete progressive program ever accomplished in a single session by any Midwestern legislature. Despite Bryan's thirty speeches in George W. Norris's district, Norris was re-elected. When he met Norris afterwards he told him frankly that he was glad he had won, thereby admitting that he placed partisanship above personal conviction and leading Norris to ask, "What explanation can be made of the psychology of such a great man when he is influenced by such a course?" Elsewhere in the Middle West progressivism was on the rise.[70]

[69] *Commoner*, December 21, 1906; Alfred E. Kahn, "The Oklahoma Constitution of 1907," (unpublished Ms.), Commager Papers; Norbert R. Mahnken, "William Jennings Bryan in Oklahoma," *Nebraska History*, 31 (December 1950), 247–274.

[70] *Commoner*, November 11, 1906; Arthur F. Mullen, *Western Democrat*, p. 127; Richard L. Neuberger and Stephen B. Kahn, *Integrity: The Life of George Norris*, p. 33; Russel B. Nye, *Midwestern Progressive Politics: A Historical Study of Its Origins and Development, 1870–1950*, p. 234; Sheldon, *Nebraska*, I, 820–824.

After the elections, when Senator Beveridge, Speaker Joseph G. Cannon, and other Republicans almost simultaneously called Bryan a dreamer, he pleaded guilty, saying that "the Democratic party even now has a dream that sooner or later will commend itself to the thinking people of the country. It is a vision of a government brought into harmony with divine will." The party needed to become a moral organization: "We cannot appeal to the conscience of the country with a conscienceless crowd in charge of the party machinery. Therefore all who would serve the public must sever their connections with the corporations, and all who remain with the corporations must sever themselves from politics." He dramatized the need for party reorganization by pointing out that the Democratic vote in Illinois was 503,061 in 1900, but that with Hopkins and Sullivan in control the vote had dropped to 360,925 in 1902, to 327,606 in 1904, and to 231,077 in 1906—a 50 per cent drop in six years.[71]

At the Trans-Mississippi Congress on Peace and Trusts held at Kansas City on November 22, Bryan won the adoption of the Interparliamentary Union's peace resolution and of his resolution opposing private monopolies and favoring the enforcement of existing antitrust laws until more stringent ones could be enacted.[72] Shortly thereafter he was pleased to compare his Madison Square Garden speech with Roosevelt's annual message. These agreed on so many counts that the press spoke of the "Roosevelt-Bryan Merger." Bryan claimed to be "more radical than ever" while Roosevelt called himself a "rational conservative" and labeled Bryan a "demagogue and agitator," but they were actually not far apart in many of their reform proposals. Agreeing with Bryan that the federal government must intervene to solve economic and social problems beyond the scope of state action, Roosevelt adopted Bryan's demands for the licensing of all interstate businesses, the federal control of railroads, the physical valuation of railroad property, the prohibition of corporations from contributing to political campaigns, the arbitration of industrial disputes, the regulation of the procedures by which the courts issued injunctions, the federal control of corporation securities, an inheritance tax, and pure food and drug legislation. Meantime he heightened his trust-busting activities and used a Democrat, Benjamin Tillman, to push the Hepburn bill through a Senate which, as Bryan had asserted a dozen years earlier, was the "Nemesis of reform." Bryan

[71] *Commoner,* November 23, December 21, 28, 1906.
[72] *Ibid.,* November 30, 1906.

cheered those items he said Roosevelt had taken from him and criticized him for not going further with others, as on railroad and trust regulation and tariff and currency reform. Roosevelt had said that to leave the present currency law unchanged meant "the liability of business disaster" and had offered the Congress a plan for a more elastic currency—temporary currency issued by the national banks that could be taxed out of existence when the emergency passed. In January 1907 Jacob Schiff predicted that if the monetary system were not reformed the country would "get a panic . . . compared with which the three that have preceded would be only child's play," and he characterized the high call money rates on the New York Stock Exchange as "a disgrace to a civilized country." Ex-Treasurer Lyman J. Gage agreed "that a stunning panic will come unless something is done," and Bryan charged that Roosevelt was "afraid" to take up real currency reform—but the Congress did nothing.[73]

"For the last eight years our party fights have furnished about all the excitement we have had in politics, but if I mistake not, your party is entering upon a struggle by the side of which our contest will seem a love feast," Bryan had written Republican Senator William E. Chandler on March 31, 1905.[74] The opposition by Nelson W. Aldrich and the rest of the Senate cabal to the Esch-Townshend and Hepburn bills and congressional opposition to Roosevelt's demand for conservation proved his point. The conservative reaction reached its boiling point when Roosevelt paraphrased Bryan and asserted that he must prevent the growth "of the least attractive and most sordid of all aristocracies," a plutocracy "which regarded power as expressed only by its basest and most brutal form, that of mere money." [75] Fear that reform "tinkering" might provoke a panic disastrous to his party's hopes led Roosevelt to tread warily. Meantime Bryan popularized the ideal of human brotherhood which made him indeed the Peerless Leader. By rigorous stumping tours and written

[73] *Ibid.,* December 28, 1906; New York *World,* December 5, 1906; H. F. Pringle, *Theodore Roosevelt, A Biography,* pp. 432–434; George E. Mowry, *The Era of Theodore Roosevelt, 1900–1912,* pp. 197–199; Matthew Josephson, *The President Makers: The Culture of Politics and Leadership in an Age of Enlightenment, 1896–1919,* p. 221; La Follette, *La Follette,* II, 202–208.

[74] Bryan Papers.

[75] Mowry, *Era of Theodore Roosevelt,* p. 210; De Witt, *Progressive Movement,* p. 52.

debates, such as his long debate with Senator Beveridge,[76] he whipped up a great deal of enthusiasm for the principles of Jefferson, Jackson, and Bryan; as a "lecturing evangelist" at Chautauqua he impressed thousands with his ideas on religion and morality; and by addresses such as those at the Holland Society and at the National Arbitration and Peace Congress held in Carnegie Hall, New York City, he continued to sponsor the cause of world peace.

According to John H. Atwood, who had supported Bryan since 1891, "The people have been surfeited with smart scamps, and cunning criminals, government grafters, and senatorial short-change men —they want honest men. They want the head to be right, but more, they want the heart to be right; and that Bryan's heart beats with them and for them, they know." [77] Bryan clearly reflected Atwood's estimate. A firm believer that God, the creator of man, had also created a moral law for his government and endowed him with a conscience with which to apprehend it, Bryan appeared as a lay prophet of the social gospel. Like the economists Richard T. Ely and Simon N. Patten, he emphasized the interrelationship between ethics and economics and the fact that a rich material life on earth was possible only if there occurred a religious reformation in which men strived to improve the lot of their brother men rather than pile up profits for themselves.[78] Therefore he undertook his "heart to heart" appeal to convince men that an enduring social transformation was impossible without changed human hearts. This was the central theme of his speeches entitled "Man," "Faith," and others which he delivered at various commencement exercises and then endless times on the

[76] The Bryan-Beveridge debate was carried in *The Reader* from March 1907 to February 1908.

[77] Richard L. Metcalfe (comp.), *The Real Bryan*, p. 21.

[78] Gabriel, *Course of American Democratic Thought*, chapter 2 and p. 306. Increasingly vigorous discussion of the monopoly question followed the exposure of the Beef Trust by Charles D. Russell in *Everybody's Magazine* and its subsequent whitewash by the Bureau of Corporations. Bryan's "extermination" doctrine was followed by Richard T. Ely's *Monopolies and Trusts* (1900) and John Moody's *The Truth About the Trusts* (1902). In "A Remedy for Trusts," *Public Opinion*, 39 (April 29, 1905), 645–648, Bryan reiterated the suggestion he first made at the Chicago Anti-Trust Conference of 1899, that "monopoly could be regulated by fixing the proportion of the total product which any corporation can produce or control . . . to 75%, or 50%, or even 25%, or at any other per cent, and that the control of more than the stated percentage should prevent the granting of a license or forfeiture of a license already granted." La Follette placed the degree of control at 40%. See *Commoner*, August 25, 1905.

Chautauqua platform. In "Faith," which attracted Woodrow Wilson to him, he said:

> Have faith in mankind. Mankind deserves to be trusted. There is something good in everyone and that good responds to sympathy. If you speak to the multitude and they do not respond, do not despise them but rather examine what you have said. If you speak from your heart you will speak to their hearts, and they can tell quickly whether you are interested in them or simply in yourself.
>
> The heart of mankind is sound, the sense of justice is universal. Trust it, appeal to it, but do not violate it. People differ in race, characteristics, in national tradition, in language, in ideas of government, and in forms of religion but at heart they are very much alike. I fear the plutocracy of wealth, I respect the plutocracy of learning, I thank God for the democracy of the heart.[79]

Part of the social transformation Bryan demanded was the proscription of war. Of particular note, in addition to his "cooling off" treaty plan and the suggestion that war should not be declared without a popular referendum except in case of actual invasion, was his demand that money be made contraband. The idea was not new, but it was supported by many who believed, as he later put it, that money was the worst kind of contraband because it controlled all other contraband, and that its control would do much to prevent the *continuance* of war.[80] Moreover, his disappointment with the results of the Hague Conference of 1907 led to his demand for unilateral United States action toward peace. The United States should announce that it would not use its navy for the collection of private debts. "This would be a beginning. Nation after nation would follow," and a public opinion would be formed which in time would compel all nations to abstain from wars for the collection of such debts.[81]

Bryan earned most of his annual income—about $1000 a week— during the crowded summer months when he spoke at Chautauqua and other meetings. Letters to Charles Bryan show that he was investing heavily in government bonds, for he refused to buy corporate securities,[82] and that he kept a sharp eye open for real estate bargains as he

[79] *Commoner*, July 19, 1907.

[80] Lawrence A. Calvo to Bryan, April 19, 1907, Bryan Papers; Willis J. Abbot to Bryan, April 29, 1907, in *Commoner*, May 3, 1907; Curti, "Bryan and World Peace," pp. 141–142.

[81] *Commoner*, October 11, 1907.

[82] Bryan to C. W. Bryan, telegram, August 26, 1907, Merchants Loan and Trust Company, Chicago, to Bryan, August 29, 1907, Silas Bryan Papers.

toured the country. He consistently refused to speak for pay on Sundays and often insisted upon paying his own expenses and more when invited to address patriotic gatherings or charitable or religious institutions. He had his set speeches but was still a masterful extemporizer. Those who knew him from his leaner years were accustomed to his manner—to his handshaking with the tremendous crowds that greeted and applauded him, the hand held high to quiet the audience so that he might speak, the vigor of his delivery and gestures, his everlasting idealism and love of humanity, his ability to end a strenuous day with a smile. Yet there were certain differences. In 1896 he had appeared as an ordinary if vocal mortal. Now he was watched by a corps of detectives and policemen in plain clothes. A heckler would be seized and locked up. To some at least he seemed to show the influence of long continued adulation and constant appearance in the limelight, to reveal himself a little theatrical and self-conscious of the important place he occupied in the public mind. At Chautauqua, those interested in the problems of the hour, particularly in how he would solve great economic problems, were disappointed. While the injection of a vital streak of piety may have done his hearers some good, his "Value of an Ideal," "Prince of Peace," "Faith," "Man," "Missions," and "The Price of a Soul" certainly did not appeal to the many Jews who came to hear him or to the larger number in his audiences who failed to find fresh light on "the mystery of life" that had been thrashed over by expert theologians for two thousand years without arriving at a definite conclusion. Moreover, he was criticized by even such supporters as Watterson for mixing a lecturing business with politics.[83] Nonetheless, Bryan proved that he could simultaneously engage in lucrative lecturing, edit a newspaper, organize the Democracy for a national campaign, provide its doctrine, and win unique recognition as one of the few men in American history to receive a third nomination from a major party.

[83] Washington *Times*, April 15, 1907; Washington *Evening Star*, April 15, 1907; Bryan, Lincoln Day Address, April 14, 1907, copy in Bryan Papers; E. F. Baldwin, *The Philosopher*, I, 99–103; W. J. Bryan, *The Speeches of William Jennings Bryan*, II, 237–238.

CHAPTER 16

"Shall the People Rule?"

I

"THREE YEARS ago we were united on the wrong side," Bryan told the faithful early in 1907. Believing that the small-town middle classes as well as the farmers of the South and West were "on fire" for a progressive revolution, he said that either the "radical" of 1896 had grown "conservative," or "something had happened to a lot of people." Again, "the radicalism of 1896 has become the conservatism of 1907. . . . The Chicago platform, denounced and laughed at by many, is so grown in favor that a Republican president has won his greatest popularity by the adoption of the principles described in that platform." [1] He rejected Thomas E. Watson's invitation to confer with him and William Randolph Hearst lest the meeting "be construed as an attempt to organize a new party," [2] spurned government ownership and metallic money as issues,[3] and averred that "The more freely you allow the people to rule, the more quickly will every abuse be remedied." [4]

In keeping with the Social Gospel movement, Bryan also concentrated on the "ethical question," the need for a "moral awakening." Using the slogan "The Brotherhood of Man," he demanded a turning away from the crass materialism of the age and a rebirth of the moral conscience so that men would "love one another instead of running riot after money and emulating men of wealth." According to the Law of Rewards, the rich should contribute generously for social purposes to churches, charities, and educational institutions, not to legislators in order to corrupt them or to foster business practices which violated

[1] *Commoner,* February 8, May 10, 1907. See also L. Satterthwait, "Bryan's Mistake," *The Arena,* 37 (March 1907), 257–259.

[2] Bryan to Watson, January 24, 1907, in C. Vann Woodward, *Tom Watson, Agrarian Rebel,* p. 398; Bryan to Watson, May 16, 1907, Henry Steele Commager Papers; Watson to Roosevelt, December 16, 1907, Theodore Roosevelt Papers; *Commoner,* June 14, 21, 28, July 12, 26, 1907.

[3] Charles W. to W. J. Bryan, July 13, 15, 1907, Silas Bryan Papers.

[4] *Commoner,* March 1, 8, 15, May 10, 24, June 14, 21, 1907; Bascom N. Timmons, *Portrait of an American: Charles G. Dawes,* pp. 141–142.

moral as well as statute law. Legitimate businessmen should separate themselves from predatory associates and "join the masses in putting an end to exploitation. . . ." The economic problem of the day was the readjustment of rewards, or "the more equitable distribution of wealth." [5] In a tilt with Joseph Pulitzer early in 1908 he extended his "conflict of interest" from the business-political world to that of the publishing-political world. The *World,* he said, was out to wreck the chances of a Democrat's being elected President and represented certain "special interests." While the editor could not be prevented from giving advice, he indicated that such advice could be judged better if Pulitzer made known what pecuniary interest, if any, he had in "railroad stocks or bonds and what in corporations commonly known as trusts." [6]

Reverting to an old practice, Bryan put principles before personalities and offered the people the names of George Gray, Woodrow Wilson, Governor Joseph W. Folk of Missouri, and Governor John A. Johnson of Minnesota as presidential candidates. He fooled no one, but at least he offered his best slate to date. Furthermore, he asserted that the sectional argument was no longer effective: Southerners should be considered, for he wanted the most available man on the best possible platform. He gave adequate coverage in *The Commoner* to Hearst's new Independence League, which drew its membership largely from dissident Democrats and which Hearst controlled more completely than Charles F. Murphy did Tammany, but did not add Hearst to the list of available candidates and ventured the prediction that members of the League would vote Democratic in 1908, just as Populists had done in 1896 and 1900.[7] As for the Republicans, why did they not take a proved reformer like Robert La Follette rather than William Howard Taft? What had Taft done to indicate that he was a reformer? What assurance did Roosevelt have that as President he would oppose predatory wealth and monopoly? [8] "What is his record?" he asked Josephus Daniels, and then answered his own question: he was a judge whose decisions had aroused the hostility of labor, a governor

[5] *Commoner,* October 11, 1907.

[6] *Ibid.,* June 28, 1907, January 10, February 14, 1908; New York *World,* January 11, February 4, 6, 1908; Edward A. Ross, *Seventy Years of It: An Autobiography,* p. 110. For the crass materialism of these years see Walter Lord, *The Good Years,* pp. 104–119, 256–271, 320–330, and Edward A. Ross, *Sin and Society, An Analysis of Latter-Day Iniquity* (Boston, 1907).

[7] *Commoner,* April 26, May 3, October 18, 1907; W. A. Swanberg, *Citizen Hearst: A Biography of William Randolph Hearst,* p. 254.

[8] *Commoner,* February 21, April 19, May 3, 1907.

of the Philippines who had made the Filipinos unhappy with American rule, a Secretary of War who had made himself popular with neither the soldiers nor the country at large. "If Mr. Taft attempts to run on his official record he will find it is important as his platform is or as his present speeches are," he concluded.[9] Bryan's brother Charles, who painstakingly studied Taft's speeches, wrote that Taft "seems [not] to favor . . . anything at present but standing pat. His speech [at Columbus, Ohio, on August 20, 1907] reminded me of what Tillman said about lynching in the South, that he did not endorse it but that he approved of it." [10]

Conservative Democrats proceeded as though Bryan were not in the running. David Bennett Hill would not even speak publicly and believed it "time for reconciliation and forgiveness." [11] The New Jersey editor of the New York *Tribune* told Woodrow Wilson that he found "little sentiment in favor of the nomination of Mr. Bryan, many of whom I have met declaring that you were their choice for the nomination and quite a few deprecating the fact that the nomination of Mr. Bryan was likely . . . unless steps were quickly taken to prevent it." [12] Others were less gentle. On April 14, 1907, George Harvey referred to Bryan as "a peerless leader who hobbles like a cripple in the wake of his successful rival, gathering as he goes the few scraps that are left of his own fallacies." [13] Wilson held similar sentiments, as revealed by his writing Adrian Joline on April 26: "Would that we could do something, at once dignified and effective, to knock Mr. Bryan once and for all into a cocked hat!" [14] Although Wilson was beginning his metamorphosis from conservative to progressive, he resisted all importunities that he run and finally told Harvey that his support for presidential candidate was not desired, in part because J. P. Morgan presumably owned the publications Harvey edited. Thus no formidable conservative threat challenged Bryan's as yet unannounced candidacy.

On August 16 a stock market panic heralded spreading economic un-

---

[9] Bryan to Daniels, n.d., but 1908, Josephus Daniels Papers; see also W. J. Bryan, "How Could the United States, if Necessary, Give Up Its Colonies?" *World To-Day*, 14 (February 1908), 151–154 and "Why the Philippines Should be Independent," *Everybody's Magazine*, 19 (November 1908), 640d–f.

[10] C. W. Bryan to W. J. Bryan, August 21, 1907, Silas Bryan Papers.

[11] Hill to George Raines, February 2, 1907, George S. Bixby Papers.

[12] W. F. Keohan to Wilson, January 7, 1907, Woodrow Wilson Papers.

[13] *Commoner*, April 26, 1907.

[14] William Jennings Bryan and Mary Baird Bryan, *The Memoirs of William Jennings Bryan*, p. 332.

rest. During October and November, by marshaling the resources of the respectable banking companies, J. P. Morgan demonstrated his leadership in American finance and helped create the community of interest, or "money trust," that continued for years thereafter. Millions in government funds placed in national banks and otherwise made available to the business community found their way into the stock market and provided only temporary relief. On October 29, Roosevelt had echoed Bryan in urging the criminal prosecution of businessmen lawbreakers. Then, probably deceived by assurances received, he promised immunity from prosecution under the Sherman Act and blessed United States Steel's acquisition of the Tennessee Coal and Iron Company.[15]

Although he realized that the inflexible currency system was a contributory cause of the panic of 1907, Roosevelt had no intention of fighting for the "elastic" currency plan he presented to the last session of the Fifty-ninth Congress. However, his annual message contained so many distinctly Bryanite suggestions that the resentment against him of the Republican as well as of the Democratic business community almost matched that against Bryan in 1896. When Congress failed to act on his reforms, he loosed a Bryanesque charge in a special message of January 31, 1908 against the "rottenness" of the American business structure, called the federal courts barriers to economic and social reform, and asserted that big unionism was as inevitable as big business. Bryan Democrats in Congress applauded him while Republicans sat glumly, and Bryan again arose to the President's support, saying that his "brave message" was a "call to arms" to which his own followers should respond.[16]

Except for tariff reform and currency reform, Roosevelt had restated demands Bryan had been making for eighteen years. Despite all his hue and cry and illusion of great activity, however, his measurable domestic achievements included only the Elkins Act (1903); the Hep-

[15] Chicago *Record-Herald,* October 27, 1907; *Commoner,* November 1, 1907; Lewis Corey, *The House of Morgan,* Chapter 17; Harold U. Faulkner, *The Quest for Social Justice, 1898–1914,* pp. 38–43; James W. Gerard, *My First Eighty Years,* pp. 111–133; William Henry Harbaugh, *Power and Responsibility: The Life and Times of Theodore Roosevelt,* pp. 311–316; Matthew Josephson, *The President Makers: The Culture of Politics and Leadership in an Age of Enlightenment, 1896–1919,* pp. 247–255; Henry F. Pringle, *Theodore Roosevelt, a Biography,* pp. 432–445; Mark Sullivan, *Our Times: The United States, 1900–1925,* III, 503–511; Robert H. Wiebe, "The House of Morgan and the Executive, 1905–1913," *American Historical Review,* 55 (October 1959), 49–57, and "Business Disunity and the Progressive Movement, 1901–1914," *Mississippi Valley Historical Review,* 44 (March 1958), 664–685.

[16] Harbaugh, *Roosevelt,* pp. 343–348.

burn, Pure Food and Drugs, Meat Inspection, and Employers' Liability acts (1906); the 1907 act prohibiting corporation contributions to campaign funds; and the 1908 law limiting trainmen's hours. He prosecuted the trusts, but they were more numerous and powerful at the end than at the beginning of his term. He could show no step taken on one single issue that the Populists and Bryan had not already advocated, nor one that the progressives had not settled in the Midwestern states; and he confessed that, with respect to action against railroads and trusts, he had "let up in every case where I have had any possible excuse for so doing." Roosevelt was potent, nevertheless, just where Bryan was impotent—in his successful dramatizing and nationalizing of the Progressive movement, in his merging of the Jeffersonian and Hamiltonian traditions, and in his ability to be practical, to compromise, rather than like Bryan or La Follette to be relentless on principles, to annihilate the enemy rather than merely to defeat him. Given the conditions under which he operated, in which conservative state legislatures sent to the Senate men purblind to elementary considerations of economic and social justice, not above using their position to promote their own interests, and self-righteously invoking the doctrine of laissez faire against reformist efforts to regulate big business or tax wealth, he had dared much to make the government control of business a "political issue." He violated his own Darwinian view of the inevitability of big business growth, and by using the federal power to regulate grave and ominous corporate abuses beyond state control, he ran afoul of the supporters of states' rights and earned criticism from those who believed that federal control would be but a few steps ahead of government ownership.[17]

Much of Roosevelt's alarming radicalism was really blustering, for he was nearing the end of his official power; and Congress, increasingly opposed to him, took his apostrophes to progressivism with a grain of salt, for he may have intended them to be "just for the record." Nevertheless, the continuing exposures by muckrakers of the "rottenness" of the business world he had condemned and the fateful juncture of agrarian and urban middle class reform pressure shook the Old Guard into realizing that their refusal to submit to some control might split their party or—as Bryan predicted—provoke Roosevelt from moderately positive action to an explosive assault upon their iniquities and the imposition of federal supervision as the only alternative to socialism if not popular violence.

[17] *Ibid.*, pp. 149–165; *Commoner*, December 6, 13, 1907.

As Bryan knew they would, the Republicans fought each other in Congress, particularly over the currency issue. To preserve the value of investments and stave off additional bankruptcies by increasing the circulation, Nelson W. Aldrich would permit banks to deposit with the Treasury the bonds of states, cities, and railroads. Eastern Republicans approved, Western Republicans split. Throughout the spring of 1908 La Follette led the West in opposing any bill that would profit the wicked railroads and in demanding that a law be passed for the physical valuation of their properties. Probably to insure the nomination of Taft, Aldrich and William B. Allison deleted the railroad bond provision just before La Follette was to deliver a prepared speech. La Follette then charged Aldrich with seeking to head off genuine currency reform. Albert J. Beveridge's suggestion of a commission to study the entire monetary system, although opposed by La Follette, was approved by Aldrich and passed the Senate. Chairman Charles N. Fowler of the House Banking and Currency Committee preferred his own asset currency bill. The House thereupon rejected the Aldrich bill and passed the radically different Vreeland bill. With the Republican national convention only a month off, the expected happened in a face-saving compromise, the Aldrich-Vreeland bill. This made possible associations of cooperating banks which could issue notes secured by either certain classes of securities or by commercial paper and also provided for the creation of a Monetary Commission. Despite La Follette's historic filibuster, the bill passed and Aldrich was appointed chairman of the commission. Now the Republicans could meet in convention and claim to be currency reformers.[18]

Bryan saw more clearly than most men the dangers of a banking system in which each bank operated independently and could neither give nor receive support from others in times of crisis. As he had said as early as 1893, a guarantee fund raised by a tax on deposits should be used to save insolvent banks, give assurance to the depositors, and prevent the spread of fear. Since the Taft plan for postal savings banks permitted no deposits greater than $250, he believed his own plan better. Moreover, he desired "to release the public from the grip of Wall Street" and therefore suggested that both national and state laws be passed to outlaw gambling on boards of trade, deals in futures and options, and bucket shops. Finally, since speculation in securities was

[18] Nathaniel Stephenson, *Nelson W. Aldrich,* pp. 324–341; Belle Case La Follette and Fola La Follette, *Robert La Follette,* II, 239–256.

not a part of the legitimate banking business, it must be separated from it. All these measures were eventually adopted—by the New Deal.

II

ROOSEVELT invited Bryan to the Conference of Governors and other representatives from the states held in Washington on May 13–14, 1908 to discuss the conservation of natural resources. Although he agreed with Roosevelt on conservation and lauded the step taken toward federal-state cooperation, Bryan disagreed with Roosevelt's centralizing tendencies and his assertion of executive leadership which usurped the power of congressional authority, saying:

> I am a strict constructionist if that means to believe that the Federal Government is one of delegated powers and that constitutional limitation should be carefully observed. I am jealous of any encroachment upon the rights of the States, believing that the States are as indestructible as the Union is indissoluble. It is, however, entirely consistent with this theory to believe, as I do believe, that it is just as imperative that the general Government shall discharge the duties delegated to it, as it is that the States shall exercise the power reserved to them. *There is no twilight zone between the Nation and the States, in which exploiting interests can take refuge from both.*

He received great applause for his "twilight zone" and was congratulated by the President, Elihu Root, and several other members of the cabinet for his stand in favor of irrigation, forest preservation, and expenditures for similar works of "permanent improvement." [19]

While Roosevelt's appreciation of Bryan increased toward the end of his term, conservative Democrats like Grover Cleveland and David Bennett Hill refused to support him or, like Woodrow Wilson, damned him long before knowing exactly what his platform would contain. Cleveland refused to join him and thus cement party unity, urged the nomination of Governor John A. Johnson of Minnesota, and told Charles S. Hamlin that "conservative and sane tariff reform" was the party's "path to success." [20] Henry Watterson also believed that John-

---

[19] Bryan to C. W. Bryan, May 15, 1908, Silas Bryan Papers; C. E. Condra, "Personal Observations and Experiences Relating to William Jennings Bryan," Ms., Nebraska State Historical Society.

[20] Cleveland to Charles S. Hamlin, October 22, 1907, Hamlin Papers; Josephus Daniels, *Editor in Politics*, p. 553; Allan Nevins, *Grover Cleveland: A Study in Courage*, p. 763; Denis Tilden Lynch, *Grover Cleveland: A Man Four Square*, pp. 539–540.

son could beat Bryan.[21] Johnson had ample funds, a following that disliked Bryan and his idealism—what Archie Butt referred to as "that Pharisaical Methodistical manner of the Peerless Leader"—and the interest of state bosses like Thomas Taggart and Roger Sullivan and of some Tammany leaders. He had supported Bryan twice. A vote getter, he had been twice elected governor by his fellow Scandinavians, mostly Republicans. A fighter, he said that he would not, as Parker had in 1904, "take nine baths a day in the Hudson [referring to Parker's frequent swimming in the river] and say the party was clean and let it go at that. If I am nominated, I'll take Bryan into the campaign with me and he'll have to show his hand in every state." "Johnson for President" headquarters were established in New York and Chicago and a publicity campaign was launched, but in his state convention in April he was crushed beneath a Bryan steamroller directed by two progressive lawyers, Fred Pike and James Manahan. He was brought out too late, and no one really bestirred himself in his behalf until Bryan's nomination was inevitable.[22]

While David Bennett Hill would not engage actively in politics he saw Roosevelt "still pursuing the *evil tenor* of his ways" and urged others to speak out against "centralizing, and in favor of legitimate state rights" and in opposition "to Roosevelt's sensationalism and hysterical legislation" and to "the colonial system of government." But it would do no good to rehash the fight in the Democratic convention of 1904. He favored letting bygones be bygones.[23] Speaking in Chicago, Wilson criticized both Roosevelt and Bryan for their demands for governmental regulation. Later in Bermuda he said he opposed woman suffrage because women would be likely to be led away by charm of manner and speech. "I have even wished at times that every fool could be also a knave instead of being, as they often are, people who possessed attractive manners and excellent intentions," he

[21] Joseph Frazier Wall, *Henry Watterson, Reconstructed Rebel,* p. 256.

[22] Watterson to Harvey, February [?], 1910, W. F. Johnson, *George Harvey, "A Passionate Patriot,"* p. 179; Arthur W. Dunn, *From Harrison to Harding, A Personal Narrative, Covering a Third of a Century, 1888–1921,* II, 50–51; James Manahan, *Trials of a Lawyer,* pp. 98, 103–104; *The Letters of Archie Butt,* pp. 6–7 (May 15, 1908); Winifred G. Helmes, *John A. Johnson, the People's Governor: A Political Biography,* pp. 226–241, 250–254, 258–265. "Poor John, poor John," Bryan was reported to have said when told of Johnson's presidential aspirations (Arthur W. Dunn, *Gridiron Nights,* p. 192).

[23] Hill to Francis Burton Harrison, February 7, 1908, Hill to William F. Sheehan, February 20, 1908, Hill Letterbooks, Bixby Papers.

added. "Take Mr. Bryan, for example. He is the most charming and lovable of men personally, but foolish and dangerous in his theoretical beliefs." To those like Joseph Pulitzer who spoke of his being a candidate he replied that "There is evidently not a ghost of a chance of defeating Bryan." He spurned with asperity the nomination as Vice President and declined an invitation to speak at a dinner where Bryan would be present.[24]

Rather than replying to his critics Bryan busied himself with organizational details. When Congress convened, on December 2, 1907, he consulted with and advised its Democratic leaders. On December 22, Bryan's brother Charles, who had cross-indexed the country, wrote that he was unhappy with the political situation in Minnesota and several Eastern states. On January 22, 1908, he reported a long talk with Norman Mack and other members of the National Committee. These men were anxious to have Bryan stop his fight against Sullivan and other "corporation Democrats," but Charles believed they would throw their machines against Bryan the moment he let up his opposition and advised him to keep up the fight. Bryan replied that he had dictated letters of advice for friends to follow in their state conventions and had suggested the organization of Democratic Clubs in each county. The election, he believed, must be won in the Western and Middle Western states. He discounted the East but concluded that "If we could get rid of Sullivan and Taggart as national committeemen, we could carry Indiana and possibly Illinois, and it would also make our fight easier in the Western states, and also in Nebraska, Kansas, South Dakota, and Ohio." [25]

During the early months of 1908 Bryan's mail increased to more than three thousand letters a day and his outgoing to four thousand, and Charles Bryan sent extra thousands of *The Commoner* into rural districts. Bryan "happened" to visit state after state just as plans were being formulated to oppose him. With great skill he frustrated most of them, often by getting young progressives to run against older con-

[24] Newspaper Clipping, March 10, 1908, Wilson Papers; Ray Stannard Baker, *Woodrow Wilson: Life and Letters*, II, 276, III, 37; J. P. Barrett, *Joseph Pulitzer and His "World,"* pp. 298, 306; Dunn, *From Harrison to Harding*, II, 7; Johnson, *Harvey*, pp. 132–135; James Kerney, *The Political Education of Woodrow Wilson*, pp. 32–33.

[25] C. W. Bryan to Bryan, December 22, 1907, January 22, 1908, Bryan telegram to C. W. Bryan, January 25, 1908, Silas Bryan Papers; *Commoner*, December 13, 1907. See B. O. Flower, "Bryan and the Would-Be Wreckers of the Democratic Party," *The Arena*, 39 (March 1908), 344–349.

servatives, who thereupon supported him as a matter of self-preservation. Moreover, he was as popular with the Democratic masses as Roosevelt was with the Republican, and to be suspected of disloyalty to him, as Arthur Dunn put it, was "almost like buying a ticket to private life." [26] As a result, convention after convention endorsed him.

On March 5 at the Nebraska Democratic state convention held in Omaha, Bryan sounded a note of hope based on the growing popularity of Democratic doctrines, the unity of the Democratic party, and the "moral awakening" brought about by the Democratic appeal, which was converting many Republicans. By frankly admitting that many of his doctrines had originated with the Populists he won their endorsement. The latter concluded that "Populists in Nebraska have but one point toward which they are working—the election of W. J. Bryan," and fusion was so close that a Populist was elected a delegate to the Denver Democratic convention. His anxiety about Nebraska nevertheless caused Bryan to send for a Western Nebraska lawyer named Arthur Mullen, who was recommended to him by his brother-in-law and general manager, Thomas S. Allen. "I am going to be a candidate again this year," Bryan told Mullen confidentially. "I think I shall be elected, but whether I am or not, I want to carry my state. I failed to carry it in 1900, and I don't want it to happen again. Will you be my Nebraska campaign manager?" Mullen accepted. While he did the field work, Christian M. Gruenther organized clubs known as the Bryan Volunteers and ran their machinery. Between them they organized seventy counties and took over what was left of the Populist organization.[27] George Fred Williams, meantime, was instrumental in getting the Massachusetts Democrats to endorse him, by three to one, but in New York, where Tammany won only after a particularly hard and rough fight, Parker was chosen to head an uninstructed delegation containing a majority against him. "It still looks like Taft's nomination by a Republican convention, although the nomination will not be very satisfactory to the Republican party," said Hill in April.

[26] Dunn, *From Harrison to Harding*, II, 51.

[27] Arthur Mullen, *Western Democrat*, pp. 129–130; J. Sterling Morton and Albert Watkins, *An Illustrated History of Nebraska*, I, 278; Addison E. Sheldon, *Nebraska: The Land and the People*, I, 829–830; Edward Stanwood, *A History of the Presidency from 1897 to 1909*, pp. 158–161. Seeing nothing in Bryan but a Democrat, the middle-of-the-road majority in the Populist national convention held on April 2–3 in St. Louis killed proposals to name him and nominated the "pure Populist," Tom Watson.

"Nevertheless, our party seems to be in worse condition than theirs. It is always so. . . ." [28]

Since Taft and Bryan were practically nominated, interest centered on the issues they would adopt. The major Eastern newspapers again opposed Bryan. The New York *Times* declared that "Republican ruin of prosperity is a better cry than Democratic promises of the millennium." Nor could Bryan obtain New York's votes by taking a New Yorker for his running mate, for they "distrust him, they fear him, they would regard his election as a national calamity." The *Times* then resurrected the platform of 1896. "There should be no compromise. Let Bryan nominate himself upon a platform of hostility to the courts, hostility to property interests, class legislation for labor, the income tax, popular election of senators, the initiative and referendum, confiscation, and all the other doctrines of Bryanite radicalism. . . . [The] election over, people will exclaim 'Thank goodness there is an end of that.' " [29]

The New York *World* practically went over to Taft, charging that under Bryan's leadership the Democratic party had become only a shadow of a once militant organization, and Pulitzer made no bones about his bitter opposition to a third nomination. "The New York *World* is willing that Mr. Bryan should be the Republican candidate for President. It is as a Democratic candidate that we object to him," he said, and in a play on 16 to 1 listed sixteen men he preferred to Bryan. As the leader, yes, the dictator, of the Democratic party for twelve years, Bryan had led it to three successive defeats. Of Jefferson's twenty-eight years of leadership the party had been in power for twenty-four; of Jackson's sixteen years for twelve; of Bryan's twelve "not a single day, a single hour, a single minute." "As an orator . . . you have few peers. As an agitator you are without a rival . . . [but] you seem to be laboring under the delusion that . . . political reform in the United States began with you and will end with you. There could be no greater error," said Pulitzer.[30]

By June 30 Bryan had the support of more than two thirds of the instructed delegates and a Committee on Resolutions that would give

[28] Hill to Denis O'Brien, April 22, 1908, Bixby Papers.

[29] New York *Times*, July 2, 3, 1908.

[30] New York *World*, July 3, 1908; C. D. Seitz, *Pulitzer*, pp. 327–328; B. O. Flower, "Bryan and the Senegambian in the New York *World's* Woodpile," *The Arena*, 39 (April 1908), 464–466, and "New York *World's* Gallant Fight for Plutocracy," *ibid.*, 39 (May 1908), 620–622.

him whatever he wanted regardless of Pulitzer, Tammany, or anyone else. Of all his issues, Eastern conservatives feared most his pronouncements on injunctions and trusts. To keep his "ultra-radicalism" out of the platform became the stated objective of at least the Pennsylvania and New York delegations. Easterners knew that they could not defeat him, but they argued that he should not be named because he could not be elected. Therefore Parker, slated for the Committee on Resolutions, prepared a resolution extolling Grover Cleveland, who died on June 24, and Martin Littleton prepared to make a fight on the floor of the convention against anything resembling a radical platform.[31]

Here was meat for a fight. No Democratic convention could praise Cleveland without disparaging Bryan, and Bryan would undoubtedly construe the Parker resolution as a personal insult. Moreover, he had defenders. Watterson had flirted with Johnson. Now he lashed out against the "ghoulish attack" on the Commoner and the "attempt to drag the body of President Cleveland from its newly-made grave to create tumult in the convention in the interest of the Murphy-Connors and Belmont-Ryan crowds. . . ." Aroused, other Bryan friends vowed that they would substitute for Parker's a resolution uncritical of Bryan. On the first day of the convention itself, a watered-down version of Parker's was adopted, after which the delegates recessed the proceedings for several hours out of respect for Cleveland.[32]

Westerners in general applauded the planks foreshadowed by Bryan's Nebraska platform and believed them quite conservative. But Bryan lost the support of those who believed he no longer represented the liberalism which bound Western Democrats and Populists together when it was whispered that he had made some kind of a deal with Eastern, particularly New York, interests. According to Richard F. Pettigrew, Bryan had asked him to see Sullivan and Murphy and Hearst's editorial writer, Arthur Brisbane. He was to tell Sullivan and Murphy that in return for their support "they should receive due and proper consideration if he were elected; that they would be consulted about offices in their localities and their political importance recognized." Sullivan and Murphy pledged support, but Brisbane did not.

---

[31] New York *Times,* July 1, 3, 1908; New York *World,* July 1, 2, 1908; *Rocky Mountain News,* July 3, 1908. Among other things, the Parker resolution stated that Cleveland had "respected the integrity of the courts" and "maintained the public credit and stood firm as a rock in defense of sound principles of finance."

[32] Louisville *Courier-Journal,* July 3, 1908; New York *Evening Post,* July 8, 1908; New York *Times,* July 3, 8, 1908; *Rocky Mountain News,* July 5, 1908.

Angered by Bryan's campaign against colonialism in 1900 and his failure to support him for the nomination in 1904, and charging that he was as conservative now as the Republicans were, Hearst had Brisbane say that "Bryan is an ignorant man. You need in the White House a good brain, and you don't need a mouth. Bryan is a mouth." [33]

In January 1908 a group of Eastern, mostly New York City, Democrats proposed to have a delegation of the most influential men in the party ask Bryan to step aside. When told the story, Bryan retorted, "Men who come to me to speak for the Democratic party must show their credentials." He knew that only those who had opposed him earlier would be bold enough to make such a demand and that among his supporters there existed the feeling that "we would rather go down to defeat with Bryan than win with another man," a feeling based on the curious logic that the more often a man was defeated the more reason to renominate him. Bryan then proceeded to Washington to "bell the cat" of the rumored opposition to him by Democrats in Congress. He found no such opposition and was thus more than ever the leader of his party.[34]

Henceforth Bryan's attitude toward opponents was dictatorial. At a meeting of Southerners, Senator John Daniel of Virginia baited him on government ownership. He replied that it was no longer an issue. "You of the South are opposed to government ownership because you are afraid your Jim Crow laws against the Negroes will be abolished by the general government." Such "personal" objections should not stand in the way of "great national reforms." "You people also complain," he continued, "because I have declared for the initiative and referendum. That ought to be an issue. I will drive every man out of the Democratic party who does not support it." In keeping with his word, his final break with Joseph Bailey of Texas came over this issue. When ex-Senator James H. Berry of Arkansas said he made defeat inevitable by adopting "impossible" issues and suggested that he stick to issues that would win, he retorted heatedly, "Win! Win! That's it! You want to win! You would sacrifice principle for success. I would not. I would not desire to be elected if the principles I stood for were not incorporated in the platform. I am not sure that defeat is not

[33] Daniels, *Editor in Politics*, p. 550; Mullen, *Western Democrat*, p. 131; Richard F. Pettigrew, *Imperial Washington*, pp. 259–260; Swanberg, *Hearst*, p. 257; Wall, *Watterson*, pp. 256–257.

[34] Chicago *Record*, July 2, 1908; Dunn, *From Harrison to Harding*, II, 71; Stanwood, *History of the Presidency*, p. 157.

better than victory, if victory comes with the sacrifice of principles. . . . I intend, if I am the candidate, that the principles shall be preserved."

"But," said Senator Daniel, "some of the things you have stood for in the past have proved wrong, and you may prove wrong again."

"I have always been right," Bryan asserted.

"What's the use?" Governor Claude Swanson later asked. "Bryan is sure to be nominated, and sure to be defeated. Let us hope that will end him and that we can then elect another man four years later." [35]

Sure of his nomination, Bryan sought to harmonize the conservative and radical wings of his party. He would agree to an Eastern vice presidential candidate and Western national chairman or vice versa, and he left the vice presidential field open to a reportedly thirty-nine possible running mates. Between July 1 and 4 many important party leaders visited him at Fairview. Ignatius J. Dunn wanted advice on the speech that would place him in nomination; Henry D. Clayton, slated to be the permanent chairman, was worried about the reportedly fifty-nine contests to be brought before the National Committee; and all sought enlightenment on his choice for Vice President. He said nothing lest he be criticized for attempting to dictate to the convention. On July 4, however, he stated explicitly that he would reject the nomination if the platform did not contain a campaign contributions publicity plank. When Herman Ridder, of the New York *Staats Zeitung*, said he could not carry New York and should withdraw in favor of one who could win, he simply replied that he could win with or without New York. Ridder, who could do so much to influence the foreign-born vote, then said he would support him, if nominated, if he adopted a conservative platform in which the tariff and trusts were made the paramount issues and wood pulp and printing paper were put on the free list. According to Ridder, Bryan accepted the free wood pulp and printing paper plank written by him.[36]

Tammany arrived in Denver more than four hundred strong but proved no match for the Bryan forces. With the prompt approval of Taft by "Wall Street circles," Bryan knew he could beat the conservative Eastern and Southern leaders who had led the party to defeat in 1904. Following his instructions, James Dahlman, his preconvention campaign manager, sat for more than three hours on the night of July

[35] Dunn, *From Harrison to Harding*, II, 47–49. See Sam Hanna Acheson, *Joe Bailey, the Last Democrat*, pp. 241–242.

[36] New York *World*, July 3, 1908; *Rocky Mountain News*, July 4, 1908.

3 listening to Murphy, Daniel F. Cohalan, Louis Nixon, and other New Yorkers, and left a happy man. The morning newspapers of July 4 announced that "HARMONY IS ASSURED." Murphy repudiated Parker's Cleveland resolution, saying that Parker spoke for himself alone; Bird S. Coler came out strongly for Bryan; and a boom started for New York's supreme court judge, William J. Gaynor, for Vice President, bringing the number of aspirants for this post to forty. Yet Murphy's failure to force Parker out as chairman of the Committee on Resolutions gave rise to the indictment of Bryan's having made a deal with Tammany, else why should Tammany be supporting him? The fact was that Murphy had known for more than a year that Bryan's nomination was inevitable. He had rejected Bourke Cockran's suggestion that New York instruct for Bryan because the heaviest contributors to Tammany were men like August Belmont and Thomas Fortune Ryan, who resented Cockran's lauding of both Bryan and Roosevelt as liberals. Soon Murphy's break with Cockran became final.[37] When Guffey asked Murphy to declare against Bryan, however, Murphy refused to commit himself. Charles Bryan opened headquarters at the Brown Hotel even as Parker himself announced that he would support Bryan, if nominated, and the practical certainty of the election of Governor Charles N. Haskell of Oklahoma as chairman of the subcommittee of seventeen on Resolutions sealed the moderately radical character of the platform.

With Charles now in command at Denver, Bryan began a front porch campaign at Fairview. He beamed upon visiting delegates, blessed them, handed them copies of "The Prince of Peace," and invited them to pass in review before the White House next March 4 —except Guffey. Again breaking his rule not to comment on fights within the party, he vigorously attacked Guffey as a "bushwhacker" who had allied himself with Standard Oil and "deliberately and willfully conspired to defeat what he knew to be the expressed will of the Democrats of Pennsylvania." He already had a hundred delegates more than the two thirds needed to nominate him. As the choice of the rank and file, he concluded, he would personally lead the fight to reform the Pennsylvania organization and unseat Guffey from the National Committee.[38]

Except for various Eastern irreconcilables supporting George Gray,

[37] Mullen, *Western Democrat*, p. 61; James McGurrin, *Bourke Cockran: A Free Lance in American Politics*, pp. 278–284.
[38] *Rocky Mountain News*, July 5, 1908.

Bryan's name was happily acclaimed at Denver. Even Pulitzer conceded that no other aspirant more nearly represented the "Roosevelt type of candidate" than Bryan. Bryan had "kept the faith." While his "excommunication" of Guffey revealed him a boss, his promise that he would do more to carry out Roosevelt's policies than Taft gave him strength with the people.

On July 5 Lincoln's Mayor F. W. "Doc" Brown, a member of the Committee on Resolutions, left for Denver with a platform written by Bryan in conjunction with many party leaders. It was basically a combination of the Oklahoma constitution, the Nebraska state platform, and the program of the American Federation of Labor. Meantime Samuel Gompers and William Mitchell conferred at length with Charles Bryan and Haskell. In June, when an AFL group headed by Gompers offered various labor planks to the Republican national convention, they were treated scurvily by Speaker Joseph G. Cannon, James Van Cleave, president of the National Association of Manufacturers, and others hostile to labor, who jeeringly and brusquely told them to "Go to Denver!" In Denver, Gompers concentrated on the injunction plank, a modification of that in the Nebraska state platform, and was pleased to have most of his ideas accepted.[39] On the evening after the adoption of the platform by the convention, Bryan telephoned Gompers to ask whether he was gratified with the labor plank and to stop at Fairview on his way back East.

In 1904 Bryan had had to fight to change a conservative platform all but adopted and had opposed a conservative candidate. Now he arranged to have the subcommittee on platform telephone him each plank as soon as it was agreed upon. As presented to the full committee, the platform would thus have his prior approval.

Bryan's control over the convention organization was equally strong. Friends in the Credentials Committee contested every important state opposed to him. A caucus of the Pennsylvania delegation spelled defeat for Guffey, and both New York and Illinois proved to be powerless because split. The threat from Hearst's Independence League, now called the Independence Party, was not considered serious, as revealed by Hearst's stating that the nomination for Vice President of Judge Samuel Seabury of New York would win his approval of the Democratic ticket.

[39] Wilfred E. Binkley, *American Political Parties, Their Natural History*, pp. 361–362; Samuel Gompers, *Seventy Years of Life and Labor: An Autobiography*, II, 255–265.

National Chairman Thomas Taggart opened the proceedings at noon on Tuesday, July 7. In about two hours Bryan's power cleared the way for his nomination, the adoption of his platform, the banishment of Guffey, the humiliation of Parker by the defeat of his original resolution praising Cleveland, and the cementing of a Western farmer–Eastern labor coalition. At the same time, however, he lost the support of the "substantial" men of his party and saw Sullivan re-elected to the National Committee.[40]

When the National Committee decided in favor of Guffey and a group of fourteen national committeemen, including New York's, protested the unseating of the Guffey men, Bryan feared the introduction of discord into a heretofore harmonious convention. He therefore wired Charles to have the Credentials Committee note the corruption in Guffey's case but to have rescinded the resolution to unseat him. "Tell them that they can trust me to take care of Guffey. I am sure that I am right about this, and I hope they will be able to look at the matter in the same light." But Haskell had electrified the convention with a sharp attack on Guffey. The day should never come, he said, when Democracy should undertake to harmonize with plutocracy, and he told Guffey to "Go back to your Standard Oil!" Looking aged, trembling with suppressed rage, and wildly gesticulating for support from friends, Guffey heard himself turned down by 615 to 387. Having eaten humble pie on his Cleveland resolution, Parker was red of face as he left the platform at the close of the session, when late leavers saw a defiant Guffey waving farewell to his party from the middle of the hall.[41]

At 5:00 P.M. Haskell read to the subcommittee on platform the suggestions brought by Mayor Brown. The preamble of the Nebraska platform and many of its planks as well were adopted in full. Then Haskell appointed subcommittees on the injunction, tariff, railroads, and guarantee of deposits planks and promised the full committee his report by Thursday, July 9. Now telegrams began flying between Bryan and Charles Bryan.

Unwilling to adjourn while awaiting the committee reports, the delegates had called for oratory. With Towne, Folk, and others absent, the blind Senator Thomas P. Gore of Oklahoma complied. There was

[40] Chicago *Record*, July 7, 1908; Josephson, *President Makers*, pp. 273–274.

[41] Bryan to C. W. Bryan, July 7, 1908, Silas Bryan Papers; New York *Times*, July 8, 1908; H. J. H., "The Democratic Convention," *The Outlook*, 89 (July 1908), 649–650; Edwin Maxey, "The Denver Convention," *The Arena*, 39 (July 1908), 152.

not a single Bryan portrait in the hall, but his casual mentioning of Bryan's name sparked an unpremeditated and spontaneous demonstration which oldsters said beat anything witnessed in twenty years. Denver was of course in the heart of the silver country, and both the delegates and spectators were friendly to Bryan. Except for those from New York, who remained silent and seated, the delegates paraded, danced about with state standards, threw everything light and harmless into the air, and cheered "Bryan! Bryan! Bryan! Bryan!" In the galleries, Ruth Bryan Leavitt and Alice Roosevelt Longworth waved their scarves and cheered. But there developed a purpose in the demonstration. Bryan's "Cross of Gold" speech had been cheered for forty-seven minutes, and that record must be broken. Alice Longworth overheard perspiring delegates inquire from one another if it had "gone over that time yet," and the delegates cheered for eighty-five minutes.[42] Yet when the Sergeant-at-Arms telephoned Bryan the details on the Guffey case and the demonstration, he found him more interested in the progress of the platform than in evidence of his personal popularity.

On Friday, July 10, the third day, keynoter Theodore A. Bell of California dutifully berated the Republican party and permanent chairman Henry D. Clayton delivered an ill-tempered denunciation of President Roosevelt. Nominations proceeded pending the report of the Committee on Resolutions. At about 9:00 P.M., following Bryan's arrangement to have Alabama yield to Nebraska for the first nominating speech, Ignatius J. Dunn of Omaha again blasted the Republicans and averred that the Democracy and the nation needed a man free from corporation influence, of positive convictions and moral courage, one who had faith in the people's capacity to govern and whom the people knew and trusted, one respected in Europe as well as in America, one known as a believer in universal Christian peace, a true progressive, a consistent champion of the reserved rights of the states and a firm believer in the doctrine of the consent of the governed—none other than William Jennings Bryan.[43]

The rush to join the Bryan bandwagon proceeded while fifteen thousand spectators ran rampant in wild confusion for more than an

[42] *Rocky Mountain News*, July 9, 1908; Willis J. Abbot, *Watching the World Go By*, p. 262; Alice Roosevelt Longworth, *Crowded Years*, p. 152; Sullivan, *Our Times*, III, 536, 538–539.

[43] Interview by the author with I. J. Dunn, Omaha, Nebraska, August 17, 1953; printed copy of speech of nomination furnished by Mr. Dunn; New York *Evening Post, Times*, July 10, 1908.

hour. When Dunn mentioned Bryan's name a dove was released. Scores of doves flew overhead as Johnson and Gray men trooped to Bryan headquarters to pledge support. Excellent seconding speeches strengthened the determination of the delegates to endorse Bryan for a third time on the first ballot. Johnson's nomination was cheered for twenty-two minutes, but Gray's bored the impatient crowd. Tammany's Murphy broke the back of the opposition by casting New York's full vote for the Commoner. At 3:40 A.M. on July 11, when the final tally was made, Bryan had 892½ votes while Johnson and Gray divided 105½, and on the motion of Minnesota Bryan's nomination was made unanimous. At 4:34, when told of his nomination, Bryan declared that if he were defeated he would not run again.

By midnight Bryan had known that the platform was just about all he desired. Charles Bryan and Governor Haskell had screened every word before telegraphing the planks to him, and he had spent about forty hours in rewording them. He asserted that "any mention of government ownership would be a mistake" and approved of criticism of Roosevelt's use of patronage to nominate Taft, the Republicans' refusal to accept a campaign contributions plank, and their acceptance of aid from the "favor-seeking corporations." He contributed the sentence, "The Democratic party speaks for the taxpayers; the Republican for the taxeaters." "Be careful that no economic issue is declared paramount," he told Charles. "We have already said that the overshadowing issue is 'Shall the People Rule'; and that this manifests itself in all questions at issue." When the anti-trust plank proved too weak, he wired Charles that he would approve the entire platform less the trust plank, on which he would offer a minority report. When the committee proved obdurate, he appealed to the delegates through Charles: "I am constrained to make this appeal to the convention for an anti-trust plank upon which I can make an honest fight in behalf of the whole people. If the convention votes down this substitute [from the Nebraska state platform] I shall at least have placed myself on record." [44] The committee rewrote the plank to suit him.

After twenty-four hours' work on the platform, Bryan had wired his brother: "How much longer had I better stay up? We are cutting our alfalfa and I shall not be in shape to work in the field unless I get

[44] Telegrams between Bryan and C. W. Bryan, July 8–10, 1908, William Jennings Bryan Papers. Some of the telegrams are printed in Bryan, *Memoirs*, Appendix, pp. 515–516.

some sleep." Charles replied: "How do you like our work? One thing said by our men was that you wanted a good platform and if they could not get it they would have to go before the delegates and ask for it, but all lovely and no bad feeling and no public knowledge. Corporation bunch trying to make changes in important planks. We have situation in hand and can put lid on any time." The alfalfa waited as Bryan continued his directions on other planks—on the Philippines, on direct election of senators as "the gateway to other reforms," on the civil service, on "cooling off" treaties, pensions, waterways, the Panama Canal, irrigation, conservation, a welcome to Oklahoma, states' rights, physical valuation of railroads and telegraphs, postal savings banks, placing the telegraphs under the Interstate Commerce Commission, and especially on the labor plank.[45]

The labor, or injunction, plank gave Bryan the most trouble. He had to placate labor yet avoid the idea that he was a visionary, and the plank proved to be a model of guarded language. It referred to the courts as "the bulwark of our liberties" and stressed the importance of maintaining their dignity before stating that "injunctions should not be issued in any cases in which injunctions would not issue if no industrial dispute were involved," and that jury trials should be provided in cases of direct contempt. Moreover, Bryan demanded an eight-hour day in all government work, a general employers' liability act, and the establishment of a Department of Labor with cabinet rank.

Adequately conservative, the platform was sparked by the leitmotif of the phrase, "Shall the People Rule?" When the Committee on Resolutions completed its sixty hours of labor and reported itself unanimously agreed, it really endorsed a platform in which Bryan's work was manifest in nearly every line. Cheering delegates unanimously approved without debate the fourth platform Bryan had written for his party.

The Vice Presidency hung on Bryan's word, but as late as July 8 he was not sure to whom to turn. "If all opposition is withdrawn [to himself] and the nomination is made unanimous . . . it may be best to take an Eastern man to show our willingness to harmonize," he wired Charles.[46] On Thursday, after Francis B. Harrison, John Mitch-

---

[45] Telegrams between Bryan and C. W. Bryan, July 8, 1908, Bryan Papers; San Francisco *Examiner*, July 11, 1908; Louis G. Geiger, *Joseph W. Folk of Missouri*, pp. 59–74.

[46] Telegram, W. J. Bryan to C. W. Bryan, July 8, 1908, Bryan Papers.

ell, and Ollie James lost interest, Taggart and John E. Lamb began booming John W. Kern, Indiana's favorite son. Early on Friday morning Taggart met for three hours with Sullivan, David R. Francis, James Dahlman, George Fred Williams, Bird Coler, Louis Nixon, and other state leaders. With no good Easterner available, eyes turned to the Middle West. Francis and James declined, saying their states were safe. When Towne released his people to Kern and Clark Howell and Archibald McNeil withdrew, the scales tipped toward Kern. Into conference with Charles Bryan went the rest of the steering committee of the convention—Haskell, Urey Woodson, and James—and Kern, Lamb, and Taggart. Taggart needed Kern's help for re-election as national committeeman, and Kern promised mutual support. After thirty minutes the die was cast.

Kern had been defeated for governor in 1900 and 1904 but had run ahead of Bryan in 1900 and far ahead of Parker in 1904. A plain, honest, unassuming Hoosier celebrated in Booth Tarkington's play *The Man From Home,* Kern epitomized farm life and agrarian morality. Although Bryan said he had no choice, Francis was directed to ask him if Kern would do. Bryan approved. Ollie James, who ran the convention with an iron hand after Clayton's voice gave out, passed Bryan's message along the convention floor, saying "Vote for Kern, boys." While Bryan wired his pleasure to have as a running mate a man in complete harmony with the platform, the New York *Times* commented that the ticket was truly consistent, "for a man twice defeated for the Presidency was at the head of it, and a man twice defeated for governor of his state was at the tail of it." [47]

Evaluation of the Denver platform varied with geography. To the East, in general, Bryan had stopped the clock and turned the party around to face his beaten policies of 1896 and 1900. In defense of conservatism and property, nine out of ten New York dailies and the *Nation, World's Work, Harper's Weekly, The Outlook, Life,* and the *American Review of Reviews,* among other periodicals, preferred Taft to Bryan. Either man would support Roosevelt's policies; therefore the real question for decision was the difference between men, not platforms. Bryan as President would bring a reign of terror, said the New York *Times,* and the New York *Tribune* caustically pointed to the omission of planks on government ownership and direct legislation from the Denver platform. More charitable, the *World* praised

[47] New York *Times,* New York *World, Rocky Mountain News,* July 11, 1908; Claude G. Bowers, *The Life of John Worth Kern,* pp. 156–166.

it as a great improvement over that of 1896 and 1900, but Pulitzer revealed his personal feelings when he wrote the editor, "Bryan is dead as a doornail." [48]

In the West, as reflected by the *Rocky Mountain News*, the Denver platform was regarded as conservatism itself. Roosevelt had adopted many of Bryan's "radical" propositions of 1896 with profit rather than destruction for the country, and he would feel almost as much at home with the platform as Bryan. The country, then, not Bryan, had changed. Paradoxically, one of the most cogent evaluations was that of the New York *Evening Post*. Bryan's third nomination was a momentous thing which it would be folly to ignore. Bryan could not be dispensed with by calling him a charlatan and adventurer. "He has not lifted himself up by his own boot-straps. He has been borne aloft by a great wave of discontent and desire for radical changes, which has swept over a large part of the country. . . . No intelligent survey of the nation's defenses against Bryanism can hide the truth that they have been greatly weakened during the last four years. A party that has appropriated Bryan's ideas can not with great effect attack his person." [49] Most of the other New York papers pronounced Bryan a marvelous and dangerous man, the strongest the Democrats could have named, and concluded that he should not be taken lightly.

III

BRYAN was sanguine of success because his platform should appeal to the farmer and also to labor in the large manufacturing states of the East and Middle West. In one of the most unique developments in American history, he had been promised the support of a labor union. "My hat's off to the Democratic party. . . . The Republicans were given the first opportunity and they ignored us," said Gompers as he left Denver.[50] Stopping off at Fairview on July 13, he promised Bryan his support even though he said he would not take the stump. Prospects of winning the foreign-born also heightened. Pleased with the free wood pulp plank, Ridder wired Bryan that "You may rely on the sincere and earnest support of the New York *Staats Zeitung*." [51]

---

[48] Pulitzer to the editor of the New York *World*, July [?], 1908, Seitz, *Pulitzer*, pp. 330–336; New York *World*, July 11, 13, 16, 1908.

[49] New York *Evening Post*, July 15, 1908.

[50] *Rocky Mountain News*, July 12, 1908.

[51] *Ibid.*, July 13, 1908.

Members of the National Committee who gathered at Fairview to discuss campaign plans with Bryan and Kern pledged themselves to Bryan's plan not to accept contributions from corporations nor to accept contributions of over $100 later than three days before elections; set $10,000 as the limit for individual contributions; and promised the publication of the names of donors of $100 or more by October 15. They also agreed that Bryan would speak only in major cities in the East and Middle West while Kern stumped the East and South.

Seizing upon a visit from a local labor organization on July 17, Bryan delivered the first speech of his campaign. This closely followed his article entitled "My Conception of the Presidency," published in *Collier's Weekly* on July 18. As President he would serve the whole people, not special groups or interests. The Vice President should be a member of the cabinet so that the President could have the benefit of his advice and provide a well-prepared successor. He wanted a Department of Labor headed by a secretary, and he wanted labor unions exempted from the anti-trust laws. Then, to a delegation of local students, he refurbished his moral argument, saying that there was a "divine law of rewards" which stated that everyone would enjoy in proportion "as that person by energy and intelligence contributes to the world." The function of government was to implement this law; the purpose of the Democratic party was to restore the government to its ancient doctrines.[52]

However, Bryan refused to state what part the prohibition question might play in the campaign. Even though county option vied with the guarantee of deposits as the prime Nebraska issue, prohibition was rapidly becoming the most far-reaching and passionately supported reform movement in the South, and George Peabody wrote him that the prohibition wave was so strong that it might grow into an important third party. When James Manahan, of the Speakers' Bureau, told him that many Democratic liquor dealers would vote for him if he would, like Taft, pledge them a square deal, Bryan's jaw grew rigid and he sat erect, stiff, and silent. Then he turned sternly on Manahan and said in low tones, "No, Jim, no. The saloons can't use me. I am against them." Manahan returned to Chicago "feeling as though I had been spanked by my father." [53]

[52] *Ibid.*, July 18, 1908.
[53] *Ibid.*, July 21, August 9, 1908; George Peabody to Bryan, January 28, 1908, George Peabody Papers; Daniels, *Editor in Politics*, pp. 521–525; Mullen, *Western Democrat*, pp. 131–132; Manahan, *Trials of a Lawyer*, p. 113; Dewey W. Grantham,

On July 20 Bryan called upon the Democratic press to raise money by dollar subscriptions, a plan designed to end the power of wealth upon government, and announced that profits of *The Commoner* henceforth to election day would be contributed to his party. His idea that the people would never control the government until they assumed the burden of supplying campaign funds caught on especially in the West, where the Republicans had trouble raising money.

In Chicago on July 25 Bryan won the election of Norman Mack as national chairman. The election of Mack granted recognition to the East, he said, and he promised a personal fight for New York. Mack would establish headquarters in Chicago, with a branch in New York. Despite Josephus Daniels's hunch that Haskell would not be a good appointee, Bryan named him the treasurer. Colonel Moses G. Wetmore, one of the few millionaires who supported him, became chairman of the Finance Committee. The vice chairman of the National Committee, Robert S. Hudspeth of New Jersey, aided by Homer Cummings of Connecticut, headed the New York headquarters, in which Herman Ridder was chairman of the Press Bureau. With few exceptions those in charge of press work had had editorial experience, for Bryan intended to depend less upon oratory than upon the printed word. While not a part of the official organization, yet most effective in getting out letters and literature, was the *Commoner* office in Lincoln.

Bryan did not talk with William Randolph Hearst, who was in the same hotel while attending the first national convention of his Independence Party. Amid red, white, and blue decorations, Hearst excoriated both older parties. "The Democratic vanguard," he said, "is . . . led by a knight arrayed in a motley of modified professions and compromised principles, of altered opinions and of retracted statements. Assuming that Mr. Bryan himself is all his most ardent admirers claim him to be—a great lawyer, an enlightened statesman, an inspired patriot, still a man is known by the company he keeps, and no decent Democrat can tolerate his free companions." Bryan was a "trickster, a trimmer, and a traitor." At the evening session, which nominated Thomas L. Hisgen and John Temple Graves, the Bryanite who tried to bring Bryan's name before the convention caused a riot and narrowly escaped physical violence at the hands of the enraged delegates.[54]

Jr., "Prohibition and the Progressive Movement in the South," unpublished Mss., courtesy Dr. Grantham.

[54] *Rocky Mountain News,* July 25, 28, 1908; B. O. Flower, "Hearst's Attack on

The evening papers of July 28 contained William Howard Taft's long acceptance speech. Taft found most of the Denver planks inconsistent, disingenuous, or destructive. He denounced trial by jury in contempt cases as anarchy and, although saying nothing about how to safeguard the nation's currency system, thoroughly condemned the guarantee of bank deposits, for it would encourage reckless banking practices by relieving the banker of his responsibility to the depositor. He predicted a "devastating panic" if Bryan were elected and absolved Roosevelt from responsibility for the panic of 1907. He tentatively favored Bryan's demand for physical valuation of railroads for the purpose of determining rates, but the roads should be valued as "going concerns," not, as Bryan desired, on reproduction cost (which would squeeze water out). Like Bryan he favored the criminal prosecution of bad trusts, but he derided Bryan's principle that "any monopoly is indefensible," for by following it "good" trusts would be destroyed with the "bad" and labor would suffer. Bryan demanded downward revision of the tariff. Taft opposed rates higher than the difference between costs of production at home and abroad and thought that some rates should be raised. While he favored a slight overall reduction after election, he disapproved of Bryan's demand for the removal of duties on trust-made articles. Moreover, he denounced Bryan's call for Filipino independence in the near future, saying that the islanders would not be ready for self-rule for another half century. Bryan called for an "adequate navy"; Taft demanded a larger Army and Navy. Bryan called for publicity for campaign contributions prior to election day; Taft would make his contributions public twenty days after election.[55]

Bryan said nothing publicly about Taft's religion, but certain Democrats reviewed Taft's negotiations in 1902 with the Vatican over the Friar Lands in the Philippines and concluded that he was favorable to Rome. Paradoxically, he was criticized because, being a Unitarian, he was not a Christian—and a man who denied the divinity of Christ should not be elected President—and Josephus Daniels, of the Publicity Committee, was hard put to dissuade the Democratic National Committee that the airing of Taft's mission to the Vatican

Bryan," *The Arena*, 40 (October 1908), 355–357; Edmond D. Coblenz (ed.), *William Randolph Hearst: A Portrait in His Own Words*, p. 37; Swanberg, *Hearst*, pp. 254–255, 257–259.

[55] Taft to Roosevelt, July 10, 1908, William Howard Taft Papers; New York *Times*, *Rocky Mountain News*, July 27, 1908.

would bring Bryan little political support. Bryan wrote Henry Watterson, who headed the Publicity Committee, that "The Republicans are making an effort to reach our Catholic Democrats, but we are planning to meet this, and will, I think, succeed measurably well, although I would not be surprised if we lost a little in this direction." In talking with Daniels, Bryan stated that he had thought it best not to turn to the South again for a national chairman but to select a Northern Roman Catholic, one who would thus counteract the tendency of the Roman Catholics to support Taft.[56] Only after Mack was chosen did Bryan discover that he was of a Roman Catholic family but was not himself a Roman Catholic.

While Bryan worked on his acceptance speech he promised to answer Taft topic by topic and warned that voting for Hearst would merely help the Republicans.[57] The withdrawal of Judge Seabury from Hearst's party and his announced support for Bryan proved to be a great boost, for Seabury confessed that Hearst was using the party to divide the opposition to Taft and so avenge Bryan's failure to support him in 1904.

On August 12, when Bryan was notified beneath the rays of an almost tropical sun, he asserted that the overshadowing issue of the campaign was "Shall the People Rule?" His third nomination could be explained only by the substantial and undisputed growth of the principles he had long advocated, he said, and he held the Republican party responsible for all abuses existing in government and with being impotent to accomplish imperatively needed reforms. For a generation it had drawn campaign funds from the beneficiaries of special legislation. "Privileges have been pledged and granted in return for money contributions to debauch elections."

Next to the corrupt use of money, the indirec: method of electing United States senators was most responsible for the obstruction of reform. Were he elected he would call Congress into extraordinary session to ask for the fulfillment of this pledge. A third instrumentality employed to defeat the will of the people was the House rules. The speaker must be divested of his great powers, which should be returned to the majority.

[56] E. L. Scharf to Mullen, October 7, 1908, Bryan Papers; Roosevelt to Taft, October 12, 1908, Taft Papers; Daniels to Mrs. Daniels, August 18, 1908, Daniels Papers; Bryan to Watterson, August 18, 1908, Henry Watterson Papers; Edgar Albert Hornig, "The Religious Issue in the Taft-Bryan Duel of 1908," *Proceedings of the American Philosophical Society,* 105 (December 1961), 530–537.

[57] *Rocky Mountain News,* July 30, 31, 1908.

If elected, Bryan concluded, he would consecrate himself "to the single purpose of making the government one in which the people ruled, in which the highest possible stimulus would be offered to great and persistent individual effort, in which everyone would enjoy his just share of his toil." The question at issue in the campaign was "whether the government shall remain a mere business asset of favor-seeking corporations, or be an instrument in the hands of the people for the advancement of the common weal." [58]

Bryan kept his promise to answer Taft topic by topic by speaking on single issues in various cities. In 1896 he had concentrated on the financial question, in 1900 on imperialism. If he was now searching for a "paramount" issue, he failed, and no single issue predominated in the campaign unless it was his vying with Taft in promising a vigorous attack on ill-gotten wealth.[59] The tariff, guarantee of bank deposits, labor, and campaign contributions questions proved to be the important ones debated, for Taft stole his thunder on the income tax by supporting it and on the direct election of senators by deeming it a nonpartisan issue, and there was really little difference between them on the Philippine question.

Deeming conditions in the Middle West encouraging, Bryan left Lincoln on September 6 for a three-week visit to the East.

Meantime Taft had been publicly silent. Not inactive, for he went fishing or played golf each day, he was plainly worried, as his correspondence with Roosevelt reveals, and he asked Roosevelt for a letter he could use against Bryan. Roosevelt wrote the letter and then practically directed him to take to the stump. ". . . you ought to be on the stump but only speak *once* or *twice* in each state you visit. Do not answer Bryan; *attack* him. Don't let him make the issues. And never *define* your religious belief! I don't believe you had best say a word about it." Taft replied: "I have your letter . . . and if anything can elect me, I believe this letter can. . . ." [60]

The announcement that Taft would stump led Bryan to state that

[58] *Ibid.*, August 12, 1908; New York *Times*, August 13, 1908.

[59] Benjamin Parke De Witt, *The Progressive Movement: A Non-Partisan, Comprehensive Discussion of Current Tendencies in American Politics*, pp. 36–37; Sheldon, *Nebraska*, I, 828; Charles Willis Thompson, *Presidents I've Known and Two Near-Presidents*, p. 52; Edgar A. Hornig, "The Indefatigable Mr. Bryan in 1908," *Nebraska History*, 37 (September 1956), 183, 199.

[60] Taft to Roosevelt, August 10, 12, 16, 1908, Roosevelt to Taft, July 11, August 12, 13, 18, September 1, 4, 1908, Taft Papers. See also Reid to Roosevelt, September 8, 1908, Reid Papers.

"GOP panic" led him to speak. Indeed, his greatest sin was being made a virtue by imitation. In 1896 and 1900 it was "demagogic" to run around hunting votes; now it was eminently proper because Taft was going to do it, "and I hope the Republican papers will make due apologies." "It is hard to keep your patents from being infringed upon this year," he added. "I'm afraid they will try to raise a campaign fund by popular contributions next." [61]

Gompers also changed his mind about stumping and on September 6 invaded the Eighteenth Illinois with the objective of defeating Cannon's re-election. He kept his *Federationist* solidly on Bryan's side and in numerous states charged that Taft favored a despotic government vested in the judiciary while Bryan favored popular government. In his Labor Day Address at Chicago, Bryan went a step further. Taft, he said, was not only known as "the father of government by injunction," hence an enemy of labor, but was also biased against the jury system as such.[62]

In Illinois and Indiana Bryan hurled the lie at Cannon, who had charged in the Illinois Republican state convention that "Bryan, a man of theories, a man who has a breaking out of the mouth," had made a million dollars by "selling wind and ink to the public." His property was worth only between $125,000 and $150,000, retorted Bryan, and he countercharged—Cannon was a "tool of privilege" who, with the aid of "Sunny Jim" Sherman, the vice presidential candidate, had strangled reform legislation in the House of Representatives despite Roosevelt's recommendations. Audiences were particularly amused by a Bryan novelty—an imaginary cross-examination of Taft in which the latter was shown to have about-faced on many issues.[63]

In 1896 and 1900 Bryan had fought Mark Hanna rather than William McKinley. In 1908 he had to fight Roosevelt rather than Taft. Roosevelt's letter endorsing Taft sat badly with him. With curious lack of understanding of a president's political functions, he said that Roosevelt was the President of all the people and should not use his position to support a particular candidate. Indeed, he was degrading a great office. A few simple sentences from Taft would be

[61] *Rocky Mountain News*, September 6, 7, 1908.

[62] New York *Times*, September 8, October 13, 1908; Gompers, *Seventy Years*, II, 269.

[63] *Rocky Mountain News*, September 12, 1908; New York *Herald*, September 15, 1908; Joseph G. Cannon, "Predatory Wealth," September 27, 1908, Cannon Papers.

worth more than all Roosevelt's eulogies, he continued. In fact the endorsement was valueless unless Roosevelt stayed on in Washington to see that Taft made good. How could Taft prevent a panic when Roosevelt already had one on his hands? he then asked. He charged that Taft was dodging and dared him to define his position on the great questions at issue. While the large crowds that greeted him in the East convinced him that all sections of the country were united in his support, he overlooked the fact that in previous elections he had drawn crowds but not votes and that the Republican campaign had not yet begun. Senator William E. Borah, known a dozen years earlier as the "William Jennings Bryan of Idaho," quipped, "Bryan is the greatest living authority on things that never happen." [64] However, the Republican vote in the September 1 election in Vermont dropped two thousand below that of 1904 and on September 15 the reduction of Maine's Republican majority of twenty-seven thousand in 1904 to less than eight thousand elated Bryan, and he renewed his challenge to Taft to speak out, also referring now to how Taft had granted franchises in the Philippines.

In Rochester, where Bryan addressed the New York Democratic state convention, Chairman Parker renewed his pledge of fealty. A deafening roar arose as he and Bryan clasped hands and faced the delegates. Bryan was greatly pleased with a convention made harmonious by the ouster of the Patrick McCarren men, who had threatened to knife the ticket, and with the selection of Lewis W. Chanler as the gubernatorial candidate. He spent an afternoon at Esopus with Parker and an evening at Wolfert's Roost talking with Mack, Edward Murphy, Hill, and others. While Hill feared that blunders might yet be made, he agreed that the campaign had started off very well and that Bryan's visit had been "very pleasant." [65] With New York apparently his, Eastern newspapers friendlier than ever before, the Republican denouement in Maine, and Republican leaders everywhere begging Taft to do something, Bryan was so hopeful of success that he was "not inclined to concede anything." Thus far things had gone his way, and in Delaware he stepped up his attack by openly charging that the United States Steel Corporation was furnishing funds to the Republican party in return for immunity from prosecution.

[64] Claudius O. Johnson, *Borah of Idaho*, pp. 77, 95.

[65] Hill to Parker, September 18, 1908, Hill to Edward Murphy, September 18, 1908, Hill Letterbooks, Bixby Papers.

Now the character of the campaign suddenly changed from a Bryan talkathon to a real scrap involving Roosevelt as well as Taft. In exposing the John D. Archbold letters to Senators Joseph Bailey and Joseph Foraker, Joseph Sibley, Hanna, and others, Hearst created a national sensation, for they referred to killing "objectionable" legislation and defeating "dangerous" men. A letter to Foraker referred to pending congressional legislation, mentioned two checks totaling $29,500 which could be regarded as a bribe by Standard Oil, and also implicated Governor Haskell, who had stopped an anti-trust suit in Oklahoma. Next day Frank S. Monnett, attorney general of Ohio from 1896 to 1900, told of an offer by alleged Standard Oil agents to pay him $50,000 to drop suits instituted by the state and that Foraker had asked him to hold up the trial of the cases. Haskell vehemently denied Hearst's charges and called him a willful liar.[66] But Foraker was through, and telegrams and letters flew between Roosevelt and Taft. Roosevelt publicly attacked Bryan through Haskell and warned Taft not to accept contributions from Standard Oil or anyone connected with it. To show that he himself had not accepted money from the company he sent copies of his letters of October 1904 in which he had directed the return of $100,000, and he told Taft to concentrate on Haskell. Parker had said that he had not collected much money in 1904, but when Mack became national chairman he announced that $300,000 had been left over. ". . . it shows that Mr. Haskell's appointment means Standard Oil money for Mr. Bryan. Bring this out, and smash and cut Bryan about it." Bryan's personal choice for Treasurer of the United States, he cried, was "an unspeakable scoundrel." [67]

In New York City on September 18 Bryan received one of the greatest ovations of his career. Speaking in Carnegie Hall on "Republican Tendencies," he accused that party of leading the nation into Socialism. Under them governmental expenditures, the number of office holders, and the size of the Army and Navy had increased faster than the rate of population growth. They sought to substitute a

[66] *Rocky Mountain News*, September 16, 18, 19, 1908; Allan Nevins, *John D. Rockefeller: The Heroic Age in American Enterprise*, II, 593; Swanberg, *Hearst*, pp. 260–263.

[67] Telegrams, Roosevelt to Taft and Taft to Roosevelt, September 19, 1908, letters, Roosevelt to Taft, September 21, 26, 1908, Taft Papers. Bryan asked Dahlman to find out how much money was in the Democratic treasury. Dahlman wrote August Belmont, the treasurer, who replied that there was on hand $419.20. Belmont to Dahlman, September 11, 1908, copy, Bryan Papers.

presidential succession for a democratically chosen executive and to centralize the federal government. In administering the Philippines they knew no constitutional limitations. Finally, they tended toward Socialism by permitting abuses which cast odium upon individualism and furnished arguments to the Socialists.[68]

In the fall of 1907, L. T. Russell, editor of the Ardmore (Oklahoma) *Morning Democrat,* had told Bryan and then written him about Haskell's connections with Standard Oil. Disbelieving the information, Bryan had thrown the letter away. Now, apparently oblivious of the implications of Hearst's exposure, he said nothing about Haskell. But Roosevelt, enraged by Bryan's attacks, defended himself and Taft by attacking Haskell. The campaign had been dull thus far, he told reporters, and he would "put some ginger in it." In Detroit, meanwhile, Bryan gave the press a telegram he had written Roosevelt demanding that he produce proof that Haskell had ever been connected with Standard Oil. He had aided Roosevelt, he added, by offering remedial measures for the public good and by urging Democrats to support such measures, but he would not permit the attitude of the Democracy to be misrepresented by Republicans.[69] The spectacle of Bryan's rebuking Roosevelt electrified the nation and provided the most sensational development of the campaign to date. Roosevelt said nothing for the moment, but Taft decided that his time to attack had arrived. Bryan, he said in his first speech, at Columbus, Ohio, was merely an eloquent and adroit public critic who had never given practical demonstration of his ability to meet and solve problems. ". . . he loves financial theories that are full of sophistries and are impractical . . . his election would mean a paralysis of business and we should have a recurrence of disastrous conditions of the last Democratic administration." The real issue of the campaign, he added, was William Jennings Bryan.[70]

So, too, thought Roosevelt, who spent almost the whole of September 23 in preparing a reply to Bryan's telegram. Haskell's connection with Standard Oil, he said, was a matter of "common notoriety" in Ohio and of court record in Oklahoma. Taft's dissolving of all connections with Foraker contrasted mightily with Bryan's sup-

[68] *Rocky Mountain News,* September 22, 1908; New York *American,* September 23, 26, 1908.

[69] *Rocky Mountain News,* September 23, 1908.

[70] *Ibid.;* Walter Wellman, "The Management of the Taft Campaign," *American Review of Reviews,* 38 (November 1908), 432–438.

port of Haskell, whose continued connection with the management of a national campaign was "a scandal and a disgrace." Haskell, "a representative leader of the Bryan Democracy . . . was unworthy of any position in our public life." With respect to Bryan's charge that the Republicans were "misrepresenting" the attitude of the Democratic party, Roosevelt retorted vigorously and flatly: "[I]n my judgment the measures you advocate would be wholly ineffective in curing a single evil, and so far as they have an effect at all, would merely throw the entire business of the country into hopeless and utter confusion. I put Mr. Taft's deeds against your words." [71]

On September 25, in Chicago, whence he had peremptorily been called by Bryan, Haskell was urged by various national committeemen to resign simply because he was embarrassing Bryan. But Haskell denied all charges of wrongdoing and shouted that he would sue his detractors. Then he was taken in hand by Josephus Daniels and others and before Bryan arrived had handed his resignation to Mack. Bryan chose Herman Ridder as his successor and then replied to Roosevelt. Until Haskell was tried in a court free of partisan bias, he would stand by him. He would dismiss the entire matter were Roosevelt not trying to make political capital out of it and, by suggesting him inconsistent in supporting Haskell and opposing trusts, questioning his sincerity. Roosevelt could search his eighteen-year record and find "not an act, a word or a thought of mine to justify your partisan charge." He then countercharged: Why had Roosevelt permitted U.S. Steel to acquire the Tennessee Coal and Iron Company and thus obtain control of more than 50 per cent of the country's steel production? Why had he shown particular favor to a monopolistic corporation? Moreover, Roosevelt must know of the contributions made by "Jupiter" Morgan, E. H. Harriman, John D. Archbold, H. H. Rogers, and other trust magnates to his campaign fund in 1904. Finally, Roosevelt was not an expert on panic preventatives, for he had a panic on his hands.[72]

On Sunday, September 27, Roosevelt tried to nail down the "main fallacies" that Bryan was expounding. Richard Olney, said Roose-

[71] New York *Times,* September 23, 1908.

[72] Bryan to Roosevelt, September 26, 1908, Roosevelt Papers. Bryan's original criticism of the acquisition of the Tennessee Coal and Iron Company appeared in the *Commoner,* November 15, 22, 1907. According to Harbaugh, *Roosevelt,* p. 227, almost 75% of contributions to the Republican party in 1904 had come from corporations.

velt, had used the anti-trust laws only against labor; he himself had instituted at least nine anti-trust cases and also seventy-five cases against railroads granting secret rebates. He was cognizant of the action of the U.S. Steel Company in acquiring the Tennessee Coal and Iron Company. "But there was no violation of law," and the action had served to prevent the spread of financial panic. "You would understand the principles on which I acted if you would rid yourself of the idea that I am trying to discriminate for or against any man or corporation because he or it is either wealthy or not wealthy. . . . I base my distinctions on conduct, not on relative wealth." Roosevelt implied that those whose interests were those of the business community and of the wageworkers would support Taft, those of special interests, like the silver barons in '96, would support Bryan, and added that ". . . your success now would be a calamity to the country both from the standpoint of business (and especially of the interest of the wageworker) and from the standpoint of morals." Roosevelt denied that those who had contributed to his campaign fund in 1904 had influenced his attitude toward the trusts. It was clearly understood that "every man shall receive a square deal" whether he gave or not. Taft had refused to support Foraker for senator, but Bryan overlooked Haskell's "gross offenses against public decency and honesty." Roosevelt promised that Haskell would obtain "justice" in the courts and concluded that Bryan's refusal to condemn "Haskellism" rested with his "moral obliquity rather than mental obtuseness." [73]

Replying to Roosevelt on September 29, Bryan dared him to match his publishing of the contributors to their parties' campaign funds in 1896 and to publicize before the current election the contributors to Taft's campaign chest. Roosevelt paid more attention to the mote in the Democratic than the beam in the Republican eye when he criticized Democratic finances. Furthermore, he well knew that "officials of the . . . favor-seeking corporations do not put up large sums of money for purely patriotic purposes." He did not assert that the President or Taft were directly influenced by funds contributed by trust magnates, but he believed the American people should know what contributions were being made "so they may judge for themselves the motive of the givers and the obligation imposed upon those who receive," and he hoped that the "honest sentiment of the country will rebuke the party whose convention refused to endorse any kind

[73] Roosevelt to Bryan, September 27, 1908, Roosevelt Papers; Oscar Straus, *Under Four Administrations*, pp. 253–254.

of publicity, and whose candidates are not willing that the people should know until after the polls are closed what predatory interests have been active in support of the Republican party." [74]

Roosevelt declined to pursue the public debate further.

According to the Bryan press, Bryan's crusade in the upper Mississippi Valley during the last week in September had attracted large and enthusiastic crowds, while Taft had addressed only small and listless groups; yet by the first days of October Taft was beginning to sense victory. "Bryan's lack of wisdom in inviting you into a discussion is shown over the West, and his claim to be the heir of your policies is now the subject of laughter and ridicule rather than of serious weight with those who might have been influenced had you not hit him between the eyes as you did upon his invitation," he wrote Roosevelt on October 3. A week later he reported that his campaign in the West had been "very satisfactory." Roosevelt urged him on. It was perfectly clear that Bryan had lost ground during the last three weeks while Taft's speeches had grown stronger. "You are making a great campaign," Roosevelt added.[75]

Unaware of the ridicule of him that Taft reported, and bolstered by the fact that every living member of Cleveland's cabinet now supported him, Bryan continued speaking to huge crowds and delivering as many as thirty speeches a day. Crying that Taft was a "dodger," Hughes a "joke," and that Cannon was backed by every predatory corporation in the country, he devoted one or two days to each of the states of the Middle West during the first half of October. In Nebraska he averaged twenty-one speeches on each of four days. In a week he traveled a thousand miles, speaking at every important town from the Kansas line to South Dakota, from the Missouri River to Wyoming. Mullen reported that after a speech he would sometimes fall down on his bed from exhaustion and sleep for a little while. "We would throw cold water on his face to wake him, and he would get up, go out on the platform, and give 'em hell, then tumble back into bed to sleep until the next performance. I have never seen such magnificent physical endurance, never heard so tireless a voice." [76]

Nor did Bryan's sense of humor or gentleness fail him despite his

[74] New York *Times*, September 29, 1908.

[75] Taft to Roosevelt, October 3, 9, 1908, Roosevelt to Taft, October 8, 1908, Taft Papers; New York *Times*, October 8, 1908.

[76] Mullen, *Western Democrat*, p. 132.

grueling undertaking. At an Aksarben initiation in Omaha, a bogus Bryan spoke for him. When called upon to speak as W. H. Taft, he delivered an impromptu speech in the character of Taft that kept the crowd roaring, as when with mock humility he apologized for omitting discussion of a particular issue because he had not found out what Roosevelt thought about it. Once, when he noticed that Charles S. Thompson, a reporter, was ill, Bryan carried his traveling bag to the train for him. In another instance, when he learned that Thompson was short of cash, he gave him twenty dollars.[77]

There was also some of the same hero worship that had begun in 1896. Mrs. Bryan recalled that in West Virginia Bryan went to speak from the rear of the train. "Near the car and at the edge of the crowd stood a thin faced woman with hands clasped convulsively and an expression of the most rapt attention. If she were standing in the presence of Christ she could not have been more worshipful. It made a tear or two drop when I watched her." Mrs. Bryan's humor also shone through her keen watchfulness. "The crowds are larger," she wrote on October 21, "the same types that I have noticed for twelve years are still extant. The long whiskered man who opens his mouth very wide and literally drinks in the speech; the long necked woman, with a small knot of hair and one tooth who waves her apron and shouts; the fond father insisting that his little son shall shake hands with the candidate; the oldest inhabitant . . . his quavering voice saying he voted first for Andrew Jackson and had never scratched a ticket since—these are here—I welcome them as old friends." But she noted certain differences. "In 1896 there was an enthusiasm approaching frenzy. I have seen men weep and tremble as they grasped [Bryan's] hand. Horny handed men have gripped my hand and breathing hard with suppressed feeling have bade me 'Take good care of him. God has raised him for this work.' In '96, too, there was a large element of good natured curiosity. Now the people are quiet and most attentive. They shout less and apparently think more." [78]

On October 15, as promised, Bryan published his roll of contributors. Ridder and his three sons gave $37,000, the largest contribution. The largest single contribution, of $5000, was made by a Denver corporation lawyer, Carl Hughes. Bryan himself came second, giving

[77] Thompson, *Presidents I've Known*, pp. 65–66, 76–77, 82–85.

[78] Mrs. Mary Baird Bryan Journal, entry of October 21, 1908, Mrs. Ruth Bryan Rohde Papers.

$4046 of the profits from his *Commoner*. William A. Clark of Montana and Norman Mack each gave $2000; others, like Hoke Smith, $250. Although Moses G. Wetmore gave liberally, he was unable to find large givers, and most of the money came in small sums. Daniels recalled that "Much of it came from people with little education, men who wrote from the farms saying they were sending a dollar with their prayers, laboring men, preachers, and men in colleges, especially small colleges, who thought there was a moral issue involved and that Bryan was a preacher of righteousness." [79] As of October 9, about fifty thousand persons had contributed $248,467.25. Only eight gifts exceeded $1000; excluding the $1000 assessment on each national committeeman, more than half the total came in sums of less than $100.

On the same date, polls taken by the *Rocky Mountain News,* New York *World,* and New York *Herald* agreed that Bryan led Taft in New York, the pivot state, and in the Ohio Valley. They listed 23 states with 100 electoral votes as doubtful and gave Bryan 178 "sure" and Taft 205 "sure." On October 18 "King Theodore" gave "Prince William" his final commands, and on October 21 he made public a letter he had written Senator Knox which contained a sweeping attack on Gompers and a defense of the Republican plank on injunctions. Meantime Bryan began his final swing about the country, from Nebraska to New York and back, and Taft invaded the South and East before returning to Ohio.

As in 1896 and 1900 Bryan appeared to be winning throughout the first two months of the campaign. As in his earlier canvasses, so again in 1908, he began late in October to level charges of evil-doing at the Republicans. In Alton, Illinois, he asserted that they would use money "as they have used it year after year . . . to purchase this election," and Mrs. Bryan noted in her Journal: "The danger now seems to be in the use of money the last days and the coercion of laborers." In Ohio he noted that the railroads were again threatening to reduce the wages of their employees if they voted for him and that there was a revival of the practice in which contracts were offered "conditional" upon his defeat, and also some ordering by Republican employers of their workers to march in parades or be fired. He repeated these charges in Louisville, Kentucky, where people packed

[79] Daniels, *Editor in Politics,* p. 543.

the streets for seven miles along his point of entry. His wild charges against the Republicans nevertheless drove many erstwhile supporters from him.[80]

Beginning with the last week in October, in response to direct orders from Roosevelt, Taft's managers reached full stride. Taft; Secretaries George von L. Meyer, James R. Garfield, and Oscar S. Straus; Senators Jonathan P. Dolliver and Robert La Follette; Representatives David J. Foster and Nicholas Longworth; and Leslie M. Shaw and General O. O. Howard would stump Ohio alone against Bryan. Roosevelt had himself interviewed in order to praise Taft; lauded a speech by Secretary Knox attacking Bryan's position on injunctions; wrote union leaders that Taft was truly a friend of labor; and ordered all cabinet members to the stump for the last week of the campaign. Governor Charles Evans Hughes and Secretary Elihu Root, particularly, pictured Bryan as a Populist whose election promised a long period of economic stagnation. Although he privately conceded that "The labor people have just cause of complaint with the Republican party taken as a whole, because Congress under the lead of Cannon treated them badly, as did the courts," Roosevelt then wrote a letter critical of Bryan and Gompers intended to smoke Bryan out. Gompers replied instead, saying that Roosevelt was attacking labor in order to win trust support. Taft, who said that workers were too intelligent to follow Gompers's advice to switch parties, believed Roosevelt's letter important less for what it said about labor than because it made people think about "what they may look for should Bryan and Gompers get into power with respect to the courts and the interference with their processes. In one aspect I think that is the most important issue of the campaign." [81]

Unbeknownst to Taft, Bryan had recently refused to pledge himself to appoint only "safe" judges to the Supreme Court if elected. Ridder and a group including Mack, Judge Morgan J. O'Brian, Charles F. Murphy, Senator Culberson, and a dozen others invited Bryan to

[80] Charles E. Ingersoll to Charles S. Hamlin, October 15, 1908, Hamlin Papers; New York *Herald*, October 20, 1908; New York *Times*, July 22, 26, October 10, 28, 1908; *Rocky Mountain News*, October 21, 25, 1908; New York *Tribune*, October 20, 1908; Hornig, "The Indefatigable Mr. Bryan in 1908," 183–189; Josephus Daniels, "Mr. Bryan's Third Campaign," *American Review of Reviews*, 38 (November 1908), 427–428; Thomas R. Marshall, *Recollections of Thomas R. Marshall: A Hoosier Salad*, pp. 175–178.

[81] Roosevelt to Taft, October 24, 27, 1908, Taft to Roosevelt, November 1, 1908, Taft Papers; Speeches and Addresses of James R. Garfield, Garfield Papers.

dinner. Ridder and O'Brian told him that New York, and thus the White House, would be his if the business interests of the city were assured that he would not disturb them. They were especially worried about what kind of men he would name to fill vacancies on the Supreme Court. If he would pledge to name men like George Gray, the business people of the country would rally to his support and elect him. Daniels sat nearly opposite Bryan and saw his jaws set and a look come into his eyes which indicated that the idea was getting nowhere. Bryan arose and politely thanked his hosts for their deep interest in him and in their party and for their undoubted sincerity—but he could not conceive that any citizen would vote for a man for President whom he could not trust to name judges of the courts without a pledge. Moreover, to exempt Gray, a bolter in 1896, would be to discriminate against all other able Democrats. Under no circumstances, not even for the Presidency, would he humiliate himself by making such a pledge. Stunned, his audience remained silent for a time. Then Murphy said, "Mr. Bryan, you are quite right. After hearing you, I am sure you ought not to make such a pledge and nobody ought to ask you to make it." Next day Ridder told Daniels that Bryan had defeated himself.[82]

Bryan set an extremely fast pace during the last days of the campaign. His giving of six days to New York revealed his determination to win the votes of that pivotal state. In the most notable gathering of the campaign, in Madison Square Garden, he hit Taft hard on the questions of labor and campaign contributions and expressed confidence in his victory by saying, "They may be able to defeat me, but they cannot cheat me of the credit that will accord me of giving an impetus to honest politics. I expect to be in Washington after the 4th of March and I want to find a Democratic Congress there."[83]

As he toured upper New York state, Bryan was extremely gratified to hear Parker reaffirm his loyalty to him and to hear Hill declare that he preferred him to Taft "because I sincerely believe he will be President himself. . . . He will not be led around with a string like a caged bear."[84] The prospect of winning the state's rural vote heightened when both Carnegie and Rockefeller announced their support for Taft on October 30. While hardly news, Rockefeller's

[82] The incident is condensed from Daniels, *Editor in Politics*, pp. 548–550, and is used by permission of the publishers, University of North Carolina Press.

[83] New York *Times, Tribune, World*, October 26, 27, 1908.

[84] New York *Times*, October 29, 1908.

pronouncement drew cries of anguish from Republicans, for it seemed to uphold Bryan's contention that their party was the haven of the trusts and that Taft would have ample money. "Mr. Rockefeller's corporation is the most notorious lawbreaker in the United States and he is for Taft because he does not want the law enforced," Bryan asserted.[85]

Nevertheless, Bryan's anti-trust program drove big business away from him. His plan to restrict corporations to less than 50 per cent of the national market would compel U.S. Steel, the American Sugar Refining Company, Standard Oil, and other large corporations to dissolve or sell some of their plants. This plan, his stand on labor and the tariff, and such skeletons in his closet as free silver and his having favored the government ownership of railroads won him the hearty hostility of most business interests. The National Association of Manufacturers, whose president Gompers swore had attempted to bribe him with a $50,000 annuity to leave the labor union movement, attacked him bitterly and strongly urged businessmen to bury him on election day.[86]

On Saturday, November 1, Bryan and Taft practically concluded their campaigns. Of 60 days actively on the stump, Bryan had spent 16 in the East; of these he had spent 10 in New York. Thirty days he devoted to the Upper Mississippi Valley, with 20 of them in Illinois, Indiana, and Ohio. Except for two days in West Virginia, he had devoted the rest to Nebraska, Kansas, Colorado, and North and South Dakota.[87] He admitted the loss of New England and of the West Coast. With the small electoral votes of the Rocky Mountain states and those of the Solid South, however, he believed he would have electoral votes to spare and a considerably large popular majority.

In eight speeches during his return from Chicago to Nebraska

[85] New York *Tribune*, October 30, 1908; New York *World*, October 30, 1908, *Rocky Mountain News*, October 31, 1908; Daniels, *Editor in Politics*, p. 521; Nevins, *Rockefeller*, II, 594.

[86] Brochure of the National Association of Manufacturers, Bryan Papers; New York *Times*, July 22, September 29, 1908. As the president of the N.A.M. put it: "It is the duty of the American business men, regardless of their party, to bury Bryan and Bryanism under such an avalanche of votes in 1908 that it will not have to be done over again in 1912 or ever." "Mr. Van Cleave's Answer to Mr. Bryan," Cannon Papers.

[87] Hornig, "The Indefatigable Mr. Bryan," pp. 196–197; Mischler Diary, Taft Papers.

Bryan spoke in great earnestness. Taft had behind him, he said, all the forces considered potent in politics—an army of officeholders, the trust magnates, most of the leading newspapers, "and an enormous campaign fund so tainted that he dare not let the people know where it comes from until after they have voted." But he himself would rather have the love of the people in whose name he fought his battles than to hold any office. In politics for eighteen years, he had "given an impulse to honest politics; I have helped create a sentiment in favor of reform, and as a candidate I have had but one thing to rely upon, the confidence of the masses in my fidelity to their interests. I've outlived the detraction of my foes." [88]

Bryan's return to Lincoln on election eve, November 2, called forth the greatest demonstration in the city's history. In his regular, tearful speech saved for such occasions he said he would win because a moral awakening had occurred. If defeated, however, he would live in the knowledge that he had left nothing undone and "find private life so full of joy that I shall not miss the presidency. . . . The affection that my countrymen have shown is to me dearer than all earthly office. And my highest ambition is to deserve the continuation of that affection." "Surely," he concluded, "the hour has come for a return of the government to the hands of the people. Let the People rule." [89]

IV

ON THE MORNING after the election, although the returns were not all in, Bryan sensed defeat and began writing letters of thanks to those who had aided him and to express incredulity. "I do not see what we could have done to have increased our vote. As far as I can see, no mistakes were made, and I am sure that every member in active charge of the campaign did his duty to the utmost," he wrote Josephus Daniels.[90] His only personal regret, he told his daughter Grace, was "that your mother will never be the First Lady of the land to the nation, as she has always been to me, and that you . . . will not make

[88] New York *Evening Post*, October 31, 1908; *Rocky Mountain News*, November 3, 1908. The great demand from the West for copies of "The Prince of Peace," which he had delivered to half a million church people in the last five years, helped convince Bryan that the campaign in the West contained religious and moral overtones. Daniels, "Mr. Bryan's Third Campaign," pp. 429–430.

[89] New York *Times*, November 3, 1908.

[90] Letter, November 4, 1908, Daniels Papers.

your debut in the White House." [91] Of course he also deplored the setback to his party. While laughing and joking with visitors to Fairview and saying that at least he had won his precinct, city, and state, he wrote Daniels that "These are crumbs of comfort which we, like Lazarus, get from the overflowing table of our rich opponents," [92] and he told Louis F. Post that he could "not understand how we were so badly beaten . . . [or] measure the relative influences of various courses but we must fight on—It is our government—we cannot be indifferent." [93]

The completeness of Taft's victory increased Bryan's perplexity. Taft had won 321 out of the 483 electoral votes and a popular majority of more than a million (7,679,006 to 6,409,106) in a voter turnout 10 per cent greater than that of 1904—but with half a million votes less than in 1896.[94] The Solid South had stood by him and he had carried Kentucky, Oklahoma, Nebraska, Colorado, and Nevada, none of them critical states. He considered making an investigation in each state, county, and precinct, then confessed that he was at a loss as how to overcome the difficulties he confronted.[95]

Unable to fathom the reasons for his defeat, Bryan used *The Commoner* and personal letters to ask for light to clear up "The Mystery of 1908." The New York *World* and other newspapers took up the chorus, and editorials and letters soon furnished many reasons. In 1908 neither party, as a party, was really ready to push the truly important issues, such as tariff revision, currency reform, railroad and anti-trust regulation, a square deal for labor, and direct elections. Instead of using one main issue, Bryan had campaigned on several, none of which had struck the popular fancy. The small returns from his dollar subscription plan could only mean that he had failed to put heart into his followers. Many believed that the panic of 1907 had been caused by economic laws over which Roosevelt had had no control. The rapidly industrializing South was lessening its opposition

---

[91] Mrs. Grace Bryan Hargreaves, "William Jennings Bryan," unpublished Ms., Bryan Papers, II, 54.

[92] Bryan to Daniels, November 4, 1908, Daniels Papers.

[93] Louis F. Post Papers.

[94] Minor parties ran badly in 1908, winning only 800,219 popular votes out of the 14,855,859 votes cast and not a single electoral vote. Populist Watson won 29,146, mostly from Georgia, and Socialist Debs earned only about 20,000 more than in 1904, for a total of 420,793.

[95] Bryan to Josephus Daniels, November 9, 1908, Daniels Papers.

to tariff protection, and he had offered no better plan for handling trusts than to extirpate them. If, as Albert Shaw said, "the business of America is business," then Bryan was *persona non grata*.[96] If, as Daniels stated, victory in the campaign hinged upon literature rather than oratory, then the Republicans had the financial advantage, for they collected $1,655,518 and the Democrats only $629,341.[97]

Still a crusader and spellbinder, Bryan nevertheless was so well known that he lacked the attraction of novelty. With few accretions to his ranks of speakers, he again had to provide most of the oratory. He had revealed great physical endurance and continued skill and attractiveness as a debater, but the greatly enlarged newspaper and magazine reading public made oratory less important than ever, and he should have known that oratory often serves to further convince those already convinced but not to win over those opposed. Moreover, little effort was made to get speakers and to hold meetings, with the result that his campaign, especially in the East, was sabotaged.

Bryan's record on many counts was held against him. Many preferred Taft because "the only alternative is Bryan, at whose approach the ghosts of '96 arise and shriek in concert of warning." [98] Consistent in 1896 and 1900, he had subsequently picked up and then dropped free silver, direct legislation, and government ownership of railroads. "Evidently he had determined to ignore dangerous problems," commented Clarence Darrow, who had declined an invitation to stump for him.[99] It also appeared that he had narrowed his radicalism in order to win the East, and his accepting of Tammany's friendship lost him Western and Southern adherents. Moreover, by persistently condemning the Bourbon reorganizers he lost the support of the states they dominated. It may well be, as George Parker noted, that his nomination had been supported by the reorganizers "not because the move was politically inevitable but for the less creditable reason that [they] hoped to be finally rid of him by assuring his overwhelming defeat for a third time." [100] Finally, he was no longer attractive to

[96] *Commoner*, October 25, 1907.

[97] Louise Overacker, *Money in Elections*, p. 38. Both National Committees made public their contributions and expenditures soon after the election, thus antedating the publicity required by a law finally enacted in 1911. *Ibid.*, p. 237; Perry Belmont, *American Democrat: The Recollections of Perry Belmont*, p. 475.

[98] New York *Sun*, October 14, 1908.

[99] Clarence Darrow, *The Story of My Life*, p. 94.

[100] George F. Parker, *Recollections of Grover Cleveland*, p. 216.

third party reformers, who took some votes away from him in closely contested states. He lost Maryland by 605 votes out of 232,000 and Missouri by 449 out of 700,000.

Bryan's reading of the returns caused him to blaze forth against Tammany. "Let Tammany Explain" where the Bryan vote had gone, his *Commoner* demanded, but Charles F. Murphy, who may have knifed the ticket, remained silent. The fact that the nation's brewing and distilling interests had again opposed him also remained firmly in Bryan's mind.[101]

Roosevelt's support of Taft was a mighty factor in Bryan's defeat, and Taft had been singularly fortunate that by November the panic of 1907 had disappeared. It rankled Bryan to be beaten by proxy, for he believed he had had much to do with the making of Roosevelt. Yet Taft's opposition had also counted, particularly when he charged that Bryan professed to be Roosevelt's heir but never made Roosevelt's policies his paramount issues and that he was a mere theorist, for what was good in Bryan's program had already been translated into law by the Republicans.

Most of the personal correspondence received by Bryan dealt with variations on the themes that he had been beaten by "Rum, Romanism, and capitalism," "Ryan, Romanism, Roosevelt, and Rockefeller," "Catholicism, Commercialism, and Coercion," or "Wall Street gold and Jesuitical conspiracy." The letters were written mostly by zealously loyal disciples and their value may be discounted to a degree. That irreconcilable gold Democrats had opposed Bryan was clear, as was the fact that Hearst's "treason" had won away some votes in the large Eastern cities. The corrupt use of Republican money was mentioned frequently, as was the use of coercion.[102] James B. Weaver spoke for

[101] Louis F. Post to Bryan, November 12, 1908, Bryan Papers; Daniels, *Editor in Politics*, p. 553; Merlo J. Pusey, *Charles Evans Hughes*, I, 246–250. Addison E. Sheldon, who spent the years 1907–1908 in New York City and who gained the confidence of some Tammany members, learned that Tammany's objective was that "Bryan was to be beaten and gotten rid of in his third campaign." Moreover, "The liquor element in New York never trusted Mr. Bryan in spite of his effort to avoid their antagonism." *Nebraska*, I, 837. Corroborating evidence of the selling out of Bryan by Tammany and Roman Catholics is furnished by C. T. Bride, "The Truth about Prohibition," Bride Collection, Bryan Papers.

[102] Letters to Bryan from Edgar L. Masters, November 11, 1908, Charles A. Wall, November 14, 1908, Henry M. Teller, November 23, 1908, Bryan Papers. In addition to the support of Roosevelt and of his half brother, Charles P. Taft, Taft noted four causes for his victory: the unanimity of businessmen, regardless of party, in distrusting Bryan; the tremendous influence of the Roman Catholic vote; the Jewish

many when he said that the monopoly and trust syndicates had "simply bought the presidency for Taft." [103] Some companies had bribed and coerced employees by promising increased wages if Taft won and reductions if Bryan won, but it was generally admitted that this sort of pressure had had little effect on the outcome. The belief that prosperity would return more quickly with Taft, who had the support of the business community, than with Bryan, had induced many workers to vote for Taft. There was not, of course, a group labor vote, but Bryan came nowhere near getting the expected 90 per cent of the votes of the million workers in the AFL. Taft had been supported solidly by the liquor forces of the nation and by most of the press, while Jim Crow laws had turned many Negroes against Bryan.[104]

Nine out of ten letters, or about a hundred in all, dealt with the religious issue. Had Bryan cared to push this matter, it would have flamed into national import in 1908 rather than in 1928, but both he and Taft sought to allay it. Some writers charged that both McKinley and Roosevelt had won Roman Catholic votes by their friendly policy toward the Roman Catholic church in the Philippines. "Judge Taft was sent to Rome to negotiate for the purchase of the Friar lands and the payment of rent and damage to church property, and as a result the Friars were established more firmly in the Islands than before. The reward for this generosity was such a proportion of the Catholic vote in this country as would throw the balance of power in favor of the Roosevelt administration," S. S. Whitney wrote Bryan.[105] Said another: "I must express the opinion that it was not the Republican party that defeated you. It was the Catholic Church. Mr. Taft was the Catholic candidate . . . and the price of their

---

vote; and breaches made in the ranks of labor by Hearst's attacks on Bryan. Letter to Roosevelt, November 7, 1908, Taft Papers. Late in 1911 Taft said, "You must remember that I was elected by Democratic votes, probably polling almost as many as McKinley did in 1896. . . ." Francis E. Leupp, "President Taft's Own View: An Authorized Interview by Francis E. Leupp," *The Outlook*, 99 (December 2, 1911), 811–818. See also O. K. Davis, *Released for Publication*, pp. 109–111.

[103] Weaver to Bryan, November 13, 1908, Bryan Papers.

[104] Among others, see the letters to Bryan by J. W. S. Thurman, November 5, 1908, W. C. Findley, November 6, 1908, J. S. Corbin, November 16, 1908, Harvey C. Garber, November 17, 1908, James S. Thomas, February 6, 1909, *ibid*. Rather than admitting that he himself had made any errors, Bryan blamed his defeat on the Republicans' use of money, newspapers, and coercion. See his letter to Thomas F. Hayden, January 2, 1909, *ibid*.

[105] Letter of November 16, 1908, *ibid*.; see also George C. Osborn, *John Sharp Williams: Planter-Statesman of the Deep South*, pp. 154–174.

support will be paid in Cabinet and Supreme Court appointments. The South was loyal to you because its [sic] the Protestant American section of the United States, free from Catholic control. Tammany is the great Catholic controlled political organization of this country. Their work is now evident. . . ." [106] Bryan found the idea repeated *ad nauseam* that "Money, Catholicism, and intimidation defeated you," and that Bryan had been "buncoed by his papal managers," including Mack, Ridder, Murphy, William J. Connors, and McCarren. Many pointed to the unusually heavy vote for Taft in the larger Eastern cities as confirmation of the obedience to an order to vote for Taft read in all Roman Catholic churches on the Sunday before election. Soon after the election Taft acknowledged that the Roman Catholic vote had helped him win, especially in cities which had large concentrations of foreign-born people, and the pope did not help matters by cabling him congratulations.

Bryan had joined Taft in trying to down religious difference as an issue in the campaign. Indeed, some correspondents took him to task for his ineptitude in handling the religious issue. His managers had circulated among Roman Catholics a tract telling of his visit to the pope during his tour around the world, but they also let it go into several Protestant Southern states. Bryan was in no way responsible for the attempted trickery, but he was held responsible for using religion to serve political ends.[107] While some Roman Catholic friends assured Bryan that "no bishop could change a vote even if he wanted to" [108] and that there was no opposition to him organized by Roman Catholic priests or bishops,[109] certain Protestant ministers were convinced that he had been crucified upon a cross of gold. "Come back to your 'Cross of Gold' argument continually," wrote one, "for on this the people are crucified. The $20,000,000 given to the Catholics in the Philippine Church affair went into the making of that cross." [110]

Bryan rejected the imputation that religion had defeated him, yet he was dismayed by its political influence and he never was completely sure of the part it played in his defeat. Not until seven months had passed was he ready to publish an editorial about it. Charles Bryan

[106] H. A. Thompson to Bryan, November 14, 1908, Bryan Papers.
[107] Philadelphia *North American,* November 11, 1908.
[108] Father James F. Nugent to Bryan, February 9, 1909, Bryan Papers.
[109] James McGuire to Bryan, January 13, 1909, *ibid.*
[110] Reverend L. H. Ruge to Bryan, November 7, 1908, *ibid.*

objected, saying that "The publication of your editorial will entirely alienate the remainder of the Catholic vote, and your argument to prove that the Catholic vote did not cause your defeat will cause Protestants to feel that you are politically interested in retaining the good will of the Catholics." [111] Bryan took Charles's advice and never published the editorial.

Eastern Democrats bade Bryan good riddance and agreed that "Disheartened, dismayed, divided, defeated for the fourth time, in debt and distress without patronage, power, prestige, or issues, it is doubtful whether the Democratic party even after the Civil War was in a more hopeless condition than after Bryan's defeat." [112] Pulitzer called for a new leader, one who had a chance to win.[113] Embittered, the New York *Times* asserted that "For Mr. Bryan this is annihilation, and in his case the crushing defeat evokes not one spark of pity. . . . Let us hope that his vocal activities will in future be confined to Nebraska, or more particularly, to Lincoln, where at least he has come out at the top of the poll." [114] One irate correspondent told Bryan that "The Democrats have in the last twelve years had enough and too much of Bossism and one man power." [115] Another said that "the Democrats who desire office . . . want you to get out of the way permanently and let some one run for the Presidency who can run. . . . Someone who can do something other than blow off hot air constantly. . . . Please accept my best wishes for a successful career as a private citizen, for the rest of your life." [116]

Republicans who felt the same way could afford to be more charitable. Writing to Whitelaw Reid, Elihu Root said that "It was a vote more against Bryan than for Taft. . . ." [117] Moreover, the Republicans had defeated Bryan rather than his party. Although the Congress remained under Republican control the Democrats had fared better than they, for the latter gained two senators but lost thirty-one representatives. Although they saved Cannon, a great strengthening of the Insurgent bloc in the Senate occurred. Republicans won seventeen governors, Democrats eleven, including five states Taft had carried. Largely because of Bryan, Democrats increased their

[111] Letters of May 7, June 6, 1909, Silas Bryan Papers.
[112] Frank R. Kent, *The Democratic Party: A History*, p. 375.
[113] New York *World*, November 4, 1908.
[114] New York *Times*, November 4, 6, 1908.
[115] Ben F. Caldwell to Bryan, November 17, 1908, Bryan Papers.
[116] Langbourne M. Williams to Bryan, November 14, 1908, *ibid.*
[117] Letter of November 23, 1908, Elihu Root Papers.

strength in almost every state legislature. The new state, Oklahoma, was resoundingly Democratic, and the Southern states generally elected progressive governors. Bryan's winning of a million and a half votes more than Parker proved that progressivism had made a permanent advance in popular favor. Those Democrats who in 1904 had supported the "radical" Roosevelt over the "conservative" Parker had returned to the fold, and Eugene V. Debs's increase of only twenty thousand votes over those of 1904 revealed that liberal Democrats who voted for Debs rather than for Roosevelt or for Parker had also returned to the Bryan camp.[118]

There was both profit and loss in Nebraska. Bryan had won the state by 12,000 in 1896, lost it by 7000 in 1900, and won it by 4500 in 1908. Out of the work of the Bryan Volunteers managed by Mullen and Gruenther came progressive Democratic governors and legislatures which from 1908 to 1918 enacted a series of truly progressive laws and the election of Gilbert M. Hitchcock to the United States Senate. But the progressives refused to follow Bryan and challenged his control of the state organization. Bryan had kept up his running feud with Representative George W. Norris by supporting his conservative Democratic opponent. If this showed Bryan a partisan, it did not explain how Norris, although a liberal, supported Taft and announced that he would even support Cannon in preference to a Democrat as Speaker.[119]

Bryan had again revealed himself an effective opposition leader. The GOP had not convinced the country that it had a monopoly on reform. Some Bryan supporters, like Folk and Henry D. Clayton, felt that he had gained in defeat;[120] others compared him with Daniel Webster and Henry Clay, who, although never President, had had great effect upon national legislation. "It is a well known fact," a minister wrote him, "that Mr. Roosevelt, in the last four years, has followed along the lines which you advocated in the campaign in which he was elected."[121] Judge W. J. Gaynor noted that "The opposition in a constitutional government does more good and achieves

[118] H. Wayne Morgan, *Eugene V. Debs: Socialist for President*, pp. 114–115.

[119] Mullen, *Western Democrat*, p. 132; Alfred Lief, *Democracy's Norris: The Biography of a Lonely Crusader*, pp. 85–86.

[120] Folk to Bryan, December 18, 1908, Clayton to Bryan, December 8, 1908, Bryan Papers.

[121] Rev. H. C. Morrison to Bryan, November 12, 1908, *ibid*

a greater reputation than those in actual control of the government," [122] and Edgar Lee Masters would have him bide his time, saying that he had "forced the imperial Republican party to admit the justice and necessity of many of the reforms you have agitated and to promise to carry them into effect. And in due season . . . all that you have contended for, which proves to be sound, will be accepted and put into practice." [123]

Although defeated again, Bryan "remained unquestionably the authentic voice of the party speaking for governmental regulation of industry and finance in order to protect agriculture and common labor. Albeit unnoticed at the time, and due to suffer some recessions, there was a distinct new trend of labor to affiliate with the Democracy, a trend that continued until it gave the party its invincible strength in the 1930's." [124] On the tariff, guarantee of bank deposits, income tax, the labor question, direct elections, and on certain aspects of the trust question, such as the prohibition of interlocking directorates, he rather than Roosevelt or Taft had foreshadowed reforms acceptable to the Democratic-Insurgent coalition that would bedevil Taft and were implemented under Wilson.

Bryan's defeat meant nothing to those who loved him. His personality and force had kept the Democratic party alive since 1896. No other man had been considered for the nomination in 1908, no other could have led the forces of Democracy as well as he, and he justly deserved the love of the millions who believed that he had kept the faith in his advocacy of Jeffersonian principles and who saw in him a cheerful and good-tempered loser. That he retained his good humor despite his defeat is revealed by his devising a story about a drunken man who attempted to pass by a doorman into a club. Gently pushed down the steps the first time, he tried again and got inside the door, only to be thrown out. On his third try he was violently ejected. Getting up and dusting off his clothes, he said, "I am on to those people. They don't want me in there." A story Bryan never heard, but which expressed the feeling of millions of voters, was that related by Charles W. Thompson. Thompson was riding a trolley car near Fairview and saw Bryan's daughter Ruth sprinting for it. She made it just in time, dropped into the seat beside him, and

[122] Letter of November 13, 1908, *ibid.*
[123] Letter of November 11, 1908, *ibid.*
[124] Binkley, *American Political Parties*, p. 360.

panted: "I seem to be the only member of the Bryan family that ever ran for anything and caught it." [125]

V

BRYAN was quite consistent and faithful to principle during his first eighteen years of political life. He had picked up and then dropped free silver and the government ownership of railroads, and he did not seek as yet to make prohibition a national political issue. However, except for that one misguided plank on free silver, by 1908 the Chicago platform of 1896 was in the process of being adopted, revealing that he had succeeded better in obtaining popular support for progressive reforms than for himself. No one during his generation agitated longer or more constantly to give political voice to social problems; few felt so deeply a compulsive inner urge to hazard denunciation, reprobation, even calumny, in honest and unpaid striving for the betterment of the American people. His avidity for political power was selfless, his support for good causes nonpartisan; unlike Roosevelt before 1912, he was willing to split his party in order to obtain needed reforms. Writing in 1910, Roosevelt boasted that "Our own party leaders did not realize that I was able to hold the Republican party in power only because I insisted upon a steady advance, and dragged them along with me." [126] His record paled before Bryan's eighteen-year pull in the progressive direction.

Bryan's greatest contribution was his insistence that political liberty could work only in the context of relative economic equality. He was unique in articulating the demands of the ordinary consumer, the average American, for the restoration of the equality of economic opportunity destroyed by a triumphant capitalism. He helped to sweep away much of the cynicism and apathy toward politics that had characterized the Gilded Age and taught men to believe that economic reformation, if not restitution, could be achieved through the ballot box. In no sense an innovator, he would restore rather than replace, re-form rather than overthrow a capitalistic system that divorced ownership and management from labor, enjoyed special legislative privilege, but assumed no social responsibility, and which

---

[125] Thompson, *Presidents I've Known*, p. 223. The late Mrs. Ruth Bryan Rohde assured the author that the tale about the trolley car is apocryphal; at least she did not recall the incident.

[126] Harbaugh, *Roosevelt*, p. 388.

had fallen in his own day into the hands of finance capitalists.[127] Basic in his thinking, as in that of other progressives, was the Jeffersonian theory of human rights, the idea that "the individual has a natural right to an existence worthy of a human being, that institutions and social arrangements are but means to the realization of this right." [128]

Bryan was often criticized after 1896 for not seeking issues to replace free silver. This criticism was only half true, for he believed that issues were created by events and circumstances and he did support new ideas, like anti-imperialism and government ownership, brought about by changed conditions. He was also criticized for being a negative voice, for providing expression of felt grievances rather than leadership, for being opposed to existing conditions or institutions but failing to offer alternative proposals.[129] In a sense this was true, for he wished to restore individualism, as envisaged in the days of Jefferson and Jackson, when material resources were so relatively easy to come by that a moderately energetic man could enjoy a competence, by ending government intervention in favor of special classes. Even more cogent was the judgment that he look back rather than forward, that the suggestions he offered were suited more for an agrarian than for the industrial nation that America had become. Nevertheless, he did propound alternative programs, many of them valid for an urban as well as a rural society. In every case these were designed to benefit individuals rather than property; moreover, he called for governmental intervention when individuals needed support beyond their capacity to provide. Although he hedged by expressing fear of the expansion of executive power, if not the usurpation of congressional power, as it had occurred under Roosevelt, he essentially demanded a welfare state, a national government powerful enough to undertake social planning to the end that the average man could earn a decent living. Hence the great opposition to him by those with vested interests, often the beneficiaries of a laissez faire that supported and encouraged but restrained not, who believed that they, the possessors of wealth, knew better than he or the common people did how to run the government.

In place of the protective tariff, for example, Bryan suggested not free trade but the reduction of rates and the extension of the free

[127] Louis M. Hacker, *The Triumph of American Capitalism*, p. 431.

[128] Merle Curti, *The Growth of American Thought*, p. 608.

[129] Richard Hofstadter, *The American Political Tradition and the Men Who Made It*, p. 190.

list until a tariff-for-revenue was obtained. Such a tariff would help win two additional objectives—a reduction in the incidence of trusts and an augmented demand for an income tax, one based upon ability to pay and hence forcing a fairer sharing of a grossly inequitably distributed national income and "compel[ling] wealth to bear its share of the expenses of the Government which protects it." [130]

Bryan believed that "A private monopoly is indefensible and intolerable," that it was "a menace to the political welfare of the country, for political independence can not long exist with industrial servitude." To restore competition, in addition to admitting competing foreign-made articles duty free, he would cause interstate corporations to obtain a federal license if they controlled as much as 25 per cent of the production of an article, restrict a corporation to 50 per cent of the total amount of any product consumed in the United States, protect the public from watered stock, outlaw interlocking directorates, prosecute corporation directors in criminal actions if they violated the anti-trust laws, and deny corporations a hiding place in the "twilight zone" between federal and state jurisdiction. Dedicated as he was to states' rights, he preferred his federal licensing plan, which left the states to administer their own laws, to Roosevelt's centralizing of the federal government with a national incorporation system.[131]

Bryan preferred to have the government control the trusts than to have them control the government. In like vein, he would have the government reign supreme in the field of banking and currency. No currency, he said, would prove adequate unless it was just to both debtor and creditor. His almost exclusive concentration on free silver in 1896 and his persistence in demanding it in 1900 proved to be erroneous, for many other problems needed solution; yet he proposed other financial reforms also. If free silver could not be obtained to provide economic justice, then some other system must be found that would preserve parity between men and property. Banks should be brought under federal control, and he remained consistent in demanding that the government rather than the banks issue and manage the currency. Moreover, to provide security for depositors during financial crises, he suggested in 1893 and more strongly in 1908 a guarantee fund created by a tax of 1 per cent on deposits; all national

[130] New York *Times*, New York *World*, August 31, 1906; W. J. Bryan, *Heart to Heart Appeals*, pp. 19–20.

[131] *Ibid.*, pp. 13, 37–38.

banks must subscribe to it, state banks could do so. The successful operation of such a fund in Oklahoma assured him that the plan was feasible. He was "simply looking at the banking question from the standpoint of the depositors," he said, "and compelling banks to make good the promise of security by which they draw deposits to the banks. . . ." [132]

In speaking of the corporation, Bryan said that "we can never become so enthusiastic over the corporation, over its usefulness, over its possibilities, as to forget the God-made man who was here first and still remains a factor to be considered." [133] No remedy for trusts would prove effective, he averred, unless the people recognized them as morally wrong. He noted that corporations were "combinations of dollars" whereas labor organizations were "associations of human beings." Since corporations dealt with inert products and labor unions with "life and with intellectual and moral forces," he wanted labor organizations to be regulated by laws that dealt with men as men, and he frequently quoted Lincoln's apt words: "Labor is prior to, and independent of, capital. Capital is only the fruit of labor, and could never have existed if labor had not first existed. Labor is the superior of capital, and deserves much the higher consideration." He therefore championed unionism, the arbitration of labor disputes, the creation of a national labor board to handle disagreements arising in interstate commerce, the absolving of labor unions from the operation of the anti-trust laws, the abolition of the labor injunction, and provision for jury trial in cases of contempt of injunction.

In the end, in these economic matters of grave import and in such other matters as the conservation of natural resources, the physical valuation of railroad properties, municipal ownership of public utilities or municipal control of public monopolies, old age annuities, and state insurance programs, Bryan consistently sought the welfare of the public rather than of property.

Bryan was equally consistent in demanding political reforms that would emancipate men from institutions or practices that denied them the exercise of their democratic rights. Even before his experiences in the House of Representatives while Thomas B. Reed was speaker he had demanded a limiting of the power of the speaker so that a minority could not tryannize a majority; from many battles in Nebraska conventions rigged by Cleveland followers and from

[132] Bryan to Woodrow Wilson, March 1, 1911, Wilson Papers.
[133] Bryan, *Heart to Heart Appeals*, p. 38.

twice seeking election as senator from a state legislature he knew of the need for direct primaries and for the direct election of senators. He had demanded the last as early as 1890; in 1892, in the House, he had sponsored his optional plan; in 1908 he called it "the gateway to other national reforms," for so long as the "exploiting interests" controlled the Senate the people could not rule. In addition he called for a single term for President, the initiative, referendum, and recall, the election of state judges, and a lame duck amendment.

Bryan's moral crusade against tainted or socially irresponsible wealth had overtones both economic and political; it was truly consistent with his belief that social problems were essentially religious in nature. He placed spiritual above mundane matters: he opposed the materialism of his age, the grubby part of the money-making process, the acquisitive instinct that drove men ruthlessly to pile up fortunes, often from dealings that wasted natural wealth, and threatened the quest by the common people for a modicum of comfort and the fulfillment of modest cultural aspirations while they revealed the Gargantuan vulgarity so vividly portrayed by Parrington and Veblen.[134] To him, Andrew Carnegie's Gospel of Wealth, which justified the free enterprise system as being in accord with natural law, was simply the law of the jungle, and he no doubt looked upon his own substantial accumulation of wealth as God's reward for his hard, honest work and clean living, in the best Puritan tradition. He repeatedly stressed the evil connection between wealth and politics, so beautifully illustrated by muckrakers from Henry D. Lloyd to Lincoln Steffens and public prosecutors from Samuel J. Tilden to Joseph W. Folk,[135] and stretched his conflict-of-interest concept to include the evils philanthropy itself could exert upon higher education, the church, and the press.

Firmly convinced that the Republicans obtained their funds from corporate enterprise by "fat-frying" tactics and repaid them with legislative largess, Bryan was among the first nationally important political figures to urge the prohibition of campaign contributions by corporations and the publication of contributions prior to elections. To prevent the power of wealth from exercising undue influence over elections, he also pioneered the idea of dollar subscriptions and of

---

[134] Curti, *Growth of American Thought*, pp. 507–511.

[135] See, for example, Geiger, *Folk*, pp. 43–58, and "Joseph W. Folk v. Edward Butler, St. Louis, 1902," *Journal of Southern History*, 38 (November 1962), 438–449,

the assumption by the government of as much as possible of the costs of campaigning.

Largely a spokesman for agrarian and sectional causes, Bryan was nonetheless a patriot and nationalist and less the isolationist than he is customarily portrayed, as revealed in his willingness to go to war with Spain in 1898, by his personal participation in the war, by his great interest in international conciliation, and by his unalterable opposition to Asiatic immigration. He objected to the Republican "large" policy on constitutional, economic, and moral grounds, established the proposition that a republic could have no colonies and, after 1905, extended his support for the arbitration of labor disputes to the "cooling off" method of settling international disputes. Eschewing the use of force, he sought the peaceful solution of controversy and the creation in the United States of a society so prosperous and happy that other peoples, of their own volition, would wish to imitate it. The American mission of achieving world peace and of extending the area of freedom and liberty, he believed, could be obtained without the use of the Army and Navy. Less the realist than Roosevelt, who understood that diplomatic success rested upon military power, he was the more consistent, for Roosevelt supported imperialism and peace at the same time.

Stubborn and commendably consistent adherence to principles which would enable the people to rule thus made Bryan an admirable leader of the opposition to Grover Cleveland, William McKinley, and Theodore Roosevelt, a "yardstick of reform" who by 1908 had convinced millions of Democrats and many Republicans that he was right and even led Roosevelt to confess that "about half" of his views were right. [136]

Roosevelt erred, for although defeated in 1908, Bryan stood on the verge of a moral victory, if not for himself, then for the Progressive movement which he had helped establish and with which he was indelibly identified, which was sweeping many states on its way to greater triumph in national legislation, and which had begun to permeate Roosevelt himself and the Republican Insurgents as well as Woodrow Wilson.

One of the few presidential candidates ever to concern himself with reforms on the state and local level, Bryan made his influence felt

[136] Paul W. Glad, *The Trumpet Soundeth: William Jennings Bryan and His Democracy, 1896–1912*, pp. 90, 108–109.

at the grass roots: Democrats like Joseph W. Folk in Missouri, Hoke Smith in Georgia, and Jeff Davis in Arkansas; Republicans like Robert La Follette in Wisconsin, Albert Cummins in Iowa, and Charles Evans Hughes in New York; and later Hiram Johnson in California and Woodrow Wilson in New Jersey could thank him for paving the way for the progressive revolutions that added fame to the names of their states. Much of the progressive legislation, social and economic as well as political in character, passed by the states had bipartisan support, and Bryan could look upon Roosevelt's filching of his reform ideas as constituting Republican endorsement for Democratic (and Populist) ideas on the national scene. By 1908, few of Roosevelt's ideas, as found in his annual messages, were new; most of them, exclusive of his demand for a larger Navy, were Bryanite in character. If Bryan had departed from a strict adherence to the traditional Jeffersonian states' rights and noninterventionist position, so too Roosevelt had departed from Hamiltonian ends, although, as Herbert Croly observed, he would employ Hamiltonian means and "use the power and resources of the Federal government for the purpose of making his country-men a more complete democracy in organization and practice. . . ." [137] By 1910 a peculiar transposition would occur, with Roosevelt out-Bryanizing Bryan with his New Nationalism, speaking of Taft's supporters as being of "the bourbon reactionary type," and calling for the limitation of armaments and a League of Peace; and the legalistic-minded and conservative Taft characterizing Roosevelt's reform proposals as "impractical" and attainable only through "revolution or revision of the Constitution."

Paradoxically, Bryan's nomination had elected Taft. Although a conservative, Taft won the Presidency because, in a campaign of personalities rather than issues, the people believed he would carry out the reforms demanded by Roosevelt. The very fact that he had been nominated three times insured Bryan a place in American history, yet the events that were to secure for him a still firmer place lay in the future. Although never again a candidate for public office, and perhaps because of that fact, he would serve his party and his country in a sensible way. A prophet of progressivism, he also had held progressive Democrats together for the twelve lean years following 1896 and brought to their attention reforms of undoubted value while insisting that an enduring social transformation was impossible without changed human hearts as well as changed minds. He would see

[137] Harbaugh, *Roosevelt*, pp. 364–365.

many of his cherished reforms adopted during the Taft administration; as a member of Wilson's cabinet he would play an important role in bringing to fruition the most vital and longest postponed reforms, including tariff and banking and currency reform, corporation control, federal laws in the interest of farmers and laborers, home rule for the Philippines, and conciliation as a widely adopted method to preserve world peace.

In 1908 Bryan had "led sublimely," as Henry Watterson said,[188] in the best organized of his three campaigns, yet he probably had concentrated too much power into his own hands. An uncompromising idealist, he had shunned political activity and personal behavior that might have rendered opponents sympathetic, with the result that he truthfully could be charged with being dictatorial. He still had a formidable following, but he failed to command the respect of many of the reorganizers, who remained loyal to the Cleveland type of laissez faire Democracy and who denied him the support of the party organization in their states.

Should or would Bryan run again? Counsel was divided. Josephus Daniels predicted that "The reforms of which Mr. Bryan has been the foremost leader will be triumphant and as editor and private citizen [he] will continue the great work to which he has consecrated his life and genius . . . but it is improbable that his name will ever again be presented for the chief magistracy." [139] Albert Shaw said that the campaign left him "in the position of a very distinguished American public man, with friends in both parties, but with no likelihood of ever running again for the Presidency." [140] However, ex-Mayor James Head of Memphis suggested that he either run again or endorse someone else; James K. McGuire advised him to leave the issue to the primaries of 1912; and Congressman Henry T. Rainey insisted that "the great mass of the people will not permit you to retire." [141] A year later Bryan announced that he would never run again. But whether he would submit to a draft in 1912 remained a moot question.

---

[188] Wall, *Watterson*, p. 257.

[139] *Editor in Politics*, pp. 552–553.

[140] "Bryan and His Future," *American Review of Reviews*, 38 (December 1908), 656.

[141] Letters to Bryan from Head, December 31, 1908, McGuire, January 3, 1909, Rainey, November 16, 1908, Bryan Papers.

Bibliography

MANUSCRIPTS

BRYAN's personal papers in the Division of Manuscripts, Library of Congress, constitute the most extensive collection of primary material on his career. Genealogical studies and the Bryan Family Bible in the keeping of the late Mrs. Thomas Stinson Allen (Mary Elizabeth Bryan), Bryan's youngest sister, in Lincoln, Nebraska, shed light on the life and times of Silas Lillard Bryan, their father. The Silas Bryan Papers, used by courtesy of the late Silas Bryan, Bryan's nephew, in Minneapolis, Minnesota, are of inestimable value for the correspondence between William Jennings Bryan and his brother, Charles Wayland Bryan. The Mrs. Ruth Bryan Rohde Papers, which were used in Ossining, New York, are not available to the public; they are valuable for Bryan's college days and courtship. A small collection of Bryan material, the John Peter Altgeld Collection, the Joseph G. Cannon Papers, and the Waldo R. Brown Collection in the Illinois State Historical Society, Springfield, Illinois, help re-create the Illinois of Bryan's youth and Altgeld's contributions to the campaigns of 1896 and 1900. The Henry Moore Teller Papers, in the State Historical Society of Colorado, Denver, also proved helpful in tracing Bryan's political career. A small collection of Bryan papers at the Nebraska State Historical Society, various studies on the history of Nebraska, and the J. Sterling Morton Collection in the Library of the University of Nebraska, Lincoln, Nebraska, give insight into Bryan's relationship to the agrarian crusade and Populist upheaval of the 1890's. The Henry Steele Commager Papers, lent to the author by Professor Henry Steele Commager, of Columbia University, contain copious extracts from the letters of William Vincent Allen, Henry D. Lloyd, George Fred Williams, and William F. Vilas, a number of special studies on Populism, and notes on secondary sources for every phase of Bryan's life. David Bennett Hill's relations to Bryan and the Democratic party are scantily sketched in the George S. Bixby Papers, New York State Library, Albany, New York. Of the other collections in the Division of Manuscripts, Library of Congress, the following were found to be very useful: William Dallas Bynum, Andrew Carnegie, Thomas H. Carter, Grover Cleveland, Josephus Daniels, Don Dickinson, Moreton Frewen, James R. Garfield, Charles S. Hamlin, John Hay, Philander C. Knox, Daniel S. Lamont, William McKinley, L. T. Michener, John T. Morgan, George W. Norris, George Peabody, Louis F. Post, Joseph Pulitzer, Whitelaw Reid,

Elihu Root, John C. Spooner, Theodore Roosevelt, William Howard Taft, Henry Watterson, Woodrow Wilson, Leonard Wood, and Robert W. Woolley. Use was also made of the extensive collections on the literature on the currency question in the Library of Congress and in the Public Library of St. Louis, Missouri; of the Judge's Docket and Bar Docket in the Circuit Court, Jacksonville, Morgan County, Illinois; and of the District Court, Justice Court, and County Court dockets at Lincoln, Lancaster County, Nebraska.

NEWSPAPERS AND JOURNALS

THE PRINCIPAL sources for Bryan's years in Salem and Jacksonville, Illinois, are the Salem *Advocate,* Centralia *Sentinel, Illinois College Rambler,* Jacksonville *Journal, Illinois Courier* (Jacksonville), Sigma Pi *Minute Book,* and the catalogue and student records of Illinois College.

For Bryan's life in Nebraska and his relationship to the agrarian crusade and Populism, the following newspapers proved to be most fruitful: Lincoln *Daily Call, Nebraska State Journal* (Lincoln), Omaha *Bee,* Omaha *Daily Herald,* and Omaha *World-Herald.* The fact that Bryan was the editor of the last from 1894 to 1896 gives it an importance perhaps out of proportion to its intrinsic merits, yet it is indispensable for a study of the life of Bryan and of the activities of Western politicians.

Viewpoints on the issues of the campaigns from 1890 through 1908 were obtained from the following newspapers: Atlanta *Constitution* and *Journal;* Miami (Florida) *Daily News;* Chicago *American, Daily News, Dispatch, Inter-Ocean, Record, Times-Herald,* and *Tribune; Illinois State Register* (Springfield, Illinois); Lincoln (Nebraska) *Herald;* Manchester (Connecticut) *Union;* New Orleans *Times-Democrat;* New York *American, Evening Post, Dispatch, Financial and Commercial Chronicle, Herald, Journal, Sun, Times, Tribune,* and *World;* Philadelphia *North American;* Louisville (Kentucky) *Courier-Journal;* Omaha *Bee* and *World-Herald;* Raleigh (North Carolina) *News and Observer; Rocky Mountain News* (Denver); Salt Lake [City] *Tribune;* Kansas City *Star;* San Francisco *Chronicle* and *Examiner;* St. Louis *Globe-Democrat* and *Post-Dispatch;* and Washington, D.C. *Evening Star, Post,* and *Times.* Bryan's activities and comments during his globe trotting were traced through *The Commoner,* Manila *American* (Manila, The Philippines), and all major London newspapers.

The *Journal of the Illinois State Historical Society* and *Nebraska History* provide details on state and local history. *Harper's Weekly, The Outlook, The Nation, Gunton's Magazine,* and *The Independent,* journals of opinion, opposed Bryan violently in 1896 and 1900. However, *The Nation* supported him on anti-imperialism in 1900. *The American Review of Reviews, Forum, North American Review,* and *Public Opinion* published articles pro and con on all major issues but generally opposed Bryan, whereas *The Arena* and the *National Bimetallist* were pro-silver and pro-Bryan. The *Congressional Record* was a never-failing source for Bryan's career in Washington, D.C. European, primarily British, opinion was ascertained from the *Contemporary Review, Fortnightly Review,* and *Quarterly Review.* Other magazines containing information about Bryan include *Agricultural History, American Bar Association Journal, American Economic Review, American Historical Review, The American Political Science Review, American Scholar, Annals of the Academy of Political and Social Science, Annals of the American Academy, Army and Navy Journal, Atlantic Monthly, The Century Magazine,* New Series, *Cosmopolitan, Current History, Current Literature, Everybody's Magazine, Illinois College Alumni Quarterly, Journal of Economic History, Journal of Political Economy, Journal of Politics, Journal of Southern History, Living Age, McClure's Magazine, National Bimetallist, Minnesota History, Mississippi Valley Historical Review, New England Quarterly, The Ohio Historical Quarterly, The Outlook, Pacific Historical Review, Pacific Northwest Quarterly, Political Science Quarterly, Proceedings of the American Philosophical Society, The Reader, Reader's Digest, Smith College Studies in History, Southern Speech Journal, Southwest Review, Transactions of the Illinois State Historical Society, The Virginia Magazine of History and Biography, Tom Watson's Magazine,* and *World To-Day.* Articles cited by author in the text and articles found useful in research from these popular and learned periodicals are listed below.

ABBOT, LYMAN. "William Jennings Bryan: A Character Study," *The Outlook,* 84 (September 8, 1906), 66–68.

ABBOT, WILLIS J. "William Jennings Bryan—a Character Sketch," *American Review of Reviews,* 14 (August 1896), 161–173.

———. "The Management of the Democratic Campaign," *American Review of Reviews,* 22 (November 1900), 556–582.

ADAMS, CHARLES FRANCIS. "What Mr. Cleveland Stands For," *Forum,* 13 (July 1892), 662–672.

ALDRICH, NELSON W. "The McKinley Act and the Cost of Living," *Forum,* 14 (October 1892), 242–253.

ALLEN, HOWARD W. "Miles Poindexter and the Progressive Movement," *Pacific Northwest Quarterly,* 53 (July 1962), 114–122.

ALLEN, WILLIAM H. "The Election of 1900," *Annals of the American Academy of Political and Social Science,* 17 (January–June 1901), 53–73.

ALLEN, WILLIAM VINCENT. "Western Feeling Towards the East," *North American Review,* 162 (May 1896), 588–593.

———. "A Western Statesman's Reasons for Supporting Hon. Thomas E. Watson," *The Arena,* 32 (October 1904), 395.

ANDERSON, PAUL RUSSELL. "Hiram K. Jones and Philosophy at Jacksonville," *Journal of the Illinois State Historical Society,* 33 (March–December 1940), 478–520.

ATKINSON, EDWARD. "Free Silver Coinage—Why Not?" *Forum,* 11 (May 1891), 350–351.

———. "Real Meaning of the Free Coinage Agitation," *Forum,* 13 (April 1892), 215–227.

———. "Jingoes and Silverites," *North American Review,* 161 (December 1895), 553–556.

———. "The Increased Production of Gold," *North American Review,* 162 (February 1896), 160–173.

BABCOCK, JOSEPH W. "The Meanings of the Election," *North American Review,* 159 (December 1894), 742–754.

BAILEY, THOMAS A. "Was the Presidential Election of 1900 a Mandate on Imperialism?" *Mississippi Valley Historical Review,* 24 (June 1937), 43–52.

BARNES, JAMES A. "The Gold Standard Democrats and Party Conflict," *Mississippi Valley Historical Review,* 17 (December 1930), 422–450.

———. "The Myths of the Bryan Campaign," *Mississippi Valley Historical Review,* 34 (December 1947), 367–404.

———. "Illinois and the Gold-Silver Controversy, 1890–1896," *Transactions of the Illinois State Historical Society, 1931* (Springfield, 1932), pp. 35–59.

BECK, C. F. "Bryan as a Soldier," *The Arena,* 24 (October 1900), 393–396.

BECKER, CARL. "What Is Still Living in the Political Philosophy of Thomas Jefferson?" *American Historical Review,* 48 (July 1943), 691–706.

BERNSTEIN, IRVING (ed.). "Samuel Gompers and Free Silver," *Mississippi Valley Historical Review,* 29 (December 1942), 394–400.

BIGELOW, PULTENEY. "What I Saw at Kansas City," *Contemporary Review,* 72 (September 1900), 442–456.

BLAND, RICHARD P. "A Janus-Faced Statute," *North American Review,* 151 (September 1890), 344–353.

———. "The Currency and the Democratic Party," *North American Review,* 156 (April 1893), 485–493.

———. "The Future of Silver," *North American Review,* 160 (March 1896), 345–351.

———. "The Duty of the Hour," *North American Review,* 163 (September 1896), 368–376.

BOUTWELL, GEORGE S. "The Income Tax," *North American Review,* 160 (May 1895), 589–601.

———. "Silver as a Circulating Medium," *Forum,* 11 (March 1891), 10–18.

BROOKS, SYDNEY. "Bryanism," *Contemporary Review,* 78 (November 1900), 633–642.

BRYAN, CHARLES W., JR. "Morgan Bryan, Pioneer on the Opequon and Yadkin," *The Virginia Magazine of History and Biography,* 70 (April 1962), 154–164.

BRYAN, WILLIAM JENNINGS. "The Currency Question: A Prophetic Utterance," *The Arena,* 16 (September 1896), 529–537.

——. "Has the Election Settled the Money Question?" *North American Review,* 163 (December 1896), 703–710.

——. "Foreign Influence in American Politics," *The Arena,* 19 (April 1898), 433–438.

——. "The Issue of the Presidential Campaign," *North American Review,* 170 (June 1900), 753–771.

——. "The Election of 1900," *North American Review,* 171 (December 1900), 788–801.

——. "The Next Democratic Nomination," *The Independent,* 55 (May 21, 1903), 1177–1180.

——. "Farming as an Occupation," *Cosmopolitan,* 36 (January 1904), 369–371.

——. "The Future of the Democratic Party: A Discussion of Moral Issues in the Pending Questions," *The Outlook,* 78 (December 19, 1904), 919–927.

——. "Has the President the Courage to Be a Reformer?" *Public Opinion,* 39 (April 15, 1905), 557–559.

——. "A Remedy for Trusts," *Public Opinion,* 39 (April 29, 1905), 645–648.

——. "Individualism vs. Socialism," *The Century Magazine,* New Series, 49 (April 1906), 856–859.

——. "Path to Peace," *The Independent,* 61 (August 30, 1906), 483–489.

——. "How Could the United States, if Necessary, Give Up Its Colonies?" *World To-Day,* 14 (February 1908), 151–154.

——. "Why the Philippines Should Be Independent," *Everybody's Magazine,* 19 (November 1908), 640d–f.

BRYAN, WILLIAM JENNINGS, JR. "My Japanese Brother," *Reader's Digest,* June 1955, pp. 17–21.

BUCK, SOLON J., "Agricultural Organization in Illinois, 1870–1880," *Journal of the Illinois State Historical Society,* 3 (April 1910–January 1912), 10–23.

BUNNELL, NEWTON L. "A Farmer's View of Free Coinage," *North American Review,* 156 (April 1893), 753–755.

CARLISLE, JOHN G. "The Tariff and the Farmer," *Forum,* 8 (January 1890), 475–488.

CARNEGIE, ANDREW. "The Silver Problem: A Word to Wage Earners," *North American Review,* 157 (September 1893), 354–370.

——. "The Ship of State Adrift, I," *North American Review,* 162 (June 1896), 641–648; "The Ship of State Adrift, II," *ibid.,* 163 (October 1896), 496–503.

CHANDLER, WILLIAM E. "Issues and Prospects of the Campaign," *North American Review,* 163 (August 1896), 175–182.

CLARK, WALTER. "Inevitable Constitutional Changes," *North American Review,* 163 (October 1896), 462–469.

——. "Free Coinage Indispensable," *The Arena,* 16 (November 1896), 934–944.

CLARK, THOMAS D. "The People, William Goebel, and the Kentucky Railroads," *Journal of Southern History*, 5 (February 1939), 34–48.

CLEVELAND, FREDERICK ALBERT. "The Final Report of the Monetary Commission," *Annals of the American Academy*, 13 (1899), 31–56.

CLEVELAND, GROVER. "Parker," *McClure's Magazine*, 24 (November 1904), 4–9.

COCKRAN, W. BOURKE. "The Financial Outlook," *North American Review*, 156 (June 1893), 738–749.

COLETTA, PAOLO E. "Silas Bryan of Salem," *Journal of the Illinois State Historical Society*, 42 (March 1949), 57–79.

––––––. "The Youth of William Jennings Bryan—Beginnings of a Christian Statesman," *Nebraska History*, 31 (March 1950), 1–24.

––––––. "William Jennings Bryan and the Nebraska Senatorial Election of 1893," *Nebraska History*, 31 (September 1950), 183–203.

––––––. "William Jennings Bryan's First Nebraska Years," *Nebraska History*, 33 (June 1952), 71–95.

––––––. "William Jennings Bryan," *Illinois College Alumni Quarterly*, 31 (January 1953), 7–11.

––––––. "The Morning Star of the Reformation: William Jennings Bryan's First Congressional Campaign," *Nebraska History*, 37 (June 1956), 103–120.

––––––. "Bryan, McKinley, and the Treaty of Paris," *Pacific Historical Review*, 26 (May 1957), 131–146.

––––––. "Governor Poynter's Interim Appointment of William Vincent Allen to the United States Senate in 1899," *Nebraska History*, 38 (June 1957), 155–163.

––––––. " 'Won, 1880–One 1884,' The Courtship of William Jennings Bryan and Mary Elizabeth Baird," *Journal of the Illinois State Historical Society*, 50 (Autumn 1957), 231–242.

––––––. "The Nebraska Democratic State Convention of April 13–14, 1892," *Nebraska History*, 39 (December 1958), 317–333.

––––––. "William Jennings Bryan's Second Congressional Campaign," *Nebraska History*, 40 (December 1959), 275–291.

––––––. "Bryan, Cleveland, and the Disrupted Democracy, 1890–1896," *Nebraska History*, 41 (March 1960), 1–27.

––––––. "Bryan, Anti-Imperialism, and Missionary Diplomacy," *Nebraska History*, 44 (September 1963), 167–187.

––––––. "William Jennings Bryan and Currency and Banking Reforms," *Nebraska History*, 45 (March 1964), 31–57.

CONANT, CHARLES A. "Plans for Currency Reform," *American Review of Reviews*, 17 (January 1898), 43–52.

––––––. "The Law and the Value of Money," *Annals of the American Academy*, 16 (1900), 189–211.

COUDERT, FREDERIC R. "The American Protective Association," *Forum*, 17 (July 1894), 513–523.

CREELMAN, JAMES. "Bryan the Man," *The Independent*, 52 (July 26, 1900), 1770–1772.

CUNNIFF, M. G. "Alton Brooks Parker," *World's Work*, 8 (June 1904), 923–932.

Current Literature. "Bryan as a Defender of Christianity," 41 (October 1906), 437–438.

CURTI, MERLE. "Bryan and World Peace," *Smith College Studies in History* (Northampton, Mass., 1931), pp. 111–258.

DAGGETT, DAVID L. Review of Frederick H. Jackson, *Simeon Eben Baldwin —Lawyer, Social Scientist, and Statesman* (New York: 1955), in *American Bar Association Journal*, 41 (June 1955), 541–542.

DANIELS, JOSEPHUS. "Mr. Bryan's Third Campaign," *American Review of Reviews*, 38 (November 1908), 423–431.

DESTLER, CHESTER MCARTHUR. "Agricultural Readjustment and Agrarian Unrest in Illinois, 1880–1896," *Agricultural History*, 21 (April 1947), 104–163.

———. "Western Radicalism, 1865–1901: Concepts and Origins," *Mississippi Valley Historical Review*, 31 (December 1941), 335–368.

———. "The Labor-Populist Alliance in Illinois, 1894," *Mississippi Valley Historical Review*, 27 (March 1941), 589–602.

———. "The Influence of Edward Kellogg upon American Radicalism, 1865–1896," *Journal of Political Economy*, 40 (June 1932), 338–365.

DIAMOND, WILLIAM. "Urban and Rural Voting in 1896," *American Historical Review*, 46 (January 1941), 281–305.

DICKINSON, G. LOWES. "Eastern and Western Ideals: Being a Rejoinder to William Jennings Bryan," *The Century Magazine*, New Series, 51 (December 1906), 313–316.

DIMOCK, ANTHONY W. "Currency Reform," *The Arena*, 19 (March 1898), 313–322.

DIXON, FRANK H. "Railroad Control in Nebraska," *Political Science Quarterly*, 13 (December 1898), 617–647.

DOSS, RICHARD B. "Democrats in the Doldrums: Virginia and the Democratic National Convention of 1904," *Journal of Southern History*, 20 (November 1954), 511–529.

DOZER, DONALD MARQUAND. "Benjamin Harrison and the Presidential Campaign of 1892," *American Historical Review*, 44 (October 1948), 49–77.

DUNNELL, ELDRIDGE GERRY. "The Rise of the 'National Democracy': The Movement for Sound Money and the Indianapolis Convention," *American Review of Reviews*, 14 (October 1896), 434–445.

DURDEN, ROBERT F. "The 'Cow-Bird' Grounded: The Populist Nomination of Bryan and Watson in 1896," *Mississippi Valley Historical Review*, 50 (December 1963), 397–423.

ECKLES, JAMES H. "The Financial Situation," *North American Review,* 157 (August 1893), 129–139.

——. "Our Experiments in Financial Legislation," *North American Review,* 159 (December 1894), 689–696.

——. "The Duty of the Republican Administration," *North American Review,* 163 (December 1896), 696–702.

ELLIS, ELMER. "The Silver Republicans in the Election of 1896," *Mississippi Valley Historical Review,* 18 (March 1932), 519–534.

——. "Public Opinion on the Income Tax, 1860–1900," *ibid.,* 27 (September 1940), 225–242.

FAIRCHILD, CHARLES S. "The United States and Silver," *Forum,* 11 (July 1891), 550–558.

FARMER, HALLIE. "The Railroads and Frontier Populism," *Mississippi Valley Historical Review,* 13 (December 1926), 387–397.

FALKNER, ROLAND P. "The Currency Law of 1900," *Annals of the American Academy,* 16 (1900), 33–55.

FITE, GILBERT C. "Republican Strategy and the Farm Vote in the Presidential Campaign of 1896," *American Historical Review,* 65 (July 1960), 787–806.

FLOWER, B. O. "Some Eastern Conservative Authorities Who Are Championing the Cause of Silver," *The Arena,* 16 (July 1896), 208–221.

——. "Four Epochs in the History of Our Republic," *The Arena,* 16 (November 1896), 928–936.

——. "Bryan and the Presidency," *The Arena,* 36 (August 1906), 189–190.

——. "Bryan and the Would-Be Wreckers of the Democratic Party," *The Arena,* 39 (March 1908), 344–349.

——. "Bryan and the Senegambian in the New York *World's* Woodpile," *The Arena,* 39 (April 1908), 464–466.

——. "New York *World's* Gallant Fight for Plutocracy," *The Arena,* 39 (May 1908), 620–622.

——. "Hearst's Attack on Bryan," *The Arena,* 40 (October 1908), 355–357.

FOSTER, CHARLES. "The Brussels Conference Reviewed," *North American Review,* 156 (April 1893), 493–500.

FRASER, HERBERT F. "Popular Tariff Fallacies," *Annals of the Academy of Political and Social Science,* 141 (January 1929), 53–60.

GAMBRELL, H. "James Stephen Hogg: Statesman or Demagogue?" *Southwest Review,* 13 (1928), 338–366.

GARLAND, HAMLIN. "The Alliance Wedge in Congress," *The Arena,* 5 (March 1892), 447–457.

GARNETT, L. A. "The Crux of the Money Controversy: Has Gold Risen?" *Forum,* 18 (January 1895), 573–586.

GEIGER, LOUIS G. "Joseph W. Folk v. Edward Butler, St. Louis, 1902," *Journal of Southern History,* 28 (November 1962), 438–449.

GIDDINGS, FRANK H. "Bryan and Our Complex Social Order," *The Century Magazine,* New Series, 51 (November 1906), 154–157.

GLADDEN, REV. WASHINGTON. "The Embattled Farmers," *Forum,* 10 (November 1890), 315–322.

GLEED, JAMES WILLIS, "Western Mortgages," *Forum,* 9 (March 1890), 93–105.

———. "The True Significance of Western Unrest," *Forum,* 16 (October 1893), 251–262.

GODKIN, E. L. "Why Bryan Failed," *The Nation,* 63 (August 20, 1896), 134

———. "The Week," *The Nation,* 63 (September 17, 1896), 203.

———. "The Week," *The Nation,* 63 (October 29, 1896), 319.

———. "Significance of the Verdict," *The Nation,* 63 (November 12, 1896), 358.

GOODLOE, DANIEL REAVES. "Western Farm Mortgages," *Forum,* 10 (November 1890), 346–356.

GRAFF, LEO W., JR. "Fred T. Dubois and the Silver Issue, 1896," *Pacific Northwest Quarterly,* 53 (October 1962), 138–144.

GRANTHAM, DEWEY W., JR. "Hoke Smith: Progressive Governor of Georgia, 1907–1909," *Journal of Southern History,* 15 (November 1949), 423–440.

GROSVENOR, CHARLES HENRY. "A Republican View of the Presidency," *North American Review,* 171 (July 1900), 41–54.

Gunton's Magazine. "Mr. Bryan's Proclamation," 19 (July 1900), 17–28.

H., J. H. "The Democratic Convention," *The Outlook,* 89 (July 1908), 649–650.

HARRINGTON, FRED H. "The Anti-Imperialist Movement in the United States, 1898–1900," *Mississippi Valley Historical Review,* 22 (September 1935), 211–230.

———. "Literary Aspects of American Anti-Imperialism, 1898–1902," *New England Quarterly,* 10 (1937), 650–667.

HARTER, MICHAEL D. "Free Coinage, the Blight of Our Commerce," *Forum,* 13 (May 1892), 281–284.

———. "The Kind of Money That Would Rule the World," *Forum,* 17 (July 1894), 603–608.

HARVEY, WILLIAM H. "The Free Silver Argument," *Forum,* 19 (June 1895), 401–409.

HEAD, FRANKLIN H. "Need of an International Monetary Agreement," *Forum,* 17 (June 1894), 455–466.

HENDRIX, JOSEPH C. "The Folly of Further Silver Agitation," *Forum,* 17 (June 1894), 467–474.

HEPBURN, A. B. "The 'Baltimore Plan' of Currency Reform," *Forum,* 18 (December 1894), 385–395.

HICKS, JOHN D. "The Birth of the Populist Party," *Minnesota History,* 9 (1928), 219–247.

Hoffman, Charles. "The Depression of the Nineties," *Journal of Economic History*, 16 (June 1956), 137–164.

Holmes, George K. "The Concentration of Wealth," *Political Science Quarterly*, 8 (December 1893), 589–600.

Hornig, Edgar A. "The Indefatigable Mr. Bryan in 1908," *Nebraska History*, 37 (September 1956), 183–199.

———. "The Religious Issue in the Taft-Bryan Duel of 1908," *Proceedings of the American Philosophical Society*, 105 (December 1961), 530–537.

Huthmacher, Joseph. "Urban Liberalism and the Age of Reform," *Mississippi Valley Historical Review*, 59 (September 1962), 231–241.

Independent. "Political Career of David B. Hill," *Forum*, 18 (November 1894), 257–269.

Johnson, Arthur M. "Theodore Roosevelt and the Bureau of Corporations," *Mississippi Valley Historical Review*, 45 (March 1959), 571–590.

Johnson, Claudius O. "The Story of Silver Politics in Idaho, 1892–1902," *Pacific Northwest Quarterly*, 33 (July 1942), 283–296.

Johnson, John R. "Imperialism in Nebraska, 1898–1904," *Nebraska History*, 44 (September 1963), 141–166.

Jones, John P. "What the Remonetization of Silver Would Do for the Republic," *The Arena*, 16 (October 1896), 736–742.

Key, V. O. "A Theory of Critical Elections," *Journal of Politics*, 17 (1955), 1–18.

Kitson, Arthur. "William Jennings Bryan," *Fortnightly Review*, New Series, 118 (October 1925), 558–567.

Knox, John Jay. "Bank Circulation and Free Coinage," *Forum*, 12 (February 1892), 772–782.

Leech, Edward O. "Would Free Coinage Bring European Silver Here?" *Forum*, 13 (March 1892), 34–44.

———. "The Fall of Silver and Its Causes," *Forum*, 13 (June 1892), 439–450.

———. "The Doom of Silver," *Forum*, 15 (July 1893), 657–665.

———. "Silver Legislation and Its Results," *North American Review*, 157 (July 1893), 42–52.

Leupp, Francis E. "President Taft's Own View: An Authorized Interview by Francis E. Leupp," *The Outlook*, 99 (December 2, 1911), 811–818.

———. "Dark Horse Convention," *The Outlook*, 101 (June 8, 1912), 297–302.

Lloyd, Henry D. "The Populists at St. Louis," *American Review of Reviews*, 14 (September 1896), 298–303.

McMasters, John Bach. "A Century's Struggle for Silver," *Forum*, 16 (September 1893), 7–10.

McMillin, Benton; John Dalzell; and W. J. Bryan. "The Coming Tariff Legislation," *North American Review*, 157 (October 1893), 493–506.

MacRae, Duncan, Jr., and Charles E. Gilbert. "Critical Elections in Illinois, 1888–1958," *The American Political Science Review*, 59 (September 1960), 669–683.

Mahnken, Norbert R. "William Jennings Bryan in Oklahoma," *Nebraska History*, 31 (December 1950), 247–274.

Maxey, Edwin. "The Denver Convention," *The Arena*, 39 (July 1908), 150–154.

Mills, Roger Q. "What Shall We Do With Silver?" *North American Review*, 150 (May 1890), 572–585.

———. "New England and the New Tariff Bill," *Forum*, 9 (June 1890), 361–370.

Moger, Allan. "The Rift in the Virginia Democracy in 1896," *Journal of Southern History*, 4 (August 1938), 295–317.

Morgan, John T. "The Danger of the Farmers' Alliance," *Forum*, 12 (November 1891), 399–409.

———. "Silver—A Money Metal," *The Arena*, 16 (October 1896), 705–720.

Morton, J. Sterling. "Farmers, Fallacies, and Furrows," *Forum*, 17 (June 1894), 385–395.

———. "Protection and the Proletariat," *North American Review*, 158 (June 1894), 641–646.

——— with W. M. Springer and Henry W. Cannon, "The Financial Muddle," *North American Review*, 160 (February 1895), 129–156.

———. "The Agricultural Problem," *North American Review*, 162 (May 1896), 638–640.

Nichols, Jeannette P. "John Sherman: A Study in Inflation," *Mississippi Valley Historical Review*, 21 (September 1934), 181–194.

———. "The Politics and Personalities of Silver Repeal in the United States Senate," *American Historical Review*, 41 (October 1935), 26–53.

———. "Bryan's Benefactor: Coin Harvey and His World," *The Ohio Historical Quarterly*, 67 (October 1958), 299–325.

Norris, George W. "Bryan as a Political Leader," *Current History*, 22 (September 1925), 859–867.

Parsons, Stanley B. "Who Were the Nebraska Populists?" *Nebraska History*, 44 (June 1963), 83–99.

Peffer, William A. "The Farmers' Defensive Movement," *Forum*, 8 (December 1889), 464–473.

Pennoyer, Hon. Sylvester. "The Financial Situation: After the Four Hundred Years, What?" *North American Review*, 157 (August 1893), 139–144.

Peterson, Merrill D. "Thomas Jefferson and the National Purpose," *Proceedings of the American Philosophical Society*, 105 (December 1961), 517–520.

Poage, George R. "The College Career of William Jennings Bryan," *Mississippi Valley Historical Review*, 15 (September 1928), 165–183.

POLK, L. L. "The Farmers' Discontent," *North American Review*, 153 (July 1891), 5–12.

POLLACK, NORMAN. "Hofstadter on Populism: A Critique of *The Age of Reform*," *Journal of Southern History*, 26 (November 1960), 478–500.

———. "The Myth of Populist Anti-Semitism," *American Historical Review*, 68 (October 1962), 76–80.

PRATT, JULIUS W. "The 'Large Policy of 1898,' " *Mississippi Valley Historical Review*, 19 (September 1932), 219–242.

QUINCY, JOSIAH. "Issues and Prospects of the Campaign," *North American Review*, 163 (August 1896), 182–194.

REED, THOMAS B. "The Political Situation," *North American Review*, 157 (September 1893), 257–267.

———. "The Present Administration of National Affairs," *North American Review*, 159 (July 1894), 1–10.

———. "Historic Political Upheavals," *North American Review*, 160 (January 1895), 109–116.

———. "A Last Tribute," *North American Review*, 160 (April 1895), 385–395.

———. "The Safe Pathway of Experience," *North American Review*, 163 (October 1896), 385–394.

RIDPATH, JOHN CLARK. "Three Epochs of Democracy and Three Men," *The Arena*, 19 (May 1898), 543–563.

ROOSEVELT, THEODORE. "The Issues of 1896. I. A Republican View," *Century Magazine*, New Series, 29 (November 1895), 68–72.

RUSSELL, WILLIAM E. "The Issues of 1896. II. A Democratic View," *Century Magazine*, New Series, 29 (November 1895), 73–77.

———. "Political Causes of the Business Depression," *North American Review*, 157 (December 1893), 641–652.

SATTERTHWAIT, L. "Bryan's Mistake," *The Arena*, 37 (March 1907), 257–259.

SCHIFF, JACOB H. "Should the Silver Law of 1890 Be Repealed?" *Forum*, 12 (December 1891), 472–476.

SELIGMAN, EDWIN R. A. "Is the Income Tax Constitutional and Just?" *Forum*, 18 (March 1895), 48–56.

SHAW, ALBERT. "William V. Allen: Populist," *American Review of Reviews*, 10 (July 1894), 30–42.

———. "Bryan and His Future," *American Review of Reviews*, 38 (December 1908), 656.

———. "William Jennings Bryan," *American Review of Reviews*, 72 (September 1925), 259–263.

———. "The American Presidential Election," *Contemporary Review*, 78 (November 1900), 609–632.

SHEARMAN, THOMAS G. "The Owners of the United States," *Forum*, 8 (November 1889), 263–273.

———. "The Coming Billionaire," *Forum*, 10 (January 1891), 546–557.

SMALLEY, EUGENE. "William McKinley—A Study of His Character and Career," *American Review of Reviews*, 14 (July 1896), 33–45.

SMITH, ROBERT W. "Comedy at St. Louis: A Footnote to Nineteenth Century Political Oratory," *Southern Speech Journal*, 25 (Winter 1959), 122–133.

SNYDER, CARL. "Marion Butler," *American Review of Reviews*, 14 (October 1896), 429–431.

ST. JOHN, WILLIAM P. "A National Platform of the American Independents of 1896," *The Arena*, 16 (June 1896), 67–69.

STANWOOD, EDWARD. "The Clamor for 'More Money,'" *North American Review*, 151 (November 1890), 634–636.

STEAD, W. T. "'Coxeyism': A Character Sketch," *American Review of Reviews*, 10 (July 1894), 47–59.

STEWART, SENATOR W. M. "Silver, and the Need of More Money," *Forum*, 11 (June 1891), 429–437.

STOCKBRIDGE, FRANK P. "Bryan, the Great Commoner," *Current History*, 22 (September 1925), 867–874.

TAUSSIG, FRANK W. "The Working of the New Silver Act," *Forum*, 10 (October 1890), 165–173.

TELLER, HENRY M. "The Loyal West," *North American Review*, 162 (June 1896), 757–758.

THOMAS, CHARLES S. "Bryan of the Nineties," *Harper's Weekly*, 58 (October 11, 1913), 6–7.

THORNBROUGH, EMMA LOU. "The Brownsville Episode and the Negro Vote," *Mississippi Valley Historical Review*, 44 (December 1957), 469–493.

TOLSTOY, COUNT LEO. "Garrison and Non-Resistance," *The Independent*, 56 (April 24, 1904), 881–883.

TRACY, FRANK B. "Menacing Socialism in the Western States," *Forum*, 15 (May 1893), 332–342.

———. "Rise and Doom of the Populist Party," *Forum*, 16 (October 1893), 240–250.

TRAYNOR, W. J. H. "Aims and Methods of the 'A.P.A.,'" *North American Review*, 159 (July 1894), 67–76.

———. "Policy and Power of the A.P.A.," *North American Review*, 162 (June 1896), 658–666.

VEST, GEORGE G. "The Real Issue," *North American Review*, 155 (October 1892), 401–406.

———. "The Coming Extra Session: A Democratic View," *North American Review*, 157 (August 1893), 240–245.

VOORHEES, DANIEL W. "A Plea for Free Silver," *North American Review*, 153 (November 1891), 524–525.

WAITE, DAVIS H. "Are the Silver States Ruined?" *North American Review*, 158 (January 1894), 24–29.

WADSWORTH, JULIAN S. "William Jennings Bryan, '81—College Days," *Illinois College Alumni Quarterly*, 15 (1939), 11–14.

WALKER, FRANCIS A. "The Free Coinage of Silver," *Journal of Political Economy*, 1 (March 1893), 163–178.

WATKINS, ALBERT. "Is Socialism an Element of Bryanism?" *The Arena*, 24 (September 1900), 225–235.

———. "The Beginnings of Bryan," *The Independent*, 52 (September 20, 1900), 2245–2248.

———. "Bryan and Jeffersonian Democracy," *Forum*, 31 (May 1901), 358–369.

WEAVER, JAMES B. "The Threefold Contention of Industry," *The Arena*, 5 (March 1892), 427–435.

WELLBORN, FRED. "The Influence of the Silver Republican Senators, 1889–1891," *Mississippi Valley Historical Review*, 14 (March 1928), 462–472.

WELLMAN, WALTER. "The Management of the Taft Campaign," *American Review of Reviews*, 38 (November 1908), 432–438.

WELLS, DAVID A. "The Downfall of Certain Financial Fallacies," *Forum*, 16 (October 1893), 131–149.

———. "The Teachings of Our Recent Economic Experience," *Forum*, 16 (January 1894), 527–543.

———. "Is the Existing Income Tax Constitutional?" *Forum*, 18 (January 1895), 537–542.

WEST, J. L. "The Recrudescence of Bryan," *Forum*, 38 (October 1906), 147–152.

WHITE, HORACE. "A Plan for a Permanent Bank System," *Forum*, 12 (December 1891), 477–482.

———. "India's Action and the Sherman Law," *Forum*, 15 (August 1893), 649–656.

WIEBE, ROBERT H. "Business Disunity and the Progressive Movement, 1901–1914," *Mississippi Valley Historical Review*, 44 (March 1958), 664–685.

———. "The House of Morgan and the Executive, 1905–1913," *American Historical Review*, 55 (October 1959), 49–60.

WILLIAMS, GEORGE FRED. "Imminent Danger from the Silver Purchase Act," *Forum*, 14 (February 1893), 789–796.

WILSON, WILLIAM L. "An Income Tax on Corporations," *North American Review*, 158 (January 1894), 1–7.

———. "The Principle and Method of the New Tariff Bill," *Forum*, 16 (January 1894), 544–548.

WILSON, WOODROW. "Mr. Cleveland as President," *Atlantic Monthly*, 79 (March 1897), 289–300.

WISH, HARVEY. "John Peter Altgeld and the Election of 1896," *Journal of the Illinois State Historical Society*, 30 (October 1937), 353–384.

———. "John Peter Altgeld and the Background of the Election of 1896," *Mississippi Valley Historical Review*, 24 (March 1938), 503–518.

WOODWARD, C. VANN. "The Populist Heritage and the Intellectual," *The American Scholar*, 29 (Winter 1959–1960), 55–72.

YATES, RICHARD. "Address at the Jacksonville Centennial, October 6, 1925,"

Journal of the Illinois State Historical Society, 18 (October 1925–July 1926), 575–635.

PERSONAL HISTORIES AND PUBLISHED CORRESPONDENCE

ACHESON, SAM HANNA. *Joe Bailey: The Last Democrat* (New York: 1932).

ADDAMS, JANE. *Hull House* (New York: 1930).

AGUINALDO, EMILIO, and ALBANO PACIS. *A Second Look at America* (New York: 1957).

ALEXANDER, D. A. S. *Four Famous New Yorkers: The Political Careers of Cleveland, Plat², Hill, and Roosevelt* (New York: 1923).

BAKER, RAY STANNARD. *American Chronicle: The Autobiography of Ray Stannard Baker* (New York: 1945).

———. *Woodrow Wilson: Life and Letters* (8 vols.; Garden City, N.Y.: 1927–1939).

BARNARD, HARRY. *"Eagle Forgotten": The Life of John Peter Altgeld* (New York: 1938).

BARNES, JAMES A. *John G. Carlisle, Financial Statesman* (New York: 1931).

BARRETT, JAMES W. *Joseph Pulitzer and His "World"* (New York: 1941).

BASS, HERBERT J. *"I Am a Democrat": The Political Career of David Bennett Hill* (Syracuse, N.Y.: 1961).

BEER, THOMAS. *Hanna* (New York: 1929).

BELMONT, PERRY. *An American Democrat: The Recollections of Perry Belmont* (2nd ed.; New York: 1941).

BISHOP, JOSEPH B. *Theodore Roosevelt and His Times, Shown in His Own Letters* (2 vols.; New York: 1920).

BLUM, JOHN M. *The Republican Roosevelt* (Cambridge, Mass.: 1954).

BOWERS, CLAUDE G. *The Life of John Worth Kern* (Indianapolis: 1918).

———. *Beveridge and the Progressive Era* (New York: 1932).

BROWNE, WALDO R. *Altgeld of Illinois: A Record of His Life and Work* (New York: 1924).

BRYAN, WILLIAM JENNINGS. *The First Battle* (Chicago: 1896).

———. *The Second Battle* (Chicago: 1900).

———. *The Speeches of William Jennings Bryan* (2 vols.; New York: 1909).

BRYAN, WILLIAM JENNINGS, and MARY BAIRD BRYAN. *The Memoirs of William Jennings Bryan* (Philadelphia: 1925).

BURNS, EDWARD M. *David Starr Jordan: Prophet of Freedom* (Stanford: 1953).

BURTON, THEODORE E. *John Sherman* (Boston: 1906).

BUSBEY, L. WHITE. *Uncle Joe Cannon: The Story of a Pioneer American* (New York: 1927).

BUTLER, NICHOLAS MURRAY. *Across the Years, Recollections and Reflections* (2 vols.; New York: 1939).

BUTT, ARCHIE. *The Letters of Archie Butt* (Garden City, N.Y.: 1924).

BYARS, WILLIAM VINCENT (ed.). *An American Commoner: The Life and Times of Richard Parks Bland—a Study of the Last Quarter of the Nineteenth Century* (Columbia, Mo.: 1900).

CAREY, FRED. *Mayor Jim: The Life of James Dahlman* (Omaha: 1930).

CHADWICK, F. E. *The Relations of the United States and Spain: Diplomacy* (New York: 1909).

————. *The Relations of the United States and Spain: The Spanish-American War* (New York: 1911).

CLARK, CHAMP. *My Quarter Century of American Politics* (2 vols.; New York: 1921).

CLEVELAND, GROVER. *Presidential Problems* (New York: 1904).

COBLENZ, EDMOND D. (ed.). *William Randolph Hearst: A Portrait in His Own Words* (New York: 1952).

COOLIDGE, LOUIS A. *An Old-Fashioned Senator: Orville H. Platt of Connecticut* (New York: 1910).

CORTISSOZ, ROYAL. *The Life of Whitelaw Reid* (2 vols.; New York: 1921).

COTNER, ROBERT C. *James Stephen Hogg: A Biography* (Austin: 1959).

COWLES, ANNA ROOSEVELT. *Letters from Theodore Roosevelt to Anna Roosevelt Cowles, 1870–1918* (New York: 1924).

COX, JAMES B. *Journey Through My Years* (New York: 1940).

CROLY, HERBERT. *Marcus Alonzo Hanna: His Life and Work* (New York: 1912).

DANIELS, JOSEPHUS. *Tar Heel Editor* (Chapel Hill: 1939).

————. *Editor in Politics* (Chapel Hill: 1941).

DARROW, CLARENCE. *The Story of My Life* (New York: 1932).

DAVIS, O. K. *Released for Publication* (New York: 1945).

DAWES, CHARLES GATES. *A Journal of the McKinley Years, 1893–1913* (Chicago: 1950).

DAWSON, THOMAS F. *Life and Character of Edmund Oliver Wolcott* (2 vols.; New York: 1911).

DENNETT, TYLER. *John Hay: From Poetry to Politics* (New York: 1933).

DEPEW, CHAUNCEY M. *My Memories of Eighty Years* (New York: 1922).

DEWEY, GEORGE. *Autobiography of George Dewey* (New York: 1913).

DINGLEY, EDWARD NELSON. *Life and Times of Nelson Dingley, Jr.* (Kalamazoo: 1902).

DUNN, ARTHUR W. *Gridiron Nights* (New York: 1915).

DUNNE, F. P. *Mr. Dooley Says* (New York: 1910).

ELLIS, ELMER. *Henry Moore Teller* (Caldwell, Idaho: 1941).

FLICK, ALEXANDER CLARENCE, and GUSTAV S. LOBRANO. *Samuel Jones Tilden: A Study in Political Sagacity* (New York: 1939).

FORAKER, JOSEPH BENSON. *Notes of a Busy Life* (2 vols.; Cincinnati: 1917).

FORD, WORTHINGTON C. (ed.). *Letters of Henry Adams* (2 vols.; Boston: 1930–1938).

FUESS, CLAUDE M. *Carl Schurz, Reformer* (New York: 1932).

GAGE, LYMAN J. *Memoirs of Lyman J. Gage* (New York: 1937).

GALE, ALBERT L., and GEORGE W. KLINE. *Bryan the Man: The Commoner at Close Range* (St. Louis: 1908).

GARRATY, JOHN A. *Henry Cabot Lodge, A Biography* (New York: 1953).

GEIGER, LOUIS G. *Joseph W. Folk of Missouri* (Columbia, Mo.: 1953).

GERARD, JAMES W. *My First Eighty Years* (Garden City, N.Y.: 1951).

GILDER, RICHARD WATSON. *Grover Cleveland: A Record of Friendship* (New York: 1910).

GILDER, ROSAMOND (ed.). *The Letters of Richard Watson Gilder* (Boston: 1916).

GINGER, RAY. *The Bending Cross: A Biography of Eugene Victor Debs* (New Brunswick, N.J.: 1949).

GLAD, PAUL W. *The Trumpet Soundeth: William Jennings Bryan and His Democracy, 1896–1912* (Lincoln, Nebr.: 1960).

GOMPERS, SAMUEL. *Seventy Years of Life and Labor: An Autobiography* (2 vols.; New York: 1925).

GRANTHAM, DEWEY W., Jr. *Hoke Smith and the Politics of the New South, 1855–1931* (Baton Rouge: 1958).

GWYNN, STEPHEN. *The Letters and Friendships of Sir Cecil Spring-Rice: A Record* (2 vols.; Boston: 1929).

HALSTEAD, MURAT. *The Illustrious Life of William McKinley* (privately printed, 1901).

HARBAUGH, WILLIAM HENRY. *Power and Responsibility: The Life and Times of Theodore Roosevelt* (New York: 1961).

HARRISON, CARTER H. *Stormy Years: The Autobiography of Carter H. Harrison, Five Times Mayor of Chicago* (Indianapolis: 1935).

HARRISON, MARY LORD (comp.). *Views of an Ex-President* (Indianapolis: 1901).

HARVEY, ROLAND HILL. *Samuel Gompers* (Stanford: 1935).

HAYNES, FRED E. *James Baird Weaver* (Iowa City: 1919).

HELMES, WINIFRED G. *John A. Johnson, the People's Governor: A Political Biography* (Minneapolis: 1949).

HERRICK, GENEVIEVE FORBES, and JOHN ORIGEN HERRICK. *The Life of William Jennings Bryan* (Chicago: 1925).

HIBBEN, PAXTON. *The Peerless Leader: William Jennings Bryan* (New York: 1929).

HIRSCH, MARK D. *William C. Whitney, Modern Warwick* (New York: 1948).

HOAR, GEORGE F. *Autobiography of Seventy Years* (2 vols.; New York: 1903).

HOOVER, HERBERT. *The Memoirs of Herbert Hoover. I. Years of Adventure, 1874–1920* (New York: 1951).

HOWE, FREDERIC C. *The Confessions of a Reformer* (New York: 1925).

HOWE, MARK A. DEWOLFE. *Portrait of an Independent: Moorfield Storey, 1845–1929* (Boston: 1932).

ICKES, HAROLD. *Autobiography of a Curmudgeon* (New York: 1943).

JAMES, HENRY. *Richard Olney and His Public Service, with Documents Including Unpublished Diplomatic Correspondence* (Boston: 1923).

JESSUP, PHILIP. *Elihu Root* (2 vols.; New York: 1938).

JOHNSON, GERALD W. *An Honorable Titan: A Biographical Study of Adolph S. Ochs* (New York: 1946).

JOHNSON, TOM L. *My Story* (New York: 1911).

JOHNSON, WILLIS FLETCHER. *George Harvey, "A Passionate Patriot"* (New York: 1929).

JOHNSON, WALTER. *William Allen White's America* (New York: 1947).

—— (ed.). *Selected Letters of William Allen White, 1899–1943* (New York: 1947).

KENWORTHY, LEONARD S. *The Tall Sycamore of the Wabash: Daniel Wolsey Voorhees* (Boston: 1936).

KERR, WINFIELD S. *John Sherman: His Life and Public Services* (2 vols.; Boston: 1908).

LA FOLLETTE, BELLE CASE, and FOLA LA FOLLETTE. *Robert La Follette* (2 vols.; New York: 1953).

LA FOLLETTE, ROBERT. *La Follette's Autobiography; A Personal Narrative of Political Experience* (Madison, Wis.: 1913).

LAMBERT, JOHN R. *Arthur Pue Gorman* (Baton Rouge: 1953).

LANG, LOUIS J. (comp.). *The Autobiography of Thomas Collier Platt* (New York: 1910).

LEACH, PAUL R. *That Man Dawes* (Chicago: 1950).

LEECH, MARGARET. *In the Days of McKinley* (New York: 1959).

LEWIS, ALFRED HENRY. *Richard Croker* (New York: 1901).

LIEF, ALFRED. *Democracy's Norris: The Biography of a Lonely Crusader* (New York: 1939).

LINK, ARTHUR S. *Wilson: The Road to the White House* (Princeton, N.J.: 1947).

LLOYD, CARO. *Henry Demarest Lloyd* (2 vols.; New York: 1912).

LODGE, HENRY C. *Selections from the Correspondence of Theodore Roosevelt and Henry Cabot Lodge, 1884–1918* (2 vols.; New York: 1925).

LONG, JOHN C. *Bryan: The Great Commoner* (New York: 1928).

LONGWORTH, ALICE ROOSEVELT. *Crowded Hours* (New York: 1933).

LOWITT, RICHARD. *George W. Norris: The Making of a Progressive, 1861–1912* (Syracuse, N.Y.: 1963).

LYNCH, DENIS TILDEN. *Grover Cleveland: A Man Four Square* (New York: 1932).

MCCALL, SAMUEL W. *Life of Thomas B. Reed* (New York: 1914).

MCCULLOCH, HUGH. *Men and Measures of Half a Century* (New York: 1889).

McElroy, Robert. *Grover Cleveland: The Man and Statesman* (2 vols.; New York: 1923).

McGurrin, James. *Bourke Cockran: A Free Lance in American Politics* (New York: 1948).

McKenna, Marian C. *Borah* (Ann Arbor: 1961).

Manahan, James. *Trials of a Lawyer* (St. Paul: 1933).

Marshall, Thomas R. *Recollections of Thomas R. Marshall: A Hoosier Salad* (Indianapolis: 1925).

Masters, Edgar Lee. *Across Spoon River: An Autobiography* (New York: 1936).

Merrill, Horace S. *William Freeman Vilas, Doctrinaire Democrat* (Madison, Wis.: 1954).

———. *Bourbon Leader: Grover Cleveland and the Democratic Party* (Boston: 1957).

Metcalfe, Richard L. (comp.). *The Real Bryan* (Des Moines: 1908).

Morearty, Edward F. *Omaha Memories* (Omaha: 1917).

Morgan, H. Wayne. *Eugene V. Debs: Socialist for President* (Syracuse, N.Y.: 1962).

———. *William McKinley and His America* (Syracuse, N.Y.: 1963).

Morison, Elting E., and John M. Blum (eds.). *The Letters of Theodore Roosevelt* (8 vols.; Cambridge, Mass.: 1951–1954).

Mullen, Arthur. *Western Democrat* (New York: 1940).

Muzzey, David S. *Thomas Jefferson* (New York: 1918).

———. *James G. Blaine: A Political Idol of Other Days* (New York: 1934).

Neuberger, Richard L., and Stephen B. Kahn. *Integrity: The Life of George Norris* (New York: 1937).

Nevins, Allan. *Henry White: Thirty Years of American Diplomacy* (New York: 1930).

———. *Grover Cleveland: A Study in Courage* (New York: 1932).

——— (ed.), *Letters of Grover Cleveland, 1850–1908* (Boston: 1933).

———. *Abram S. Hewitt, With Some Account of Peter Cooper* (New York: 1935).

———. *John D. Rockefeller: The Heroic Age in American Enterprise* (2 vols.; New York: 1940).

——— (ed.). *The Letters and Journal of Brand Whitlock* (2 vols.; New York: 1936).

Noblin, Stuart. *Leonidas LaFayette Polk, Agrarian Crusader* (Chapel Hill: 1945).

Norris, George W. *Fighting Liberal: The Autobiography of George W. Norris* (New York: 1945).

Oberholtzer, Ellis P. *Jay Cooke, Financier of the Civil War* (Philadelphia: 1907).

Olcott, Charles S. *The Life of William McKinley* (2 vols.; Boston: 1912).

OLSON, JAMES C. *J. Sterling Morton* (Lincoln, Nebr.: 1942).

ORCUTT, WILLIAM DANA. *Burrows of Michigan and the Republican Party* (2 vols.; New York: 1917).

OSBORN, GEORGE. *John Sharp Williams: Planter-Statesman of the Deep South* (Baton Rouge: 1943).

PALMER, GEORGE T. *A Conscientious Turncoat: The Story of John M. Palmer* (New Haven: 1941).

PALMER, JOHN M. *Personal Recollections: The Story of an Earnest Life* (Cincinnati: 1901).

PARKER, GEORGE F. *Recollections of Grover Cleveland* (New York: 1909).

PEPPER, CHARLES M. *The Life and Times of Henry Gassaway Davis, 1823–1916* (New York: 1920).

PERKINS, DEXTER. *Charles Evans Hughes and American Democratic Statesmanship* (Boston: 1956).

PRINGLE, HENRY F. *Theodore Roosevelt: A Biography* (New York: 1931).

———. *The Life and Times of William Howard Taft* (2 vols.; New York: 1939).

PROCTER, BEN H. *Not Without Honor: The Life of John H. Reagan* (Austin: 1962).

PUSEY, MERLO J. *Charles Evans Hughes* (2 vols.; New York: 1951).

PYLE, JOSEPH GELPIN. *Life of James J. Hill* (2 vols.; New York: 1917).

RICHARDSON, LEON BURR. *William E. Chandler, Republican* (New York: 1940).

RICHBERG, DONALD R. *My Hero: The Indiscreet Memoirs of an Eventful But Unheroic Life* (New York: 1954).

RIDGE, MARTIN. *Ignatius Donnelly: The Portrait of a Politician* (Chicago: 1962).

ROBINSON, WILLIAM A. *Thomas B. Reed, Parliamentarian* (New York: 1930).

ROOSEVELT, THEODORE. *Autobiography* (New York: 1913).

ROPER, DANIEL C., in collaboration with Frank H. Lovette. *Fifty Years of Public Life* (Durham: 1941).

ROSEWATER, VICTOR. *Life and Times of Edward Rosewater* (privately printed, n.d.).

ROSS, EDWARD A. *Seventy Years of It: An Autobiography* (New York: 1936).

ROSS, THOMAS RICHARD. *Jonathan Prentiss Dolliver: A Study in Political Integrity and Independence* (Iowa City: 1960).

ROSSER, CHARLES M. *The Crusading Commoner* (Dallas: 1937).

RUSSELL, CHARLES EDWARD. *Bare Hands and Stone Walls: Some Recollections of a Side-Line Reformer* (New York: 1933).

SCHURZ, CARL. *The Reminiscences of Carl Schurz* (3 vols.; New York: 1907–1909).

SHERMAN, JOHN. *Recollections of Forty Years in the House, Senate and Cabinet* (2 vols.; Chicago: 1895).

Sievers, Harry J. *Benjamin Harrison: Hoosier Statesman* (2 vols.; New York: 1959).

Simkins, Francis B. *Pitchfork Ben Tillman, South Carolinian* (Baton Rouge: 1944).

Smith, Rixey, and Norman Beasley. *Carter Glass: A Biography* (New York: 1939).

Stahl, John M. *Growing with the West: The Story of a Busy, Quiet Life* (Toronto: 1930).

Stealey, Orlando O. *Twenty Years in the Press Gallery* (New York: 1906).

Stephenson, Nathaniel. *Nelson W. Aldrich* (New York: 1930).

Stevenson, Adlai E. *Something of the Men I Have Known* (Chicago: 1909).

Stoddard, Henry L. *As I Knew Them; Presidents and Politics from Grant to Coolidge* (New York: 1927).

Stoddard, Lothrop. *Master of Manhattan: The Life of Richard Croker* (New York: 1931).

Stone, Candace. *Dana and "The Sun"* (New York: 1938).

Stone, Irving. *Clarence Darrow for the Defense: A Biography* (New York: 1941).

———. *They Also Ran* (New York: 1943).

Stone, Melville E. *Fifty Years a Journalist* (Garden City, N.Y.: 1921).

Straus, Oscar S. *Under Four Administrations* (Boston: 1922).

Sturtevant, Julian M., Jr. (ed.). *Julian Monson Sturtevant: An Autobiography* (New York: 1896).

Sullivan, Mark. *The Education of an American* (New York: 1938).

Summers, Festus P. *William L. Wilson and Tariff Reform* (New Brunswick, N.J.: 1953).

——— (ed.). *The Cabinet Diary of William L. Wilson, 1896–1897* (Chapel Hill: 1957).

Swanberg, W. A. *Citizen Hearst: A Biography of William Randolph Hearst* (New York: 1961).

Syrett, Harold C. (ed.). *The Gentleman and the Tiger: The Autobiography of George Brinton McClellan, Jr.* (New York: 1956).

Tarbell, Ida M. *All in the Day's Work* (New York: 1939).

Tebbel, John. *The Life and Good Times of William Randolph Hearst* (New York: 1952).

Thayer, William Roscoe. *The Life and Letters of John Hay* (2 vols.; Boston: 1915).

Thompson, Charles Willis. *Party Leaders of the Time* (New York: 1906).

———. *Presidents I've Known and Two Near-Presidents* (Indianapolis: 1929).

Timmons, Bascom N. *Portrait of an American: Charles G. Dawes* (New York: 1953).

VILLARD, OSWALD GARRISON. *Fighting Years: Memoirs of a Liberal Editor* (New York: 1939).

WALL, JOSEPH FRAZIER. *Henry Watterson, Reconstructed Rebel* (New York: 1956).

WALTERS, EVERETT. *Joseph Benson Foraker: An Uncompromising Republican* (Columbus, Ohio: 1948).

WATTERSON, HENRY. *"Marse Henry": An Autobiography* (2 vols.; New York: 1919).

WERNER, M. R. *Bryan* (New York: 1929).

WHEELER, EVERETT P. *Sixty Years of American Life: Taylor to Roosevelt, 1850–1910* (New York: 1917).

WHITE, HORACE. *The Life of Lyman Trumbull* (New York: 1913).

WHITE, WILLIAM ALLEN. *Masks in a Pageant* (New York: 1928).

WHITE, W. L. *Bernard Baruch* (New York: 1950).

WHITLOCK, BRAND. *Forty Years of It* (New York: 1914).

WILLIAMS, CHARLES R. *The Life of Rutherford Birchard Hayes* (2 vols.; New York: 1914).

WILLIAMS, WAYNE C. *William Jennings Bryan, A Study in Political Vindication* (New York: 1923).

———. *William Jennings Bryan* (New York: 1936).

WINKLER, JOHN K. *W. R. Hearst, An American Phenomenon* (New York: 1938).

WOODWARD, C. VANN. *Tom Watson, Agrarian Rebel* (New York: 1938).

WORKS OF GENERIC VALUE

ABBOT, WILLIS J. *Watching the World Go By* (Boston: 1933).

ALTGELD, JOHN PETER. *Live Questions* (Chicago: 1899).

ARNETT, ALEX M. *The Populist Movement in Georgia* (New York: 1922).

BALDWIN, E. F. *The Philosopher* (Chicago: 1906–1913).

BEER, THOMAS. *Mauve Decade* (New York: 1937).

BINKLEY, WILFRED E. *American Political Parties, Their Natural History* (New York: 1943).

BRYAN, WILLIAM JENNINGS. *Under Other Flags* (Lincoln, Nebr.: 1904).

———. *British Rule in India* (Westminster: 1906).

———. *Letters to a Chinese Official* (New York: 1906).

———. *The Old World and Its Ways* (Lincoln, Nebr.: 1907).

———. *Guaranteed Banks* (Chicago: 1908).

———. *Heart to Heart Appeals* (New York: 1917).

BUCK, PAUL H. *The Road to Reunion* (Boston: 1937).

BUCK, SOLON J. *The Granger Movement, 1870–1880* (Cambridge, Mass.: 1913).

———. *The Agrarian Crusade: A Chronicle of the Farmer in Politics* (New Haven: 1920).

BURNHAM, W. DEAN. *Presidential Ballots, 1836–1892* (Baltimore: 1955).

BURNS, EDWARD MCNEIL. *The American Idea of Mission* (New Brunswick, N.J.: 1957).

CARNEGIE, ANDREW. *The Gospel of Wealth and Other Timely Essays* (New York: 1900).

CASE, VICTORIA, and ROBERT ORMOND CASE. *We Called It Culture: the Story of Chautauqua* (Garden City, N.Y.: 1948).

Centennial Celebration of the Founding of Illinois College, October 12–15, 1929, Jacksonville, Illinois (Chicago: 1929).

CHICAGO CIVIC FEDERATION. *Conference on Trusts* (Chicago: 1899).

CLARK, JOHN B. *Populism in Alabama* (Auburn: 1927).

COCHRAN, THOMAS C. *The American Business System: A Historical Perspective, 1900–1955* (Cambridge, Mass.: 1957).

COMMAGER, HENRY STEELE. *The American Mind: An Interpretation of American Thought and Character Since the 1880's* (New Haven: 1952).

COMMONS, JOHN R. and ASSOCIATES. *History of Labour in the United States* (New York: 1918).

COREY, LEWIS. *The House of Morgan* (New York: 1930).

CROLY, HERBERT. *The Promise of American Life* (New York: 1910).

CROZIER, W. A. (ed.). *Virginia County Records* (New York: 1895). Vol. I.

CURTI, MERLE. *The Growth of American Thought* (New York: 1943).

DE WITT, BENJAMIN PARKE. *The Progressive Movement: A Non-partisan, Comprehensive Discussion of Current Tendencies in American Politics* (New York: 1915).

DEGLER, CARL N. *Out of Our Past: The Forces That Shaped Modern America* (New York: Harper Colophon ed., 1962).

DEMOCRATIC NATIONAL COMMITTEE. *Democratic Campaign Book. Congressional Election, 1890* (Washington: 1890).

———. *Democratic Campaign Book. Presidential Election, 1896* (Washington, D.C.: 1896).

———. *Democratic Campaign Book. Presidential Campaign, 1900* (Washington, D.C.: 1900).

———. *Democratic Campaign Book. Presidential Election, 1904* (New York: 1904).

———. *Democratic Campaign Book. Presidential Election, 1908* (Washington, D.C.: 1908).

DESMOND, HUMPHREY JOSEPH. *The A.P.A. Movement* (Washington, D.C.: 1912).

DESTLER, CHESTER MCARTHUR. *American Radicalism, 1865–1901: Essays and Documents* (New London: 1946).

DEWEY, DAVIS R. *Financial History of the United States* (11th ed.); (New York: 1931).

———. *National Problems, 1887–1897* (New York: 1907).

DICK, EVERETT E. *The Sod-House Frontier, 1854–1890* (New York: 1937).

DORFMAN, JOSEPH. *The Economic Mind in American Civilization* (5 vols.; New York: 1946–1959).

DOUGLAS, PAUL H. *Real Wages in the United States, 1896–1928* (Boston: 1930).

DUNN, ARTHUR W. *From Harrison to Harding: A Personal Narrative, Covering a Third of a Century, 1888–1921* (2 vols.; New York: 1922).

ELLIOTT, CHARLES BURKE. *The Philippines to the End of the Military Regime* (Indianapolis: 1916).

EWING, CORTEZ A. M. *Presidential Elections, From A. Lincoln to F. D. Roosevelt* (Norman: 1940).

——. *Congressional Elections, 1896–1944: The Sectional Basis of Political Democracy in the House of Representatives* (Norman: 1947).

FAULKNER, HAROLD U. *The Quest for Social Justice, 1898–1914* (New York: 1931).

——. *Politics, Reform, and Expansion, 1890–1900* (New York: 1959).

FELS, RENDIGS. *American Business Cycles, 1865–1897* (Chapel Hill: 1959).

FILLER, LOUIS. *Crusaders for American Liberalism* (New York: 1939).

FINE, SIDNEY. *Laissez Faire and the General Welfare State: A Study of Conflict in American Thought* (Ann Arbor: 1956).

FONER, PHILIP S. *History of the Labor Movement in the United States* (2 vols.; New York: 1955).

FORBES, W. CAMERON. *The Philippine Islands* (2 vols.; Boston: 1928).

FORD, H. J. *The Cleveland Era* (New Haven: 1921).

GABRIEL, RALPH H. *The Course of American Democratic Thought: An Intellectual History Since 1815* (New York: 1940).

GLAD, PAUL W. *McKinley, Bryan, and the People* (Philadelphia: 1964).

GOLDMAN, ERIC. *Rendezvous with Destiny: A History of Modern American Reform* (New York: Vintage Books, 1956).

GOSNELL, HAROLD F. *Boss Platt and His New York Machine* (Chicago: 1924).

HACKER, LOUIS M. *The Triumph of American Capitalism* (New York: 1940).

HAGEDORN, HERMANN (ed.). *The Works of Theodore Roosevelt. National Edition* (20 vols.; New York: 1926).

HAY, JOHN. *The Platform of Anarchy: An Address to the Students of Western Reserve University, October 6, 1896* (Cleveland: 1896).

HAYNES, FRED E. *Third Party Movements Since the Civil War with Special Reference to Iowa* (Iowa City: 1916).

HAYS, SAMUEL P. *The Response to Industrialism, 1885–1914* (Chicago: 1957).

HEALY, DAVID F. *The United States in Cuba, 1898–1902: Generals, Politicians, and the Search for Policy* (Madison, Wis.: 1963).

HECHLER, KENNETH. *Insurgency: Personalities and Politics of the Taft Era* (New York: 1940).

HICKS, JOHN D. *The Populist Revolt: A History of the Farmers' Alliance and the People's Party* (Minneapolis: 1931).

HOFSTADTER, RICHARD. *The American Political Tradition and the Men Who Made It* (New York: Vintage Books, 1954).

——. *The Age of Reform: From Bryan to F. D. R.* (New York: 1955).

HOLLINGSWORTH, J. ROGERS. *The Whirligig of Politics: The Democracy of Cleveland and Bryan* (Chicago: 1963).

HOLT, W. STULL. *Treaties Defeated by the Senate* (Baltimore: 1933).

HOPKINS, C. H. *The Rise of the Social Gospel Movement in American Protestantism, 1860–1915* (New Haven: 1940).

ILLINOIS, STATE OF. *Debates and Proceedings of the Constitutional Convention of the State of Illinois, Convened at the City of Springfield, December 3, 1869* (vol. I; Springfield: 1870).

——. *Judge's and Bar Dockets, Circuit Court, Jacksonville, Morgan County* (1883–1887).

ILLINOIS COLLEGE. *Minutes of Board of Trustees.*

JONES, STANLEY L. *The Presidential Election of 1896* (Madison, Wis.: 1964).

JOSEPHSON, MATTHEW. *The Robber Barons: The Great American Capitalists, 1861–1901* (New York: 1934).

——. *The Politicos, 1865–1896* (New York: 1938).

——. *The President Makers: The Culture of Politics and Leadership in an Age of Enlightenment, 1896–1919* (New York: 1940).

KENT, FRANK R. *The Democratic Party: A History* (New York: 1928).

KERNEY, JAMES. *The Political Education of Woodrow Wilson* (New York: 1926).

KIRKLAND, EDWARD C. *Industry Comes of Age: Business, Labor, and Public Policy, 1860–1897* (New York: 1961).

KOHLSAAT, H. H. *From McKinley to Harding* (New York: 1923).

KNOLES, GEORGE H. *The Presidential Campaign and Election of 1892* (Stanford: 1942).

KROCK, ARTHUR (ed.). *The Editorials of Henry Watterson* (New York: 1923).

LAUCK, W. JETT. *The Causes of the Panic of 1893* (New York: 1907).

LAWSON, THOMAS W. *Frenzied Finance* (New York: 1905).

LEWIS, EDWARD R. *A History of American Political Thought from the Civil War to the World War* (New York: 1937).

LINDSEY, ALMONT. *The Pullman Strike: The Story of a Unique Experiment and of a Great Labor Upheaval* (Chicago: 1942).

LORD, WALTER. *The Good Years* (New York: 1960).

LOWRY, EDWARD G. *Washington Close-ups. Intimate Views of Some Public Figures* (Boston: 1921).

MACLAREN, GAY. *Morally We Roll Along* (Boston: 1938).

McGUIRE, JAMES K. (ed.). *The Democratic Party of the State of New York* (3 vols.; New York: 1905).

McPHERSON, EDWARD. *A Hand-Book of Politics* (Washington, D.C.: 1874–1892).

MASTERS, EDGAR LEE. *The New Star Chamber and Other Essays* (Chicago: 1904).

MERRILL, HORACE S. *Bourbon Democracy of the Middle West, 1865–1896* (Baton Rouge: 1953).

MILLIS, WALTER. *The Martial Spirit* (Cambridge, Mass.: 1931).

MINOR, HENRY. *The Story of the Democratic Party* (New York: 1928).

MORGAN, H. WAYNE (ed.). *The Gilded Age* (Syracuse, N.Y.: 1963).

MOOS, MALCOLM. *The Republicans: A History of Their Party* (New York: 1956).

MORISON, SAMUEL ELIOT, and HENRY STEELE COMMAGER. *The Growth of the American Republic* (3rd ed.; 2 vols.; New York: 1942).

MORTON, J. STERLING, and ALBERT WATKINS. *An Illustrated History of Nebraska* (3 vols.; Lincoln, Nebr.: 1910–1920).

MOWRY, GEORGE E. *Theodore Roosevelt and the Progressive Movement* (Madison, Wis.: 1946).

————. *The Era of Theodore Roosevelt, 1900–1912* (New York: 1958).

MYERS, GUSTAVUS. *History of Tammany Hall* (New York: 1917).

NATIONAL ANTI-TRUST CONFERENCE. *Official Report of the National Anti-Trust Conference Held February 12, 13, 14, 1900* (Chicago: 1900).

NATIONAL DEMOCRATIC PARTY. *Proceedings of the Convention of the National Democratic Party, Indianapolis, September 2 and 3, 1896* (Indianapolis: 1896).

NEBRASKA, STATE OF. *District Court Dockets, Lincoln, Nebraska* (vols. R–X, I–II).

————. *Justice Court Dockets, Lincoln, Nebraska* (vols. 15–22).

————. *County Court Dockets, Lancaster County* (vols. 13–20).

NEVINS, ALLAN. *The Emergence of Modern America, 1865–1878* (New York: 1927).

NEW YORK STATE LEGISLATURE. Joint Committee on Investigation of Life Insurance. Armstrong Committee. *Testimony, Exhibits, Report, 1905* (7 vols.; Albany: J. B. Lyon Co., 1906).

NYE, RUSSEL B. *Midwestern Progressive Politics: A Historical Study of Its Origins and Development, 1870–1950* (East Lansing, Mich.: 1951).

OGG, FREDERIC AUSTIN. *National Progress, 1907–1917* (New York: 1918).

OLSON, JAMES C. *History of Nebraska* (Lincoln, Nebr.: 1955).

OVERACKER, LOUISE. *Money in Elections* (New York: 1932).

PECK, HARRY THURSTON. *Twenty Years of the Republic: 1885–1905* (New York: 1906).

PERKINS, WHITNEY T. *Denial of Empire: The United States and Its Dependencies* (Leyden: 1962).

PERLMAN, SELIG. *A History of Trade Unionism in the United States* (New York: 1950).

PETERSON, MERRILL D. *The Jefferson Image in the American Mind* (Galaxy Books ed.; New York: 1962).

PETTIGREW, RICHARD F. *Imperial Washington* (Chicago: 1922).

POLLACK, NORMAN. *The Populist Response to Industrial America; Midwestern Populist Thought* (Cambridge, Mass.: 1962).

PORTER, KIRK H., and DONALD B. JOHNSON. *National Party Platforms, 1840–1956* (Urbana: 1956).

PRATT, JULIUS W. *Expansionists of 1898* (Baltimore: 1936).

RAMMELKAMP, CHARLES H. *Illinois College: A Centennial History, 1829–1929* (New Haven: 1928).

RATNER, SIDNEY. *American Taxation: Its History as a Social Force in Democracy* (New York: 1942).

RAUSCHENBUSCH, WALTER. *Christianity and the Social Crisis* (New York: 1910).

REGIER, C. C. *The Era of the Muckrakers* (Chapel Hill: 1932).

RHODES, JAMES FORD. *History of the United States from the Compromise of 1850* (9 vols.; New York: 1893–1928).

———. *The McKinley and Roosevelt Administrations, 1896–1909* (New York: 1922).

ROBINSON, EDGAR E. *The Presidential Vote, 1896–1932* (Stanford: 1934).

ROSEBOOM, EUGENE H. *A History of Presidential Elections* (New York: 1957).

ROSS, EDWARD A. *Sin and Society: An Analysis of Latter-Day Iniquity* (Boston: 1907).

RUSSELL, CHARLES EDWARD. *These Shifting Scenes* (New York: 1914).

SALOUTOS, THEODORE. *Farmer Movements in the South, 1875–1933* (Berkeley, Calif.: 1960).

——— and JOHN D. HICKS, *Agricultural Discontent in the Middle West, 1900–1939* (Madison, Wis.: 1951).

SANDOZ, MARIE. *Old Jules* (Boston: 1935).

SCHLESINGER, ARTHUR M. *The Rise of the City, 1878–1898* (New York: 1933).

SCHULTZ, WILLIAM J., and M. R. CRANE, *Financial Development of the United States* (New York: 1937).

SCOTT, ROY V. *The Agrarian Movement in Illinois, 1880–1896* (Urbana: 1962).

SEYMOUR, MARY J. *Lineage Book. National Society of the Daughters of the American Revolution* (Washington, D.C.: 1898), vols. VII, XII, XIX, XXI.

SHANNON, FRED A. *The Farmer's Last Frontier, 1860–1897* (New York: 1945).

SHANNON, JASPER B., with RUTH McQUOWN. *Presidential Politics in Kentucky, 1896–1948* (Lexington: 1950).

SHARKEY, ROBERT P. *Money, Class, and Party: An Economic Study of Civil War and Reconstruction* (Baltimore: 1959).

SHELDON, ADDISON E. *Nebraska: The Land and the People* (3 vols.; Chicago: 1931).

SILVER CONVENTION, FIRST NATIONAL. *Proceedings of the First National Silver Convention* (St. Louis: 1889).

SMITH, HENRY NASH. *Virgin Land: The American West as Symbol and Myth* (Cambridge, Mass.: 1950).

STANWOOD, EDWARD. *A History of the Presidency* (New York: 1898).

———. *American Tariff Controversies in the Nineteenth Century* (2 vols.; Boston: 1903).

———. *A History of the Presidency from 1897 to 1909* (New York: 1912).

STEEVENS, G. W. *Land of the Dollar* (New York: 1897).

STUDENSKI, PAUL and HERMAN E. KROOS. *Financial History of the United States* (New York: 1952).

SULLIVAN, MARK. *Our Times: The United States, 1900–1925* (6 vols.; New York: 1926–1935).

TAFT, PHILIP. *The A.F.L. in the Times of Gompers* (New York: 1957).

TARBELL, IDA M. *The Nationalizing of Business, 1878–1898* (New York: 1936).

TAYLOR, CARL CLEVELAND. *The Farmers' Movement, 1620–1920* (New York: 1953).

TAUSSIG, FRANK W. *The Tariff History of the United States* (New York: 1923).

TRUMBULL, LYMAN. *The Cause and Suggestion of the Cure of Labor Troubles* (Chicago: 1894).

TUTTLE, CHARLES RICHARD. *Illinois Currency Convention* (Chicago: 1895).

UNION COLLEGE OF LAW. *Circular of the Union College of Law for the Year 1883–1884* (Chicago: 1883).

VAN RIPER, PAUL P. *History of the United States Civil Service* (Evanston, Ill.: 1958).

WALTON, W. C. *Centennial History of McKendree College* (Lebanon, Ill.: 1928).

WARD, ESTELLE FRANCES. *The Story of Northwestern University* (New York: 1924).

WECTER, DIXON. *The Hero in America: A Chronicle of Hero-Worship* (New York: 1941).

WERKMEISTER, W. H. *A History of Philosophical Ideas in America* (New York: 1949).

WEYL, WALTER E. *The New Democracy* (New York: 1912).

WHITE, LEONARD D., with the assistance of Jean Schneider. *The Republican Era: A Study in Administrative History, 1869–1901* (New York: 1958).

WILDE, ARTHUR HERBERT. *Northwestern University: A History, 1855–1905* (4 vols.; New York: 1905).

WILLIAMS, D. R. *The United States and the Philippines* (New York: 1924).

WILLIS, HENRY PARKER. *The Federal Reserve System: Legislation, Organization and Operation* (New York: 1923).

WILSON, GEORGE H. *Centennial Celebration of the Founding of Illinois College* (Jacksonville: 1929).

WILTSE, CHARLES M. *The Jeffersonian Tradition in American Democracy* (Chapel Hill: 1935).

WOLFF, LEON. *Little Brown Brother* (New York: 1961).

WOODWARD, C. VANN. *Origins of the New South, 1877–1913* (Baton Rouge: 1951).

WORCESTER, DEAN C. and RALSTON HAYDEN. *The Philippines, Past and Present* (New York: 1930).

SELECTED TITLES FROM THE LITERATURE ON THE MONEY QUESTION

ANDREWS, ELISHA BENJAMIN. *An Honest Dollar* (New York: 1889).

Annual Reports of the Director of the Mint (Washington, D.C.).

BARRETT, D. C. *The Greenbacks and the Resumption of Specie Payments, 1862–1869* (Cambridge, Mass.: 1931).

BOLLES, ALBERT S. *Financial History of the United States, 1861–1885* (New York: 1886).

BOOKWALTER, JOHN WESLEY. *If Not Silver, What?* (Springfield, Ohio: 1896).

BROUGH, WILLIAM. *The Natural Law of Money* (New York: 1894).

BULLOCK, CHARLES J. *Essays on the Monetary History of the United States* (New York: 1900).

CHANDLER, LESTER V. *An Introduction to Monetary Theory* (New York: 1940).

CHAPMAN, E. O. *Silver Question in a Nutshell* (c. 1896).

DAWES, CHARLES G. *Banking System of the United States and Its Relation to the Money and Business of the Country* (Chicago: 1894).

DE KNIGHT, WILLIAM G. *History of the Currency of the Country* (Washington, D.C.: 1897).

DELMAR, ALEXANDER. *History of Monetary Systems* (London: 1895).

———. *Barbara Villiers; or, A History of Monetary Crimes* (New York: 1899).

DONNELLY, IGNATIUS. *American People's Money* (Chicago: 1896).

DUNBAR, CHARLES F. *Laws of the United States Relating to Currency, Finance, and Banking from 1789 to 1891* (Boston: 1891).

DUNNE, GERALD T. *Monetary Decisions of the Supreme Court* (New Brunswick, N.J.: 1960).

EMERY, MRS. S. E. V. *Seven Financial Conspiracies Which Have Enslaved the American People* (Lansing: 1888).

EVLIS, R. *Uncle Sam's Dream* (Chicago: 1896).

FISHER, IRVING, assisted by R. L. COHRSSEN, *Stable Money: A History of the Movement* (New York: 1934).

FONDA, ARTHUR I. *Honest Money* (New York: 1895).

FOOTE, ALLEN R. *A Sound Currency and Banking System; How It May Be Secured* (New York: 1895).

HAMMOND, BRAY. *Banks and Politics in America from the Revolution to the Civil War* (Princeton, N.J.: 1957).

HARVEY, WILLIAM HOPE. *Coin's Financial School* (Chicago: 1894).

———. *Coin Up-to-Date* (Chicago: 1895).

———. *Coin on Money, Trusts, and Imperialism* (Chicago: 1899).

———. *The Book* (Monte Ne, Ark.: 1932).

——— with W. J. BRYAN and OTHERS. *The Money of the People* (Chicago: 1895).

HEPBURN, ALONZO B. *History of Coinage and Currency in the United States and the Perennial Contest for Sound Money* (New York: 1903).

———. *History of Currency in the United States* (New York: 1915).

History of the Coinage Act of 1873. Senate Misc. Doc., No. 132, 41st Congress, 2d Sess. (Reprint; Washington, D.C.: 1900).

HODGSON, J. G. (comp.). *Stabilization of Money* (New York: 1933).

International Monetary Conference 1892. Senate Ex. Doc. No. 82, 52d Congress, 2d Sess. (Washington, D.C.: 1892).

JONES, JOHN P. *Resumption and the Double Standard; or, the Impossibility of Resuming Specie Payments in the United States Without Restoring the Double Standard of Gold and Silver* (Washington, D.C.: 1876).

KELLER, BRONSON C. *History of Demonetization* (St. Louis: 1896).

KEMMERER, EDWIN WALTER. *Money: The Principles of Money and Their Exemplification in Outstanding Chapters of Monetary History* (New York: 1935).

KITSON, ARTHUR. *A Scientific Solution of the Money Question* (Boston: 1895).

KNOX, JOHN JAY. *United States Notes: A History of the Various Issues of Paper Money by the Government of the United States* (New York: 1884).

———. *A History of Banking in the United States* (New York: 1903).

LARSON, HENRIETTA M. *Jay Cooke, Private Banker* (Cambridge, Mass.: 1936).

LAUGHLIN, J. LAURENCE. *Facts About Money* (Chicago: 1895).

———. *Gold and Prices Since 1873* (Chicago: 1895).

———. *The History of Bimetallism in the United States* (3rd ed.; New York: 1898).

———. *The Principles of Money* (New York: 1903).

———. *Money and Prices* (New York: 1919).

———. *A New Exposition of Money, Credit, and Prices* (2 vols.; Chicago: 1931).

LEIGHTON, GEORGE E. *Why We Oppose the Free Coinage of Silver; Address before the Trans-Mississippi Commercial Congress, 1894* (St. Louis: 1894).

LOCKWOOD, GEORGE R. *Some Facts and Figures Against the Unlimited Coinage of Silver* (St. Louis: 1896).

McPHERSON, LOGAN C. *The Monetary and Banking Problem* (New York: 1896).

MITCHELL, WESLEY C. *A History of the Greenbacks* (Chicago: 1903).

MORGAN, H. WAYNE. *Western Silver and the Tariff of 1890* (privately printed, 1959).

NOYES, ALEXANDER DANA. *Forty Years of American Finance, 1865–1907* (New York: 1909).

Roberts, George E. *Coin at School in Finance* (Chicago: 1895).

Russell, H. B. *International Monetary Conferences* (New York: 1898).

Shannon, Frederick F. *A Moneyless Magnate and Other Essays* (New York: 1923).

Spahr, G. B. *The Present Distribution of Wealth in the United States* (New York: 1896).

Taussig, Frank W. *The Silver Situation in the United States* (New York: 1896 ed.).

Walker, Francis A. *Money* (New York: 1891).

———. *International Bimetallism* (New York: 1897).

White, Horace. *Money and Banking Illustrated by American History* (Boston: 1896).

Willem, John M., Jr. *The United States Trade Dollar* (New York: 1959).

Willis, Henry Parker. *A History of the Latin Monetary Union* (Chicago: 1901).

UNPUBLISHED SOURCES

Binkley, Wilfred E. "The Man in the White House," Ms.

Boell, Jesse F. "The Career of William Jennings Bryan to 1896," M.A. thesis, University of Nebraska, 1929.

Buckner, Philip F. "Silver Mining Interests in Silver Politics, 1876–1896, with Special Reference to the Organized Agitation and the Independent Silver Party Movement," M.A. thesis, Columbia University, 1953.

Condra, C. E. "Personal Observations and Experiences Relating to William Jennings Bryan," Ms., Nebraska State Historical Society.

Flower, Edward. "Anti-Semitism in the Free Silver and Populist Movement and the Election of 1896," M.A. thesis, Columbia University, 1952.

Glynn, Herbert L. "The Urban Real Estate Boom in Nebraska during the 1880's," M.A. thesis, University of Nebraska, 1928.

Goldberg, A. A. "Public Opinion and the Acquisition of the Philippine Islands," M.A. thesis, Yale University, 1937.

Grantham, Dewey W., Jr. "Prohibition and the Progressive Movement," Ms.

Harmer, Marie U. "The Life of Charles H. Van Wyck," M.A. thesis, University of Nebraska, 1929.

Hummel, Ray Orvin, Jr. "William Jennings Bryan, 1896–1900," M.A. thesis, University of Nebraska, 1931.

Johnson, Arthur M. "The Anti-Trust Law, 1901–1909," Ms.

Johnson, Henry T. "History of the Beet Sugar Industry in Nebraska," M.A. thesis, University of Nebraska, 1934.

Johnson, John R. "Nebraska in the Spanish-American War and the Philippine Insurrection: a Study in Imperialism," Ph.D. thesis, University of Nebraska, 1937.

JONES, VIRGINIA BOWEN. "The Influence of the Railroads of Nebraska on Nebraska State Politics," M.A. thesis, University of Nebraska, 1927.

KUESTER, FRIEDA C. "The Farmers' Alliance in Nebraska," M.A. thesis, University of Nebraska, 1927.

McINTYRE, KENNETH E. "The Morton-Bryan Controversy," M.A. thesis, University of Nebraska, 1943.

MAHNKEN, NORBERT R. "The Nebraska Congressional Delegation and Tariff Legislation, 1880–1900," M.A. thesis, University of Nebraska, 1939.

MARGULIES, HERBERT. "Bryan's Democracy: A Study of His Writings and Speeches," M.A. thesis, University of Wisconsin, 1951.

MARSHALL, HELEN E. "The Social Philosophy of William Jennings Bryan: An Interpretation," M.A. thesis, University of Chicago, 1929.

RAAB, KENNETH D. "Henry T. Rainey," Ms.

ROSEWATER, VICTOR. "Life and Times of Edward Rosewater," Nebraska State Historical Society.

SCOTT, MITTI YOUNG. "Life and Political Career of William Vincent Allen," M.A. thesis, University of Nebraska, 1927.

SILVEUS, MARIAN. "The Antecedents of the Campaign of 1896," Ph.D. thesis, University of Wisconsin, 1932.

STORMS, ELIZABETH. "A Study of the Nebraska State Election of 1890," M.A. thesis, University of Nebraska, 1924.

STOUGH, RUTH KNOX. "The American Protective Association," M.A. thesis, University of Nebraska, 1931.

Index

Abbot, Willis J., 103, 146, 188, 281, 340, 341; names Bryan the "Great Commoner," 152
Aguinaldo, Emilio, 235, 363
Alcott, Bronson, 9
Aldrich, Nelson W., 215, 303, 386, 395
Allen, Thomas S., 380, 399
Allen, William Vincent, 113, 376; supports Bryan on the income tax, 59; elected Senator, 76; institutes suit to enjoin sale of gold bonds, 91; as permanent chairman of the Populist national convention of 1896, 153, 155–156; appointed to the Senate, 1900, 247–248
Altgeld, John Peter, 162, 242, 257, 263, 281, 305, 309; calls unofficial silver convention, 106; supports Bland as presidential candidate, 1896, 117, 125, 128, 129, 141–142, 145–146
American Bimetallic League: convention of July–August 1893, 82; convention of Memphis, Tenn., June 1895, 107–108; creates National Silver Committee, 107; merges into American Bimetallic Union, 110
American Bimetallic Union, 110, 113
American Federation of Labor, 93, 405
American Protective Association, 46, 102, 281
Andrews, E. Benjamin, 180
Anti-trust issue, 334, 385
Archbold, John D., 419, 421
Atwood, John H., 115, 128, 129, 131, 387

Bacon, Senator Augustus O., 235
Bailey, Senator Joseph, 96, 123, 127, 331, 373, 374, 375; breaks with Bryan, 402
Baird, John, 22, 23
Baird, Mrs. John, 21, 23
Baird, Mary Elizabeth, 16, 18; enrols at Jacksonville Female Academy, 21; meets Bryan, 21; courtship with Bryan, 21–23, 27–29; marriage, 30
Bank notes: Bryan opposes repeal of state bank note tax, 70, 77, 78, 92–93
Belmont, O. H. P., 273, 340, 345
Belmont, Perry, 238–239, 268
Bennett, Philo Sherman: and the Bennett case, 314–316

Beveridge, Senator Albert J., 13, 276, 339
Bimetallic Democratic National Committee, 118, 120
Blackburn, Senator Joseph C. S., 128, 150, 242, 305; as Democratic presidential aspirant, 1896, 121, 144, 145
Bland, Representative Richard Parks, 83, 86, 90, 97, 110, 117, 161, 213; as chairman of the Committee on Coinage, 69; as Democratic presidential aspirant, 1896, 121, 131, 144–146; as possible Democratic vice presidential candidate, 1896, 149–150
Bland-Allison Act, 83, 86; passed, 63–64; vetoed, 64; passed over Hayes's veto, 64
Bliss, Cornelius, 165, 349
Boies, Horace, 67; supported by Bryan as presidential candidate, 1896, 70, 117; as Democratic presidential aspirant, 1896, 121, 144, 145; as possible Democratic vice presidential candidate, 1896, 149, 161
Borou, Brian, 1
Bowbray, Baron William De, 1
Boyd, James E., 34, 44, 122
Bride, Cotter T., 328
Brisbane, Arthur, 249, 401–402
Broady, Jefferson H., 34; collects money in silver states for Bryan, 1892, 73
Brown, Charles W., 42
Bryan, Charles Wayland, 4, 341, 398; as business manager of The Commoner, 290; at the Denver convention, 405–410
Bryan, Frances, 4
Bryan, Grace Dexter, 49, 429
Bryan, John, 1
Bryan, Mary Elizabeth, 4
Bryan, Nancy Lillard, 4
Bryan, Russell Jones, 4, 16, 24
Bryan, Silas Lillard, 1, 2; ideas on education, 2; academic and legal education, 2; elected to Illinois state senate, 2; as state senator, 3; begins judicial career, 3; builds farm mansion, 3–4; children, 4; gentleman farmer, 4; influence on William J. Bryan, 5, 7–8; in congressional campaign, 1872, 7; on William J. Bryan as a college student, 15; death, 23; legacy, 24

Bryan, William Jennings
—Early life and education: born 1860, 4; named, 4; home education, 4; work on home farm, 5; early ambitions, 5; religious conversion, 6; credits father's influence, 6–7; early interest in politics, 7; father's influence upon, 7–8; joins Presbyterian church, 10; and his college curriculum, 10; as a student, 11–12; work in literary society, 13–15; wins prize for oratory, 15–16; early political work, 16; first mentions Jefferson, 16; outstanding characteristics, 17–18; follows Jefferson, 19–20; courtship, 19–23, 27–29; marriage, 30; attends law school, 24–27; obtains master's degree, 29; law practice, Jacksonville, Ill., 27–31; moves to Lincoln, Nebraska, 32
—And early Nebraska politics: law practice, 33–35; supports tariff reform and Cleveland, 1888, 35–37; helps determine Democratic party policy, 38–39; accounts for Populist revolt, 39–41; first congressional campaign, 41–48
—As congressman: appointed to Ways and Means Committee, 50; introduces legislation, 50–52; on his direct election bill, 52; on tariff reform, 52d Congress, 52–55; on tariff reform, 53d Congress, 56–60 (see also Wilson-Gorman tariff); on the income tax, 56–60; on currency reform, 62–70, 77–86; campaign for re-election, 70–76
—As competitor with Grover Cleveland: in campaign for United States Senate, 1893, 76; wins control of the Nebraska Democracy, 90; opposes sale of gold bonds, 91, 93–96; compared with Cleveland, 97–98
—And the preconvention campaign of 1896: declines to run again for Congress, 1894, 99; aided by Nebraska Democratic Free Coinage League, 99; issues senatorial platform, 100; as editor of Omaha World-Herald, 100–101; seeks fusion with Populists, 100–102; senatorial campaign, 1894–1895, 102–103; delivers the Nebraska Democracy to the Populists, 101–102; begins lecture tours, 104; address at Memphis, Tenn., May 1895, 106; finds Cleveland's monetary views contemptible, 106, 111; address at Springfield, Ill., convention, June 1895, 107; opposes Britain on gold and imperialism, 111–112; suggests compromise on free silver ratio, 112; on bolting and need for fusion, 113; preconvention letter campaign, 113–114; victorious in Nebraska primary convention, 1896, 114–115; declines presidential endorse-

ment by Nebraska Democrats, 115; on "Principles First," 115–116; woos support from Altgeld, 117–118; at the Republican national convention, 118–119
—At the Democratic national convention of 1896: insists that the silver majority rule, 120, 128; mentioned as presidential possibility, 121–122; defeated for temporary chairman, 121, 123; fails to win seat in the convention, 122; fails in election as chairman of Committee on Resolutions, 123–124; predicts his nomination, 124–125, 132–133; availability to all parties, 125–126; defeated for permanent chairman, 128; speech on evening of July 7, 128; seated in the convention, 129; reads the platform, 129–130; lobbies on convention floor, 131; arranges for debate on platform, 132; delivers "Cross of Gold" speech, 137–141; absents himself during the balloting, 143; nominated, 146; on the Democratic vice presidential candidate, 149–150
—In the campaign of 1896: suffers defections, 150–151; refuses to comment on actions in Populist national convention, 155–156; accepts Populist presidential nomination, 158–159; nominated as presidential candidate of National Silver Party, 159; accepts Democratic nomination in Madison Square Garden, 161–164; on first tour, 165–174; accepts nomination of National Silver Party, 174; accepts Democratic nomination, 174; on second tour, 174–188; electioneering technique, 175–176; on last tour, 188; receives returns, 189–190; congratulates McKinley, 190; declines to contest the election, 193–194
—And the Spanish-American War: shifts attention to Cuban crisis, 220; opposes issue of gold war bonds, 220–221; favors war in behalf of a free Cuba, 221, 222; offers service, 223; delivers speech on "Imperialism," 224–225; commissioned volunteer colonel, 226; as colonel, 226–227; experiences as soldier, 227–232; resigns from army, 232; speaks against imperialism, 232–233, 237; and the Treaty of Paris, 233–236
—And the campaign of 1900: as a political evangelist, 207–208; as a Jeffersonian, 209; starts campaign for 1900, 213; displeased with McKinley's administration, 215; and the Dingley tariff bill, 215; in Smyth v. Ames case, 216; opposes the "reorganizers," 216–217; opposes Hanna for Senator, 217–218;

refuses to change issues of 1896, 218–
220; Jackson Day speech, January 8,
1897, 219; and the preconvention campaign, 239–240, 249–252; at the Chicago
Anti-Trust Conference, 1899, 240–241;
and the elections of 1899, 241–244; refuses to desert free silver, 243; promised
support of anti-imperialists, 245; and
the Nebraska senatorship problem,
1899–1900, 247–248; and the issues for
1900, 253–254; and the Kansas City
convention, 255–262; and the campaign
of 1900, 263–284; accounts for his defeat, 284–285; compared with Cleveland, 288–289; and his issues after 1900,
292–293; increases his religious work,
293–294
—On "tainted money," 294–295, 357–
360; compared with Theodore Roosevelt, 297–299, 385–386; as leader of the
opposition, 299, 443; on Roosevelt and
the trusts, 301–302; on Roosevelt and
tariff reform, 302; on Roosevelt and
the coal strike of 1902, 302–303; on
Roosevelt and currency reform, 303–
304, 394–396; on Roosevelt and foreign
policy, 304; criticizes Cleveland, 308–
309, 310, 311–312, 319; criticizes the
"reorganizers," 311, 312, 313, 319; opposes A. B. Parker as presidential candidate, 312; and the Bennett case, 314–
316; visits Europe, 1903–1904, 316–318;
and the preconvention campaign of
1904, 318–325; and the St. Louis convention, 327–343; in the campaign of
1904, 345–350; offers a reorganization
plan, 345–346, 351–352; regains leadership of the Democracy, 351–352; increases emphasis on morality, 353–354,
356–357, 387–391, 412, 442; urges support of Roosevelt by Democrats, 354–
356, 360–361, 378–379, 393; resigns as
trustee of Illinois College, 358–360; on
world tour, 1905–1906, 360–375; meets
J. P. Morgan, 366; talks with George
Harvey, 367–369; tries to win Cleveland over, 369; on government ownership issue, 369–370, 375–378; battle
against Roger Sullivan, 370, 380; and
the Oklahoma constitution, 383–384;
on the Chatauqua circuit, 387–389
—And the campaign of 1908: in preconvention campaign, 390–405; at the
Conference of Governors, 396; drops
government ownership as issue, 402,
408; breaks with Joseph Bailey, 402;
and the Denver convention, 405–410;
and the campaign, 411–437; debates
with Roosevelt, 417–423; refuses to
make pledges, 426–427; and "The Mys-

tery of 1908," 429–435; contributions
to American life, 438–445
Bryan, Mrs. William Jennings: studies
law, 30, 33; cofounder of Lincoln
Sorosis, 38; passes bar examination, 38;
helps husband in Congress, 49; suggests
Bryan resume law practice, 104; attends
Chicago convention, 120, 127; on the
campaign of 1908, 424, 425
Bryan, William Jennings, Jr., 38
Bryan, William Smith, 1
Buckner, Simon Bolivar, 171
Bullard, E. F., 22
Butler, Marion, 113, 156, 203, 268; as
leader of middle-of-the-road Populists,
153; as temporary chairman of Popu-
list national convention, 1896, 155 n.;
as chairman of Populist national com-
mittee, 159
Butt, Archie, 397

Caffery, Senator Donelson, 170
Campaign of 1896: and defections from
Bryan's leadership, 150–151; compared
with Civil War, 151; significance, 211
Campaign of 1900, 263–289
Campaign of 1904, 345–350
Campaign of 1908, 390–439
Cannon, Joseph B., 184, 303–304, 405, 417
Carlisle, John G., 80, 82, 95, 105, 150,
187, 307
Carmack, Senator Edward, 340, 341
Carnegie, Andrew, 222, 233, 234; critical
of Bryan in 1896, 195
Castor, Tobias, 71, 73
Chandler, Senator William E., 247, 386
Chautauqua, 387–388
Clark, Champ, 13, 280, 305, 331, 337
Clark, John Bates, 240
Clayton, Henry D., 403, 407
Cleveland, Grover, 82, 87, 89, 90, 99, 110,
163, 369, 378; opposes Bryan's income
tax plan, 56, 59–60; refuses to sign
Wilson-Gorman tariff, 60; defeats silver bills in first administration, 64;
warns against a free silver bill, 66; renominated for president, 72; uses
patronage power against Bryan, 77,
79; opposes silver in inaugural address,
1893, 79; opposes Bryan as a "Populist,"
79; calls extraordinary session to repeal Sherman Act, 82; sells gold bonds,
91, 93; submits currency and banking
reform plan, 1894, 94–96; compared
with Bryan, 97–98, 288–289; repudiated
in elections, 1894, 103; buttresses the
Democracy in the South, 106; marks
unofficial Illinois silver convention as
beginning the battle of the standards,
106; offers banking and currency plan,

Cleveland, Grover (*continued*)
111; Venezuelan message, 1895, 111;
last bond sales, 112; on the Democratic
national convention of 1896, 151; re-
jects presidential nomination by National Democratic Party, 171; critical
of Bryan, 216, 308, 319, 345; opposes
war with Spain, 221; opposes Bryan
in 1900, 264; refuses to run in 1904,
319; endorses Parker, 319–320; praises
Parker, 343; refuses to support Bryan
in 1908, 396; death, 401
Cockran, W. Bourke, 166–167, 246; on
Ways and Means Committee, 53; opposes Bryan's income tax bill, 57–58;
bolts Bryan in 1896, 151; opposes war
with Spain, 221; at the Chicago Anti-
Trust Conference, 240; supports Bryan
in 1900, 265, 272, 273, 404
Cockrell, Senator Francis M., 122, 329,
336, 337, 340, 341
Coler, Bird S., 271, 404
The Commoner, 290–292, 313–314, 316,
361, 370, 371, 372, 398, 432
Conant, Charles A., 333
Conciliation treaties. *See* "Cooling Off"
treaties
Conference of Governors, 1908, 396
Connell, William J., 41–47
"Cooling Off" treaties, 371, 385, 387
Cortelyou, George B., 348–349, 350
Coxey, Jacob, 162
Creelman, James, 175, 190, 243, 251–252,
305, 329
Crisp, Charles F., 50–51, 69
Croker, Richard, 218, 219, 243, 252, 258,
260, 261, 271, 273–274, 279, 374
"Cross of Gold" speech, 137–141; ana-
lyzed, 147
Culberson, Senator Charles A., 340, 375
Currency reform: and the demonetiza-
tion of silver, 62–63; and the Bland-
Allison Act, 63–64; and the Sherman
Silver Purchase Act, 64–65; and the
battle over repeal of Sherman Act,
82–86, 89–90; and Cleveland's gold
bond sales, 91, 93–96, 112; and Lyman
Gage's currency reform plan, 219; and
Lyman Gage's gold bond program, 220;
and the Gold Standard Act of 1900,
246–247. *See also* Bank notes, Free silver, Gold bonds, Greenbacks, Guarantee of bank deposits, *and* Seigniorage
legislation

Dahlman, James, 103, 114, 352, 403
Danforth, Elliott, 163
Daniel, John, 115, 331, 332, 334, 341,
402–403; as Democratic presidential
aspirant, 1896, 121; as temporary chairman of Chicago convention, 127; as
possible Democratic vice presidential
candidate, 1896, 149
Daniels, Josephus, 149, 426–427, 431;
favors Bryan as presidential candidate,
1896, 116–117, 123; accompanies Bryan
in campaign, 1896, 181
Darrow, Clarence, 113, 117, 337
Davidson, Mariah Wood, 2
Davis, Henry Gassaway, 182, 340; as Democratic vice presidential candidate, 340,
343
Dawes, Charles Gates, 2, 33, 38, 119, 349
Debs, Eugene V., 153, 154, 162, 169, 351;
and the Pullman Strike, 105; declines
Populist presidential nomination, 1896,
157; endorses Bryan, 1896, 157
Democratic National Convention: 1896
presidential aspirants, 121–122; battle
over temporary chairman, 122–123;
majority report of, 129–130; debate
over platform, 135–143; balloting for
presidential candidate, 143–146; choice
of vice presidential candidate, 149–150
Democrats, gold: decide to establish
separate party, 1896, 162; criticize
Bryan, 166–167; organize third party,
170–171; labeled "reorganizers," 216;
make poor showing in elections of 1897,
218; oppose Bryan in 1900, 264, 282; de-
mand gold in St. Louis platform, 336–
343. *See also* National Democratic Party
Depew, Chauncey, 168, 192–193
Dewey, Admiral George, 227, 246
Dickinson, Don, 118
Dingley, Nelson, 53
Direct election of Senators, 42, 52, 416
Donnelly, Ignatius, 113, 169
Douglas, Stephen A., 3, 148
Dubois, Frederick T., 118, 329
Dunlap, Millard F., 117, 370, 380
Dunn, Ignatius J., 403, 407–408

Edgerton, Joseph A., 41, 42, 88
Elections: 1896, 190–192; 1898, 231–232;
1900, 277–298; 1901, 308; 1902, 310;
1903, 313; 1904, 350–351; 1906, 380–382,
384; 1908, 429–430, 435–437
Emerson, Ralph Waldo, 9

Fairbanks, Charles W., 276, 305
Field, Allen W., 72, 74, 185
The First Battle, 212–213, 285
Folk, Joseph W., 348, 373, 391
Foraker, Senator Joseph B., 276; and the
Archbold letters, 419
Francis, David R., 307, 374
Free silver: and the Bland-Allison Act,
63–64; and the Sherman Silver Pur-
chase Act, 64–65; in President Har-

rison's annual message of 1891, 69; and defeat of Bland silver bill, 69; Sherman wishes to repeal own bill, 72; battle to repeal Sherman Act, 82–86, 89–90; as Bryan's paramount issue in 1896, 205–207; as the Democratic party's paramount issue in 1900, 245; as Bryan's Jonah in 1900, 279–280; dropped by Bryan, 431, 438

Frewen, Moreton, 172, 316–317, 369

Garland, Hamlin, 188
Gaynor, William J., 404
George, Henry, 127, 134, 218
Gere, Charles H., 45, 263
Girdner, John H., 250, 261
Glass, Carter, 145
Godkin, E. L., 164, 172, 194, 221, 265, 345
Goebel, William, 242, 243, 243–244 n.
Gold bonds: Cleveland's offer to sell, 78, 91, 93–96, 112; Bryan's opposition to sale of, 78, 91, 93–96, 112
Gold Standard Act of 1900, 246–247
Gompers, Samuel, 405; remains aloof from politics in 1896, 169; refuses Bryan's tentative offer of a cabinet post in 1896, 170; supports Bryan in 1908, 411, 417, 426
Gorman, Senator Arthur Pue, 59, 236, 244, 307
Government ownership: as an issue in 1908, 369–370, 375–378, 438
Gray, Senator George, 128, 234, 319, 336, 391, 408
"Great Commoner": origin of title, 152
Greenbacks, 63, 78, 87, 109, 111
Gruenther, Christian M., 399
Guarantee of bank deposits, 85, 87, 412, 414, 416
Guffey, James M., 256, 328, 404–405, 406

Hamlin, Charles S., 307, 308, 335, 347
Hanna, Marcus A., 118, 119, 162, 165, 167, 183, 189, 253, 270–271, 281, 417, 419; spurns cooperation with gold Democratics, 1896, 151; and the management of the Republican campaign of 1896, 192–202; wins a Senate seat, 217–218
Harmon, Judson, 322, 329
Harris, Senator Isham G., 128
Harrison, President Benjamin, 69
Harrison, Carter, 247, 265, 307, 309, 370
Harrison, Francis B., 409
Harrity, William F., 79, 127, 216–217
Harvey, George, 365, 367–369, 392
Haskell, Governor Charles N., 404, 406; and the Archbold letters, 420–421
Hay, John, 162, 187, 194
Hayes, President Rutherford B., 64

Hearst, William Randolph, 373, 415; supports Bryan in 1896, 146; supports Bryan in 1900, 251; as Democratic presidential aspirant, 1904, 322; and the Independence League (party), 391, 413; criticizes Bryan, 413; and the Archbold letters, 419
Hill, David Bennett, 163, 166, 251, 252, 255, 261, 271, 307; as one of the Senate's "Big Four," 59; as temporary chairman of the Chicago convention, 1896, 122–123, 127; defeated as permanent chairman of Chicago convention, 128; makes minority report to the Chicago convention, 129, 132, 136, 143; bolts Bryan in 1896, 150; at the Kansas City convention, 258, 259, 260; at the St. Louis convention, 320, 332–333, 336, 340, 341; drops politics, 347
Hinrichsen, William H., 106, 117
Hitchcock, Gilbert M., 88; supports Bryan for Congress, 1890, 45, 48; warns Bryan against free silver, 66; breaks with Bryan, 248, 276, 277, 348; defeated for re-election to Congress, 351
Hoar, Senator George F., 233, 245
Hogg, James, 113, 116, 123, 145, 243, 248
Holcomb, Silas A., 101, 102, 153
Hopkins, John P., 268, 307, 322, 328
Howell, Clark, 115, 136, 384
Hughes, Charles Evans, 426

Illinois College, 9; curriculum in Bryan's day, 10; literary societies, 12–13; Bryan resigns as trustee, 358–360
Income tax: bill introduced by Bryan, 56–60; declared unconstitutional, 105; and the St. Louis Democratic platform, 333–334
Independence League (party), 391, 405
Ingersoll, Robert, 10
Injunction, labor: see Labor injunction
Interparliamentary Union, 371
Irvine, Frank, 88, 89

Jackson, Andrew, 168
Jacksonville, Illinois, 9, 17, 18, 19, 26; and Bryan's law practice threat, 27–31
James, Ollie, 246, 410
Jefferson, Thomas, 111, 169, 182, 209; first mention by Bryan, 16; model for Bryan, 19–20
Jennings, Israel, 2
Jennings, Mariah Elizabeth, 2; marries Silas Lillard Bryan, 2; family ancestry, 2; character, 3; educates children, 4
Johnson, Governor John A., 391, 396, 408
Johnson, John G., 256
Johnson, Tom L., 248, 254, 375
Johnson, William E., 38

Joline letter, 392
Jones, Charles H., 129
Jones, Dr. Hiram, 23, 306; provides college home for Bryan, 9; places Bryan with law firm, 26
Jones, Senator James K., 116, 256, 280; at the Chicago convention, 120, 124, 132, 133, 135; as chairman of the Democratic National Committee, 155–156; at the Populist national convention, 1896, 162–163; predicts Bryan's victory, 183; concedes defeat, 189–190; as campaign manager, 204

Kern, John W., 340, 410, 412
Kirby, Brown, and Russell, 26, 27
Knox, P. C., 301, 426

Labor injunction, 105–106, 405, 409, 417
La Follette, Robert, 351, 373, 381, 391, 395, 426
Lease, Mrs. Mary E., 75, 277
Leupp, Francis E., 134–135
Lillard, Nancy, 1
Lincoln, Abraham, 3, 148
Lodge, Senator Henry Cabot, 172, 180–181, 225–226, 235
Lodge, Mrs. Henry Cabot, 196
Lloyd, Henry D., 153, 154, 169, 284

McBride, John, 169
McClellan, George Brinton, Jr., 145, 313, 369
McGuire, James K., 307
Mack, Norman, 257, 258; as Democratic national chairman, 413, 415
McKinley, President William: originally favored silver, 64; helped pass Bland-Allison Act over Hayes's veto, 64; stumps against Congressman Bryan in Nebraska, 72, 102, 118, 119; incredulous that Bryan should be named for president, 143; accepts currency question as paramount issue, 1896, 151, 161; conducts front porch campaign, 1896, 162, 200–201; refuses to stump against Bryan, 167; promises Cleveland to oppose free silver, 214; renominated, 1900, 252; makes free silver the paramount issue, 1900, 266; and his letter of acceptance, 271; on tariff reciprocity, 296–297
McLean, John R., 121, 144, 149–150, 241, 244, 296, 356
McMillin, Benton, 50–51, 56, 181–183
Mahoney, Thomas J., 109, 122, 129
Manahan, James, 397, 412
Martin, Euclid, 73, 77, 101, 171
Mason, Senator William E., 185, 233
Masters, Edgar Lee, 137

Matthews, Governor Claude, 121, 144, 149
Metcalfe, Richard L., 49, 257, 258
Miller, Dr. George L., 34, 42, 48, 68, 69
Mills, Roger Q., 50–51, 69
Mitchell, John, 405, 409–410; and the coal strike of 1900, 270
Monetary conferences, international, 70, 80, 214
Morgan, John P., 366, 393, 421
Morgan, J. P., and Company, 93–95, 383
Morton, J. Sterling, 69, 99, 171, 284, 307; as leader of the Nebraska "slaughterhouse Democrats," 34; as Bryan's political patron, 35–36, 38–39, 48; warns Bryan against free silver, 66, 68; as gubernatorial candidate, 1892, 73; supports Bryan for re-election to Congress, 1892, 75; as Secretary of Agriculture, 76–77, 79; appeals to railroads for aid against Bryan, 1893, 89; critical of farm leaders, 89; opposes Bryan in 1900, 264
Mullen, Arthur, 399, 423
Murphy, Charles F., 310, 345, 401–402, 404, 432

National Anti-Imperialism League, 268
National Anti-Trust Conference, 1900, 245
National Association of Manufacturers, 405
National Bimetallic Union, 105; merged into American Bimetallic Union, 110
National Democratic Party: select candidates for campaign of 1896, 170–171; praised by Grover Cleveland, 171; influence on campaign of 1896, 192. See also Democrats, gold
National Silver Committee (of the American Bimetallic League), 107, 109, 110
National Silver Convention, First, 64
National Silver Party: created, 110; national convention of 1896, 153, 159–160
Nebraska Democratic Free Coinage League, 99, 100, 102
Nebraska People's Independent Party, 41
Nebraska Sound Money League, 108
Norris, George W., 13, 283, 351, 384
Norton, S. F., 157

Ochs, Adolph, 172, 328, 339
Ogden, Judge Joseph, 71
Olney, Richard, 270, 319
Omaha World-Herald, 100–101, 108

Palmer, Senator John M., 170–171
Panic of 1893, 80–81; Bryan's cures for, 81–82; worsens, 90

Panic of 1907, 392–393, 414, 430
Parker, Judge Alton B., 259, 271, 307, 319, 320, 399, 401, 418, 427; as Democratic presidential aspirant, 1904, 320–343; in 1904 campaign, 347–350; declines ever to run again, 352
Patterson, Thomas M., 153
Pattison, Governor Robert E., 144, 270, 328
Peffer, Wiliam A., 153, 155
Pennoyer, Governor Sylvester, 121, 144, 146
Pershing, John J., 38
Pettigrew, Senator Richard F., 118, 183, 305, 329, 401
Philippine Islands, 232–234, 363
Phillips, Wendell, 11
Platt, Senator O. H., 215, 303
Poindexter, Miles, 150–151
Populist national convention, 1896, 153–159
Populist Party: wins state of Nebraska, 1894, 101–103; gains in 1892 over elections of 1890, 103; nominates Bryan in 1896, 157; nominates Bryan in 1900, 249–250; national convention of 1904, 326
Prohibition: as a Nebraska issue, 1889, 38–39; as a Nebraska issue, 1890, 44, 46–47; not an issue in 1908, 412, 438
Publicity for campaign contributions, 373, 412, 416, 421–423, 424–425, 442
Puerto Rican tariff, 247, 248
Pulitzer, Joseph, 321, 327, 374, 391

Rainey, Congressman Henry T., 380
Reciprocal tariffs, 296–297
Reed, Thomas B., 53
Reid, Whitelaw, 49, 152, 194; as Bryan's host in London, 1906, 366–367
Reorganizers, Democratic: See Democrats, gold, and National Democratic Party
Republican national convention: of 1896, 118–119; of 1900, 252–253; of 1904, 325–326
Republicans, silver: bolt the Republican national convention of 1896, 118–119; name Bryan for president, 1900, 261
Ridder, Herman, 403, 411
Rockefeller, William, 165, 295, 427–428
Roosevelt, Theodore: as Civil Service Commissioner, 49; criticizes Bryan in 1896, 151–152, 163, 194; as vice presidential candidate, 1900, 253, 269, 274, 275, 283; compared with Bryan, 297–299, 385–386; and his debate with A. B. Parker, 1904, 348–350, takes over some Bryan policies, 354, 372–373, 378–379, 444; critical of Bryan, 379–380; and

currency reform, 386, 393, 395–396; and trust busting, 394; helps Taft in campaign, 1908, 416–426; in newspaper debate with Bryan, 1908, 417–423
Root, Elihu, 283, 325, 426, 435
Rosewater, Edward, 48, 72, 75, 277, 283
Rosewater, Victor, 47
Ross, Edward A., 185, 202, 289
Rosser, Dr. Charles M., 110, 116, 123, 132–133, 147, 188, 263
Round Table Club, 38
Russell, Governor William E., 129; defends minority report in the Chicago convention, 132, 137
Ryan, Thomas F., 326, 345, 367–369, 380

Salem, Illinois, 2, 4, 5, 18
Sawyer, Andrew J., 42
Schiff, Jacob H., 345, 386
Schurz, Carl, 172, 194, 221, 265, 284
Seabury, Judge Samuel, 405, 415
Sectionalism: as an issue in the campaign of 1896, 133, 135–136, 148, 151, 152, 153
Seigniorage legislation, 86, 91–92
Sewall, Arthur: as Democratic vice presidential candidate, 1896, 149–150; rejected as vice presidential candidate by the Populists, 1896, 156; nominated as vice presidential candidate by National Silver Party, 159, 203
Seymour, Horatio, 19
Shamp, Jerome, 73–75
Sheehan, William F., 340, 341
Sherman, Senator John, 64, 65
Sherman Silver Purchase Act: passed by compromise, 64; opposed by Sherman, 65; Sherman introduces repeal bill, 72; Bryan opposes repeal without a substitute, 77; battle to repeal, 82–86, 89–90
Sibley, Joseph, 107, 111, 150
Sigma Pi, 12, 13–15, 16–17, 18
Simpson, Jerry, 153, 155, 268
Smyth, Constantine J., 41, 42, 122
Sovereign, James R., 169, 272
Spooner, Senator John C., 215, 276, 303
Springer, Congressman William M., 49, 50–51, 53
Stanchfield, John B., 271, 273
Stevenson, Adlai: as Democratic presidential aspirant, 1896, 121; as Democratic vice presidential candidate, 1900, 260–261, 266, 272
Stewart, Senator William M., 67, 276
Stone, Governor William J., 146, 155, 156, 163, 255, 256
Storrs, Dr. Henry E., 9
Sturtevant, Julian Monson, 10–11, 11 n.
Sugar trust decision, 105
Sullivan, Mark, 13, 197, 214

Sullivan, Roger, 322, 370, 380, 397, 401–402, 406
Swanson, Claude, 115, 403

Taft, William H., 304, 313, 391–392; and the campaign of 1908, 414–434
Taggart, Thomas, 322, 349, 351, 397, 406, 410
"Tainted money," 294–296
Talbot, Adolphus, 33, 38, 260
Tammany Hall, 252, 274, 279, 403–404, 432 n.
Tariff reform: in Bryan's first congressional campaign, 41–48; "Pop gun" tariff reform, 52–55; and the Wilson-Gorman tariff, 56–60; and the Dingley tariff, 112, 215; and McKinley on reciprocity, 296–297; as an issue in the St. Louis platform, 334; as an issue in 1908, 416. See also Reciprocal tariffs
Taubeneck, Henry E., 153, 154
Teller, Senator Henry M., 117, 263–264; endorses free silver, 111, 112, 117; threatens to bolt if silver not endorsed in 1896, 118, 119; as possible Democratic presidential choice, 121; supports Bryan in 1896, 146–147; urges Populists to support Bryan, 153, 203, 213; supports Bryan's demand for war with Spain, 221
Teller Amendment, 222
Tennessee Coal and Iron Company, 393, 421
Thacher, John Boyd, 178
Thomas, Senator Charles S., 114, 128, 142, 257, 258
Thompson, Judge Owen P., 370, 380
Thompson, William H., 71, 122, 248, 276, 310, 380
Thurston, John M., 102, 103
Tilden, Samuel, 19
Tillman, Benjamin, 110, 143, 145, 162, 258, 259, 296, 327, 329, 341, 342, 385; criticizes Cleveland, 111, 113, 116, 127; defends majority report of Chicago convention, 129, 130–131, 135–136
Tolstoy, Count Leo, 317–318
Tomlinson, John W., 109, 183
Towne, Charles A., 269, 281, 305, 340; supports Bryan in 1896 campaign, 183; nominated for vice president by Populists, 1900, 250, 258, 260, 261; declines the Populist and silver Republican nominations, 261, 266–268
Trans-Mississippi Congress: of 1890, 80; of 1894, 93; of 1895, 110
Treaty of Paris, 233–236, 268, 274, 284
Trumbull, Lyman: hires Bryan as law clerk, 24; influence on Bryan, 25; writes Populist declaration of principles, 93; death, 120

Union College of Law, 24; curriculum in Bryan's day, 24 n.
United States Steel Company, 301, 418, 421

Van Cleave, James, 405
Van Wyck, Augustus, 252, 258
Van Wyck, Charles H., 41, 44, 72
Van Wyck, Judge Robert, 218, 243
Vardaman, James K., 341
Vilas, Senator William F., 132, 137, 374

Waite, Davis H., 113, 153
Wall, Edwin C., 322, 337
Warner, General Adoniram J., 66, 218
Watkins, Albert, 42, 69, 226, 307
Watson, Thomas E., 88, 162, 203–204, 266, 327, 344, 347, 351, 380; as leader of the middle-of-the-road Populists, 1896, 153; as Populist presidential candidate, 1896, 156; opposes war with Spain, 221; refuses to stump for Bryan in 1900, 266
Watterson, Henry, 171, 242, 307, 319, 381, 396–397, 401
Weaver, General James B., 82, 101, 102, 113, 432–433; as Populist presidential candidate, 1892, 72; stumps for Bryan in Nebraska, 1892, 75; as Populist fusionist leader, 1896, 153, 155, 156–157, 161, 162, 213
Wells, Rolla, 307
Western Silver Miners' Association, 104
Western States Commercial Congress, First, 66
Whipple Academy, 9, 12
White, Henry, 316, 317, 371–372
White, Senator Stephen, 122; as permanent chairman Chicago convention, 1896, 128, 129, 131, 133
White, William Allen, 142
Whitney, William C., 49; assumes charge of Democratic gold forces, 1896, 116; leadership in Chicago convention, 127, 246
Williams, George Fred, 142, 143, 180, 257, 258, 261, 399
Williams, John Sharp, 329, 340, 341, 343, 345, 369, 375
Wilson, William L., 83, 89; as member of Ways and Means Committee, 53; as Chairman of Ways and Means Committee, 56; presents bond sale bill, 95; supports Bryan in 1900, 270
Wilson, Woodrow, 346–347, 365, 391, 392; refuses to support Bryan in 1908, 396, 397–398
Wilson-Gorman tariff, 56–60, 309
Wood, General Leonard, 363–364

Yamashita, Yachichiro, 362